# More advance praise for
## *The Second World Wars*

"I couldn't put it down. It is rare to encounter a view of the war from the multiple perspectives of the six powers, three on each side, who were the prime combatants, in the elemental theaters of sea and air and land. The analysis is excellent. *The Second World Wars* is a major work of historical narrative and deserves to meet readers receptive to its riches."

—David Lehman, author of *Sinatra's Century*

"Victor Davis Hanson's comprehensive account of World War II is a wonder. Where others have supplied a narrative, he provides analysis. He explores the war's origins; the role played in its conduct by air power, sea power, infantry, tanks, artillery, industry, and generalship; and the reasons why the Allies won and the Axis lost. This is an eye-opener and a page-turner."

—Paul A. Rahe, author of *The Grand Strategy of Classical Sparta*

# THE
# SECOND
# WORLD
# WARS

Also by VICTOR DAVIS HANSON

*Warfare and Agriculture in Classical Greece*
*The Western Way of War*
*Hoplites* (editor)
*The Other Greeks*
*Fields Without Dreams*
*Who Killed Homer?* (with John Heath)
*The Wars of the Ancient Greeks*
*The Soul of Battle*
*The Land Was Everything*
*Bonfire of the Humanities*
      (with John Heath and Bruce Thornton)
*An Autumn of War*
*Carnage and Culture*
*Between War and Peace*
*Mexifornia*
*Ripples of Battle*
*A War Like No Other*
*The Immigration Solution*
      (with Heather MacDonald and Steven Malanga)
*Makers of Ancient Strategy* (editor)
*The Father of Us All*
*The End of Sparta: A Novel*
*The Savior Generals*

# THE
# SECOND
# WORLD
# WARS

---

HOW THE FIRST GLOBAL CONFLICT
WAS FOUGHT AND WON

VICTOR DAVIS HANSON

BASIC BOOKS
New York

Basic Books
Hachette Book Group
1290 Avenue of the Americas, New York, NY 10104
www.basicbooks.com

Printed in the United States of America

First Edition: October 2017

Published by Basic Books, an imprint of Perseus Books, LLC, a subsidiary of Hachette Book Group, Inc.

The publisher is not responsible for websites (or their content) that are not owned by the publisher.

Print book interior design by Amy Quinn

Library of Congress Cataloging-in-Publication Data
Names: Hanson, Victor Davis, author.
Title: The second world wars : how the first global conflict was fought and won / Victor Davis Hanson.
Description: New York, NY : Basic Books, an imprint of Perseus Books, LLC., a subsidiary of Hachette Book Group, Inc., 2017. | Includes bibliographical references and index.
Identifiers: LCCN 2017024227| ISBN 9780465066988 (hardcover) | ISBN 9780465093199 (ebook)
Subjects: LCSH: World War, 1939–1945. | World War, 1939–1945—Campaigns.
Classification: LCC D743 .H329 2017 | DDC 940.54—dc23
\LC record available at https://lccn.loc.gov/2017024227

LSC-C

10  9  8  7  6  5  4  3  2  1

For Susannah Merry Hanson (1986–2014)

*Amata nobis quantum amabitur nulla.*

# Contents

# Maps

# THE
# SECOND
# WORLD
# WARS

# Preface

THE MORE THAN three dozen missions carried out by my father, William F. Hanson, in a B-29 bomber over Japan, were a world apart from his cousin's experience. Victor Hanson's war ended in a fatal May 19, 1945, rendezvous with a Nambu machine gun nest on the crest of Sugar Loaf Hill with the 6th Marine Division on Okinawa. Both fought in a way foreign to their other cousin, Robert Hanson, who worked as a logistician in Iran, ferrying American military freight to the Russians.[1]

All three Hansons experienced different wars from that of my maternal cousin Richard Davis. He "rolled" across France as part of Patton's Third Army. Dick's war in turn was unlike that of another maternal cousin, Beldon Cather. As a boy I remember an occasionally feverish Beldon on the farm as a lifelong semi-invalid, suffering neurological disabilities from serial bouts with dengue fever contracted while fighting in the Pacific. Beldon did not battle in the same manner or against the same enemies or in the same places as his brother Holt, killed while serving in combat with an artillery battalion of the Seventh Army in November 1944, and buried in France at the Epinal American Cemetery.

World War II sent the youth of American, British, German, Japanese, Italian, and Russian families across the globe in odd alliances against each other. They battled in the air, at sea, and on the ground for all sorts of expressed reasons, employing machines that were often new and fighting in ways still not fully understood, and against a variety of enemies. When the veterans of my family shared stories about their service at holiday gatherings in the early 1960s, we eavesdroppers listened to their descriptions of exotic locales and situations, wondering whether they had even fought in the same war.

They insisted that they were kindred soldiers in a shared struggle against a common evil with a variety of faces. How fighting different enemies, alongside disparate allies, in greatly different ways across the globe coalesced into one war is a paradox—and the subject of this book. Its aim is to explain why a single conflict encompassed global fighting in ways not true of most prior wars, fought in limited locales between predictable enemies and through familiar methods.

I TITLE THIS book *The Second World Wars* for two reasons. One, no supposedly single conflict was ever before fought in so many diverse landscapes on premises that often seemed unrelated. And, two, never had a
war been fought in so many different ways—to the extent that a rocket
attack on London or jungle fighting in Burma or armor strikes in Libya
seemed to belong to entirely different wars.

World War II, however, began traditionally enough in 1939–1940 in
Europe as a series of border conflicts exclusively between European powers, including Britain. As is true of much of European history, aggressive
states attacked their perceived weaker neighbors, usually through surprise
and in reliance on greater preparation and armament. By the end of 1940,
what had so far seemed to be familiar European infighting had achieved
a Caesarian or Napoleonic scale. But by the end of 1941, something quite
cataclysmic followed: all the smaller conflicts compounded unexpectedly
into a total, global war, in which the Axis powers of Germany, Italy, and
Japan were soon materially outmatched, strategically unprepared, and
likely to lose in catastrophic fashion. Advances in Western technology
and industrialization, when married with both totalitarian zealotry and
fully mobilized democratic states, also ensured that the expanded war
would become lethal in a way never before seen.[2]

Three unexpected events explain why the border fights that had begun periodically—and sometimes ended and started again—between
1939 and 1941 were no longer seen as a series of separate wars but had co-
alesced and became redefined as part of what we now know as World War
II in the United States, or as the Second World War in the Anglosphere.
First, Germany without warning invaded its partner, the Soviet Union
(June 22, 1941). Second, in addition to its long war with China, Japan
took on new enemies by conducting surprise attacks on the Pacific and
Asian bases of Great Britain and the United States (December 7–8, 1941).
Third, both Germany and Italy then declared war against the Americans
(December 11, 1941).

Only these unforeseen developments in the single year of 1941 recalibrated prior regional conflicts in Europe and Asia into a continuous and now interconnected global war that drew three new powerful
participants—Japan, the Soviet Union, and the United States—into the
two formidable alliances, with a vast array of aircraft carriers, sophisticated planes, artillery pieces, and vehicles. The new worldwide fight
was rebranded as one of Germany, Italy, and Japan against Britain, the
Soviet Union, the United States, and China—with smaller and weaker
allied states on both sides. Thus the holistic idea of a Second World War
was born.[3]

Despite the wartime propagandas that followed, there were few common fault lines of religion, race, or geography to make sense of this confusing conflict—much less common methods of conducting the fighting. Being victims of Axis aggression, most often through unprovoked attacks, was about the only common bond that held the Allies together, a tripartite alliance that initially hinged on retaliating against Adolf Hitler and that thus dissipated months after his death almost as quickly as it had been formed.

THIS BOOK DOES not follow a strict chronological sequence. Nor does it offer a comprehensive narrative history of all the diverse theaters and campaigns of the war. Rather, it focuses on particular battles emblematic of the larger themes of how the respective belligerents made wise and foolish choices about why, how, and where to fight the war. It is not, then, an operational history of the war that provides detailed accounts of day-by-day fighting, advances, and retreats.

Instead, the book's chapters analyze the diverse methods and effectiveness of combat—the role of civilians, industry, air power, navies, infantry, armor, siegecraft, and military leadership—to assess how these different investments and strategies led one side to win and the other to lose, and how the war's diverse theaters, belligerents, and ways of fighting came eventually to define a single war.

A general theme also transcends the chapters: the once ascendant Axis powers were completely ill-prepared—politically, economically, and militarily—to win the global war they had blundered into during 1941. Simply killing the far greater number of soldiers and civilians over the next four years—the vast majority of them Russians, Eastern Europeans, and Chinese—never equated to destroying their enemies' ability to make war.

I THANK MANY for help in completing this book. The Hoover Institution, Stanford University, has offered continued support since my appointment in 2003, especially from John Raisian, director emeritus, and the current director, Thomas Gilligan. I have learned a great deal on war and peace from my colleagues at Hoover, especially Peter Berkowitz, Peter Robinson, Shelby Steele, and Thomas Sowell. Eric Thomas Wakin, head of archives at Hoover, along with his staff, generously helped with assembling photographs from the trove of World War II material at Hoover. I thank Bill Nelson for drafting the maps. David Berkey, a research fellow in classics and military history at Hoover, has proven an invaluable research assistant, and I owe him considerable gratitude for his help in editing the manuscript, finding obscure books and periodicals, and bringing to my attention both facts and ideas that I otherwise would have missed. My assistant, Megan Ring, also offered timely organizational help, especially in matters of editing and bibliography.

Martin Anderson and his wife, the late Illie Anderson, generously supported my tenure as the Martin and Illie Anderson Senior Fellow in classics and military history at Hoover. Each September I have spent my vacation teaching for a month as the Wayne and Marcia Buske Distinguished Fellow in History at Hillsdale College, where over the past decade I sought to draw out my colleagues about World War II, especially President Larry Arnn and Professors Tom Connor, Mark Kalthoff, and Paul Rahe. I also thank colleague Al Phillip of Hillsdale, who has partnered with me in leading annual military history tours of Europe over the last ten years, and helped to arrange visits to many of the major World War II battlefields and cities of conflict in war-torn Europe.

My friend of over thirty years, Professor Bruce Thornton, gave me his characteristic insight about the war and literature of the 1930s. My former editor at Encounter Books, Peter Collier, kindly read a rough draft of the manuscript, and I have profited greatly from his accustomed good sense and astute editorial advice—as well as from Professor Williamson Murray, whose vast knowledge of World War II is unmatched, and who generously offered a number of insightful suggestions, saving me from a number of wrong notions. Neither is responsible for any errors that have remained. Roger and Susan Hertog have been staunch supporters, and for over a decade I have valued Roger's sound judgment on foreign affairs and security issues, past and present.

Lara Heimert, publisher of Basic Books, inspired me to write on World War II. Otherwise, I might never have undertaken this book. I thank Roger Labrie, a senior editor at Basic; Karl Yambert, my copyeditor; and Lara, for carefully editing the manuscript and helping me to clarify my thoughts and approaches. My literary agents of three decades Glen Hartley and Lynn Chu of Writers' Representatives, along with Lara, encouraged me to think about writing a different history of World War II; once again I am indebted to Glen and Lynn for their expertise and my link with the publishing world from the distance of rural California.

My son Bill Hanson and daughter Pauli Steinback as usual offered steady encouragement and support, especially during the sudden and shared loss of our dear Susannah, daughter and sister, whose love of the past was matched by her constant enthusiasm and advice to persevere in the present, and whose weekly calls about the progress of this book helped me to finish it. I was so fortunate to have had the love and friendship of such a kind and gentle person, even for so brief a time.

Throughout the two years of writing and research, my wife and friend, Jennifer, offered her steady guidance and good sense—and lots of ideas when walking battlefields, whether on Omaha Beach, at Bastogne, or across Sicily.

I finish this book in my sixty-third year in the farmhouse of my great-great grandmother, Lucy Anna Davis. My own more recent memories of all who have lived here before me—grandparents Rees and Georgia Davis, parents Pauline and William Hanson, siblings Alfred and Nels Hanson, and cousins Maren and Rees Nielsen—and their shared love of the land have always made it a perfect place in which to write, remember, and commemorate. It was here as a small boy that I first learned to appreciate the terrible sacrifices of World War II from the dining-room discussions of family, agrarians, neighbors, and veterans who believed that their various Second World Wars were tragic and hellish—but still worth fighting even in such faraway and often deadly places.

*VDH*
*Selma, California*
*August 2017*

# PART ONE

---

# IDEAS

When, where, and why did they fight?

*In a war of ideas it is people who get killed.*

—Stanisław Jerzy Lec[1]

# 1

# The War in a Classical Context

S OME SIXTY MILLION people died in World War II.
On average, twenty-seven thousand people perished on each day between
the invasion of Poland (September 1, 1939) and the formal surrender of Japan (September 2, 1945)—bombed, shot, stabbed, blown apart, incinerated, gassed, starved, or infected. The Axis losers killed or starved to death about 80 percent of all those who died during the war. The Allied victors largely killed Axis soldiers; the defeated Axis, mostly civilians.

More German and Russian soldiers were killed in tanks at Kursk (well over 2,000 tanks lost) than at any other battle of armor in history. The greatest loss of life of both civilians and soldiers on a single ship (9,400 fatalities) occurred when a Soviet submarine sank the German troop transport *Wilhelm Gustloff* in the Baltic Sea in January 1945. The costliest land battle in history took place at Stalingrad; Leningrad was civilization's most lethal siege. The death machinery of the Holocaust made past mass murdering from Attila to Tamerlane to the Aztecs seem like child's play. The deadliest single day in military history occurred in World War II during the March 10, 1945, firebombing of Tokyo, when a hundred thousand people, perhaps many more, lost their lives. The only atomic bombs ever dropped in war immediately killed more than a hundred thousand people at Hiroshima and Nagasaki together, most of them civilians, while tens of thousands more ultimately died and were maimed from radiation exposure. World War II exhausted superlatives. Its carnage seemed to re-invent ideas of war altogether.

YET HOW, WHY, and where the war broke out were familiar factors. The sophisticated technology and totalitarian ideologies of World War II should not blind us to the fact that the conflict was fought on familiar ground in predictable climates and weather by humans whose natures were unchanged since antiquity and thus who went to war, fought, and forged a peace according to time-honored precepts. Reformulated ancient ideas of racial and cultural superiority fueled the global bloodbath between 1939 and 1945, which was ostensibly started to prove that some ideologies were better, or at least more powerful, than others. Nazi Germany certainly believed that other, supposedly inherently spiritually weaker Western nations—Britain and France in particular—had conspired since World War I to prevent the expression of naturally dominant German power. In his memoirs, Grand Admiral Karl Doenitz, Commander-in-Chief of the Kriegsmarine, the German navy, after January 1943, summed up accurately the German justification for the war: "Britain went to war in 1939 because Greater Germany, growing in strength and united with Austria, was becoming a menace to British imperial and economic interests." Notice how Doenitz's key phrase, "Britain went to war," assumes that the German invasion of Poland was the result of victimization and grievance and thus should not have provoked a wider war.[1]

By 1939, Germans had concluded that the postwar policies of the Western European nations were unfair, vindictive, and, with some tolerable sacrifices, correctible, given the rebirth of Germany under a uniquely powerful National Socialism. An unfettered Germany would establish hegemony throughout Europe, even if that effort might require dramatic changes in current borders, substantial population exchanges, and considerable deaths, though mostly of non-Germans. In time, both Fascist Italy (which had invaded both Ethiopia and Albania prior to September 1, 1939) and Japan (which had invaded China well over two years before the German attack on Poland) felt that if Hitler could take such risks—as he had throughout 1939–1941 in apparently successful fashion—then they too might take a gamble to share in the spoils. Perceived self-interest—and a sense of the ancient Greek historian Thucydides's realist notion of honor and fear—as much as ideological affinity, explained which power entered the war, or left it, or chose to remain neutral.

World War II was conceived and fought as a characteristic Western war in which classical traditions of free markets, private property, unfettered natural inquiry, personal freedom, and a secular tradition had for centuries often translated to greater military dynamism in Europe than elsewhere. If the conflict's unique savagery and destructiveness can only be appreciated through the lenses of twentieth-century ideology, technology, and industry, its origins and end still followed larger contours of conflict as they developed over 2,500 years of civilized history. The Western military's essence had remained unchanged but it was now delivered at an unprecedented volume and velocity, and posed a specter of death on a massive scale. The internecine war was largely fought with weaponry and technology that were birthed in the West, although also used by Westernized powers in Asia. The atomic bombs, napalm, guided missiles, and multi-engine bombers of World War II confirmed a general truth that for over two millennia the war making of Europe and its appendages had proven brutal against the non-West, but when its savage protocols and technology were turned upon itself, the corpses mounted in an unfathomable fashion.

STARTING WARS IS far easier than ending them. Since the Peloponnesian War (431–404 BC) between Athens and Sparta and their allies, winning—and finishing—a war was predicated on finding ways to end an enemy's ability to fight, whether materially or psychologically. The Axis and the Allies had radically different ideas of how the wars of World War II would eventually conclude—with the Allies sharing a far better historical appreciation of the formulas that always put a final end to conflicts. When World War II broke out in 1939, Germany did not have a serious plan for defeating any of those enemies, present or future, that were positioned well beyond its own borders. Unlike its more distant adversaries, the Third Reich had neither an adequate blue-water navy nor a strategic bombing fleet, anchored by escort fighters and heavy bombers of four engines whose extended ranges and payloads might make vulnerable the homelands of any new enemies on the horizon. Hitler did not seem to grasp that the four most populous countries or territories in the world—China, India, the Soviet Union, and the United States—were either fighting against the Axis or opposed to its agendas. Never before or since had all these peoples (well over one billion total) fought at once and on the same side.

Not even Napoleon had declared war in succession on so many great powers without any idea how to destroy their ability to make war, or, worse yet, in delusion that tactical victories would depress stronger enemies into submission. Operation Sea Lion, Germany's envisioned invasion of Britain, remained a pipe dream—and yet it offered the only plausible way to eliminate Britain from the war that Hitler had started. Grand Admiral Erich Raeder, then head of the Kriegsmarine, repeatedly warned Hitler that an amphibious invasion of Britain in 1940 was quite impossible. After explaining why the German navy was unable to transport hundreds of thousands of troops across the Channel, Raeder flatly concluded, "I could not recommend a landing in England." After the war, Field Marshal General Wilhelm Keitel agreed that the military was not up to the task and was relieved that Hitler finally conceded as much:

"I very much worried. I fully realized that we would have to undertake this invasion with small boats that were not seaworthy. Therefore, at that time I had fully agreed with the decision of the Fuehrer." The invasion of Russia, codenamed Operation Barbarossa, would prove a rerun of the early successes of blitzkrieg in precisely the one theater where it would be nearly impossible to conduct it effectively—an operation that Raeder in hindsight claimed to have opposed, desperately but vainly advising Hitler that "under no circumstances should we go to war with Russia."[2]

War's eternal elements—a balance between powers, deterrence versus appeasement, collective security, preemption and preventive attacks, and peace brought by victory, humiliation, and occupation—still governed the conflict. As was true in most past conflicts, the publics in Axis countries, regardless of the odiousness of fascist ideology, supported the war when Germany, Italy, and Japan were deemed to be winning. Even the liberal German historian Friedrich Meinecke was caught up in the German euphoria following the sudden collapse of France in 1940: "And to have regained Strasbourg! How could a man's heart not beat a little faster at this? After all, building up an army of millions in the space of only four years and rendering it capable of such achievements has been an astonishing and arguably the greatest and the most positive accomplishment of the Third Reich." The classical Greek historian Thucydides, who so often focused on the Athenian public's wild shifts in reaction to perceived battlefield victories or defeats, could not have captured any better the mercurial exhilaration at the thought of decisive military success.[3]

The pulse of the war also reflected another classical dictum: the winning side is the one that most rapidly learns from its mistakes, makes the necessary corrections, and most swiftly responds to new challenges—in the manner that land-power Sparta finally built a far better navy while the maritime Athenians never fielded an army clearly superior to its enemies, or the land-power Rome's galleys finally became more effective than were the armies of the sea-power Carthage. The Anglo-Americans, for example, more quickly rectified flaws in their strategic bombing campaign—by employing longer-range fighter escorts, recalibrating targeting, integrating radar into air-defense networks, developing novel tactics, and producing more and better planes and crews—than did Germany in its bombing against Britain. America would add bombers and crews at a rate unimaginable for Germany. The result was that during six months of the Blitz (September 1940 to February 1941), the Luftwaffe, perhaps the best strategic bombing force in the world in late 1939 through mid-1940, dropped only thirty thousand tons of bombs on Britain. In contrast, in the half year between June and November 1944, Allied bombers dropped twenty times that tonnage on Germany.[4]

The same asymmetry was true at sea, especially in the Battle of the Atlantic. The Allied leadership made operational changes and technological improvements of surface ships and planes far more rapidly than could the U-boats of the Kriegsmarine. America adapted to repair and produce aircraft carriers and train new crews at a pace inconceivable in Japan. The Allies—including the Soviet Union on most occasions—usually avoided starting theater wars that ended in multiyear infantry quagmires. In contrast, Japan, Germany, and Italy respectively bogged down in China, the Soviet Union, and North Africa and the Balkans.

The importance of the classical geography of war is also unchanging. Ostensibly the Mediterranean should not have mattered in a twentieth-century war that broke out in Eastern Europe. The nexus of European power and influence had long ago shifted far northward, following the expansion of hostile Ottoman power into the western Mediterranean, the discovery of the New World, the Reformation, the British and French Enlightenments, and the Industrial Revolution. But the Mediterranean world connected three continents and had remained even more crucial after the completion of the Suez Canal for European transit to Asia and the Pacific. The Axis "spine" was predicated on a north-south corridor of fascist-controlled rail lines connecting ports on the Baltic with those on the Mediterranean. Without the Mediterranean, the British Empire could not easily coordinate its global commerce and communications. It was no wonder, then, that North Africa, Italy, and Greece became early battlegrounds, as did the age-old strategic stepping-stones across the Mediterranean at Crete, Malta, and Sicily that suffered either constant bombing or invasions.

British, American, Italian, and German soldiers often found themselves fortifying or destroying the Mediterranean stonework of the Romans, Byzantines, Franks, Venetians, and Ottomans. Gibraltar still remained unconquerable. Without a viable plan to attack it on land and from its Iberian rear, the Axis gave up taking the fortress, as had every aggressor that had coveted it since the British annexation of 1713. That Germany and Italy would try to wage war on the Mediterranean and in North Africa without serious attempts to invade Gibraltar and Malta is a testament to their ignorance of history.[5]

Still other classical precedents were forgotten. Western military history showed, but was apparently again dismissed by Allied planners, that it was often difficult to start a campaign northward up the narrow backbone of the Italian Peninsula. What usually started in Sicily petered out in mid-peninsula, given the ease of defense in the narrow mountainous terrain of the Apennines with seas on both flanks. Hannibal and Napoleon alone seemed to have believed that Italy was best conquered from the north rather than the south. Nor had Europeans ever had much success trying to attack Russia from the west. Despite the grand efforts of Swedes, French, and Germans, the expanses were always too wide, the barriers too numerous, the window of good weather too brief—and the Russians were too many and too warlike on their own soil. Planes and tanks did not change those realities. Germany's problem in particular was that its two most potent enemies, Britain and Russia, were also the hardest to reach. While Germany's central European location was convenient for bullying the French and Eastern Europeans, its British and Russian existential enemies enjoyed both land and sea buffers from the vaunted German army.

The Allies were surprised that Hitler staged two invasions through the Ardennes in southeast Belgium. But in addition to the examples of World War I, the critically located rough terrain had been a nexus for passing armies since it was first mentioned in Caesar's *Gallic Wars* and later became a favorite campaign ground of Charlemagne. Invading a united Britain historically had also usually proved a bad idea. Not since the Romans and William the Conqueror had any military seriously tried an amphibious landing on the British coasts. Far more easily, the British and their allies—from the Hundred Years' War to World War I—landed troops on the Western European Atlantic coastline, which, being longer, was harder to defend and not often politically united. Motor vehicles and bombers did not reinvent the military geography of Europe during World War II.

After the age of Napoleon, no southern European power on the Mediterranean was able on its own to match northern European nations. World War II was again no exception. Italy was the first of the Axis to capitulate. The Iberians wisely stayed out of the war. Greece was easily defeated by the Germans. North Africans were largely spectators to lethal European warfare taking place in their midst. Turkey remained neutral for most of the war. If World War II was fought across the globe, its ultimate course was still largely determined by northern European states and their former colonies in a way that was true of all European wars since the late eighteenth century.

Over twenty-four hundred years ago, the historian Thucydides had emphasized the military advantages of sea powers, particularly their ability to control commerce and move troops. Not much had changed since antiquity, as the oceans likewise mattered a great deal to the six major belligerents in World War II. Three great powers were invaded during the war: Germany, Italy, and Russia. Three were not: America, Britain, and Japan. All the former were on the European landmass, the latter were either islands or distant and bounded by two vast oceans. Amphibious operations originating on the high seas were a far more difficult matter than crossing borders, or in the case of Italy, crossing from Sicily onto the mainland.

The protection afforded Great Britain and the United States by surrounding seas meant that containing the German threat was never the existential challenge for them that it always was for the Western Europeans. The generals of the French may have always appeared cranky to the Anglo-Americans, but then, neither Britain nor America had a common border with Germany. The only way for Germany to strike Britain was to invade and occupy the French and Belgian coasts, as reflected both in the German *Septemberprogramm* of 1914 and in Hitler's obsessions with the Atlantic ports between 1940 and 1945. Since the fifteenth century, European countries that faced the Atlantic had natural advantages over those whose chief home ports were confined to the North, Baltic, and Mediterranean Seas.

Even if weaker than Germany, the islands of Japan nevertheless made an Allied invasion a far more difficult proposition than would crossing the Rhine or Oder into Germany. In fact, no modern power had ever completed a successful invasion of the Japanese homeland, a fact well known to Allied planners who wished to, and did, avoid the prospect through dominant air power.

Japan's various strategic choices in 1941 were predicated a great deal on traditional geographical considerations. Japan could further reinforce its decade-long presence in China, or in June 1941 join Hitler by attacking the Soviet Union from the east, or absorb more orphaned colonial territory in Asia and the Pacific, or allow the Imperial Navy to begin new wars against the United States and Britain because it was an island sea power with few immediate worries about ground invasions or enemy amphibious landings. Left unspoken was the fact that in almost all these geographical scenarios, an often xenophobic and resource hungry Japan had few friends. It had alienated the Western powers during the 1930s, invaded China in 1937, fought the Soviets in 1939, and been aggressive toward India; it was disliked and distrusted in the Pacific and unable to partner effectively with its own Axis allies.

Any eastward expansion of twentieth-century Japan into the Pacific depended also on the status of its western geography. If either Russia or China were to be hostile—and both usually were—by definition Japan would be faced with an uninviting two-front war. In World War II, the bulk of Japanese ground forces—over six hundred thousand at any given time—was fighting in China, where over a half-million Japanese soldiers eventually perished. Japan was willing to risk a two-front war after its nonaggression pact with the Soviet Union in April 1941, given that the Chinese front was mostly stalemated, but it never envisioned the possibility that Pearl Harbor would lead to a three-theater conflict in which Japan would be fighting China, the United States, and finally the Russians. Because pulling out of the Chinese morass was deemed unacceptable by the government of General and Prime Minister Hideki Tojo, and given that the Imperial Japanese Army had already fared poorly against the Russians from 1932 to 1939 along the Mongolian border, Japan felt its best choice of aggression was a surprise "preemptory" naval air attack on the geographically distant Americans, who allegedly might soon have attacked Japan or would eventually have strangled its importation of key resources. General Tojo told the Japanese war cabinet that he had thought of all the alternatives "until it makes my head ache, but the conclusion always is that war is unavoidable."[6]

Weather was also never superseded by twentieth-century technology, but as in ancient times it often shaped the battlefield, as it had in the storms that sank much of King Xerxes's fleet at Artemisium during the Persian invasion of Greece (480 BC), the scorching heat that sapped the Crusaders at Hattin (1187) and cost them a catastrophic defeat against Saladin and the Muslims, or the rain-soaked ground that hampered Napoleon's artillery and cavalry movements in his defeat at Waterloo (1815). To the end of the war, Germans argued that the early and unusually harsh winter of 1941 had robbed them of two critical weeks at Moscow— and when that window closed, so did any chance of victory. Inhuman cold stymied airlifts to German troops at Stalingrad and the attempts at evacuation of units that became surrounded there. Fog stalled airborne reinforcements to British forces at Arnhem in 1944, contributing to the German repulse of a major Allied initiative. Strong winds and clouds in part forced General Curtis LeMay to change tactics by taking his B-29s to lower elevations and dropping incendiary rather than general-purpose bombs, thereby setting Tokyo afire with napalm. Generals and admirals, like their ancient counterparts, often predictably blamed the weather for their failures, as if they assumed in their plans that nature should be predictably compliant rather than fickle and savage.

BY 1939, GERMANY had entered its third European war within seventy years, following World War I (1914–1918) and, before that, the

Franco-Prussian War (1870–1871). Conflicts throughout history become serial when an enemy is not utterly defeated and is not forced to submit to the political conditions of the victor, whether in the two Peloponnesian or three Punic Wars, or the later Hundred Years' and Seven Years' Wars. Such was the case with the preludes to World War II, when many of the major familiar nations of the European world were again at war. Germany was once more the aggressor. That fact also helped spawn the familiar idea of "World War II" and its alternative designation, the "Second World War." Yet this time around, both sides tacitly agreed that there would not be a World War III—either Germany would finally achieve its near century-long dream of European dominance or cease to exist as a National Socialist state and military power. Yet the Allies understood history far better: in any existential war, only the side that has the ability to destroy the homeland of the other wins.

The war, also like many conflicts of the past, was certainly chronologically inexact, with two official denouements known in the Anglosphere as V-E and V-J Day. The war, like many, was also ill-defined, especially for a country such as Bulgaria, to take one minor example, which had no common interests or communications with its nominal Pacific ally Japan. Likewise, the Greeks were indifferent to the war against fascism in China, and in the same way the Soviet Union cared little whether Italy had invaded France.[7]

Often border disputes on the periphery of Germany, ethnic hatreds in Eastern Europe and the Balkans, and political grievances and national ambitions set off regional wars that were only with hindsight lumped all together as World War II, at least in Britain and the United States. Most sides had hopes of allying their parochial causes to larger ideological crusades. But far more important, they just wanted to join the right side of strong allies that might be likely winners and divvy up spoils. General Francisco Franco's fascist government in Spain was emblematic of such opportunism that transcended ideological affinities. During 1939–1941, Franco—despite horrendous recent losses in the Spanish Civil War and despite Hitler's occasional rebuffs—considered possible entrance into the war on the Axis side. Franco assumed that the Allies would likely be defeated and there might be colonial spoils in North Africa allotted to Spain. He often boasted that Spain might unilaterally take Gibraltar or enlist hundreds of thousands of warriors to the Axis cause. But between 1943 and 1944, Spain increasingly began to reassert its neutrality, in recognition that the Axis powers would now likely lose the war and their war-won territories—and prior allegiance might earn an Allied invasion and with it a change of government. By late 1944, Fascist Spain was no longer exporting tungsten to Germany and was instead reinvented as sympathetic to British and American democracy and eager to become an anticommunist ally after the war.[8]

At any given time, any given people—the Finns in 1939, the Italians, Russians, and Chinese in 1940, the Americans in summer 1941—found it difficult to define the world war that had really been triggered by the German invasion of Poland. After the war began in 1939, America imposed a boycott on the Soviet Union over its surprise invasion of Finland, only soon to reverse course and provide arms to the once-blacklisted Russians to defeat the once-noble victim, Finland. Both Britain and Germany had long courted Italy and the Soviet Union as allies and vice versa. Japan occupied Vichy-held Indochina, although both Japan and Vichy France were nominal allies of Germany. Soviet leader Joseph Stalin signed pacts or came to formal and informal agreements of nonaggression with *all* the major belligerents at one time or another.

WHAT QUALIFIES A conflict as a world war? Despite its title, World War I had never really been truly global. Africa was largely left out of it, save for small, regional battles in the interior and the hundreds of thousands of Africans who joined colonial armies in Europe and the Middle East. Outside of the Middle East and Turkey, mainland Asia was also mostly immune from the carnage. There was little frequent surface fighting on the high seas, apart from the waters around Europe and Britain, and in the Mediterranean. Air power was in its infancy. Neither North American nor Australian territory was attacked. The Arctic saw little combat.

In fact, until 1941 there had never been a global war. Even the bloodiest wars of the past were theater conflicts. The so-called Persian Wars (490–479 BC) were really only about the annexation of Ionia and the Greek mainland as the westernmost provinces of the Persian Empire. Alexander the Great fought a Greek, Asian, and North African war (335–323 BC), yet left the western Mediterranean alone. Carthage versus Rome was mostly a Mediterranean affair that drew in only local North African tribesmen, southern Europeans, and the vestiges of Macedonian power in Greece (264–146 BC). The Crusades were essentially one-dimensional campaigns across the eastern Mediterranean to the Middle East. The Hundred Years' War (1337–1453) or the destructive American Civil War (1861–1865) never became global.

Rome's legions and galleys from the first and second centuries BC had been deployed in Africa, Western Europe, Asia, and throughout the Mediterranean. But they did not fight all at once and not much elsewhere.

Although Winston Churchill described the Seven Years' War (1754/1756–1763) as "the first world war," it was not, given that China and Japan were not involved, and most peoples in India, Asia, South America, and Africa were only tangentially affected. Napoleon's twelve years of warring (1803–1815) perhaps came closest to becoming a worldwide conflict among dozens of enemies. Its subsidiary and affiliated conflicts spread beyond Europe and Russia to some major fighting in North Africa, the Middle East, the Mediterranean, the Atlantic, and North America. Perhaps five million perished in the two decades of the Napoleonic Wars. But in general, the idea of world wars has been absent in history. Even the few intercontinental conflicts that took place were not necessarily any more destructive than more frequent border conflicts. World War II changed all that.[9]

Only in retrospect did historians and veterans begin to equate the various wars around the world between 1939 (or perhaps as early as 1931–1937 in the case of Japan) and 1945 as part of a thematic conflict. And yet not everywhere. The French who were defeated in June 1940 never warmed to the idea of a World War II that they had bowed out of for four years. The Soviets—who believed that they alone had defeated Nazi Germany, which was the only real focus of their war—saw the "Great Patriotic War" as theirs alone. But then in the past, the tsars likewise had used the same self-referential nomenclature for their "patriotic" wars against Napoleon of France and Kaiser Wilhelm II of Germany.

Such reformulations and rebranding happen frequently throughout history. The "Peloponnesian War," for example, was an invention largely of Thucydides in the late fifth century BC. Unlike many of his contemporaries, the Athenian veteran and ex-admiral saw in hindsight that lots of successive wars and interludes—the Archidamian War, the Peace of Nicias, the Sicilian War, the Decelean War, and the Ionian War—were all fought between 431 and 404 BC as a single, if episodic, conflict. The decade-long Persian Wars and the century-long Punic Wars likewise came to be known in such comprehensive fashion only *after* the final battles in the defeat of Persia and Carthage, respectively. In that sense, some have seen World War II as properly part of a continual transatlantic versus German "Thirty Years' War" that broke out in 1914, quieted down in 1918, then went through Thucydidean cycles of calm and tension before being renewed in 1939 and ended, it seems, for good in 1945.[10]

CONFUSION CHARACTERIZED PRELUDES to war during the 1930s. Initially the democracies had naively assumed that even non-democratic

European nations such as Nazi Germany and Fascist Italy might at least share a common age-old Western religion, pedigree, and history and thus be familiar, somewhat rational, and have no desire to repeat the appalling bloodletting of the Somme and Verdun in 1916. Given the tragedy of World War I, Hitler's Germany surely would appreciate the need for negotiation and concessions and thus agree to iron out differences through diplomacy, without again resorting to suicidal violence. Such patience and naiveté only eroded classical deterrence and encouraged further Nazi aggrandizement.

Most wars since antiquity can be defined as the result of such flawed prewar assessments of relative military and economic strength as well as strategic objectives. Prewar Nazi Germany had no accurate idea of how powerful were Great Britain, the United States, and the Soviet Union; and the latter had no inkling of the full scope of Hitler's military ambitions. It took a world war to educate them all.

Throughout history, conflict had always broken out between enemies when the appearance of deterrence—the material and spiritual likelihood of using greater military power successfully against an aggressive enemy—vanished. From Carthage to the Confederacy, weaker bellicose states could convince themselves of the impossible because their fantasies were not checked earlier by cold reality. A stronger appearance of power, and of the willingness to employ it, might have stopped more conflicts before they began. Put another way, deterrence in the famous formulation of the seventeenth-century British statesman George Savile, 1st Marquess of Halifax, meant that "men are not hanged for stealing horses, but that horses may not be stolen."[11]

But once thieves were not hanged and more horses were indeed stolen, who is strong and who weak became confusing, and the proper recalibration that pruned rhetoric and posturing from knowledge of real strength returned only at the tremendous cost of a world war. Hitler's *Mein Kampf*—"the new Koran of faith and war" according to Winston Churchill—was in truth a puerile rant that gained credence only through German rearmament and aggressiveness, at least before Stalingrad. After that battle, Hitler was no longer read widely and was only rarely heard by Germans, as the ambitions of the Third Reich waned and Nazi Germany was exposed as far weaker than its enemies and led by an incompetent strategist. The prewar reality was that Russian armor was superior to German. Inexplicably, the Soviets had not been able to communicate that fact, and in consequence lost deterrence. Hitler later remarked that had he just been made aware of the nature of Russian tank production, and specifically about the T-34 tank, against which standard German anti-tank weapons were ineffective, he would never have invaded the Soviet Union. Maybe. But it took a theater war in the East that killed over thirty million people to reveal the Soviets' real power. Accordingly, leaders and their followers are forced to make the necessary readjustments, although often at a terrible price of correcting flawed prewar impressions.[12]

In the case of the timidity of the Western democracies in 1938–1939, General Walter Warlimont explained Hitler's confidence about powers that easily could have deterred Germany: "(1) he felt their [the Allies'] Far Eastern interests were more important than their European interests, and (2) they did not appear to be armed sufficiently." What a terrible cost ensued to prove Hitler wrong.[13]

Only after the disastrous battles of Leipzig (1813) and Waterloo (1815) did Napoleon finally concede that his armies had never been a match for the combined strength of Russia, Prussia, Austria, Sweden, and England. Had all those states combined in a firm coalition a decade earlier, Napoleon might well have been deterred. Churchill without much exaggeration said of Hitler's military agenda, "up till 1934 at least, German rearmament could have been prevented without the loss of a single life. It was not time that was lacking."[14]

By any fair measure, Germany in 1939—in terms of the number and quality of planes, armor, manpower reserves, and industrial output—was not stronger than the combined French and British militaries—or at least not so strong as to be able to defeat and occupy *both* powers. The later German-Italian-Japanese axis was far less impressive than the alliance that would soon emerge of Great Britain, America, and Russia—having only little over a third of the three Allies' combined populations, not to speak of their productive capacity. After all, the United States by war's end in 1945 would achieve a wartime gross national product nearly greater than that of all of the other Allied and Axis powers combined.[15]

In sum, sixty million dead, twentieth-century totalitarian ideologies, the singular evil of Adolf Hitler, the appearance of V-2 rockets, the dropping of two atomic bombs, the Holocaust, napalm, kamikazes, and the slaughter of millions in Russia and China seemed to redefine World War II as unlike any conflict of the past—even as predictable humans with unchanging characteristics, fighting amid age-old geography and weather patterns, continued to follow the ancient canons of war and replayed roles well known from the ages.

Why the Western world—which was aware of the classical lessons and geography of war, and was still suffering from the immediate trauma of the First World War—chose to tear itself apart in 1939 is a story not so much of accidents, miscalculations, and overreactions (although there were plenty of those, to be sure) as of the carefully considered decisions to ignore, appease, or collaborate with Adolf Hitler's Nazi Germany by nations that had the resources and knowledge, but not yet the willpower, to do otherwise.

# 2

# Grievances, Agendas, and Methods

THE CAUSES OF World War II were many. Age-old border and national grievances sparked tensions. There was not just general unhappiness of both the winners and losers of World War I over the Versailles Treaty that had supposedly ended the conflict and established a lasting peace, but also real furor at a settlement variously labeled as either too soft or too hard—and increasingly seen on all sides as unsustainable.

Neither of the prior two German wars—the Franco-Prussian War and World War I—had solved the perennial problem of a unified, dynamic, and nationalist Germany in the heart of Europe. And by the 1930s these tensions were energized by twentieth-century fascist technologies and ideologies. The result was a veritable fantasyland that grew up in the late 1930s in both Europe and Asia, in which citizens of the intrinsically weaker Axis powers, both industrially and technologically, were considered supermen, while real Allied supermen lost their confidence and were despised by their enemies as unserious lightweights.

What followed was the central tragic irony of World War II: the weaker Axis powers proved incapable of defeating their Allied enemies on the field of battle, but nevertheless were more adept at killing far more of them and their civilian populations. World War II is one of the few major wars in history in which the losing side killed far more soldiers than did the winners, and far more civilians died than soldiers. And rarely in past conflicts had the losers of a war initially won so much so quickly with far less material and human resources than was available to the eventual winners. In sum, World War II started in a bizarre fashion, progressed even more unpredictably, and, in the technological sense, ended in nightmarish ways never before envisioned. The shock of the war was not just its historic devastation and brutality, but that such unprecedented savagery appeared a logical dividend of twentieth-century technology and ideology—a century in which enlightened elites had promised at last an end to all wars, and shared global peacekeeping as well as new machines and customs to make life wealthier, more secure, and more enjoyable than at any time in history.

WORLD WAR II is generally regarded to have begun on September 1, 1939. Germany invaded Poland—for the third time in seventy years crossing the borders of its European neighbors. Hitler's aggression prompted a declaration of war on Germany by Britain two days later. Most of the British Empire and France joined in, at least in theory. Seventeen days later, the Soviet Red Army, assuming that it would not be fighting Japan simultaneously, entered Poland to divide the spoils of this ruined and soon-to-disappear nation with Nazi Germany.[1]

The later Axis of Germany, Italy, and Japan had participated in small wars prior to September 1939 in Spain, Abyssinia, and Manchuria. But none of those aggressions—nor even the Nazi 1938–1939 absorption of much of Czechoslovakia—had prompted a collective military response from the European democracies. Throughout history larger states have more frequently blamed their smaller and often distant allies for entangling them in wars than they have rushed to prevent or end those wars. In 1938 few in Paris or London had wished to die for Czechoslovakia, or to stop the Axis agenda of incrementally absorbing borderlands far from the Western capitals. In September 1939 few wanted to fight for Poland—at least if they believed that the war itself would end with the end of Poland. The Soviet ambassador to Britain, Ivan Maisky, recorded a conversation in November 1939 he had with Lord Beaverbrook, who illustrated British fears just ten weeks into the war: "I'm an isolationist. What concerns me is the fate of the British Empire! I want the Empire to remain intact, but I don't understand why for the sake of this we must wage a three-year war to crush 'Hitlerism.' To hell with that man Hitler! If the Germans want him, I happily concede them this treasure and make my bow. Poland? Czechoslovakia? What are they to do with us? Cursed be the day when Chamberlain gave our guarantees to Poland!"

If recorded accurately, Beaverbrook's words were in fact not that different from Hitler's own initial feelings about Britain, which, he felt, should have stayed out of a European land war, kept its empire, and made a deal with the Third Reich about their respective hegemonies: "The English are behaving as if they were stupid. The reality will end by calling them to order, by compelling them to open their eyes." Being neutral is by design a choice, with results that either harm or hurt the particular belligerents in question—with neutrality almost always aiding the aggressive carnivore, not its victim. Or as the Indian statesman and activist

V. K. Krishna Menon cynically once put it, "there can be no more positive neutrality than there can be a vegetarian tiger."[2]

Still, Hitler was for a moment dumbfounded—"unpleasantly surprised," in the words of Winston Churchill—that the supposedly enfeebled Allies had at least nominally declared war over Poland. It was
natural that Hitler should be taken aback, given the fact that his new nonaggression pact, signed with the Soviet Union on August 23, 1939, had
eliminated, he had hoped, the specter of a World War I–like, two-front
continental war. After all, Poland's fate had always been to be divvied up,
given that it had been partitioned on at least four previous occasions. Hitler soon recovered as he sensed that even though the Allies had declared
war, there was little likelihood that they would ever wage it wholeheartedly. Moreover, Hitler envisioned something different for Poland: not just
a quick defeat, but the "annihilation" of the state altogether in a manner
that would be "harsh and remorseless." Poland would disappear before
the dithering Allies could do much about it, and would teach them of the
unpredictable nihilism of the Third Reich.[3]

Yet the duplicitous German and Russian attack on Poland, digested
over the ensuing eight months of occupation, slowly did change ideas of
going to war in France and Britain. Poland's quick end was seen as the
final provocation in a long series of Hitler's aggressive acts that had left

Growth of the Third Reich, 1933–1941

the Western enemies of Germany deeply angered but also abjectly embarrassed and terribly afraid. For the shamed Western Europeans who were for a time snapped out of their lethargy, Hitler's stopping at Poland in September 1939 was suddenly seen to be as unlikely as the earlier beliefs that the Nazis would have ceased their aggressions after Germany's 1938 annexations of Austria or the Sudetenland, Czechoslovakia's German-speaking areas bordering Germany and Austria. Certainly, Hitler had an agenda that transcended even that of the Kaiser's and that could not be accommodated through concessions and diplomacy. The combined invasion of Poland also destroyed the unspoken democratic assumption that the evils of Nazism nonetheless would prove useful in shielding the West from the savagery of Russian Bolshevism. If Hitler had now made arrangements with the Soviet Union, then little was left of the amoral realpolitik that had excused Nazi brutality in exchange for keeping Stalinism away from the Western democracies.[4]

Hitler went to the trouble of dropping leaflets over Britain to convince the British not to see the loss of Poland as a legitimate cause to pursue their declared war against Germany. But the potential for a wider war was already looming. Aside from the pivotal global role of the British Empire, there were soon alliances with, and enemies against, Germany on several continents—Australia, Asia, North America, and eventually South America. Nations declared war on one another without full appreciation of the long-range potential of any of them to conduct a world war. This time around, the conflict grew far wider and far more deadly than in 1914, in part because the war of 1939 soon transcended the nineteenth-century European problem of containing the continental agendas of a dynamic, united, and aggrieved Imperial Germany, and technology had reduced both time and space. The new war after 1941 involved the political futures of hundreds of millions, far beyond the paths of the Rhine and Oder, and on all the continents, as battles on rare occasions reached the Arctic, Australia, and even South America. At one time or another, most of the world's greatest cities—Amsterdam, Antwerp, Athens, Berlin, Budapest, Leningrad, London, Moscow, Paris, Prague, Rome, Rotterdam, Shanghai, Singapore, Tokyo, Vienna, Warsaw, and Yokohama—could be reached by either bombers or armor, and were thus either bombed or besieged. By 1945 almost every nation in the world, with only eleven remaining neutral, was involved in the conflict.[5]

A STRANGE CONFLUENCE of events had not made the prewar reality of German, Italian, and Japanese collective weakness clear to the Allied powers until perhaps late 1942, after the victories at Stalingrad, El Al-amein, and Guadalcanal. That was some time after Adolf Hitler—then Benito Mussolini, and finally the Japanese militarists led by Hideki Tojo—had foolishly gambled otherwise in Russia, the Balkans, and the Pacific, earning the odd Allied alliance of common resistance against them. The Germans and Italians had cheaply earned the reputation of im-mense power by intervening successfully against a weak Loyalist army in the Spanish Civil War (1936–1939). They had showcased their late-model planes, artillery, and tanks—rightly seen as cutting-edge in the late 1930s but rarely acknowledged as near obsolete by 1941. Their power seemed to have illustrated to the world a desire to use brute force recklessly and to ignore moral objections or civilian casualties. Franco's Nationalists had won. The Loyalists, backed mostly by the Soviet Union and by Western volunteers, had lost.[6]

The Axis paradigm, at least in terms of infrastructure and armaments, seemed initially to have survived the Great Depression better than had the democracies of Western Europe and, in particular, the United States. In truth, America, for all its economic follies, had probably done as well as Germany in combatting the Depression, even though Hitler's showy public works projects received far more attention. Confident Axis powers boasted of a new motorized war to come on the ground and above. This gospel seemed confirmed by a parade to Berlin of visiting American and British military "experts," from aviator Charles Lindbergh to British tank guru J.F.C. Fuller. Most were hypnotized by Nazi braggadocio and pag-eantry rather than examination of precise armament output and relative quality of weapons. Few guessed that the hugely costly Nazi rearmament between 1934 and 1939 had nearly bankrupted the Third Reich but still had not given it parity in heavy bombers or capital ships with its likely enemies.

Mussolini and Hitler were far more frenzied leaders than those in Western Europe and America, and were able to feign a madness that was a valuable asset in prewar geopolitical poker. Both were wounded and bemedaled combat veterans of World War I from the enlisted ranks. A generation later, they now posed as authentic brawlers more willing to fight than their more rational Western Allied counterparts, who were led by aristocrats of the 1930s who had either been administrators or officers in the First World War. The antitheses were reminiscent of the historian Thucydides's warning about the insurrection on the island of Corcyra, where the successful "blunter wits" were more ready for prompt action than their more sophisticated opponents.[7]

By the 1930s, the aftermath of the so-called Great War had given birth to a sense of fatalism among the generation of its noncommissioned veterans. In almost all of Hitler's nocturnal rantings, he invoked the realism of the trenches of World War I, but in terms in which that nightmare steeled character rather than counselled caution. His lessons were quite different from the surrealism and occasional dark absurdity of Guillaume Apollinaire, Wilfred Owen, and Siegfried Sassoon, whose antiwar work found far larger international audiences than did that of their German counterparts. Perhaps more philosophical victors could afford to reflect on the war in its properly horrendous landscape; dejected losers by needs both romanticized their doomed bravery and found scapegoats for their defeat.

To the extent that they were prepared, the Allies for much of the 1920s and early 1930s seemed resigned, at least tactically, to refight the return of another huge slow-moving German army. They feared a future conflict as another mass collision of infantries plodding across the trenches (a conflict they had nonetheless won). As a result of such anxiety, the reconstituted allied powers in theory sought solutions to the Somme and Verdun in mobility and machines to avoid a return of the trenches. In reality, the preparations of those nations closest to Germany, such as France and Czechoslovakia, were more marked by reactionary static defensive fortifications. Concrete was impressive and of real value, but antithetical to the spirit of the mobile age and the doctrine of muscular retaliation. A geriatric French officer class and lack of tactical innovation and coordination meant that even had the Germans' main thrust targeted the concrete fortifications of the Maginot Line, it might well have succeeded.

The Depression-era democracies were also without confidence that their industrial potential would ever again be fully harnessed, as it had been in 1918, to produce superior offensive weapons in great numbers. The 1920s were a time for finally enjoying the much-deserved peace dividend, not for more sacrifices brought on by rearmament that could only lead to endless war with the same European players. Luftwaffe head Hermann Goering scoffed to the American news correspondent William Shirer in Berlin in November 1939, just two months after the invasion of Poland, "if we could only make planes at your rate of production, we should be very weak. I mean that seriously. Your planes are good, but you don't make enough of them fast enough."

Goering typically was quite wrong, but his errors at least reflected the German sense that the Allies had lost the power of deterrence, which is predicated not just on material strength but the appearance of it and the acknowledged willingness to use it. Even today, few note that French, British, and American plane production together in 1939 already exceeded that of Italy and Germany. The British were already flying early Stirling (first flight, May 1939) and Handley Page (first flight, October 1939) four-engine bomber prototypes, and the Americans were producing early-model B-17s (delivered as early as 1937). These antecedents were slow and sometimes unreliable (especially the British aircraft), but they gave the Allies early pathways to the use of heavy bombers that would soon be followed with improved and entirely new models. Most important, Allied aircraft factories were already gearing up to meet or exceed German fighter and bomber designs, even before America entered the war. Later the delusional Goering himself would deny that Allied fighter escorts could ever reach German airspace—at a time when they were routinely flying through it and were occasionally shot down inside the Third Reich.[8]

No matter. Almost every public proclamation that the Allies had voiced in the 1920s and early 1930s projected at least an appearance of timidity that invited war from what were still relatively weak powers. For the decade after Versailles, France, Britain, and the United States scaled back their militaries. All sought international agreements—the Washington Naval Conference (1921–1922), the Dawes Plan (1924), the Locarno Treaties (1925), the Kellogg-Briand Pact (1928), and the London Naval Conference (1930)—to tweak the Versailles Treaty, to limit arms on land and sea, to pledge peaceful intentions to one another, to showcase their virtue, to profess invincible solidarity, and even to declare war itself obsolete—anything other than to rebuild military power to shock and deter Germany. The prior victors and stronger powers yearned for collective security in the League of Nations; the former losers and weaker nations talked about unilateral action and ignored utopian organs of international peace. Democratic elites reinterpreted the success of stopping Germany and Austria in World War I as an ambiguous exercise without true winners and losers; Germans studied how clear losers like themselves could become unquestioned winners like their former enemies.

By the late 1920s, the victors of World War I were still arguing over whether the disaster had been caused as much by renegade international arms merchants as by aggressive Germans. Profit-mongering capitalists, archaic alliances, mindless automatic mobilizations, greedy bankers, and simple miscalculations and accidents were the supposed culprits—not the inability in 1914 once again to have deterred forceful Prussian militarism and German megalomania. British and French statesmen dreamed that Hitler might be an economic rationalist, and that new trade concessions could dampen his martial ardor. Or that he might be a realist who could see that a new war would cost Germany dearly. Or they downplayed Nazi racialist ideology as some sort of crass public veneer that hid logical German agendas. Or they saw Hitler as a useful—and transitory—tool for venting the frustrations of soberer German capitalists, aristocrats, and the Junker class. Or they believed National Socialism was a nasty but effective deterrent to Bolshevism.[9]

Consequently, when Chancellor Hitler acquired absolute power and was ratified as Führer on August 29, 1934, Allied statesmen assumed that the Germans would soon tire of their failed painter and Austrian corporal. Elites sometimes equate someone's prior failure to gain social status—or receive a graduate degree or make money—with incompetence or a lack of talent. Yet the pathetic Socialist pamphleteer and failed novelist Benito Mussolini, and the thuggish seminary dropout, bank robber, and would-be essayist Joseph Stalin—traditional failures all—proved nonetheless in nihilistic times to be astute political operatives far more gifted than most of their gentleman counterparts in the European democracies of the 1930s. The British statesman Anthony Eden lamented that few in Britain had ever encountered anyone quite like Hitler or Mussolini:

> You know, the hardest thing for me during that time was to convince my friends that Hitler and Mussolini were quite different *from British business men or country gentlemen* as regards their psychology, motivations and modes of action. My friends simply refused to believe me. They thought I was *biased* against the dictators and refused to understand them. I kept saying: "When you converse with the Führer or the Duce, you feel at once that you are dealing with an animal of an entirely different breed from yourself."[10]

The Western democracies at first failed to appreciate the extent to which Hitler's string of earlier spectacular diplomatic successes and easy initial blitzkrieg victories enthralled a depressed German people proud of a profound artistic and intellectual heritage. Cultured as they might have been, millions of the *Volk* saw no contradiction between High Culture and the base tenets of a National Socialism that steamrolled its opponents. Or, if anything, perhaps they sensed a symbiosis between the power of the German armed forces, the Wehrmacht, and the supremacy of Western civilization, as Hitler himself often ranted about opera, art, and architecture as the fruits of his victories deep into the night to his small, captive dinner audiences.

Panzer commander Hans von Luck related just such a cultural-military intersection, even during the dark December 1944 German retreat from the old Maginot Line on the French border. As Luck walked among the ruins of a bombed-out church, in the heat of battle, he suddenly saw an organ, and immediately showed himself to be a soldier of culture and sensitivity. "Through a gaping hole in the wall we went in. I stood facing the altar, which lay in ruins, and looked up at the organ. It seemed to be unharmed. A few more of our men came in. 'Come,' I called to a lance-corporal, 'we'll climb up to the organ.' On arriving above, I asked the man to tread the bellows. I sat down at the organ and—it was hardly believable—it worked. On the spur of the moment I began to play Bach's chorale *Nun danket alle Gott*. It resounded through the ruins to the outside." There was no apparent disconnect between fighting to protect National Socialist Germany and seeking to play Bach amid the wreckage of battle.[11]

EMOTIONS PUSH STATES to war as much as does greed. Materialists might argue that all three resource-starved Axis powers simply went to war for more natural wealth—ores, rubber, food stocks, and especially fuels. They wanted additional territory that belonged to someone else, usually someone weaker, in order to expand their influence and population beyond their recognized borders. Yet it did no good to point out to National Socialist leaders that Germany's large population, robust industry, and relatively little damage from the Great War made it likely to resume its role as a European powerhouse even without, for example, incorporating Austria, the Sudetenland, and western Poland. Nor would Hitler believe by late August 1939 that the Third Reich was already in Germany's best geostrategic position since its founding, with its largest population and territory since the birth of the German state. Germany had far more territory in September 1939 than it has today with a similarly sized population.

There was no longer a hostile Tsarist Russian Empire. There was no rivalry with an Austria-Hungary, no antagonistic and interventionist United States. France and Britain were both willing to compromise. Nazi Germany freely bought oil on the open market, often from North America. It had either renegotiated or reneged on, without consequences, any international agreement that it felt detrimental to its expansionist agenda. Germans were not starving. *Lebensraum* ("we demand land and territory for the nourishment of our people and for settling our surplus population") was not based on an existing shortage of arable land.[12]

Likewise, it would have been fruitless to point out that Japan did not need half of China to fuel its industries, or that the backward areas of East and North Africa were not the answer to Italy's chronically weak economy. Instead, all three fascist powers resented, in varying degrees, and especially during the hard times of the early 1930s, the Versailles

Treaty and its aftermath—especially that their honor had been impugned and their peoples had not received respect and commensurate deserts. They went to war to earn global power and especially to be recognized as globally powerful. The irrational proved just as much a catalyst for war as the desire to gain materially at someone else's expense.

Japan and Italy nursed nagging grievances from 1919. As veterans of the winning side then, both now felt that they had not been rewarded with sufficient territorial spoils from Germany and Austria by the Big Power architects of the Versailles Treaty. Japan did not feel appreciated for its yeoman work of helping British naval forces in the Indian and Pacific Oceans, and occasionally in the Mediterranean, and was not satisfied by the acquisition of a few German holdings in the Caroline, Marianas, and Marshall archipelagos. Italy did not see much territorial profit in gaining South Tyrol in the Alps, at least as compensation for its loss of nearly a million lives on the Austrian border in World War I. It viewed Versailles as proof of a "mutilated victory."[13]

For all their bluster, the future Axis powers were anxious too. Germany remained deeply suspicious of the Soviet Union and of the Western democracies' ability to hem it in with the global alliances, trade embargoes, and blockades. Italy feared the French and British navies: with eventual help from the Americans, both fleets might easily shut Mussolini out of his envisioned Roman imperial role in the Mediterranean. Japan was fearful of the omnipresence of the British and American fleets in the Pacific, which was seen as an affront to its sense of imperial self and its grandiose imperial agendas.[14]

If Hitler's second greatest mistake—after the first of invading Russia in June 1941—was declaring war on the United States on December 11, 1941, it was for a few months understandable, given the still meager size of US ground forces on the eve of a global war that would inevitably involve a struggle for the European landmass. In Hitler's fevered strategic calculations, he apparently assumed that after Pearl Harbor (according to Foreign Minister Joachim von Ribbentrop, "the most important event to develop since the beginning of the war") an underarmed America would have its hands full with the Imperial Japanese Navy. It would be unlikely even to find the ships to transport an entire army to Europe across submarine-infested waters.[15]

The advantages of sinking British-bound American convoys in the ensuing year 1942 were seen as worth the risk of tangling with the US Navy. America was now confronted with a two-front war. And if the United States had been content to watch Britain in flames, the end of France, and mass murder in China, it likely would not fight well if at all when faced with the specter of a Germany allied with Japan. In Hitler's warped view of World War I, he never appreciated the miraculous efforts of the United States to have transported almost two million men to Europe in less than two years while producing an enormous amount of war materiel, despite being largely disarmed before 1917. As late as March 1941, Hitler had expressed no worries about serious US intervention in the war, given that America was at least "four years" away from its optimum production and had problems with "shipping." Japan would whittle down the US fleet—or, even if Japan could not do so entirely, Fortress Europe nonetheless offered no friendly shores on which green American amphibious forces might land.[16]

No one, except a few German generals like Ludwig Beck, had dared to point out to Hitler the delusions on which such views were based. With a declaration of war on America, Hitler may have felt that at last he was to settle up with Jews worldwide. In any case, General Walter Warlimont claimed that Hitler scoffed at the idea of the United States as a serious enemy. America's war potential "did not loom very large in Hitler's mind. Initially, he thought very little of the United States' capabilities." Hitler did not grasp that by 1941 America had already begun to tap unused productive capacity from the Great Depression. Fifty percent of the US workforce was not fully employed during the 1930s, but easily could be if the nation were mobilized to confront a "total war."[17]


HITLER'S GERMANY IN the late 1930s was seen by the democracies either as not much of an existential threat or as so great an existential threat that it would require another senseless war to stop it. While there were plenty of starry-eyed fans of fascism in the democracies of Western Europe and America, there were few vocal democratic zealots under the German, Italian, and Japanese tyrannies. It would have been unthinkable—and likely fatal—for German students in 1933 to proudly announce their collective unwillingness to fight for the newly installed Nazi government in the manner that the students of the Oxford Union had passed a resolution "that this House refuses to fight for King and Country." The memoirist Patrick Leigh Fermor, who was at that moment aged eighteen, walking through Germany on his way from Rotterdam to Istanbul, noted of the vote:

> I was surrounded by glaring eyeballs and teeth. Someone would shrug and
> let out a staccato laugh like three notches on a watchman's rattle. I could
> detect a kindling glint of scornful pity and triumph in the surrounding eyes

which declared quite plainly their certainty that, were I right, England was too far gone in degeneracy and frivolity to present a problem. . . . These undergraduates had landed their wandering compatriots in a fix. I cursed their vote; and it wasn't even true, as events were to prove. But I was stung still more by the tacit and unjust implication that it was prompted by lack of spirit.[18]

Between the two wars, the European democracies—Britain especially, in which free expression thrived—sought to explain the horrors of the Great War within a general theory of Western erosion. British and French literature reflected the pessimism of national decline and civilizational decadence, and saw rearming as reactionary and coming at the expense of achieving social justice. We now talk generally of appeasement in the modern era, but it is difficult to grasp just how firmly embedded active pacifism was within the Western European democracies. In France during the 1920s, teachers' unions had all but banned patriotic references to French victories (which were regarded as "bellicose" and "a danger for the organization of peace") and removed books that considered battles such as Verdun as anything other than a tragedy that affected both sides equally. In the Netherlands, the few larger ships that were built were called a *flottielje-leider* ("flotilla leader") rather than a cruiser, apparently to avoid the impression that they were provocative warships. As the French author Georges Duhamel put it, "for more than twelve years Frenchmen of my kind, and there were many of them, spared no pains to forget what they knew about Germany. Doubtless it was imprudent, but it sprang from a sincere desire on our part for harmony and collaboration. We were willing to forget. And what were we willing to forget? Some very horrible things."[19]

Perhaps Horace Wilson, advisor to British Prime Minister Neville Chamberlain, best expressed the mood of British appeasement in 1938–1939: "Our policy was never designed just to postpone war, or enable us to enter war more united. The aim of appeasement was to avoid war altogether, for all time." Across the Channel, Germans had seen appeasement in a different light. Of the *Anschluss*, Germany's forced annexation of Austria, Chancellor Franz von Papen later concluded, "not only had there been no armed conflict, but no foreign power had seen fit to intervene. They adopted the same passive attitude as they had shown toward the reintroduction of conscription in Germany and the reoccupation of the Rhineland. The result was that Hitler became impervious to the advice of all those who wished him to exercise moderation in his foreign policy."[20]

In the late thirties Winston Churchill was playing the hand of the Athenian statesman Demosthenes, although a weaker one, in his warnings about Hitler—a far crueler despot than Philip II of Macedon. If there was squabbling in Britain and France over the inability of the Allies to stop Hitler's serial provocations between 1936 and 1939, there was increasing unanimity inside Nazi Germany. Once-skeptical German generals, who had feared the endpoint of Hitler's trajectory, were soon silenced by his seemingly endless and largely cost-free diplomatic successes.[21]

When the French did not move against Germany's vulnerable western flank in September 1939, and when Prime Minister Édouard Daladier made it clear that Hitler, to achieve a peace, would have to give up most of his easy winnings in Austria, Czechoslovakia, and Poland, and when the French and British could not win over the Soviet Union with either bribes, concessions, or appeals to common decency, a massive invasion of France was all but certain, but not necessarily irresistible. From the German performance in the Spanish Civil War to its annexation of Austria and its incorporation of the Sudetenland, the consequences of blitzkrieg were too often vastly exaggerated and falsely equated with inherent military superiority—a fact true even later of the so-so operations of the German military in Poland and Norway at the beginning of the war itself.

Most overly impressed observers ignored the fact that such lightning-fast German attacks were hardly proof of sustained capability. They were no way to wage a long war of attrition and exhaustion against comparable enemies, especially fighting those with limitless industrial potential across long distances, in inclement weather, and on difficult terrain. Few pondered what would follow once Germany ran out of easy border enemies or guessed that it would predictably have to send Panzers across the seas or slog in the mud of the steppes. That proved an impossible task for a nation whose forces relied on literal horsepower and had little domestic oil, no real long-range bombing capability or blue-water navy, and a strategically incoherent leadership. German blitzkrieg would never cross the English Channel. It would die a logical if not overdue death at Stalingrad in the late autumn of 1942.

Of all the services of the Wehrmacht, the air force should have been the most critical. In fact, it was the most incompetently led, by a cohort of energetic but mentally unstable grandees—most prominently the World War I veterans Hermann Goering, Erhard Milch, and Ernst Udet. The Luftwaffe hierarchy carved out bureaucratic fiefdoms that impeded aircraft production. For too long it was wedded to a bankrupt idea that bombers should focus on dive bombing. Luftwaffe commanders had designed a superb ground-support air force that could facilitate surprise attacks against small vulnerable states, but had not committed to creating a truly independent strategic arm. In a larger sense, the early Nazi war machine, like that of the Japanese, had grown confident in the prewar era that new sources of military power—naval air power, strategic bombing, and massed tank formations in particular—if used in preemptory fashion, could wipe out enemy counterparts and thus end the war before it had started. Even the new weapons and strategies of the Allies would cede the battlefield to the technological superiority and strategic sophistication of the Axis powers, rendering the greater industrial potential of the larger states immaterial.[22]

The Kriegsmarine—predicated on the idea that battleships might one day challenge Britain at sea (along with Admiral Doenitz's insistence that U-boats could do what surface ships could not)—possessed not even a single aircraft carrier. It built just enough heavy surface ships to siphon off precious resources from the army and U-boat fleet, but not enough to pose a serious threat to the Royal Navy. Admiral Raeder illustrated the abyss between Hitler's braggadocio and the military resources of the Third Reich: "There were 22 British and French battleships against our 2 battleships and 3 pocket battleships. The enemy had over 7 aircraft carriers; we had not one, as the construction of our *Graf Zeppelin*, though nearing completion, was stopped because the Air Force had not even developed suitable carrier planes. The allied enemy had 22 heavy cruisers to our 2, and 61 light cruisers to our 6. In destroyers and torpedo boats the British and the French, combined, could throw 255 against our 34." Indeed, Germany started the conflict with not one heavy bomber. Its navy could deploy only five battleships. There were only fifty submarines that were ready for service, and only three hundred Mark IV tanks, the only German model comparable to most French or Soviet counterparts.[23]

Hitler, for all his talk of Aryan science, could not even brag that German researchers and industry had given him superior weapons on the eve of war. The Messerschmitt Bf 109 was not markedly better than the British Supermarine Spitfire fighter. In 1939, the French Char B1 tank was better armed and armored than its German Mark I, II, and III counterparts; so was the lighter but reliable French Somua S35 (over 400 produced). Hitler had little idea that the Soviet Union had vastly more planes, tanks, and divisions than he did—and soon of a quality equal to or better than the Wehrmacht's.[24]

Before August 1939, it was still more likely that if neutrals like the United States or even the Soviet Union were to intervene in the war, they would do so against Nazi Germany. Each might eventually bring to the war far larger and more diverse militaries than Germany, Japan, or Italy. The most widely read prewar prophets of new armored and air power—Giulio Douhet, J.F.C. Fuller, B. H. Liddell Hart, Billy Mitchell, James

Molony Spaight, and Hugh Trenchard—were not German. Although France first turned for its security to massive border fortifications and dubious friendship pacts with the fickle Soviet Union and weak Eastern European states, finally it began to rearm. As early as 1930, the British ambassador to France supposedly confessed to André Maurois, the novelist and later veteran, why the British had not listened to the French worries over an angry and possibly ascendant Germany: "We English, after the war, made two mistakes: we believed the French, because they had been victorious, had become Germans, and we believed the Germans, through some mysterious transmutation, had become Englishmen."[25]

The French army—the supposed bulwark of the West—with help from the other smaller European democracies and Britain, outnumbered German troops in the West. Yet the stronger France became, the more it seemed to fear using its assets even in a defensive war against Germany. A sense of dread had loomed since right after Versailles, when the always prescient Marshal Ferdinand Foch had warned, "The next time remember the Germans will make no mistakes. They will break through northern France and seize the Channel ports as a base for operation against England."[26]

The future Allies understandingly were in no mood to sacrifice more of their youth so soon after the tragic losses of World War I. When stung by the growing realization that the Peace of Versailles had solved very little, the democracies resorted to charades. Perhaps they must not offend Benito Mussolini, given their need for his allegiance against Hitler. Anthony Eden quotes a pathetic diary entry of Neville Chamberlain weirdly blaming the Austrian *Anschluss* on Eden, who had resigned as foreign secretary, for supposedly alienating Mussolini—in a manner that his successor, the appeasing Lord Halifax, would never have: "It is tragic to think that very possibly this [the *Anschluss*] might have been prevented if I had had Halifax at the Foreign Office instead of Anthony at the time I wrote my letter to Mussolini."[27]

Aside from the failure to recognize that past victory is a quickly wasting asset, some in Britain, France, and the United States privately felt that Germany had some legitimate grievances about the loss of territory from World War I. Japan—a member of the Allied councils in the aftermath of World War I—perhaps also had reasonable claims. Even by Western colonial reckoning, the Japanese, more so than distant European colonial powers, deserved the greater sphere of influence among their Asian brethren. Japan chafed under European condescension. So it quietly continued its efforts to establish a first-rate navy and trained superb naval aviators on the assumption that it would expand a new Pacific sphere of influence that would be protected by a fleet of aircraft carriers. In response, British and Americans continued to dream that such emulative peoples could hardly master Western technology and tactics.[28]

Such confusion ensured that should the Axis powers be content with their occupations and limit their annexations to just a few neighboring and weaker states—Abyssinia, Austria, Czechoslovakia, Manchuria, and Korea—then there would be no good reason to resort to another world war to stop them. The democracies wrongly believed that their laxity would be seen as magnanimity. Meanwhile, the Axis rightly interpreted Neville Chamberlain's popular reference to Czechoslovakia as "a faraway country" as a window into democracy's moral weakness.

Unfortunately, most British statesmen, including luminaries like Lord Halifax and David Lloyd George, Britain's successful prime minister during the second half of World War I, privately were relieved by the Munich Agreement—forgetting Aeschylus's truism that "oaths do not give credibility to men, but men to oaths." As France later collapsed in early June 1940, a French newspaper publisher lamented to the American journalist A. J. Liebling how unnecessary was the imminent French defeat:

> We spoke with no originality whatever of all the mistakes all the appeasers in the world had made, beginning with Ethiopia. We repeated to one another how Italy could have been squelched in 1935, how a friendly Spanish government could have been in power in 1936, how the Germans could have been prevented from fortifying the Rhineland in the same year. We talked of the Skoda tanks, built according to French designs in Czechoslovakia, that were now ripping the French army apart. The Germans had never known how to build good tanks until Chamberlain and Daladier presented them with the Skoda plant. These matters had become for every European capable of thought a sort of litany, to be recited almost automatically over and over again.[29]

"Our enemies are little worms," Hitler supposedly would later scoff at Allied peacemaking efforts. "I saw them at Munich." He apparently had read the well-intentioned naïf Neville Chamberlain accurately. Whereas Winston Churchill told the House of Commons on October 5, 1938, that Munich was "a defeat without a war," at about the same time Anthony Eden recorded a conversation in which Prime Minister Chamberlain had apparently remarked to a British colleague right after Munich, "you know, whatever they may say, Hitler is not such a bad fellow after all." Chamberlain and other grandees had been taken in for years by Hitler's lies, all to the effect of convincing them that he spoke for a victimized people with legitimate grievances and that he abhorred war as much as did the democracies. In an interview with the British *Daily Mail* correspondent and Hitler aficionado George Ward Price in August 1934, Hitler had assured that "Germany's present-day problems cannot be settled by war. . . . Believe me, we shall never fight again except in self-defense."[30]

ALL NATIONS GO to war thinking that they can somehow win. Had Germany won World War I, of course, there would likely not have been a Second World War twenty-one years later. Only Germany's defeat and the postwar settlement that failed to deal with the "German Problem" ensured a replay. Nonetheless, it is at first glance surprising that the German-speaking peoples believed so soon after an earlier and catastrophic defeat that the outcome of a second and eerily similar aggressive effort might turn out any differently. Why exactly was Hitler assured he could succeed where Kaiser Wilhelm II had failed?[31]

When Hitler initially went to war in 1939 against Poland, he did so confident that Germany this time around would be fighting only on one front at a time, and could cease the conflict unilaterally when its appetites were satiated. As a self-taught student of history, Hitler felt that he had proceeded, in an episodic and carefully circumscribed fashion, in direct opposition to Kaiser Wilhelm II's past nightmare of recklessly incurring an immediate two-theater war. "Who says I am going to start a war like those fools in 1914?" Hitler sometimes bragged. Like Hannibal who thought he could reverse the verdict of the First Punic War, and like Hannibal's Carthage, which had been defeated but not emasculated in 241 BC, so Hitler and the Third Reich were convinced that the second time around they would not repeat the strategic mistakes of an earlier generation.[32]

Later, Nazi Germany would eventually find itself in a conflict on both its borders and in the skies above the homeland that it could not win. But in 1939 Hitler at least had believed that his nonaggression pact with the Soviet Union and the facts of a temporizing France, an isolated Britain, and a still-neutral United States had ensured that this time around there would be only a single enemy to fight at a single time. In other words, Poland would prove a short, limited, and likely successful war, and would be followed periodically by other short border conquests. He was initially correct in nearly all of his assumptions. That over the course of the disastrous year 1941, the Third Reich unilaterally chose a three-front war with Britain, Russia, and the United States perhaps still meant for Hitler that the war against the Allied superpowers somehow was still a sort of one-front active war with the Soviet Union: Britain was quiescent on the ground in Western Europe, and the United States had its hands full with Japan.

Under the partnerships of the Anti-Comintern Pact of 1936–1937, both the sea powers Japan and Italy were likely to flip to Germany's side should it appear to be winning its war in Europe, especially at the expense of the British Empire. The old German-Austrian partnership would reappear. But this time the alliance was accomplished through the German forced annexation of Austria and the coercion of its old subordinate subject states. Hitler had other reasons to believe World War I would not repeat itself. True, Italy's military assets were thought to offer only dubious advantage to a German-led alliance. But its Mediterranean geography was nevertheless a valuable asset not available in 1914. Benito Mussolini's original model of the fascist state also inflated its importance, as did Rome's iconic religious and historical resonance. So Germany had almost all its allies from World War I, and had also flipped new ones as well in Italy and Japan.

Hitler was inordinately impressed by the naval power of his two fellow Axis powers, as if the Mediterranean and the Pacific might become Axis lakes in a way inconceivable in World War I. He accepted that the German navy was far weaker in a relative sense in 1939 than it had been in 1914, and the so-called naval parity achieved by the Z-Plan (the Kriegsmarine's ten-year agenda to create a huge fleet) was still nearly a decade away. At the beginning of the war a prescient Admiral Raeder lamented that his far-too-small surface fleet could do little against the British navy except "die with honor." At a later point Hitler assumed that eventually the Japanese navy and its martial audacity could tie down both the European colonials and the United States in a Pacific slugfest. The fear of Soviet communism, or, after 1940, the allure of rich orphaned European colonies in the Pacific, or the resentment of serial British and American bullying—any or all would ensure Japan's eagerness to fight alongside Germany.

Yet fighting a common enemy separately was not quite the same as fighting it in synchronized and complementary fashion. The use of the vaguer *Axis* rather than *Allies* to describe the German relationship with Italy and Japan was revealing. It is hard to cite major examples of any serious Japanese-Italian-German strategic coordination. General Warlimont of the OKW (*Oberkommando der Wehrmacht*, Supreme Command of the Armed Forces) confessed to a late 1942 agreement to coordinate with the Japanese: "This document was characterized by the same degree of deception and insincerity as had become the rule for relations with Italy.

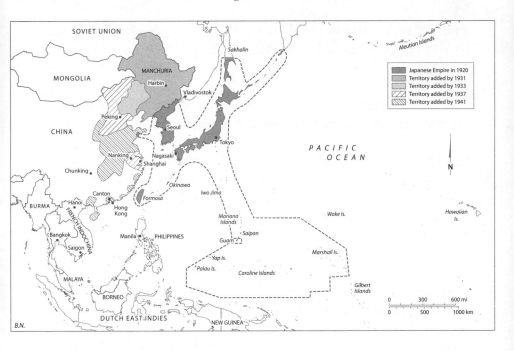

Expansion of Imperial Japan, 1932–1941

The OKW Operations Staff had no part in its drafting and did not even see it. Subsequent German-Japanese military contacts were limited to occasional visits by Japanese officers to German Supreme Headquarters."

Count Galeazzo Ciano, Mussolini's son-in-law and minister of foreign affairs, lamented of the invasion of the Soviet Union in June 1941 that "we were informed of the attack on Russia half an hour after German troops had crossed the eastern border. Yet this was an event of no secondary importance in the course of the conflict, even if our understanding of the matter differed from that of the Germans." Ciano failed to note that Italy likewise gave Hitler no forewarning of its invasions of Albania and Greece, given that deception was the mother's milk of tyrannies. One of the ranking German liaison officers with the Axis partners remarked, "Mussolini feeling himself poorly situated, attacked Greece through Albania without telling us anything in advance—an episode that developed into a major disaster. . . . When the Italian adventure led to disaster, it was the Germans who had to pull Mussolini's chestnuts out of the fire in the Balkan operations, which were a drain on us for the rest of the war." Likewise, the Pearl Harbor attack caught Germany off guard; without it, Hitler might never have declared war on the United States. Hitler thought he had learned the lessons of World War I, but soon only

amplified its mistakes by setting a model of arrogant deceit that was emulated by his equally arrogant and deceitful allies.[33]

OVER ITS TWENTY-YEAR lifespan, the Versailles Treaty of 1919 had been
systematically violated by Germany and psychologically orphaned by the
British, French, and Americans. Like the Treaty of Lutatius (241 BC)
that had ended the First Punic War—and supposedly all future Roman-
Carthaginian conflicts—Versailles had tragically combined the worst
possible aspects of a peace settlement. The 440 articles within the treaty
are often still interpreted as vindictive and thus cited as culpable for the
rise of Hitler that followed. But the problem was far more complicated
than that. Versailles was psychologically humiliating in its attribution of
guilt for the war solely to Germany while, in fact, it was hardly punitive
at all—at least in the sense of permanently and realistically preventing
German rearmament. In contrast, after World War II the Allies' postwar NATO agenda was roughly summed up by its first secretary general,
General Hastings Ismay, as "to keep the Russians out, the Americans
in, and the Germans down." Had the victors of 1918, the so-called Big
Four of Britain, France, Italy, and the United States, followed something
analogous to the later NATO accord, Hitler might well have not come to
power, a divided Germany would not have rearmed to the degree that it
did under him, and the nascent Soviet Union would have been kept out of
European power politics.

Such an effective paradigm was impossible, given that the Versailles
Treaty of 1919 did not follow anything like the unconditional surrender
of 1945. By November 1918, the German people had not suffered war on
their own soil. Germany was tired and hungry, but it was not ruined. It
was shamed by the victors for starting (and losing) the war but it had not
been prevented from soon starting another one like it. No Allied power
was unilaterally willing to monitor all the treaty's provisions and to insist
that Germany abide by the treaty's arms-limitations accords. In a paradoxical way, precisely because Germany was not ruined by World War I,
the Allied powers were subsequently hesitant to occupy it, rightly suspicious of the likelihood of German pushback.[34]

Worse still, Germany emerged after 1918 in better geostrategic shape
than either of its traditional rivals, France or Russia. The latter by 1919
was torn apart by revolution, had large parts of its territory fought over,
occupied, and liberated, and was now separated from European affairs by
the creation of a number of Eastern European buffer states. France, with
well over twenty million fewer citizens than Germany, could much less

than Germany afford the losses of World War I and it had suffered cata-strophic damage from the four-year occupation of swaths of its territory by the Kaiser's army. And with the destruction of the Austro-Hungarian, Ottoman, and Russian Empires, Germany was much more easily able to fill the vacuum of power in the East.[35]

The Versailles summit began in January 1919, months after the ces-sation of hostilities. Perhaps 75 percent of the victorious Allied ground forces were already demobilized. They were not easily called back to enforce terms placed on an already resentful Germany. Germans cited the global dangers of a spreading Bolshevism, and warned the arbiters at Versailles that any punitive occupation would only lead to Russian-style communism all the way to the Rhine. Ostensibly there were real indemni-ties (when and if enforced), but they came without commensurate Allied efforts to guarantee either German impotence or its permanent transition to a more viable democratic system. The departure from the battlefields quickly after the armistice may have instilled among the victors a sense of discord, weakness, and shame, while empowering those among the de-feated who thought that the winners were neither confident nor strong. It was not the unwillingness of the United States to join the League of Na-tions that helped doom the former Allies, but America's refusal to remain well-armed and ready to conduct a mutual defense treaty with France and Britain that likely encouraged Hitler.[36]

In sum, by the standards of the era, Versailles was mild. The treaty was not as harsh as the peace Germany had imposed on France in 1871. It was softer than the terms Germany forced on the nascent and defeated Soviet Union in February 1918. The surrender package that German dip-lomat Kurt Riezler's plan had envisioned for France in the heyday of late summer 1914, the so-called *Septemberprogramm*, was far more punitive than Versailles. Humiliating but not emasculating a defeated enemy is far risk-ier than showing magnanimity to a beaten adversary that is then occu-pied, politically reformed, and stripped of its ability to renew war.

Germans could accept culpability if they were soundly beaten and shamed—that was clear after 1945—but not if their homeland was al-lowed to remain sacrosanct, as it was in 1918. Soon almost all German politicians monotonously blamed their subsequent economic miseries on reparations, or on the Danzig Corridor, or on the War Guilt Clause of the treaty, rather than on their own inept economic policies or social instabil-ity. They listened to Hitler when he reminded them that the Fatherland had remained largely untouched during and after the war. While there had been far fewer riots and less unrest back home than Hitler later alleged, the collapse of the magnificent army was blamed on backstabbers—Jews or communists who did to the German Army what the Americans, British, and French could not. The angst was not that Germany had started the war by invading neutral Belgium, but only that it had somehow lost the war while still occupying foreign territory, east and west.[37]

Hitler's generals later conceded that the Allies, even by 1939–1940, had been better armed than Germany, but lost their initial border wars due to poorer morale. Defeatism had infected the French aristocracy, and some of the French Right saw Hitler as a preferable alternative to the French Left ("Better Hitler Than Blum" was a slogan expressed against French Socialist Léon Blum). Or as Field Marshal Erich von Manstein explained the conquest of Western Europe in 1940, "indeed, as far as the number of formations, tanks and guns went, the Western Powers had been equal, and in some respects even superior, to the Germans. It was not the weight of armaments that had decided the campaign in the West but the higher quality of the troops and better leadership on the German side. While not forgetting the immutable laws of warfare, the Wehrmacht had simply learnt a thing or two since 1918." Or perhaps not entirely. In World War I, Imperial Germany had waged a traditional war that was ended by armistice without occupation of the Fatherland. Hitler's second attempt at remaking the map of Europe was a war of annihilation that would end in the destruction of Germany itself. Berlin in May 1945 did not look at all like it had in November 1918.[38]

IN SUM, GERMAN humiliation and shame, and French, British, Russian, and American laxity, along with other shadows of World War I all explain why a war broke out twenty years after Versailles. But the vast differences between 1914 and 1939 also account for why it progressed so differently. The next time around the greatest disconnect would prove to be found in civilian casualties. The majority of the seventeen million who perished in World War I were combatants (59 percent), and there were roughly even losses among the Allied and Central powers. More telling, World War I noncombatant deaths were largely a result of either war-related famine or disease—most commonly the horrific Spanish flu pandemic of 1918 and the often inept efforts to combat it—or from blockades and agricultural disruptions.

World War II was largely a deliberate effort to kill civilians, mostly on the part of the Axis powers. Most of the fatalities were not soldiers: perhaps 70–80 percent of the commonly cited sixty million who died were civilians. Noncombatants perished mostly due to five causes: (1) the Nazi-orchestrated Holocaust and related organized killing of civilians and prisoners in Eastern occupied territories and the Soviet Union, as well as Japanese barbarity in China; (2) the widespread use of air power (especially incendiary bombing) to attack cities and industries; (3) the famines that ensued from brutal occupations, mostly by the Axis powers; (4) the vast migrations and transfers of populations, mostly in Prussia, Eastern Europe, the Soviet Union, and Manchuria; and (5) the idea prevalent in both totalitarian and democratic governments that the people of enemy nations were synonymous with their military and thus were fair game through collective punishments.[39]

The first war had remained a conflict of European familial nations that shared roughly the same assumptions about limited parliamentary government and the rule of the aristocracy. That was true of both the more authoritarian leaders of Germany and more socialist French and British democratic politicians. The actual or symbolic supreme commanders of three of the most powerful belligerents—King George V of Britain, Kaiser Wilhelm II of Germany, and Tsar Nicholas II of Russia—were all related (the British monarch was first cousin to both the Kaiser and the Tsar) and indeed were almost identical in appearance and dress. With the exception of the Ottomans, all major powers had prayed to the same god. All claimed the same shared European past. Only within those common parameters would individual national character, ethnic pride, glorious history—call them what you will—galvanize one side or the other to greater effort.

That traditional European commonality had long imploded by the eve of World War II. National Socialism was to be a force multiplier of Prussian militarism. Italian fascism boasted it alone could restore the old Roman Empire. In Asia, the samurai code of Bushido gave credibility to warlords in Tokyo who had destroyed Japan's incipient parliamentary government and promised a new Asian order under a Japanese-led Greater East Asia Co-Prosperity Sphere. Imperial Russia of the tsars was to be reinvented as the Soviet Union, trumpeting a new man and a new national secular religion based on state coercion and moral relativism—and especially the Red Army and American-style methods of mass industrial production. Mass popular movements in Germany, Japan, Italy, and Russia defined themselves in antitheses to monarchy and bourgeoisie republican government. National armies became ideological and revolutionary armed forces. Prussian militarism by 1918 had arguably proved to be more savage than that of any of the Allies. But German mercilessness was nonchalantly accepted as a given by late autumn 1939. The Wehrmacht was not just formed from German-speakers residing on ancestral soil but was now reinvented as a mythological pure *Volk* that deserved superior status, in the way that the *razza* best captured Mussolini's new Italy and *Yamato-damashii* entailed more than just those who spoke Japanese or lived under Japanese auspices. Weaker indigenous peoples in Africa, Asia, and the Americas would fall because, in Darwinian terms, they deserved to be enslaved. Western Europeans likewise would concede, not because they were necessarily inherently inferior, but because they had become decadent in their leisure and wealth, without a national ethos or muscular religion—or dynamic leader.

When warned by his generals in August 1938 that the so-called Westwall (known in English as the Siegfried Line and later the site of the bloodbath in the Hürtgen Forest), a defensive fortification built between 1938 and 1940 opposite to the Maginot Line, would not prevent attacks from France and its allies if Germany attacked Czechoslovakia, Hitler scoffed: "General [Wilhelm] Adam said the Westwall would only hold for three days. I tell you, it will hold for three years if it's occupied by German soldiers." When pondering whether Italy should join the war on the side of Germany in April 1940, Mussolini pontificated, "it is humiliating to remain with our hands folded while others write history. It matters little who wins. To make a people great it is necessary to send them to battle even if you have to kick them in the ass."[40]

Given these realities, Churchill and Roosevelt insisted that the totalitarian and nationalist ideologies that drove the Axis to war in a way unlike past bellicosity must be destroyed. Sober Germans, Italians, and Japanese, in the Allied way of thinking, had to be freed from their own hypnotic adherence to evil, even if by suffering along with their soldiers. Armistices this time around would not do. Nor would a second round of the Versailles Treaty. The Allied victory must be unconditional. Death was commonplace in World War II because fascist zealotry and the overwhelming force required to extinguish it would logically lead to Allied self-justifications of violence and collective punishment of civilians unthinkable in World War I. The firebombing of the major German and Japanese cities, the dropping of two atomic bombs, the Allied-sanctioned ethnic cleansing of millions of German-speaking civilians from Eastern Europe, the absolute end of the idea of Prussia—all by 1945 had earned hardly a shred of remorse from the victors.

Despite German brutality in 1914, there had been nothing quite similar to the *Waffen SS* (the military arm of the *Schutzstaffel* or "protective squadron") and nothing at all akin to Dachau or the various camps at Auschwitz. The Kaiser's Germany would not have exterminated seventy to ninety thousand of its own disabled, chronically ill, and developmentally delayed citizens, as the Third Reich had by August 1941. The idea of

Japanese kamikazes might have been as foreign in 1918 as it was largely unquestioned in late 1944. In 1918, Imperial Germany at least surrendered without the occupation of its homeland—a scenario impossible to envision in 1944–1945. Some eleven thousand American and Filipino troops gave up Corregidor to avoid starvation and needless losses in May 1942. In contrast, the subsequent 6,700 Japanese occupiers did not similarly quit the island fortress in February 1945, but had to be killed nearly to the last man. The destruction of populist ideologies, especially those fueled by claims of racial superiority, proved a task far more arduous than the defeat of a sovereign people's military.[41]

There were still other catalysts that would explain the second war's singular loss of life. The technology of mass death was more developed than it had been in 1918. True, the mass use of poison gas, submarines, warships, artillery, machine guns, repeating rifles, grenades, and mines all predated 1939. The ground soldier at the war's beginning in 1939 was superficially similar to his 1918 counterpart. Both often carried bolt-action rifles and grenades. They likewise fell prey in droves to artillery shelling and machine guns. Steel helmets continued to offer inadequate head protection. There was still no practical and universally worn body armor that could deflect rifle bullets. In history's endless cycle of challenge and response, the shift toward the offensive brought about by industrial weaponry still remained in control. Infantry still had not many choices other than foxholes and trenches to survive artillery barrages. Field guns were larger, more numerous, and more accurate, yet they appeared to the eye similar to the artillery of World War I. At sea, the guns of battleships were more accurate but not always that much larger. Destroyers and cruisers were faster and often greater in size, but nonetheless were still recognizable as destroyers and cruisers. Most World War II surface ships were superficially indistinguishable from their World War I counterparts—many would see service in both wars—even if their armament, engines, and artillery were superior. Submarines, torpedoes, and depth charges were improved over those of World War I, but they were not new.

More important, the ability to move men and materiel and to travel far more easily by land, air, and sea proved a catalyst for turning a European border dispute into a global war. Compared to what had seemed the ultimate in lethal weaponry in World War I, these scientific and industrial revolutions ensured tens of millions of more deaths in the second war. And the majority of the innovations favored the Allies, who nonetheless would lose far more lives than the Axis. The first breakthrough was in air power. By 1939, the evolution of fighters and fighter-bombers helped to make trench warfare rarer, while augmenting the ability to clear the advance and protect the flanks of fast-moving motorized columns. Tactical air support of ground troops vastly increased their lethality. Strategic bombing brought the war home to civilian populations, raising questions about the level of civilian culpability for the war effort unknown in past conflicts. By war's end, the destruction wrought by Allied tactical and strategic aircraft, mostly American and British, simply dwarfed any similar air efforts achieved by the Axis powers. The belated success of bombers from mid-1943 through 1944 and onward wrecked the German petrochemical and transportation industries and diverted huge numbers of planes and artillery from the Eastern Front to the homeland.[42]

Armored and transport vehicles in no way resembled the erratic, clunky machines that had achieved temporary tactical advantages between 1916 and 1918. Just two decades later, sophisticated vehicles appeared in the tens of thousands, and were increasingly mechanically reliable and far more powerful, as well as far better armed and protected. A Jeep or tank in 1945 looked more like its counterpart in 2016 than in 1918. Shock-and-awe tactics allowed independent groups of Panzers to spearhead infantry advances and achieve breakthroughs otherwise impossible in the past. Rapid envelopments, particularly on the Eastern Front, would result in vast captures of prisoners on a scale unknown in World War I.

One lesson of the conflict was that speed kills. When soldiers could cover more distance and at greater speeds, they inflicted more death. Entire divisions could now move over thirty miles a day and be supplied from hundreds of miles to the rear. The access to refined fuels was critical to all logistics and governed strategies about long-term supply. At the end of World War I, the British foreign secretary, Lord Curzon, had summed up the victory with the quip, "we swam to victory on a sea of oil." The same would prove true of the Allies in World War II.[43]

Over four million military trucks were produced in World War II. Despite the greater numbers of combatants, there were probably fewer horses employed in World War II than in World War I, and after 1940 most were confined to the German and Soviet armies. The latter had largely evolved to motorized transport by late 1944 (near the end of the war, Nazi propaganda minister Joseph Goebbels called the Soviet army "motorized robot people"), in part due to the gift of 457,561 American trucks and armored vehicles. By contrast, until the end of the war the fuel-short Wehrmacht still depended on the horse for the majority of its infantry's transportation needs. Journalists by 1941 had mythologized blitzkrieg. But more often Germans conducted a *Pferdkrieg*, a war relying on horses—and plentiful spring and summer pasturage.[44]

Aircraft carriers proved critical naval assets at the very beginning of the Pacific war. They rapidly ensured the obsolescence of the battleship, which was to all but disappear as a decisive asset by the end of the war. The vast majority of ship losses in World War II were to torpedoes or bombs launched from submarines, planes, and destroyers. In comparison, few ships sank due to the thundering broadsides of behemoth battleships or heavy cruisers. Naval and occasionally land-based air power turned the great sea battles—the fighting near Singapore, the chase of the *Bismarck*, the Coral Sea, Midway, the fight over the Marianas, Leyte Gulf, and Okinawa—mostly into contests of carrier-based aircraft attacking with impunity any enemy ships except like kind. During the entire war, only two light carriers and one fleet carrier (HMS *Glorious*) were destroyed by surface ships. The vast imbalance between Axis and Allied total carrier production (16 to 155) meant that tactical air superiority over the Atlantic, Mediterranean, and Pacific was far easier for the Allies to achieve than for their enemies. Neither the Russians, the Germans, nor the Italians deployed aircraft carriers. Their respective modest surface fleets were hampered by ineffective air cover. That absence hurt the Kriegsmarine far more than it did the Soviet military. The Soviet Union remained primarily an infantry power with a land-based air force, without obligations abroad—but with two allies in the European theater with large carrier forces. Axis carriers and naval air pilots were exclusively Japanese. But by war's end they were dwarfed by the huge production totals of the Anglo-Americans. Apparently, Germany had always believed that its future wars would be confined to the continent and thus naval air power would be less important, and that the seas of the Baltic and Atlantic were not conducive for air operations. Admiral Raeder in lunatic fashion early on summed up the German appraisal of carriers as "only gasoline tankers."[45]

Even if its Kriegsmarine had come to its senses and reordered its priorities, Germany had too few resources to build a respectable carrier fleet. Hitler's invasion of the Soviet Union had ensured a great need for Axis ground troops, trucks, and armor. Back home over the skies of Germany, Luftwaffe fighter aircraft soon became critical to intercept the growing number of Allied bombers. Given those obligations in the air and on the ground, German and Italian carriers again remained a fantasy. Meanwhile, Axis surface ships were never replaced in the ratios they were lost, often to Allied naval air power. After 1943, the British and Americans alone kept building larger surface ships, frequently used to support amphibious operations.

Breakthroughs in electronics, medicine, and high technology also favored the Allies. Britain and the United States did not so much display preponderant inventive genius as a pragmatic sense of how to deploy new scientific inventions on the battlefield more quickly and in the greatest quantity. Radar and sonar ended the idea of stealthy invulnerability in the clouds or in the ocean depths. By 1940, the trajectories of planes and submarines could be identified in advance of visual sighting. War was unleashed from at least some of its traditional weather-related restraints.

The British and Americans outpaced the Germans in all these critical technologies that made war far deadlier. Or, when the Allies fell behind in development, they quickly caught up and rendered initial Axis breakthroughs irrelevant. The introduction of plasma, sulfa drugs, mass vaccinations, and belatedly, penicillin, meant that septicemia, tetanus, gangrene, and other bacterial infections were not always fatal. The old category of "wounded" was no longer necessarily a step on the way to "killed in action." In all areas of medicine, the British and American armies proved the most efficient in treating soldiers' combat injuries and preventing disease, although the Germans were more effective (or brutal) in returning wounded soldiers to combat.

Jet engines and rocketry would eventually revolutionize warfare. Both were on the horizon but neither arrived in time nor in enough numbers to change the course of World War II. In the case of much faster Luftwaffe jets, huge numbers of superb piston-driven Allied fighters, especially British Spitfires and American Mustangs, overwhelmed fuel-short and often poorly piloted Messerschmitt Me 262 Swallows. That the Axis produced rockets, jets, and superior torpedoes, and yet were the most reliant on horse transportation, is emblematic of their lack of comprehensive industrial policy and pragmatic technological planning—an area where America, Britain, and the Soviet Union excelled. We often forget that the Third Reich was postmodern in creative genius but premodern in actual implementation and operations.

Two final unforeseen inventions, the atomic bomb and the ballistic missile, were used only at the end of the fighting to eerie, if controversial, effect. In contrast to Germany's squandered scientific breakthroughs, the atomic bombs were primarily responsible for the avoidance of an invasion of Japan. If the body counts at Hiroshima and Nagasaki were less than those who perished from the conventional firebombing of the other Japanese cities, and if V-2 missiles killed far fewer British than plodding Flying Fortresses and Lancasters did Germans, the new weapons' aggregate potential for mass death on the immediate horizon was also far greater. Had the war gone on for a few more years, it was possible that huge fleets of missiles, and perhaps even atomic-tipped projectiles (albeit only by the United States), would have become feasible and freely used.[46]

Finally, all of the belligerents would subordinate military decision-making to civilian leaders. There were to be no Alexanders, Caesars, Napoleons, or even de facto supreme military leaders such as Generals Erich Ludendorff and Paul von Hindenburg, who by the last year of World War I were making most of Imperial Germany's military and strategic determinations, unfettered by much civilian oversight. Both decided to quit the war in panic when they saw their armies losing. Likewise, in the latter months of World War I, Generals Douglas Haig, Ferdinand Foch, and John J. Pershing, without much audit, crafted most of the Allied strategic decisions on the Western Front. In contrast, in World War II all of the war's greatest battlefield luminaires—General George Marshall, General Georgy Zhukov, General Bernard Montgomery, General Dwight Eisenhower, Admiral Isoroku Yamamoto, and German generals Franz Halder, Erich von Manstein, and Erwin Rommel—followed strategic initiatives set out by Churchill, Roosevelt, Stalin, and Hitler, as well as Tojo (though himself an active army officer) with guidance from Emperor Hirohito. It may sound counterintuitive, but generals are usually more sparing with their troops than are their civilian overseers.

Hitler and Stalin in 1941 and 1942 adopted militarily unsound strategies that added to the horrific body counts of World War II. Unnecessary entrapment of Soviet armies had led to over four million Russian dead by the end of 1941. Nearly as disastrous were the no-retreat German sacrifices such as that at Stalingrad at the end of 1942 and those throughout much of 1943–1945. World War II partly disproved Georges Clemenceau's famously paraphrased line, "war is too important to be left to the generals." In fact, a global war was too important to be left in the hands of a civilian ex-corporal.

In sum, World War II was in some sense a traditional conflict that was fought over familiar military geography of the ages. It was sparked by age-old human passions such as fear, honor, and self-interest, and more specifically by the loss of classical deterrence that can be predicated on impressions and appearances almost as much as hard military power and resources. However, its twentieth-century incarnations of totalitarianism, whether German Nazism, Italian fascism, Soviet communism, or Japanese militarism, often made the aggressors erratic rather than circumspect and predictable. All the warring parties assumed that the end of the war would not be achieved through armistices and concessions but through the existential destruction of their enemies. Such resolution accepted not just that the Axis powers were skilled killers, but also that Germany and Japan in particular would likely concede defeat only when ruined, thus requiring their Allied opponents to embrace commensurate levels of violence. Totalitarianism, when married to twentieth-century industrial technology, logically led to general destruction on a global scale.

If it is mostly clear why the war was fought and how it became so lethal, why then were the alliances so unstable, the belligerent partnerships often so unalike, and their respective visions of victory so different?

# 3

# Old, New, and Strange Alliances

THE PREWAR AMBITIONS of every warring nation are not set in stone. They expand and contract during the conflict according to the perceived pulse of the battlefield. Setbacks scale down aspirations; success creates ad hoc fantasies of grand conquests—the common denominator being fickle public opinion, even in totalitarian nations. Hitler could not stay off German radio before 1942, blustering and threatening; after Stalingrad, Propaganda Minister Joseph Goebbels could hardly get him back on the air. Ecstatic German crowds met Hitler's return from Paris in 1940. Fewer Germans welcomed his sheepish reemergence from his high-security retreat at the Wolf's Lair in late 1944. Hitler did not deliver a radio address to the German people during the entire critical year of 1944.[1]

Neutral Spain and Sweden were as generous to the Third Reich in 1940 as they were hesitant to trade with it in 1945. Many Allies joined the cause after 1943. Many of Germany's partners quit the Axis after 1944. There were only a few exceptions in the war to these age-old human tendencies, such as the renunciation of the victorious Winston Churchill at the British polls in July 1945, or the effort to invade India in March 1944 by an already-spent Japanese military.

A more rational Germany, Italy, or Japan might have envisioned consolidating and digesting its successful aggressions. Despite Hitler's schizophrenic rhetoric of wishing for supremacy only on the European mainland, and his occasional allusions to pan-continental conquest, it is telling that by mid-1941 Germany could have lorded over a Nazi-occupied and mostly unified Europe without turning on its de facto ally Russia. Yet a few years later, amid a crumbling Third Reich, a petulant Hitler—who had invaded France, bombed Britain, waged a surprise attack on the Soviet Union, and declared war on the United States—by 1945 still claimed that he had never desired a war beyond Poland.

The role of the rapid fall of France in expanding the war is sometimes not appreciated. The implosion of Republican France made the heroic sacrifices of the West in World War I seem as if they were, in the end, all in vain, and thereby created deep depression among the old Allies. The world had turned upside down, as the mystique of the indestructible French army of 1914–1918 vanished along with France itself. Hitler himself now wrongly believed anything was possible, and probably expanded his previously repressed agendas accordingly. A military that could do in six weeks what the grand army of Hindenburg and Ludendorff had not in four years, need not worry too much about Britain, despite the pesky persistence of the Royal Navy and Royal Air Force. Had France just survived even as an autonomous rump state, most of Hitler's freedom of action in the East and elsewhere would have been postponed indefinitely.[2]

On the eve of the Blitz in 1940, Hitler supposedly bragged to Albert Speer, his state architect and later munitions minister, "London will be a rubble heap, and three months from now, moreover! I have not the slightest sympathy for the British civilian populace." Hitler was convinced that his proven formula of adding territory to Greater Germany without much cost was also valid for global wars against the United States and the Soviet Union. One reason was that war, for Hitler, the wartime creature of the bunker, was not only politically useful but also spiritually nourishing for a great race. "War does not frighten me," he boasted as early as 1934. "If privation lies ahead of the German people, I shall be the first to starve and set my people a good example."[3]

Overreach after even the smallest victory was in the fascist DNA. A weak Italy, temporarily victorious only in British Somaliland, ensured that it could not secure its position in North Africa once it had invaded Greece. Throughout the 1930s the Japanese had no prewar realistic strategic plans to hit the homelands of likely future enemies Britain and the United States. Had they just sidestepped Singapore, the Philippines, and a distant Pearl Harbor, and consolidated their gains in China, they might have carved out, without a general war, a hegemony that extended from China to the orphaned Pacific colonies of the defunct Dutch and tottering French empires.

So there were plenty of strategic options for each of the Axis powers to consolidate holdings without involving the Western democracies and the Soviet Union in a global war. All the Axis powers were oil short. But there were ways of obtaining sufficient fuels from allies and in partnership with the Soviet Union without war, or in the case of Japan, in the Dutch East Indies without attacking Pearl Harbor and Singapore.[4]

The Axis powers had various schemes. At first, they simply accepted anything that was given to them; then took most anything that could be taken without great cost; and next retained as much of the territory that they had stolen as possible; and finally focused on nothing except the very survival of their regimes. As for the Allies, by 1942 three facts had shaped their war aims and became the subtexts for a series of three summits between the Americans, British, and Soviets, and additional bilateral meetings between Britain and the United States. First, there was a shared but mostly unspoken assumption that their collective prior policies of appeasement (what Anthony Eden once called "peace at almost any price"), indifference, or de facto alliance with the Axis had utterly failed, to the point of humiliation. That was an easier recognition for the democratic leaders of Britain and America than for Stalin. Europeans had blamed America for staying out of Europe's war; America had blamed Europeans for not preparing for their own war. Yet the Russian leader had no one to blame but himself for Hitler's drive eastward, having previously come to formal agreement with Nazi Germany while directly abetting Hitler's aggressions. In any case, by late 1943 in various prior meetings and agreements the Allies agreed that there could be no separate negotiated armistice with any of the Axis leaders, given that past diplomacy had led only to more humiliation and war.

Second, in an ironic twist, the Allies went further and conceded that they had once been unprepared for Axis duplicity, and in some sense should not be surprised at what they had wrought. That belated recognition of being duped made the Allied powers all the more determined to mobilize for war in a manner that their increasingly naive enemies could scarcely imagine, much less match. Such acceptance of prior laxity and its failure to appease the Axis did not just mean an eventual call for unconditional surrender—formalized as such between Churchill and Roosevelt at the 1943 Casablanca Conference—but, again, also the de facto destruction of the ideologies that drove the Axis.[5]

Third, annihilation of the Axis powers would require a cost in blood and treasure unforeseen in past wars, and demand a temporary unity of purpose quite at odds with the Allies' own perceived differing postwar agendas. Churchill, Roosevelt, and Stalin after 1941, at first singly and then collectively, were each prepared to wage the war as one of annihilation and far more existentially than had Lloyd George, Woodrow Wilson, and Tsar Nicholas II, and were in far better positions to do so. The Allies fought World War II to rectify the mistakes made at the end of World War I and to avoid circumstances that would lead to a World War III. They solved the former problem, but the latter required another half century of enormous sacrifices and "unconditional responsibilities."[6]

The strange alliances of World War II opened a Pandora's box of mass death that transcended six years of formal fighting, largely because the most fanatical of the major belligerents (Germany and Japan) attacked great populations in Russia and China who at least initially were easily accessed near their respective borders and whose militaries initially could not protect their own people. And just three belligerent powers (China, Germany, and the Soviet Union) before, during, and not long after World War II, had exterminated or would kill more people off the battlefield—many of them their own citizens—than their enemies did on it between 1939 and 1945.

The Soviet Union entered the war and then the democratic Western alliance after killing perhaps ten million of its own without foreign intervention or even much global censure during the so-called Red Terror and Great Purge following World War I, and the collectivizations and ensuing famines of 1932–1933. With near impunity, Hitler slaughtered six million Jews in the heart of Eastern Europe—the vast majority of them in occupied territory of the Third Reich as it was collapsing, with the Allies closing in on both fronts and their aircraft with near complete control of the skies. Mao Zedong, who came to power after the liberation of China from the Japanese, systematically murdered and starved to death perhaps forty to seventy million Chinese in concentration camps, purges, famines, the Great Leap Forward, and the Cultural Revolution, beginning not long after the war and not ending until the 1970s. World War II and its aftermath were variously linked to these three great holocausts of the twentieth century.[7]

The war gave Hitler both the resources and the general backdrop for mass murder so necessary to engineer the Final Solution, especially on the Eastern Front. Absorbing Poland, unifying Eastern Europe, occupying the Baltic states, and invading Russia stripped millions of Jews of any chance of state defense against Hitlerian savagery.[8]

Prior to 1939, the world was slowly beginning to fathom the sheer brutality of Stalin's purges, forced relocations, and famines from the 1920s to the early 1930s that had led to the state-orchestrated deaths of millions of Russians. Such revelations, along with the later nonaggression pact between Nazi Germany and Communist Russia, at least politically had tended to weaken any support abroad for the idea of state-coerced communism. But that fact changed after Hitler's invasion of the Soviet Union and the ensuing partnership between Stalin and the Western democracies that changed a bloody dictator into "Uncle Joe."[9]

It is hard to envision Mao Zedong coming to absolute power separate from the circumstances during and right after World War II. Mao's postwar toll over the subsequent two decades may have been larger than Hitler's and Stalin's combined, and trumped even the genocide attributable to the Japanese militarists. Mao's leftist revolutionary credentials established by his early postwar defeat of the often incompetent and exasperating Chiang Kai-shek regime tempered Western criticism, even through the 1950s and 1960s. Again, the origins of his subsequent genocides can be traced to his rise in stature during and as a result of World War II.

IN SEPTEMBER 1939 few observers would have predicted the Allied and Axis alliances that arose in late 1941. Aside from the evils of expansionist German, Italian, and Japanese fascism, the conniving of the Soviet Union was most responsible for the outbreak of World War II and for the strange shifts in alliances that followed. Before 1939, its antifascist propaganda and prior shared history of conflict against Germany seemed to offer the Soviet Union the chance of at least a cynical alliance with Britain and France, which in the past had seen no problems allying with traditional Russian autocracy as a critical deterrent to German expansionism to the west. In contrast, one of World War II's greatest paradoxes was how Stalin's hope that Germany and the Western European nations would wear each other out in 1940 boomeranged on his country after June 1941. As a result of Stalin's former empowerment of the Nazis, some in Britain and the United States had quietly argued that there was no hurry to open a second ground front in Western Europe, given that the totalitarian Soviets and their doppelganger Nazis were destroying each other in the East. In a related irony, only by dividing up Poland in September and October 1939 did the Soviet Union create a common border with the Third Reich. An even greater disconnect was that the postwar allies ratified Soviet ownership of the Baltic states and parts of Eastern Europe that Stalin had grabbed while partnering with Hitler before June 1941.[10]

After 1939, Germany's ally Russia was so close to East Prussia that it still seemed inconceivable that Hitler could ever attack westward with such a historically and ideologically hostile "partner" at his immediate rear. Nor could he move eastward against the Soviet Union with France and Britain mobilized on his western border. A despairing Admiral Raeder on the eve of Operation Barbarossa purportedly sighed about Hitler, "I expressed myself as incredulous of any intent on his part to unleash a two-front war after his own constant denunciation of the stupidity of the Imperial Government in doing this identical thing in 1914. The Russo-German Treaty should not be violated and under no circumstances, since the treaty itself guarded us against a war on two fronts." Raeder's exasperation may well have been postwar mythmaking, inasmuch as most of the Wehrmacht elite supported Barbarossa and assumed it would be a continuation of the easy success seen in Western Europe.[11]

The Soviet state, not Germany, by 1941 fielded the world's greatest number of soldiers, armored vehicles, and airplanes. Russia, not Germany, had the world's best tanks and artillery. Between 1939 and the eve of the German invasion, the Soviets had produced eighty thousand mortars and guns, seventeen thousand aircraft, and 7,500 tanks, including nearly two thousand late-model T-34s and KV-1s. Russia, not Germany, was both a fuel and food exporter. The Soviets could field more army divisions than all of the Axis powers combined. Yet again Hitler ignored or downplayed those realities. Instead he relied on massaged German intelligence that was ignorant of the advanced state of Russian armaments. The Nazi hierarchy was sorely out of date in its assessments of the modern Red Army. It had focused on Stalin's 1938–1939 purges of the Red Army's officer corps, the lethargic Soviet advances into Poland in 1939, and problems subduing Finland in 1940 as confirmation of the Russian army's chronically poor performance, dating back to the Russo-Japanese War of 1904–1905 and the collapse of the tsarist ground forces in 1917. None of that, however, was necessarily a referendum on the wisdom of fighting on Russian soil in mid-1941.[12]

Germany had humiliated the Soviets at Brest-Litovsk in 1918. Hitler likewise knew that Soviet-German military cooperation in the 1920s and 1930s was supposedly predicated on the notion that Soviet industry and technology had more to learn than to teach. In 1940, Hitler also apparently had relied on ossified World War I west-east equations: if France had proved unconquerable in World War I and Russia was defeated in less than three years, then the fall of France in 1940 in six weeks might mean that this time around Russia would crumble in a month—as if a still-ascendant Russian communism in 1939 was similar to a tottering Tsarist Russia of 1917, or the confident French of 1914 were the same people as those in 1939–1940.

In May 1941, Karl Bremer, the director of the German-controlled press during the occupation of France, supposedly got drunk during a reception at the Bulgarian embassy in Berlin. He soon blurted out German plans to invade Russia that reflected the illusions that the abrupt collapse of the once-vaunted French army had encouraged: "Inside of two months our dear [Nazi ideologue Alfred] Rosenberg will be boss of all Russia and Stalin will be dead. We will demolish the Russians quicker than we did the French." Bremer was just channeling more Hitlerian mythmaking. During his victory tour of Paris in June 1940, Hitler scoffed to General Wilhelm Keitel, head of OKH (*Oberkommando des Heeres*, Supreme

Command of the Army), how much easier defeating Russia would be than the just-completed conquest of France: "Believe me, Keitel, a campaign against Russia would be like a child's game in a sandbox by comparison."[13]

As for leaving Britain unconquered to the rear, the experience of World War I weighed on Hitler. For all his grand talk of eastern *Lebensraum* and strategic minerals, farmland, and oil, Hitler's wartime experience was entirely in the West; the brutal battles of the Somme and Passchendaele convinced him that the Western Front would always be the tougher nut to crack. Hitler therefore found consolation in the idea that, just as Imperial Russia had not survived the Kaiser even though Britain had, so too would Stalin fall even if Churchill would not.

Russia's leadership worried only about the survival and expansion of Soviet communism and the Stalinist regime. To the degree the British and French conceivably could have made ironclad anti-German assurances to Russia before 1939, Stalin might have cemented negotiations with them on a common front, thereby most likely delaying or even preventing what would become a world war. But Stalin could not forge a partnership, given the French and British unwillingness to sell out quite so brazenly the idea of self-determination in Eastern Europe that was already sacrificed to German and Soviet agendas. The Soviets then were quite prepared to cut a better deal with Hitler to divide Poland and to pledge mutual nonaggression. That pact was seen as a continuance of both their own renegade military cooperation and their mutual loathing of the idea of an independent Poland.[14]

Russia could now face down Japan; Hitler was freed eventually to eye France. Stalin might well have preferred a pact all along with a fellow totalitarian like Hitler ("only a very able man could accomplish what Hitler had done in solidifying the German people, whatever we thought of the methods") to one with Western democrats. For his part, Hitler appreciated that those who had mastered the absolute use of power were likely to be more sympathetic to similar aggrandizing dictators. Hitler came to idolize Stalin, even late in the war as the Red Army was destroying the Wehrmacht: "Churchill has nothing to show for his life's work except a few books and clever speeches in parliament. Stalin on the other hand has without doubt—leaving aside the question of what principle he was serving—reorganized a state of 170 million people and prepared it for a massive armed conflict. If Stalin ever fell into my hands, I would probably spare him and perhaps exile him to some spa; Churchill and Roosevelt would be hanged."[15]

After the pact, Russia looked to the Baltic states and the borderlands with Eastern Europe and soon displayed an appetite for conquest that even Hitler found inordinate. In Soviet thinking, the communists were only recovering what had properly belonged to Russia under the tsars but had been liberated or plundered during the chaotic transition to communism. In addition, the Soviets did not always deliver all the promised resources to the Third Reich, and continually upped their demands for German technology and industrial goods, convincing Hitler that perhaps the nonaggression accord shorted German interests, especially in terms of receiving Russian oil. Stalin grew ever more worried that France, as the traditional bulwark to German expansionism, collapsed much too quickly. He shortly thereafter formally annexed the Baltic states, cut out swaths of Romanian territory, and stepped up rearmament. Germany put up with all this to be free to war against the Western European democracies, which Stalin had assumed would put up a much tougher fight than his own targeted acquisitions. Ironically, democracies did nothing for Czechoslovakia and little more for Poland, rendering void all their prior principled unwillingness to agree to Stalin's realpolitik as the price of alliance.[16]

Any long-term partnership between Stalin and Hitler was bound to fail. Communism was not a kindred ideology of Nazism. With general class rather than particular racial enemies, Marxism had proven far more dynamic and with more international appeal than had the Aryan racial obsessions of National Socialism, and was thus seen by Hitler as Nazi Germany's chief existential threat. Both nations still nursed recriminations from the prior war. The Soviets still chafed under the humiliating terms of Russia's capitulation in 1918. The Germans remembered that the atrocious behavior of tsarist armies in 1914 in East Prussia had rivaled their own savagery in Belgium. If a Soviet pact with the West might have deterred war, one with Hitler ensured it in the long term.

Russia likewise was critical to the cause and evolution of the Pacific war. Its victory over the Japanese army in a series of Manchurian border wars between May and September 1939 convinced many in the Japanese military that it was unwise to fight the Soviet Union unilaterally on its eastern boundaries. Marshal Georgy Zhukov's ground forces were better led, better equipped, and more numerous than those of the Japanese army. In addition, Stalin, at the end of the border fighting, had enhanced his military advantages by signing a nonaggression pact with Japan's supposedly anticommunist Axis partner, Nazi Germany. Subsequent Japanese realpolitik, and a bitter sense of betrayal by Germany, would lead Tokyo to formalize its own nonaggression pact with Stalin in April 1941.[17]

That tit-for-tat double cross would have two fundamental consequences to the nature of the alliances of World War II, and explain the expansion of the war into a worldwide conflict. One, Japan in June 1941, without an invitation to join the initial invasion, would not subsequently aid Hitler's Operation Barbarossa with a simultaneous attack from the east along the Manchurian border. The reluctance arose partly out of both Japanese self-interest and pique, but also partly because a greedy and ascendant Hitler had snubbed the Japanese in June 1941 (he would not by late 1942) because he had wished to claim all his envisioned winnings alone. Indeed, when the Germans were apprised of the Japanese decision in April 1941 to form their own pact with Stalin just weeks before Operation Barbarossa, General Warlimont noted the indifference, or even the relief, at the accord among German officers: "We don't need anyone just to strip the corpses." By September, after three months of mostly German success, Hitler bragged, "today everybody is dreaming of a world peace conference. For my part, I prefer to wage war for another ten years rather than be cheated thus of the spoils of victory." Perhaps Hitler also quite wrongly figured that a Japanese attack in the East against a lightly populated Siberia was not of much immediate help against the centers of Russian industry and commerce, at least in comparison to the Japanese tying down Anglo-American naval forces and some ground troops in the Pacific and Asia.[18]

Japan's nonintervention nonetheless guaranteed that the beleaguered Soviet Union would avoid a two-front war and would have Vladivostok free to receive unimpeded US Lend-Lease aid from West Coast ports of America. In response, by December 1941, Stalin had rushed almost twenty divisions westward for the defense of Moscow, which helped to stall Hitler's siege and the successful German blitzkrieg of 1941. After the war, the incompetent Field Marshal Keitel confessed that even rapid German advancement and historic victories had not translated to a rapid victory, as was true between 1939 and 1941: "After the decisive battles at Bryansk, which was a terrific beating for the Russians, or perhaps, after the siege of Moscow and Leningrad, or after the battles on the Donetz Basin, one had to realize that it would come to a long war."[19]

Two, the armistice with the Japanese on September 14, 1939, also had assured the Russians of a safe rear and so greenlighted their invasion of Poland, in the manner that a more formal Soviet-Japanese nonaggression pact on April 13, 1941, had likewise unleashed Japan upon Britain and the United States. Given the choice of a slugfest with Russia or, after June 1940, the lure of poorly defended Dutch, French, and perhaps British colonies now ripe for the plucking, the Japanese, especially the army, logically preferred resource-rich Asia and the Pacific. Note that for the most part Stalin honored both his promises with the Nazis and the Imperial Japanese far more assiduously than he would his postwar agreements with Britain and the United States. Perhaps it was worse even than that: Stalin kept to the letter of his nonaggression pact with Japan to ensure that Soviet-bound ships could leave American ports safely and reach Vladivostok through Japanese-controlled waters. The Soviets would eagerly accept US Lend-Lease and ensure its delivery by abetting America's archenemy. In the hierarchy of autocratic deceit, it was hard to determine which dictatorship was the chief offender—Japan, which had made assorted deals with Hitler's archenemy to avoid a three-front war; Germany, which had earlier made a deal with Japan's archenemy to avoid a two-front war; or Russia, which had at various times had made deals with both Germany and Japan that harmed Britain and America, whose supplies would help to keep it alive.

Nazi Germany, Japan, and the Soviet Union for nearly two years had all jockeyed with one another to prevent a two-theater conflict, the fear of all six major belligerents of World War II. Yet when the war finally ended in 1945, only an opportunistic Stalin had achieved his aim of largely avoiding such a war. During the destruction of Poland, Winston Churchill had presciently said of the Soviet Union's 1939 double cross, "I cannot forecast to you the action of Russia. It is a riddle wrapped in a mystery inside an enigma; but perhaps there is a key. That key is Russian self-interest."[20]

THE STRENGTHS AND weakness of the various major belligerents, the nature of their governments, and their decisions to exploit perceived weakness or to punish unprovoked aggression explain the memberships of the respective wartime alliances by late 1941. Russia was the only belligerent that mostly eschewed naval warfare and systematic strategic bombing to focus on its infantry by fielding the war's largest army. For all Stalin's machinations to gain territories without cost, in the end Russia paid by far the highest price of any of the belligerents. Historians still seek to sort out the degree to which the Soviets' catastrophe was a result of their own duplicity. Note as well that while Stalin, between 1941 and 1944, constantly berated the British and Americans for failing to open an immediate second front against his former partner Hitler, he nonetheless rejected outright any counter-suggestion that the Russians might at least do something on their own Asian borders against Japanese occupiers to relieve their allies from the pressures of a two-front war against the Axis, and to facilitate the transport of aid to China. In fact, Stalin enumerated various reasons why he would not engage the Japanese—all of which boiled down to the reluctance to fight the dual-enemy conflict that his own allies were engaged in, even if they were pitted against far fewer Axis soldiers.

It might not be entirely fair to Stalin but it nonetheless remains an accurate generalization that no other single individual was responsible for more deaths between 1925 and 1945, whether by forced famines, mass executions, the aid to and empowerment of Hitler until June 1941, the reckless wastage of the Red Army in 1941–1942, and the political cleansing of Eastern Europe between 1945 and 1946. The Soviet Union entered the war seeking to grab territory with Hitler and ended the war acquiring more than it had ever envisioned by warring against him.[21]

GREAT BRITAIN WAS the only Allied power that fought the entire war against Germany and its Axis partners from September 3, 1939, to Japan's formal surrender on September 2, 1945, in Tokyo Bay. Of what would become the Big Three allied nations of Great Britain, the Soviet Union, and the United States, only Britain had begun hostilities against an Axis power without being directly attacked itself when it nominally went to war on behalf of its ally Poland. Great Britain and its empire—not France, the United States, or the Soviet Union—was also the only Allied nation that ever faced Germany alone, from the fall of Western Europe in May 1940 to the invasion of Russia in June 1941. With well less than half the material and human resources of the United States, it would nonetheless fight in Europe, Italy, Sicily, and North Africa, on and below the high seas, in the Pacific, and along with the United States would conduct a costly strategic bombing campaign over Europe. Its expanding economy was the most underrated of the three Allied powers. The Dominions—especially Australia, Canada, New Zealand, and South Africa—offered steady supplies and many of the war's best soldiers, who were central to the British strategy for fighting a global war. More than half of all British divisions as well as 40 percent of RAF crews were raised in the Dominions, colonies, and India. Hitler talked grandly of the British Empire, but he had no idea of the resources—industrial, agricultural, financial, military, and human—that Britain might exploit in a world war, or of how loyal such diverse British subjects would prove to be in supplying hundreds of thousands of troops to the British military.[22]

Hitler did not fully appreciate the obvious fact that Britain had a far greater navy than any of the three Axis powers in 1939, or that British air forces were rapidly evolving to become better balanced and coordinated than was the Luftwaffe. The need to fight over vast distances and to protect imperial ground made it natural for the British to emphasize air and naval power, and to avoid a meat-grinder ground war in France and Belgium. The Nazi regime seemed to be completely clueless about the vast transformation in British military preparedness that had begun in late 1938. In Hitler's obsessions with land warfare, the fact that Britain had not mobilized a huge expeditionary army in the fashion of 1916 apparently deluded him about the importance of growing British sea and air power, and their abilities to ensure supply lines for troops and imports.[23]

From the outset of World War II in September 1939, Great Britain best of the Allies also articulated the nature of the Axis threat, predicted the course of Nazi aggression, and anchored the future alliance—largely because of the singular leadership of Winston Churchill after May 10, 1940, and the inherent resilience of the British people. As early as 1937, Churchill had warned the haughty German ambassador to Britain, Joachim von Ribbentrop, that the British were not as comparatively weak as their prior appeasement might otherwise have indicated. At the German embassy in London, Churchill had refused to be complicit with Germany's designs on Eastern Europe and the USSR, earning threats from Ambassador Ribbentrop. In reply, Churchill offered, "do not underrate England. She is very clever. If you plunge us all into another Great War, she will bring the whole world against you like last time." The Germans did not grasp that appeasement was not necessarily static, but rather a momentary wish not to suffer moderate casualties in exchange for the hope of avoiding them altogether—a mood that could eventually lead to frustration and with it war with righteous indignation and zeal. Or as George Orwell and others noted, "in international politics . . . you must be either willing to practise appeasement indefinitely, or at some point be ready to fight." Nor was appeasement necessarily a barometer of military preparedness. An appeasing nation can often enjoy military superiority over an aggressor, albeit with a far greater desire not to use the superior assets it enjoys.[24]

After mid-1944, Britain fought, if briefly, over some of the same battlegrounds anyway. The much longer and greater American role between 1941 and 1945 than in 1917–1918 meant that the British lost fewer lives than they had in World War I. By 1945 Russia had borne the bulk of infantry fighting against the German colossus, unlike the Tsar's army that had dissolved well before the Western Armistice of November 11, 1918. The resurgent Red Army in 1942, fighting on a single front, allowed Britain to free up more of its resources to expand air power and to fight a second front against the Japanese—the sort of global outreach that exceeded expeditionary efforts in World War I.

Had Winston Churchill made an agreement with Germany in June 1940, as Hitler and some British grandees sometimes fantasized, or had he not become prime minister in the prior month, then Nazi Germany either might not have turned on Russia or might conceivably have beaten it. Only the survival of Britain meant the resurrection of a second European front against Hitler in the West, albeit by air power and Mediterranean fighting prior to June 1944. Without a free Britain there would have been neither an early American bombing campaign nor an eventual American landing in Western Europe. At the least, without Britain the United States would have lacked a forward staging area from which to retake the continent. The remarkable resistance of Britain in 1940 did much to convince the United States to invest the greater share of its efforts in the European theater of operations. The British expertise accrued from fighting the Germans from September 1939 onward proved invaluable to the United States in 1942.

The least powerful and populous of the three major Allies, Great Britain proved in many respects the most principled and the most effective, given the resources at its disposal and always with the acceptance that the burdens of the global and often lonely war might leave postwar Britain reduced in power, as a postwar world gravitated to the Soviet Union and the United States. Americans may have tired of British lectures and their imperial pretensions, but the British were crucial to the Allied alliance— dependable, courageous, ingenious, and talented in ways no other power could match.

Of the six major powers in World War II, America alone did not in any substantial way have its traditional continental homeland invaded or bombed. Two oceans with thousands of miles of seas between the United States, Asia, and Europe protected American industry, as Hitler himself soon lamented. But if such distance ensured uninterrupted American military production, it also meant that America did not have a close affinity with European and Asian politics. For far too long it lacked an accurate up-to-date appraisal of the nature of the Axis militaries. As was true in World War I, the confident Americans would arrive in Europe, whether in Sicily, Italy, or at bases in Britain, convinced that they had the answers to defeat Germany in a way the far more experienced British did not.

America prior to Pearl Harbor freely offered advice, but despite budding rearmament was also shockingly ill-prepared for an extended land or air war. While the British and the Europeans had all but disarmed by the early 1930s, they had rather rapidly wised up after Munich. By 1939, both

France and Britain had neared Germany's annual defense outlays, investing between 21 and 23 percent of their respective gross national product in rearming. By 1940, the combined defense spending of the two economies exceeded Germany's. In contrast, despite a massive naval expansion program, America still spent only 1 percent of GNP on defense in 1939 and a mere 2 percent in 1940, even as the war was raging in Europe. As a percentage of America's budgetary dollars, defense expenditure dipped between 1932 and 1939, and often the money spent was not efficiently allotted but reflected congressional pork-barrel interests.[25]

America's secure geography was also a double-edged sword. Whereas the fronts were safely distant from the United States, they also were hard and costly to reach, and sometimes dangerous to supply. Throughout the war, the United States had the largest supply and transportation overhead of the conflict. It dispatched soldiers and materiel across the globe, often under dangerous skies and in perilous waters. Because the American public was the only wartime populace not under attack, it was more difficult to rally the country on the premise that military defeat would equate with the extinction of America as a nation.[26]

Yet the United States was the only belligerent on either side of the conflict to have fought fully in every conceivable theater and manner against Japan, Italy, and Germany. Those extraordinary commitments were reflected in the transformation of the American economy. By the end of 1944, it was allotting over $80 billion per year, well over 40 percent of its GNP, to the war effort. And by 1945, 93.5 percent of annual budget outlays went to the military forces or defense-related investments. It spent 20 percent more of its much larger budget on military forces than did Nazi Germany. For all the Axis talk of decadent Americans, the working men and women of the United States produced far more per capita industrial output than any nation of the war.[27]

Mobility was critical to overcoming innate disadvantages of sending troops thousands of miles from home to initiate offensives against far more experienced Axis troops. In response, America invested considerable capital and manpower in its naval and air forces, and focused on producing inexhaustible numbers of reliable, easy-to-use, and mostly effective weapons. A twelve-million-man military had vast obligations, from supplying the Soviet Union to securing Australia to eroding Axis and Japanese industry by air and sea. The two most expensive weapons programs of the war, the Manhattan Project and the B-29 bomber, were both designed to bring destruction to faraway enemies, by air. By the early twentieth century, the US military had never envisioned starting a major war by rolling across its borders into Mexico or Canada, and so it

America built the greatest number of aircraft, launched the largest tonnage of ships, fielded the largest and most efficient medical services, and finally by mid-1945 produced a greater gross national product than all the other four warring nations combined.

The United States did not enter the war to grab new territory in the manner of Germany, Italy, Japan, and the Soviet Union. America ended up eventually returning most of what it had conquered. The initial American strategy was to strike as quickly as possible at the heartland of the Third Reich, defeat the Wehrmacht, remove the Nazis, and then invade Japan. Americans had met and defeated a tiring German army in 1917–1918, and had not experienced something like Verdun or the Somme. Their leaders knew the fickle and impatient nature of the American public, eager for rapid decisive victories and equally quick to tire and turn on long-drawn-out engagements that did not bring rapid and unambiguous results. Just a month after Pearl Harbor, the Roosevelt administration sought seemingly impossible yearly production goals of twenty thousand anti-aircraft guns, forty-five thousand tanks and armored vehicles, and sixty thousand aircraft. By the war's end, it had sometimes achieved those targets.[30]

IN SUM, THE idea of the "Allies" shifted throughout the war. Before June 1940, the plural noun *Allies* denoted Great Britain and the Western democracies of Europe. After the collapse of France, Scandinavia, and the Low Countries in 1940, and the invasion of Russia in June 1941, the Soviet Union and Great Britain, now loosely aligned with China, were the only Allied powers left actively fighting the Axis powers.

By December 1941, some twenty-seven months after the start of the war, the Allied alliance was again recalibrated by the Pearl Harbor attack and the Axis powers' respective declarations of war on the United States. What bound together the new so-called Big Three of America, Britain, and Russia was certainly not ideological brotherhood (much less liberal values and consensual government) or a willingness of each to fight all three Axis powers. Instead, the common bond of the Big Three, although a strong one, was the shared experience of having Nazi Germany either invade a member's homeland, preemptively declare war on a member, or attack a member's ally, as well as a shared existential desire to destroy Nazi Germany.

For their part, the Axis powers, despite prewar professions of solidarity, genuine fascist commonalities, and empty talk of pacts of "steel" and the like, changed their own coalition just as radically. Unlike the Allied alliance, the Axis league was predicated not in reaction to what the enemy had done but entirely on ephemeral perceptions of Germany winning the war and ensuring a favorable postwar settlement. Germany was the lone Axis power actively at war in Europe between September 1939 and June 1940. As France was overrun in June 1940, Mussolini's Italy belatedly joined Germany, in the expectation of easy spoils from already beaten or weakened enemies. After December 7, 1941, the notion of the Axis expanded yet again to include Japan and a few Eastern European nations, when the Japanese Imperial Navy attacked the United States and Great Britain in the Pacific in anticipation that a reeling Britain and Russia would soon be defeated, leaving a neutral, supposedly disarmed, and isolated United States to make concessions. Tragic irony was always a trademark of World War II. The Allies had little ideological affinity and yet fought as partners in pursuit of righteous revenge; the Axis were kindred fascists, but waged aggressive war often at cross-purposes and as individual belligerents in dreams of their own particular aggrandizement.

How the war was fought across the globe proved just as paradoxical as how it started—and as ironic as how and why the belligerents had formed their respective alliances. Many of the decisions involving strategy, weaponry, industrial policy, manpower, technology, and leadership were derived from the same mindset and assumptions that had led the Axis powers to go to war in the first place—and the Allies to seek a terrible response.

# PART TWO

—·—

# AIR

The follies and brilliance of air power

*And in the air are no streets, no channels, no point where one can say of an antagonist, "If he wants to reach my capital he must come by here." In the air all directions lead everywhere.*

—H. G. Wells[1]

# 4

# The Air Power Revolution

T HE AXIS AND the Allies produced eight hundred thousand military, transport, and trainer planes during World War II—an astonishing development given that air power had only come of age during World War I. Almost three hundred thousand planes were lost to combat or accidents, or were too badly damaged to be salvaged. The Allies built three times as many aircraft as the Axis. In the critical categories of heavy bombers, transports, and fighter-bombers, the aircraft of the Allies very quickly proved as superior in quality as they were greater in quantity, and they gave the victors advantages in mobility, deployment, and offensive reach undreamed of by the Axis.

Recordkeeping was predictably sporadic, especially on the Eastern Front. Many of the documents of the German Luftwaffe, for example, were lost by war's end, both by intent and in the flotsam and jetsam of the chaos of spring 1945. Nonetheless, a good guess is that about 350,000 pilots and air crewmen on all sides died, although air fatalities in most militaries were lumped in with army losses. Perhaps nearly two million European and Asian civilians perished from strategic bombing raids, at least half of them women and children. World War II began with the bombing of Warsaw and ended with the atomic bombing of Hiroshima and Nagasaki. Despite the impressive advances in air power, perhaps only 3 percent of military casualties during World War II were related to the use of aircraft. Still, air power proved the greatest single expenditure of all military investments, comprising on average 30 percent of the major belligerents' outlay and over 40 percent of America's wartime budget. The costly venture—one especially favored by the democracies as a way of reducing infantry losses—was predicated not on killing lots of the enemy per se, but on destroying its machines and its ability to produce war materiel. Air power required building and maintaining complex machines, airfields, and communications, the unprecedented consumption of expensive aviation fuels, and the costs of aircraft maintenance, as well as an extraordinary outlay in training pilots and crews in a way not true of ground troops.[1]

The cost effectiveness of air power was always hard to calibrate. By 1941, air forces were so deeply embedded within tactical army and navy operations, logistics, and transportation that it was almost impossible to isolate them as either a separate budgetary cost or a single strategic dividend. There was also the psychological component—how to calibrate the terror instilled by shrieking Stukas in Poland and France, or what the incineration of Tokyo and destruction at Hiroshima and Nagasaki did to the Japanese commitment never to surrender. It is canonical that air power in and of itself cannot end a war, but the Japanese gave up without being invaded, arguably in large part due to the B-29 fire raids and the dropping of two atomic bombs rather than just the Soviet invasion of Manchuria.[2]

Armored operations were not critical to the Japanese army. Amphibious assaults were not routine German naval operations. The Soviets did not conduct much strategic bombing. However, every belligerent employed some sort of tactical air force and diverted key resources from both the army and navy to fund it. Likewise, military aircraft spawned ancillary weapons and technologies completely unseen in the past, from huge aircraft carriers and airborne troops to guided missiles, semi-smart rocket bombs, and jet fighters. The two deadliest breakthroughs of the war—napalm and atomic bombs—were weapons of the air. Over Tokyo on March 9–10, 1945, and Hiroshima on August 6, 1945, they accounted for the two most lethal days in the history of warfare.

Until the twentieth century, fighters were either soldiers or sailors: the hoplites of Marathon, the sailors on triremes at Salamis, the men both on and beneath the walls of Vienna, the sailors at Lepanto, the cavalry at Waterloo, and those manning ships of the line at Trafalgar. All missiles—arrows, sling balls, javelins, and artillery projectiles—were launched from the ground or ships. During most of the Age of Gunpowder until the late nineteenth century, the attacker was usually within sight of the intended target. In 1939 all that changed forever.[3]

Of course, fighting in the air was not entirely novel in 1939. A rare use of hot-air balloons in the Napoleonic Wars (1799/1803–1815) and the later famous 1849 Austrian "bombing" of Venice caused consternation but had no effect on the course of those wars. Thousands of biplanes in World War I put combatants above the earth in a way only dreamed about since the myth of Icarus or the sketchbooks of Leonardo da Vinci. Aerial fighting after 1914 escalated rapidly, often involving thousands of planes. Yet, even then, airplanes were still considered unreliable or even dangerous machines and thus had little influence on the strategic pulse of the conflict, despite the production by late 1918 on all sides of an aggregate two hundred thousand war and transport planes. Nonetheless, in World War I the French and British only sporadically bombed Germany. Berlin remained almost completely untouched.[4]

German zeppelins and bombers inflicted slight damage and loss of life in Britain and France during World War I, far less than a single typical Allied bombing raid twenty-some years later. Air power by 1918 finally had grown to be important tactically over France and Belgium, but had yet to evolve into an effective strategic weapon. But by the outbreak of World War II, just four decades of aviation had already led to monoplanes so powerful and fast that those directing the air war suddenly began making astounding promises of air supremacy over the battlefield. These theories were grounded on a central premise: soldiers would not just transfer their fighting to the skies, but by doing so would reinvent battles below.


As is commonly the case during cycles of radical technological breakthroughs, interwar euphoria over air power soon led to fantastic claims that air power would eliminate most fighting on the ground altogether. The prewar Italian air theorist General Giulio Douhet in dramatic fashion warned that

> to have command of the air means to be in a position to wield offensive power so great it defies human imagination. It means to be able to cut an enemy's army and navy off from their bases of operation and nullify their chances of winning the war. It means complete protection of one's own country, the efficient operation of one's army and navy, and peace of mind to live and work in safety. In short, it means to be in a position *to win. To be defeated* in the air, on the other hand, is finally to be defeated and to be at the mercy of the enemy, with no chance at all of defending oneself, compelled to accept whatever terms he sees fit to dictate. (italics in original)

The failed German Blitz over Britain would early on prove Douhet absolutely wrong in almost every claim. The problem with such air and armor prophets was not that they were mistaken per se, but that their exaggerated and melodramatic forecasts made no allowances for the age-old challenge and response cycles: for every "unstoppable" tank or bomber that "always got through," World War II proved that there would emerge a new counterweapon, such as a cheap, hand-held Panzerfaust anti-tank weapon or high-performance fighter.[5]

Grandiose theories about omnipotent air power were understandable, given the lingering trauma arising from the Western European trenches and subsequent vows never to fight such a static infantry battle again. The utopian efforts of well-meaning statesmen in the 1920s to outlaw certain planes and bombing strategies conversely also meant exaggerating public fears of air power, while also stoking their own militaries' desires to possess air forces as lethal as possible. The technological breakthroughs of the interwar period in aviation science—the payload, range, and speed of fighters and bombers tripled between 1935 and 1940 alone—also frightened European publics. The rapid growth of air power in the 1920s and 1930s was analogous to the specter of nuclear weapons in the early Cold War, which was another argument that new weapons had grown so terrible that wars of any sort could never be fought again without the utter destruction of civilizations.[6]

A new generation of fast and high-flying planes, it was believed, would bypass the battlefield to attack the civilian rear. Warplanes alone would end an enemy's economic ability to make war, or at least would terrorize a population into calling off its military effort altogether, thereby diminishing the loss of life. In other words, no theorist or politician quite knew what to expect of air power in the next war.

"I think it is well also for the man in the street to realise that there is no power on earth that can protect him from being bombed. Whatever people may tell him; the bomber will always get through. The only defence is in offence, which means that you have to kill more women and children more quickly than the enemy if you want to save yourselves." So on November 10, 1932, British prime minister Stanley Baldwin infamously offered his pessimistic assessment of air defenses to the British House of Commons. True, Baldwin might have been correct that a majority of bombers on most missions might usually "get through." But they would do so only at such a high cost, and often with such questionable results, that doubt would arise over the sustainability and efficacy altogether of strategic bombing. Later, Baldwin would accept that fighter and bomber production could provide Britain deterrence against the German threat of invasion, but his successor Neville Chamberlain eventually returned to the earlier view that massive rearmament was wasteful and provocative, even though to his credit he maintained fighter production and encouraged air force development. The problem with Baldwin and Chamberlain was not that they had unilaterally disarmed Britain, but that both did not accelerate and expand British fighter production at a rate that was attainable, given British industrial and technological advancement and what was warranted by the rise of the Third Reich.[7]

The major prewar prophets of the air—Clément Ader (*Military Aviation*), Giulio Douhet (*Command of the Air*), Colonel William "Billy" Mitchell (*Winged Defense*), Royal Air Force Marshal Hugh Trenchard, and General Walther Wever—had in varying degrees predicted not just that air power would be integral to all land and sea tactical operations of the future, but also that strategic bombing could radically diminish enemy production. Among them, Wever perhaps was the least dogmatic; he tried to ensure a multifaceted tactical and strategic capability for the Luftwaffe rather than having it become an independent branch of the military that possessed the ability to win wars for Germany entirely through air operations against the industrial and population centers of the enemy. Again, some of the air determinists later were to be proven partly right by the cinders of Berlin and Tokyo, and perhaps by the dropping of the atomic bombs, but quite wrong by the horrendous losses of the Luftwaffe, RAF Bomber Command, and the US Army Air Forces, as well as the need of the Allies to invade the homelands of Germany and Italy to end the war. Even after prolonged bombing campaigns, cities and their inhabitants were surprisingly resilient. Planes, it turned out, were like catapults and crossbows: their effectiveness hinged on technological challenge and response, and evolving proper tactics and strategies.[8]

Soon flak guns, barrage balloons, radar, and fighter aircraft checked the raw offensive power of the bomber—along with nature, in the form of fog, ice, clouds, and high winds that were often the best defenses of Berlin and Tokyo. By late 1940, the prewar dreams of new uncontested weapons of the skies had been brought back to earth. Air power, it turned out, could not level the industries of island fortress Britain any more than nightly appearances of German Heinkel, Dornier, and Junkers bombers could terrorize the London public into giving up. Thousand-plane British area-bombing raids might have engulfed Hamburg in flames but nonetheless did not initially much curb the German production of new Tiger and Panther tanks that would blast apart their Russian counterparts.[9]

Humans, after all, live not in the air but on the ground, and sometimes underground, during bombing attacks. As deadly as strategic bombing might eventually become in World War II, it might never replace the Neanderthal need to meet the enemy on the ground, destroy his will to resist, defeat him, and occupy his territory. Air power could not see soldiers hiding in reinforced buildings or interrogate prisoners or talk with civilians. Critics of air power argued over whether bombers and fighters were simply assets transferred to another theater of operations—and one less relevant than ground warfare in forcing an enemy to surrender.

Yet, by 1943, once air power was freed from its fantastical prewar promises and with the continual appearance of far better engines, airframes, guidance, and sighting systems, strategic bombing and tactical air support slowly had begun to substantiate some of the wild claims of its prewar messiahs. Improved fighters became instant force multipliers of armor and infantry in a way not seen before 1939. Multitudes of long-range escort fighters, rather than new advanced bomber designs per se, finally empowered the deep penetrations of air squadrons. With air supremacy—destroying the enemy's air forces to gain a monopoly of the skies and thus to attack with near impunity everything below—anything was possible. Without it, the airplane was simply nullified by another airplane.

As air advocate Alexander P. de Seversky put it, "only air power can defeat air power. . . . The actual elimination or even stalemating of an attacking air force can be achieved only by a superior air force." Again, the great controversy of air power in World War II was not that planes created great damage on the ground. (By 1945 many parts of the great industrial and capital cities of the defeated Axis—Berlin, Bremen, Dusseldorf, Hamburg, Kobe, Mainz, Milan, Tokyo, and Yokohama—lay in rubble, and the culprit was most often air power.) Instead, the question hinged on the degree to which warplanes brought enough military dividends to justify their high costs—and if so, exactly how they were to be employed.[10]

By 1945, the rough consensus was that when air supremacy (effective enemy air opposition no longer exists) or perhaps even superiority (enemy air opposition is consistently defeated) was finally achieved, then a new force might be unleashed in spectacular fashion to destroy armies, navies, industries, and civilian centers in ways otherwise impossible. (It was assumed that naval and ground anti-aircraft systems could not nullify the offensive punch of aircraft.) Yet should belligerents find themselves almost evenly matched, stalemate in the skies became a diversion of resources perhaps otherwise better spent on the ground, especially given that the losses of pilots and crews often exceeded the fatality rates of foot soldiers.

PILOTS WERE AS important as planes, and sometimes good pilots in mediocre planes could match bad pilots in superior aircraft. Airmen were also not just combatants but technicians of sorts, who had to become more attuned to the workings of their machines than those who drove internal combustion engines below. Most important, airmen could target the enemy almost anywhere they pleased. The battle space was now to be gauged in cubic, not square, yards. It seemed as if the practical elements of all the classical military handbooks from Aeneas Tacticus, Vegetius, Sun Tzu, and the Byzantine Emperor Maurice to Generals Carl von Clausewitz and Antoine-Henri Jomini were suddenly to be rendered irrelevant. Air zealots were convinced that they were creators of an entirely new military science and doctrine.[11]

Ships before the twentieth century had fought only at sea level. Seasoned Alpine troops who fought in Scandinavia between 1939 and 1940, or Anglo-American and Japanese troops who climbed through the high ground of the China-Burma theater, rarely fought much above ten thousand feet. In contrast, airplanes now battled from near ground level to thirty thousand feet, in a three-dimensional fashion unknown among earth- and sea-bound soldiers and sailors, and in an atmosphere unobstructed by coastlines or mountains. The Allies sought to send out bombing squadrons—especially with the advent of the B-29 Superfortress in late 1944—that flew so high at five-and-a-half miles above the earth that they were almost immune from both artillery fire and most enemy fighters. But that assumption sometimes failed to reckon that the increased power and fuel required to reach such altitudes radically impaired bombing accuracy, payload capacity, speed, and both human and mechanical performance. If air power was freed from the impediments of terrain, it was also far more constrained by a nascent and not altogether understood technology.

When a Tiger tank stalled or a British destroyer lost power, trapped crews still had some recourse to fight on land or the surface of the sea. In the air, the failure of machines sent crews spiraling to earth in parachutes, at best, or free falling to their deaths, at worst. In other words, airplanes, like submarines, were intrinsically more dangerous modes of transport than either surface ships or wheeled vehicles, especially in the terrible weather of the northern latitudes. War at sea was treacherous. But that danger was why most of history's greatest sea battles—Salamis, Lepanto, and Navarino, for example—took place near land.[12]

Aeronautics evolved far more rapidly than even the most radical improvements in naval and land warfare. If it had taken three hundred years for clumsy matchlocks and harquebuses to displace crossbows and longbows, in just the twenty years between the world wars, air power was completely reinvented. True, the new American *Essex*-class aircraft carriers that by early 1944 had ensured naval supremacy over the Japanese were far more sophisticated than the smaller and simpler USS *Wasp* (CV-7) (1940–1942) or even the huge battle-cruiser converts like the USS *Lexington* (CV-2) (1927–1942) and USS *Saratoga* (CV-3) (1925–1946). Tiger tanks were far more powerful (if hardly more reliable) than their tiny and mostly underarmed German Mark I and II predecessors that crushed Poland. All these improvements nonetheless were incremental evolutions rather than pathbreaking innovations. Turrets, tracks, armor, and internal combustion engines marked the parameters of tank technology.[13]

In contrast, World War II began with plodding biplanes like the British Fairey Swordfish torpedo bomber and ended inconceivably with the deployment of Me 262 German jet fighters and V-2 ballistic missiles. Air power saw the greatest technological breakthroughs of any theater of the war. The allure and potential of such a radically new technology initially seemed to have drawn the top engineering and scientific minds in Europe in a way not true of artillery, tanks, or surface vessels. America's air lords—Hap Arnold, Jimmy Doolittle, Curtis LeMay, and Carl Spaatz—proved among the most capable generals of any military in the war.[14]

The experience of air battle was also far more solitary. Even in the largest of planes—the behemoth B-29 that burned down much of the urban core of Imperial Japan, for example—only eleven crewmen fought within a single airframe. That was a far different experience from, say, even that of a small *Fletcher*-class destroyer, which usually required over three hundred officers and men, or the tank crews that were accompanied by hundreds of infantrymen and grenadiers at their side. The fighter pilot depended on his own machine far more than other warriors below, and usually had far more ability at his own fingertips to kill and destroy than foot soldiers and sailors. And yet the pilot's own aircraft required a squad of mechanics to fuel, fix, and arm the plane—numbers vastly greater than those to the rear that supplied and equipped a single foot soldier. Esprit de corps was pyramidal, not lateral, as a host of unseen support soldiers was needed to empower a single pilot or bombing crew.[15]

Admiral William "Bull" Halsey Jr., sixty-two when the war ended, was on the bridge of his warships during the Battle of Leyte Gulf, and sixty-three-year-old General Gerd von Rundstedt motored about the front during the 1939 invasion of Poland. In contrast, supreme air marshals rarely flew routine fighter missions and only occasionally were observers on bombing missions. No one expected General Henry Harley "Hap" Arnold, commanding general of the US Army Air Forces, to lead B-17 squadrons over Germany, or General Curtis LeMay, veteran of some of the most dangerous B-17 missions and a few B-29 flights from China, to lead the B-29s on the fire raids—as much as either might have liked to. Air power was different: a middle-aged or old man could lead from the bridge or jeep, but not so easily from behind the controls of a fighter or high-performance bomber. Either the greater odds of death in air combat or the rigors of air pressure and altitude made leading from behind far more common among air marshals. Of course, too, a general in a cockpit was more isolated from his men in other bombers than was an army commander in a jeep on the ground. The old World War I ace, rotund Hermann Goering, like Field Marshal Albert Kesselring staring out from Cap Gris Nez across the Channel, had no firsthand and updated knowledge of British Spitfires or of much else above the ground.[16]

Remote and distant supreme command—in the manner of Admiral Doenitz's unfamiliarity with the constantly changing threats facing his U-boats—may explain in part why airplanes (like submarines) for much of the war were often so unwisely deployed. Often air campaigns were waged against the recommendations of pilots themselves, whether in the German decisions to turn back from attacking British airfields in 1940 to the area bombing of cities or in the largely disastrous American daylight precision bombing campaigns of 1942–1943. Over twenty American generals and admirals died due to enemy action during combat operations during World War II; the few Army Air Force generals who perished were lost in crashes (e.g., Lieutenant General Frank Maxwell Andrews, Lieutenant General Millard Fillmore Harmon Jr., and Brigadier General James R. Anderson) rather than shot down leading missions.

By 1945 aircraft carriers, not battleships, were recognized as a navy's most lethal attack arm. The two largest American offensive operations in the European theater—Normandy and the Arnhem campaign—all saw airborne troops play major, if not always successful, roles. Without British Mosquitoes and Typhoons, and American Thunderbolt fighter-bombers, the Allied ground offensive of July and early August 1944 might well have stalled in Normandy. Between D-Day and the end of the European war on May 8, 1945, American fighters and fighter-bombers flew an incredible 212,731 sorties against German forces, and expended twenty-four million rounds of .50 caliber ammunition at the German army—over seventy thousand rounds every day and about twenty bullets per enemy combat soldier. German Panzers, at any rate, considered it dangerous to be transferred from the Eastern Front to the Western, largely because American and British armor had far more lethal fighter air support than did superb Soviet armor.[17]

Ships operated amid squalls and storms. Vast amphibious operations like the D-Day invasion of Normandy went ahead in the middle of rough seas. British cruisers, battleships, destroyers, and carriers in May 1941 closed in on the *Bismarck* despite fog and high seas. Army Group Center continued its desperate march on Moscow even when late autumn temperatures dipped to almost minus 50 degrees Fahrenheit.

Routine cloud cover and the jet stream, however, doomed the early campaigns of high-altitude, precision bombing by B-29 Superfortresses. Without the confident expectation of serial snowstorms, fog, and overcast skies over Belgium, Hitler would never have ordered his December 16, 1944, "Watch on the Rhine" campaign through the Ardennes that hinged, for a moment successfully, on inclement weather that grounded British and American fighter-bombers. Even with crude radar sets, weather patterns governed the effectiveness of World War II air power in a way not true of either naval or infantry operations. "If weather at the target area was not suitable to bombing," wrote American Brigadier General Haywood S. Hansell, "then a whole mission had been wasted and perhaps the lives of many crewmen had been lost to no effect."[18]

The epic poet Homer's bowman Paris was deemed less heroic than the spearman Achilles. A medieval knight's death by a crossbow bolt was somehow felt to be tragic in a way being hacked in face-to-face combat by an aristocrat's broadsword was not. Transferred to the twentieth century, that same dichotomy played out with a rookie pilot in a strafing Typhoon or Thunderbolt above Normandy easily wiping out a crack German veteran Waffen SS platoon that had survived three years of nightmarish battle on the Eastern Front. The lamentations of German generals over the hordes of fighter-bombers that shredded their Panzers were predicated not just on anger at the Luftwaffe's comparative impotence but also on the ancestral notion that missile troops—in this case American and British kids in their teens and early twenties piloting *Jäger Bombers* ("hunter-bombers")—should not so easily from afar and anonymously kill their supposed veteran infantry betters on the battlefield.[19]

World War II infantrymen and sailors objected that aircrews' food, accommodations, and hours were far preferable to the alternatives of the trench and foxhole, or the mess hall and hammock on rolling seas. Most airfields were to the rear of the front lines. Relative calm between missions allowed a break from the stress of combat that sailors on a cruiser never had because they could never be quite sure whether there were enemies below, above, or on the surface. Soldiers complained that they waited weeks for rest and relaxation, but "flyboys" enjoyed both every day. Such perceptions had nothing to do with the reality of death. B-17 crews, for example, suffered higher casualty percentages than did most infantry units or seamen below. By late 1944 and early 1945, the Luftwaffe on average was losing to accidents and enemy action more than 30 percent of its deployable fighter force *per month*.[20]

Three to four times as many ground soldiers were wounded as killed. But in the air the ratio was reversed: three times as many were killed as injured—no doubt because of the ubiquity of larger-caliber machine guns, cannon, and flak, the added enemy of the altitude, and the lack of accessible medical attention. Thin skins of a metal plane offered almost no protection for pilots and crews. Hundreds of machine gun and cannon rounds, usually in calibers larger than those of infantry rifles, often left little flesh remaining. Other than occasional armor behind the seat, most planes did not have the horsepower to accommodate reinforcement of their aluminum airframes. Planes were far faster than land vehicles and their crashes therefore far more lethal. Flying in a bomber was the equivalent of manning a tank or ship without armor. Harold Bird-Wilson, air vice marshal and veteran of the Battle of Britain, relates the gruesome story of his squadron commander, who mistakenly attacked a heavy German Messerschmitt Bf 110 fighter: "Jerry got the better of him and all we found of him was his shirt." No poem of World War II has been more haunting than Randall Jarrell's "The Death of the Ball Turret Gunner," with its eerie last line, "When I died they washed me out of the turret with a hose."[21]

Successfully bailing out of a B-17 or B-29 was no guarantee of survival. Along with the rigors of capture and detention, there were occasional summary executions by civilians showered daily by incendiaries. My father, a central fire control gunner of more than three dozen B-29 missions, once remarked that he sometimes did not even wear a parachute on a low-level fire raid, given that either the inferno or irate civilians below meant instant death if he ever descended from the plane. Fighter-bombers often unloaded their magazines on civilian trains, ordinary car traffic, and houses and farms—a fact not forgotten by those on the receiving end when pilots bailed out or ditched. Aircrews did not overly worry about the effect of their operations on civilians thousands of feet below. As one B-29 tail gunner remarked years later of the fire raids, "unlike men on the ground, we were far removed from the suffering we caused far below. We engaged in anonymous destruction." No one lamented, for example, that a British fighter strafed the car of Field Marshal Fedor von Bock—who claimed privately that he had no sympathy for the Nazism that he so eagerly served—killing the general, his wife, and stepdaughter, who were all fleeing the front in the closing days of the war.[22]

HISTORICALLY, CAVALRY HAD played five chief roles on the Western battlefield. They served as prebattle reconnaissance forces to scout enemy formations. They covered the exposed flanks of vulnerable infantrymen. As heavier mounted lancers, cavalry blasted a hole for infantry to exploit.

Horsemen were also used as rapid pursuers against the vulnerable and fleeing defeated. Occasionally en masse they conducted full-scale attacks on enemy infrastructure. The new air cavalry of World War II followed all five of those agendas. During the breakout from Normandy in late July 1944, Allied reconnaissance apprised the American army of the position of dug-in German formations. In "Operation Cobra," launched seven weeks after the D-Day landings, some three thousand American heavy and fighter-bombers during the last week of July 1944 blasted a hole through German Panzer divisions. That massive aerial assault allowed the US First Army to break out from its stagnation within the hedgerows.

Once the newly formed American Third Army joined the race eastward from Normandy, General George S. Patton relied on the tactical air cavalry of General Elwood "Pete" Quesada's fighter-bombers to protect the flanks of his fast-moving force from encirclement by superior German Panzers. Operation Barbarossa three years earlier had been predicated on Panzer thrusts that ranged far ahead of infantry, their vulnerable flanks also being protected by the Luftwaffe. Even if American fighter-bombers could not always easily stop Panzers, they systematically destroyed supply trucks, interrupted logistics, terrified armor and artillery crews, and slaughtered infantry. Weeks later at the so-called Falaise Pocket, it was the pursuing air formations, in the manner of Napoleonic chasseurs, that inflicted much of the damage on fleeing remnants of Army Group B that had sought to escape from the closing Allied pincers. By war's end, packs of fighters were free-ranging over the enemy's homeland, destroying anything that moved.[23]

Air power was revolutionary and traditional all at once. It brought cavalry to the heavens as well as the machine gunner and heavy artillery. Speed and distance were redefined by air power. Bombs came from distances undreamed of by artillery, while airborne weapons were fired not by slow-moving vehicles or ships but from platforms that were gone by the time their shells hit their targets.

Common air parity did neither side much good. Occasional air superiority allowed planes to attack those below with mixed results. But rare air supremacy meant air power ruled the seas and the ground. The effect of air power may not have been the only cause of the Axis defeat. But as a general rule, when German and Japanese planes enjoyed supremacy in Western Europe, Russia, and Asia and the Pacific until mid-1942, the Axis were ascendant. When they did not, Axis forces between 1943 and 1945 across the globe quickly went from stalemate to defeat to absolute ruin, as Allied aircraft flew and attacked wherever they wished.

# 5

# From Poland to the Pacific


T HE GREATER PREWAR arming and mobilization of Germany and Japan, and to a lesser extent Italy, had given the Axis a head start over
the Allies in air operations. They strafed and bombed mostly underpre-
pared and nearby neighbors, creating overconfidence that soon led inevitably to laxity. Japan, for example, in 1939–1940 spent 72 percent of its entire
annual budget on military expenditures. Germany produced more planes
in the mid-1930s than either the United States or Great Britain. Even Japan
built twice as many aircraft in 1939 as did America. Yet a far more massive
Allied effort to match and surpass early Axis leads in both the quality and
quantity of fighters and fighter-bombers had already achieved parity by the
end of 1942 and clear superiority in transports, fighters, and bombers by
late 1943. Again, the entire pulse of World War II mirror-imaged the relative production of and improvements in aircraft between 1939 and 1944.[1]

Italian and German aircraft deployed in the Spanish Civil War, and
Japanese airplanes over Manchuria, were reportedly both superior and
more numerous than those available to the Western democracies. German prewar air transportation was among the world's best. Yet, quite
ominously for the Axis, even by the end of 1940 Japan and Germany together still produced only 60 percent as many aircraft as did a neutral
United States and a beleaguered Britain combined, a gap that would
widen in 1941. Early border campaigns by Germany had misled the world
into believing that the Luftwaffe's initial edge in the number and quality
of planes might be permanent, a reflection of intrinsic Nazi technological,
industrial, or even ideological superiority. The ensuing air war over Britain and in Russia and the Mediterranean questioned all such notions by
early 1941, and utterly refuted them by late 1942.[2]


THE LUFTWAFFE, OFFICIALLY little more than four years old, swarmed
over Poland from the north, south, and west on September 1, 1939. More

than two thousand fighters and dive bombers accompanied the Panzers. German Panzerkampfwagen Mark I and II tanks were already obsolete, but due to close air support these lightweight machines were able to plow through Polish forces and blast supply depots and transportation hubs. The easy victories were declared to be confirmation of the verdict from the recent Spanish Civil War that it was pointless to resist tactical German air power when used in conjunction with armor.

Few critics in late 1939 had bothered to note that a largely disarmed United States possessed, in its peacetime air force, a contemporary four-engine bomber, the B-17, that even in its earliest incarnations was probably as good as or better than the smaller two-engine workhorses of the Luftwaffe. Quite logically the Wehrmacht had assumed a medium bomber might be adequate for hitting its most likely adversaries on either border. Nor was there even much need for an intensive German strategic bombing campaign for the first two weeks of the war. Poland's assets were almost all deployed in the field and were steadily being destroyed, and were not likely to be quickly or easily replaced by existing Polish reserves or industrial production. Those Polish troops who could not immediately be attacked in eastern Poland would be left to the Soviets.[3]

Still, both Hitler and Goering saw the propaganda advantages of bombing Warsaw, terrorizing the population, and sending a message to the Western Europeans, who would likely be horrified at the thought of such incendiaries soon raining down on their own civilians. In September 1939, Germany possessed the best-organized and best-professionally trained strategic bombing force in the world. Its fighter-escorted, two-engine bombers awed immediate neighbors. Between September 24 and 27, the first European city to be bombed since 1918 was methodically hit with the chief purpose of killing civilians and eroding morale. Between five hundred and one thousand Luftwaffe light and medium bombers ruined about 40 percent of Warsaw's mostly undefended urban center, resulting in some twenty-five to forty thousand civilian deaths. In the generalized dread of German air power that followed, few speculated whether the Luftwaffe would have had such an easy time had Poland had flak batteries, barrage balloons, and fighter squadrons, or late-model radar stations.

The American aviation hero Charles Lindbergh—himself accorded occasional choreographed visits to the Luftwaffe from 1936 to 1938—had warned the military establishments of Britain and America of the excellence and diversity of the new German aircraft models, supposed reflections of the vitality of Nazism itself. In a personal letter to General "Hap" Arnold written in November 1938, Lindbergh implied wrongly

that the Luftwaffe had become nearly invincible: "Germany is undoubt-
edly the most powerful nation in the world in military aviation and her
margin of leadership is increasing with each month that passes. In a number of fields, the Germans are already ahead of us and they are rapidly
cutting down whatever lead we now hold in many others."

Lindbergh, in delusional admiration for German professionalism,
was overly impressed by the daring of the Third Reich's experienced and
skilled pilots, and the brilliance of its ground-support tactics. Yet the
Luftwaffe hardly warranted his hyperbole, which seemed based more on
romantic notions of relative national will and purpose than on military
capacity. "The organized vitality of Germany," Lindbergh still gushed in
his autobiography four decades *after* his visit, "was what most impressed
me: the unceasing activity of the people, and the convinced dictatorial
direction to create the new factories, airfields, and research laboratories."

It seems odd that by late 1938 Lindbergh did not seek fundamental
comparisons between Luftwaffe bombers and the new American B-17
Flying Fortress, or German transports versus the converted American
civilian airliner the DC-3—soon to be rebranded by the military as the
C-47—or how well the long-range Focke-Wulf Fw 200 Condor stacked
up against the more versatile and practicable Consolidated PBY Catalina.
The Messerschmitt Bf 109 was not all that superior to the new British Supermarine Spitfire. Lindbergh also ignored the fact that German avionics
and radar were behind those of their British rivals. German industry did
not have a history of mass-assembly production comparable to that of
the American automobile industry. And Hermann Goering was certainly
not a competent air marshal in the fashion of his prewar counterparts in
Great Britain and the United States.[4]

Nonetheless, in the first days of World War II, the Polish campaign
seemed tailor-made to frighten the French and British publics. Junkers
Ju 87 Stukas, sirens shrieking, made near vertical dives before pulling
up from the ground in the last seconds to unload bombs with murderous accuracy on outmanned Polish infantry. Late-model Bf 109 fighters
achieved air superiority in a matter of hours, destroying all eight hundred
planes of the hapless Polish air force in less than two weeks.[5]

German advances clamped down south from East Prussia and east
from eastern Germany and German-annexed Czechoslovakia. There
would soon be no chance of strategic withdrawal to the east across the
vast expanses of Poland, given that the Soviet Union was set to attack the
Poles in just three weeks. That one of the weaker nations on the Eurasian
mainland was nearly simultaneously invaded, in surprise fashion by the
two neighboring and strongest land powers in the world, was not much

considered. Instead, an air-augmented *Blitzkrieg*—"lightning war," a term the German strategists themselves did not normally employ—ipso facto was deemed unstoppable by those likely to be next in its path.

German Panzers and infantry could have defeated Poland even without two thousand planes in the skies. Until he met the British Royal Air Force, Goering scarcely grasped that the number of enemy aircraft and pilots destroyed meant little if they could be easily replaced or even expanded at rates comparable to or exceeding those of the Luftwaffe. The blame for such naiveté was mostly Hitler's, who, despite upping German military expenditures in 1939 to over 20 percent of GDP, never prepared the Wehrmacht or German industry, even psychologically, for something of a quite different magnitude than the European border wars of 1939–1940.

Hitler's next air assaults against Denmark (April 9, 1940) and Norway (April 9–June 10, 1940) further upped the deadly reputation of German air power, again regardless of the actual quality and number of planes in the skies. The Danes capitulated in six hours and the Norwegians in two months, but the Germans still had not met a comparable air rival. The Luftwaffe could not stop Norwegian shore batteries and British warships from sinking several Kriegsmarine ships, including ten destroyers, almost half of the existing German destroyer fleet. The harsh climate and rough weather of Scandinavia, and the complexity of covering large amphibious operations without carrier forces, suggested that in any offensive operation other than a clear-weather border incursion against a weak neighbor, the Luftwaffe would face real difficulties.[6]

For a variety of reasons, Hitler's Luftwaffe never could produce en masse heavy bombers similar to the superb American B-17 and the later B-24, or even to first-generation British Stirlings and Halifaxes, and ultimately the remarkable eight-ton-carrying workhorse Avro Lancaster. In a few months after the Norway campaign this shortcoming would prove one of the great weaknesses of the Luftwaffe, and perhaps ensured that it would never be able to bomb Britain into submission, or even much reduce British industrial output. Having impressive medium bombers in 1939 that surprised and terrified outgunned neighbors did not mean competence in long-range strategic bombing across the sea or a thousand miles into the Soviet Union.

German industry had introduced the excellent four-engine Focke-Wulf Fw 200 Condor as a civilian airliner in 1937, proving that it could build four-engine aircraft with wingspans over one hundred feet. Yet the failure to master heavy bomber production was as much tactical as technological, and was often later blamed on early Luftwaffe air marshals who for a time were supposedly wedded to the flawed idea that the dive-bombing capability of medium bombers could substitute for high-altitude strategic bombing. German strategists had also assumed that blitzkrieg resulted inevitably in short wars that precluded the need for long-term strategic pounding of faraway enemy industry. In part, Hitler was already thinking of miracle weapons such as guided missiles and jet aircraft that might preclude the need for heavy bombers. Yet paradoxically the huge investment in 1943 in jets and the V-rockets made it difficult to continue to fund adequately a heavy bomber program. In part, the dead-end ex-perience of the flawed Heinkel He 177—a rather brilliant experimental design using just two nacelles for what were, in fact, two pairs of cou-pled engines—perhaps soured designers on the entire idea of pursuing four-engine aircraft. Few aircraft were as theoretically sophisticated and innovative—and unworkable—as the 177.

Early slow and vulnerable four-engine British bombers like the Short Stirling and the Handley Page Halifax were gradually superseded by heavier Avro Lancasters by late 1942. Nonetheless, in terms of reliability, payload, and speed, these early heavies were probably still at least as good as any medium bombers that Germany built until the emergence of the Dornier Do 217 in early 1942. Almost every subsequent German effort at producing reliable four-engine or beefed-up two-engine strategic bomb-ers en masse—whether the Messerschmitt 264 Amerika, the Junkers Ju 290, or the Heinkel He 177 Griffin—would prove wanting. The fact that the Germans kept trying to build heavy bombers suggests that they fi-nally assumed four engines to be usually superior to two-engine designs. Despite the tendency for ever-greater horsepower of individual power plants throughout the war, two engines never supplied quite enough power for heavy bomb loads and extended range.

Hitler himself raged about the failure of the 177: "The garbage plane is, of course, the biggest piece of junk that was probably ever pro-duced." The Heinkel cost just as many man-hours of labor as the B-17, but, despite possessing impressive payload, speed, and range, was never produced in comparable numbers and lacked the workmanlike reliabil-ity of the American bomber. Goering's idea of deploying four hundred heavy bombers by 1942, and an operational bomber fleet of one thou-sand planes (largely with the inclusion of problem-plagued Heinkel He 177s) by 1943 remained a fantasy, and a bitter fantasy at that, given the unreliable Heinkel's marked inferiority to its Allied counterparts. Often the Germans resorted to mythmaking about their unproven prototypes, at times naming the ill-conceived Griffin (and an entire series of failed models) the "Ural Bomber" and the Me 264 the "Amerika," as if mere brand names could translate into real bombers that would reach Soviet or American industry. It was typical of Nazi Germany's mythologies that it built a few six-engine prototype bombers (e.g., Junkers Ju 390) but not a single mass-produced practicable four-engine one.[7]

In his dinner conversations Hitler turned to magical solutions to his bomber dilemma: "If I had a bomber capable of flying at more than seven hundred and fifty kilometres an hour, I'd have supremacy everywhere. . . . I'd annihilate the enemy—for it would be impossible for him to catch up with his loss of production during the period." Hitler dreamed of uses for weapons that he (and his enemies) never possessed; in contrast, Allied leaders did not fantasize of four-hundred-mile-per-hour bombers, but instead found ever new strategies of utilizing their assets already in production, whether using heavy strategic B-17s and B-24s as tactical ground-support bombers to blast holes in German lines during Operation Cobra in late July 1944 or employing high-level B-29s beginning in March 1945 on low-level incendiary raids over Japan.[8]

Four-engine bombers—given their greater drag, complexity, and maintenance—were not always intrinsically better than two-engine models. Intercontinental airliners today, for example, are trending back to employing two, rather than four engines, given the vast increases in individual engine power and efficiency. But given the status of aeronautical science in the 1940s, to achieve greater bomb tonnage and longer ranges, it was usually necessary to design heavy bombers with four of the standard engines of the era. The excellent German Daimler-Benz DB 603 power plant produced over 1,700 horsepower and allowed the new relatively compact, two-engine Dornier Do 217 bomber to match many of the performance characteristics of heavier American bombers until the emergence of the B-29 (its four mechanically plagued Wright R-3350–23 and R-3550–23A Duplex-Cyclone engines still produced 2,200 hp each). But fewer than two thousand two-engine Do 217s were built. The theory that high-performance two-engine bombers could match their larger four-engine counterparts in speed, range, and bomb load again was never quite proven in World War II.

Finally, in early 1944, the Germans accepted that they simply did not have the ability to build both bombers and fighters, the latter so necessary to protect the homeland from Allied B-17s, B-24s, and Lancasters. Luftwaffe head Goering explained why German bombers virtually ceased to exist later in the war: "But you have to consider that I can always build four or five fighters instead of a four-engine bomber. . . . For example, what was the drop in production of heavy and medium bombers as compared to the increase in small fighters." Goering was, of course, correct.

But the dilemma was worse than that, given that much of the later astonishing increase in German fighter production while the Third Reich was being bombed was somewhat illusionary: the fighters were often hastily and shoddily manufactured, and the Luftwaffe was not able to provide pilots and fuel for the planes it received.

Despite Hitler's grand prewar plans, there were no deployable German aircraft carriers at all, and thus no naval aircraft comparable to either the American, British, or Japanese carrier air fleets. Apparently, Hitler believed that naval surface war would always be waged close to the shores of Germany and Italy, and not against the United States and the British Empire, and would thus be within range of Axis land-based aircraft. Like battleships, carriers were expensive to build. They would only draw resources away from both Admiral Raeder's commitment to battleships and battle cruisers and to an increasingly influential Admiral Doenitz and his dreams of deploying a huge transoceanic fleet of sophisticated U-boats. Unlike other navies, rivalries in the Kriegsmarine were not just between the new advocates of carriers and the defenders of traditional surface ships like battleships and cruisers, but also between U-boats and *all* types of surface ships.

THE MAY 10, 1940, invasion of France and the Low Countries proved a replay of Poland on a vast scale. Again without warning, Hitler attacked neighbors in relatively clear weather. The relatively brief fighting did not tax supply and logistics. The combined French, Belgian, and Dutch air forces were far more impressive than the Polish, but not enough to alter the results: Germany gained air superiority within days for the advancing Panzers.[9]

In a controversial decision that marked the unambiguous beginning of bombing exclusively civilian targets, the Germans sent 110 Heinkel two-engine bombers to hit Rotterdam. Because of winds and the lack of effective firefighting, the wooden high-rises of the city's historic center burned and nearly one thousand Dutch citizens were killed and a large but unknown number left homeless—supposedly another clear warning of what resistance to the Wehrmacht might entail for Britain and France in the new age of strategic bombing. RAF Air Commodore Wilf Burnett remembered the event:

> When the invasion of Holland took place I was recalled from leave and went on my first operation on 15th May 1940 against mainland Germany. Our target was Dortmund and on the way back we were routed via

Rotterdam. The German Air Force had bombed Rotterdam the day before and it was still in flames. I realised then only too well that the phony war was over and that this was for real. By that time the fire services had extinguished a number of fires, but they were still dotted around the whole city. This was the first time I'd ever seen devastation by fires on this scale. We went right over the southern outskirts of Rotterdam at about 6,000 or 7,000 feet, and you could actually smell the smoke from the fires burning on the ground. I was shocked seeing a city in flames like that. Devastation on a scale I had never experienced.[10]

By May 10, when the Germans crossed the French border, over four hundred British fighters and bombers were flying over France, with Hurricane fighters and Fairey and Bristol bombers based on French soil near Rheims. While outnumbered and often fighting above hostile ground, British fighters had nearly matched, dogfight for dogfight, the Luftwaffe's best. German pilots were surprised to discover in initial air fights over Dunkirk that a few of the newly appearing British-based Supermarine Spitfire Mk Is—unlike the more numerous and better-known Hawker Hurricanes—were almost comparable (despite their short range) to the heralded workhorse of the Luftwaffe, the Messerschmitt Bf 109E, in terms of speed, reliability, and climbing rate. In regard to maneuverability and ease of handling, Spitfires were perhaps even superior to, and their less experienced pilots as good as or better than, their German counterparts and veterans of the war in Poland. Spitfires each month were also being produced in greater numbers than 109s, and British pilots were schooled and deployed at a far more rapid rate in superb aircraft requiring less training and skill to operate.

The point is not that in brief encounters British Spitfire pilots proved consistently superior either over Dunkirk or the Channel to their German Bf 109 counterparts. Instead, the lesson is that the Luftwaffe finally met a serious enemy. And this new experience demonstrated that German air power—Stuka dive bombers, fleets of medium and often unescorted bombers, adequate pilot training programs, moderate aircraft production, first-generation radar, ground-breaking use of radio navigation and pathfinder units—was no longer exceptional. And yet it had to be extraordinary to fulfill Hitler's agendas on the relative cheap. Fortunately for the Germans, the Royal Air Force over France continued to conduct unescorted bomber attacks against German ground deployments, at one point losing two hundred bombers in three days.[11]

Churchill, in a controversial but ultimately wise decision, at last chose not to reinforce the RAF's fighter fleet over a sinking France. About a third to a half of the RAF deployable fighters and over two hundred pilots and planes had already been lost in May and early June. The long-expected full showdown between the two air forces would come a few weeks later in mid-summer 1940.

Even in defeat, outnumbered French pilots flying the supposedly outclassed and outnumbered Curtiss P-36 Hawk and the often problem-plagued but superbly maneuverable new Dewoitine D.520, along with British Hurricanes, had lost fewer planes than the Bf 109s they shot down—a harbinger of things to come for the Luftwaffe over Britain. In fact, French fighters outfought the Luftwaffe in almost all categories of fighter performance, albeit largely because many Luftwaffe squadrons were absorbed with ground support of an advancing army. Unfortunately, the Allies did not deploy their excellent planes, superb pilots, and home terrain to full advantage, failing to ensure that their aircraft were well serviced and maintained—and in the air. Numbers and quality of planes were not the only criteria of success. Throughout World War II, far more important were questions of operational efficacy: how many sorties each particular plane flew and to what degree it coordinated its efforts with ground troops. In that regard, the Luftwaffe sent up its planes far more frequently each day, and it used them in ground support of the Panzers far more effectively than did the French in support of their armor.

To the south, French pilots did well against the fighters and bombers of Mussolini's Regia Aeronautica that soon had been opportunistically sent across the border to France in expectation of piling on a collapsing France and nearly defeated Britain. Again, France's defeat was not due to substandard French fighters, poor pilots, or a lack of aircraft, but rather to faulty command, sloppy organization, and low morale that had resulted in only a quarter of three thousand available French fighters being deployed in actual battle. Planes flew too infrequently and were not properly serviced; too many were prematurely sent to sanctuaries in North Africa; and too many were held in reserve. Even so, the Germans lost somewhere around 1,400 aircraft to French and British fighters in the air and on the ground, almost as many planes as they would lose in the ensuing defeat in the skies over Britain—losses that would haunt the Luftwaffe a year later in Russia. More important, a complacent Luftwaffe took away another wrong lesson from its air victories in France: German organization, training, and élan could easily nullify disadvantages in aircraft numbers and performance—a myth to be exposed during the Blitz and for the rest of the war.[12]

THE BATTLE OF Britain is often defined as the relatively brief but fierce air war over Britain between July 10 and October 31, 1940. In fact, the "battle" was a yearlong, on-off slog that had begun earlier, in June 1940, and continued until June 1941, when unsustainable German losses and the invasion of Russia ended serious further Luftwaffe efforts to bomb Britain into submission. Other than some temporary setbacks in Norway, a few minor successful French armored counterattacks, and a period of U-boat losses, the utter failure of the Luftwaffe over Britain was the first clear-cut defeat of the German military. The verdict also seemed final: Nazi Germany had no fallback plans for obtaining air superiority over Britain. For the next five years, Hitler looked in vain for miracles to recalibrate the war against Britain. The numerous 1941–1942 defeats of the British in overseas theaters and the later use of V-1 and V-2 rockets against England were never to achieve what the Luftwaffe in 1940 could not.

The Luftwaffe had planned to quickly clear the Channel of the British navy, assure air superiority over the British fighter fleet, and then with impunity systematically bomb British war industries, with particular emphases on ports, shipping, docks, and storehouses. All that was to be the prelude to an amphibious invasion of Great Britain. Germans also might occasionally bomb civilian centers in the manner of Warsaw or Rotterdam to hasten the collapse of British morale. The supposed result would be a veritable walk-in victory by amphibious German forces (Operation Sea Lion). Or, a demoralized and blockaded Britain, without sufficient food or weaponry, would be forced to sue for peace—a reminder to the United States that only accommodation with the Third Reich could exempt it from such an eventual reckoning as well. Absent from the Luftwaffe calculus were intangibles that transcended pilot skill and plane excellence but that were so central in achieving air supremacy: the relative rates of replacing pilots and planes, an air command's innovation and response to daily changes, the distance of the target from air bases, typical weather conditions, and the concurrent responsibilities of air power in other theaters. In addition, the Germans failed to appreciate that the supremacy of British radar was not so much technological but organizational and practical in placing radar sites in key seams while having the properly trained staffing to interpret the results accurately and then to make the intelligence quickly available to commanders of fighter squadrons.

On the eve of the attack, the British had about three hundred fewer serviceable fighter aircraft than the Germans. The Luftwaffe was wildly optimistic. It had a mostly short trip to British targets from new bases in occupied France and a more distant Norway (which almost immediately proved too far for Bf 109 fighter escorts and too taxing on crews, even

for the rarer bombing missions against northern Britain and Scotland).
The late summer weather of 1940 should not have posed too much of
an impediment. Britain's air arm was all that was left of Allied air resources, with little chance that Commonwealth planes and pilots, a
neutral America, or a pro-German Soviet Union could quickly alter the
balance of rival air power. No plane in neutral America's fighter arsenal
of the time—not the P-36, P-39, or P-40—offered any advantage over
existing British frontline fighters; production of the adequate P-38 Lightning was stalled, and the two-engine fighter would not see widespread
combat until April 1942.

Yet, astonishingly, the British not only defeated the Luftwaffe's strategic bombing campaign but also dealt it such a crippling blow that by
late spring 1941 Hitler would miss especially the 1,600 German aircraft
and nearly three thousand Luftwaffe pilots and crews lost over Britain—
coming on top of more than 1,400 lost planes in the battle for France.
Despite the enormous forces arrayed for Operation Barbarossa and the
stepped-up plane production, the Luftwaffe started the campaign markedly weakened, with at least two hundred fewer bombers than it had at
the beginning of the May 1940 war against France. While the Soviets had
sent supplies to Hitler to fuel his efforts to destroy Britain, British fighters
in contrast had eroded the Luftwaffe in a way that lessened the odds of an
easy victory in a few months against Russia—one of most important but
least heralded contributions of the war.[13]

Conventional wisdom suggests that just a few more days of concentrated German attacks on radar installations and fighter bases might have
broken, at least for a while, the RAF fighter screens. But then suddenly,
the traditional explanation continues, Hitler, enraged over British retal-
iatory bombing of Germany—particularly the August 25, 1940, inconsequential raid against Berlin—ordered Goering and his subordinates
to switch to nocturnal attacks on London. That unwise early September
change in strategy caused much death and destruction, but still did not
knock out British industry, while giving the reeling RAF a critical respite
from further attack on its airfields and radar.

That conventional explanation for the cause of German defeat over
Britain is surely incomplete. More likely, the German failure was ultimately due as much to Hitler's air marshals' own flawed strategic and
operational thinking, much of which predated the war, as it was to Hitler's petulant outbursts. German fighter pilots and planes, while more
numerous, were not particularly qualitatively or quantitatively superior to
British Spitfire squadrons, and in many cases were inferior. In fact, when
the battle began in earnest on July 10, 1940, the number of battle-ready,

late model, top-flight fighters—Bf 109s versus Spitfires and Hurricanes—favored the British. By late 1940, the Germans were losing more planes per month than were the British, and building fewer—hardly a sustainable proposition for an aggressor soon to invade the Soviet Union.

German bombers were mostly medium, two-engine Heinkel 111s, Dornier Do 17s, and the excellent Junkers 88s—all without impressive bomb loads. German planes over Britain faced worries over fuel shortages. British fighters had more time for interception and dogfighting, and pilots could bail out over friendly territory. British airfields were better developed and perhaps more likely to be paved than German runways in many forward bases of occupied France, which were often makeshift dirt, grass, and gravel. The Germans had unwisely planned an air offensive in late summer on the expectation of an easy victory before the weather worsened and targets became obscured with cloud cover. The British knew their own fickle weather and the unpredictable conditions over Britain better than did the Germans. The latter often assumed that they were intrinsically well acquainted with the vicissitudes of the northern latitudes, only to find the weather to be an unanticipated enemy both over Britain and deep in Russia.[14]

London was also not Warsaw or Rotterdam but was outfitted with superior anti-aircraft forces from searchlights and flak batteries to barrage balloons and sophisticated firefighting capabilities. And it was a vast metropolis. In 1939, London was still the largest city in the world, with a population slightly larger than New York's, at well over eight million inhabitants in the Greater London area. It was also the symbolic center of resistance to the Third Reich and drew in some of the most gifted and courageous pilots from the Dominions as well as volunteers who had escaped from occupied Eastern Europe. Unlike the Poles and Dutch, the British Isles could assume that German bombing was entirely strategic and not designed to accompany ongoing infantry and armor attacks. In other words, they knew in advance that every plane in the sky that crossed the Channel had agendas of bombing their cities or airfields, or defending bombers.

The Blitz was not just the first (and last) German strategic attempt to defeat an enemy entirely with air power, but the first in the history of warfare. Early air power was being asked to do on its own—destroy the British ability to resist—what neither the German army nor navy could come close to doing. The problem was not so much that the Luftwaffe misjudged the obstacles to a successful Blitz, but that in 1940 no air force quite understood what would be required by strategic bombing to reduce an enemy's entire war-making potential.

RAF Air Chief Marshal Sir Hugh Dowding was an authentic if often underappreciated tactical genius, who carefully customized the RAF fighter reserve by focusing his high-performance Spitfires on German fighters, and the steadier-firing Hurricanes against slower German bombers. Dowding was willing to endure short-term criticism as British cities sometimes went up in flames and Spitfires ceded initial opportunities to go after the vulnerable and finite number of bombers. Yet by the end of the battle, Hermann Goering's premier 109s, the backbone of German air power, still suffered more losses than any other Luftwaffe aircraft.[15]

In contrast to the steady-handed Dowding, Goering was serially erratic. One postwar American interrogator summed him up thusly: "Lazy, superficial, arrogant, vain, and above all, a *bon viveur*." General Heinz Guderian noted of his visits with Goering at his Karin Hall castle: "He either wore red boots of Russian leather with golden spurs—an item of dress scarcely essential to an aviator—or else he would appear at Hitler's conferences in long trousers and black patent-leather pumps. He was strongly scented and painted his face. His fingers were covered with heavy rings in which were set the many large gems that he loved to display." No such character would have enjoyed supreme air command in either the British or American air forces. Nor would a Dowding or Hap Arnold take on additional responsibility, as did Goering, for everything from economic planning to occupation policy.[16]

In knee-jerk response to Hitler's own mercurial fits that ignored intelligence reports of bombing effectiveness, Goering alternated his choice of strategic emphases between radar sites and airfields, and industries and civilian centers. Dowding bet correctly that the Luftwaffe bomber fleet, with dwindling fighter escorts, would suffer unsustainable losses before it broke British morale or ruined England's cities and industries. For almost a century British industry had lagged behind its German counterpart and now had a fraction of the theoretical resources of German-occupied Europe. Nevertheless, throughout the battle it exceeded German aircraft production by more than a two-to-one margin (2,354 to 975 new planes). During the war itself, Britain outproduced Germany in aircraft five of the seven years from 1939 into 1945.[17]

German strategic bombing forces never recovered from their utter defeat, and essentially ended their operations over Britain in June 1941, in fear they would have no support to provide to the upcoming German effort in Russia had they continued to battle the RAF. To achieve a mere 5 percent reduction in British military production, the Luftwaffe had lost somewhere between three thousand and four thousand pilots and crews killed, captured, or missing. Whereas the civilian and military casualties of the Battle of Britain were substantial—well over 44,652 British subjects killed, 52,370 wounded—the toll represented less than 10 percent of the Axis casualties in the Stalingrad campaign alone. The British air victory helped to persuade Hitler to turn eastward in his long-standing desire to attack Russia, even without sustainable air supremacy. That blunder ensured the survival of Western resistance. Britain and its army and navy had not suffered the fate of Poland and Western Europe, largely due to its superb pilots and planes and the leadership of Winston Churchill, Hugh Dowding, and an array of British air marshals. It is no exaggeration that the Spitfire ruined Hitler's entire strategic timetable of 1940–1941 and thereby altered the course of the war.[18]

OVER THE NEXT four years, both the Germans and the Russians sought to bomb each other's economic infrastructure and civilian centers only occasionally. The Luftwaffe in autumn 1942 helped to level Stalingrad—purportedly at one point dropping scrap metal on the defenders when bombs ran low—a distant provincial Soviet city without adequate air defenses. Otherwise the Germans focused their strategic bombing attacks on Leningrad and Moscow, as well as on Russian transportation, oil, and manufacturing sites. In these operations, more than fifty thousand Russian civilians were to die from German bombers, an unheralded number that was greater than the noncombatant toll of the Blitz in Britain.

German bombers could never reach most of the Russian industry that before and during the war had been transferred beyond the Urals, and the Luftwaffe thus had almost no ability to substantially curb Russian military production. The cities that the Germans did target were usually bombed in tactical support of nearby and ongoing infantry attacks, in a blinkered way unimaginable to British and American strategic bombing planners. Similarly, after a few futile attempts to hit Berlin, the occupied cities of Eastern Europe, and especially the oil facilities in Romania, the Soviet Union virtually ignored strategic air operations. Unlike Germany, it could afford to. Due to the expanding Anglo-American air campaign beginning in 1942, Stalin never felt a need to devote more than 15 percent of his aircraft production to multi-engine bombers.[19]

Neither of the belligerents on the Eastern Front had developed bombers akin to second-generation Anglo-American heavy Lancasters, B-17s, and B-24s—much less the later huge American B-29 Superfortress. The Russian four-engine Tupolev TB-3 bomber was obsolete—slow, with a small carry weight, and low service ceiling—when the war broke out but was never superseded before the end of the war.[20]

Even by summer 1941, the Luftwaffe had learned that its limited-range medium bombers could hardly operate successfully against a country about a hundred times larger than Great Britain. The harsh Soviet winter snows hampered high-altitude bombing, hid targets, and compounded maintenance problems. German supply lines lengthened, making it hard to deliver fuel to bombers. A soon-to-be-outnumbered German army meant that the Luftwaffe could hardly spare fighters for escorting sporadic bombing missions against Soviet cities. Once Soviet industry began to supply thousands of top-flight T-34 tanks by late 1942, the Luftwaffe had little choice but to concentrate almost exclusively on ground support and to protect the transportation of armored vehicles and guns from distant German factories to the front.[21]

The Germans had lost the Battle of Britain, but the preeminence of blitzkrieg on the ground still remained largely unquestioned. Russia was no island with surrounding seas impeding the approach of Panzers, so Hitler assumed that rapid armor thrusts, huge encirclements, and tactical air support would still destroy Russian defenses in just a few weeks, just as they had forced the collapse of Polish and Western European ground forces. In the Second Punic War, Hannibal through a bold double pincer movement had surrounded and destroyed a larger Roman army at the Battle of Cannae (216 BC) in southeast Italy. Cannae-like encirclements leading to annihilation had been the dream of every German commander since the birth of the German state, and were apparently embedded into the DNA of the general staff. If the Panzers were let loose on a vast landscape with tactical air superiority, then the Wehrmacht could at will repeat decisive victories like Sedan in the Franco-Prussian War (1870) or Tannenberg in World War I (1914) and destroy the Red Army.

Again forgotten was the fact that the Soviets' newfound allies, the British and Americans, soon established an ability to bomb Germany, in lieu of an immediate second ground front in the West. The Luftwaffe, in contrast, had no such strategic air partners. The Italians or Japanese were hardly able to take up the slack and bomb Russian or British plants. In the Armageddon of the Eastern Front, the Soviet Union simply had far better and more useful allies than did the Third Reich.

On the first day of invasion the Luftwaffe, in perhaps exaggerated style, claimed that it had destroyed over two thousand Soviet aircraft. Within a week the toll rose to over four thousand. By winter 1941, much of the original Russian air force of summer had ceased to exist. The Germans boasted that they had destroyed over twenty thousand Russian planes in 1941 alone. Although Russia would eventually lose almost ninety thousand combat aircraft on the Eastern Front, its industry would produce 150,000 planes in addition to eighteen thousand Lend-Lease models sent from Great Britain and the United States. The Luftwaffe racked up astounding numbers of destroyed Russian aircraft, suffering far fewer lost planes that were nonetheless far less easily replaced.[22]

The initial Russian air losses were mostly obsolete planes. Unfortunately for the Luftwaffe, by late 1942 an array of Soviet Yakovlev, Lavochkin, and Ilyushin fighters and fighter-bombers began appearing by the thousands. They were nearly comparable to the Germans' Bf 109, and in some cases, even to newer Fw 190 models. Nearly five thousand of the supposedly obsolete P-39 American Airacobra were provided through Lend-Lease and became a favorite Russian ground-support fighter, given its durability and 37 mm cannon—yet another example of how close Allied cooperation maximized collective resources in a way unimaginable among the Axis. As in the manner of the German shock at the superb Russian T-34 tank, the Luftwaffe had no inkling that Soviet science and industry could produce thousands of first-rate Russian aircraft to fly ground-support roles. The Russians often ignored conventional doctrines of achieving air superiority as a first priority. Soviet air planners were not overly worried about destroying the Luftwaffe in higher-altitude dogfights but instead sought to overwhelm German planes nearer the battlefield, regardless of the staggering cost in Russian pilots and planes.[23]

The rest of the air war in the East followed a familiar script: Russians—fighting over familiar terrain and initially enjoying shorter interior lines, more plentiful fuel, greater production of quality aircraft, and vastly superior manpower—finally matched the Luftwaffe, and by 1944 were eventually able to overwhelm it. Two additional unexpected developments contributed to the Soviet air rebound. By early 1943, Anglo-American bombing sorties over occupied Europe and Germany had tripled. That now-existential threat forced the Luftwaffe to redeploy thousands of fighters to defend the homeland, along with thousands of anti-aircraft batteries, just as next-generation, medium-range American Thunderbolt and Lightning fighters were beginning to enter the war. German weapons production increasingly was forced to focus on air defenses, with less emphasis on tanks and field artillery, at precisely the time German armies in the East were desperately in need of more armor and big guns. Stalin harped on the absence of a second front in Western Europe in 1943, but he largely kept silent about the help that the Anglo-American strategic bombing campaign offered in reducing numbers of German anti-tank guns and Luftwaffe ground-support sorties, not to mention the necessity of redeploying Wehrmacht air and anti-aircraft assets to meet the Allied invasions of North Africa, Sicily, and Italy.[24]

THE ASSUMPTIONS OF 1939–1940 that there could be a "moral" and scientifically precise targeting of military-industrial complexes soon gave way to the area bombing of civilian centers, a few of them without much strategic importance. That alarmists and appeasers were wrong in 1939 about the likely damage from strategic bombing did not mean that they would not be right by 1944.

Through 1941, effective precision bombing was beyond the technological capacity of either Allied or Axis contemporary bombers. A prewar French bombing manual had warned (and had been largely ignored) that there was little more than a one in nine chance of hitting a target with any accuracy from even ten thousand feet. In Germany, there was little angst about indiscriminate bombing of Warsaw, Rotterdam, or Paris, given that there was little air defense and less likelihood of retaliation against the Third Reich. Later during the initial phases of the Battle of Britain, Hitler did temporarily restrict Luftwaffe targeting because of fears of reprisals against German cities by the RAF Bomber Command. But he quickly dropped that reluctance, in anger over inconsequential British bombing attacks on Berlin, and, even more likely, because the Luftwaffe believed that firebombing the British capital might either break British will or consume British dock facilities and industry.[25]

Undeterred by the prior Blitz, the British began hitting western Germany in earnest in early 1942, even with fleets still dominated by often outdated or inadequate medium two-engine bombers (Wellingtons, Whitleys, Hampdens, and Manchesters), and almost exclusively at night. Apparently the retreat from Dunkirk, the Russian demands for a second front, the current American investment in strategic air power, and the sheer force of personality of volatile Air Marshal Arthur Harris had steadily upped Bomber Command's share of scarce resources.

For all the impediments to these early attempts at strategic bombing, Harris sometimes achieved frightening early results. In operations like the "thousand plane" raid over Cologne on May 30–31, 1942, Bomber Command razed six hundred acres of the urban center and sent over a hundred thousand civilians fleeing the city, while losing around forty-three bombers. An elated Harris—to be known widely to the public as "Bomber" Harris—felt that he now had hit on the right formula to destroy the Third Reich, especially given that the new superb Lancaster four-engine bombers (that composed only 7 percent of the bomber fleet over Cologne) were scheduled to appear in even greater numbers by early 1943. In the March 1943 raid on the Ruhr city of Essen, home to the Krupp arms works, a huge force of 442 British bombers put most of their bombs, the majority of them incendiaries, squarely on the urban center with small losses of their own.

The British believed that the Germans could not stop Bomber Command when its heavy bombers flew with maximum bomb loads (often with incendiaries mixed in) at night, guided by hyperbolic navigation (based on differences in the timing between the reception of two radio signals) called Gee, and with radar H2S enhancement, a method of radar scanning of ground targets while airborne. Night missions meant less need for offensive armament, and thus less weight and smaller plane crews (seven crewmen, on average, for most four-engine bombers) than on the American B-17s (usually ten crewmen) bombing in daylight. There were certainly fewer British losses when a heavy bomber went down. Harris's arguments could at times become hard to refute: if area bombing did not tangibly disrupt an urban center's contribution to the war effort, then it was justified on intangible grounds of ruining enemy morale, "dehousing" civilian workers, causing civic havoc, and forcing huge expenditures in civil defense and diversions of ground assets.

Still, at least for the first years of the bombing campaign, there was little evidence that the German public was turning against Hitler because of British incendiaries. As Hitler himself supposedly put it, "these air raids don't bother me. I only laugh at them. The less the population has to lose, the more fanatically it will fight. . . . People fight fanatically only when they have the war at their own front doors. That's how people are. Now even the worst idiot realized that his house will never be rebuilt unless we win."[26]

Left unsaid was Harris's Old Testament sense of righteous anger that fueled Bomber Command, as well as a feeling of vengeance that the bullying Germans were finally receiving long overdue payback in the only way that the British were able to provide at that point in the war. In his most famous remark of the conflict, Harris presciently summed up his future directive: "The Nazis entered this war under the rather childish delusion that they were going to bomb everyone else, and nobody was going to bomb them. At Rotterdam, London, Warsaw and half a hundred other places, they put their rather naive theory into operation. They sowed the wind, and now they are going to reap the whirlwind."

Harris was not exaggerating. When he took over Bomber Command in mid-1941, he had just sixty-nine heavy four-engine bombers at his disposal. When the war ended he could easily put two thousand in the air. From March 5 to July 13, 1943, mostly British bomber forces pounded the entire Ruhr Valley, eventually torching Bochum, Cologne, Dortmund, Duisburg, Dusseldorf, Essen, Gelsenkirchen, Krefeld, Muelheim, and Wuppertal, as well as dams on the Moehne and Eder Rivers. Despite the ongoing reorganization of German industry by Albert Speer, key production in steel and armaments declined at precisely the time new armor and artillery were desperately needed on the Eastern Front.[27]

The Americans (who knew little of what the Luftwaffe had done to Warsaw or Belgrade) initially disagreed with area bombing, even though they arrived in Britain in midsummer 1942 without the precision bombing experience of either the British or Germans. They quickly began to

Strategic Bombing in Europe

hit Europe during the day with allegedly high-precision "Flying Fortress" B-17s, setting the stage for both a unified Allied strategy of twenty-four-hour, day-and-night attacks and an acrimonious clash of air doctrines. The Americans argued that their better-armed B-17Gs, equipped with a specialized crew of ten, and with nine heavy machine guns, exempted them from serious fighter attack. (In aggregate, some seven hundred .50 caliber machine guns of a collective bombing group were directed at fighters.) Americans also pointed to their vaunted (though overhyped) Norden bombsights, claiming that they could hit strategic industries with near pinpoint accuracy. Yet the British continued to achieve more lethal results through area bombing, and ignored American pretenses of targeting only military targets to spare collateral damage.

The later week-long incineration of Hamburg ("Operation Gomorrah") in July 1943, by nighttime British Lancasters and, to a lesser extent, daytime American B-17s, was supposedly a successful model of Allied cooperation to come, given the frightening fact that forty thousand Germans lost their lives and thousands more were displaced. In fact, the Americans played only a supporting role in the city's destruction. A perfect, if not somewhat accidental, storm of disasters seemed to have accounted for the horrendous German losses. The element of surprise and unusual high summer winds, as well as unexpected approaches over the empty ocean and the first widespread use of chaff as a radar counter-measure, allowed the bombers to arrive often undetected and to create a singular firestorm that would not normally occur over other targets. The British offered little moral posturing about their area bombing. In contrast, the Americans stuck to the pretense that they were bombing only industrial targets with precision accuracy, even though the vast majority of their ordnance missed the assigned targets due to the frequent reliance on unreliable radar targeting as well as the inability of the Norden bombsight to correct adequately for wind and clouds under combat conditions.[28]

By employing technological breakthroughs, like detachable auxiliary gasoline drop tanks to increase the range of fighter escorts and better radar that improved navigation, the Americans became more like the British than the British like the Americans. In fact, at war's end, the use of the world's most sophisticated bomber, the gargantuan B-29, had not evolved much beyond British-style night area bombing. The B-29s were designed as high-altitude, daylight mission precision bombers, but by 1945 they had become huge incarnations of Lancasters, and they were achieving the same fiery results on the unfortunate enemy below.

At the November 1943 Tehran Conference, the United States announced that its two strategies for defeating the Third Reich were an

Allied landing in 1944 on the French coast, and both night and day bombing deep into the German homeland by the Americans and the British. Both were responses to the impossible Russian demands for an immediate opening of a second front in Western Europe against the Germany army. Years after the war, Marshal Vasilii Chuikov, one of the liberators of Berlin, still illustrated deep-seated Soviet suspicions and ignored the role of Allied bombing: "The long delay in the opening of the second front caused us, Soviet soldiers, to understand the actions of our Western allies much more correctly than they were represented in the messages full of endless soothing promises which the statesmen of the West fed to us." Nonetheless, the more the Soviets complained of inaction, the more the Western Allies bombed.[29]

As late as mid-1943 the air war was still going poorly for the Allies, as both bomber losses and German munitions production climbed. British bombers for a while were surprised by the effective combination of German night fighters, sophisticated searchlights, flak batteries, improved radar grids, and the transfers of experienced fighter pilots, mostly flying later-model Fw 190s and Bf 109s, from the Russian front. In any case, the assertions of British air marshal "Bomber" Harris that by late 1943 or early 1944 strategic bombing might win the war proved impossible. As bombers flew far more deeply into Germany, their exposure to fighters only increased and losses mounted. Later, the "Black Sunday" raid of August 1, 1943, by B-24 Liberators based in Libya against the Romanian oil fields and refineries at Ploesti proved an ungodly disaster. The Americans believed that they could come in low at one hundred feet or less, in full surprise, and thus with certainty of hitting their flammable targets. In fact, the Germans and Romanians were waiting with one of the most sophisticated anti-aircraft defenses of the war. Of the 178 B-24s that took off, fifty-three were lost and fifty-five were damaged. Around 660 crewmen were killed, captured, missing, or interned in neutral countries. Only thirty-three of the 178 bombers returned to Libya without damage; the majority of the survivors landed with nearly ruined planes or made emergency landings throughout the Mediterranean. The ill-named Operation "Tidal Wave" was one of the few strategic bombing raids of the war in which more crewmen were lost to air defenses than civilians to bombs. Damage to Ploesti from the August 1 raid was neither lasting nor severe enough to curtail German oil supplies.[30]

Not much later, the "Black Week" of October 9–14, 1943, should have rendered the entire American heavy bomber campaign ineffective, or at least the idea of long-range and mostly unescorted daylight bombing operations deep into the Reich and its allies. One hundred and forty-eight B-17s were shot down or damaged on a second great mission over Schweinfurt (after losing sixty bombers and another ninety damaged on the initial August 17, 1943, raid)—20 percent of the entire force. Six hundred American crewmen were killed or captured. In October alone, twenty-eight bombers on average were lost on *every* mission. B-17 gunner Elmer Bendiner later wrote, "all across Germany, Holland and Belgium the terrible landscape of burning planes unrolled beneath us. It seemed that we were littering Europe with our dead."[31]

Long-range missions may have been somewhat curtailed, but they were not stopped entirely, especially since there were few other avenues before June 1944 of fulfilling Allied promises to the Soviet Union of opening a major second front. The bombers did occasionally inflict considerable strategic damage, and relief was felt to be on the horizon with the advent of longer-range escorts. Even the costliest and most infamous of the long-range precision raids—the first Schweinfurt-Regensburg mission of August 17, 1943, against the ball-bearing and Bf 109 aircraft works—probably resulted in disrupting half the production at both plants. American replacement crews and planes may have made up for the losses, as the US architects of bombing felt that they were at least hitting targets or thinning out the Luftwaffe, or both.[32]

A year later, by summer 1944, the British and Americans were clearly winning the air war. They were losing far fewer bombers per raid, and upping the numbers of fighter escorts, while German fighter forces lost half their strength each month, nullifying their own huge increases in fighter production. By focusing far more on attacking fuel supplies (mostly oil and synthetic oil plants), transportation, and the aircraft industry, sizable formations of British and American bombers—escorted by hundreds of high-performance Thunderbolts and Mustangs with drop tanks and permission to range widely to hunt down German fighters rather than stay close to their bombers—finally wore the Luftwaffe out. Spitfires, with drop tanks, should have played a far more prominent role over Germany. But a series of wrong-headed decisions kept them out of long-range escort service until 1944, largely due to old prejudices, dating back to the Spanish Civil War, that bombers, especially at night, could get through without fighter support. In addition, the British lapse was stubbornness on the part of senior RAF commanders who ignored evidence quite early on that, with rather easy adjustments and modifications, the Spitfire could have become an excellent long-range escort fighter. By contrast, the Americans had never experienced the trauma of a Blitz and felt no need to hold back their fighters to protect their own homeland.[33]

In May 1944 alone, the Luftwaffe wrote off half of its total single-engine fighter aircraft and a quarter of all its vaunted Bf 109 and fw 190 pilots. In the first five months alone of 1944, the Luftwaffe lost the equivalent of its entire pilot strength. For the last nine months of the war, the Allies enjoyed complete air supremacy. They systematically destroyed over 60 percent of the largest German cities, even if they were still unable to prevent increases in German production of war materiel brought on by radical changes in the German economy and workforce. Nevertheless, by war's end about 1.8 million German workers had been transferred out of factories to repair bombing damage to the Third Reich's oil facilities and transportation networks. Bombing did not just stop the mobility of trains and tanks but also disrupted German productivity by turning skilled factory laborers into repair workers.[34]

The final successful nine months of Allied bombing must be balanced against the prior failures of the British (other than the Battle of the Ruhr) and then of the Americans between 1940 and 1943. That savage trade-off has framed the postwar controversy about strategic bombing for the past seventy years. Altogether, over 160,000 British and American bomber crewmen were killed, wounded, or captured. In the case of British Bomber Command, about half of all bomber crewmen deployed over Europe were casualties, rates that exceeded trench warfare in World War I and even topped the fatality percentages of those Japanese who volunteered (or were forced) to join kamikaze forces. The Americans lost forty thousand dead airmen and six thousand destroyed bombers, and spent $43 billion on strategic bombing. The catastrophic losses of Allied bomber crews have in part deflected (along with recent more optimistic reassessments of damage done to German industry) the moral question of incinerating hundreds of thousands of German civilians, many of them not directly involved in the war effort. Deciphering the ethical calculus of strategic bombing is almost impossible, given the ongoing slaughter of nearly twenty-seven million on the Eastern Front, the smokestacks of Auschwitz, the inability of the Allies to invade France until mid-1944, the need for a second front to placate Stalin, and the relative ineffectiveness prior to the summer of 1944 of seriously hurting the operation of the Third Reich in other Western theaters such as Italy.[35]

The Allies accepted that their ultimate campaign against German synthetic fuel and transportation facilities had been as effective in weakening the Wehrmacht as area bombing of cities to "dehouse" civilians probably had not been. For Allied ground commanders who advanced through the wreckage of bombed-out German urban areas, area bombing did not make strategic sense, and seemed a barbaric and vain enterprise. A month before the Germans surrendered, General George S. Patton noted in his diary the common consensus of Army generals: "We all feel that indiscriminate bombing has no military value and is cruel and wasteful, and that all such efforts should always be on purely military targets and on selected communities which are scarce. In the case of Germany, it would be on oil."[36]

Neither the Russians, the British, nor the Americans would have reached Germany in March and April 1945 had not Allied bombers first nearly wrecked German oil and transportation, and ended Luftwaffe ground support, making it impossible for Panzer divisions to travel by day. Bombing was to be assessed not just in often cruelly curtailing German production but also in wasting Wehrmacht assets from the Atlantic to the Eastern Front and hastening the liberation of millions from the slave and extermination camps of the Third Reich. Or as the historian Williamson Murray—who has argued that strategic bombing ranked with the Eastern Front as one of the two chief causes of the Allied victory—summed up the effect of the Anglo-American strategic bombing effort on the Luftwaffe: "There were no decisive moments or clear-cut victories. Rather, the American pressure put the German fighters in a meat-grinder battle of attrition both in terms of pilots and of materiel. It was the cumulative effect of that intense pressure that in the final analysis enabled the Western Powers to gain air superiority over Europe; that achievement must be counted among the decisive victories of World War II."[37]

THE MEDITERRANEAN LIES at the intersection of three continents, where three great religions arose, and it is the gateway to global commerce from Gibraltar through the Suez Canal. Its historical importance should have made it an immediate Axis air priority, one enhanced by early momentum. The Iberian coast was pro-German. After summer 1940, the southern French shoreline was likewise nominally allied to Hitler. Italy was an Axis power. Germans, Italians, and Bulgarians occupied Greece in June of 1941. Turkey was neutral but, until the battle at Stalingrad, seemed to lean toward Germany. Palestine's Arabs were pro-German as well. Italy and Vichy France initially controlled most of North Africa from the Atlantic to the Egyptian border. Not since Roman times had so much of the Mediterranean Sea and coastline been in the orbit of a single alliance.

Yet the Axis powers never consistently obtained sustained superiority and never at all supremacy in the skies. That fact doomed all their subsequent efforts to occupy North Africa from Morocco to Suez, either to cut off British imperial trade or to link up with the Japanese. After the Operation Torch landings in Algeria and Morocco in November 1942, the Americans and the British quickly were able to bring in a great number of aircraft, either directly on escort carriers from the United States or from existing bases in Great Britain. By spring 1943, the Americans and the British had over two thousand operational fighters and bombers in North Africa alone.[38]

Hitler's invasion of Russia in June 1941 had originally drawn some Luftwaffe squadrons eastward, and shorted German air power in North Africa and Italy, although not as much as one would have thought, given the growing quagmire in the Soviet Union. In addition, the Italians and later the Germans ignored the chances of an early and perhaps easy invasion of Malta, and, with mounting troubles in Russia, seem to have lost any chance to coerce Fascist Spain to allow a land attack on Gibraltar. Despite the seesaw Mediterranean air war and the long-term forces arraying against Germany, Hitler had transferred Field Marshal Kesselring and the air power of Luftflotte 2 on November 15, 1941, from the Soviet Union to Italy. Kesselring, over the ensuing months, gradually reestablished parity and occasionally even air superiority over Malta. He had planned to assault the island (Operation Herkules) in a stepped-up effort to supply German Field Marshal Erwin Rommel, at least until the plan was abandoned in November 1942 after Rommel's failure at El Alamein.

Even before the arrival of the Americans, the British had developed several fighter bases from Gibraltar to Cyprus. Those centers made Mediterranean Sea routes more dangerous to Axis transports than the counterpart Axis air bases on Sicily and Crete were to the Allies. Before Operation Barbarossa, the Germans had demonstrated that they could invade and occupy Mediterranean islands from the Dodecanese to Crete; after December 1942, they fought mostly a Mediterranean war to stabilize the North African front and interrupt Allied maritime trade rather than to absorb Egypt and Suez. But by May 1943, some 230,000 German and Italian soldiers had surrendered, ending the air war for North Africa and robbing the Third Reich of some of its best divisions in a loss of manpower nearly comparable to that in the final weeks at Stalingrad. Allied air power was the one constant that initially kept ill-prepared British troops alive and later kept well-prepared British and American forces on the offensive.

The Americans were not so interested in protecting imperial trade as in bombing new targets in Europe. They saw their bases in the Allied Mediterranean as especially suited for conducting long-range bombing against eastern portions of the Third Reich. Fewer Luftwaffe fighters were deployed on the southern trajectories into Germany. The weather pathways from Allied home bases in the Mediterranean were often clearer or at least more predictable. Targets in Eastern Europe—especially oil fields in Romania—were well in range in a way not so true for sorties from Britain. And B-24 Liberators, which enjoyed greater range but were more vulnerable than the B-17s to German fighters, were well suited for the southern bases. By November 1943, there were nearly a thousand four-engine American bombers operating out of North Africa, Sicily, and Italy, giving the British-American round-the-clock bombing campaign yet another dimension.[39]

Allied Mediterranean forces, however, failed to use enormous advantages in tactical and strategic air power to affect in any significant degree ground operations in Italy. The Mediterranean Allied Air Forces (MAAF) of 1944–1945 controlled the skies over Italy; by 1944, over five thousand strategic and tactical Allied aircraft were operational. German armored forces increasingly were obliged to travel only by night. By 1944, most rail shipments southward through the Brenner Pass were subject to steady air assault. Any German troops not entrenched risked serial strafing. Nonetheless, the Allies were never able to translate such air supremacy into strategic victory in Italy, largely because of rough terrain; frequent rain and flooding; diversions of troops to France; brutal but inspired German ground leadership under Field Marshal Kesselring; the lack of a coordinated supreme Allied air, land, and sea command; and the often questionable American generalship of Lieutenant General Mark Clark, who oversaw American and later Allied operations. Italy became a sad case study on the limitations of even overwhelming advantages in tactical air power.[40]

NAVAL AIR POWER played a limited role in the European theater despite the greater concentrations of forces. France was defeated before it could finish its two planned aircraft fleet carriers.* Despite grandiose plans, Germany and Italy never launched any of their envisioned flattops. In contrast, Britain started the war with six fleet carriers under construction, and six to seven in operation. At Taranto (November 11–12, 1940) and Cape Matapan (March 28, 1941), British naval aircraft helped to damage the Italian battleship fleet, which had unfortunate consequences for the

---

*Fleet carriers* usually displaced between eighteen and thirty-five thousand tons and were armed with about eighty to one hundred aircraft; *light carriers* were much smaller (about ten to fifteen thousand tons), and carried about half the number of aircraft. *Escort* or *jeep carriers* were even smaller—about ten thousand tons in displacement with fifteen to twenty-five planes.

Italian effort in North Africa and against Malta by discouraging offensive operations beyond Italian waters. British Swordfish biplane torpedo bombers also helped to sink the German marquee battleship *Bismarck* (May 27, 1941). The Italian fleet was rendered largely impotent by the end of 1942, and German surface ships by early 1943. Carriers were free to provide air cover for Allied amphibious operations in North Africa, Sicily, and elsewhere in the Mediterranean. After D-Day there was little need for naval air support for ground troops, and British and American escort carriers were mostly used to hunt down vestigial German U-boats and protect convoys between North America and Great Britain.[41]

The vast—and often calmer—expanses of the Pacific were a far different story. Japan started the war with ten aircraft carriers, a number that exceeded the combined Pacific carrier fleets of the British and Americans. The American Pacific carrier fleet was fortuitously at sea on the day of the Japanese attack on Pearl Harbor, but the Allies' strategy of island hopping on the way to the Japanese mainland ensured that American carriers participated in almost every major land and naval engagement after that.

One theme perhaps characterized the entire naval air war in the Pacific: in major carrier air encounters—the battles of the Coral Sea, Midway, the Eastern Solomons, Cape Esperance, Santa Cruz, the Philippine Sea, and Leyte Gulf—the result was either an American tactical or strategic victory, or at least a draw. In fact, American carriers never lost a single carrier-to-carrier air battle against their Imperial Japanese enemies, despite entering the war in December 1941 with only four fleet carriers (USS *Hornet*, USS *Enterprise*, USS *Lexington*, and USS *Saratoga*) in the Pacific. (The USS *Wasp* was not transferred from the Atlantic until June 1942.) Yet by November 1942, despite the great victory at Midway and the loss of four Japanese carriers, for a time only the *Enterprise* was left operational in the Pacific.

Several consistent themes characterized the spectacular American naval air success. First, like Japan and Great Britain, the United States was a pioneer in naval aviation and had long experience with carriers between the wars. American admirals were widely trained, did not craft overly complex plans involving ruse and deception, in the manner of the Japanese, and managed even in hard-fought battles to avoid catastrophic losses. As a result, the Americans never lost more than one fleet carrier in any single engagement. Altogether, during four years of war, the Americans sank twenty Japanese carriers of various sizes and models, while losing eleven carriers, only four of which were fleet carriers.

Second, the United States built some twenty-two fleet carriers to Japan's sixteen of all categories (light and fleet) during the war. America's new *Essex*-class carriers—ninety aircraft, thirty-three knots maximum speed, 27,100 tons standard displacement, and nearly nine hundred feet long—were qualitatively superior to any carrier in the world. Even more important, the Americans in astounding fashion built on the eve and during the war over 150 fleet, light, and escort carriers. They also continually increased their number of carrier pilots, while Japan's naval aviation forces insidiously decreased, due both to greater carrier and plane losses and to far shorter and less successful pilot training.[42]

Japanese carriers faced far more enemy submarines and surface ships than did their American counterparts. The Americans were far more adept at repair and maintenance of their carrier fleet and replacement of lost aircrews. After the Battle of the Coral Sea (May 4–8, 1942), the badly damaged *Yorktown* was made seaworthy and refitted in just sixty-eight hours at Pearl Harbor. In contrast, the crippled *Shokaku* and the plane-depleted *Zuikaku* took months to be repaired or refitted with aircrews—a fact with terrible consequences for the Japanese a month later at the Battle of Midway. Had the fallout from the Battle of the Coral Sea been reversed, the Imperial Japanese Navy might have fought at Midway with six fleet carriers to the Americans' two.

America could also afford to commission new battleships (10 between April 1941 and April 1944) without shortchanging its carrier fleet. The Japanese did not come close to matching that number. Japan entered the war with ten battleships, while building just two more, the seventy-two-thousand-ton behemoths *Musashi* and *Yamato*. They were the two largest, most costly warships in the world, but proved relatively useless in battle before being swarmed by American carrier planes and sunk. The estimated construction costs of a *Yamato* or *Musashi* battleship were around 160–170 million Japanese yen each. For such a sum, the Imperial Japanese Navy might have built ten of its latest excellent *Akizuki*-class destroyers (approximately 18 million yen apiece), invaluable in escorting merchant ships and waging antisubmarine warfare, and considered among the best destroyers built during the war. A fleet of twenty of them would have done far more damage than the twin *Yamato*-class white elephants that sucked resources from Japanese naval air programs and often sat idle for want of fuel.[43]

Japan began the war with fighters and torpedo bombers that were largely as good as or better than their American counterparts. Yet in less than two years after Pearl Harbor, American carriers were mostly supplied with Hellcat fighters, updated Dauntless and Helldiver dive bombers, and Avenger torpedo planes. In terms of speed, armament, performance, and survivability, these second-generation fighters and bombers were mostly superior to all their Japanese fighter, dive, and torpedo bomber counterparts.

The comparative rate of production of new naval aircraft made it utterly impossible for Japan to achieve numerical parity. In Japan's peak production year of 1944, it manufactured a total of 28,180 military aircraft, quite an impressive number had Japan been at war only with China or perhaps just Britain or the Soviet Union. Although budgeting for a two-front war, that same year America sent ninety-six thousand new planes abroad to Europe and the Pacific. By war's end, the US Navy's carrier fleet and support bases alone had received eighty thousand planes, which was more aircraft than Japan produced for all branches of its military during the entire war. Such production reflected vast industrial disparities. In terms of steel and coal, America had outproduced Japan by margins of well over ten-to-one. Oil output was even more dramatically one-sided: the United States entered the war pumping over seven hundred times more domestic oil per year than Japan. Japan ranked twenty-second in the world in oil production in 1941; the United States, first. Without adequate supplies of refined fuels, the Japanese could never build, operate, or train carrier forces comparable to those of the British and Americans.[44]

Japan increasingly shorted its ground forces in order to seek parity with the American and British air and naval forces in the Pacific. Although the output and productivity of the Japanese economy (more analogous to the Soviet than the Italian) is sometimes underrated by historians, Japan's huge investment in air and naval power still did not achieve parity with the Anglo-Americans, but it helped to explain why a chronically ill-supplied Japanese army in China and Burma was never quite able to achieve any of its long-term objectives.[45]

By mid- to late 1943, the US Navy had attained complete air superiority in the Pacific. American carrier pilots were free to engage in critical multifaceted missions without much worry of competing enemy naval air power. They hunted down Japanese ships and transports, raided Japanese land facilities on islands and the homeland, and provided air support for American amphibious operations and bombing missions. In fact, American carriers and their aircraft suffered more losses from Japanese surface ships, submarines, and land-based kamikazes than from Japanese naval air attacks. Not a single American fleet carrier was lost after 1942.

Carrier planes also facilitated the creation of land-based air forces. American carriers for eight months continually supplied Wildcats and dive bombers to the Marines' "Cactus Air Force" on Guadalcanal. The key conquest of the Marianas (June–August 1944) was due entirely to American naval air superiority; no territorial loss so hurt Japan's war effort as the establishment of B-29 bases on Guam, Saipan, and Tinian, which soon would guarantee fire raids on the Japanese mainland. When news reached Fleet Admiral Osami Nagano of the loss of the Marianas, he lamented, "Hell is on us."[46]

Carrier war completely inverted the logic of aviation. As a general rule, planes had to become more powerful and better designed to achieve greater attack ranges. That fact was ostensibly true of naval aircraft as well as land-based planes. But carriers could uniquely advance the air base closer to the enemy—even while planes were in the air—thus adding a second dimension to the operational range of carrier-based fighters and tactical bombers that was impossible for land-based aircraft.

The air wars in the Pacific and Atlantic were, of course, radically dissimilar. Japanese naval air power posed an entirely different and originally greater threat to British and American ships than did Axis land-based air forces. But in both theaters, the Allies by mid-1944 had largely neutralized all sources of Axis air power and achieved air supremacy. That reality ensured that the British and Americans were increasingly free to use their huge fleets to mount amphibious invasions and strike enemy bases almost anywhere they chose.

Voltaire reportedly wrote that "God is not on the side of the big battalions, but on the side of those who shoot best."[47] In the case of the air war, by 1944 the Allies had sent out both the most planes and the best-trained pilots, and crushed what had been the best air forces in the world when the war began in 1939. That achievement unleashed hundreds of thousands of planes against unprotected civilians and soldiers on the ground and at sea, which had been the intent of air power in the first place.

In traditional ground and sea theaters of World War II, technological and operational progress continued at an astonishing pace. Because air power was a revolutionary weapon and in constant cycles of technological change and response, weapons of the air—rockets, jets, huge four-engine bombers—by 1945 seemed from another planet in comparison to those of 1939. Likewise, air munitions and tactics matched revolutionary changes in aircraft, with the result that no one in 1939 could have dreamed of atomic bombs and kamikaze suicide planes used as veritable cruise missiles. In the next chapter, a paradox arises about how air power ended the fighting in the Pacific in World War II: at precisely the moment when air forces had at last dominated the war and were savagely used to incinerate hundreds of thousands of workers and civilians, their existential lethality also abruptly finished the conflict, saving millions more.

# 6

# New Terrors from Above

THE MOST DEADLY weapon of the entire war was the huge American B-29 bomber. It turned on its head the bankrupt idea of gigantism, as seen in the examples of the battleship *Yamato* or German so-called Royal or King Tiger tanks. In the B-29's case, perhaps uniquely of all new World War II weaponry, vastly bigger indeed proved vastly better. The B-29 squared the circle of gigantism by being both huge and numerous—the only gargantuan weapons system of its class that was nonetheless built in plentiful numbers (about 4,000). The Boeing Superfortress is forever remembered as conducting the lethal napalm raids over Japan and as the first and only plane in history to drop atomic bombs during wartime. From the beginning of the war, the Americans had accepted that it would be far harder to bomb island Japan than mainland Germany and Italy with their existing land-based multi-engine bombers. The Japanese home islands were surrounded by concentric archipelagoes, all fortified and defended by hundreds of thousands of veteran Japanese troops and fighter hubs. Friendly air bases in China and India were distant and not easily supplied. The weather in the Far East was unpredictable and its patterns less well studied than in Europe.

Japanese industry was largely still untouched by serious raids until early 1945. Even as Japan was losing the war—suffering unsustainable fighter losses and lacking adequate fuel stocks even for pilot training—its industries by mid-1944 were still producing more combat aircraft than at any time during the war. In late February 1945, Tokyo was still virtually unharmed, even as Berlin was in veritable ruins.

For the Americans, the only effective way to ruin Japan's production was to deploy an innovative, ultra-long-range heavy bomber from great distances, stationed on any island within a radius of roughly 1,500 miles from the Japanese homeland. The round-trip ranges of existing Allied heavy bombers—B-17s, B-24s, and Lancasters—were adequate to reach most of the Third Reich from various bases in Britain and Italy, but in the

Pacific they lacked an additional thousand miles for round-trip missions from any conceivable island base.[1]

The solution, contemplated even before the beginning of the war, was not cheap. The B-29 Superfortress program probably cost more than the Manhattan Project to build the atomic bomb: somewhere between $1 billion and $3 billion, depending on how various associated research and development costs were allotted. The most sophisticated plane in aviation history to that point entered mass production less than two years after the flight of the first prototype on September 21, 1942. The bomber was enormous. Its 141-foot wingspan (well over twice that of most German bombers) and over 130,000-pound maximum loaded weight dwarfed its large B-17 Flying Fortress predecessor (103-foot wingspan, 54,000-pound loaded weight). With a crew of eleven, just one more than on most models of the B-17, the Superfortress was faster (top speed 365 mph), normally carried almost twice the payload (10 tons), and vastly extended the nature of round-trip operations (in theory between 3,200 and 5,800 miles).[2]

Use of the revolutionary but temperamental plane hinged on massive support and logistics. It guzzled so much fuel—between four and five hundred gallons of gasoline per hour—that logisticians eventually grasped that B-29 fleets in war zones could only be supplied by sea. The bomber's four Wright R-3350–23 Duplex-Cyclone turbosupercharged—but problematic—radial engines, the new innovative computerized and synchronized gun systems, and a novel pressurized cabin all required constant maintenance, expensive spare parts, and skilled ground crews. In the words of General Curtis LeMay, who by January 1945 was in command of all American strategic bombing operations against the Japanese homeland, the novel B-29 "has as many bugs as the entomological department of the Smithsonian Institution. Fast as they got the bugs licked, new ones crawled out from under the cowling." The nose segment alone, for example, required over a million rivets and some eight thousand parts. Some 1,400 subcontractors supplied parts for the plane.[3]

Although the American public expected missions against the Japanese home islands as quickly as possible, the initial B-29 bases in India and China were not so easily accessed, much less supplied, and at times were vulnerable to Japanese counterattacks. By the end of the war, B-29 losses had totaled well over four hundred of the monster planes, the majority of them probably from accidents and mechanical failure—a statistic not necessarily indicative of unreliable planes per se, as much as the novel doctrine of taking off from distant islands in new aircraft, flying mostly over water, often at night, and encountering rough weather over Japan, with a continuous flight time of sixteen hours and longer.

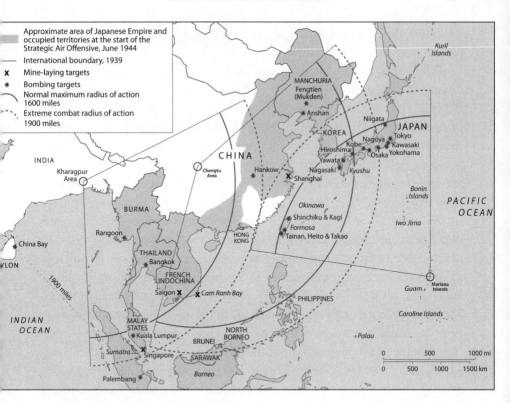

Strategic Bombing in the Pacific

Indeed, the long 1,500-mile flight from the Mariana bases—ready for frequent missions by November 1944—to the Japanese mainland often resulted in navigation errors and lost planes. And while the loss rate per individual sortie was "tolerable" (approximately 1.4 planes lost per 16-hour mission), given the thirty-five-mission service requirement (later often increased) and long distances over sea in darkness, it was likely that a third of the crews would not survive. Altogether, over three thousand B-29 crewmen were killed or went missing.[4]

The plane's ability to fly above thirty thousand feet when heavily loaded, at theoretical operational speeds of nearly three hundred miles per hour, was supposed to make the B-29 almost invulnerable to flak and enemy aircraft as it methodically blew apart Japanese industry with precision bombing. Although the huge bomber was never used against Germany, news reports of the B-29's performance characteristics terrified Hitler himself, being the concrete manifestation of his pipe dreams of "Amerika" and "Ural" bombers. And when four B-29s came into Stalin's hands, he immediately ordered them reengineered as the Tupolev Tu-4, the Soviet Union's first successful, long-range heavy bomber. Between

1947 and 1952, over eight hundred Tu-4s were built and then later deployed as nuclear bombers well into the 1960s.[5]

The gargantuan bomber entered service in May and June 1944, just months after the black weeks of nearly unsustainable losses of B-24s and B-17s in Europe. As a result, there were growing worries that the European experience of four-engine heavy bomber vulnerability might prove catastrophic to the B-29 program, given that each plane initially cost between two and three times more than the complex B-24 Liberator—and much more when all the research costs of the innovative plane were prorated.

High winds were a near constant over usually cloudy China, occupied Southeast Asia, and Japan. The India- and China-based B-29s were neither able to fly with regularity nor bomb with accuracy, in part due to inexperienced crews. Only about 5 percent of their aggregate bomb loads ever hit the intended targets. Almost no accurate intelligence existed about the exact location of particular Japanese munitions industries. Prior to the March 9–10, 1945, incendiary raids, only 1,300 Japanese had died as a result of US bombing of the Japanese homeland. The B-29 project was on the verge of being the most expensive flop in military history, making Hitler's catastrophic investment in the V-2 guided ballistic rocket look minor by comparison.[6]

The eventual solution settled on by General Curtis LeMay—who previously had flown extensively as a B-17 group and division commander in Europe, and formally took over from General Haywood S. Hansell the B-29 XXI Bomber Command based on the Mariana Islands in January 1945—was contrary to the entire rationale of the huge plane's design and proved as brilliantly counterintuitive as it was brutal, simplistic—and controversial. Rather than flying high and relatively safely in daylight as intended, LeMay's B-29s would now go in low at between five and nine thousand feet. The squadrons, in British fashion, would bomb mostly at night, and, at least during the first three incendiary missions, without their standard full defenses or reliance on precision bombsights. Staying at low altitude spared the temperamental engines, saved fuel by obviating climbing to required higher altitudes, and upped the payload of bombs to ten tons and more, an incredible load for prop-driven bombers. Mixed loads of new M-69 napalm incendiaries, combined with explosive ordnance, meant that the notorious Japanese jet stream was now an ally, not an impediment, to the B-29s' destructiveness, spreading the inferno rather than blowing conventional bombs off target.

Payload, not accuracy per se, played to the strengths of the B-29. Japanese anti-aircraft defenses were short of rapid-firing, smaller-caliber guns and thus were mostly unable to deal with nocturnal low-flying bombers arriving at fast speeds. In addition, the American capture of Iwo Jima was ongoing, and by the time of the March fire-raids the Americans were near to mopping up the island. Its capture would at last allow a more direct (and fuel-saving) B-29 route to Tokyo without the worry of hostile fighter attacks on the way.[7]

None of LeMay's superiors would later object to such a radical change of tactics on either moral or operational grounds. In part, their silence reflected the reality that, even before Pearl Harbor, Army Chief of Staff General George C. Marshall had ordered research into firebombing Japanese cities as part of contingency plans to wage war against Imperial Japan, given that nearly four in ten Japanese lived in cities. In part, it was a mark of respect for LeMay, who had led some of the most dangerous missions on B-17s over Europe and flew early and hazardous B-29 sorties over the Himalayas from China. In addition, there was recognition that traditional high-altitude missions were ineffective, or as LeMay characterized his role, "you go ahead and get results with the B-29s. If you don't get results, you'll be fired. If you don't get results, there'll never be any Strategic Air Forces of the Pacific."[8]

As in the case of the other architect of Allied incendiary bombing, British Air Marshal Arthur Harris, LeMay would face caricature and censure in the postwar era, at least some of it originating from the firebombing of Japan. Torching civilian centers was contrary to the entire moral pretenses of the US precision strategic bombing thus far in the war. And LeMay's predecessor, General Haywood Hansell, had argued that his precision strikes were improving and had at least forced the Japanese to disperse industry, thus impairing productive efficiency.

Unlike "Bomber" Harris, LeMay wisely made few extravagant claims, at least at first, about "dehousing" the Japanese population and ending the war outright, but rather insisted that incendiaries were unfortunately necessary to compensate for the fact that dispersed factories were embedded among the civilian population. When Japanese production dropped, LeMay logically took credit and defended the high civilian death tolls. He enjoyed the role of a take-no-prisoners general, but beneath his crusty exterior, like George S. Patton, he was one of the most introspective, analytical, and naturally brilliant commanders of the war. If he was a frightening man in his single-minded drive "to put bombs on the target," he was also an authentic American genius at war.[9]

The March 9–10, 1945, napalm firebombing of Tokyo remains the most destructive single twenty-four-hour period in military history, an event made even more eerie because even the architects of the raid were initially not sure whether the new B-29 tactics would have much effect on a previously resistant Tokyo. The postwar United States Strategic Bombing Survey—a huge project consisting of more than three hundred volumes compiled by a thousand military and civilian analysts—summed up the lethality of the raid in clinical terms: "Probably more persons lost their lives by fire at Tokyo in a 6-hour period than at any time in the history of man." Over one hundred thousand civilians likely died (far more than the number who perished in Hamburg and Dresden combined). Perhaps an equal number were wounded or missing. Sixteen square miles of the city were reduced to ashes. My father, who flew on that mission, recalled that the smell of burning human flesh and wood was detectable by his departing bombing crew. A half century later, he still related that the fireball was visible for nearly fifty miles at ten thousand feet and shuddered at what his squadron had unleashed.

After the horrendous raid, there was no way to stop the new B-29 deliveries of mass death, except for shortages of napalm at the Marianas depots. In the next five months, LeMay destroyed more than half the urban centers of the largest sixty-six Japanese cities, as he used the B-29 in exactly the opposite fashion for which it was designed. Japanese on the ground believed that it was the firebombing of the medium- and smaller-sized cities that finally broke civilian morale, given that the damage was increasingly widely distributed. As one firsthand observer put it: "It was bad enough in so large a city as Tokyo, but much worse in the smaller cities, where most of the city would be wiped out. Through May and June [1945] the spirit of the people was crushed."[10]

American B-29s probably caused well over a half-million civilian deaths in toto, although the exact number can never be accurately ascertained. Certainly, the bombing helped to ensure that the production of both Japanese weapons and fuels came to a near standstill. Crews might fly up to 120 hours per month, far more than normally scheduled B-17 missions in Europe. On days when the B-29s did not firebomb, they hit key Japanese harbors, dropped mines, and soon reduced shipping by over half. The bombers may have damaged Japanese industry as much by shutting down its transportation, ports, docks, and factory supplies as by the firebombing of industrial plants. Over 650,000 tons of Japanese merchant shipping was destroyed and another 1.5 million tons rendered useless, given the inaccessibility of ports and Allied control of the air and sea.[11]

Area and incendiary bombing over Europe had finally turned controversial, yet after February 1945 there was hardly any commensurate moral concern about burning down Japan. A variety of reasons explained the paradox, apart from the oft-cited racial animus against Japan that had surprise-attacked the United States and the growing fatigue from the continuation of the war after the surrender of Germany. The weather and jet stream made precision bombing far more difficult over Japan, while the nature of Japanese wooden and paper construction ensured that fire-bombing would be unusually effective. The Great Kanto earthquake and fire of 1923 had consumed the wooden buildings of Tokyo and Yoko-hama and killed 140,000—a fact not lost on American air war planners.[12]

Whereas the British had embraced area bombing in Europe early on in the war, and the Americans had clung stubbornly to the idea of more precision attacks, in the Pacific the moral calculus now worked quite differently. The Americans alone conducted the entire strategic campaign. They were no longer in the convenient position of being able to both criticize and learn from the efforts of an ally. The astronomical investments in the B-29 and its continued inability to serve as a precision bomber over Japan argued for immediate results at any costs, even if that meant nullifying some of the bomber's original reason to be: its high-altitude invulnerability to flak and fighters and its accurate bombing of heavy industry. Finally, the bloody Iwo Jima (February 19–March 26, 1945) and Okinawa (April 1–June 22, 1945) campaigns had convinced American strategists that only air power could avoid an even deadlier ground invasion of the Japanese mainland. The net result was a near unanimous though often unspoken willingness to burn up the cities of Japan.

As for the morality of the fire raids, the Americans argued that they could not be entirely blamed, given that before impending incendiary attacks began they dropped generic leaflets warning civilians to vacate: for example, "Unfortunately, bombs have no eyes. So, in accordance with America's humanitarian policies, the American Air Force, which does not wish to injure innocent people, now gives you warning to evacuate the cities named and save your lives." But how exactly evacuating Japanese families were to survive in the countryside during March and April was another story, as was knowing exactly when a Japanese city on the list was actually to be targeted. It was also doubtful that entire populations would have been able to obtain permission to leave from the Japanese military.

LeMay and his generals also cited the dispersed nature of the Japanese industrial war effort, which deliberately sought to integrate war production with civilian centers, and thus paradoxically ensured that the fire raids hit both civilian and military-industrial targets. They also pointed out that, while the final outcome of the war was not in doubt, nevertheless, thousands of American, British Commonwealth, and Asian soldiers were dying each day, fighting the Japanese and suffering from disease and maltreatment in Japanese prison camps. Later, Japanese accusations of genocide by air rang hollow to the Americans, given that the Imperial Japanese Army was responsible for perhaps fifteen million dead in China alone, a theater that the Allies had no real ability to enter with force before 1945. Nonetheless, the blunt-spoken LeMay confessed, "I suppose if I had lost the war, I would have been tried as a war criminal."[13]

Firebombing probably shortened the Pacific war by nearly destroying Japanese industry and commerce. B-29s may have eroded civilian morale in a way not true of the European bombing, although after the terrible Tokyo raid, firefighting and civil defense improved and Japanese civilian losses went down in other cities under attack. Still, a Japanese reporter, pressed to deny American boasts of damage to Japanese cities from the fire raids, instead conceded, "Superfortress reports of damage were not exaggerated: if anything, they constitute the most shocking understatement in the history of aerial warfare." By summer 1945, only four major cities—Kyoto, Hiroshima, Nagasaki, and Sapporo—remained largely undamaged.[14]

Both atomic bombs were dropped from B-29s, the only American bomber capable of carrying the ten-thousand-pound weapons and reaching the Japanese mainland from the Mariana bases. Most controversy over the use of the two bombs centers on the moral question of whether lives were saved by avoiding an invasion of the mainland. The recent Okinawa campaign cost the Americans about twelve thousand immediate dead ground, naval, and air troops, and many more of the fifty thousand wounded who later succumbed, with another two hundred thousand Japanese and Okinawans likely lost. But after the bloodbaths on Iwo Jima and Okinawa, those daunting casualties might well have seemed minor in comparison to the cost of an American invasion of the Japanese mainland.

The ethical issues were far more complex and frightening than even these tragic numbers suggest. With the conquest of Okinawa, LeMay now would have had sites for additional bases far closer to the mainland, at a time when thousands of B-17 and B-24 heavy bombers, along with B-25 and B-26 medium bombers, were idled and available after the end of the European war. Dozens of new B-29s were arriving monthly—nearly four thousand were to be built by war's end. The British were eager to commit Lancaster heavy bombers of a so-called envisioned Tiger Force (which might even in scaled-down plans have encompassed 22 bomber squadrons of over 260 Lancasters). In sum, the Allies could have been able to muster in aggregate a frightening number of over five thousand multi-engine bombers to the air war against Japan. Such a force would have been able to launch daily raids from the Mariana Islands as well as even more frequently from additional and more proximate Okinawa bases against a Japan whose major cities were already more than 50 percent obliterated.

A critical consequence of dropping two atomic bombs on Hiroshima and Nagasaki may have been not just precluding a costly American invasion of Japan, but also ending a nightmarish incineration of Japanese civilization. Otherwise, by 1946 American and British Commonwealth medium and heavy bombers might have been able to mass in numbers of at least two to three thousand planes per raid. Just two or three such huge operations could have dropped more tons of TNT-equivalent explosives than the two atomic bombs. Within a month, such an Allied air force might easily have dropped destructive tonnage equivalent to ten atomic bombs, following the precedent of the 334-plane March 9–10 fire raid of Tokyo that killed more Japanese than either the Hiroshima or Nagasaki nightmares.

"It seemed to me," Japanese prime minister Kantaro Suzuki remarked after the war, "unavoidable that, in the long run, Japan would be almost destroyed by air attack, so that, merely on the basis of the B-29s alone, I was convinced that Japan should sue for peace. On top of the B-29 raids came the atomic bomb, which was just one additional reason for giving in. . . . I myself, on the basis of the B-29 raids, felt that the cause was hopeless." LeMay was not far off the mark when he said of the use of the atomic bombs, "I thought it was anticlimactic in that the verdict was already rendered."

Without the decisive B-29 fire raids and the dropping of the atomic bombs, the American legacy of strategic bombing in the postwar era would have remained much more problematic, given the huge losses of bombers over Europe and the need for ground troops storming Germany. In contrast, the lethality of the B-29s led to a postwar consensus, rightly or wrongly, that huge manned bombers could win a war, in the manner of the fire raids, by destroying the enemy's heartland without the need to invade the enemy homeland with infantry forces. That checkered tradition was highly influential in the Cold War, particularly in the Korean and Vietnam Wars, until the onset of laser- and GPS-guided precision weapons in the 1980s gave planners greater strategic—and apparently ethical—latitude.[15]

In unmistakable irony, it took the genius of LeMay to reinvent the B-29 into a low-level, crude fire-bomber (somewhat in the German tradition of the 1930s of envisioning two-engine medium bombers for low-altitude or dive-bombing missions), exploiting its singular advantages of range, load, and speed while ignoring its great strengths of high-altitude performance, pressurization, and sophisticated gunnery that had accounted for its huge research, development, and production costs. That the bomber was rushed into full production with largely untested technologies, and yet proved the most lethal conventional weapon of the war, was one of the great scientific marvels of the conflict.

IN SUMMER AND early autumn 1944, three radically new Axis aerial weapons made their appearance: the German V-1 and V-2 rockets, and the Japanese kamikaze suicide dive bombers. All reflected last-ditch efforts to nullify Allied air defenses through new technologies and strategies. They were admissions both that Allied aircraft dominated the skies and that there was no conventional remedy to redress that fact. Yet, apart from those shared assumptions, Hitler's postmodern missiles and the Japanese premodern suicide planes could not have been more different.

The precursor to the V-2 rocket was the V-1 cruise missile (both were known as *Vergeltungswaffen* or "vengeance weapons" on the apparent logic that they were paybacks for Allied bombing, which itself was payback for initial German aerial aggression). The German propaganda ministry had persuaded the German public that at last the British would account for the firing of Hamburg and Cologne, which led to unrealistic expectations that the V-weapons might translate into fewer bombings of the homeland and a slowdown in the Allies' progress on the ground. Instead, the initial hype about wonder weapons only ensured a general disappointment once it became clear to the Germans that the rockets had not led to any discernable letup in the British effort.[16]

The V-1 flying bomb was recognized by its peculiar engine noise as the "doodlebug" or "buzz bomb" to the British against whom it was predominately aimed. This early version of a cruise missile was little more than a self-propelled five-thousand-pound flying bomb with 1,900 pounds of actual explosive. A brilliantly designed and reliable pulse-jet engine ensured a subsonic speed of 350–400 mph, at relatively low altitudes of two to three thousand feet. The main drawback of the V-1 was not necessarily its relatively slow speed or payload or even range (not much over 150 miles), but its primitive autopilot guidance system, which was governed by a gyroscope, anemometer, and odometer that were only roughly calibrated by considerations of direction, distance, fuel allotment, winds, fuel consumption, and weight. At their peak almost a hundred V-1s were launched at Britain per day. When launched from across the Channel in occupied coastal Europe, most buzz bombs were intended to hit somewhere within the vast London megalopolis, but without much certainty where. In the end, the V-1s proved even more inaccurate than the bombs dropped during American "precision" daylight raids over Germany.

Exact figures on V-1 production and deployment remain murky and controversial. The Germans eventually may have built or partially assembled almost thirty thousand V-1s and actually launched over ten thousand of them at various targets in Britain, of which well over 2,400 struck London. After the Normandy invasion, almost another 2,500 were aimed at Allied-occupied Antwerp and other sites in coastal France and Belgium, where a far larger percentage made it through air defenses. Even though about half of all V-1s launched misfired, went off course, or were knocked down by Allied ground and air anti-aircraft efforts, over six thousand British civilians were killed by them, and nearly eighteen thousand were injured. But if the V-1 was less sophisticated and more vulnerable than the V-2 that followed, it also delivered a similar payload far more cheaply. The Germans could produce well over twenty V-1s for each V-2 built. Even though the slower V-1 was far more vulnerable to British defenses, there was still a better chance that the aggregate thirty-eight thousand pounds of explosive of a collective twenty V-1s might hit strategic targets than the 2,200 pounds of a single, albeit unstoppable, V-2. If just 25 percent of the V-1s arrived near a target, then the cost per payload ratio still bested a successful V-2 launch by a factor of five. But in the end, the productive capacity of the British munitions industry was completely unaffected by either of the two V-weapons.[17]

Despite the V-1's short range, in terms of the cost of delivering a ton of explosives to a well-defended target, these early cruise missiles were not entirely ineffective for a side that was clearly losing the war. Unlike the terrible expense in crews and planes incurred in the 1940 failed German bombing of Britain, or the so-called Baby Blitz for four months in early 1944, the flights of the V-1s entailed few if any German military personnel losses, although thousands of starving slave laborers perished making the missiles. When weighed against the prior conventional need for fighter escorts and bomber crews, cruise missiles could be built and deployed relatively cheaply, and thus made the V-1 at least a formidable terror weapon.

True, the missiles did not harm British industry, but for months the buzz bombs diverted about a quarter of British bombing sorties to hunt down V-1 sites (reminiscent of Saddam Hussein's 1991 use of inaccurate SCUD missiles against Israel that likewise, for a time, redirected critical air resources from US and coalition bombing missions). At war's end, V-1s, despite their rather small aggregate tonnage, had achieved almost the same casualty rates and (admittedly unimpressive) structural damage on the enemy, per ton of explosive delivered, as did earlier German bombers, but without the human cost to the Luftwaffe.[18]

Some of the V-1's terror arose from the timing of its appearance. The new weapon was deployed in force in June 1944, without warning, and more than three years after the end of the major air battles of the Blitz. (The 1944 Baby Blitz had killed around 1,500 British civilians and mostly ended in May.) The shocked British public had by then finally thought their homeland to be relatively safe from air attack, especially as Allied ground forces in Normandy would soon eliminate most German forward air bases in occupied Europe. Ultimately the V-1 threat against British cities ended only when sufficient European territory was occupied to render the short-range weapon ineffective, forcing the last generation of V-1s to divert to the port of Antwerp and its environs.[19]

The successor V-2 rocket was quite a different matter. A true ballistic missile, the V-2 proved to be a poor weapon in terms of the costs necessary to deliver explosives across the Channel. While many more of the cheaper V-1s were launched against British and European targets than the later V-2s (approximately 5,000–6,000 V-2s were built or partially assembled, and between 2,500 and 3,200 launched), there was absolutely no defense against the latter supersonic weapon. The rockets reached altitudes at their apex of fifty-five miles and hit the ground at speeds up to 1,800 miles per hour.

Only 517 V-2s were confirmed to have hit London proper. Nonetheless, they killed over 2,500 civilians and injured thousands more. On average, for every V-2 successfully launched against London, about five civilians were killed. Nonetheless, unlike the case of the V-1, Londoners soon accepted that there was no defense against the random hits of the supersonic V-2. The American playwright S. N. Behrman remarked of the V-2 effect on London in January 1945: "I had arrived late in the day, and the British government official who met me remarked casually that the first V-2s had fallen earlier. They had made deep craters, my host said, but had been far less destructive than had been anticipated. There were no instructions about how to behave if you were out walking when the V-2s came, he said, because there were no alerts. You just strolled along, daydreaming, till you were hit."[20]

The comparison with traditional bombers was instructive. Just four or five large Allied bombing raids late in the war (500 planes carrying 4,000 pounds of ordnance each) delivered as much explosive as *all* of the V-2 launches combined. Yet both V-weapons proved evolutionary in a way that piston- and propeller-driven bombers did not. The V-weapons were respectively the antecedents of the late twentieth-century cruise missile and Cold War intercontinental ballistic rocket. Given the programs' huge research and development budgets and their lack of precision targeting and relatively small payloads, what supported the use of at least the V-1 flying bomb (but not the far more expensive V-2 rocket) was its psychological effect upon the Allies in late 1944, when they were confident of victory. The vengeance weapons were launched at a time when Germany was short of trained pilots and the fuel to train them, and they were the only viable mechanisms for both delivering ordnance over enemy targets and diverting Allied raids away from German cities.

Nevertheless, frightening though the V-weapons were, had Hitler earlier invested commensurate resources in a long-range strategic bomber, he would have had far more chance of causing havoc over Britain. Alternatively, the postwar US Strategic Bombing Survey estimated that the huge resources devoted to the V-weapons program could have produced an additional twenty-four thousand fighters. German sources put the costs of the programs somewhat higher, and suggest that just for the full investment and production costs of making, for example, five thousand V-2s at twenty thousand man-hours per rocket, the Luftwaffe might have instead built well over twenty-five thousand additional Fw 190 top fighters—a figure greater than the twenty thousand 190s that were built—and that might have changed the air war over Germany, had the planes been supplied with good pilots and adequate fuel.

The German Supreme Command of the Armed Forces (OKW) was originally not told of the extent of the V-weapon programs. But even when later briefed on both the V-1 and V-2 programs, it seemed, quite understandably, underwhelmed, concluding that "the quantity of explosive which can be delivered daily is less than that which could be dropped in a major air attack." Alternatively, had Hitler canceled the V-2 program and used its resources to focus solely on the V-1s, he might have produced well over a hundred thousand more such cruise missiles, with a far greater likelihood of inciting terror among the British population. The misplacement of resources into the V-2 program, as in a litany of other grandiose German projects, proved a disaster of enormous proportions for the Wehrmacht that even today is not fully appreciated.[21]

THE JAPANESE TOOK a much more macabre (albeit fiscally wiser) approach for combating Allied air superiority by substituting human lives for the staggering costs of scientific and material investment. Suicide pilots, or kamikazes ("divine winds")—a reference to the providential storms that sank a portion of the Mongols' fleet in the attempted invasion of Japan in

1281—probably made their inaugural systematic appearance at the Battle of Leyte Gulf in October 1944, a few months after the first use of V-weapons against Britain. Japanese suicide missions, like the German rocket attacks, arose from the now-shared Axis inability to penetrate Allied air defenses to deliver bombs on Allied targets—in this case, largely the expanding US Pacific Fleet.[22]

Exact information on the number of attacks, losses, and results achieved is somewhat uncertain, given that only about 14–18 percent of the kamikazes that initially took off ever reached and hit their intended targets. Some missions were mixed with conventional bombing sorties. It was often difficult to attribute damage exclusively to kamikaze strikes, or even to know exactly the number of planes that were officially assigned to suicide missions, or to count as kamikazes those traditional bombers and fighters that were crippled and in ad hoc fashion crashed into their targets. Both Japanese naval (65 percent of all sorties) and army aircraft participated in the suicide attacks.[23]

The threefold differences between the German V-weapons and the kamikazes are instructive about the nature of strategic wisdom in World War II. First, in contrast to the terrorizing V-weapons, the Japanese attackers were capable of tactical and strategic precision, inflicting considerable damage on the American naval fleet. On average, 10 percent of the planes in each kamikaze operation were forced to turn back due to mechanical problems. Another 50 percent were shot down or crashed before nearing their target. Many either missed entirely or did little damage once they struck. Nonetheless, in the ten months of kamikaze attacks, Japanese suicide pilots struck 474 Allied warships. They killed about seven thousand Australian, British, and American sailors at a cost of 3,860 pilots and aircrews. Kamikazes accounted for about 50 percent of all US Navy losses after October 1944. Their success rate in sinking ships and killing sailors was about ten times higher than that of traditional Japanese naval bombers.[24]

Second, the material cost per kamikaze mission was miniscule compared to the V-weapons. Even in late 1944, Japan still possessed thousands of obsolete fighter planes. They may well have been no match for American Hellcats and Corsairs but they could make perfectly good kamikaze cruise missiles. The suicide bomber campaign in that sense drew on existing military assets and entailed far less investment in pilot skill, training, and fuel than did the conventional uses of military aircraft.

Third, given their one-way missions, the kamikaze pilots of mostly Mitsubishi A6M Zero fighters were capable of a range of over a thousand miles from their homeland bases, more than five times the range of the

V-weapons. The threat of suicide attacks was eliminated only when the airfields on Japanese islands were destroyed and kamikaze access to fuel, planes, and spare parts ended. Ultimately, realizing those conditions required the surrender of the Japanese government.

The kamikazes achieved their greatest successes during the US invasion of Okinawa. Given the huge concentration of American ships and their relative proximity to Japanese airfields on the mainland, the kamikazes were able to sink seventeen US warships and to kill nearly five thousand sailors—all without altering the course of the campaign. In comparison to a V-1, what the kamikaze pilot may have sometimes lacked in airspeed and size of payload was more than made up with a greater range and vastly superior accuracy. The human brain proved far more adroit in finding a strategic target than did the primitive guidance systems of the V-1 or V-2. In the narrow strategic sense, like the V-weapons, kamikazes were evolutionary and would reappear decades later (albeit in a bizarre form), most prominently in the West on September 11, 2001, when Middle Eastern suicide hijackers of passenger jets were able to do more damage at little cost inside the continental United States than any foreign enemy since the British torching of the White House during the War of 1812.[25]

Even with an often unskilled pilot at the controls, a kamikaze-piloted Zero fighter, equipped with a five-hundred-pound bomb, full of flammable aviation fuel, and diving at targets at speeds of over three hundred miles an hour, proved a formidable weapon. Had the kamikazes been used earlier at the Battle of Midway against just three American carriers and their thin screens of obsolete F4F Wildcats, the Imperial Navy might have forced radical changes in American Pacific strategy and prolonged the war.

There was one final kamikaze paradox. Suicide bombings were effective, but they reflected a loss of morale and desperation that indicated that the war was already irrevocably lost before they appeared.[26]

GERMANY AND JAPAN embraced revolutionary war planning by devoting record percentages of their military budgets to air power. Yet by war's end Hitler was desperately searching for miracle air weapons like the V-1 and V-2 rockets and jet fighter-bombers, while the Japanese were resorting to kamikazes. This was the efflorescence of despair. Both the Germans and the Japanese conceded that it had become impossible to match American, British, and Russian conventional air fleets that had evolved to more sophisticated, and far more numerous, fighters and bombers.

The Axis regression was due to various reasons, some of which applied equally well to their eventual loss of early advantages in ships, armor, artillery, and infantry forces. Production counted. The air war was supposed to follow the pattern of many of the successful regional German and Japanese border conflicts of 1939 and 1940. Given these remarkable early successes and the inferior forces of their proximate enemies, there was less urgency to bring new fighters and bombers into mass production or to train new pilots or to study the quality and quantity of aircraft that America, Britain, or Russia was producing. Axis overconfidence was fed by ignorance of not only the aeronautical and manufacturing genius of British and American industry, but of Russian industrial savvy as well.

Take the superb Messerschmitt Bf 109 fighter (33,000 built), which was partially superseded only by the Fw 190 (20,000 built). These were the two premier fighters that Germany relied on for most of the war. In contrast, in just four rather than six years of war, initial workmanlike American fighters such as the P-40 Warhawk were constantly updated or replaced by entirely new and superior models produced in always greater numbers. The premier American fighter of 1943, the reliable two-engine Lockheed P-38 Lightning (10,000 built) was improved upon by the Republic P-47 Thunderbolt (15,500 built). The excellent ground-support Thunderbolt fighter, in turn, was augmented by the even better-performing North American P-51 Mustang (15,000 built) that had been refitted with the superb British Rolls-Royce Merlin engine to become the best all-around fighter plane of the war. No fighter plane made a greater difference in the air war of World War II than did the Mustang, whose appearance in substantial numbers over Germany changed the entire complexion of strategic bombing. The idea that Nazi Germany and Imperial Japan might have collaborated to produce a hybrid super fighter, in the way that the British and the Americans coproduced the P-51, was unlikely.

At the same time, in the Pacific theater, initial Marine and carrier fighters like the Grumman F4F Wildcat (7,800 built) were replaced on carriers mostly by the Grumman F6F Hellcat (12,000 built) and on land by the Vought F4U Corsair (12,500 built). The Corsair had proved disappointing as an American carrier fighter, but the British, in the manner they had up-gunned the Sherman tank into a lethal "Firefly" and reworked the Mustang into the war's top escort fighter, modified the Corsair to become a top-notch carrier fighter. Neither Germany nor Japan had any serious plans to bring out entirely new models of superior fighters built in larger numbers than their predecessors. After the war, Field Marshal Keitel admitted that the Third Reich had not just fallen behind in fighter production but in quality as well: "I am of the opinion that we were not able to compete with the Anglo-Americans as far as the fighter and bomber aircraft were concerned. We had dropped back in technological achievements. We had not preserved our technical superiority. We did not have a fighter with a sufficient radius. . . . I refuse to say that the Luftwaffe had deteriorated. I only feel that our means of fighting have not technically remained on the top."[27]

Resources and geography played key roles. German industry was bombed systematically by late 1942, and Japanese factories by late 1944 and 1945. For all the problems with the Allied bombing campaign, no one denied that, in its last months, heavy Allied bombers finally took a terrible toll on Axis aircraft production, transportation, and fuel supplies. The availability of fuel proved the greatest divide between Axis and Allied air power. Once the Americans and the British by 1944 had successfully focused on targeting German transportation, oil refineries, and coal conversion plants, and the US Navy had made it almost impossible for Japanese tanker ships to reach Japan from the Dutch East Indies, and as Axis prewar fuel stocks were exhausted, then pilot training hours, the key for maintaining air parity, plummeted. The Germans and Japanese soon fielded green pilots, often in planes that were poorly maintained, against far better trained American and British counterparts.

Given the transfer of much of the Russian munitions industries across the Urals, the end of most serious Luftwaffe conventional bombing of Britain by 1941, and the safety of the American homeland, Allied aircraft production was always secure. It did not matter much that by 1944 the Germans and Japanese were miraculously turning out nearly seventy thousand airframes per year, when the Allies were producing well over twice that number and usually of better quality. German and Japanese aircraft and pilot increases were perhaps sufficient to maintain control of an occupied Europe and the Pacific Rim, but not to wage global war against the industrial capacities of America, Britain, and Russia.[28]

While the quality of planes was always crucial, even more important was the quantity of good enough warplanes put into the air. At the beginning of the Pacific war, the Japanese Zero, and at the end of the European wars, the jet-powered Me 262 Swallow, proved the best fighters in the world. But the former was of relatively static design and was obsolete by 1943. The latter was unreliable and scarce. The fact that the vastly superior American F6F Hellcat and F4U Corsair were produced in twice the numbers in half the development time of the Japanese Zero does a lot to explain the early American acquisition of air supremacy in the Pacific.[29]

German Me 262 jet fighters—the air equivalent of the superb but often overly complex and far too expensive Tiger tank—were never produced en masse (1,400 built) nor were they supplied with sufficient fuel or maintenance crews. Their runways were by needs long, and thus made easily identifiable targets for marauding American and British fighter-bombers. The novel jet engines of the Me 262 had a short lifespan, and repair and maintenance were complicated and expensive. It took German pilots precious months to calibrate the proper use of jet aircraft, and, against Hitler's initial wishes, to focus on destroying Allied heavy bombers rather than using the Me 262 as a multifaceted bomber, ground supporter, or dogfighter. The relationship between early jet aircraft in World War II and late-model, high-performance, piston-driven fighters was analogous to fifteenth-century firearms and archery: gunpowder weapons were harbingers of a military revolution, while bows were at an evolutionary dead end. Nonetheless, as far as cost-benefit analyses and ease of use and maintenance, bows for a while longer were preferable to early clumsy harquebuses for widescale use.

Superb German fighters such as the Bf 109 and Fw 190 were updated and built in enormous numbers (almost 55,000 total aircraft). Yet their combined totals were still inferior in aggregate to Supermarine Spitfire, Yakovlev Yak-9, North American P-51 Mustang, and Republic P-47 Thunderbolt fighter production—aircraft that proved roughly comparable in combat.[30]

The vaunted Luftwaffe, in truth, was the most poorly prepared branch of the German military, both on the eve of and during the war, and it eroded as the war progressed and its allotment of German resources declined. Its various planners from Ernst Udet to Hermann Goering were incompetent and often unstable. (The drug-addicted, obese, and sybaritic Goering, for example, once purportedly floated the idea to Albert Speer of building concrete locomotives, given shortages in steel production.) German air planners were too long taken with the idea of using large two-engine bombers as tactical dive bombers. German strategic bombing was not so much an independent entity as an adjunct to tactical ground support. The Luftwaffe was asked to make up for the intrinsic deficiencies of the nearly four-million-man ground force that invaded the Soviet Union in June 1941. Had the invaders been fully motorized and uniformly and amply equipped with the latest German tanks, an independent Luftwaffe might have been freed to range ahead of the army to attack industry and transportation and swarm over the landscape to hit Soviet airfields, given that Soviet air defenses paled in comparison to what the Germans had just faced over Britain.[31]

Poorly designed planes like the two-engine heavy fighter Me 210 (fast, unreliable, and dangerous, only 90 finished), or its better-performing successor the Me 410 (about 1,200 produced), were rushed into production to replace increasingly obsolete heavy fighters like the Me 110, but usually proved vastly inferior to single-engine, high-performing, late-model Spitfires and Mustangs. For all its ingenious designs, experimental aircraft, and habitual gigantism, the Luftwaffe still had no workhorse transport comparable to the superb multifaceted American Douglas C-47 Skytrain ("Dakota" in the RAF designation), which was reliable, mass-produced (over 10,000 built), and rugged. The otherwise adequate German Junkers Ju 52 transport was slower, carried less payload, and was built in less than half the numbers of the C-47. Most aeronautical breakthroughs—navigation aids, drop tanks, self-sealing tanks, chaff, air-to-surface radar—were put to the greatest and most practical effect by the Allies.[32]

By 1943 the Allies had far more effectively concentrated on the training and the protection of their pilots. They focused on using their most experienced airmen to instruct new cadets, rather than sacrificing their accumulated expertise through continuous frontline service until they inevitably perished. Far larger air academies and longer training regimens often meant that more American, British, and even Russian pilots by the end of 1943 had more air time than their Axis counterparts. By war's end, US fighter pilots, for example, had three times more precombat solo flight time than their Axis enemies. That fact may help explain why they had shot down their German counterparts in air-to-air combat at a three-to-one aggregate ratio.

The ability to take off from and land on a rolling carrier deck required lengthy training. Japan never quite recovered from the slaughter of its superb veteran first-generation carrier pilots in 1942 at the Coral Sea, Midway, and a series of carrier encounters off Guadalcanal. It made no adequate long-term investment in expanding new cohorts to replace the diminishing numbers of the original "Sea Eagles," Japan's elite corps of highly trained carrier pilots, or hundreds of the navy's land-based fighter pilots, even though the destruction of American carrier forces was key to long-term Japanese strategy.[33]

In moral terms, there is no difference in the losses of soldiers in particular branches of the military. In a strategic calculus, however, the deaths of skilled pilots represented a far greater cost in training and material support than did the losses of foot soldiers. Somewhat analogous to lost skilled naval aviators at the Coral Sea and Midway, for instance, were the high fatalities of trained Turkish bowmen at the sea battle of Lepanto between a coalition of Christian polities and the Ottomans. While the Ottoman sultan was able to replace his galley fleet that was all but destroyed in 1571 off the western coast of northern Greece, it proved far more difficult to train and replace thousands of skilled archers, a fact that may explain the reduced Ottoman offensive operations in the central and western Mediterranean over the next few years. This was a lesson that the Japanese began to learn, to their sorrow, only during late 1942.[34]

The ability to build runways ex nihilo in newly conquered territory became an American specialty. The huge bases on the Marianas, Iwo Jima, and Okinawa, or in recaptured France, Italy, and Sicily, were unmatched by any comparable Axis effort. When the Germans began the Battle of Britain, many sorties operated from makeshift French bases that lacked concrete runways and made takeoffs and landings unnecessarily hazardous. Japanese veteran pilots and aircraft engineers lamented the vast differences between US and Japanese air base construction: "It was obvious that the ability of American engineers to establish air bases wherever and whenever they chose, while Japan struggled against the limitations of primitive methods and a lack of material and engineering construction skill, must affect the final outcome of the war to no minor degree in favour of the United States."[35]

Only carrier planes had allowed Japan to attack American assets from Pearl Harbor to Midway, in a way impossible with its infantry or battleships and cruisers. In turn, later US island hopping that led to an encircled Japan was spearheaded by a huge naval air force. Similarly, once air supremacy was achieved in the months before the D-Day landings in Normandy, the presence overhead of far more numerous and often better fighters made it possible for the American army to reach Germany in less than ten months, in a way perhaps otherwise impossible given the numbers and quality of its armor and infantry.

There was no better investment for the Allies by late 1944 than putting a young pilot of twenty-one years, with nine months of training, in excellent, mass-produced, and relatively cheap fighters and fighter-bombers such as the Supermarine Spitfire, Hawker Typhoon, Yak-9, Lavochkin La-7, P-47 Thunderbolt, or P-51 Mustang. The latter light, all-aluminum, and low-cost plane could fly as high as forty thousand feet, and when equipped with drop tanks enjoyed a roundtrip range of two thousand miles, while achieving maximum speeds of 437 miles per hour at twenty-five thousand feet. Roving packs of such fighters helped to neutralize superior German armor and more experienced infantry, and finally allowed heavy bombers to devastate Germany. After arriving at the Western Front in 1944, the veteran German Panzer strategist Major General F. W. von Mellenthin despaired that German Panzers could not operate in

France as they had in the East, given American fighter-bombers: "It was clear that American air power put our panzers at a hopeless disadvantage, and that the normal principles of armored warfare did not apply in this theater." Meanwhile, in the vast expanses of the Pacific, Corsair and Hell-cat fighters in about a year systematically reduced the Imperial Japanese naval and land tactical air forces to irrelevancy, and rendered the Pacific a mostly American and British domain.[36]

Strategic bombing has become perhaps the most contentious issue of all the controversies surrounding the conduct of World War II. Neverthe-less, on some points the use of high-altitude bombers solicits surprising unanimity. Its use by all sides in the early war was not initially as cost-effective in terms of achieving immediate results as the employment of fighters and fighter-bombers in tactical and ground-support operations. It failed to defeat Britain, either materially or psychologically. It did not play much of a role in the initial success of the German invasion of the Soviet Union or the Russian defeat of the ground forces of the Third Reich in East Europe. Japan never bombed China into submission. The Anglo-American strategic bombing effort over Europe did weaken and finally ruin Germany, but mostly in the last months of the war, and after enormous losses of aircraft that were the result of often wrong-headed and anti-empirical Allied dogmas.

The United States Strategic Bombing Survey released findings that the American bombing of the Third Reich had been successful but costly: forty thousand aircrew members dead, six thousand aircraft lost, and $43 billion spent. It found bombing was quite successful in some areas (e.g., oil, truck production, transportation), while less so in others (e.g., ball bearings, aviation production), prompting the debate to grow heated and yet more nuanced, raising far more questions than providing answers. Assessments of the role of strategic bombing sometimes became par-adoxical: the victims on the ground often claimed that it had won the Allies the war, while the victors in the air downplayed their own achieve-ments. Tracking German monthly industrial output was not an accurate assessment of Allied air power if it did not consider models of what Ger-man production might have been without the damage done by strategic air power. In other words, the infamous efforts of Albert Speer to draft forced labor and disperse factories ultimately proved unsustainable, given that the enormous disruptions in the German economy caused by bomb-ing would have led to its eventual collapse anyhow had the war gone on beyond mid-1945.[37]

The Allies launched a number of disastrous attacks between 1939 and early 1944, including especially the failed British raids against Berlin in

November 1943 through March 1944 (2,500 bombers damaged or lost), the calamitous American raid in August 1943 on the Romanian oil fields at Ploesti (100 B-24s damaged or lost), and the twin American attempts in August and October 1943 to knock out the ball-bearing factories at Schweinfurt, Germany (nearly 350 B-17s damaged or lost). In a tragic sense, the failures may have provided some of the lessons and experience that improved Allied bombing operations and eventually led to the destruction of German cities in late 1944 and 1945. Without a major second front against German-occupied northern Europe, it was unclear exactly what the Allies were to do—aside from North Africa, Sicily, and Italy—to convince the Soviet Union and their own publics that they were in equal measure damaging the Third Reich.

The bombing campaign in geostrategic terms helped to keep together the Allied alliance, especially at a time when an early cross-Channel invasion promised to Stalin would have been a disaster. Moreover, the sudden improvement of the Red Army's westward advance in late 1943 and 1944 often correlated to transfers from the Eastern Front of thousands of German artillery platforms and Luftwaffe fighters to defend the Third Reich from Anglo-American bombers. That the Nazis reallotted new military production and manpower to the anti-aircraft missions rather than to bolstering ground forces against the Russians was also fundamental to the Red Army's recovery.

In the West, a rather small and sometimes inexperienced Allied expeditionary force was able to reach central Germany in less than a year largely because German industry was short on fuel and rail facilities, and because even its most sophisticated new armored vehicles became constant targets of air assaults from their fabrication in factories to their transport to the front. In addition, the investment in planes, fighters, and support personnel, along with the vast losses accrued, nevertheless caused the enemy to incur astronomical air defense and civil defense costs, even in areas that were not further targeted for assault. By 1943, for example, Britain had spent the equivalent of nearly $2 billion in its civil defense forces, largely in reaction to fears of another Blitz; Germany invested even more on defense against bombing.

Allied area bombing not only led to the dispersal of factories and disrupted transportation hubs in Axis cities but also wore on the social cohesion necessary to fuel the war effort. Without the bombing it is hard to envision how the Allies could otherwise have thwarted the Axis war economies before their ground forces reached the homelands of Japan and Germany. By 1944 thousands of innocent civilians in Eastern Europe, the Soviet Union, China, Southeast Asia, and the Pacific were daily being gassed, shot, starved, and tortured by occupying German and Japanese ground forces. Without area bombing—that is, had the British emulated American daylight "precision" bombing operations, and likewise had the Americans kept B-29s at high altitudes on traditional precision missions over Japan in 1945—the war may well have been prolonged to 1946. If so, the additional combat casualties and civilian executions and deaths could have approximated the numbers of German and Japanese civilians who did perish in Allied area bombing.

There are still no definitive answers to these strategic and humanitarian dilemmas. Until there are, it remains difficult to dismiss the contribution of strategic bombing to the accelerated ruination of Germany and the surrender of Japan. In reductionist terms, the side that flew heavy bombers in numbers (and had the oil to fuel them) won, and the side that did not, lost; even more starkly, the side that could not build a four-engine bomber sacrificed strategic range and lost the war. For all its qualifications, the Strategic Bombing Survey offered a guarded final verdict of success:

> The achievements of Allied air power were attained only with difficulty and great cost in men, material, and effort. Its success depended on the courage, fortitude, and gallant action of the officers and men of the air crews and commands. It depended also on a superiority in leadership, ability, and basic strength. These led to a timely and careful training of pilots and crews in volume; to the production of planes, weapons, and supplies in great numbers and of high quality; to the securing of adequate bases and supply routes; to speed and ingenuity in development; and to cooperation with strong and faithful Allies. The failure of any one of these might have seriously narrowed and even eliminated the margin.[38]

When one side built three times as many quality aircraft as the other, and by war's end trained more than ten times as many pilots, then victory in the air from the mid-Atlantic to the Chinese border was nearly assured—and with it victory on the ground as well.

PLANES CHANGED THE face of battle in World War II, but ancient ideas of sea power and maritime control still governed how a nation's assets, air bases included, would be supplied and protected, as well as enhanced across the oceans. The planet was surrounded by atmosphere, the unlimited space of air power; yet the seas still covered 70 percent of the earth's surface. Whereas even the longest-ranged aircraft of World

War II could rarely fly more than three thousand miles without landing to refuel, capital ships could range five times that distance on their original fuel allotments. When navies did refuel, it was often while in transit—an operation impossible in the air for World War II aircraft—insuring ships an independence and autonomy unavailable to air power.

When the war broke out in 1939, the British and the Americans possessed respectively the largest and second-largest fleets in the world. A mystery of relative sea power in World War II is why the Axis powers, which all believed in the strategic goal of some sort of naval supremacy, assumed on the eve of their respective aggressions that they could defeat superior navies. In that context, a theme of the following three chapters is again incongruity: both Germany and Japan thought that technological superiority—manifested in the first case by a sophisticated U-boat fleet, and in the second by the world's largest carrier force—might trump British and American numbers, especially as expressed in battleships. In the end, however, the supreme commands of the Axis powers wasted their scarce assets in building huge and nearly obsolete battleships and cruisers, while their more innovative enemies deployed the most modern and powerful submarines and carriers in the world.

An early-model American P-51 Mustang fighter. When it was later reequipped with the supercharged British Rolls-Royce Merlin 61 engine and six .50 caliber machine guns, the P-51 became the best long-range fighter of the war. *World War II Pictorial Collection, Envelope CG, Hoover Institution Archives*

The most famous mission of the North American B-25 Mitchells was the Doolittle raid that bombed Tokyo on April 18, 1942, just four months after Pearl Harbor. Here B-25s of the Mediterranean-based 12th American Army Air Force fly through flak to bomb the German-occupied railyards at Sibenik, Croatia. *World War II Pictorial Collection, Envelope CG, Hoover Institution Archives*

At peak strength in 1944, some seventeen B-17 bombing groups (at full strength of about 72 planes each) were based in Great Britain. Here a B-17 takes off from a British airfield to the cheers of fellow aviators and crewmen. *World War II Pictorial Collection, Envelope AV, Hoover Institution Archives*

Saint-Lô en ruines.

Operation Cobra, the late July 1944 American breakout from the Normandy hedgerows, was predicated on using heavy and medium bombers to blast holes in German lines near the French city of Saint-Lô. The bombardment worked but left the historic city in ruins. *World War II Pictorial Collection, Envelope CP, Hoover Institution Archives*

The city of Caen, in Normandy, was supposed to be taken on D-Day, June 6, 1944. More than a month later the British and Canadians finally liberated most of the city, but only after Allied bombing and shelling and German counterattacks had all but destroyed the historic municipality. *World War II Pictorial Collection, Envelope FG, Hoover Institution Archives*

The USS *Lexington* (CV-2, sunk at the Battle of the Coral Sea) and USS *Saratoga* (CV-3) were originally laid down as battle cruisers but converted to become among the largest aircraft carriers in the world when they were commissioned in 1927. The nearly identical carriers were uniquely outfitted with four sets of twin 8-inch naval guns, in case inclement weather prevented air patrols. Here the prewar *Saratoga* handles planes on patrol in 1938. *Stephen Jurika Papers, Box 2, Hoover Institution Archives*

The US deployed more than 140 new fleet, light, and escort carriers in World War II, more than those in all other navies combined during the conflict. Pictured here at its launching in September 1943 is the light carrier USS *San Jacinto*. Future president George H. W. Bush was a TBF Grumman Avenger torpedo bomber pilot on the *San Jacinto*. *Robert B. Stinnett Miscellaneous Papers, Envelope A, Hoover Institution Archives*

Even the Allied inability to capture the French Atlantic ports intact, and the destruction of one of the two artificial Mulberry harbors by a violent storm, did not stop the seaborne supply of Operation Overlord. Huge Allied LST (Landing Ship, Tank) amphibious craft such as these were driven right up onto the beaches to unload tanks and heavy equipment. *World War II Pictorial Collection, Envelope FF, Hoover Institution Archives*

In October 1944 the beach at Leyte Island was turned into a huge supply depot, key to the American reconquest of the Philippines. Here huge American LSTs dot the beachhead, while smaller amphibious boats aid in ferrying in supplies and manpower. LSTs could carry 18 Sherman tanks, 32 heavy trucks, or over 200 troops—or a mixture of vehicles and manpower. *World War II Pictorial Collection, Envelope AX, Hoover Institution Archives*

The Americans were stunned by the superb German light machine guns, the dreaded Maschinengewehr 34, superseded in 1942 by the even more rapid-firing MG 42. Here an American soldier (Pfc. Ralph H. Kolberg of Stevensville, Michigan) on Okinawa holds the Browning M1919A6 light machine gun. Unfortunately, the A6, while reliable, could fire only about 400–600 rounds per minute—about half the rate of the MG 42. *World War II Pictorial Collection, Envelope A, Hoover Institution Archives*

Her contribution helped win.
Her services have been recognised by the people.

Russian women, unlike the women of almost all other major powers, served in combat roles throughout the Eastern Front. First Lieutenant Anastasiya Kurchenko was decorated with the Order of the Red Star and Medals for the Defence of Odessa, the Defence of Sevastopol, and the Defence of Leningrad. *Russian Pictorial Collection, Box fBW, Hoover Institution Archives*

Under Hitler's infamous "commissar order" of June 6, 1941, issued just two weeks before the start of Operation Barbarossa, German officers themselves routinely ordered the execution of all Soviet commissars who surrendered. *Russian Pictorial Collection, Box fBW, Hoover Institution Archives*

General Douglas MacArthur *(center)*, with arms around emaciated and recently released POWs British general Arthur Percival *(left)* and American general Jonathan M. Wainwright *(right)*, ensured that both were present at the Japanese surrender in Tokyo Bay on September 2, 1945. *World War II Pictorial Collection, Envelope CG, Hoover Institution Archives*

After the German surrender at Stalingrad on February 2, 1943, the city was left completely ruined. Thousands of Soviet citizens returned to Stalingrad to rebuild, living in a vast tent city during the reconstruction. *Russian Pictorial Collection, Box fBW, Hoover Institution Archives*

After the German retreat from Sevastopol (May 1944), Russian soldiers return to the center of the city to commemorate those who had fallen during General Erich von Manstein's brutal and successful siege in 1942. *Russian Pictorial Collection, Box fBW, Hoover Institution Archives*

The Red Army took 61,587 German
in the Crimea

Hitler's stand-fast orders proved disastrous for the Wehrmacht during its gradual withdrawal from Soviet territory. At Sevastopol, German and Romanian forces under the command of German general Erwin Jaenecke eventually withdrew, against Hitler's orders. But the delayed retreat led both to Jaenecke's court-martial and the capture of over sixty thousand German prisoners, such as those pictured here. *Russian Pictorial Collection, Box fBW, Hoover Institution Archives*

# PART THREE

# WATER

Naval power at sea, in the air, and on the ground

*Therefore the history of sea power, while embracing in its broad sweep all that tends to make a people great upon the sea or by the sea, is largely a military history.*

—Alfred Thayer Mahan[1]

# 7

# Ships and Strategies

O N JANUARY 30, 1945, the Soviet submarine S-13 torpedoed and blew up the German ship *Wilhelm Gustloff*, instigating the worst loss of life on a single ship in human history. The Russian crew had written on their deadly torpedoes, "For the Motherland," "Stalingrad," and "For the Soviet People."

The former passenger liner was named for an assassinated prewar Swiss Nazi. As a makeshift converted troop carrier, the *Gustloff* was evacuating some 10,500 German civilians and military personnel from Gotenhafen (modern Gdynia, Poland) to northern Germany, just days ahead of the arrival of the Red Army into western Poland. The transport was unarmored and only lightly armed—and far too small to hold adequately its vast cargo of refugees and troops. More unfortunate, it was steaming at night in the frigid winter waters of the Baltic Sea without much escort. At least three of the S-13's torpedoes tore apart the ship. The *Gustloff* quickly turned over and sank within forty-five minutes. The desperate escape attempt from the *Gustloff* resulted in 9,400 fatalities, including five thousand children.[1]

The fate of the *Wilhelm Gustloff* reminds us of the paradoxes of naval warfare, ancient and modern. Hundreds or even thousands of people, crammed into single vessels, surrounded by often turbulent seas, could find death in seconds. Yet because of the dispersion of fleet strength among numerous ships, and the sheer expense of taking large numbers of people to sea, it was also far harder to kill tens of thousands at sea than on land. So the *Wilhelm Gustloff* remains the exception rather than the rule of naval warfare. The great one-day jaws of death in World War II were not usually catastrophic ship sinkings but rather the firebombing of cities like Hamburg, Dresden, and Tokyo. The Tokyo fire raid took ten times more civilian lives than were lost on the *Gustloff*. There was a *Gustloff*-sized death toll nearly every day at Auschwitz between April and July 1944. Of the major belligerents—Germany, Great Britain, Japan, Italy, the Soviet

Union, and the United States—the fewest fatalities by far were in their respective navies. For all the faces of death at sea, water can still be a refuge from fire, the great killer of people.

History's most lethal sea encounters in the age of oar and sail— Salamis (480 BC), Ecnomus (254 BC), or Lepanto (1571)—saw only about the same number of deaths as their contemporary land counterparts, for example, at Plataea (479 BC), Cannae (216 BC), or the first Ottoman siege of Vienna (1529). Victorious Athenian, Roman, or Christian sailors could finish off hundreds of enemy triremes and galleys, and put all the defeated to death—especially with the aid of an unforgiving sea against those who could not swim—and still not exceed the death tolls of the far more common infantry battles. Much later at the largest and most decisive sea battles of the nineteenth and twentieth centuries—Trafalgar (1805, almost 15,000 combined British, French, and Spanish fatalities), Jutland (1916, 8,500 dead), Midway (1942, 3,300 killed), and Leyte Gulf (1944, 15,300 fatalities)—not much had changed: the number of fatalities did not approximate the combined death tolls of contemporary infantry battles such as Napoleon's defeat at Leipzig (1813, perhaps 92,000 killed and wounded) or at the death throes of the Sixth Army and its affiliated forces at Stalingrad (as many as 1.7 to 2 million dead through January 1943). What was true in ancient times has remained valid in the modern era: the most lethal battles at sea have been nowhere near as deadly as those on land.[2]

Although hundreds, even thousands of men could be lost in seconds when a ship blew apart or went down—just three of 1,418 crewmen survived when the battle cruiser HMS *Hood* exploded, apparently hit by a shell from the *Bismarck* on May 24, 1941—most sailors of defeated fleets in World War II survived. That is the eternal paradox of sea battle: the sea can become both a tomb for a single ship and a sanctuary for an armada.[3]

Often, violent storms did more damage to a navy than did the enemy. Gales were lethal, partly because normally sound seamanship and caution were subordinated to military risk-taking. Even more important, warships—whether Roman galleys with their clumsy boarding devices like the *corvus,* or top-heavy American and Japanese carriers and cruisers—were primarily designed to damage other ships. Warships were never engineered for stability or to enhance the chances of cargoes safely reaching port.

With the advent of steel ships, oil-fired engines, and sophisticated navigation, navies no longer needed to fight near land. Often they battled far away from shore and routinely braved the rough seas of the mid-Atlantic and Pacific. In September 1935, for example, during the so-called

Fourth Fleet Incident off the Kuril Islands, elements of the Japanese Pacific fleet were caught in a typhoon that severely damaged newly designed heavy cruisers and destroyers, as well as carriers, leading to a revamping of Japanese naval design and construction.[4]

Typhoon Cobra of December 1944 caught Admiral William Halsey's Third Fleet operating off Luzon in the Philippines. Despite radar, radio communications, and air reconnaissance, Halsey plowed right into the typhoon of over one-hundred-mile-per-hour winds. The storm killed 793 men, sank three destroyers, and damaged over thirty carriers, battleships, cruisers, and destroyers. The US Navy suffered more loss of life and far more ships damaged from Typhoon Cobra than at either its signature battles of the Coral Sea or Midway. Admiral Halsey was more in danger from a subsequent court of inquiry than from the audit of his controversial but less costly chase of the Japanese carrier arm at the Battle of Leyte Gulf.[5]

The purpose of investing in navies to win sea battles was not necessarily to kill large numbers of enemy combatants, given that the homeland was usually well guarded by land troops when the fleet went to sea. Rather, the duty of a fleet was to sink and disable expensive merchant ships and warships, kill or drown skilled seamen, and thereby destroy an enemy's capital investment, while neutralizing an adversary's ability to move troops by sea and import resources. The loss of a single battleship like the *Bismarck* was the rough equivalent of the loss of seven to eight hundred Tiger I tanks, or about 60 percent of the entire number of Tigers *ever* produced.[6]

Still, even a superior fleet could hardly starve most enemies into submission, at least in any reasonable amount of time. Sea power, like an air force, was always an ancillary to infantry. In the final days of the Peloponnesian War, the Spartans and their growing alliance finally destroyed the Athenian fleet and sailed victoriously into the harbor of Piraeus. Yet even that triumph required a simultaneous hoplite infantry occupation of the Attic hinterland and the omnipresence of the Spartan army outside the walls of Athens. In the American Civil War, the Union blockade sorely crippled the Confederacy and denied it the import of key armaments and the export of cotton, its most valuable commodity, but ultimately General William T. Sherman had to march through the South to defeat Confederate armies and devastate Southern ground on his way to join General U. S. Grant's Army of the Potomac in Northern Virginia. The British blockades of Germany in both World Wars weakened German resistance, but Imperial Germany and the Third Reich surrendered only once their infantry enemies had shattered German armies. The Americans destroyed the Imperial Japanese Navy fleet, but it was atomic bombs and incendiary attacks that most likely precluded the need for an amphibious invasion of Japan. In sum, once fleets neutralized their maritime enemy counterparts, their goal, even if it were largely to strangle imports and blockade the coasts, was ultimately to enhance land operations.[7]

Ships can make even the most naturally poor states rich, but only if they control lands and commerce far beyond their own shores. That is why far-off naval defeats for a maritime power can set in motion huge commercial and fiscal tsunamis in mere hours that will eventually cripple the ability to mobilize infantry. The Japanese defeat at Midway and the loss of four fleet carriers meant that just seven months after the Pacific war commenced, Japan was no longer in a strategic position to keep the American fleet out of her vital sea-lanes that linked the newly acquired, resource-rich Greater East Asia Co-Prosperity Sphere with Tokyo. Japan had neither the capital nor the labor to quickly replace several lost capital ships that had protected oil deliveries from the Dutch East Indies to Japanese factories. Without naval superiority, mostly defined by 1942 as hundreds of planes ranging unimpeded two to three hundred miles from their carriers, the Japanese could not stop the US Marines and even greater numbers of army forces from cutting off dozens of their forward garrisons while island hopping their way toward the Japanese mainland.[8]

As with the exercise of air power to achieve command of the air, human conflict at sea always hinged on achieving maritime superiority. Hitler sputtered that what was left of his expensive surface fleet was mostly worthless after 1942, given British air and naval mastery. He threatened to turn his few remaining cruisers and battleships into scrap, given their idleness and uselessness. With superiority at sea, however, a power can send its forces wherever it wishes; without it, a nation is confined only to ground operations—and largely of an enemy's choosing. It is not impossible for a continental empire to achieve naval superiority—Sparta accomplished that feat in 404 BC with the help of Persian capital, and Rome built a superior fleet in the First Punic War—but it is unlikely. Most imperial land powers—Turkey, France, Russia, Austria-Hungary, Germany—always had difficulty subduing their rival maritime enemies whose capital and long traditions of expertise made up for their otherwise inferior manpower.[9]

Building the wrong kind of ships or not enough of the right kind—especially for a naval power with limited industrial resources—could prove a colossal and sometimes fateful waste of investment. Commander Minoru Genda, perhaps Japan's foremost expert on naval air power, ridiculed the all-powerful battleship lobby of the Imperial Japanese Navy and its responsibility for the squandered outlay in monster battleships. He scoffed, "such ships are the Chinese Wall of the Japanese Navy." Genda equated the idea of grand collisions of battleships as "exercises in masturbation." Despite their formidable guns, the *Bismarck*, *Tirpitz*, *Yamato*, and *Musashi* were the stuff of prewar romance and collectively achieved relatively little in the war; even Hitler deprecated his mostly useless new battleships as "the last of the knights in armour." Supposedly, they would blow like kind out of the sea. In fact, the monster, oil-guzzling ships could be bombed, often with near impunity, by planes from either carriers or land bases, and torpedoed as well by far more economical submarines and destroyers.

Super-battleships in World War II achieved fame largely by establishing records of being the largest warships ever to sink due to hostile action. The twin Japanese behemoths gulped oil at such a rate that the *Yamato* ("hotel Yamato") often stayed in port. Even before the war, the Japanese had fretted that "battleships without oil cannot move," a worry that soon became reality. It was to the credit of the US Navy that it finally resisted prewar calls to build so-called super-dreadnoughts of some seventy thousand tons, fearful that such behemoths would inordinately drain the naval budget. Proof of the romance of the super-battleship was illustrated by the plans of all the major navies at the outset of the war to build even larger dinosaurs, such as the envisioned American *Montana* class (about 70,000 tons, with twelve 16-inch guns), the Japanese A-150 class (70,000 tons, with five 20-inch guns), the British *Lion* class (43,000 tons, with nine 16-inch guns; one ship of the class built), and some of the huge German H class (H-42: 90,000 tons, eight 20-inch guns). All were eventually canceled either because of staggering projected costs or due to the growing evidence of battleship obsolescence during the war, mostly in terms of not being able to protect these huge projected investments from fleets of cheap naval fighter-bombers.[10]

Even the size and quality of a fleet at the beginning of a war were not always predictive of naval success or failure. Far more critical was a sea power's ability to expand, improve, and maintain fleets during the course of the war. The sixteenth-century Ottoman Empire usually had more ships in the Mediterranean than its archrival Venice, but it lacked the productive and innovative capacities of the Venetian Arsenal's shipyards to turn out superior replacement galleys at a far greater rate. Sparta's eventual maritime alliance of Corinthian, Spartan, and Syracusan triremes at times nearly matched the size of the Athenian fleet. But for decades— until the entrance of the wealthy Persian Empire on the side of Sparta— the Athenian navy could still construct far more triremes, more rapidly, and equipped with better crews than its aggregate enemies.[11]

Between 1939 and 1941, the German, Japanese, and Italian fleets in their entirety were already inferior to the combined British and American theater fleets. The margin would widen. The Axis powers had a fraction of the shipbuilding capability of the Allies. They also suffered from far less naval experience and were without sure supplies of oil. A *Bismarck* or *Yamato* might appear more impressive in 1941 than the *Arizona* or *Pennsylvania*. Yet the former capital ships were to be followed by just one more battleship of their class, whereas the latter were forerunners of an entire generation of ten fast modern battleships of the *North Carolina*, *South Dakota*, and *Iowa* classes to appear in 1941 through 1944 (*North Carolina* and *Washington*; *South Dakota*, *Indiana*, *Massachusetts*, and *Alabama*; *Iowa*, *New Jersey*, *Missouri*, and *Wisconsin*). All had plentiful oil and abundant air support and, most important, performed key roles as floating artillery in support of amphibious landings. Again, the survival of all battleships depended on which side had achieved naval air supremacy; after 1942 it was always the Allies.[12]

GERMANY AND ITALY never had much of a chance of landing on British, much less American, soil. For all the majesty of Japan's prewar fleet, it was still inferior to Anglo-American combined naval power and was never able to endanger the homelands of its American or British enemies. Rarely has an existential war broken out that would decide the fate of all nations involved, in which one side so eagerly accepted the impossibility of ever being able to invade the homeland of its main enemy.[13]

In the war to come, Germany, to the degree that it ever wished even to deploy its troops in the Mediterranean, dreamed that it might rely on the Italian surface fleet to keep the Afrika Korps supplied. Hitler came to know the prohibitive costs of building battleships and cruisers, and thus appreciated Mussolini's stubbornness (or foolishness?) for squeezing out of a much weaker Italian economy a far larger surface fleet than his own. Likewise, Hitler, with his armies stuck outside of Moscow in December 1941, declared war on the United States after Pearl Harbor for lots of alleged reasons, including his naive assessment that the Japanese might tie down a considerable part of the British and American fleets and thereby curb aid to his British and Russian enemies, a conjecture that showed scant appreciation of Allied shipbuilding or of the full nature of the Soviet-Japanese nonaggression pact. The Pacific war, in that view, would ideally divert US and British warships away from the Battle of the Atlantic and the Mediterranean so that Hitler's U-boats might finally cut the Anglo–North American umbilical cord.[14]

Hitler's fantasies about the Italian fleet were soon dispelled by British admirals. His concerns about easy access to nearby sources of natural wealth—the oil of the Caucasus, Spanish tungsten, Swedish iron ore, Ukrainian grain—illustrate his admission that he had gone to war without an adequate navy to ensure importation of such needed goods from anywhere in the world. Germany's neglect of a blue-water navy reflected all sorts of decisions beyond just limited shipbuilding resources: financial constraints, Hitler's preference for a continental and short war, a trust in the greater value of land-based air power, the proximity of Great Britain and Scandinavia to the Luftwaffe bases, the past disappointments and later losses of the Kaiser's imperial surface fleet, and the late start in shipbuilding due to the limitations imposed by the Versailles Treaty. Yet if Germany was not fully able to exploit Eastern European and Russian sources of oil, to take one example, and if synthetic oil plants proved insufficient, he would not be able to fuel the Wehrmacht if cut off from oil that was imported by sea.[15]

In desperation Hitler was finally reduced to dreaming of an anti-navy, one that could do damage to other fleets but not in and of itself guarantee advantageous maritime commerce for the Third Reich. A small but well-built fleet of surface ships and a growing armada of submarines, coupled with the Italian navy, might tie down the British fleet in particular key strategic landscapes, choking off sea-lanes to Britain, and complemented by the threat that Japan might eventually siphon off Allied ships to the Pacific. Meanwhile, Hitler would hold on to a huge continental empire from the Volga to the Atlantic, without much need of imported resources. In the contemporary example of a much weaker Chinese navy seeking to deny the much stronger American navy freedom of action at key choke points in the South China Sea, so the small (and hypothetical) German counterforce would negate the ability of Allied warships in the Atlantic to profit fully from naval superiority on the surface.[16]

Hitler remembered that although the U-boat fleet had failed at just such a strategy in World War I, it nonetheless had terrified the British. Almost half of the U-boats and their crews by late 1918 were lost to British countermeasures, but U-boats had nonetheless sunk a quarter of the world's entire merchant tonnage, some 5,708 ships. Such a gargantuan effort had still failed to stop Great Britain: the British merchant fleet was larger at the end of World War I than at the beginning. But no matter. Some World War I German strategists pointed to the fact that the Kaiser's U-boat fleet had done far better than the more costly investments in the dreadnoughts of the Imperial Fleet.[17]

By late 1941, even disrupting intercontinental sea-lanes, integrating grand strategy with Japan, and invading island nations like Britain or distant powers like the United States were far beyond the abilities of the Kriegsmarine, at least in the manner that both the rival admirals Erich Raeder and Karl Doenitz had once dreamed. On the eve of the war, Raeder had warned Hitler that Germany's naval rearmament program (the so-called Z-Plan) would not even approach parity with the British for at least five years and not achieve superiority for ten. And prewar German studies had concluded that the U-boat fleet was in no position to change the failed verdict of World War I in the Atlantic, assuming British submarine defenses had the edge in 1939.

In the end, the huge German investment in large prestige surface ships—at the war's beginning, ten modern battleships, pocket battleships, and heavy cruisers, and another seven under construction—brought few returns. Their costly presence helps to explain why Admiral Doenitz began the war with a pathetic fifty-seven deployable submarines. Germany's dreams of a surface fleet to match Britain's were comparable to Napoleon's earlier and similarly expensive fantasies that the French could build better and more powerful ships of the line to overcome British numerical superiority and greater command, ability, and experience.[18]

The preferable strategic solution for the Third Reich would have been never to go to war at all against the world's two greatest fleets, given that it was already near financial insolvency by late 1939. The next best alternative would have been to wait until 1944–1945 in the slim hopes that Great Britain and the United States would not have increased their naval assets while Germany quadrupled its own. The only remaining realistic choice would have been to achieve by 1939 Admiral Doenitz's dream of a huge U-boat fleet of some three hundred submarines, while scrapping all plans to deploy battleships and cruisers. Hitler had rejected all three scenarios and so never had a serious plan to defeat two of his likely enemies.[19]

JAPAN WAS A different story. It entered the war with a larger surface fleet in the Pacific than the United States or Great Britain. The Japanese possessed the third-largest navy by tonnage in the world. By January 1, 1942, Japan outclassed the United States Pacific Fleet in every category of warship. Right after Pearl Harbor, the Japanese could immediately deploy double the number of US fleet aircraft carriers stationed in the Pacific (6 to 3), though the United States would soon bring over both the *Wasp* (from the Atlantic and Mediterranean) and the *Hornet* (from Norfolk). The Japanese had more light carriers (4 to 0). Their surface fleet was far more formidable in battleships (10 to 2), cruisers (38 to 16), and destroyers (112 to 40), the latter ships armed with the dreaded Type 93 Long Lance oxygen-fueled torpedoes.

Although Japan's carrier fleet was the world's largest, the Imperial Japanese Navy had put great trust in its battleships as the final arbiter of naval superiority. This reactionary impulse did not arise just from emulation of Western obsessions with large surface ships, but rather also from its own fabled experience in the Russo-Japanese War (1904–1905). Admiral Heihachiro Togo had blown the Russian imperial fleet out of the war in the Battle of Tsushima (May 27–28, 1905), largely because Japan's smaller number of battleships and greater number of cruisers still had combined superior tonnages, better rangefinders, more guns, and more advanced gunnery. The lessons from the victory were to put faith in more, bigger, and better naval artillery, and in torpedoes fired from smaller destroyers.[20]

Imperial Japan's submarine fleet was also the largest in the Pacific, well-designed and equipped with excellent torpedoes. Yet Japan had no serious initial plans to enter Suez and link up with the Axis in the Mediterranean, much less to fight in the Atlantic. It was quite enough for the imperial fleet to fight three Pacific enemies simultaneously—supplying troops in Manchuria and patrolling the Chinese coast; battling the British and Americans in Burma and Malaysia, and threatening India; and stopping American island hopping to Japan.

The Americans—and many Japanese—had thought that any attack on the distant American base at Pearl Harbor was impossible, given the inability of the Japanese fleet to conduct such distant operations due to refueling challenges and the need for radio silence along the long route to Hawaii. The strike on Pearl Harbor was an anomaly, a gamble that would never quite be repeated—a singular example of brilliant seamanship and organization, as well as luck and the fact that the Americans were militarily drowsy, not as vigilant during winter, and not at war. Without peacetime surprise, it would have been difficult for *any* carrier fleet to have hit its enemy's distant territory to any great effect before 1943. The Americans later could not quite emulate the earlier Japanese surprise attack. Their Task Force 18, including the *Hornet* that was to launch the Doolittle raid on April 18, 1942, was detected about 170 miles short of what was planned. As a result, the B-25 bombers took off some ten hours early.[21]

Even in late 1942, after losses in the Coral Sea and off Midway Island, and suffering attrition at a half-dozen engagements around Guadalcanal, Japan still enjoyed superiority in its total number of carriers, battleships, and cruisers. At one point, after the sinking of the *Hornet* in September

1942, just one American fleet carrier, the damaged *Enterprise*, was operating in the Pacific—against eight Japanese carriers carrying five times as many aircraft.

The Imperial Japanese Navy was jubilant over the scorecard of the first six months of the war against the United States, especially the clearcut victories at Pearl Harbor and Singapore, and in the Java Sea and Indian Ocean. Much of its success was attributable to superb carrier pilots. Japanese analysts felt that "in the first six months of the war, therefore, our naval aviation alone had sunk two aircraft-carriers and seriously damaged a third, sent to the bottom one seaplane tender, either sunk or heavily damaged ten battleships, destroyed four and heavily damaged two cruisers, and sunk ten destroyers. . . . Compared to the losses sustained by the Allied powers in the Pacific, therefore, we suffered very lightly, indeed." And they were certainly justified in thinking that Japan had achieved tactical victories, albeit without any guarantees of eventual strategic success: "The tally of the enemy and Japanese ships lost in the first six months of the war was a literal realization of the Navy's concept of 'ideal combat conditions,' to 'wage a decisive sea battle only under air control.' For the ten years prior to the Pacific War we had trained our airmen implicitly to believe that sea battles fought under our command of the air could result only in our victories. The initial phase of the Pacific War dramatically upheld this belief." Taking Manila, Rabaul, Singapore, Malaya, Burma, and their surrounding territories in just six months may have been unprecedented. In such a short period, "Japan took more territory over a greater area than any country in history and did not lose a single ship."[22]

Even if the Imperial Japanese Navy could not match US ship production and pilot training, its initial cohort of far more seasoned pilots and carrier crews would have to be killed off before the Allies could achieve parity. Americans, for their part, talked grandly of a tactical win at the Battle of the Coral Sea (May 7–8, 1942) and a strategic blowout at Midway (June 4–7, 1942). But neither battle had yet brought them naval superiority. That goal was not achieved until late 1943, mostly because the Americans built an entire new fleet of capital ships, and ceased losing assets as it had at Pearl Harbor, the Coral Sea, Midway, and off Guadalcanal. It is often forgotten that the American humiliation and defeat off Savo Island in the Solomon Islands in early August 1942—four Allied cruisers sunk or scuttled, against no Japanese ship losses—came two months *after* Midway. At Savo—a much smaller version of the great Japanese battleship and cruiser victory at the Battle of Tsushima nearly forty years earlier—the Japanese inflicted a twenty-to-one casualty ratio of seamen, ten times greater than the American advantage at Midway.[23]

The apparent Japanese prewar strategy for winning the naval war was to degrade both American and British fleet strength in a series of surprise attacks throughout December 1941 and early 1942, and then, in a subsequent classic showdown between battleships, cruisers, and carriers, to destroy the hoped-for impulsive Anglo-American response. Japanese naval supremacy would then force the Allies to sue for peace rather than spend the blood and treasure necessary to build entire new Pacific fleets and raise combat divisions necessary to root out the Japanese from their newfound acquisitions in such a distant empire. Yet the Japanese had never envisioned having three naval enemies on their hands by mid-1943: a surviving British fleet (to be vastly expanded by 1944), the sizable remnants of the old prewar US Navy, and a newly built American Pacific Fleet larger than all the surviving navies of the world combined.[24]

The Imperial Japanese Navy also had little conception of the irrepressible fighting spirit of the US Navy or of its superb officers, especially its admirals of the caliber of Chester Nimitz, Raymond Spruance, William Halsey, and Charles Lockwood, who were in their late fifties and early sixties and had spent a lifetime at sea. There were plenty of incompetent American captains and admirals, which was no surprise, given the huge and sudden expansion of the US Pacific Fleet. But the key decision-making at the top proved consistently superior to that of the Japanese admiralty.

Japanese admirals often dreamed up complex naval operations to disperse American warships—evident in their campaigns at Midway and, later, Leyte Gulf—while neglecting the more mundane but far more important tasks of attacking US merchant vessels in the Pacific. Japanese admirals also had a fatal habit of curtailing successful operations at critical moments of near victory, apparently in fear that they might lose their mostly finite and irreplaceable naval assets. Such was the case of inexperienced Admiral Chuichi Nagumo's indecision at Pearl Harbor; Admiral Takeo Takagi's unwillingness to use the full air fleet of the *Zuikaku* to destroy the wounded retreating *Yorktown* after sinking the *Lexington* at the Battle of the Coral Sea; the sudden withdrawal of Admiral Hiroaki Abe at the successful first naval battle of Guadalcanal; the failure of Vice Admiral Gunichi Mikawa to use his famous night victory at Savo Island to finish off the American supply ships off Guadalcanal; and Admiral Takeo Kurita's inexplicable sudden departure from the successful engagement off Samar Island during the Leyte Gulf showdown. Timidity is not a trait we usually associate with the aggressive Japanese Imperial Navy, but it nonetheless was endemic among its admiralty in a way not true of the Americans.[25]

By January 1945, after just three years of war, the United States not only outclassed the Imperial Japanese Navy in the Pacific in every category of naval strength, but had completely overwhelmed it in numbers of deployable fleet carriers (14 to 2), light and escort carriers in service (66 to 2), active battleships (23 to 5), cruisers (45 to 16), and, perhaps most important, a staggering 296 destroyers against the Japanese's surviving 40. Such lopsided figures, however, were only a part of the equation. Already by mid-1943 American naval fighters, dive bombers, and torpedo planes—Hellcats, updated Dauntlesses, Avengers, and Helldivers—had proven superior to their Japanese counterparts, were far more numerous, and were increasingly more expertly piloted. In fact, the greatest flaw in the operational concepts of the Imperial Japanese Navy was its inadequate training of new carrier pilots. It turned out naval aviators in the mere hundreds each year rather than in the thousands, and after six months of even successful operations was unable to keep pace with its losses. This dearth of experienced carrier airmen to match strategic ambitions was already apparent by the early Battle of the Coral Sea, where Japanese bombing accuracy was dismal.[26]

Prewar Japanese naval strategy was predicated on an array of unlikely assumptions that were soon rendered little more than fantasies. American commitments to convoy duty and amphibious landings in the Atlantic and Mediterranean theaters did not much hamper the Pacific reach of the US Navy. Prior American isolationism was a result of choice, not of any intrinsic lack of potential to wage war or rearm. There was no evidence that Japanese prewar surface ships and carriers were necessarily superior to American designs. Even Japan's vaunted carrier dive bombers and fighters—the Val and Zero—were not all that much better than prewar American Dauntlesses and Wildcats. Nor would they be updated and improved as rapidly as their American counterparts. Large fleet carriers like the *Lexington* and *Saratoga*, commissioned in the mid-1920s, were comparable or superior to their contemporary Japanese counterparts such as the *Kaga* and *Akagi*, and were among the largest and most lethal ships in the world for most of the 1930s.

The Japanese had no realistic plans for the conquest of Hawaii as they did for the Philippines or Malaya, perhaps because of Pearl Harbor's proximity to the United States and the impossibility of fueling and supplying such an outpost so far from Japan. Even after their auspicious beginning of the Pacific war, the Japanese had no realistic systematic plan to absorb additional strategically important Allied territory such as Midway, Australia, and southern New Guinea. Japanese tankers and freighters had no idea how to conduct the effective convoy system implemented by the

British and later the Americans in the Atlantic, and were extremely vulnerable to submarines, mines, surface ships, and bombers.[27]

The Japanese navy ostensibly started the war with a number of technological and material advantages: experienced naval air forces, effective nocturnal gunnery, excellent destroyers, and intimate knowledge of the Pacific. They built superb submarines and possessed the world's most lethal torpedoes. The Type 93 Long Lance oxygen-driven torpedo, although flammable and hazardous to use, was superior in every category of performance. It was some fifteen miles per hour faster than its American counterpart, with three times the range, and had three hundred more pounds of explosive. Unfortunately, the Imperial Japanese Navy rarely used its submarine fleet strategically against vulnerable Anglo-American shipping. Too often Japanese submarines were used as ancillaries to the main surface fleet. Just as Hitler was unable to consolidate and exploit the natural and manmade resources of an occupied continental Europe, so too the Japanese were naive in thinking they had enough ships to protect and exploit a far-flung, newly acquired Greater East Asia Co-Prosperity Sphere, predicated on the invincibility of a navy that had theretofore only been able to bully its inferiors. In characteristic Axis fashion, Japan simply did not have the naval means to match its grandiose strategic ends.[28]

To THE DEGREE that Benito Mussolini's Italy even had a coherent and sustained naval strategy, it was the idea that the Regia Marina could conduct autonomous operations in the Mediterranean. Mussolini assumed that German U-boats would keep the British and later the Americans busy in the North Atlantic, ensuring their absence or weakness in the Mediterranean, which the Italians construed as a *Mare Nostrum* to connect a new Rome stretching from southern Europe to the Aegean and North Africa. Mussolini's success in bluffing the far stronger British and French navies in 1934–1935 to allow him access through the Suez Canal for his colonial wars in eastern Africa had further convinced some of the more delusional in Fascist Italy that its superior morale and spiritual fiber could make up for its numerical inferiority and material shortcomings at sea. If the greatest navy in the world had not stopped Mussolini's aggrandizements in East Africa in 1935, fear of a vastly smaller fleet of Italian battleships must have been the ostensible cause. That the British fleet could easily have blown the entire Italian expeditionary force out of the water before 1940 was a fact ignored.[29]

Italy never built a carrier force. It apparently relied on air bases in Southern Italy, Sicily, and North Africa to provide cover for its

Mediterranean fleet. Still, on paper the Italian navy was impressive. The Regia Marina boasted six battleships, led by the huge flagships *Littorio* and *Vittorio Veneto,* each over forty thousand tons and armed with nine 15-inch guns. They were supported by nineteen heavy and light cruisers as well as fifty-nine destroyers and 119 submarines. Without responsibilities in the Atlantic or Pacific, the Italian navy after 1940 became the largest force in the Mediterranean. With the exception of an absence of carriers, the Italians outnumbered the British Mediterranean fleet of Admiral Andrew Cunningham in almost every category of warship, while enjoying greater air support from large Axis bases in Sicily and, after April 1941, Crete.[30]

But the capital ships of the Regia Marina lacked modern radar. The fleet had little night-fighting capability. It had neither the oil stocks nor material support comparable to the infrastructure of the Royal Navy. The Italian navy had no realistic plans to strike comprehensively at the heart of British sea power in the Mediterranean at Suez, Malta, and Gibraltar. It could not cut off the British from their oil supplies in the Middle East.[31]

When Italy entered the war on June 10, 1940, its apparent path to victory was predicated on three developments, two of which were largely out of its own control. The first was that the impending German defeat of France meant the end of the rival and superior French Mediterranean fleet, an advantage confirmed by the British destruction of key Vichy French warships in their harbors in Algeria at Mers-el-Kébir and at Dakar in French West Africa. For about five months, Italy therefore enjoyed a flukish Mediterranean preeminence entirely not of its own making.[32]

Second, Germany, so Mussolini prayed, would continue to focus on Britain in 1940 and 1941, and either invade and occupy the country, or through a U-boat campaign destroy the British ability to import food, fuel, and materiel and bring an island nation to terms. Either way, the Royal Navy would soon be forced to weaken its forces in the Mediterranean. When Mussolini went to war against France and Great Britain, he had no expectations that just weeks after the evacuation from Dunkirk, Britain would survive the Blitz. He also had no real interest in or concern over whether Hitler would invade the Soviet Union in June 1941, a surprise act that eventually diverted German air strength from the Mediterranean.

Third, Mussolini declared war on the United States on December 11, 1941, with only vague ideas about the reach of American naval power, an act likely never imagined when it went to war against Britain in June 1940. Given American struggles with isolationism during 1939–1940, he apparreckoned that the United States either could not or would not deploy in the distant Mediterranean, especially with the huge Imperial Japanese Navy threatening its Pacific interests. Overestimation of the reach of the Japanese fleet would prove a fatal assumption by all the Axis powers.[33]

In other words, the Italian fleet could supply its expeditionary forces in North Africa only as long as Germany was not at war with Russia, as long as Britain was besieged by the Luftwaffe and U-boats, and as long as the United States stayed neutral or at least was preoccupied by Japan. As early as autumn 1942, all those conditions had mostly altered. Mussolini's prewar naval hierarchy had focused on cruiser and battleship tonnage, speed, gun size, and armor. In such categories, Italy's fewer ships on paper were roughly comparable to their British enemies. But in less romantic criteria—night-fighting ability, radar, communications and intelligence, crew training and morale, officer experience, maintenance, and fuel and ammunition supplies—the Italians were woefully inadequate. They could not fulfill key objectives that would have crippled the Allies, such as bottling up the entrance to the Mediterranean, shutting down the Suez Canal, keeping the sea-lanes to North Africa open, or capturing Malta. Most tragic of all for the Italians, their navy—the fourth largest in the world when the war broke out—was ossified. Its huge size had represented an investment of well over two decades' worth of unsustainable capital and labor expenditure. Italy's naval experience can be summed up by the fact that it did not start from the keel up, much less finish, a single new major capital ship during its brief war in the Mediterranean. Rarely in military history had such a large powerful fleet played almost no helpful role in a war and disappeared so quickly.[34]

THE BRITISH BEGAN World War II with the largest surface fleet in the world: twelve battleships, seven carriers, fifty-six light and heavy cruisers, and over 180 modern and older destroyers. They had pioneered the very concept of the modern battleship with their launching of the 1906 HMS *Dreadnought* and first deployed planes at sea off the converted flattop HMS *Hibernia* in 1912. As an island power, Britain enjoyed numerous ice-free, deep-water ports that looked out to the North Sea, English Channel, and North Atlantic.

The British assumed, correctly, that with preservation of their naval superiority and air parity in the Atlantic and Mediterranean, German forces could never invade their island nation or even starve it into submission. To the contrary, one day the Western Allies would use a secure Britain as a base from which to land troops on the continent to reach Berlin and end the war. In 1940 Churchill had also assumed that if the USSR were to become an ally, it would siphon off the resources of the Third Reich away from Britain and its interests. Until then, naval superiority and the continued enlargement of the fleet through an extensive ship-building industry would allow Great Britain to conduct sea operations from Burma to North Africa and the Mediterranean. Its ships would ensure continued access to overseas resources and its empire, and the ability to land troops on the periphery of Axis-controlled Europe and Japan.

British sea power would seek to neutralize the large, but inexperienced Italian navy, strand the Axis in North Africa, allow amphibious landings anywhere in the Mediterranean, and ensure the end of almost all Atlantic imports into Germany. It would also be able to land troops in Burma and elsewhere in the Pacific because of the lack of coordination between Japan and Germany that was the result not just of Hitler's megalomania or the incompetence of his diplomatic team, but also of his lack of sufficient ships and easy maritime access to Asia through Suez or around the Cape of Good Hope.

Almost all British strategic maritime objectives of the war were achieved by 1943. The cost was not cheap: over fifty thousand dead seamen (nearly double the number of British sailors lost in World War I), five battleships and battle cruisers sunk, along with eight fleet and light aircraft carriers, an astonishing thirty-four cruisers, 153 destroyers, and seventy-four submarines. By the end of six years of fighting, the Royal Navy had lost nearly half of its prewar warship strength, and almost a third of all ships in its wartime fleet—manpower and ship losses far greater than what was suffered in the four-year experience of what would become a much larger American navy. Nonetheless, the British military, through its reliance on naval and air power, and alliances, had managed to win a much longer and bloodier conflict than World War I while suffering about 40 percent of the aggregate combat fatalities incurred in the earlier war.[35]

In sum, naval success helps explain why Britain could fight World War II longer than any other warring power and yet suffer the fewest number of combat casualties of the six major belligerents. Churchill and his advisors saw the British navy, the American and Russian armies, and British and American bombers as the best way to avoid another Somme. They were largely proven right. The RAF and the Royal Navy did not guarantee that Britain would win the war, only that it could not be defeated—a key to understanding the course of the war during the critical year between the fall of France and the invasion of the Soviet Union, when Britain had no active allies and lots of enemies. By late 1940, the British position miniscent of that described in 1801 by Admiralty First Lord, John

Jervis, 1st Earl of St. Vincent, concerning a nearly unstoppable Napoleon's threats to reach the English coast: "I do not say, my Lords, that the French will not come. I say only they will not come by sea."[36]


THE UNITED STATES entered the war after a relatively recent naval rearmament campaign in the late 1930s that had almost achieved naval parity with the Japanese fleet in the Pacific and had ensured—well apart from the British navy—superiority over both the Italian and German fleets. America was worried that should the British navy fail in 1940, then its own naval assets could hardly stop a Kriegsmarine that might have absorbed the fleets of both Great Britain and France, and was allied with Italy and Japan. The American predicament after Pearl Harbor was not that its prewar fleet was too small or had neglected naval air power and submarines. Instead, the challenge was that the ambitious strategic aims of a rearming United States—unconditionally defeating and eventually occupying all three quite distant Axis powers while supplying the Soviet Union and Great Britain—initially outstripped the available means to achieve them. In response, soon after Pearl Harbor America adopted a naval strategy as simple as it was ambitious: keep Great Britain viable by ensuring that the Atlantic remained open to shipping; achieve naval superiority in the Mediterranean to ensure landings on Axis-occupied territory; and hold the Japanese at bay for a year until new ship production would allow the destruction of the imperial fleet and amphibious landings on Japanese-held Pacific islands and eventually the mainland itself.

American naval planners at first struggled with a paradox of priorities. The supposedly lesser enemy, Japan, possessed the far more formidable fleet, had successfully attacked the United States, and therefore posed the greater threat to American-held territory. Yet Tokyo was considered of secondary importance, at least officially, to the European theater by the War Department. It would take at least a year before America's newly formed Joint Chiefs recognized that a "Germany first" policy did not necessarily apply to the navy in the same fashion it affected the army and air forces. In other words, America could prioritize sending armor, airborne, and motorized divisions and strategic bombers to Europe, while deploying the great bulk of US submarines, surface vessels, aircraft carriers, Marines—along with several crack Army infantry divisions—to the Pacific, where the US Navy would achieve near preeminence quite unimaginable in the European theater.[37]

After the loss of the Philippines and the British defeats in Malaysia and Burma, short-term US naval agendas in 1942 were aimed at keeping a viable line of supply from Australia to Midway Island and Hawaii without losing entirely the shrinking Pacific fleet to a numerically superior Imperial Japanese Navy. Within two years, new merchant fleet production, a vast expansion in the size of the US Navy, and the attrition of the German and Italian navies in the Atlantic and Mediterranean, with commensurate transfers of American ships to fight Japan, would guarantee American naval superiority in the Pacific and the ability to peel back the concentric layers of the Greater East Asia Co-Prosperity Sphere.[38]

Such American hopes hinged on several assumptions: that naval superiority would allow Marines and eventually over twenty-one Army divisions to be transported and supplied while island hopping to Japan; that cruisers and battleships were not antiquated assets, given that their firepower offered ideal mobile artillery support for island amphibious assaults; that American carriers and submarines would whittle down Japanese warships and render them irrelevant; that new American island bases would allow air forces, along with carrier planes, to bomb and mine the mainland and provide air cover for the growing fleet; and that submarines would destroy the Japanese merchant fleet.

The United States did not fight a single major surface sea battle with either Germany or Italy, and never lost a battleship after Pearl Harbor or a fleet carrier after 1942. By the time America entered the war in December 1941, Britain had already offered preliminary outlines of how to neutralize the German U-boat fleet through the convoy system, superior intelligence, new technology, and air and surface fleet superiority— although for the first six months of 1942 German U-boats were poised to cut off Britain from North America. Despite initial resistance to British strategy, the United States was able to help Britain defeat the U-boats not much more than a year after entering the war. Victory in the Battle of the Atlantic allowed Allied surface ships to ensure the viability of amphibious landings in North Africa, Sicily, and Normandy.[39]

How the US Navy by just midway through the war had become the world's largest and most accomplished sea power is a complex story, but the general outlines are clear enough. Early on it had commissioned its first carrier, the converted *Langley* (11,000 tons) in 1922, and had designed the *Ranger* (14,500 tons, commissioned in 1934) from the keel up as a carrier. As noted earlier, the carriers *Saratoga* and *Lexington*—converted from battle cruiser hulls, commissioned in 1927–1928 at thirty-eight thousand tons, with speeds up to thirty-five knots, and armed with over ninety fighters and bombers—were the prewar navy's largest and most prestigious ships. Although clumsy, they were perhaps the best carriers in the world at the outbreak of the war. In their long prewar careers, the carriers had helped attract innovative officers to naval aviation, such as future admirals Ernest King, Bill Halsey, and Marc A. Mitscher. Americans had also cultivated a symbiosis between carrier and battleship strategies, as the idea of a carrier battle group was seen as a natural extension of the previous though soon-to-be obsolete practice of massing cruisers and battleships with escorting vehicles. The Americans had more affinity with the British fleet than with those of the Germans, French, or Italians; the latter all had lacked the proven carrier expertise of Great Britain, which had also commissioned the world's first truly modern aircraft carrier, the *Argus*, in 1918.

The wartime commissioning of twenty-four *Essex*-class carriers—the most sophisticated aircraft carriers of the war—was the natural evolution from the *Lexington* and *Saratoga*. It is often forgotten that the American fleet that broke the back of the Imperial Japanese Navy in 1943–1944 was largely designed and approved for construction before Pearl Harbor, and mostly through the efforts of one naval visionary, Congressman Carl Vinson, chairman of the House Naval Affairs Committee, who from 1934 to 1940 pushed through five successive landmark bills to expand and reconfigure the US Navy. The novelist and Guadalcanal veteran James Jones once wrote of the emergence of the new huge American fleet, "in 1943 alone the war effort at home had brought into service: 2 fast battleships; 6 fleet carriers; 9 light carriers; 24 escort carriers; 4 heavy cruisers; 7 light cruisers; 128 destroyers; 200 submarines. . . . If the Japanese naval staff could have seen the list they would have shuddered."[40]

The United States did not devote its submarines just to attacking warships, as the Japanese largely did, but also to focusing on merchant shipping. In this regard, it gained invaluable knowledge and operational know-how from the long British antisubmarine experience. Unlike the Japanese, American submariners operated nearly autonomously in hunting down enemy merchant convoys, and thus cutting off the Japanese mainland from its newly acquired territory in the Greater East Asia Co-Prosperity Sphere.

Both the *Gato* and *Balao* classes of American submarines became the finest of the war to be built in large numbers. Vice Admiral Charles A. Lockwood, the head of the US Submarine Force Pacific Fleet, was the most innovative submarine admiral of the war, primarily because he gave great latitude to his commanders, ensured they had superb ships and (eventually) torpedoes, and urged them to take risks to concentrate on curtailing Japanese supplies to its far-flung empire. By 1943, after initial problems with prewar torpedoes were worked out, the subs went on to all but destroy the Japanese merchant fleet.[41]

The Americans also found ways to employ otherwise ossified battleships and heavy and light cruisers that transcended classic shootouts
between capital ships. Their four *Iowa*-class battleships were the fastest
and best-designed of the war. Although many of the twenty-four American battleships successfully fought at least two major battles against their
Japanese counterparts—off Guadalcanal (November 14–15, 1942) and
the Philippines (October 25, 1944)—the United States more often deployed such capital ships as floating artillery platforms, in a manner that
the Germans, Italians, and Japanese never quite could.

New *Baltimore*-class heavy cruisers (displacing over 14,000 tons)
bristled with nine 8-inch (over 200 mm) and twelve 5-inch (127 mm)
guns. Superb light cruisers like those of the *Cleveland*-class (12,000-ton
displacement, twelve 6-inch guns and twelve 5-inch guns) ensured that
at every major American amphibious invasion after 1942—Sicily, Italy,
Normandy, and southern France, as well as the far more numerous island assaults in the Pacific—American surface ships provided critical
pre-landing bombardment and targeted enemy artillery during the assault. Their huge main batteries were usually far larger than any Japanese
or German land counterparts, even if naval gunfire sometimes lacked the
necessary trajectories for direct hits on the vulnerable roofs of reinforced
concrete and coral fortifications. Still, with ranges of well over twenty
miles, American battleship guns could pound the invasion beaches and
rear areas while staying immune from most counterfire. The 14-inch
(350 mm) and 16-inch (approximately 400 mm) guns of American battleships were far larger than the US Army's own heavy 240 mm howitzers (short-barrel artillery pieces that lobbed shells at high trajectories).
Sometimes the Navy was faulted for firing hundreds of shells at fortified Japanese positions without eliminating resistance when Marines and
Army units hit the beaches. But the point of such barrages was never to
eliminate Japanese positions entirely, but to enhance ground advances.
All ground troops complained of the inadequacy of naval fire; none suggested that it was irrelevant to their success.

In sum, Axis ships like the *Bismarck*, *Tirpitz*, *Yamato*, *Musashi*, *Roma*,
or *Vittorio Veneto* were majestic examples of nautical engineering, but they
remained largely wasted assets and were never utilized in amphibious operations in the fashion of the *Tennessee* or *New Jersey*.[42]

THE SIZE OF the Soviet Union, and its almost complete self-sufficiency in
oil, ores, and coal, allowed the Russians to believe they could fight both
offensive and defensive wars without much of a need to transport many

Red Army troops by sea or to ensure steady maritime imports—if food could be imported somehow to make up for the possible wastage and loss of croplands. Thanks to Allied naval superiority, such assumptions in large part proved correct. The huge size of the Red Army was proof that the Soviet navy—and for that matter Russia's strategic air forces—did not compete with its ground forces for resources as did American naval (3.4 million servicemen, with half a million in the Marines) and air (2.4 million) investments. By the beginning of the war with Germany in 1941, the Soviets had no carriers and only three aged battleships. By 1944 the Red Fleet's allotment had been reduced from prewar levels even further to only about 6 percent of the Soviet defense budget.[43]

The Soviet Union, for all its talk of worldwide communist expansion in the 1920s, did not prepare for it militarily, focusing instead on the defense of the motherland. Privately, Soviets assumed that they would have to deal with the armies of Japan to the east and Germany to the west—or another possible intervention from the Western powers—while conducting offensive ground operations against their own immediate land neighbors, such as Poland and Finland. Given such strategic objectives and its self-sufficiency in oil, food, and ores, it made less sense to invest in a navy comparable to its enemies or allies, especially after postponing earlier ideas of promoting worldwide communist expansion by force. While Russia entered the war with the largest numbers of submarines, for instance, it had the smallest surface fleet of the six major combatants.

Given poor weather in the Baltic and North Seas, and given that Germany did not often bring what was left of its fleet into Russian waters, there was to be no major battle between the German and Russian northern fleets. The other two Soviet naval forces—in the Black Sea and the Pacific—played small roles in the Allied victories. The Japanese remained loyal to the terms of their nonaggression pact with the Soviets to such a degree that almost half of US Lend-Lease materiel was shipped safely from West Coast ports on Soviet vessels directly to Russia at the port of Vladivostok. This alternate so-called Pacific Lend-Lease route of Russian merchant vessels became one of the safest transit paths of the entire war. Russian submarines by 1944 were sometimes sinking Axis freighters and small surface ships in the Black Sea and eastern Baltic, but no Russian (or German) warship altered the course of Operation Barbarossa. When Russia finally piled on Japan days before the ending of the Pacific war, it had to borrow over 250 small ships from the United States just to occupy Sakhalin Island and a few Japanese islands in the Kuril archipelago.[44]

Before the USSR was invaded in June 1941, Stalin looked fondly on the idea of German U-boats tying down Britain and slowly starving it into submission. After Operation Barbarossa, Stalin flipped, hopeful that the British navy would nullify the German fleet, interrupt scheduled supply convoys for Germany's Army Group North, and supply the Soviet Union with war materiel. After December 7, 1941, Stalin further assumed that the British and American fleets would consume Japanese naval attention, thus precluding both a second Axis ground front against the Soviet Union and the need for Russia to conduct a two-theater offensive war. There would be plenty of time, after the war, when Soviet ambitions turned global, to invest in a blue-water fleet to promote Russian imperial expansionism.[45]

As EARLY AS 1939, strategists had warned their publics that the looming war would be fought on all fronts far differently than was World War I. Such apprehensions largely arose because of new medium strategic bombers and the use of reliable, fast tanks that might turn static warfare into a conflict of mobility and encirclement. Whereas observers expected U-boats once again to seek to strangle Great Britain and isolate it from its overseas suppliers, while breaking the blockade of Germany, almost no naval expert foresaw the predominant role that aircraft carriers were almost immediately to play. America's war began with a devastating attack of enemy carriers on "Battleship Row" at Pearl Harbor. Yet almost all senior American naval officers sighed relief that the three Pacific theater carriers—*Enterprise*, *Lexington*, and *Saratoga*—were out to sea at the time of the attack. Rarely in military history had an iconic asset—the battleship—metamorphosed so rapidly from an irreplaceable emblem of national maritime strength into an ossified anachronism. There may not have been a prewar "Carrier Row" at Pearl Harbor, but if there had been, and if it were severely damaged, there would *not* have been a sigh of relief that at least the Japanese had missed three battleships out to sea.

Prewar carriers mostly were fashioned from converted ocean liners, battle cruisers, or battleship hulls—sometimes an ironic reaction to the 1922 Washington Naval Treaty's restrictions on battleship tonnages—with no consensus on optimum designs, armament, speed, or size. While post-treaty ships like the *Akagi*, *Kaga*, *Lexington*, and *Saratoga* were undeniably large, their designs were not emulated by later models that were conceived from the hull up as carriers. Early naval biplanes were neither fast nor reliable enough to place their ordnance consistently on targets, in a way that would ensure that enemy surface ships (in the age before radar) could not sneak up and blast vulnerable carriers out of the water. As a result, many early carriers were armed with 8- and 5-inch gun batteries.

Perhaps it was more tolerable for the battleship interests to envision pre-war carriers as veritable battle cruisers with an array of turret batteries in addition to a flight deck.

The maximum ranges of most battleships' main batteries—14-, 15-, 16-, or even 18-inch guns—varied from sixteen to twenty-five miles, depending on the size of the charge, type of projectile, elevation of the gun, and velocity of the shot. The shell's destructive power was not just determined by the caliber of the gun but depended on additional factors such as velocity and the payload, which in turn were also predicated on the quality and length of the barrels. The 16-inch guns of an *Iowa*-class battleship, for example, were probably as destructive as the *Yamato*'s 18-inch batteries due to the former's heavier and faster-moving—but smaller-diameter—projectiles. Most World War II guns could fire salvoes every thirty-five or forty seconds, and keep that rate of fire up either until their ammunition was depleted or the barrels began to wear out (somewhere between 150 to 400 shots, depending on the nature of the shell, the size of its propellant, and the quality of the ship's barrels). Battleships were the masters of the seas—in their tiny radiuses of about twenty miles.[46]

A standard fleet carrier, in contrast, might easily send off three or four sorties of thirty or forty bombers and fighters per day against an enemy two hundred miles away (over an hour's flight, depending on weather conditions), with the high likelihood that some of its dive- and torpedo-bombers would place ordnance on the target, while the vigilant mother carrier stayed out of range of an enemy's big guns. The problem with battleships was not that they could not do more destructive damage to ships and shoreline installations than carriers—and at a cheaper cost and in less time than a carrier's planes—but that they lacked naval aviation's range and were far more vulnerable to counterattack. A torpedo hit from a carrier plane was usually more likely to damage a battleship than was a barrage from another surface ship.

Carriers, then, could also offer a far greater array of techniques for damaging a ship, from strafing to dive-bombing to aerial torpedo attacks. Naval fighter screens offered far better defenses against air attack than those of a battleship's anti-aircraft batteries, and with good radar naval aircraft could spot potential attacks and prepare for them with sophisticated air patrols. Aircraft carriers were also cheaper to build, a flight deck costing less capital and labor than a battleship's massive and intricately machined gun turrets. The new *Iowa*-class battleships that entered the Pacific in 1943–1944 each cost about $20 million more than the late-model *Essex*-class fleet carriers, and required almost as many crewmen (nearly 3,000) as carriers. Their nine 16-inch guns could theoretically fire collectively over a thousand huge shells an hour (each weighing nearly 3,000 pounds) at targets well over twenty miles distant. But they had no ability to hit anything two to three hundred miles away, as could the ninety to one hundred planes on a new *Essex* carrier. Anything a battleship could do—blow up surface ships, bombard shore positions, show the flag—a carrier could usually do better and almost as cheaply.

In the six years of World War II, on only three occasions did a battleship sink, or even help to sink, a carrier. During the Norway campaign, the obsolete and relatively small HMS *Glorious* (converted to a carrier in the late 1920s) was surprised on June 8, 1940, and sunk by the German battleships *Scharnhorst* and *Gneisenau*, due to the utter incompetence of the captain, who had failed to provide customary air patrols. Likewise, the small escort carrier *Gambier Bay* was destroyed on October 25, 1944, by the Japanese heavy cruiser *Chikuma* and the battleship *Yamato*. The Japanese converted light carrier *Chiyoda* was finished off in the Battle of Cape Engano (October 25, 1944) by American cruisers after suffering damage from aerial attack. In contrast, carrier aircraft during the war sank well over a dozen battleships as well as hundreds of cruisers, destroyers, and submarines. The Axis's four largest and most expensive battleships— *Bismarck*, *Musashi*, *Tirpitz*, and *Yamato*—were all sunk, or severely damaged, by naval aircraft.

Battleships proved an evolutionary dead end in World War II, and after a century of preeminence gradually disappeared from most of the world's fleets in the postwar era. The firepower of the grand ships of "Battleship Row" that were put out of commission at Pearl Harbor— most of them first deployed during and right after World War I—was not all that different from that of their modern successors of 1943. Until the age of guided missiles, it was difficult for a conventional World War II surface ship, given problems of accuracy, to consistently hit another ship at ranges much over fifteen miles. Yet the mystique of battleships still prevailed for a while—a two-centuries-old romantic image of British and French men-of-war lining up to blast each other apart at close ranges during the Napoleonic Wars. Battleships were beautiful, "sacred" vessels. Their size and guns were a testament to national power. Rare though battleship duels were, there was something about such raw, unambiguous displays of lethal force that captivated admirals and tended to cloud their judgment about the cost-to-benefit values of such majestic dinosaurs.[47]

What preserved the idea of a postwar surface cruiser was the introduction of guided missiles in the 1960s. For the first time, they gave larger surface ships the ability to hit targets at ranges of hundreds of miles, comparable to carriers' air fleets. And while we assume that cruisers and battleships are now long-obsolete notions, today's new American *Zumwalt*-class "destroyers" in reality are pocket battleships of a sort, displacing some 14,500 tons, larger than most World War II heavy cruisers.

In contrast to World War II surface ships' more-or-less fixed armaments, naval aircraft were upgraded constantly and often radically so. By 1943 American Hellcats, Helldivers, and Avengers were qualitatively different planes from their earlier counterparts. Both battleships and carriers often shared the same basic hull substructures. Yet the latter updated its offensive reach in a way impossible for the former's guns. The limits of a battleship's gun range, whether it was of the *North Dakota* or the newer *Iowa* class, were static. In contrast, in 1942 a standard carrier torpedo plane's theoretical total range was about 450 miles (e.g., the Douglas TBD Devastator), with a combat radius of about half that distance. Yet just a year later most carriers could deploy torpedo bombers with a range of a thousand miles, when equipped with auxiliary tanks, and an active combat radius of almost four hundred miles (e.g., the Grumman TBF Avenger). In other words, carriers could double their targeting range without substantially modifying their hulls, engines, or decks. Had Germany and Italy finished a carrier for each of their battleships and battle cruisers—for example, a *Graf Zeppelin*–class carrier carrying twelve or so modified Bf 109s and perhaps thirty adapted Ju 87 Stukas—they would have had a far better chance of winning the battles for the Atlantic and Mediterranean.[48]

THE SECOND GREAT revolution in naval warfare was under the sea. Even early model submarines, especially German U-boats—had proven deadly in World War I. They could be built and manned far more cheaply than cruisers and battleships, and yet had the potential to be far more lethal to merchant shipping, especially until the Allies developed effective mines, depth charges, convoys, and air patrols. Quick dives by U-boats usually were better defenses against air attack than were a surface ship's antiaircraft batteries.

A U-boat fleet for a rearming Germany offered a fast-track method of attacking British shipping, without the expense of seeking parity with the Royal Navy's huge surface fleet. For most of World War I—before and after the Battle of Jutland—the Germans had parked their surface fleet, but their submarine fleet had attacked the Allies all over the globe and sunk over five thousand ships. By 1939, the promise of improved submarines seemed to guarantee greater success in World War II, given superior ranges, speeds, depths, and armament.

German submarines accounted for far more sunken enemy merchant shipping and warships—well over fourteen million tons worth—than all the battleships, cruisers, air power, and mines of the Third Reich combined (7 million tons). The cost-to-benefit ratios of submarines versus large surface ships explained why subs proliferated and battleships became calcified, and why the Germans soon regretted diverting precious resources from submarine construction to their surface fleet. When the *Bismarck* went down in May 1941, so too did an investment of some 200 million Reich marks and 2,200 sailors. Its sister ship, the slightly larger *Tirpitz,* may have been even more expensive; one thousand German seamen were lost when British bombers finally blew up the battleship in a Norwegian fjord in November 1944. The combined but paltry efforts of the two huge battleships resulted in one destroyed British battle cruiser, the iconic HMS *Hood,* some damage to a British battleship and a few cruisers, and on one occasion the shelling of British installations on the island of Spitsbergen. The *Tirpitz* never fired its main battery at any seagoing vessel—nearly similar to the experience of the wasted assets of the even bigger Japanese white elephant *Musashi.* Yet submarines sank some seventeen aircraft carriers in World War II, far more than the three carriers lost to salvos from surface ships. Years after the war, Admirals Doenitz and Raeder, while together as inmates of Spandau prison, still argued over naval allotments, with Doenitz blaming his onetime superior for shorting the U-boat fleet to build glamorous but otherwise relatively "bloated" surface ships.[49]

In defeat in the Battle of the Atlantic, Germany's expense in U-boat construction and service was about a tenth of the costs that the Allies lost in sunken cargoes, ships, and investments in antisubmarine warfare. The Kriegsmarine suffered horrendous losses (781 of over 1,100 U-boats built, entailing about 33,000 of some 40,000 deployed U-boat crewmen). Nonetheless, this was less than Allied lives lost on merchant ships and warships (approximately 72,000). All German losses from U-boats—men and equipment combined—proved a fraction of what was consumed in a number of major land battles. Yet German submariners came closer than any of the Wehrmacht's air or land forces to curtailing the war effort of Great Britain.[50]

German submarines could easily have been even more astutely deployed. The Kriegsmarine sank some 14.5 million tons of American, British, and Russian shipping (or 18,565 tons sunk for each U-boat lost). In contrast, the American submarine fleet in the Pacific lost just fifty-two boats while sinking 5.2 million tons (about 102,000 tons sunk for every submarine lost). While German submarines sank almost nine million aggregate tons of shipping more than did the American submarine fleet, the U-boat force was also nearly four times larger and fought almost two years longer. The reason for the superior efficiency of the American submarine fleet lay in the Allied ability to conduct antisubmarine operations far more effectively than either the Japanese or Germans. But additionally, American submarines were larger, with superior radar, and were better suited for the conditions of the Pacific than were U-boats for the Atlantic. Most important, German U-boat operations were micromanaged by Admiral Karl Doenitz in a way untrue of his American counterpart in the Pacific, Admiral Charles Lockwood.[51]

Prior to World War II, the prevailing naval logic dictated that all surface ships should become more deadly as they became larger, given the greater number of 14- to 16-inch guns they mounted and the increases in their armor belts. More utilitarian submarines and destroyers were customarily an afterthought in prewar assessments of naval power. The average early twentieth-century destroyer—of about 1,200 to 1,500 tons of displacement, four to six 4-inch guns, and speeds over thirty knots with ten to twelve torpedo tubes—originally came into modern use just prior to World War I to protect the fleet by screening more valuable ships from surface or submarine attack. Destroyers also served as scouts that could radio back information on enemy positions. They were especially valuable in patrolling enemy shorelines, sinking merchant craft, and deterring attacks from fast torpedo boats. During World War I, destroyers had come into their own as the antisubmarine ship of choice, which could be built in great numbers, and whose depth charges and light guns could escort a convoy at far less cost than cruisers.[52]

Destroyers' 3-, 4-, or 5-inch guns were considered too small to do much damage to larger surface ships. Their torpedoes could sink battleships and cruisers but they were usually too vulnerable to get within accurate torpedo range. In the interwar period, the size of individual destroyers grew. In part, they were not, as were cruisers, subject to the initial limitations of ship class tonnage in various naval agreements, at least until the London Naval Limitation Treaty agreements of the latter 1930s. But for reasons of economy it soon made more sense to expand upon a cheaper destroyer hull than to downsize a light cruiser. In terms of a cost-to-benefit analysis of comparative naval tonnage required for patrolling the seas, it would have made far greater sense, for example, for the German Kriegsmarine to disperse twenty versatile destroyers across the Atlantic than to send out the single battleship *Bismarck*.

World War II revolutionized the use of the destroyer. Equipped with radar and sonar, better torpedoes, and far more anti-aircraft guns and multiple depth-charge throwers, destroyers were by war's end the most versatile vessels. By cramming such diverse weapons systems into such a small and inexpensive ship, the destroyer became essential in escorting convoys, hunting down and screening the fleet from submarines, and serving as radar pickets posted on the circumference of a fleet to ward off air attacks, both conventional and kamikaze. The small size of destroyers made them hard-to-hit targets. And because as "tin cans," destroyers had thin metal skins, often huge armor-piercing shells from cruisers and battleships went right through their infrastructures without exploding, as in the engagement off Samar (October 25, 1944) during the Battle of Leyte Gulf. In contrast, on rare occasions, destroyer torpedoes sank enemy cruisers and battleships, such as the Japanese battleship *Fuso* that was probably torpedoed by the American destroyer *Melvin* at the Battle of the Surigao Strait (October 24–25, 1944).

As in the case of fighter aircraft and tanks such as the French Dewoitine fighter and the Char B1 tank, a navy's theoretical technological superiority did not necessarily equate to maritime efficacy. In the prewar period, the French, who deployed some of the most impressive cruisers and battleships on the seas, had also redefined the ideal destroyer with the six ships of its pathbreaking *Le Fantasque*–class: displacing 2,600 tons, reaching incredible speeds of over forty miles an hour, and equipped with five 5.4-inch guns. Yet French command, organization, experience, and morale did not match French nautical engineering skill, and French industry never turned out late-model ships and planes in sufficient numbers. Like the rest of the French fleet, most of the *Le Fantasque*–class destroyers sought refuge in North African ports and became irrelevant after June 1940.[53]

In total, 490 destroyers were sunk during the war, more than all other classes of surface ships combined. The United States alone lost sixty-eight destroyers—but not a single battleship after Pearl Harbor or a fleet carrier after October 1942. Building hundreds of destroyers instead of dozens of battleships or carriers spread risk, protected the greater investment of larger ships, and allowed an American naval presence in areas of marginal concern. The British, desperate for help in the Battle of the Atlantic in September 1940, had traded basing rights in the Caribbean and Newfoundland to the Americans in exchange for fifty old US destroyers—*not* in hopes of receiving a battleship or two or a dozen cruisers. From the first to the last year of the war, it was the destroyer that proved the most economical investment in terms of cost to build and man versus the benefits that accrued.[54]

When the war was over, the contours of postwar fleets were established for the next seventy years, anchored by submarines, destroyers, and carriers. Battleships and World War II type cruisers all but vanished from the seas.

IN THE NEXT two chapters concerning sea battles in the Atlantic and Pacific, six years of naval warfare in World War II are defined by three constant themes. First, the Axis powers before the war did not build enough ships of the sort that might have saved them, especially superb German U-boats and Japanese fleet carriers. Instead, they invested in far too many expensive battleships and heavy cruisers that brought them little advantage. Second, the victorious British and American navies were authentic two-ocean fleets, with the ability to send warships equally against the Japanese, Germans, or Italians and supply vessels around the globe; the Axis armadas, in contrast, rarely ventured beyond their respective seas. Third, Great Britain and the United States both started and ended the war with the world's largest navies for logical reasons: sustained naval supremacy rested on the less-romantic advantages of industrial capacity and policy, accumulated experience, and the ability to train quickly and competently thousands of naval officers and sailors.

# 8

# From the Atlantic to the Mediterranean

THE FIRST, MOST evenly matched, and longest theater of naval battle in World War II was in the North Atlantic and, on occasion, the North and Baltic Seas. It was fought largely by U-boats and a few surface ships of the Kriegsmarine against British and North American convoys, escort warships, and long-range aircraft. The so-called Battle of the Atlantic began as a partial replay of the German U-boat effort in World War I. Once again, German naval strategists thought they might starve Britain into submission, a nation that now needed fifty-five million tons annually of imported food and natural resources to survive. Barring that, the planners of the U-boat war dreamed of disrupting the Allied blockade of German ports, or at least obtaining naval superiority near the shores of occupied Europe, thereby precluding any future Allied effort to stage amphibious landings.

Despite revolutionary breakthroughs in German nautical communications and engineering during the interwar period, what had doomed the Imperial German U-boat effort of World War I would mostly do the same to the U-boat fleet of the Third Reich. Once more, the Allies—again with the belated entry of the United States—would produce far more merchant ships than the U-boats could sink, and thus win the "tonnage war." Once more, the Allies would develop new antisubmarine technologies and countermeasures faster and more efficiently than the Germans could improve submarines. Whereas the Imperial German U-boat fleet destroyed nearly thirteen million tons of Allied shipping by November 1918 at the cost of 178 submarines and five thousand crewmen lost in combat, the Third Reich, at war for six, not four, years, would do little better (14 million tons) while losing over five times as many crews (approximately 33,000 submariners) and over four times as many U-boats (781).[1]

The Battle of the Atlantic was fought over six years, from the first days of the war in 1939 to mid-1943, with residual sparring until the war's end in spring 1945. Along with the warships of its Commonwealth allies, Britain's fleet from mid-1940 to December 1941 was the only credible Allied navy still fighting the Kriegsmarine. The British navy tried to blockade Germany and its territories in occupied Europe as well as to starve out its armies. But such a time-tested strategy initially assumed that Germany would fight largely along its borders as it had in World War I, with its maritime access traditionally limited to the North and Baltic Seas and without access to the Atlantic. Neither assumption proved true in World War II.

Two factors are constant throughout naval history. First, the location and security of bases greatly determine the effectiveness of forwardly deployed fleets. Second, the security of such bases depends on the pulse of the land war, or at least on the status of ground forces in the surrounding territory that can transcend battle at sea. As war began in Europe in 1939, the British navy never imagined that within a year the Kriegsmarine would soon control, either through outright occupation or alliance, nearly all of the coasts of continental Europe. By autumn 1941 the Wehrmacht had absorbed much of European Russia. In contrast, Britain remained as vulnerable by sea as it had been in World War I, but with some substantial disadvantages this time around. Germany quickly obtained the shorelines of Norway and France as windows on the Atlantic for its fleet. Britain, with the exception of Gibraltar, soon lost all its prior friendly ports on the European Atlantic coastline. Hitler now also had the Italian Mediterranean fleet as an ally. Britain lost the French navy, the world's fourth largest, as a partner. Suddenly, cutting off Britain from its imports should have been far easier than in World War I, and far more practicable than the British efforts to stall the Wehrmacht by restricting maritime imports into Germany.[2]

A number of general turning points would determine whether the Germans could cut off Britain. First was the Axis-Allied race to create the larger navy. More specifically, the Germans sought to replace lost U-boats and crews faster than the British and Americans could build new merchant ships and convoy escort ships. The tonnage war depended not just on relative economic strength but also on the exposure of shipping yards, pens, and related factories to enemy air attacks, and the respective strategic choices over allotment of key resources.

Second, each power sought to incorporate breakthroughs in ship design, communications, intelligence, armament, and detection more rapidly than did its adversary. The rather sudden emergence of credible German and Italian fleets by 1939 was not necessarily an accurate barometer of what would follow, given that the Allies had not been updating commensurately their own larger navies in the decade prior to the

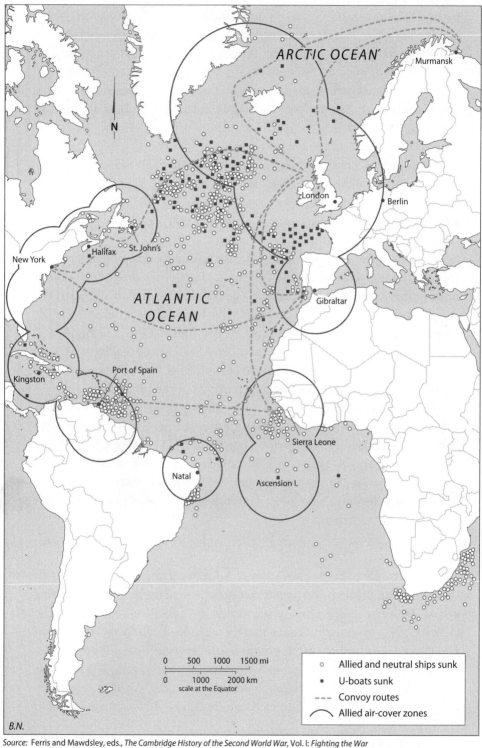

The Battle of the Atlantic

Source: Ferris and Mawdsley, eds., *The Cambridge History of the Second World War*, Vol. I: *Fighting the War*

outbreak of the war. Germany and Japan eventually produced some highly innovative new nautical technologies—ranging from sophisticated torpedoes, nocturnal optics, the Type XXI U-boat, and mines, to the snorkel and complex cryptology—but they rarely shared enough of their scientific advancements in submarines. They were ill-prepared to rush new breakthroughs into mass production, at least in the brilliant fashion of the British. And they lacked the capital and manpower of the Allies' counterintelligence and scientific agencies.[3]

Third, it was unclear whether air power more likely aided U-boats in sinking merchant ships or helped convoys to destroy U-boats. Comparative advantage would hinge both on the ability to make more and better long-range planes and the strategic choices of when and how to use such air power.[4]

Fourth, either the German or British admiralty would benefit more from the cooperation of its allies. Although Italy dispatched a few submarines to the Atlantic, there was zero chance that the Italian and Japanese surface fleets would play any prominent role in the Atlantic. And while Germany occasionally sent a U-boat to the Indian Ocean or South Pacific, German submarines of the so-called Monsoon Group were of little help to Japan. In contrast, the Americans and British were full partners at sea in the European theater and rival partners in the Pacific.[5]

Fifth, the ongoing and constantly changing pulse of the war on land would better aid either the German or the British naval effort. Either British or German war obligations beyond the Atlantic would likely siphon off critical naval resources to a greater comparative degree. Most important, changes in strategic geography, prompted by the entrance of the United States and the Soviet Union into the war, would likely alter operations in the Atlantic.

THE SEESAW BATTLE of the Atlantic underwent several phases. All of them were predicated on sudden changes in the five defining moments above. The first months of the submarine war went well enough for the Allies, despite assorted disasters elsewhere on land and in the air. Britain had started the conflict with far more antisubmarine vessels (over 180 destroyers) than the Third Reich had U-boats. The weaker naval power was tasked with going on the offensive not just against the world's largest navy but also against the enormous merchant marines of North America and the British Empire at large.

Oddly, given all the lessons of U-boat lethality in World War I and talk of Nazi rearmament, Germany began the war with a comparatively insignificant fleet of submarines, many of which were smaller, obsolete Type II coastal boats. The Type IIs lacked the range, speed, size, armament, and communications of the newer Type VII series, which themselves were never really fit for effective service across the vast Atlantic. In addition, well into 1941 the Germans were plagued by faulty magnetic torpedoes, a large percentage of which failed to explode on contact, nullifying the best efforts of U-boat captains and thereby nearly ruining morale.[6]

From their experience in World War I, the British almost immediately began escorting convoys from North America. The Germans had not yet perfected the strategies of, or had the resources for, massed wolf packs deployed deep into the Atlantic, safe from air attack, that laid in wait for slow-moving convoys. For such a small U-boat fleet, the chances that individual submarines would find ships far out in the Atlantic were slim. Nonetheless, Britain immediately saw the need to increase its already-large destroyer fleet by any means necessary. By September 1940 it had pressed the United States for the stopgap measure of an additional fifty World War I mothballed destroyers as part of swaps for bases in Newfoundland and the Caribbean. The deal is often ridiculed today as one-sided and ungenerous on the part of the United States. True, many of the destroyers of the *Caldwell* and *Wickes* classes may have been less than modern and in terrible shape. But the majority of them would see plenty of service against U-boats and survive the war. Nineteen of the ships were quite adequate *Clemson*-class destroyers, which the United States itself used throughout the conflict. Meanwhile, Germany was losing surface ships as Britain was now adding them. Hitler's two-month-long assault on Denmark and Norway (April 9–June 10, 1940) ended up costing the Kriegsmarine three heavy and light cruisers and ten destroyers, while siphoning off U-boats from the Battle of the Atlantic at precisely the time Britain increased its antisubmarine fleet.[7]

Britain also held the early technological edge, due to much longer experience with early radar and sonar sets (or ASDIC, "Anti-Submarine Detection Investigation Committee"). Together such systems could offer newfound advantages in locating subs on and beneath the surface. British grand strategies for dealing with U-boats—convoys, sonar detection, depth charges, and air surveillance and attack—had primarily been tested since the last year of World War I and had been institutionalized in the fleet. Winston Churchill, as First Lord of the Admiralty, had provided his full support for addressing the U-boat peril. In contrast, German naval strategy still remained confused. Admirals Doenitz and Raeder still vied for Hitler's attention to focus on either surface ships or U-boats.

In addition, from September 1939 to June 1940, the French fleet had joined the British in patrolling the European Atlantic coasts. The German navy, however, was still confined to its original North and Baltic Sea ports. For much of the winter there, harbors froze over, and the distance from the Atlantic routes vastly limited U-boat ranges. By early 1940 the brief U-boat offensive had largely failed. For most of 1939 Doenitz was scarcely able to ensure that more than ten U-boats were actually out in the Atlantic on patrol at any given time. He needed new bases, far more late-model U-boats, and a different way of using them if he were to avoid the verdict of the past war.[8]

In the second year of the war, the pulse of the tonnage battle radically changed. The numbers of Allied ships sunk by U-boats in the North Atlantic soared. From an average of about twenty-eight merchant ships destroyed per month in the last four months of 1939, the tally grew to a monthly rate of about forty ships throughout 1940. This was largely due to improved German U-boat production. Only 1.5 ships had been built per month in 1939. But output reached over four per month in 1940 and up to an incredible 16.5 in 1941.

Just as important, newer Type VIIC U-boats slowly entered service. They would eventually become the mainstay of the new U-boat fleet: 568 of them were to be commissioned during the war. The Type VIICs were faster, had longer ranges, and were stocked with more torpedoes than all earlier German models. Nevertheless, their efficacy by global standards was often exaggerated. In comparison to American *Gato*-class subs of 1941–1942 (which were rapidly replaced and improved upon by the *Balao* and *Tench* classes), the nimble and easily maneuverable VIIC was outclassed in a variety of categories: far fewer torpedoes, far smaller, far less range, far more uncomfortable, and slower. The superiority of American submarines and the relative inferiority of German U-boats is rarely noted, given their vastly different theaters of operation.

Doenitz also soon perfected the strategy of wolf pack attacks, in which several U-boats lay in ambush for plodding convoys. Since the mid-1930s the Germans also had broken some British naval codes and often had advance warning of the timing and routes of many convoys. Doenitz carefully charted his zones of attack so that they were well out of range of first-generation British air patrols. Now with months of aggregate experience, dozens of U-boat commanders had vastly improved and refined their operational tactics. The odds were slowly beginning to favor the Germans.[9]

Events on land also helped the Kriegsmarine. The fall of the Western European democracies in June 1940 completely redefined the U-boat war.

New bombproof sub pens on the French coast at the warm-water harbors of Bordeaux, Brest, La Rochelle, Lorient, and Saint-Nazaire gave refuge to the Atlantic-bound U-boats some five hundred miles closer to the battle zone than their former North Sea bases. U-boats used that savings in distance to range farther out into the Atlantic. Lufthansa's premier prewar airliner, the pathbreaking four-engine Focke-Wulf Fw 200 Condor, with wartime adaptations, could stay aloft for fourteen hours with occasional ranges over two thousand miles. Once based on the French coast, small fleets of radar-equipped Condors scoured the mid-Atlantic, providing valuable intelligence to U-boat commanders. By war's end, the planes, equipped with bomb racks and crude bomb-sights, had also accounted for the sinking of over 350,000 tons of Allied shipping. Yet, inexplicably, fewer than three hundred Condors were to be built—about a tenth of the number of the somewhat smaller two-engine American Consolidated Catalina PBY flying boats—too few to change the tempo of the Atlantic war.[10]

The perfect storm of 1940 only grew worse for the British. What was left of the French fleet after July 1940 now was rendered largely irrelevant. A month later, an opportunistic Mussolini would send twenty-six of his own submarines to Bordeaux to aid German U-boats in the Atlantic. The British suddenly found themselves at war in Norwegian waters and in the Mediterranean, at a time when they were forced to send more supply convoys to their distant Pacific colonies in increasing fear of Japan. Meanwhile, fear of German invasion for most of 1940 argued for the Royal Navy to remain closer to home. These added responsibilities conspired to disperse and weaken British antisubmarine strength throughout the North Atlantic. The net result was increasing German confidence that the U-boats might succeed where the Luftwaffe had not in forcing their sole remaining enemy, Great Britain, to accept a negotiated armistice.[11]

Yet by spring 1941, against all odds and mostly alone, the British slowly began to check German submarine advances. For the third time in two years, the momentum of the seesaw Battle of the Atlantic once again began to reverse. Despite more experienced captains, improved torpedoes, and more submarines, Germany was again on the defensive, as U-boats were rendered little more effective than in 1939. The geostrategic responsibilities of the two adversaries had once again flipped. Germany was now forced to deploy ever more of its manpower from the Arctic Circle to the Sahara, without yet fully exploiting Europe's aggregate industrial potential. For the first six months of 1941 the Wehrmacht focused on planning Operation Barbarossa, as critical resources were directed to the army and Luftwaffe in an anticipated land and air war well over a thousand miles distant from the North Atlantic.

In contrast, by spring 1941 Great Britain no longer had any Western European exposure. In the months before the Japanese attack on Singapore, its responsibilities had shrunk largely to a one-front war in North Africa, the failed defense of Greece, and a still-anemic air campaign over the continent. As was true during even the worst months of the Blitz, when a supposedly beleaguered Britain outproduced Germany's aircraft industry, the British and Canadians built more merchant ships, destroyers, and corvettes than the Third Reich could produce U-boats per month, even at the Kriegsmarine's new accelerated rate.

With the sinking of the German flagship *Bismarck* in May 1941, the prior twenty-month effort of the Third Reich's surface fleet to harass the Royal Navy and weaken the British merchant marine for all practical purposes came to an end. Many of Admiral Raeder's once-promising new cruisers and battleships were at the bottom of the Atlantic, damaged, hiding, or bottled up by British ships in French, German, or Norwegian ports. The responsibility of containing what was left of the German surface navy was largely outsourced to British fighter and bomber forces, freeing up yet more Royal Navy ships to focus on U-boats.[12]

Equally important, improved British radar sets were not yet matched by German countermeasures. Their effectiveness was further enhanced after May 1941 when the British Navy salvaged from two U-boats—one captured, one sunk—cryptographic tables and elements of the Enigma cipher machine itself. For the last six months of 1941, British code breakers were able to read German naval communications routed through the Enigma cipher, an effort enhanced by Admiral Doenitz's micromanagement of his fleet that required a vast corpus of daily coded radio transmissions. The British admiralty could either route North American convoys well around wolf pack rendezvous points, or intercept and destroy lone U-boats heading to and from their engagement areas. Again, the key to British cryptological superiority in the U-boat war was not just technological or predicated on chance capture of German codes and coding machines, but rather on a much more sophisticated and comprehensive approach to deciphering and disseminating such knowledge to the armed forces in a rapid and pragmatic fashion.[13]

Germany was not quite done yet. By early 1942 the Axis and Allies had opened yet a fourth—and the most lethal—chapter to the Battle of the Atlantic, once again hinging on vastly changed strategies, geography, technology, and productive capacity. In February 1942 German naval intelligence introduced a so-called fourth wheel and greater complexity to the Enigma cipher machines that all but ended the ability of the Allies to listen in on U-boat communications for several months. At about the same time, the German naval surveillance service (B-Dienst) also made greater inroads in cracking the so-called British and Allied Merchant Ships code (BAMS). For a critical few months of 1942, most communications about planned Allied convoy operations and routes were known in advance to the Kriegsmarine, suggesting that U-boat commanders now knew far more about the plans of their intended targets than their British targets knew about them.

The entry of the United States into the war in December 1941 should have offered immediate and unequivocal advantages for the British. The prewar US fleet was still the second largest in the world and now could operate freely against U-boats. Unfortunately, for the first six months of the American war the very opposite proved true. Germany enjoyed newfound advantages precisely because America's mostly unprotected merchant fleet at last became fair game. For a variety of reasons, Admiral Ernest King, Chief of Naval Operations, did not immediately deploy American warships to escort Britain-bound convoys. In the initial months of outrage over Pearl Harbor, King resisted diverting too many US ships from the war against Japan. And in truth, for all his anti-British posturing, King did not yet have many American destroyers and long-range bombers on hand to focus on the U-boats. The result was that U-boats could feast on American merchant ships as they first set out from their East Coast ports. Slow-moving transports were often easily silhouetted against brightly lit cities that were not subject to blackouts. Month after month, cargoes of food, gas, and war materiel were blown up, often with most of their crews, in sight of the American coast.[14]

In the first eight months of the new U-boat war against America, the Germans in Operation *Paukenschlag* ("Drumbeat") sank over six hundred ships, totaling over three million tons of shipping, at a loss of little more than twenty U-boats. Such lopsided totals should have broken the back of any incoming belligerent without sizable reserves of merchant ships.

Doenitz was able to deploy scarcely more than a dozen submarines off the American East Coast, a fact that makes the U-boat achievement even more astonishing. By marginally custom-fitting Type VIIs for extended ranges, and deploying a handful of the larger, new Type IX U-boats, the Battle of the Atlantic now sought to expand permanently into American waters. Over two hundred of the Type IX U-boats would eventually be built. If they were less agile and submerged far more slowly than earlier models, they also had a greater range of operation, as well as six torpedo tubes (rather than the five of most Type VII models) and more powerful engines.[15]

As autumn 1942 approached, Doenitz believed that at last he was harvesting Allied ships faster than they were being built—the most important calculus of the Battle of the Atlantic—while Britain's factories and armies were running out of vital resources. He assumed likewise that the Japanese fleet—unbeaten in a string of victories from December 1941 to May 1942—was drawing off American surface ships to the Pacific. The need to supply the Soviet Union likewise meant that additional American merchant ships were diverted from the North Atlantic route. The result was that as the Allies spread their strength, a refocused German U-boat fleet found advantage against North American convoys. Yet the blinkered Doenitz did not grasp that his startling success after the entry of the United States into the war was a temporary aberration that was due less to German prowess than to American inexperience and poor choices. Once Admiral King released convoy escorts, and new, long-range B-24 Liberators began air escorts (though never in enough numbers), the U-boats would find 1943 as terrible a year as much of 1942 had proved uplifting.[16]

The greatest obstacle to the success of the U-boats was the unprecedented US production of destroyers, corvettes, and more merchant ships. By the last three months of 1942, less money was spent on building battleships, carriers, and cruisers, as well as armored vehicles, due to the urgent need to win the war against U-boats. American strategists saw that if their supply ships could not reach Great Britain and keep the sea-lanes open for troop transport, then the size of the American expeditionary army targeted to land on the shores of Mediterranean and Western Europe would not much matter.[17]

The brief German resurgence had also been based on a transitory intelligence advantage. But in October 1942, the British once again cracked the modified German naval code after the salvaging of Enigma key sheets and settings from another wrecked U-boat, and by December were once again reading Admiral Doenitz's communications. The British also appointed a new antisubmarine commander, Admiral Sir Max Kennedy Horton, who continued the key innovations of his predecessor, Admiral Percy Noble. The two together had fashioned novel tactics, among them more independent killer antisubmarine ships that were able to range more widely to focus on convoys under attack by U-boats, as well as providing support vessels to help save crews.

The hunters then soon permanently became the hunted. As was true of General James Doolittle's command decision of February 1944 to release American fighters from their direct bomber-escort duties so that they might range freely in search of German airfields and distant Luftwaffe fighters, so too British surface ships increasingly proactively took the war to the U-boats. Whether in the air or on the seas, the rationale was similar: individual pilots and captains, when freed from direct proximity to bombers and merchant ships, could find all sorts of multi-dimensional ways to hunt down their adversaries where and when they were most vulnerable. The best defense proved to be an audacious offense freed from preset doctrine.[18]

While Germans worked on long-term technological breakthroughs like snorkels and hydrogen-powered propulsion, the Allies implemented more incremental and practical advances: multiple-firing depth-charge throwers, powerful new airborne searchlights, small escort carriers that could bring their own air cover along with the convoy, and, always, improved radar and sonar. By mid-1943 these changes had at last all but doomed the entire U-boat effort.

Convoy ONS 5 that crossed the Atlantic in April and May 1943 is often viewed as emblematic of the final Allied victory in the Atlantic. The ensemble steamed across the Atlantic with one accompanying warship for every three merchant vessels. Despite being attacked by wolf packs of nearly forty U-boats for over a week, at least thirty of forty-two Allied merchant ships got through. Six of the attacking U-boats, however, were lost, and more were damaged. In later weeks, Atlantic convoys suffered minimal losses, or at least far fewer than did the U-boat packs that attacked them. The Battle of the Atlantic had all but ended by autumn 1943. In May alone, the Germans had lost a quarter of all their deployed U-boat fleet (43 in one month), while sinking only fifty-eight ships, a mere fraction of the Allied monthly new production. Meanwhile, American shipyards were turning out hundreds of *Liberty* and larger *Victory* merchant ships, totaling well over thirty-two hundred by the end of the war.[19]

Although U-boats remained an irritant throughout the war, they posed no serious threat in the conflict's final twenty-four months. Admiral Doenitz confessed that by early 1943, "radar, and particularly radar location by aircraft, had to all practical purposes robbed the U-boats of their power to fight on the surface. . . . I accordingly withdrew the boats from the North Atlantic. . . . We had lost the Battle of the Atlantic." Despite monthly increases in Allied convoys, the transatlantic route for the vast majority of merchant ships in 1944 and 1945 from North America to Britain was nearly risk free.

Although he had destroyed an enormous amount of Allied shipping at sea, Doenitz never curtailed Allied convoys nor, of course, could he extinguish factory production at the source—the most economical method of destroying the means to conduct a war. Consequently, the Allied merchant fleet was larger after the Battle of the Atlantic than before. The best that could be said for the German U-boat campaign was that it was the only theater of the war where Germany may have won in the narrow terms of a relative cost-to-benefit analysis of men and materiel, even as it lost the Battle of the Atlantic.[20]

NAVAL SUPREMACY IN the eastern Mediterranean determined critical entrance to and exit from the Suez Canal, the proclivities of a neutral but always opportunistic Turkey, and the fate of key British supply bases in Egypt. Yet after the bold German capture of Crete in April 1941, the eastern Mediterranean remained largely static: Germans and Italians went on to occupy the Dodecanese Islands that remained Axis controlled until the end of the war, and from there used their air power to control much of the Aegean. Yet Germany and Italy were never able to exploit that propitious beginning to alter the course of the Mediterranean theater, much less permanently alter transit via Suez from the Atlantic to the Pacific. The Axis failure, again, was attributable to the vast superiority of the Royal Navy, which, protected by RAF squadrons, continued to operate freely out of Alexandria and Cyprus. Neither base was ever systematically bombed by the Germans or Italians. And after the December 1941 attack by Italian frogmen on two British battleships in Alexandria and the German failure at El Alamein, British bases in the eastern Mediterranean were all but secure for the rest of the war. Far from using Crete and the Dodecanese Islands as starting points for further conquests that might result in strategic advantage, Germany's earlier eastern Mediterranean acquisitions died on the vine, becoming irrelevant by the end of 1943.

Fantasists in Japan and Germany had earlier dropped their illusions of ever meeting at Suez. Yet Churchill's grand plans in autumn 1943 of retaking the Greek Aegean and Dodecanese Islands also proved a failure on all counts. The Germans enjoyed air superiority from Aegean island air bases. America was not interested in the Dodecanese campaign. And it was hard to see how replacing Germans with British in the Aegean would much aid the Allied cause that was soon to be determined in Western and Eastern Europe. In sum, the Mediterranean east of Greece, despite occasional bitter fighting, to the end of the war became a backwater without much change after summer 1941. It was a veritable Mediterranean Norway—another occupation that had idled needed German troops since 1940—that cost the Third Reich capital and manpower without offering much strategic recompense.[21]

The central and western Mediterranean were quite a different story. Unlike British-held Egypt, North Africa from eastern Libya to the Atlantic was soon the scene of constant battle, especially as southern France and Italy became the focus of Allied amphibious landings. Malta

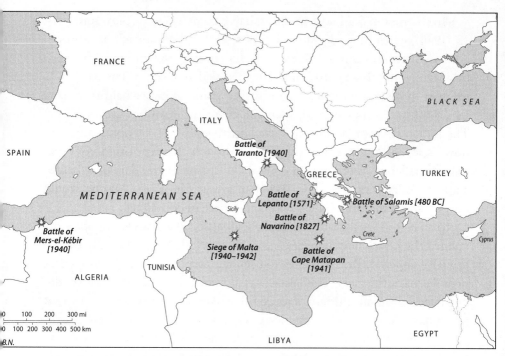

Major Naval Battles in the Mediterranean

and Sicily—closer to Germany's borders and the ultimate nexus of the war—were as violently fought over in 1942 and 1943 as Cyprus and Crete remained quiet. Despite initial British victories in a series of encounters with the Italian surface navy, from 1940 to mid-1942 the Axis still enjoyed the advantage. The French fleet was either sunk or retired by June 1940. The United States had little presence in the Mediterranean until late 1942. British airfields at Gibraltar, Malta, and Alexandria were offset by Axis fighter bases in Crete, Libya, and Sicily. There were still more Italian surface ships and German U-boats in the Mediterranean than there were British vessels. Against such odds, somehow Britain maintained a Mediterranean passage to its beleaguered troops in Malta and Egypt.[22]

The reason was again superior British operational skill. In a series of showdowns with the British Mediterranean navy, the larger Italian fleet—lacking good radar, secure fuel supplies, and familiarity with night fighting—was often port-bound or limited to brief breakouts. Like the Imperial Japanese Navy's initial parity with the American Pacific fleet, numbers proved deceiving. Whereas Britain could transfer warships from the Atlantic and Pacific, and build more ships, Italy's resources were ossified, and its shipbuilding industry was static. Britain risked battleships and cruisers, and most survived; Italy hoarded and lost them.

In the first major battle at the Italian base at Taranto (November 11–12, 1940), carrier-based British aircraft, under their audacious admiral, Andrew Cunningham, torpedoed the Italian fleet in its home port, seriously damaging three battleships (two disabled, one sunk). The battle was the first in history in which carrier-based planes without help from surface ships had sunk battleships, and its effect on Mussolini was dramatic. The Italian fleet was soon transferred northward from its opportune, but now exposed, Mediterranean perch. Although the fleet often ventured out to challenge Malta-bound convoys, and two of the damaged battleships were back in service in less than a year, the Regia Marina would never take on the British fleet with any degree of confidence.

Ironies followed from the landmark battle. The Japanese supposedly studied the attack closely in planning for Pearl Harbor, especially the innovative ability of British planes to use their torpedoes in a shallow-water port. Perhaps this close emulation was also why they, like the British, did not later follow up initially successful strikes with further attacks that could have destroyed the American fleet and its facilities entirely. Meanwhile, even the British had apparently learned little from their own revolutionary success. A little over a year later, the battleship *Prince of Wales* and the old, but still powerful battle cruiser *Repulse* would be sent to Singapore without fighter escort and would easily be blown apart by Japanese land-based planes in even more dramatic fashion than the manner in which British carrier pilots had earlier trounced Italian battleships.[23]

Admiral Cunningham struck again at Cape Matapan (March 27–29, 1941) off the Greek Peloponnese a little over four months later. His Commonwealth fleet sank three Italian cruisers and two destroyers—all without radar capability—without suffering serious losses. Again, better British seamanship, audacity, radar, and intelligence explained the lopsided result. The only way for the Axis powers to destroy the British Mediterranean fleet was through air power and U-boats, and not through the numerical superiority of their Italian cruisers and battleships. For example, in fights off Crete in May 1941, the Luftwaffe sank two British light cruisers and six destroyers with minimal losses. In the constant struggle to isolate Malta and disrupt British supplies to North Africa, Axis air power, along with U-boats and mines, seemed close to winning the battle of the Mediterranean by the end of 1942, sinking two British carriers, a battleship, over ten cruisers, and more than forty destroyers, along with forty submarines.[24]

To aid the U-boats, the Italian fleet was supposed to whittle down British destroyers that could be used for antisubmarine operations. Yet once again, the Italian navy would not take risks. The British, even with far greater resources deployed elsewhere, did. The British Mediterranean fleet grew larger than the Italian throughout 1942 and 1943, even as it lost more ships. Until the late arrival of the Americans in November 8, 1942, the British had envisioned three aims in winning the Mediterranean naval war: ensuring that reliable supply routes to their troops in North Africa could soon be maintained, diminishing Axis sea power enough to ensure amphibious landings in North Africa and southern Europe, and reestablishing a much safer route from Britain through the Suez Canal to the Indian and Pacific Oceans. In achieving these agendas, Admiral Cunningham proved to be not just a better sea lord than his German and Italian counterparts, but perhaps the premier admiral of the entire European theater.

In contrast, it would be hard to come up with a worse Axis maritime strategy in the Mediterranean than what Hitler and Mussolini had crafted. Malta, not Crete, was the strategic linchpin between the continents, and yet it was never seriously assaulted by land. Again, the Dodecanese Islands were a strategic dead end. Seizing Gibraltar should have been the overriding concern of Hitler. Yet he failed in negotiations with Spain's Francisco Franco—who, after the cataclysm of the Spanish Civil War, wanted to stay out of Hitler's war or, barring that, wanted much of Vichy France's North African territory. Hitler's failure to win over Spain created the anomaly of British Gibraltar controlling the western entry into and exit from the Mediterranean, despite being surrounded on all shores by hostile neutrals or Axis enemies. It was perhaps ironic that had Germany not supplied Franco during the Spanish Civil War, and had the Republicans won, Hitler in autumn 1940 likely could have simply invaded an exhausted Spain shortly after the fall of France and might well have taken Gibraltar.

The Pacific war in 1942 drew off British naval assets to Burma and for the protection of India, but not to the same degree that Operation Barbarossa shorted the Axis Mediterranean, an area that Hitler himself once scoffed that the Germans "had no interests in." As was true almost everywhere else in the war, the disastrous decision to invade the Soviet Union ensured that the Axis could never marshal the wherewithal to drive the British out of the Mediterranean for good.[25]

After late 1942, the Italian fleet was almost out of both oil and ships. It could play no real role in salvaging the North African Axis expeditionary forces. German U-boats on occasion would sink Allied ships even in the very last days of the war, but the era of wolf pack attacks crippling

Mediterranean commerce were long over. The British and American fleets by mid-1943 could land on Mediterranean shores anytime and anywhere they chose. Of the some sixty U-boats that at one time or another entered the Mediterranean, only one survived the war.[26]

Mussolini's pipe dream of an ever-growing ("whoever stops is lost") North African empire and refashioned *Mare Nostrum* vanished. So did Erwin Rommel's brief hope of heading to Suez and perhaps even meeting up with Army Group South—the southern prong of Hitler's three armies that had invaded the Soviet Union in June 1941—to drive through the Middle East to the Caspian Sea. The key to success in the Mediterranean was never how much area a power controlled—a map of Italian versus British territory in 1942 proved lopsided in favor of the former—but the *location* of the territory. As long as Gibraltar, Suez, and Malta—the entry, exit, and midway valves of the Mediterranean—remained British, they proved far more important Mediterranean bases than did Rhodes, Crete, and Sicily. Given growing Allied fleet and air power, the only Axis hope in the Mediterranean was a swift German victory over the Soviet Union, the addition of allies such as neutral Turkey and Spain, greater availability of ships and planes, and Japanese naval approaches to the Suez Canal. All were still possible in late 1941, unlikely by autumn 1942, and impossible by early 1943.

Still, the Mediterranean never quite panned out for the Allies, at least as Churchill originally envisioned, as the entry point into Austria and Germany through the "soft underbelly" of Europe. At best, Allied naval superiority in the Mediterranean meant that Sicily, Italy, and southern France were all to be invaded, with the stationing of long-range Allied bombers in Italy for deeper penetration into eastern Germany and its Eastern European partners. In addition, once the Kriegsmarine and the Regia Marina ceased to exist as viable navies, Britain could ensure relatively easy transport of supplies and troops through the Mediterranean to the Pacific.[27]

THE ANOMALY ABOUT naval war in the European theater was that it largely ended two years before the collapse of Germany and Italy. Despite occasional losses to vestigial U-boats, after late 1943 Allied ships were largely free to go where they wished and do what they wanted—in a way not so true of land operations until late 1944 or early 1945.

The Pacific naval war should have progressed with far more difficulty for the British and the Americans, given the greater resources of the

Japanese imperial fleet and the ostensible Allied "Europe first" policy of allotting resources. Instead, the British and American fleets achieved parity in six months, naval superiority in two years, and outright supremacy in less than three. By 1944 Allied naval power was free to turn nearly all its attention to ensuring supply and enhancing ground and air power—the chief objectives of putting a fleet to sea.

# 9

# A Vast Ocean

T<small>HE</small> S<small>OUTH</small> P<small>ACIFIC</small> was part of a far larger ocean, considerably more distant from the centers of Allied naval command in Washington and London than either the Mediterranean or the Atlantic. To a far greater degree, naval operations hinged on air power, amphibious landings, the acquisition of island bases, and the availability of fuel depots, all of which ensured that supply ships, troop transports, tankers, and convoys took on enormous importance. The three largest fleets in the world—the British, American, and Japanese—collided in the Pacific, and it was no accident that the largest sea battles of the war—Pearl Harbor, the Coral Sea, Midway, off Guadalcanal, the Philippine Sea, and Leyte Gulf—were all Pacific engagements.

In late February 1942, just two months after Pearl Harbor, a patched-together Allied fleet of American, British, Dutch, and Australian cruisers and destroyers—the so-called ABDA command—collided with a Japanese force of about the same size in the Java Sea. The Allied ships had come to sink Japanese convoys and thereby stop the invasion of Java and therefore the Japanese momentum. But when the main battle and its follow-up skirmishes were finally over—the largest surface ship encounters since the Battle of Jutland—two Allied cruisers and three destroyers were sunk. Over twenty-three hundred seamen were killed, including the commander of the fleet, the audacious Dutch admiral Karel Doorman, who went down with his flagship the *De Ruyter*. The Allies failed to sink a single Japanese warship. Only thirty-six Japanese sailors were lost. The slaughter at the Battle of the Java Sea dispelled any of the Allies' ethnocentric doubts about Japanese control of the Pacific after Pearl Harbor. Indeed, the Allies now thought Japanese sailors were supermen, and feared that their own initial defeats near Singapore and at Pearl Harbor may have been unavoidable rather than aberrant.

When the war began, in almost every area of naval operations the Japanese seemed to hold the advantages in the Pacific. Their cruisers and destroyers were generally larger and often better armed than their Allied counterparts. Japanese naval gunfire was more accurate, especially at night. Allied ships were not as well led, coordinated, or organized. One would have thought that Japan, not Britain, enjoyed a five-hundred-year naval tradition of global supremacy and had invented dreadnoughts, large-caliber naval guns, and steam propulsion. By the end of 1942, six months after the American victory at Midway, four of the six Pacific-based US carriers—*Hornet, Lexington, Yorktown,* and *Wasp*—were sunk, and a fifth—*Saratoga*—was damaged and out of action.[1]

The naval war in the Pacific never followed patterns of sea fighting in the Atlantic and Mediterranean. For one, the matchup between the combatants was far different. Both sides had carrier fleets. The war started in earnest not in autumn 1939 but over two years later, when aviation and carrier technologies were already adapting to wartime conditions and vastly improving, and the larger lessons from the Atlantic and Mediterranean could be digested. The British and Americans for the most part fought only one naval enemy—the Japanese—not two, as in Europe. After 1943 the Axis European powers offered little indirect aid in drawing off Allied ships from the Pacific. Except for some initial and final joint operations, the British and Americans found no immediate need to coordinate many ship-to-ship or amphibious operations against Japan, as had been true in the Mediterranean and Atlantic. In British eyes, Singapore's fall was psychologically catastrophic but perhaps insignificant in comparison to the incendiary burning of London. In contrast, the only American territory directly and seriously attacked in the war was by Japan, not Germany. Great Britain had no Pacific coastline; America's was over 1,200 miles in length.

These paradoxes also helped to explain why the American navy would take the lead in the Pacific as the British initially had in the Atlantic. If the American admiral Ernest King appeared to the British cantankerous and obstinate in a way General George Marshall did not, it was partly because British admirals could offer him far less valuable advice about Japan than seasoned British generals could to Marshall about Germany and Italy. Britain was essential as a bomber base and launching pad for the invasion of Europe; no such British strategic asset existed in the Pacific, likewise leading to far greater American autonomy. In the end, the British and American fleets communicated enough during the Pacific war to avoid working at cross-purposes, but otherwise did not always worry about clearing operations with one another. That independence seems to have worked successfully enough in a way it had not initially in the Atlantic.[2]

Three key themes characterized the mutual racial stereotyping of the naval war in the Pacific. First, the Japanese believed, wrongly, that Western seamen, naval aircrews, and Marine and army ground troops lacked the ferocity and martial spirit of the sailors and amphibious troops of the Imperial Japanese Navy. They were surprised, for example, that the pilots flying outclassed TBD Devastator torpedo bombers equipped with defective torpedoes—the inadvertent sacrificial pawns at the Battle of Midway—unflinchingly flew on to their certain deaths. When Japanese veterans on Guadalcanal met defeat at the hands of untried and initially ill-equipped 1st Marine Division soldiers and several subsequent army regiments, they were shocked by the discovery that they were fighting a power that was even stronger spiritually than materially.

Second, the British and Americans falsely assumed that the Japanese were mere emulators of Western science, copycats always one step behind in all categories of naval design, aviation, and technology. Americans were soon to be stunned, for example, by Japanese optics and skilled night gunnery in their one-sided victory at Savo Island. For a supposedly parasitic power, Japan's navy, despite the usual absence of onboard radar, had somehow started the Pacific war with more numerous carriers, the world's largest battleships, the best torpedoes and destroyers, and the most skilled aviators flying in naval bombers, fighters, and torpedo planes that were all comparable with or superior to American models.

Third, in part because of the racial dimension, there was often little quarter given in the Pacific and Asia. The Japanese executed captured American seamen, often after harsh interrogations, both as a reflection of their own martial code and as a way of terrifying Western soldiers. Yet while mostly following the rules of Westernized warfare, the Americans proved more brutal. They relied on their overwhelming firepower against the vast majority of their Japanese enemies who were reluctant to surrender, and did not worry about the collateral damage that their martial might visited upon civilians in Japanese industrial zones.

Ultimately, it was the Japanese who were the more mistaken in their stereotyped assumptions. By late 1942, British and American seamen and ground troops were fighting as audaciously as the Japanese, while Japan's technology and industry ultimately proved inferior by 1943. For all of their prewar mastery, the Japanese could never quite match the rapid breakthroughs and industrial mobilization of their Western enemies, who were far more experienced in the rapid challenge-response cycle of technological innovation than the Japanese. In addition, the premodern brutality of the Japanese did more to galvanize their enemies than the horrific use of American bombs and shells did to win the Japanese any sympathy as victims.

Also, unlike the European theater, the Allied naval war in the Pacific was not an auxiliary to land and air operations. Most American infantry fighting was by definition amphibious, relying on ships landing, and then supporting, expeditionary army units and Marines. In contrast, British and American navies in the Atlantic and Mediterranean had sought to achieve maritime superiority as a means to plant conventional infantry and armor on German-occupied territory, or to stop Axis amphibious or airborne invasions. This combined strategy ensured that continental armies fought their way into the heart of the German homeland and thus quickly left the protection of naval artillery and air cover.[3]

In the Pacific, warships were more autonomous and less commonly subordinated to infantry operations. The Allies targeted the Japanese navy and merchant fleet and thereby hoped to starve the vast and over-extended Japanese maritime empire into submission. Their efforts were akin to the Kriegsmarine's efforts against Great Britain, but with two important differences. First, unlike the Germans, the British and American hunters enjoyed far more naval assets—more ships, planes, and late-model technology—than did their targets. Second, the Americans were more confident that they could occupy or destroy mainland Japan, while the Germans had long given up on doing the same to the British homeland by mid-1941.

The Allies weren't the only ones to fight a two-front war. Japan diverted precious resources away from its Pacific operations because of its army's decade-long quagmire in Manchuria, Burma, and China—all theaters that also relied on maritime superiority to ferry weapons and men from mainland Japan. The Pacific war was also far more unpredictable than the Battle of the Atlantic. The Mediterranean had been familiar to Western powers since the hegemony of the classical Athenian and Roman imperial navies. Despite major Allied bases at Singapore and in the Philippines, much of the South Pacific remained a blank slate to the Allies. The routes across the North Atlantic had been fought over for centuries by Europeans and their colonial subjects, but the American fleet knew little about the maritime landscape around Guadalcanal or off Java. Everything from ocean currents and shoals to tropical diseases and little-known indigenous peoples made fighting in the Pacific a far more mysterious enterprise than steaming in the non-exotic Atlantic or the Mediterranean. James Michener could never have written a best-selling novel titled *Tales from the North Atlantic,* nor Rodgers and Hammerstein an idyllic musical about Americans based amid those same frigid waters.

Nicholas Monsarrat's epic postwar novel of the Battle of the Atlantic, *The Cruel Sea*, is a quite different, nightmarish elemental story of men at sea amid furious weather and wily German U-boaters.

The Pacific naval war saw over forty separate engagements between Japanese and American warships. For all the talk of the ruthlessness of the Bushido code, the Japanese were captives to American admiral Alfred Thayer Mahan's grand idea of seeking one great battle to destroy an enemy navy and thereby gain maritime superiority, and with it a negotiated rather than an absolute victory. That idea had worked with the near destruction of the Imperial Russian fleet at the great Battle of Tsushima thirty-six years prior to Pearl Harbor that pressured the Russians to seek peace. The overly complex strategies of the Imperial Japanese Navy from the Battle of Midway to the Battle of Leyte Gulf shared that common theme of hoping to lure the Americans into a trap and then decimating their fleet, resulting in paralysis of the American war machine. Yet that nineteenth-century strategy had failed utterly even at Japan's greatest tactical victory at Pearl Harbor. The problem was not just that they had not destroyed enough of the right sort of ships or bypassed infrastructure and oil depots or had failed to goad the wounded Americans into a follow-up shootout in the mid-Pacific. The real flaw of the operation was that even in victory the Japanese were still quite unable to reach the sources of manpower and production in North America. Japan did not fully appreciate that Pearl Harbor's fleet was merely a proximate tactical expression of remote but nearly unlimited and impregnable American strategic power.

Rarely in history have even lopsided naval victories—at Salamis, Syracuse, Lepanto, or Trafalgar—led outright to the end of a war. In contrast to the Japanese victory, the Americans aimed instead not just at blasting apart the enemy fleet in one decisive interaction of battleships and carriers, but also at insidiously severing Japanese maritime supply lines, securing bases for long-range strategic bombers, and cutting off and isolating Japanese island garrisons. Destruction of the Japanese people's ability to wage war was the American navy's aim, not a large and symbolic blow that would convince the Japanese that Pearl Harbor had been a mistake and could be rectified by concessions and peace talks.

THE PACIFIC WAR fell into three distinct phases. The first year of the war—from December 7, 1941, to January 1, 1943—was fought by Japan against the prewar Pacific fleets of the United States and, to a lesser extent, Great Britain and its Commonwealth allies, along with orphaned ships of the Netherlands. Before Pearl Harbor, the US Pacific Fleet was impressive enough, boasting nine battleships, three carriers, twenty-four heavy and light cruisers, eighty destroyers, and almost sixty submarines. Nonetheless, on December 7, 1941, the Americans in the Pacific were outnumbered in every category by the Imperial Japanese Navy, especially in the number of fleet carriers.

The greater number of ships, much longer experience and training, superior naval aircraft, far better torpedoes, and skilled night-fighting ability earned the Japanese a cumulative draw, in terms of surviving naval tonnage, in a series of wild engagements in the Java Sea, the Coral Sea, Midway, and at five sea battles off Guadalcanal. By the end of 1942, despite substantial losses at Midway, the Japanese still had salvaged rough parity, at least in the sense that the Imperial Japanese Navy had destroyed about as many ships as it had lost. It still had the greatest number of undamaged fleet carriers in the world, and thereby was still able to defend the outer defensive rings of its Greater East Asia Co-Prosperity Sphere.

At the beginning of 1943, however, a second, quite different war followed between what soon amounted to a mostly new American fleet and a now fossilized, prewar Imperial Japanese Navy, increasingly hampered by oil shortages and the cumulative losses of highly skilled carrier pilots. At the precise time that Japan was declaring supremacy in the Pacific, it was largely ignorant that the United States could increasingly tap into not only a supply of ships from the large Atlantic fleet, but also an entirely new armada that had been under construction since 1940–1941. This aggregate force would soon prove not just larger than the prewar American Pacific fleet of 1941, but more than double the size of the entire Imperial Japanese Navy. As noted earlier, in addition to a new fleet of escort (122) and light carriers (9), the US also turned out twenty-four large, *Essex*-class fleet carriers (each some 27,100 tons, with 90–100 planes). The carriers were soon aided by new generations of Hellcat, Helldiver, and Avenger fighters and torpedo and dive bombers—each model superior to their Japanese counterparts. By war's end, the US Navy would train over sixty thousand naval pilots and deploy some ninety thousand naval aircraft of all types.

Of special note were the escort carriers (8,000–10,000 tons, 17 knots), designed not to replace but to augment light and fleet carriers. They were small, unarmored, unstable in rough seas, uncomfortable for sailors, and slow, but were still perhaps the most innovative naval idea of the war. Aside from their cheaper cost and rapidity of construction, escort carriers were in many ways more cost-effective than either larger light or fleet carriers. It took just three-and-a-half escort carriers to match the air power of a standard fleet carrier. And in terms of the size of the crew needed to deploy naval aircraft, escorts were again far more economical (850 versus 3,500). With the 122 escort carriers it launched during the Pacific war, the US Navy found a rapid method of beefing up and dispersing the air fleet's arm, and covering the huge ocean, in a way that otherwise would have required the enormous expense of adding thirty-four additional fleet carriers. And as new-model and heavier naval aircraft were deployed on frontline *Essex*-class fleet carriers, thousands of first-generation and lighter F4F Wildcats and Dauntless dive bombers found second careers on escort carriers.

In less than four years, American shipyards not only produced a staggering tonnage of warships, but ships of superior quality in every category currently deployed by any of the major combatants. In addition to two new *North Carolina*–class battleships (36,000 tons, nine 16-inch guns), the US Navy added four even faster and more powerful battleships of the *South Dakota*–class (35,000 tons, nine 16-inch guns) and, most astonishingly, four huge *Iowa*-class battleships (45,000 tons, nine 16-inch guns), all to be augmented by refloating six older battleships that had been submerged at Pearl Harbor. The Germans publicized the launching of the *Bismarck* as a seminal moment in the history of German sea power; the Americans yawned as they launched their four *Iowa*-class battleships, all superior in quality to *Bismarck* and *Tirpitz*.[4]

The new American carriers and battleships were flanked by an additional fleet of fourteen new *Baltimore*-class heavy cruisers (14,500 tons and nine 8-inch guns) and an extraordinary destroyer arm of 175 *Fletcher*-class, fifty-eight *Sumner*-class, and over ninety-five advanced *Gearing*-class ships. Whereas the Japanese had shorted their smaller ship fleet by an unwise investment in huge battleships, the Americans were far more flexible in building an unglamorous but huge armada of over four hundred destroyer escorts (approximately 1,400 tons, 24 knots), the majority by 1943 deployed in the Pacific. This brilliantly versatile ship could stop merchant vessels with its 3-inch and (on some later models) 5-inch guns, provide anti-aircraft support for the fleet, launch torpedoes against larger ships, and sink submarines with depth charges. Along with the escort carrier, the destroyer escort helped to explain why the Japanese submarine force never achieved the results of its American counterpart, why American merchant ships in the Pacific suffered relatively minimal losses, and why American warships could go after even the smallest Japanese trawler.[5]

After Pearl Harbor the United States also built and deployed an entire new armada of large, long-range, and sophisticated fleet submarines— over 70 of the *Gato*-class and 122 *Balao*-class fleet boats, which along with other classes represented some 228 new submarines that joined the fleet, again with the vast majority deployed in the Pacific. American subs would sink over half of all Japanese ships lost, and shut down Japanese supply lanes, doing as much in unheralded fashion to destroy the Japanese economy as the napalm and mines dropped by the B-29 bomber fleet. The *Balao-* and later *Tench*-class submarines were superior to any other submarine produced in number during the war.

These assets allowed a third and utterly destructive phase of the war to be conducted by US surface ships and submarines from early 1943 to August 1945 against Japanese merchant shipping. In addition, US surface ships provided constant artillery support to amphibious operations and granted near immunity to American merchant vessels supplying a burgeoning number of air and naval bases reaching ever closer to the Japanese mainland. The net result was the strangulation of the import-based Japanese mainland economy and the orphaning of hundreds of thousands of Japanese soldiers on scattered Pacific islands without much hope of either resupply or evacuation.

No navy in military history had started a war so all-powerful as the Japanese and ended it so utterly ruined and in such a brief period of time—not the Persians at Salamis, nor the Athenians at Aegospotami (405 BC), the Ottomans at Lepanto, the French at Trafalgar, or even the Russians in 1905.

THE PEARL HARBOR attack was brilliantly conceived and conducted, although in prewar scenarios the United States supposedly had anticipated just such a surprise carrier attack on Hawaii. A huge Japanese fleet of six aircraft carriers and their capital ship escorts (2 battleships, 3 cruisers, and 11 destroyers, all except one to be later sunk by 1945) somehow made their way undetected to within two hundred miles of the Hawaiian shore. Then, even more amazingly, the First Air Fleet—some 353 planes strong, in two waves—completed the utter surprise, ruining in just two hours the battleship strength and much of the air power of the Pacific command, while departing with only marginal losses. Not since the Battle of Trafalgar had one navy so damaged its enemy (2,403 Americans killed, four American battleships submerged, four damaged) at so little cost to itself (64 killed), and yet achieved so few strategic results.[6]

The Japanese somehow believed that if they cut off North American supply lines to Australia, held off the US fleet for two years in the eastern and South Pacific, and consolidated their newly won empire, the British and Americans—faced with a losing war in Europe—would finally sue for accommodation. By needs, the Pearl Harbor attack also was operationally blinkered. Vice Admiral Chuichi Nagumo, who had little experience commanding carriers, did not order third and fourth strikes on Pearl Harbor that might have ruined the port facilities, destroyed much of the existing fuel supplies of the fleet, taken out valuable support ships and submarines, or blown up arms depots and workshops. Nagumo, despite his past ignorance of naval air operations, had perhaps some legitimate reasons for not doing so. The Japanese fleet's own fuel supplies were tenuous. Nagumo could ill afford losses to his small and irreplaceable cadre of naval aviators. He had no sure idea about the whereabouts of three American carriers or an unknown number of submarines. Unpredictable December weather—it was no easy task refueling on the high seas in winter—likewise added to the Imperial Japanese Navy's traditional anxiety. Many of Nagumo's aviators privately were relieved that the fleet was playing it safe and going home after just two strikes at Pearl Harbor. Perhaps most important, the fleet commander knew that many in the reactionary Japanese admiralty would consider Pearl Harbor a success by virtue of the destruction of the prestigious American battleship fleet.[7]

In the seven months following Pearl Harbor, the Japanese fleet ran wild, easily erasing the old European colonial and American spheres of influence. Naval superiority meant virtually unopposed landings at the Philippines, Thailand, Malaysia, the Dutch East Indies, Wake Island, New Britain, the Gilbert Islands, Guam, and Hong Kong. The Japanese are often scolded by historians for becoming infected with the "Victory Disease" early in the war. Yet in just four early naval battles preceding the Battle of the Coral Sea—at Pearl Harbor, Singapore, in the Indian Ocean and the Java Sea—they sank or grounded six Allied battleships, one carrier, one battle cruiser, six cruisers, and five destroyers, and killed over six thousand British, Dutch, Commonwealth, and American seamen, all without suffering a single ship lost and fewer than two hundred dead. However, despite tactical naval victories and strategic acquisitions, the Japanese navy still had not accomplished its main goal of destroying the American carrier fleet. More important, as the Japanese steamrolled through the Pacific, the further the Greater East Asia Co-Prosperity Sphere expanded, the more undermanned and undersupplied Japanese naval and merchant forces became.[8]

At the Battle of the Coral Sea (May 4–8, 1942), conditions in the Pacific theater insidiously began to change, although it was not so apparent at the time. A relatively weak American fleet, centered around just two carriers—with largely inferior planes—fought the Japanese to a rough draw. The interruption of Japan's prior record of success was an astounding achievement just five months after Pearl Harbor. The Imperial

Japanese Fleet lost more seamen and key aviators at Coral Sea than did the Americans. Moreover, as a result of Coral Sea, the Japanese called off the planned invasion of Port Moresby on New Guinea, the first time in the war that the Imperial Navy had cancelled an amphibious operation. The sinking of the light carrier *Shoho*, the damage to the fleet carrier *Shokaku*, and the near destruction of the air arm of the fleet carrier *Zuikaku* were far more grievous to Japan than were the sinking of the *Lexington* and the damage to the *Yorktown* to the Americans—especially given the greater American ability to repair capital ships and get them back into battle far more quickly.[9]

The next major encounter, at Midway (June 4–7, 1942), was, to paraphrase Churchill of the British win at El Alamein, not the beginning of the end of the Japanese fleet, but rather the end of the beginning of the American effort to blunt Japanese aggression. At the cost of the sinking of the previously wounded *Yorktown*, and the loss of much of the American torpedo bombing force, the Americans destroyed four Japanese fleet carriers along with nearly 250 naval aircraft.[10]

There were many reasons for the American victory at Midway, beyond the unplanned sacrifice of the obsolete American Devastator torpedo bombers that diverted Japanese fighters away from the faster, higher flying,

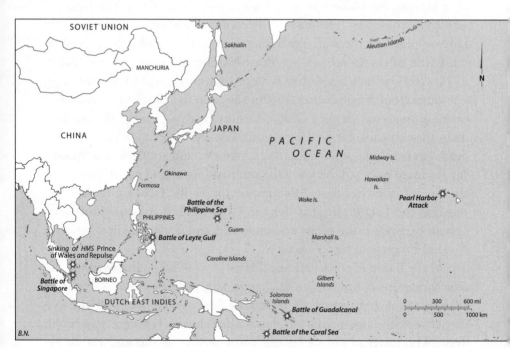

Major Naval Battles in the Pacific

and mostly unnoticed Dauntless dive bombers. The overall commander Admiral Isoroku Yamamoto unwisely had divided up his huge fleet, ensuring that his battleships, additional carriers, and cruisers would be sent on a strategically nonsensical invasion of the Aleutians, and thus were not present at Midway. Yamamoto's prebattle overconfidence also was undone by intelligence failures. He not only received little accurate information about the general whereabouts of the *Enterprise* and *Hornet,* but also assumed that the *Yorktown* had been sunk or rendered disabled at the Battle of the Coral Sea. In the end, Yamamoto did not seem to believe that two American carriers of not much more than twenty thousand tons displacement posed an existential threat to his grand fleet wherever they were.[11]

Superb naval intelligence and codebreaking gave the Americans some advance warning about where, when, and in what strength the Japanese would strike next. Land-based aircraft from the island of Midway harassed the carriers of Admiral Nagumo, in command of the Carrier Striking Task Force, and caused them to lose focus on the American carriers. The Americans took risks to win, the Japanese were too careful not to lose. The loss of four Japanese fleet carriers at Midway would almost equal the sum total of *all* new replacement fleet carriers built by Japan during the entire war. The verdict at Midway now meant that the Japanese could no longer expect accustomed naval superiority in any of its projected expansions in the South Pacific.[12]

But Japan's naval power was such that it could not be so easily neutralized in just two battles at the Coral Sea and Midway. Japanese battleships and cruisers remained adept at night fighting. Despite their losses, the Japanese still retained through 1942 a slight edge in naval air strength. The Japanese did not take long to prove their resilience. In their efforts to supply their battling forces on Guadalcanal between August and November 1942, the American and Japanese navies fought a series of brutal naval battles and several smaller engagements off the island: Savo Island (August 8–9), the Eastern Solomons (August 24–25), Cape Esperance (October 11–12), the Santa Cruz Islands (October 25–27), the Naval Battle of Guadalcanal (November 12–15), and Tassafaronga (November 30). When the protracted five-month sea conflict was over, the Americans had won the island but suffered losses at least comparable to the Japanese: about 440 planes, over five thousand naval casualties, and well over twenty ships. During the sustained fighting, the carriers *Saratoga* and *Enterprise* were damaged and the *Wasp* and *Hornet* sunk. With the earlier losses of the *Lexington* and *Yorktown* at the Coral Sea and Midway, the United States had effectively no fleet carriers that were undamaged in the South Pacific until the full repair and refit of the *Enterprise* and the arrival of new *Essex*-class ships in mid-1943. Such carrier losses would hamper aggressive use of carrier forces for much of 1942–1943. For a brief moment before the arrival of a new generation of carriers, Japan's strategy of nullifying American naval air power while occupying dozens of Pacific islands and using their land air bases as immovable "aircraft carriers" to harass the vulnerable US fleet seemed to be working.[13]

Yet after all the destruction, the Japanese still lost Guadalcanal. With the American conquest of the island went any chance the Japanese had of cutting the Allied supply lines to Australia, much less to making inroads into the Indian Ocean. Japan's destroyer and naval air strengths were now irreplaceably damaged. Guadalcanal, not Midway, was the true turning point of the Pacific naval war.[14]

By MID-1943, THE tide had turned for good against the Japanese. By the end of 1944, the new American fleet deployed not just the largest air arm in the world, but one larger than all contemporary carrier air arms combined. Proof of such overwhelming superiority was clear at the next great battle in the Philippine Sea (June 19–20, 1944), fought in conjunction with the American landings on the Mariana Islands. When the so-called Great Mariana Turkey Shoot was over, just a single American fleet (a fast carrier force of seven fleet carriers, eight light carriers, and seven battleships) had destroyed the bulk of Japanese naval air power in the Pacific, downing over 450 carrier aircraft while sinking three Japanese carriers without losing a single ship. There were lots of reasons for the American victory. But chief among them was that the US Navy simply sent out far more numerous and better aircraft—many of them superb F6F Hellcat fighters—piloted by better-trained and more experienced aviators.

Later at the Battle of Leyte Gulf (October 24–25, 1944), which was likely the largest sea battle in naval history in terms of the combined tonnage of the some 370 assembled ships, the Americans in just four days ended the Japanese navy's ability ever again to wage conventional offensive operations. The Imperial Japanese Navy, which probably had fewer naval aircraft at the battle than the Americans had ships, lost a fleet carrier, three light carriers, three battleships, and an incredible ten cruisers and nine destroyers, while sending its first suicide planes against the American fleet. In less than six months, Japan would turn systematically to kamikaze attacks, and at Okinawa used them to inflict the worst losses on the US Navy in its history. But after Leyte Gulf, Japanese warships never again constituted a strategic threat and were incapable of sustained operations. The loss at Leyte was Japan's version of Aegospotami, the catastrophic naval defeat of 405 BC that left the city of ancient Athens open to attack and siege, and ended its last vestiges of empire.[15]

WHAT ELIMINATED THE Japanese fleet in just three years was not just the huge and skilled American fleet of carriers and surface warships. Americans also had mostly secure supply lines from the West Coast to the South Pacific, and an endless fleet of merchant ships that ensured that US Marine and Army divisions were always better supported than their Japanese opponents.

Japan had no such security. One reason why was that in less than four years American submariners sank over two hundred Japanese warships and 1,300 merchant vessels—well over 50 percent of all Japanese ships lost to the Americans. That was a remarkable feat, given that the Americans entered the war without much actual submarine wartime experience and had to cover a far larger area of operations than in the Atlantic, even as their supply lines lengthened throughout the war as those of the retreating Japanese shrank.

The Japanese were far less adept in antisubmarine operations than the British and Americans in the Atlantic. By one method of calculation, the American submarine offensive proved to be the most cost-efficient method of war making of the entire war: Japan paid more than forty times the cost, both in conducting antisubmarine operations and in making up for lost shipping to submarines, than the combined US expense of conducting its submarine offensive and suffering its own merchant losses. That proved an unsustainable ratio, given that the US economy at the start of the war was already ten times larger than the Japanese.

The Pacific naval war might be summed up with one final irony. At the beginning of the war, off Singapore, the Japanese had taught the navies of the world about the futility of sending battleships and cruisers like the HMS *Prince of Wales* and *Repulse* into battle without air cover. Less than four years later, the Imperial Japanese Navy was reduced to dispatching on a one-way suicide mission the world's largest battleship, the *Yamato,* to Okinawa as a behemoth maritime kamikaze without sufficient fuel or air support against the world's greatest carrier air arm. What Britain had taught the Italians at Taranto in 1940 about the vulnerability of battleships to dive bombers and torpedo bombers had been forgotten by the British off Singapore in 1941. And the same lesson Japan had embraced at Singapore, they likewise ignored by needs off Okinawa in 1945.[16]

As in the case of Germany and Italy, Japan's expeditionary ambitions were far too large to be met by its existing naval forces or by its potential to build and man new ships. The Imperial Japanese Navy might have fought and matched either the Royal Navy or the American Pacific Fleet in the eastern Pacific under the conditions of a limited war, perhaps like the Russo-Japanese conflict of 1904–1905. But it could not fight the two largest fleets in the world simultaneously, much less in engagements ranging from the Aleutians to the Indian Ocean, while also ferrying armies throughout the Pacific and protecting the sea-lanes of a newly acquired empire far larger than Japan itself.

For all the traditions of national seamanship, admiralty, and courage, World War II at sea was ultimately predicated on which side built the most merchant tonnage and warships, and put the largest number of men at sea in good ships under competent commanders. The British and Americans would end the Axis's ability to move materiel and troops across the seas. And after 1942, they, not Japan and Germany, would choose how, when, and where the theaters of World War II would unfold. Ships were the foundation of Allied cooperation. Britain would send help to Russia and give the United States a huge depot and base from which to cross the English Channel to Europe. The United States would keep Britain and Russia supplied with critical food supplies and resources, wage an existential war against Japan, and partner with Britain to prune off German appendages in the Mediterranean and Italy.

At war's end, the Allies had fielded more planes, tanks, and infantrymen than had the Axis. But the greatest disproportionality was in naval and merchant marine vessels. Whether by measuring aggregate tonnage or individual ships, total Allied naval construction exceeded that of the Axis by at least seven- to tenfold. Of the sixty million who perished in World War II, naval operations claimed the least number of casualties, far fewer than either those lost to air power or fighting on land. Yet it was Allied superiority at sea that had saved all three Allied nations millions of lives and ensured that they could never lose the war.

IN THE NEXT five chapters, a few recurring themes resonate about the relative effectiveness of ground troops: the size of armies, the quality of fighting men, the nature of arms and equipment, and the effectiveness of supreme commanders, both in the tactical and strategic sense. None was a static benchmark; all evolved as belligerents sought to adapt, change, and improve. Yet the final story of Allied victory on the ground was found in eventually fielding far larger armies than those of the Axis powers, which by late 1943 at last roughly matched the fighting ability, weapons and supplies, and generalship of those who had started the Second World Wars.

# PART FOUR

# EARTH

## Armies on the ground, in the air, and at sea

*The military history of the half-century following the fall of
France in 1940 can, without too much oversimplification,
be boiled down to the story of Western armies allowing their
infantry to deteriorate until, in the moment of truth, they
discover the folly of such neglect.*

—John A. English and Bruce I. Gudmundsson[1]

# 10

# The Primacy of Infantry

INFANTRYMEN HAVE ALWAYS been the most important of soldiers, from Homer's Achaeans and Trojans who battled beneath the walls of Troy to the legionaries who finally stopped Hannibal at Zama. Civilization is grounded on land. Outside of Aristophanic comedy, cities are not perched in the clouds, in a reality unchanged by technology or social upheaval. It was, is, and will always be far easier and cheaper to feed and arm men on the ground than at sea or in the heavens.

Overwhelming naval power can nearly starve an island or smaller land power of its resources, and on occasion force it into submission. The Allied navy almost did that with Japan by 1945 and could have finished the job by 1946 or 1947 if it had been necessary. At one time Germany believed that its U-boat fleet might do the same to Britain by late 1942. Instead, the British and American fleets by 1942 had stopped almost all maritime importation by the Third Reich and ensured oil shortages. Sustained strategic air power reduced cities to veritable ruins in Germany and Japan. Yet ultimately in a total war, if an enemy was to be thoroughly defeated and its politics changed to prevent the likelihood of renewed resistance, hostile armies had to be routed and land occupied by infantrymen. The fact that Japan and Germany had no ability to invade and occupy Britain and the United States, while the Allies most certainly did intend to put boots on the ground in all their enemies' homelands, is yet another reason why the Axis lost the war.[1]

Even the great sea and air battles of ancient and modern times—Ecnomus, Actium, Trafalgar, Jutland, the fire- and atomic bombing of Japan, the detrition of Iraq in 1991, and the removal by air power of Slobodan Milosevic and his government from the Balkans in 2000—did not eliminate the need for infantry. Only the great hoplite battle of Plataea, not just the brilliant sea victory at Salamis, finally rid Greece of Xerxes's invading Persians. The victorious Holy League fleet of 1571 never besieged Istanbul, and thus the Ottomans continued to threaten the West even after their crushing naval defeat at Lepanto. In modern times, Great Britain's air and sea power helped win back the Falklands in 1982. Yet ultimately British troops still had to land on the island and physically force Argentine infantrymen to surrender and depart. Saddam Hussein was not removed until an army rolled into Baghdad in 2003, even though he had been subject to withering air assault during the previous twelve years. Air and naval power can win limited wars, but, barring the use of nuclear weapons, not total wars in which occupation of the defeated's land is central to permanent victory and a lasting peace.

In World War II the need for infantry primacy was an unfortunate reality for the Allies, given the central and advantageous geographical position of Germany and the long-proven superiority of the German army. At its peak, Hitler's land forces would reach five million active frontline soldiers, who would largely have to be destroyed or captured if the Third Reich were to vanish from Germany.[2]

Even the three great naval powers on the eve of World War II— Great Britain, the United States, and Japan—eventually had larger armies than navies. Those interservice disparities grew ever wider throughout the war, especially with the demise of major naval battles in the European theater by 1943. Luftwaffe and Kriegsmarine personnel by 1944 were routinely fighting as foot soldiers. As horrific as air and sea battle became in World War II, well over 75 percent of the aggregate combatants killed and missing on all sides were foot soldiers. The Battle of Midway was a historic Allied naval victory. Yet the total American and Japanese fatalities (approximately 3,419) over four days were less than a third of the *daily* fatalities of German and Russian dead at the two-week Battle of Kursk.[3]

FOOT SOLDIERS SURVIVED the technological and organizational revolutions of the twentieth century in a variety of ways. Most important, by 1945 a soldier's arms had proven far more deadly than at any time in history. The greatest revolution in arms of World War II was neither in armor nor more-lethal artillery, but in the pedestrian rifle that spewed bullets at rates unimaginable in prior wars. The United States alone produced over forty billion rounds of small-arms ammunition in World War II. And by late 1942, the chief weapon of most American soldiers was increasingly the gas-operated M1 Garand caliber .30 rifle with an eight-bullet clip. The semi-automatic rifle, the first reliable model of its kind to be mass-produced, proved to be one of many World War II precursors to such lethal postwar assault weapons as the AK-47 and M16. Unlike its workmanlike World War I predecessor, the M1903 Springfield bolt-action rifle, the new American M1 had far less recoil. If it was not as accurate as the Springfield at long distances, it also did not require the shooter to move his hands from round to round. That convenience ensured more rapid and, with training, precise-enough sustained fire. A trained American soldier could fire and reinsert clips to achieve forty to sixty shots per minute, with good results within three hundred yards. Quite unlike the earlier, heavy, and specialized M1918 Browning Automatic Rifle (BAR), with a twenty-bullet detachable magazine and a five-hundred-rounds-per-minute rate of fire, the easy-to-use M1 was a light general-issue weapon. When General George S. Patton called for troops to use "marching fire" ("one round should be fired every two or three paces"), he assumed that such rapid shooting was possible only with weapons like the M1, "the greatest battle implement ever devised."[4]

The excellence of the M1 surprised the world in 1942 and set a standard, prompting a small-arms race to mass-produce semi-automatic and fully automatic rifles with even greater rates of fire, greater penetration, and larger magazines. In 1944, the appearance of the frightening German *Sturmgewehr* (StG) 44 ("storm rifle")—over four hundred thousand produced—marked the world's first assault weapon. It combined the accurate range of a carbine (300–400 yards) with the theoretical rate of fire of a heavy machine gun (500–600 rounds per minute)—albeit in bursts of twenty-five to thirty shots from its detachable magazines. The *Sturmgewehr* was preceded by the German light machine gun, the *Maschinengewehr* (MG) 42 (400,000 produced between 1942 and 1945), which could fire at an average rate of 1,200 rounds per minute. It may well have been the most feared infantry weapon of the war and refined the grotesque art of killing in ways unimaginable in the past. The Allies were fortunate that the German army was not equipped with both weapons in mass numbers in 1941–1942.[5]

By the end of World War II, millions of infantrymen of almost every major power had access either to hand-held machine guns, semi-automatic rifles, or first-generation assault weapons, resulting in a storm of bullets that far outpaced the gunfire of the trench warfare of World War I. World War II infantry was also equipped with a number of auxiliary weapons undreamed of just twenty years prior. Grenades were both more powerful than World War I models and far more plentiful; when launched from rifles, their range increased tenfold to over 350 yards. All the major armies by 1944 had access to hand-held flamethrowers, to be used against entrenched positions.

Soldiers in World War II employed land mines in numbers and varieties never previously even imagined, from small anti-personnel to large anti-tank models. These portable explosive devices gave the infantrymen the ability to lay down fields of fire that could stop the progress of entire armored columns. The use of mines and anti-tank weapons in campaigns in North Africa and in Asia and the Pacific led American planners to conclude that tanks were hardly invincible and that the number of once-planned armored divisions might better be reduced. All of these infantry weapons were easy to operate and required little training.[6]

Most of these advances were in offensive weaponry, but not entirely. Among the sixty to ninety pounds of gear that autonomous soldiers now carried, they had greater access to nonperishable rations and medical supplies, as well as compact tools and navigation aids. While the weight of personal gear soared, so did the availability of motorized transport, at least on the Allied side. By 1944, the typical American infantry division was outfitted with nearly 1,400 motor vehicles, a fact that helped explain why the foot soldier was now expected to carry more weight than any infantryman in history, including Greek hoplites and their servants of the past. A constant criticism of the American military, both during and after the war, was the extraordinary weight carried by the GI—although his heavy pack, in terms of percentage of his body weight (around 50 percent), was in fact, in proportional terms, lighter than what Japanese soldiers carried (their packs could approach 100 percent of body weight). The American soldier's heavy gear was not so much just a reflection of American abundance as the fact that all World War II foot soldiers had access to food, clothing, weapons, and supplies undreamed of in the past, but without the personal "batmen" of antiquity who sometimes accompanied heavy classical infantry.[7]

Steel helmets—especially the German *Stahlhelm* (M1935 and its later iterations) and the American M-1 models—covered more head and neck area than did World War I versions. They were sometimes made from stronger nickel- and manganese-steel alloys and tended to reduce head and neck wounds. But all attempts to craft body armor, both sufficiently tough to prevent penetration of bullets and shrapnel and yet light enough to wear, had failed. As in World War I, but unlike in post–Vietnam War conflicts, infantry casualties spiked in World War II as the arts of offensive weaponry flourished and defensive protection stalled. Only in the late twentieth century did the advent of new ceramics and hybrid metal fibers offer the infantrymen body armor that could protect against high-velocity modern bullets and some shrapnel. In contrast, World War II was part of an unfortunate cycle in which offensive rifles, machines guns, grenades, artillery, and bombs were becoming ever more lethal and numerous without a commensurate development in personal armor. Traditionally, technological breakthroughs in the defense of infantrymen accelerate in more affluent societies of static populations, in which foot soldiers are scarcer and battle more conventional on the open plains. Greek and Roman foot soldiers were probably the best-protected infantry until the rise of the modern age, and enjoyed a rare period in history in which their armor actually turned away a variety of offensive weapons.[8]

The new lethality of infantrymen—together with the increasing number of aircraft carriers and U-boats, and the rapid growth of strategic and tactical air power—all worked to diminish the relative percentages of ground soldiers in most World War II armies. Increased logistical support and greater mechanization also made it more expensive to field an army division than in the prior world war; far more support troops and mechanics were needed to attend not just to soldiers but to the array of their machines as well. The United States, for example, although it had mobilized a far larger active military than during World War I (12.2 million versus about 4 million), and deployed it in far more theaters of operation, nevertheless for a variety of understandable reasons (most prominently the huge size of air and naval forces and the need for skilled workers in the vast archipelago of American industry) fielded fewer active US combat infantry soldiers on its central front in Europe by May 1945 than it had by November 1918.[9]

Unlike the static trench warfare in World War I, there were far more varied modes of infantry battle in World War II, mostly because of the diverse geography of Europe, the Mediterranean region, and the Pacific. First arose the large and small continental ground wars that characterized Germany's multiple border invasions. Hitler soon followed the destruction of Poland with a second wave of brief border wars to the west and south that saw roughly the same sort of combined blitzkrieg attacks and familiar logistical support. Again in surprise fashion, the Wehrmacht would steamroll in succession over nearby Eastern and Western Europe in a way unimagined even by the Imperial German Army twenty-five years earlier.

However, after the April–June 1941 invasion and occupation of Greece and Crete, the landscape of continental battle changed and expanded in frightening fashion. On June 22, 1941, the Third Reich sought to extend its range of European operations by invading the Soviet Union. The German military with its allied armies mobilized nearly four million strong for the campaign, but when it went into the vast expanse of Russia in June 1941 it faced novel obstacles, well aside from prior considerable air and vehicle losses in Poland, France, and the Balkans, and over Britain and Crete that were never rectified. The army was now responsible for occupying almost all of Europe, a burden that siphoned off tremendous German manpower. The lull after the victories over France, Belgium, and the Netherlands in June 1940, and the availability of the flotsam and jetsam of millions of rifles, artillery, shells, motor vehicles, and planes scavenged from defeated European militaries, along with the reluctance to go on to a total war footing, had all made it seem unnecessary to expand the Germany army and its supplies enough to meet the unprecedented challenges of entering the Soviet Union.

Certainly, Hitler had added more divisions, and the OKW had made inroads in refining its combined air, armor, and infantry operational doctrine. The quality and number of its aircraft, tanks, and artillery likewise had improved somewhat. Nonetheless, in terms of its size versus the expanse to be covered and the magnitude of enemy forces to be defeated, the Germans who invaded the USSR were perhaps proportionally at a greater disadvantage in Russia than they had ever been in Western Europe, especially given the loss of ground-support aircraft and veteran pilots in the wars of 1939–1940. The German army's multiphase Eastern and Western European wars between 1939 and 1945 accounted not only for most infantry casualties of World War II, but for more aggregate combat causalities than in all other theaters combined, as well as nearly matching the war's total of civilian and military fatalities.[10]

Although both the British and Americans had sent large expeditionary armies to France and Belgium in World War I, there also arose a quite greater variety of World War II infantry battles that involved large expeditionary forces on all sides that were foreign rather than native to the continent, including the Anglo-Americans, Italians, and Germans in North Africa, the Allied invasions of Sicily, Italy, and Western Europe, and the British and Japanese expeditionary forces in Burma and China. Armies sent far abroad differed chiefly in the nature of their origins and methods of supply, and demanded far closer intraservice cooperation. Expeditionary forces started at the enemy coastline. Because they could not always rely on the land transportation of supplies directly from their home soil, logistics became even more important than fighting power. The homeland, at least in the case of one of the belligerents, was always distant, and thus not usually immediately in danger should invading armies be thrown back. New York, for example, was not directly threatened by the outcome of the Battle of the Bulge in a way that Paris was by the first German invasion through the Ardennes, or Moscow had been in December 1941, or Berlin in 1945. Oddly, at such a late date on the eve of the Battle of the Bulge, Hitler reminded General Wolfgang Thomale how much more vulnerable was Germany than America: "If America says: 'We're off. Period.

We've got no more men for Europe,' nothing happens; New York would still be New York, Chicago would still be Chicago, Detroit would still be Detroit, San Francisco would still be San Francisco. It doesn't change a thing. But if we were to say today 'we've had enough', we should cease to exist. Germany would cease to exist."[11]

Expeditionary warfare required constant attention to morale and spirit. Troops knew they were not defending their homes but had instead crossed the seas to attack those of others. The French felt differently about the German invasion of May 1940 than did their allied British expeditionary forces. The most civilized theater of war—if we dare use that adjective for the horrors of North Africa—was fought from Egypt to Morocco, where none of the European combatants (e.g., Italians, Germans, British, and French) or the Americans were fighting on their home ground. Traditionally, every expeditionary army—Xerxes in Greece, Alexander the Great in Bactria, the consul Crassus's Roman legions at Carrhae, the Byzantines in Italy, the Crusaders outside Jerusalem— eventually experienced difficulties once the campaign transcended a few set battles. It is generally forgotten that American, British, Canadian, and Commonwealth infantries in World War II rarely fought on their home ground (aside from Hawaii and the Aleutians), a fact that might explain their greater investments in air and naval power, and one that should nullify some of the criticism that their relative ferocity was sometimes not comparable to that of German, Soviet, or Japanese ground forces.[12]

Given that Britain and Japan were island powers, given that a distant America enjoyed a two-ocean buffer from its enemies, and given that Italy's opportunities for aggrandizement would largely be found across the Mediterranean, amphibious operations loomed large in World War II. Logistics was the key for the Italian, German, British, and American efforts in North Africa, and also for the Allied invasion of Italy, southern France, and Normandy. Such fighting was predicated on transporting armies safely across the seas, a fact that governed even the size and nature of shipped artillery and tanks. There was little chance that American planners and logisticians would have considered sending any weapon comparable to the awkward German rail guns or ponderous King Tiger tanks across the seas and unloading it at ports or the Allies' artificial harbors, called Mulberries, at Normandy. The need to transport weapons long distances by sea was both an additional expense and also a catalyst for innovation and experimentation. Such shipping limitations on weapon size and design are also rarely computed when assessing the quality of national arms in World War II. It was perhaps easier to deploy Tiger tanks to Kursk by rail than to Tunisia by Italian or German freighters.

Another sort of expeditionary warfare centered on island and littoral fighting, where amphibious forces stormed ashore after assuming both naval and air superiority. Given the relatively small landscape of the targeted territory, invaders usually had to advance no more than a hundred miles, and usually far less, from the coastline. The aim of these ground operations was to eliminate strategically hostile strongholds, while providing naval bases and air bases to carve away the air and sea space of the enemy. Throughout World War II there were only a handful of failed island operations where the attackers were forced to re-embark or surrender. All such relatively quick defeats were British or Dominion endeavors in Europe: in Norway (April–June 1940), Dieppe (August 1942), and the Dodecanese landings (September–November 1943). They were largely a result of strategic confusion, poor operational planning, and an inability to achieve prior air and naval superiority.

Otherwise in almost every case—the Japanese invasion of the Philippines and much of New Guinea, Singapore, or the Aleutians, or the American island hopping from Tarawa to Okinawa—initial success was assured by controlling the skies and seas. Japanese expeditionary forces were successful only until late 1942, or as long as Japan enjoyed a brief window of superiority in the air and at sea. Japan failed in almost all its amphibious efforts shortly after that window closed, or lost almost all the ground that it once occupied.

The opposite trend characterized America's steady ascendance. After losing Guam, Wake Island, and the Philippines in late 1941 and early 1942 to Japanese seaborne attackers, the US Marines and Army went on the offensive in late 1942 at Guadalcanal and thereafter established a successful, though costly, record of amphibious operations. They were never repelled in a single effort, largely because of their careful attention to ensuring pre-invasion material superiority, auxiliary aerial bombing, and naval gunfire.

At times when a landing stalled or an inland thrust was stymied, as at Omaha Beach, the first dark hours at Tarawa (November 1943), or at the Shuri Line on Okinawa in May 1945, the Americans nonetheless pressed ahead, convinced in part that it was critical to their mystique never once to abandon men on the beach after landing. In that sense, their confident resoluteness was reminiscent of the imperial Athenians who reminded the doomed besieged islanders of Melos that they would not abandon their blockade, because they "never once yet withdrew from a siege for fear of any."[13]

There were only a small number of airborne assaults during World War II, largely because prewar fantasies of mass drops of parachutists proved unrealistic. It was difficult to anticipate winds, or to be sure that paratroopers would land where intended rather than drift off course or even into enemy positions. It was almost impossible to protect a parachutist from both hostile ground and air fire while dangling in the air. Once they landed, such light troops could hardly muster sufficient heavy weaponry, artillery, and armor to resist inevitable enemy counterattacks, or hope to be supplied if they were behind enemy lines or far ahead of friendly positions. Nonetheless, for a while the attractions of airborne forces seemed enticing, especially the idea of surprise, the ability to overcome natural obstacles such as rivers and fortresses, and the promise of trapping the enemy between airborne troops and advancing infantry—without the enemy quite knowing where its enemy might appear next.[14]

After some use of airborne troops in Poland and against Norway, the Germans first mounted a serious use of their *Fallschirmjäger*, or "parachute hunters," when three airborne regiments were dropped against the Western Europeans during the battle for France. In successive daring operations—against the Moerdijk Bridge in the path to Amsterdam and some airfields near Rotterdam and The Hague during the May 10–14 German advance, the capture of the supposedly impregnable Belgian fortress of Eben-Emael (May 10), and at bridges in the Ardennes—German paratroopers created the illusion that this new paradigm would help speed up the collapse of the weak Western democracies.

The early airborne successes of the *Fallschirmjäger* soon prompted a much more ambitious and dangerous effort, Operation *Merkur*, to spearhead the invasion of Crete on May 20, 1941. Almost everything went wrong with the German drops, given that they were now no longer operating over land, but over seas against an experienced British navy. Well over 350 aircraft were destroyed. Such losses were not easily made up and would later partly explain the chronic shortage of German supply aircraft in the subsequent critical first two years of Operation Barbarossa. In addition, the Germans suffered almost seven thousand casualties, and for the first time in a major battle may have lost more dead in victory than the enemy did in defeat.[15]

Three thousand ninety-four paratroopers were killed, perhaps one reason why the subsequent German occupation of Crete proved especially savage. The debacle reminded Hitler that airborne troops, when not quickly supplied and followed by Panzers and infantry, were nearly defenseless, especially if neither air nor naval superiority had been achieved before they were dropped. The cost of Crete may have persuaded him not only to avoid landing paratroopers on the more strategically valuable Malta, but also to relegate all future airborne forces to minor operations in North Africa and Italy and during the Battle of the Bulge. Germans both created modern major airborne strategy and then gave up on it before the Allies had even sought to emulate them.[16]

Two years after the bitter German experience in Crete, the Allies' first attempt to send a division of airborne troops against Sicily on July 10, 1943, likewise was seen as successful, but also similarly almost ended in calamity. High winds wrecked and scattered gliders. Parachutists were dispersed far off their assigned targets. In the case of the 504th Regimental Combat Team, Allied troops on the beaches and at sea mistook them for Germans and shot up their gliders and transports, inflicting over two hundred friendly casualties. Airborne apologists, as was their wont, argued that such confusion and misdirection achieved the unintended effect of panicking German and Italian defenders as well.

Some success with the highly trained 82nd Airborne Division at Salerno, Italy, in September 1943 had encouraged the Allies to risk deploying nearly fifty thousand paratroopers for the D-Day landings of June 6, 1944: the 82nd and 101st American Airborne divisions, and the British 6th Airborne. The plan was to secure bridges in advance of the Allied troops' breakout from the beaches, as well as to knock out German artillery emplacements, disrupt communications, create confusion, and hamper German reinforcements headed to the landing areas. Due to bad weather, German anti-aircraft guns, and poor intelligence, nothing much happened as planned and yet the drops succeeded in securing the critical Orne River and Caen Canal bridges. As early as the airborne drops in Sicily, seasoned German soldiers when taken prisoner had asked American paratroopers whether they had previously fought the Japanese, in amazement at their courage and audacity.[17]

The most disastrous use of airborne troops was the infamous Operation Market-Garden against the Rhine River bridges in Holland in September 1944, a misconceived effort to leapfrog the Rhine, punch a narrow hole through German defenses, and pour into the Ruhr, thus ending the war before 1945. Due to popular literary and cinematic reconstruction of the operation, the campaign is now unfortunately known as "A Bridge Too Far"—as if the failure to take the final bridge at Arnhem meant that the operation was otherwise 90 percent successful. It was not.

The planning was flawed. General Bernard Montgomery had ignored his own intelligence that the British drop on Arnhem would land amid sizable German forces that included undermanned but spirited SS Panzer divisions, the 9th and 10th. Both were deployed under the fervent and capable Nazi field marshal, Walter Model, while undergoing refit and recovery.

The key British drop zone at the last bridge before Germany at Arnhem was sited far too distant from the river. Bad weather in England
delayed reinforcements. The two American divisions that would take
the initial bridges were veteran, but the paratroopers of the British 1st
Airborne—assigned the hardest task of holding the "bridge too far" at
Arnhem—were valiant yet had not yet attempted an airdrop on such a
scale. The idea that a narrow exposed road could facilitate fast transit
of the advancing Allied armor column was absurd. Montgomery had little reputation for risky mobile advancement in the manner of a Rommel
or Patton. And one of his subordinates, General Frederick Browning,
was both blinkered and incompetent, lacking precisely the rare gifts that
the passed-over Major General Matthew Ridgway possessed to salvage
an otherwise bad idea. General Brian Horrocks was an admirable armor
commander with a stellar war record, but he lacked the near maniacal
aggressiveness required to push through a long armored column to connect and secure the bridges. Oddly, despite the disastrous implementation
of an inherently flawed plan, Market-Garden still might have succeeded
had the overland component—the advance of Horrocks's British XXXth
Corps armored column—taken more risks and forgone rest stops.[18]

A final lavish Allied airborne operation involving three American
and British airborne divisions was Montgomery's monumental crossing
of the Rhine (Operation Varsity) in March 1945, the war's largest single-
day drop at a single location. But by then the outcome of the war was
foreordained and the end just seven weeks away. Other Allied commanders such as Generals Courtney Hodges and Patton crossed the Rhine at
about the same time without the help of airborne troops. And the entire drop seemed almost more ceremonial than necessary to grab Rhine
bridges and riverside towns. The irony is that the complex Operation
Varsity was the most professional of all the Allied drops, as its landings
were far closer to friendly lines, while Montgomery's ground forces had
started their advance before, not during or after, the parachute landings.
Ironically, Market-Garden had been ineptly conceived, but at least it had
the potential to change the course of the war in the West. In contrast,
six months later, the more professionally conducted Operation Varsity
did not much matter to the Allied crossing of the Rhine or the Anglo-
American advance into Germany.[19]

Other than the initial German landings in France and Belgium and
the American operations on the morning of D-Day and to retake Corregidor in 1945, it became hard to justify the increased cost of deploying
paratroopers, despite the fact that their rigorous training and élan usually made them superb fighters in more traditional roles as infantry. The

Soviets both created the war's largest airborne units and used them the least in major operations: two major airborne drops at Vyazma (January 18–February 28, 1942), and the Dnieper/Kiev operation (September 1943), which largely proved to be failures. Like the Japanese and Italians who also formed smaller airborne contingents, high casualties persuaded the Soviets that parachutists were better employed as rifle divisions on the ground.

A final theater of ground operations was the siege, the age-old effort to storm cities and garrisons. Massive new siege guns and air bombardment neither altered the methods of siegecraft nor reduced the importance of the classical requisites of favorable supply, circumvallation, numbers, and weather conditions. As in the past, lengthy sieges became psychologically obsessive, often expending blood and treasure in either attacking or defending fortified positions that were not worth the commensurate costs. When civilian met soldier in confined landscapes, the death toll spiked, and it was no surprise that the greatest carnage of World War II—at Leningrad and Stalingrad—was the result of efforts to storm municipal fortresses.

Foot soldiers ultimately decided every theater in World War II except the final defeat of the Japanese homeland forces. The war, which had once promised to reinvent how and where conflicts were fought, instead validated the ancient supremacy of land forces, but with one important caveat. Infantrymen were no longer just defined by their guns, artillery support, and vehicles, but equally by the ships that delivered, supplied, and communicated with them, and the aircraft that protected and enhanced them. The Allied soldier had far greater naval and air support than did his Axis counterpart, so much so that these twentieth-century considerations redefined age-old criteria about infantry excellence itself.

Superficially, the national armies of World War II appeared similar. To the naked eye, infantry uniforms, organization, and equipment of both the Axis and the Allied ground forces reflected a common Western genesis, even in the case of a Westernized Japan. But on closer examination, the respective armies were starkly different, a reflection of distinct cultures and unique political histories. The next chapter notes how throughout the war national stereotypes usually stayed constant: the Soviet juggernaut that relied on overwhelming numbers and firepower; the organization, logistics, and superb air and naval support of the American army; the professionalism of the British officer corps and Britain's unique ability to galvanize former colonial and Commonwealth troops for a single purpose; the ferocity of the Japanese soldier that was not matched by adequate support or weaponry; and the terrifying lethality of the Wehrmacht that sent its soldiers into battle with the expectation that their combat superiority could trump their enemies' superior numbers and supply. Whereas these generalizations were often borne out, frequently armies were forced to fight in a mode inconsistent with their stereotypes because the singular objectives of their supreme commanders required ground forces to adapt to unique geographical, industrial, and strategic realities. For the most part, an immutable army did not drive the nation to war, the nation drove the army, and the army soon adapted accordingly, sometimes in accustomed character, sometimes not.

# 11

# Soldiers and Armies

N O ONE QUITE knew what made an excellent foot soldier in World
War II. Endless considerations factored into such comparisons: the
length of time in combat, the nature of the equipment, the type of enemy
that an army usually faced, the strategic demands placed on armies, the
caliber of tactical and strategic leadership, the relative size of the armies,
the ratios between deaths inflicted and received, the logistical challenges
faced, and the particular status of the theater in which an army fought.
Armies were also not static. Their effectiveness waxed and waned in accord with ongoing losses and commensurate reinforcements, logistical
support, and new weapons. Combat effectiveness was also a relative assessment: armies were defined as effective, not just in absolute terms, but
in comparison to the constantly changing criteria and the status of their
enemies. The German soldier had better guns and armor in 1944 than in
1941, but the Wehrmacht also proved far weaker in comparison with the
much more rapidly growing and improving Red Army.

The difference between losses inflicted and incurred is sometimes
defined loosely as "fighting power." Yet the percentage of casualties suffered versus caused is not always a valid criterion of infantry excellence.
The United States achieved startling kill ratios in Vietnam, but without
destroying the North Vietnamese army or saving an autonomous South
Vietnam. The Japanese army slaughtered Chinese soldiers at a sickening
rate and yet never secured China.

The best armies of World War II were simply those that had marshaled the most material and human assets and wisely used them to win
the majority of their battles and ultimately the war, often integrating air
and naval forces to enhance their superior strategies. Germany, as was
true in World War I, is largely considered to have produced the most effective infantry fighting power, even as it once again started a war that
it would lose relatively rapidly and with disastrous results. That paradox
suggests that either its supposed infantry supremacy had again lulled

Germany into adopting impossible strategic objectives that required far more diverse assets and numbers than were available, or that its infantrymen, in fact, were actually not as exceptional as their reputations—or both.

As a general rule, the age-old calculus of fighting power often proved irrelevant in World War II. It was not just that hundreds of thousands of troops perished due to air power or armor rather than hand-held weapons, but that even millions of soldiers—sacrificed in the Kiev pocket, trapped at Stalingrad, or cut off and expected to perish on Japanese-held islands—were wasted through the nihilist directives of their own leaders, who were often captives of fascist or communist ideologies that were not always grounded in strategic or tactical reality.[1]

OF THE SIX major belligerents, the United States devoted comparatively the smallest percentage of available military manpower to the US Army: only about 48 percent (excluding the Army Air Force). Yet because the US military itself became so huge so rapidly, second in size only to the Soviet armed forces (12.5 million versus 12.2 million), the Army nevertheless grew to six million. However, only about a third of the Army's manpower (or about 2 million) were assigned to ground-combat units. That percentage did not change much throughout the war. By May 1945 there were scarcely over sixty US infantry and armored divisions in Europe, and about ninety Army divisions in all, including those deployed in Italy, the Mediterranean, and the Pacific. During the 337 days between D-Day and the German surrender, half of all American infantrymen in Europe had been in combat for 150 days, 40 percent of them for 200 days, which was considered the point at which most soldiers displayed symptoms of combat fatigue. Alone among the armies of the six major belligerents, the US Army was exclusively an expeditionary force and almost always on the offensive; it suffered stalls and setbacks at the Kasserine Pass in early 1943, and more seriously in the Hürtgen and Ardennes Forests in late 1944, but American ground forces neither entrenched for long periods nor suffered long retreats in the fashion of the thousand-mile withdrawals of the Red Army in 1941, or the Wehrmacht in 1944–1945 on the Eastern Front, or the occasional defensive retirement of the British in North Africa and Greece in 1941, or the retreating Italians in 1940–1941. This idea of constant motion forward explains why the US military invested so heavily in air and sea power, logistics, and mobility.

Only about 16 percent of all American uniformed personnel fought on the ground in combat. The staggering size of the American military, and yet the relatively small percentages who were front line ground soldiers, also explains the legendary paradoxes of the US armed forces: Why, compared to other powers, did the American military in toto suffer relatively fewer casualties? Why was it chronically short of infantry divisions? Why were its combat infantrymen exhausted, thus suffering high losses? Why was it able to project power in so many places and in so many diverse ways? In sum, the fewer uniformed personnel who were fighting in frontline army combat units, the more were freed to conduct naval, air, and logistics operations. But again a paradox arose of enhancing infantry lethality by marshalling air and naval support while thus ensuring long combat and eventual exhaustion to a far-too-small number of ground troops.[2]

As was the case prior to America's entry into World War I in 1917, the US Army had fewer than two hundred thousand active-duty soldiers before the outbreak of World War II in Europe in September 1939. Unlike most continental armies, the United States did not have bellicose neighbors in North America for most of the twentieth century up to this point and had felt itself largely immune from worry over invading foreign expeditionary armies—facts that also explained its army's traditionally small peacetime size. The US Army of 1939 was also utterly ill equipped. The .50 caliber machine gun was considered an anti-tank weapon. The 1903 bolt-action Springfield remained the standard rifle. There were few artillery pieces over 75 mm in size. Rarely in the history of civilization had so mammoth an economy and so large a population fielded so small a military.

Yet at the end of hostilities in 1945, the army had grown to well over eight million soldiers and airmen, reaching its peak in 1945 (8,276,958) as it ascended from the nineteenth-largest army in the world to the second largest of the war. The number of officers in the US Army was larger in 1945 than the number of soldiers in the entire Cold War American army of 1960. And yet of the major belligerents, US ground forces had the smallest number of actual combat divisions (under 100 army and Marine divisions by late 1944), in comparison to the aggregate size of the actual army and in relation to the US military in general—and thus again the highest ratios of noncombat personnel. Even as late as 1943, the faltering Italian army (3 million) was nearly as large as the number of all American Army soldiers stationed abroad in ground and air combat theaters (3.7 million), even though Italy's population was only a third that of the United States. Nearly 40 percent of the twelve-million-man US military was deployed in rear-echelon tasks far distant from combat zones.[3]

Implicit in such a strategy of devoting so many American resources to supply and logistics and to air and naval power in a two-front war was the reality that the Soviets finally had over five hundred active divisions tying down well over three million Axis ground troops. The subtext to the unholy alliance with the Soviet Union, despite its record of prewar genocide and active cooperation with Nazi Germany until June 1941, was that the American public accepted that German infantrymen would kill, and be killed by, far more Russian than American foot soldiers. The Red Army by 1943 had allowed the United States—the most distant of the major powers from the front lines of battle—to invest lavishly in supply and logistics, as well as in tactical and strategic air forces and a huge two-ocean navy. Specialization among the three major Allied powers is an underappreciated reason why the Allies turned the tide of war so quickly after 1942.[4]

Why the American Army was small, in relative terms, is also illustrated by how diverse and spread over the globe the American military had become by the latter part of the war. For example, on the single day of the invasion of Normandy (June 6, 1944), around the world other US forces were just as much on the attack at sea and in the air. As part of the ill-fated Operation Frantic shuttle-bombing operations between US air fields in Italy and refueling bases in the Soviet Ukraine, over 150 B-17s and their P-51 escorts attacked the oil fields at Galati, Romania. Another five hundred B-17s and escorts hit the often-targeted Romanian fields at Ploesti. Meanwhile, the 12th Air Force conducted continuous tactical air strikes on German positions in Italy. Allied ground troops also had just occupied Rome two days earlier and were garrisoning the city in preparation for offensives against the Gothic Line in northern Italy. In the Asian and Pacific theaters on this same landmark day of June 6, the US Pacific Fleet was making preparations to invade the Mariana Islands within a week, with a combined force almost as large as had landed at Normandy. Meanwhile, B-29 bombers prepared for their first raid against Japan from forward bases in China, while six B-25 Mitchell medium bombers and ten P-51 fighter escorts conducted operations against Tayang Chiang, China. B-25s were also attacking Japanese troops moving on Imphal, India. Meanwhile, the submarine *Raton* was tracking a Japanese convoy near Saigon. The submarine *Harder* sank a Japanese destroyer off Borneo, while the *Pintado* torpedoed and destroyed a cargo vessel off the Marianas. B-24 heavy bombers hit Ponape Island in Micronesia as tactical strikes were conducted against the Japanese on Bougainville, New Britain, and New Guinea.

In other words, even as the American Army and its supporting naval and air forces participated in the largest amphibious landing in history, the US military was on the offensive against the Germans in Italy, conducting long-range bombing from Italy and Britain, torpedoing convoys in the Pacific, assembling forces to storm the Marianas, and carrying out air strikes from bases in China all the way to New Guinea. On such a single typical day of combat, diverse fleets of B-17s, B-24s, B-25s, B-26s, B-29s, A-20s, P-38s, P-39s, P-40s, P-47s, and P-51s were all in the air from Normandy to the China Sea.[5]

Of the ground forces of the major combatants, the American Army had the lowest percentage of fatalities: less than 3 percent of all US Army soldiers were killed, although the figure rose to nearly 4 percent of the nearly seven hundred thousand US Marines who, along with Army units, fought the Japanese between 1942 and 1945. The relatively low fatality rate again probably reflects, inter alia, that the United States was the best-supplied army in the war, at least in terms of air and artillery support forces, medical organization, and food and fuel. The American army also limited its casualties by fighting less than four years, compared to the roughly five-and-a-half years of the British and German armies, the nearly five years of the Soviets (both as an ally and an enemy of Germany), and the more than six years of the Japanese in China and the Pacific. Critics point out that the US Army had a far higher percentage of what was formerly known in the First World War as "shell-shock" cases—a malady referred to in World War II as "combat fatigue" and more recently as "post-traumatic stress disorder" (PTSD)—as well as lower ratios of wounded soldiers returning to full duty than either Axis armies or the Soviet Red Army. More starkly, only one US soldier was shot for desertion and cowardice. A variety of reasons may explain the unprecedented concern for injured and psychologically traumatized soldiers, but in pragmatic terms, the United States treated its soldiers more humanely because it could afford to, given America's vast material advantages and the sanctity of the US homeland.

American armies were never threatened with utter annihilation as in the case of the Wehrmacht, the Japanese army, the Italian army, and the Red Army. Rommel made the following observation of American soldiers in February 1943:

> Although it was true that the American troops could not yet be compared with the veteran troops of the British Eighth Army, yet they made up for their lack of experience by their far better and more plentiful equipment and their tactically more flexible command. In fact, their armament in anti-tank weapons and armoured vehicles was so numerous that we could look forward with but small hope of success to the coming mobile battles. The tactical conduct of the enemy's defence had been first class.[6]

In other words, no other army in the world to the same degree knew how to produce, maintain, repair, and use machines.

In Germany and Japan, the respective branches of the armed forces fought incessantly and blamed each other for catastrophic losses. In contrast, the Americans possessed the operational art and doctrine to combine widely disparate forces in staging repeatedly successful amphibious landings throughout the Pacific—the common bond among the rival services being a fascination with and mastery over machines. B-29 heavy bombers strategically and routinely mined Japanese harbors in complementary fashion with ships and naval aircraft. Carriers sustained catastrophic damage from Japanese kamikaze attacks to achieve air superiority over Okinawa that ensured air and naval battery support for Marine and Army units. B-17 four-engine high-level bombers played the role of tactical aircraft and blasted holes in German lines to stage the breakout of stalled US land forces in Normandy. Or as General Dwight D. Eisenhower, supreme commander of all British, Canadian, and American forces that landed in Normandy in 1944, summed up in bureaucratese the American way of war: "War is waged in three elements; but there is no separate land, naval, or air war. Unless all assets in all elements are efficiently combined and coordinated against a properly selected, common objective, their maximum potential power cannot be maximized."[7]

It did little good to unleash a veteran German grenadier, with over three years past experience on the Eastern Front, against an American soldier if he were first strafed or bombed, or went into battle hungry and without medical care, or found his supporting Panzers either burning or sitting on the side of the road out of gas. Postwar interviews with German soldiers may have revealed a far greater respect for individual Russian soldiers than for Americans, and Russians for Germans rather than American, on the understandable principle that the existential nature of war on the Eastern Front was far harsher than in the West. Yet what makes an army effective is not just the heroism or combat zeal of individual soldiers, but also the degree of assets—artillery barrages, air support, food, medicine, and supplies—at its disposal.[8]

The American emphasis was not so much on creating a fierce individual warrior, bound with strong ties of loyalty and honor to fellow men of arms (although the GI was often just that), as on making sure that he was supported with enough materiel, and acquired sufficient expertise, to defeat any adversary he faced, and to reassure him that he had a good chance to survive the conflict. The system rather than the man was what would win the war. It was in some ways a throwback to the first centuries BC and AD, when standardized and far better-equipped

Roman legionaries near the Rhine and Danube occasionally tangled with Germanic tribes that put a much higher premium on individual warriors' weapons prowess, courage, and skills, but usually lost.[9]

In contrast to the American Army, the Wehrmacht far more emphasized unit loyalty, individual pride and honor, and extensive combat training. The German soldier was seen as a sort of craftsman, a human extension of the pride in workmanship that had produced a Panther tank that was technically superior to the American Sherman but that could never have been built in similar numbers or with commensurate reliability and ease of use. When American generals such as George S. Patton sought to recreate the American foot soldier as a deadly killer analogous to the German ("Americans love to fight—traditionally! All real Americans love the sting and clash of battle"), his speeches and rules became the stuff of popular caricature that for many explained his later near-career-ending slapping incidents.[10]

The US Army in every one of its major land operations battled far more experienced German and Japanese armies that after 1942 largely enjoyed the advantages of being on the defensive and had at least marginally better knowledge of local geography, and were far closer to their ultimate sources of supply. It should have been ostensibly far easier, for example, to defend a Guadalcanal or Tarawa than to capture it, or to repel than conduct an amphibious landing in Sicily or Normandy, or to defend inside the Hürtgen Forest rather than attack through it, or to shoot down from rather than climb up to Monte Cassino, or to block rather than mount a crossing of the Rhine, or to take down a bomber over the homeland rather than to fly it a thousand miles over enemy territory and get home.

The US Army—except for some inaugural defeats in Tunisia (February 1943)—did not just win its offensive wars, but won them with far fewer aggregate losses than almost any other infantry force of the war. Again, mobility was an American trademark. Imagine the idea that any German expeditionary army might have embarked from southern France in early summer 1941, crossed the Atlantic in safety, and landed over thirty thousand Wehrmacht troops in the Caribbean Sea—in the similar manner that General Patton's Western Task Force had left its convoy assembly points off Newfoundland, crossed the Atlantic Ocean, and disembarked at Casablanca, Morocco, in November 1942. Such comparable German operations would have been impossible.[11]

American campaigns were not predicated just on martial excellence, but prepped in advance by what supply could and could not do, by intelligence about how the enemy might react to any offensive, and by the ultimate strategic objectives for which armies were led. General Patton's

Third Army outran its supply train in late August 1944, like Rommel's Afrika Korps in midsummer 1942. But unlike the German experience, Patton was not forced into a long retreat, inasmuch as he could rely on air support, continuance of minimum supplies, and help if need be from other Allied armies. He also knew his clear-cut mission was eventually to cross the Rhine, whereas no one in the German High Command ever quite knew where Rommel's Afrika Korps was ultimately headed. When Hitler unwisely chose to send the German army into the Soviet Union in June 1941, the flawed decision was considered by most German field marshals to be unassailable. In contrast, when Franklin Roosevelt equally unwisely had wished to land American armies on the western coast of France in 1943, many of his own civilian and military experts quickly tabled the idea through rational argument and overwhelming data concerning shortages in landing craft, insufficient air superiority, worries over U-boats, and lack of experience in amphibious operations. Roosevelt calmly gave in to advice; Hitler in tantrums threatened his advisors.[12]

American land forces also were brilliantly bifurcated to accommodate the geography of a global two-theater war. Only the British and the Americans fought both a long European and Asian war; no other Axis or Allied nation could have done both at such great distances successfully and simultaneously. The US Marine Corps—eventually six combat divisions, along with auxiliary and air forces—together with twenty-one Army divisions, assumed responsibility for leading the ground war against the Japanese on the natural assumption that Pacific amphibious operations uniquely required more integration with naval forces. Island hopping usually involved briefer but more frequent major battles than continental warfare. Such specialization allowed select Army divisions and Marines and their supporting naval and air arms to gain familiarity with the Japanese way of war. The sterling reputation of the US Marines for the next seven decades was largely established in the Pacific and the savage hellholes—Guadalcanal, Tarawa, Iwo Jima, Okinawa—out of which it emerged bloodied but triumphant. The same was true of the US Army in the Pacific, which was involved in more amphibious landings than even the Marines.[13]

Fighting in the Pacific proved far different than battling Germans or Italians. Combat on the Pacific islands usually involved far more hand-to-hand encounters. Small-arms fire caused a greater percentage of American deaths in the Pacific than had been true in European theaters, where artillery fire was far more lethal. The more Americans employed naval gunfire, tanks, flamethrowers, napalm, and sophisticated amphibious tactics in storming the Pacific islands from Tarawa to Okinawa, also the more premodern became battle with grenades, rifles, bayonets, and knives in the rough terrain and often monsoon weather of the islands.[14]

Marines did not fight in Europe, and US carrier forces rarely did after 1943. There was a "Europe first" American strategy, based on the initial worry that the fall of Britain would win Hitler the war and preclude any chance for an American base of operations to retake the continent. But quite soon after it had become clear that Britain would not be invaded, operations became even more divergent. America's World War II allotment doctrine, even if initially described as 70–30 percent Europe to the Pacific, soon de facto became the Navy and Marines first to the Pacific, 75 percent of Army divisions and armor first to Europe. Even US arms production followed such specialization. Hellcats did not escort B-17s in Europe. *Essex* carriers were not built with the Mediterranean in mind. Battleships proved important in the Pacific, not so much in the Atlantic. Given the virtual impregnability of the American homeland, the United States was the only nation of the major Allies that had a choice about which theater it chose to focus upon. Neither Britain nor the Soviet Union shared such latitude, given their proximity to the Third Reich.[15]

On the operational level, no army was so well supplied with trucks as the American. The United States produced nearly 2.4 million military transport vehicles, a greater number than the entire combined production of the Axis, British, and Russians. It was not just that American soldiers did not march to battle to the same degree as other armies, but once there they moved far faster and covered more ground than other land forces. Trucks—not tanks—in large part explain why the Allies won the ground war, a fact never fully appreciated by the Third Reich, Italy, and Japan. That every American truck had to be shipped across the Atlantic or Pacific makes the achievement even more wondrous.[16]

American infantrymen could count on adequate grenades, mines, and machine guns that were better than those of the Italian and Japanese armies. By 1943 US artillerymen and US field guns—given their numbers, the nature of the ammunition, the training and communications of the gunners—were among the deadliest of the war. Increasingly, 105 mm and 155 mm artillery guns, and huge 8-inch guns and 240 mm howitzers, were easily mobile and sometimes self-propelled, adding to their lethality in ways often underappreciated by other militaries. And by 1945, American proximity fuzes, when combined with preexisting superb targeting and communications, gave the American infantryman the most accurate artillery support of the war.[17]

In terms of relative efficacy, the US Army proved especially devastating when fighting the Italians and Japanese. In part, that effectiveness was due to the frequent large-scale surrenders of the former, and the complete absence of such capitulations by the latter. It is often pointed out that the German army, whether in 1942 or 1945, whether on the defensive or offensive, whether outnumbered or not, whether in pure ground slugfests or in combined operations, on average killed about 1.5 GIs for every German soldier lost, a startling ratio (though not as lopsided as the American Army Air Force's three-to-one superiority in aerial combat over its German counterparts). The reasons for such a surprising statistic concerning German infantry superiority may be many, but some may be related to the fact that Americans were more likely tasked with riskier offensive invasions and landings than with exclusively defensive operations.

Germany prior to 1939 had fought no more frequently in the last century than had America on average. Postwar psychological studies did not detect a greater degree of authoritarian impulses on the part of the German public that translated into more obedient or disciplined soldiers. By mid-war, American draftees were trained just as long as their German counterparts. Neither the Kriegsmarine nor the Luftwaffe matched the kill ratios of the army.

The achievement, aside from the critical infantry experience gained from 1939 to 1943, is partly explained by ideological indoctrination and superior officer training and professionalism. By 1941, Hitler's propaganda machine had infused the foot soldiers of the Wehrmacht with the tenets of National Socialism since their adolescence. Such inspirational doctrine may well have improved battlefield morale of the German soldier in ways well beyond that of his World War I imperial German counterpart. The foot soldiers of the Wehrmacht probably believed that they were innately superior to their enemies and that their culture and system of war making had been preeminent in the recent past and ultimately would be again, and they consequently had far fewer worries about committing violence or often atrocities. But it was also true that the German soldier's superb weapons and battlefield leadership, at least in the late 1930s and the first years of the war, reinforced confidence among the ranks. Being an infantryman in Germany also brought greater social prestige than being a GI in the United States, from the rank of private to general, a fact that might have led to superior recruits, or at least to higher morale. Of the three services, it was clear that only the German army rivaled the armies of its enemies and was superior to those of its allies.[18]

If there were weaknesses at the highest levels of American command, the US Army nonetheless produced the greatest numbers of excellent brigadier, major, and lieutenant generals, as well as a mostly underappreciated logistical and support staff. The number of officers involved in

Operation Overlord who planned the Normandy landings dwarfed the cadre of Axis officers who designed Operation Barbarossa, and they were more likely left alone from interference from their civilian overseers. Of the German landings in Norway, General Walter Warlimont of OKW contrasted negatively the German "disorder in the military sphere created by authoritarian leadership with the exemplary simplicity of the command organization adapted by the democracies for the great Anglo-Saxon landing operations in North Africa in November 1942 and in Normandy in June 1944."[19]

Soldiers of every army in World War II at times shot considerable numbers of prisoners and committed atrocities against civilians. But no army of World War II committed so few war crimes in relationship to its size as the Americans, with the exception perhaps of the British and Dominion armies. The US Army as a general rule did not allow the deaths of hundreds of thousands of its prisoners as did the Germans on the Eastern Front, and it did not rape, loot, and murder civilians on the scale of depredations of the Red Army or the Japanese. It had no record of institutionalized brutality as did the Italians in Somaliland and Ethiopia; it did not coerce comfort women as did the Japanese, or shoot its former allies as did the Germans with Italians in Greece. It did not help to organize death squads nor participate in genocide as was true of both the German and Japanese armies. In the end, most enemies preferred surrendering to the Americans or British; most allies sought American support; and most civilians welcomed the presence of Americans.[20]

The general critique of the American foot soldier in World War II was that he was never as hard pressed as his German, Japanese, Russian, or even British counterpart. GIs were supposedly promoted far too easily to noncommissioned officer status (eventually 50 percent of all enlistees). There may have been almost as many officers in the Army (10 percent) as the percentage of troops assigned to frontline combat. Too many soldiers were diagnosed with psychiatric disorders (9 percent of all army personnel); indeed, in combat theaters, the US Army treated soldiers for psychiatric disorders at a rate ten times higher than its German counterparts. The American combat soldier stayed in the hospital for a long duration of time when wounded (an average of 117 days), and often was not required to return to his combat unit when released (36 percent). He required too many supplies (over 80 pounds per day) and had too many men to his rear who should have been at the front. He was too reliant on artillery barrages to advance, and assumed he should ride rather than march to the front. Replacements were sent piecemeal to the front as individuals, rather than as cohesive groups arrayed in regional or local units. And yet he fought heroically without having his army execute well over twenty-five thousand of its own soldiers as happened in the Wehrmacht, and perhaps well over a hundred thousand as was true of the Soviet army.[21]

Criticisms of the GI ignore the fact that no other army had to be raised so quickly from virtual nonexistence. No other army had to be transported to all its fronts over the oceans at such great distances, or was expected almost always to take the offensive on arrival on the battlefield. No other army competed so much with other branches of the military for talent. No other military, of which the army was the chief component, suffered such a small absolute number of casualties in comparison to those it inflicted upon the Axis ground forces.

The GIs of 1941 may have been somewhat different from those of the past—or future—American armies. Most young recruits had grown up during the Depression, a time that tended to lower material expectations and made even the spartan conditions of army life seem preferable to civilian poverty. Times were harder in the late 1930s than in the Roaring Twenties or the 1950s and 1960s. The army of 1941 was also the first in which millions of Americans had grown familiar with first- and second-generation internal-combustion engines, from tractors and delivery trucks to cars and motorcycles. No generation of men in their twenties before or since has been more adept at mechanics, or mechanics that could at least be mastered by shade-tree apprentices. General Patton saw this ability as critical to the American army: "The Americans, as a race, are the foremost mechanics in the world. America, as a nation, has the greatest ability for mass production of machines. It therefore behooves us to devise methods of war which exploit our inherent superiority. We must fight the war by machines on the ground, and in the air, to the maximum of our ability." And the American army did just that.[22]

THERE WAS NOTHING like the Soviet Red Army before World War II, nor has there been since. A number of characteristics made it utterly exceptional, aside from the fact that the Soviets were surprise attacked by a savage enemy that gave no quarter on Russian home soil. First, the Soviet army was already huge at the beginning of the war, having well over five million men in both its Western and Eastern theaters when the Germans invaded. On the vast front against the Wehrmacht it may initially have numbered in toto well over two hundred combat divisions, with over one hundred additional divisions spread throughout the Soviet Union. And the Red Army never stopped growing: the Soviets processed thirty million conscripts during the entire course of the war, as the army reached peak operational strength of well over ten million soldiers in a military of over twelve million.

At its zenith, the Soviet Union could in theory deploy well over five hundred divisions. It was regarded as a great feat of mobilization that the Americans had created nearly a hundred-division army in less than a year and a half, but in nearly the same time period the Soviets mobilized over four hundred new and replacement divisions, albeit smaller in size, far less equipped and motorized, and without need to transport them across thousands of miles of ocean to the front or simultaneously to supply vast naval and air forces.[23]

No other army experienced such losses. About 4.5 million Russians died in the first full year of the German invasion alone, a number almost as large as the size of the German army itself in 1941. By war's end the Soviet army had suffered far more killed in action (7 million) than its original size. The figure may have soared to over an aggregate eleven million military dead when the wages of disease and capture were factored into the equation, a number that still does not include at least another ten to sixteen million civilian dead. General Eisenhower related a comment from Soviet marshal Georgy Zhukov concerning land mines that reflected the Soviet Union's stereotyped indifference to the losses in its conscript army: "Marshal Zhukov gave me a matter-of-fact statement of his practice, which was, roughly, 'There are two kinds of mines; one is the personnel mine and the other is the vehicular mine. When we come to a minefield our infantry attacks exactly as if it were not there. The losses we get from personnel mines we consider only equal to those we would have gotten from machine guns and artillery if the Germans had chosen to defend that particular area with strong bodies of troops instead of mines' . . . I had a vivid picture," Eisenhower noted, "of what would happen to any American or British commander if he pursued such tactics."[24]

German generals, who otherwise had great respect for the power of the Red Army, noted of Soviet tactics that "it was usually safe to encourage the Russians to attack, so long as the defence was elastically designed. The Russians were always very bull-headed in their offensive methods, repeating their attacks again and again. This was due to the way their leaders lived in fear of being considered lacking in determination if they broke off their attack." There are no exact figures of how many German soldiers were killed by the Red Army, but a good guess is that between 70 percent and 80 percent of all its killed, missing, captured, and wounded were due to Russian action (somewhere around 5 million casualties). Even in the first days of their invasion of Russia, the Germans learned that Soviet soldiers were quite unlike the Poles, Scandinavians, Western Europeans, and Balkan enemies that they had previously steamrolled. A German officer remarked of Russian resistance: "The way of waging war had completely changed; it was completely unfamiliar to us. We soon found the first reconnaissance patrols had fallen into Russian hands. They had their genitals cut off while still alive, their eyes gouged out, throats cut, or ears and noses cut off. We went around with grave faces, because we were frightened of this type of fighting."[25]

Hitler had assured the Wehrmacht that the Russians would fold in less than three months, in the manner of all previous targets of his ground forces. But as early as August 1941, after two months in Russia, German morale was ebbing, largely because it seemed that the more Soviet soldiers were killed or captured, the more enemies appeared with adequate equipment and fierce determination. A young German lieutenant Hellmuth Stieff wrote in despair to his wife in August 1941, when things were still going well enough for the invaders: "All these conditions, which we see and experience day in, day out . . . slowly create a state of resentment in you, so that you would really rather withdraw into your own shell. If some sort of change does not occur shortly in all this, there will be a catastrophe. Having to watch this go is awful."[26]

Despite the assumed prewar backwardness of Soviet science and industrial capability, the Red Army fielded the greatest number of excellent tanks (over 80,000 T-34s of various types) and larger numbers of howitzers, rockets, artillery, and anti-aircraft guns (over 500,000) than any other army of World War II. Even at the moment of the German invasion, the Soviets in mid-1941 possessed more armored vehicles than Britain, France, Germany, Italy, and the United States combined. Thanks to its own adequate production of heavy trucks (almost 200,000) and the enormous number of American and British Lend-Lease imports (another 375,000), the Soviet army in sheer numbers eventually fielded the most motorized divisions of the entire war. By early 1943, the Red Army had over twenty thousand tanks at the front, and were adding them at the rate of two thousand a month, and did this after losing almost all their existing prewar fleet of armored vehicles in 1941 and reconstituting much of their tank production beyond the Urals.[27]

The United States, Britain, and the British Dominions sent over fourteen thousand tanks to the Soviet Union from 1942 to 1945, at least a few of them upgraded diesel Shermans with the British 17-pounder gun, which was more than all German Panther and Tiger tank production combined. The individual Soviet infantryman after mid-1942 was often armed with the superb PPSh-41 submachine gun (over 6 million produced during the war) or the SVT-40 semi-automatic rifle (1.6 million).

While neither may have quite matched counterparts in other armies, such as the German StG 44 assault weapon or American M1 carbine, both weapons by 1943 ensured that the much larger Soviet army was equipped enough to do real damage to the German army.

Soviet industrial efficiency was achieved by concentrating on munitions (tanks, artillery, machines guns, rifles, etc.) while relying on Allied Lend-Lease imports for food, trucks, locomotives, rails, radios, and critical natural resources, especially aluminum, without which the Soviets could not build tank engines or aircraft frames. Also, in the late 1930s Soviet central planners had finally invited in Western, particularly American, companies to participate in technical assistance programs, which gave them expertise in assembly-line mass production and standardization of parts that would refashion the nature of Soviet industry. In terms of artillery, by mid-1944 the Soviet army typically had ten times the number of large guns as the Germans. By January 1945, the Red Army had available over a hundred thousand large artillery pieces and heavy mortars, with over a million men in artillery units, at precisely the time German supplies were diminishing as a result of both production and transportation dislocations and transfers of artillery and aircraft back to the homeland for air and ground defense.[28]

Such huge numbers, iron-clad discipline, little effective popular pressure to curb infantry losses, the largest population base of all the major and affiliated combatants with the exception of China and India, and near endless supplies of tanks, trucks, and artillery pieces made the Soviet army the deadliest and most terrifying infantry force of the war. As long as the Russian military was kept out of the Pacific and Mediterranean wars, had no obligation to supply other allies, and did not have to initiate strategic bombing and major naval operations, infantrymen were free to focus on a single enemy on a single front in what turned out to be the largest and most lethal battle line in military history. Even the backwardness of the interior of the Soviet Union tended to favor Russian defenders over European invaders. Germans claimed that they were unfamiliar with the weather, terrain, transportation structure, and geography of Mother Russia (although many of their officers had fought deeply inside and occupied Russian territory in 1917–1918). In August 1941, a German officer summed up the bewildering landscape: "I've already had it up to here with this much-vaunted Soviet Union! The conditions here are prehistoric. . . . We're suffering a lot from artillery fire here, and we have to live day and night in foxholes for protection from shrapnel. The holes are full of water. Lice and other vermin creep in too." He might have asked of his veteran senior officers if anything had changed much from 1918.[29]

The Germans actually faced two Red Armies. The initial Soviet force slowly disappeared between June 1941 and spring 1942, suffering well over four million dead in roughly a year of fighting and losing much of its armor, planes, and artillery. But to the bewilderment of the German army, the devastated original Red Army had never quite collapsed. Instead, the Soviets retreated over eight hundred miles into the interior of Russia, an option never available to the reeling French, Dutch, or Belgian armies a year earlier. The expanse of Russia offered the Red Army endless inland Dunkirks from which it could withdraw and reequip.

As the attenuated German army expanded to occupy a million square miles of European Russia, destroying or acquiring 7,500 factories and over half of Soviet electrical production, the remnants of the original Soviet Army were absorbed by a replacement force of 4.5 million soldiers. This second-generation force was more frequently equipped with new T-34 tanks, larger caliber and more plentiful artillery, and semi-automatic weapons. It was also increasingly protected by improved fighter aircraft and, by 1943, the beneficiary of American and British trucks, radios, and other material support. Aside from massive aid from the British and Americans, the Soviet salvation was found in the fact that the communist government still remained intact, had an entire protected industrial state beyond the Urals, demanded sacrifices unimaginable in the West, governed a population already used to serial depravations, and fought a uniquely existential war in which both sides accepted that defeat was tantamount to death. If the average life of a Soviet tank was less than six months at the front, it mattered little when two thousand new T-34s a month were joining the Red Army, along with nearly ten thousand crewmen. In sum, what the Red Army did to the Wehrmacht in 1944–1945 frightened Europeans for the next half century.[30]

THE BRITISH ARMY made up only 56 percent of all British uniformed forces, only a slightly greater ratio than in the American military. From the outset it faced a myriad of unique operational and strategic dilemmas, especially following the fall of France. That unforeseen disaster of June 1940 ended the army's century-long strategy of having at least one major European land power as a buffer and partner to enable the British to concentrate on naval power. From June 25, 1940, to June 22, 1941, the British army and its Commonwealth cousins were the only active national land forces of any repute facing the Axis powers. Britain's entire expeditionary army in France (nearly 400,000 soldiers and support staff) had been beaten, humiliated, and evacuated before and during the

Dunkirk operation, after over sixty thousand had been killed, captured, or wounded. The army by July 1940 should have been rendered largely combat ineffective after losing most of its equipment by the time it embarked from Dunkirk. Yet somehow in the ensuing year before Operation Barbarossa, the British military alone took on both the Italians and the Germans in North Africa and the Balkans, while maintaining mastery of the Atlantic and neutralizing the Italian fleet in the Mediterranean.[31]

The failed effort in Norway (April–June 1940) to stop the Nazi invasion and occupation (over 4,000 British casualties) and the evacuation from Dunkirk (June 1940) had sobered British planners by late 1940, reminding them again why the empire instead might be more wisely defended by air and sea power. At most, a comparatively small professional expeditionary army would avoid the mistake of 1914 of colliding with the continental German army, and instead check smaller and weaker Axis forces on the periphery of Europe, at least until the hoped-for arrival of a huge American overseas army. Unless there were a falling out between the Soviet Union and Nazi Germany, and unless the United States came into the war, there was little chance that the British army could return to Western Europe. And there was no chance that Britain alone could fight its way into Germany and defeat the Wehrmacht. Yet at the same time, given British industrial power, naval and air strength, morale, military professionalism, and superior supreme command, there was even less likelihood that Hitler could successfully invade Britain or bomb it into submission. Either new wonder weapons or major new belligerents would have to enter the war in 1941 to end what seemed to be an approaching German-British deadlock.

By summer 1940 the British Army and its imperial allies faced a global crisis. Aside from protecting its home soil from a possible German invasion, it sought to secure overseas interests from Suez to Burma that were soon threatened by Germans, Italians, and, increasingly, the Japanese. From July 1940 until autumn 1942, the British army suffered a series of further withdrawals or surrenders at Singapore, in Greece and Crete, and at Tobruk, which threatened to demoralize the public and undermine confidence in Winston Churchill's leadership. Even the prior initially successful operations against the Italians in Egypt and Libya (autumn 1940) were reversed by the infusion of German reinforcements in early 1941 and British redeployments to Greece. The surprise Japanese attacks and declaration of war on December 8 would naturally drain huge assets of the British Empire away from its mostly stable position by late 1941.[32]

Army prospects improved after the active American entrance into the European theater in November 1942. The British were quickly ensured a new partnership that, for the first time in the war, might lead to Allied logistical, air, and naval superiority over the Axis in the Mediterranean. After the final victory in North Africa (May 1943), except for the Market-Garden fiasco, the British army did not lose outright another campaign in the European theater. Despite its disparate deployments, the British army suffered the fewest combat dead of the six major nations at war, at 144,079 (along with 239,575 wounded, 33,771 missing, and 152,076 captured), in defeating the Italians, Germans, and Japanese on simultaneous fronts.[33]

The army's eventual success was not due to superior supplies or a pantheon of brilliant Napoleonic field marshals. Although quite adequate, British rifles, artillery, and tanks were not better than what was found in other Allied or Axis armies, except perhaps among the Italians and at times the Japanese. The key to the overtaxed army's resilience was found in its professionalism, generally high morale, and workmanlike office corps, although the officers' first concern was often not to engage in risky operations in which casualties were sure to spike and losses could not be easily replaced. British troops were equipped with the slow-firing but extremely accurate bolt-action Lee-Enfield .303 rifle (Rifle No. 4), and soon the various models of the Sten submachine gun (over 4 million produced). The latter could prove a deadly weapon at short ranges and was steadily improved. The World War I–vintage water-cooled .303 caliber Vickers machine gun was still lethal. British artillery by the time of Normandy was nearly as good as the German. The British army was far more motorized than were its enemies. Perhaps with the exception of the adequate Churchill, its tanks before 1943 were subpar. But the incorporation of the American Sherman, especially after mid-1944 when sometimes equipped with the British 17-pounder gun, gave British infantry adequate armor support. Infantry ground-to-air coordination by 1943 was superior to any force except the Americans, due largely to excellent communications and superb Spitfire, Hurricane, and Typhoon fighter-bombers.[34]

A few British army generals—Bernard Montgomery and William Slim especially—were among the best planners and most professional commanders of the war. Montgomery was both the most celebrated for his victory at El Alamein and the most culpable for his sluggish pursuit after a beaten and retiring Rommel, the failure to close promptly the Falaise Pocket, the inability to take quickly the key port of Antwerp, the ill-starred Operation Market-Garden assault, his silly editorializing after the Battle of the Bulge, and his over-prepped and publicized crossing of the Rhine. Yet Montgomery was a favorite of both Churchill and General Alan Brooke (later 1st Viscount Alanbrooke), chief of the Imperial

General Staff, who nonetheless both privately conceded that he was an irritant, a disrupter of the alliance, and a plodder—but not one to suffer a disastrous defeat. Oddly, for all their complaints about Monty, generals like George S. Patton developed respect for his talents and worked well with him when necessary.[35]

Insightful British supreme command avoided a premature Allied landing in Western Europe before 1944 as well as some of the more eccentric Aegean plans of Winston Churchill, and in large part guided the Americans' strategic thinking between 1942 and 1943, from North Africa to Italy. That Britain alone of the Western democracies did not fall in 1940, how it nearly matched the military production of a much larger Germany, and why it exercised political clout comparable to far larger allies, is attributable to its excellent military, and in particular the ability of the British army to inflict more losses on the Axis than it incurred. The Axis defeated the British at particular battles and in individual theaters at Singapore, Burma, Greece, Crete, and Libya. Yet these periodic tactical victories did not lead to lasting strategic advantages, given British naval superiority, strategic bombing capability, and relative immunity from attack on its industrial base.[36]

THE GREAT ISSUE in World War II was the degree to which the superior fighting power of the German foot soldier would translate into sustained strategic victories. In terms of training, unit command, and morale, no other infantry force for the duration of the war proved its match. German army training manuals may have stressed that "superior combat power can compensate for inferior numbers," but the issue hinged on the definition of "inferior numbers," as a disadvantage of two to one was quite different from five or seven to one, as became the reality in many theaters by late 1944. German prowess was defined in part by anachronistic ideas that infantry superiority was achieved by ground troops killing more ground troops than they lost, and downplayed the more important Allied advantages of numbers, equipment, supplies, ships, and planes.[37]

The German army's operational excellence was often rendered irrelevant by nihilistic decisions of the supreme command, such as Hitler's redirecting entire army groups on the Eastern Front between 1941 and 1942, issuing no-retreat, no-surrender orders at Stalingrad and El Alamein, and subsequently in 1943–1944, or mounting doomed offensives such as the attack through the Ardennes in late 1944 or the Operation Spring Awakening relief of Budapest in March 1945. Hitler's blinkered view of geostrategy was abetted by the blinders of the German General

Staff at both OKW (the Supreme Command of the German Armed Forces) and to a lesser degree at OKH (the Supreme Command of the German Army). By training and nature, few of even the best German generals were equipped to think of war in terms of grand strategy or geopolitics, and were flummoxed by Hitler's often esoteric talk of critical strategic resources, contours in changing alliances, and cultural nonsense. His pseudohistorical ranting worked well on a professional Prussian military class that so often could not distinguish his disastrous from its own mediocre strategic thinking, and whose legacy theretofore had been largely a free wartime hand from its political overseer. (Kaiser Wilhelm II at the beginning of World War I had supposedly quipped, "the General Staff tells me nothing and never asks my advice. I drink tea, saw wood and go for walks.")

When the Wehrmacht no longer delivered victories in Russia by late 1941 as easily as it had in France, Hitler began the erratic removal of generals like Gerd von Rundstedt, Erich von Manstein, and Heinz Guderian. It would have been unthinkable of Churchill similarly to fire Montgomery after the failure to close the Falaise Pocket or after Market-Garden, or of Roosevelt to bring home General Courtney Hodges after he entered the Hürtgen Forest. By 1943 the German army had devolved from an aggressive and competent regional offensive force into an outmanned and out-supplied global occupation army that could no longer win the ground wars it had started, and that often was at the mercy of superior enemy air and naval power. Its mission had changed to a wholly defensive one, in the manner of the Japanese resistance that hoped to inflict such losses on advancing infantry forces, so as to convince them that their demands for unconditional surrender were not worth the inevitable human or material costs. Both high- and medium-ranking Waffen SS officers like Oberst-Gruppenführer (roughly, "General") Sepp Dietrich, Standartenführer (Colonel) Joachim Peiper, or Obersturmbannführer (Lieutenant Colonel) Otto Skorzeny were not so much doctrinaire Nazis as unquestioning vicious fighters who eagerly embraced the Nazi idea of giving no quarter and fought as savagely without hope of victory as they once had when assured of conquest.[38]

German infantrymen recalled the Spartans of World War II. The *Heer*, or German army, like the ancient *homoioi* ("The Similars") of Sparta was highly trained and terrifyingly professional. Like Spartans, Wehrmacht soldiers were effused with militarist doctrine, chronically short of men, brilliantly led on the battlefield—and often deployed for imbecilic strategic ends. Like the Spartan maverick generals Brasidas, Gylippus, and Lysander, there were also plenty of inspired officers in the German army, but in addition to a rare Manstein or Rommel, there were also far more unimaginative versions of dullard Spartan kings (Generals Alfred Jodl, Wilhelm Keitel, and Walter Warlimont) who as overseers at OKW would, along with Hitler, waste their deadly assets.

Before the encirclement at Stalingrad (November 1942), the German army was mostly undefeated, either by the Soviets or by any of the dozen national armies it had steamrolled since September 1939, and its training and operational doctrines were regarded as unimpeachable. The chief theme of the *Truppenführung*, the German Army Manual for Unit Command in World War II, was officer initiative ("mission command," *Auftragstaktik*), the freedom for even junior officers to fulfill a defined mission as they saw fit on the ground, without micromanagement from above. It was ironic that the autocratic Nazis gave more initiative to their junior officers than the democratic British and Americans did to their majors and colonels.[39]

Given relatively weak opposition and the serial use of surprise attack against neighbors, it is hard to determine to what degree between 1939 and 1941 so-called blitzkrieg was either a myth or truly a revolutionary tactic of using motorized divisions, backed by concentrations of tanks in tandem with air support, to race ahead to encircle and collapse the morale of more static enemies. Nonetheless, until 1941 most of the German army remained plodding. It was largely moved by horses and outfitted mostly with light Mark I and Mark II tanks that were substandard and inferior to most of their French counterparts: over eight hundred were lost in the Polish campaign alone and were labeled by the Germans themselves as "unsuitable for combat." Even German armored divisions had relatively few tanks. On the eve of Operation Barbarossa, General Heinz Guderian's Second Panzer Group was equipped with only 930 tanks to accompany its 148,554 men. The army that invaded the Soviet Union was premodern: fifteen thousand Polish peasant wagons, seventy-five divisions powered only by horses, hundreds of different types of looted and often obsolete European vehicles, seventy-three different models of tanks, and fifty-two different makes of anti-aircraft guns. A standard motorized German division had begun the war with nine hundred trucks— and five thousand horses.[40]

The German army entered the war with more firepower per infantry division—twenty-four howitzers, seventy-two anti-tank guns, 135 mortars, and 442 machines guns—than its Polish, French, or British counterparts. In 1939, none of Germany's enemies even fielded formal independent armor divisions. The Wehrmacht's intrinsic weaknesses would be clear the first time Germany's huge army met a roughly matched enemy. The 37 mm anti-tank gun was ineffective against French heavy tanks, and would often prove useless against early-model Russian T-34s. Due to fuel shortages and inadequate vehicle output, along with growth in the size of the army, by the end of the war there was probably a greater percentage of German divisions relying on horse-drawn transport (approximately 85 percent) than in September 1939. If the Allies worried about gasoline supplies, the German army was dependent on grass and hay. And during the last two years of the war, the army reverted to the older tradition of leadership by unimaginative top-down directive (*Weisungsführung*), as it back-peddled on two fronts along clearly defined lines and in accordance with Hitler's own orders.[41]

Hitler's serial interference in operations hamstrung the military, as he stocked OKW with sycophants such as Generals Wilhelm Keitel, Alfred Jodl, and Walter Warlimont to monitor the more meritocratic and professional staff at OKH. After his firing of General Walther von Brauchitsch as head of OKH in December 1941, Hitler took direct control of the army himself, essentially ending such autonomy of the army as it was and making the Army High Command nearly irrelevant. After the war, Albert Speer told his interrogators that Hitler's takeover of OKH "was the most unfortunate decision taken in this war."[42]

Had Hitler kept out of operational decision-making, there was some chance that Leningrad, Moscow, and perhaps even Stalingrad would have been taken and the front stabilized along the Volga River. The problem was not just that Hitler in unhinged fashion prohibited tactical retreats that would have saved hundreds of thousands of German troops. He was just as prone to periods of timidity, when he lost his nerve and ordered halts in German advances when daring and rapidity might have brought far greater success. Agreeing with some of his generals to halt the Panzers before the Dunkirk evacuations was one such instance. General Franz Halder of OKH remarked even early on in the war that when events were going well in France, Hitler at times became "terribly nervous" and "frightened of his own success" and "became unwilling to take any risks." The failure to destroy the entire British expeditionary army at Dunkirk may have been the most calamitous mistake prior to the invasion of Russia, given that the psychological toll on the British public and the new Churchill government of losing well over three hundred thousand soldiers in one fell swoop would have been enormous.

Only three of some thirty-six full German generals survived the war in command, and thereby avoided what became a standardized unfortunate fate. Only one of the army's seventeen field marshals retained a command at war's end; the other sixteen were relieved of command, removed from the active army, executed, killed in action, or captured. The army's problem was not just that a professional officer class was audited by an incompetent General Staff, but also that the German General Staff had been completely absorbed by an increasingly irrational Hitler.[43]

As in the case of the Red Army, there were two German armies. The first was a smaller elite core of about a half-million soldiers equipped with excellent weapons by contemporary standards and staffed by brilliant officers. Until 1942 it was rarely opposed by any infantry force of similar caliber and was mostly employed only on Germany's borders. The other and largely replacement German army was vast but uneven. It was often underequipped and poorly supplied, deployed in far distant and foreign geography, lacking adequate air support, corrupted by auxiliary death squads, and forced to rely on reluctant conscripts, many of them poorly trained and too young or too old. It was tasked with occupying conquered territory of about 1.5 million square miles—far larger than the Roman Empire at its greatest extent—that by 1944 was often openly hostile.[44]

Still, as Germany's fortunes were on the wane after 1943, it often remained difficult for allied forces to defeat the core elements of the German army, even as the vast second German force was steadily pushed back on all fronts and had collapsed in North Africa, was withdrawing from Normandy, and was on the defensive after Kursk. So Hitler was in part correct to rely on the operational excellence of the German army—"the German soldier can do anything"—to nullify Allied numerical superiority and his own confused strategic orders. German soldiers' morale arose not necessarily just from enthusiasm with the tenets of National Socialism and the rebirth of German pride and nationalism that it had helped create. There was the added factor of unbelievable successes from September 1939 to April 1941 that bred a sense of fated destiny to the army's efforts. Only after the surrender at Stalingrad (February 2, 1943), when there were no more unprepared neighbors to be surprise attacked, did Propaganda Minister Joseph Goebbels demand "total war" against a supposedly wounded USSR.[45]

What best characterized the German army of World War II— eventually growing to more than five million men—was paradoxically a chronic shortage of manpower, or at least far too few men for the grand strategic objectives that Hitler had set out for the Wehrmacht. The anomaly is easily illustrated by the army's status on the eve of the invasion of the Soviet Union. In less than a year, Hitler had added eighty-four divisions to the Field Army. It soon numbered 3,800,000 men, in addition to 150,000 SS troops, for a grand total of 650,000 new soldiers added to the army since the fall of France in June 1940. These appear to be impressive numbers, especially when eventually augmented by hundreds of thousands of allied troops from Finland, Romania, and Hungary, and later Italy and Spain. In fact, they were insufficient for a Third Reich that sought to occupy and defend Poland, Norway, Denmark, the Netherlands, France, Greece, and Crete, while deploying troops to North Africa and garrisoning the homeland. All this while the Wehrmacht was attacking a Soviet army with more men and equipment, across a million square miles of battle space, and waging existential wars in the Atlantic and the skies of Europe—just six months before Germany then also declared war on the United States.[46]

On the battlefield it could be a terrifying experience for any Russian soldier to face his German counterpart, well apart from matters of experience and operational and organizational doctrine. By 1944 thousands of German soldiers in the East were equipped with the war's most lethal hand-held machine gun, the *Sturmgewehr* (StG) 44, the world's first true assault rifle. Some German infantry units since 1942 had also been equipped with the best light machine gun of the war, the twenty-five-pound *Maschinengewehr* (MG) 42, which could hit targets up to two thousand yards away. German infantrymen were generally equipped with more MG 42s than their Allied counterparts were with comparable light machine guns, which typically offered only half the rates of fire. Both the StG 44 and the MG 42, along with Panther and Tiger tanks, were desperate attempts to provide shrinking German infantry forces with more firepower and thus overcome quantity with superior quality—a formula, however, that rarely has had much success in a war between like Western powers. World War II was not an asymmetrical colonial war in the fashion of the Anglo-Zulu Wars in South Africa (1879–1896) or the Mahdist War in the Sudan (1881–1899), where Westerners had modern munitions and indigenous enemies almost none. While the Germans for a time may have found some preeminence in personal weapons and armor, their margin of technological superiority over Allied guns and tanks was hardly enough to offset their increasing numerical inferiority in men and machines.[47]

The atrocities committed by the Wehrmacht during the war were not just the domain of the Waffen SS, especially on the Russian front. For the first seven months of that campaign, the regular German army oversaw on average ten thousand deaths of Soviet prisoners *per day* from execution, disease, or starvation—a total of nearly two million deaths by the end of 1941. In part, the carnage was attributed to the Germans' own surprise by Soviet mass surrenders and their own ill-preparedness to cope with the hordes of captured soldiers amid poor supplies, partisans, and inclement weather. But only in part, given that the German army was constantly reminded that in the National Socialist creed, Russians and Slavs were *Untermenschen*, subhumans who were to have no viability in postwar Nazi-occupied Russia. The army had earlier worried very little about the fate of the defeated Soviets in the General Staff's planning of Operation Barbarossa. The Wehrmacht was more than willing to abide by the infamous "Commissar Order" on entry into the Soviet Union. (Article II: "The originators of barbaric, Asiatic methods of warfare are the political commissars. So immediate and unhesitatingly severe measures must be undertaken against them. They are therefore, when captured in battle, as a matter of routine to be dispatched by firearms.")[48]

THE JAPANESE ARMY, unlike all the other infantry forces of the six major belligerents, was both a military and political force that set national policy. The minister of war, an office controlled by the army and often independent from or identical to the prime ministry, was ultimately subordinate only to the emperor himself. Prior to 1941, Japan's recent land wars against Manchuria (1931), China (1937), and the Soviet Union (1939) were primarily army operations, but proved either quagmires or failures. The fact of army supremacy, then, was ironic, given that the navy, and the naval and army air forces, were far better equipped according to Western standards than was the army itself. Prior to World War II, the Imperial Japanese Navy had largely been responsible for the country's more dramatic victories in the Russo-Japanese War, despite some inspired army campaigns in Manchuria.[49]

In 1941 the Japanese army, with 1,700,000 soldiers organized in some fifty-seven combat divisions and various auxiliary units, was larger than any Allied land force other than the Soviet Red Army. But most Japanese manpower was stationed in China and along the Mongolian border, where it had become bogged down since 1932 in a chronic, low-level conflict with the Russians. By 1938 there had been over 2,800 incidents between the Japanese and Soviet armies. In a series of intensified border wars in 1939, the Japanese had suffered a climactic defeat at Khalkhin Gol by General Zhukov's superior Red Army armor and artillery.

The logical move in 1941 would have been to deploy new units—the Japanese army would steadily grow to over five million by 1945—to stabilize China, and in conjunction with Nazi Germany to invade the Soviet Union. Instead, manpower shortages would continue to dog Japanese strategic ambitions on land. Despite Japan's huge army and its large prewar population of over seventy million, only about 20 percent of eligible

Japanese were at some time to serve in the military, a smaller ratio of mobilization than was true of Nazi Germany.[50]

Until late 1941, the Japanese had not yet fought the British or the Americans, and had some contempt for both despite their own tepid performance against the Soviet Union and China. The apparently dismal infantry performances of France and Britain in May and June 1940 helped to persuade the Japanese army that the democracies were far less formidable than had been the Russians. Timing also was important. The Japanese were still under the impression by late November 1941 that the Wehrmacht would likely take Moscow. The elimination of the Soviet Union might free up more European Axis resources against Britain and thus argue against the deployment of British, or even American, forces in the Pacific. Ironically, that decision of the Imperial Japanese Army to forgo another land war with the Soviet Union in 1941 in conjunction with Nazi Germany, and instead to allow the Imperial Japanese Navy to begin a naval conflict with the United States, may have saved Russia and doomed Japan. What advantages accrued from surprise, prior Japanese involvement in Asia, and general Allied inexperience quickly dissipated by late 1942. Even the inaugural effort of the American 1st Marine Division at Guadalcanal in late 1942, less than a year after Pearl Harbor, demonstrated that the Japanese soldier was no braver than inexperienced American Marines, and much less well supplied, fed, and armed.[51]

Until it had met the Russians along the Mongolian border (May–August 1939), Japanese infantry had never fully been tested by modern Western armor, artillery, and air support. The Japanese army's victories thirty-five years earlier in the Russo-Japanese War at the Yalu River and Mukden were over poorly equipped and badly led tsarist forces—armies not comparable to the later mechanized Red Army of the industrial Soviet state.

Japan had never produced a medium much less a heavy tank that approximated even early British or American models. It did not fully understand the value of centrally coordinated heavy field artillery. The Japanese were far behind in areas such as self-propelled guns, transport trucks, jeeps, heavy machine guns, and radio-directed artillery fire. Its divisions on average were not motorized, much less in reliable radio contact with air support. There was nothing comparable in the Japanese military to the US Navy Seabees, whose mechanized ingenuity proved invaluable in crafting bases and airstrips amid harsh climate, rough terrain, and jungle in the Pacific.

Japanese commanders often thought more in operational terms, as if tactical successes at Singapore or the Philippines would ipso facto result somehow in strategic victories. Japan, like Britain, was an island power.

But before 1941 it had no real experience in seaborne operations on a scale comparable to the Allied Mediterranean invasions of late 1942. The Japanese lacked the amphibious craft and logistical support to ensure the army easy passage and adequate supplies, failings that in part doomed the Japanese on Guadalcanal. Whereas the Japanese army could conduct simple transport of expeditionary forces to ports in China, it had little facility for numerous small amphibious landings against Pacific islands, unless they were largely uncontested. Aside from Pearl Harbor, Singapore, and the Philippines, the Japanese army's mode of operation was to grab territory relatively unopposed, fortify it, and then demonstrate to the Allies that the cost to recover it exceeded its value. Yet less than six months after Pearl Harbor, and after the draw at the Battle of the Coral Sea, the Japanese already had given up on their planned amphibious assault on Port Moresby on the southern coast of New Guinea. The Imperial Japanese Army remained an enigma. It could fight fiercely in the manner of the Wehrmacht, but was organized and supplied in the fashion of the Italians. It shared both Axis partners' propensity to overrate the value of martial zealotry, deprecate the role of motor vehicles and supplies, and downplay the war-making potential of the Allies.[52]

Nevertheless, in a series of island campaigns, as well as during the invasion of Burma, from late 1942 to the last months of the war on Okinawa, the Imperial Japanese Army was able to inflict terrible casualties on Allied forces for a variety of reasons. The army and its officer corps were far more experienced from a near-decade-long struggle in China than were either their British or American counterparts, at least until 1942–1943. Aggressive and savvy Japanese generals of the caliber of Masaharu Homma, Tadamichi Kuribayashi, Mitsuru Ushijima, and Tomoyuki Yamashita (all of whom either were hanged or shot for war crimes at war's end or perished with their troops in defeat) found success early in the war against poorly prepared and demoralized, though not necessarily numerically inferior, Allied troops. Later they proved masters at studying American amphibious protocols and learning how to exact huge costs while dug in on the defensive. Anytime the mechanized mobility and firepower of Allied infantry could be nullified by static Japanese defenses, jungle and mountainous terrain, and elaborate fortifications—beneath concrete and coral in idyllic Pacific island landscapes—American, British, and Dominion casualties skyrocketed.[53]

By the 1930s Japanese militarism had combined traditional strains of samurai culture, Bushido, Shinto Buddhism, and emperor worship with contemporary fascism to excuse military atrocities. A cult arose of modern, supposedly racially superior warriors whose moral worth was calibrated by battlefield prowess and cruelty toward enemies. Since the victories of the Russo-Japanese War of 1904–1905, Westernization had a paradoxical effect on the Japanese military: encouraging modernist dreams of reaching mechanized parity with Western powers, while engendering a sense of reactionary contempt for those who saw war in terms of materiel and machines rather than manhood.

No army had a smaller ratio of wounded to dead than did the Japanese. Nihilistic banzai charges that were suicidal and brought little tactical advantage were institutionalized, from the Battle of the Tenaru on Guadalcanal to bloodier charges on Saipan and Okinawa. In the manner that German soldiers of World War II were probably more enthused about the idea of war than their predecessors in the German Imperial Army, so too the Japanese army that invaded China was indoctrinated in ways not necessarily true during the earlier twentieth century, even during its startling successes over the Russians at the Yalu River and Mukden in 1904–1905. As General Kojiro Sato put it in his prewar popular fantasy, *If America and Japan Fight*, "courage or cowardice was the decisive factor, strength or weakness only of subsidiary importance." Strength, however, mattered quite a lot. Despite Sato's fantasies, the Japanese ended up losing ten soldiers for every British and American soldier they killed.[54]

For troops that were soon on the defensive, often immobile and dug in, Japan's light weaponry in theory was not all that much inferior to commensurate Western models. The family of light Nambu machines guns, the Type 89 grenade launcher, the 38 Arisaka rifle, and Japanese 75 mm artillery were all dependable and easy-to-use weapons. But without Western opposition until 1939, Japan's armored forces stagnated and remained too light and too small. There were also not enough artillery pieces larger than 75 mm. Japanese motorized vehicles were a fraction of what was used by the British and Americans. Although the combined Japanese military reached over seven million men in arms, reflecting the fact that Japan's population (73 million at the time of Pearl Harbor) was nearly as large as Greater Germany's (80 million), the army was outproduced by its Allied enemies in every category of weapon system. The United States produced over 2.5 million machine guns, the Japanese less than a fifth of that number. The British turned out four million pistols, the Japanese eight thousand. The Americans deployed a hundred thousand tanks and self-propelled guns, the Japanese less than five thousand. Even the Italian army, which disbanded in 1943, had twice as many mortars (17,000) as the Japanese (8,000).[55]

Over a decade, the Japanese army may have been largely responsible for the loss of over twenty million Chinese, Indian, and Indochinese unarmed civilians. Yet in nearly four years of war, the Japanese military managed to kill only about 120,000 British and American soldiers, and capture some seventy thousand, while losing in the process nearly two million dead to enemy arms. The Imperial Japanese Army fairly earned the reputation for cruelty: no army in World War II killed so many civilians while being so inept at killing its better-armed enemies.

THE ROYAL ITALIAN Army literally ceased to exist little more than three years after Mussolini declared war on Britain and France on June 10, 1940. Italian infantrymen, like the soldiers of the Wehrmacht, experienced the misfortune of suffering casualties at the hands of almost every major belligerent of World War II: the French in June 1940 and again in early 1943, the Russians between 1941 and 1943, the British from 1940 to 1943, the Americans from 1942 to 1943, and, in isolated cases, during the German-Italian fighting from 1943 to 1945. After an initial victory over the outnumbered British colonial forces in East Africa and in western Egypt, the Royal Italian Army never won another major battle unassisted.

Over four million Italians would serve in the Royal Army; almost a half million were either killed or went missing in combat. Mussolini began the war as a staunch ally of Hitler. Yet more Italians would eventually die in German prisoner-of-war camps as military detainees or as forced laborers in Germany after 1943, than were captured and held in camps by the Americans. If the Italian army had the least resources of the major powers—inadequate air support, poor supplies, outclassed armored vehicles and artillery—it also took on one of the most ambitious and far-reaching roles of any army in the war. Italy (approximately 45 million people) fielded over ninety divisions, almost nearing the size of the ground combat forces of the United States with its population of over 130 million.[56]

By the time Mussolini had declared war on the French and British, the Italian army was already short of supplies and still recovering from its draining expeditionary fighting in Ethiopia (1935–1936), the Spanish Civil War (1936–1939), and Albania (1939). Yet another of the many ironies of Mussolini's foreign policies was that he had so overextended his forces in "peace" that he was entirely unprepared for the German war that broke out in 1939, a paradox that Hitler never quite appreciated, given his apparent ebullience at Italian bullying in the 1930s and chronic disappointment in Italy's incompetence after June 1940.

Unfortunately for Italy, Mussolini's initial successes in his prewar minor interventions against outnumbered and obsolete forces had convinced the fascist government that the Royal Italian Army was somehow a serious, albeit junior, partner to the Wehrmacht. In fact, in every category of military assessment, the Italian army was far inferior to initial British and French armed forces. The Italian wartime economy was the weakest of all the major nations fighting in Europe, taxed especially by Mussolini's insistence on building a huge Mediterranean surface fleet of battleships and cruisers that would ultimately prove of little strategic advantage. Italian industry produced little more than 10 percent of the vehicles turned out in France and Britain. Italy had only a fraction of the strategic materials—oil, coal, and iron ore—that were available to its enemies.[57]

The Italian army had not necessarily deteriorated since 1918 when as an Allied partner and member of the Big Four it had finally defeated the Austrians in savage fighting, after losing well over a half-million men. Rather, the problem this time around was both political and strategic, manifesting itself in at least two pernicious ways. First, Mussolini saw no need to confine the army largely to its proximate northern borders, assuming instead that his new German-Austrian ally provided a valuable buffer that freed his expeditionary forces to be sent to East and North Africa, France, the Balkans, the Soviet Union, and Greece. But that was a role well beyond Italian maritime transportation and logistical abilities at any time. Second, Germany was a poor substitute for Italy's far more powerful former British, French, Russian, and American allies of World War I. The latter coalition had far better matched limited Italian means with their common strategic ends. Mussolini dubbed his far more ambitious Mediterranean agendas in World War II a "Parallel War;" and initially he had been as apprehensive of German encroachment as he was of British resistance.[58]

While Italian military craftsmanship was always superb and would produce some excellent ground weapons and prototypes—the Carro Armato P26/40 tank, SPA-Viberti AS.42 armored car, assorted 75 mm and 100 mm medium field-artillery pieces, or the Beretta Model 38 submachine gun—the fascist state had no serious concept of mass production, much less the resources to fuel it. The few competitive weapons that Italy produced either came into production too late in 1943 or in too few numbers.[59]

In succession, Mussolini sent the army across the border into France on June 10, 1940, where it was soon soundly beaten even by the collapsing French army. In July it invaded British Somaliland, and enjoyed some success by expelling depleted British garrisons. (Yet a year later, most Italian forces were defeated in East Africa.) On September 13, 1940, the Royal

Italian Army invaded Egypt and was soon repelled by a much smaller British army and forced to retreat five hundred miles through Libya, saved for a while only by the arrival of Rommel and the dispersion of victorious British forces to Greece. What was left of the Italian army in North Africa was reinforced in 1942 and partnered with the German Afrika Korps. It too ceased to exist after the general Axis surrender of May 1943 in Tunisia. The late October 1940 invasion of Greece had proved a disaster, tying down a half-million Italian soldiers in the Balkans until the arrival of the Germans, while the army was short of manpower and supplies in East and North Africa. Italy suffered nearly ninety thousand casualties in the effort to invade and occupy Greece alone.[60]

In his greatest blunder of the war—and such an assertion is always controversial given the nearly endless choices—Mussolini had sent over ten divisions to the Russian front. At least eighty-five thousand soldiers were killed there, and another thirty thousand wounded. Perhaps twenty to thirty thousand died in Russian prisoner-of-war camps. The Royal Italian Army, which was chronically short of supplies in partnership with the Afrika Korps, nonetheless lost 1,200 artillery pieces and eighteen thousand motor vehicles on the Eastern Front. Mussolini had been more worried about losing prestige if the Hungarians and Romanians had joined the Germans without Italians present (Italy "must pay our debts to our allies"), and no doubt he also sensed an easy German victory and wished to scavenge the anticipated Soviet carcass, especially oil supplies from the Caucasus.[61]

In partnership with the German defenders in Sicily, the Royal Italian Army suffered enormous casualties (140,000 killed, wounded, and missing of its quarter-million-man home army). The army was soon disbanded with the general defection of Italy from the Axis cause in September 1943.

Had Mussolini not sent forces into Russia and the Balkans, he would have been able to deploy a million-man army in North Africa at a time of relative British weakness and thereby set back Allied progress in southern Europe by at least a year. Mussolini saw willpower as the ingredient for army success. He was oblivious to the fact that morale is often built or eroded by the competency of military leadership and the ability of the home front to provide soldiers with weapons of greater quantity and quality than those of their enemies.

Ultimately, the Italian soldier did not wish to fight World War II. If he were forced to, he would have preferred either to deploy on Italy's northern borders or to fight East Africans and small colonial forces in East and North Africa. Instead, Mussolini chose a European war against modern forces and former allies with no history of animosity toward Italy. The army would become expeditionary and thus logically cease to exist just little more than three years after going to war.[62]

IN CONCLUSION, ASSESSMENTS of the respective armies of World War II involved far more than just evaluating infantry forces themselves. By nineteenth-century standards of foot soldiers largely fighting foot soldiers, the German and Japanese armies may be ranked as preeminent in World War II, given their respective martial zeal and operational competence. But a number of important twentieth-century developments nullified their professionalism and thereby explained systematic Allied victories on the ground by mid-1943. First, the Allies did not just enjoy superior air power in support of their ground troops, but also attained air supremacy through the quantity and quality of their fighters and fighter-bombers, unlimited fuel supplies, and the better training of far more numerous pilots. When Messerschmitt Bf 109s and Mitsubishi A6M Zeros controlled the skies over Poland, France, or the Pacific, the Japanese and German armies often were unstoppable; when they ceased dominating the air by 1943, they stalled. The German and Japanese foot soldiers usually did not fight just their Allied counterparts but also an array of strafing and bombing planes, as well as vast convoys of freighters that brought food, ammunition, and weapons to Allied armies in a manner completely unmatched by the Axis powers.

Second, the limited industrial base and vulnerable merchant marine of all the Axis powers made it difficult to support expeditionary armies, and yet fighting far from home became the focus of Axis aggression. When the Axis nations sent their ground forces into North Africa, the Soviet Union, Southeast Asia, and the Pacific Islands, they quickly discovered challenges and landscapes far different from their past fighting in their own environs, including far stronger enemies who far better understood the key role of distance in modern warfare as it applied to logistics and mechanized transportation.

Ideology, for good or evil, was a force multiplier of German, Japanese, and Soviet armies. Stalin's iron will and murderous regime led both to disastrous encirclements in 1941–1942 and to costly but unstoppable offensives in 1944–1945. In contrast, the German and Japanese armies could ill-afford the no-retreat orders of their fascist leaders at Stalingrad and in the Pacific. The vast expanse, industrial base, and rich allies of Russia gave it tactical and strategic latitudes not available to Germany and Japan. Stalin's stubbornness could lead to the loss of millions of soldiers without collapse, in a way that the obduracy of Hitler and Tojo could not. In an ironic sense, Germany and Japan may have fielded the best individual foot soldiers but the worst armies.

In the next chapter, the string of Germany's successful border wars between September 1939 and April 1941 conspired to ensure the Wehrmacht's later catastrophe in Russia after June 1941. The more that the German army swallowed up weak Western neighbors, the more it believed that its spirit and élan had been the catalysts for its success, rather than the age-old criteria of good weather, easy logistics, and a head start in rearmament and munitions production. Hitler should have learned from the Battle of Britain that the defeat of the Luftwaffe in 1940–1941, against an Allied power completely unlike his previous victims, offered a lesson applicable to impending fighting on the ground in Russia—a nation likewise enjoying geographical advantages, foreign sources of supply, sophisticated weaponry, and a population that was willing to perish rather than surrender. Instead, the episodes from Dunkirk to Stalingrad proved a Greek tragedy for the German army. The hubris arising from surprise attacks on weaker nations ensured a terrible nemesis from doing the same against the one power, the Red Army, that could inflict on the German army ten times the casualties that it had suffered from all previous conflicts.

# 12

# The Western and Eastern Wars
# for the Continent

BETWEEN 1939 AND February 1943 Germany launched a number of successive ground offensives, nine of which involved countries that the German army had either surprise attacked successfully or had belatedly intervened into during ongoing conflicts: Poland, Denmark, Norway, the Low Countries (Belgium, the Netherlands, and Luxembourg), France, Yugoslavia, Greece, the British in North Africa, and the Soviet Union. Meanwhile, the so-called Winter War saw the Red Army invade Finland (November 30, 1939–March 13, 1940). Yet two continent-wide offensives radically changed the course of the entire war, one ending in June 1940 at Dunkirk on the Atlantic Ocean and the other at Stalingrad in February 1943 on the Volga River, over two thousand miles distant.

Because Germany had started World War II and was the most powerful member of the Axis alliance, how its ground forces fared in these two campaigns on the European continent determined the course of the war. Whereas the Americans, Italians, Japanese, and Russians all had watched carefully the pulse of the Third Reich's initial border wars that took place in a circumference around the Third Reich, it was the defeat of France and the later surprise assault on the Soviet Union that determined the trajectory of the war in Europe and to some extent in the Pacific as well. As a general rule, when the German army ground up its neighbors, it earned the eventual participation in the war of its opportunistic partners, Italy and Japan, and for a time the Soviet Union as well. And when the army stalled in Russia, its hold on its alliance weakened and its operations elsewhere in North Africa, Sicily, and Italy felt the aftershocks.

Another theme characterized the two great European continental wars against France and Russia: the French army, the presumed principal obstacle to German expansionism, crumbled in weeks, while the assumed incompetent Red Army ended up in Berlin. Never in military history had a great power so overestimated the ability of one existential enemy while so underestimating the capability of another. The meat grinder of the Western Front in World War I was replayed in World War II in the East, and the collapse of the Eastern Front in 1917 and the ensuing vast German occupation of 1918 was somewhat repeated in the West in 1940.

The "strange defeat" of the huge French army in June 1940—a catastrophe still inexplicable nearly eighty years later—recalibrated the entire strategic course of World War II. When the war broke out in September 1939, the Wehrmacht had been fixated on one chief enemy: the indomitable French army that had two decades earlier spearheaded the Allied victory over the Kaiser's forces on French and Belgian soil. France, as Hitler frequently expressed in *Mein Kampf,* was considered the chief stumbling block to German efforts to reassert European preeminence, and it was determined to put its resources into ground forces at a time when other democracies like the British (and soon the Americans) were investing more in strategic air power and carriers. The French, it was felt, might bend but once more would be hard to break. They certainly would fight on their home soil (they had no intention of a serious preemptory attack on Germany's western flank in 1939) far more fervently than did the Danes, Norwegians, or Poles. In the Finns' dogged resistance to the often poorly planned and conducted Soviet invasion during the Winter War, the Germans had already seen what highly motivated troops on the defensive might do to a much larger, modern-equipped invader. But defeat the French army in the North, the Germans believed, and much of the country would then be neutralized, while the rest of continental Western Europe would fall to the Third Reich and the specter of a two-front ground war would all but end. The chief German paradox of World War II was that it feared the French in 1940 far more than it did the Russians in 1941. But by any fair material or spiritual barometer, the Red Army had greatly improved over the tsar's military—just as Napoleon had reenergized the calcified armies of the ancien régime—and was demonstrably the far greater danger to the Wehrmacht.

French population (50 million) and industry (1938 GDP of about $186 billion) were smaller than the Third Reich's (80 million, GDP of $351 billion), even before the second round of German conquests and occupations of 1939 and early 1940. The French understood demography as fate, and so had begun to rearm earlier than had either the British or Americans. By May 1940, they fielded an extraordinarily large army of over three million men and nearly 3,500 tanks. On paper, the French armed forces appeared just as formidable as their heroic predecessors that stood at Verdun, especially in the quality of their fighter planes and tanks. The investments in the Maginot Line were controversial but nonetheless had resulted in a nearly impenetrable three-hundred-mile wall of defense from Switzerland to Luxembourg, protecting the most accessible pathway into France from Germany. The bulwark also freed up greater numbers of French troops to deploy to the north and east on the mostly unfortified Belgian border. Paradoxes followed: the general defensive mentality instilled by the Maginot Line hampered the offensive spirit needed where its protection stopped, even as the French feared walling off and isolating their Belgian ally to the north that nonetheless could offer no guarantee of keeping the Germans away from France. Even Hitler had assumed that avoiding the Maginot Line and barreling through the top-third of France in May 1940 would be only the first phase in a long war of attrition lasting well into 1942. Most at OKW envisioned occupying northern France with a static front against a rump state to the south.[1]

Much of Hitler's fear of France and dismissal of the Soviet Union derived from his own past experiences as a foot soldier and the lack of reliable intelligence about the interior and defenses of the Soviet Union. In World War I, Hitler had fought and lost in the West and assumed that other Germans, no better than he, had won on the Eastern Front due only to weaker opposition.

He and his generals understood Western Europe well and feared the technology of the Allied militaries, especially French tanks and fighters, and British bombers. In contrast, the Nazi leadership was later continually amazed about the source of Russian weapons, as if the unimaginable Soviet losses of 1941–1942 should have magically exhausted the huge reserves of the Red Army. In a March 2, 1943, diary entry, Goebbels noted of a conversation with Goering, head of the Luftwaffe, that "he [Goering] seemed to me somewhat helpless about Soviet war potential. Again and again he asked in despair where Bolshevism still gets its weapons and soldiers." The Nazis also prioritized France because they hated socialist democracy at the same time that they had a perverse admiration for Soviet totalitarianism, Bolshevik though it was. Hitler repeatedly expressed his respect for the career and methodologies of his onetime collaborator Joseph Stalin, whose connivance between August 1939 and June 1941 had allowed him to turn westward, but he held only contempt for Western statesmen, consistent with his system of values that calibrated morality by degrees of perceived ruthlessness.[2]

Western Europe represented less than 20 percent of the landmass of the Soviet Union. Most important, it possessed good roads and standardized rails, and lacked the room of Russia in which invading armies might be swallowed up pursuing retreating forces. The battlefields in the West were near the German Ruhr. Resupply was easy compared to sending material across the expanse of the Ukraine. Familiarity between the French and the Germans, both being of a kindred Western European heritage, meant that the war likely would lack the barbarity of the later Eastern Front. Those surrounded would likely surrender, because they had hopes of being treated with "European" humanity. Hitler apparently believed that in any future war the Soviets would fight well, and yet the Wehrmacht would easily prevail because of Russian backwardness; in contrast, the French might not fight as well, but might still hold out because of their comparable arms and experience. That mostly the opposite occurred explains much of the strange war that followed.

On May 10, 1940, Hitler invaded Belgium, France, and the Netherlands with over three million men, nearly twenty-five hundred tanks, and over seven thousand artillery guns. Yet the targeted Allied western democracies in response could in aggregate muster *more* men, armor, and planes. That fact had initially spooked the planners of the German High Command, who also were concerned that half their conscript invading army had little experience or training. And they had further reasons to worry, because two-thirds of German tanks had proven already obsolete after just nine months of war. Mark I and II Panzers, still the vast majority of German armor, were clearly inferior to the majority of French armored vehicles.

France, given its far smaller territory and lack of sizable Lend-Lease shipments, by itself was incapable of rebounding to mobilize the vast manpower or industrial reserves that later characterized the Soviets' recovery from invasion in 1942–1945. For a variety of self-interested reasons, Belgium, Britain, Denmark, France, the Netherlands, and Norway had never coordinated well their respective forces or munitions industries, and so their paper strength always proved a chimaera. After the destruction of Poland and Czechoslovakia, the small Western democracies had either hoped to fight from fixed positions or expected that Hitler would turn his attention mostly to their British or French neighbors.

It was never the prewar British intent to deploy vast ground forces in the West for a joint defense of French soil at the levels characteristic of 1914–1918 (between 1.5 and 2 million troops), and so Britain kept its air and expeditionary ground commitments at somewhat over three hundred thousand soldiers by May 10, 1940. Most of the divisions that were sent were hastily mobilized, largely untried, and ill-prepared. General Alan Brooke, commander of the British II Corps, admitted in November 1939: "On arrival in this country [France] and for the first 2 months the Corps was quite unfit for war, practically in every aspect. . . . To send untrained troops into modern war is courting disaster such as befell the Poles."[3]

The French military had poor communications, with few radios to coordinate armored infantry and air support. Confused and aged officers were not nearly as able to use their formidable assets as were the Germans. Later General Wilhelm Ritter von Thoma attributed the German armored victory to concentrations of force, especially to tanks and planes blasting away corridors of resistance, rapid movement during the night, and autonomous mobile columns that brought their own fuel and food. Marc Bloch, the legendary French historian and combat veteran of the defeat, agreed: "The ruling idea of the Germans in the conduct of this war was speed. We, on the other hand, did our thinking in terms of yesterday or the day before. Worse still: faced by the undisputed evidence of Germany's new tactics, we ignored, or wholly failed to understand, the quickened rhythm of the times."[4]

The German General Staff had advanced and rejected various (and mostly predictable) plans of attack before agreeing on a more unexpected approach, in part due to fears that original, traditional agendas of a broad assault had been compromised and that their plans had fallen into the hands of the Allies. The quite radical element of the new version of attack, the so-called Manstein Plan, was a central strike through the supposedly rugged Ardennes Forest into Belgium—well *above* the Maginot Line—and an assumption that once the Allies saw that they were not so much outflanked to the north in Belgium but rather sliced by sickle cuts from behind through the Ardennes, strategic chaos would follow. Sending the smaller Army Group C to the south against the Maginot Line would cause most of the French forces not trapped near Belgium to fear being caught in another pincer. Cutting the larger Allied defenses in two, the Germans would emerge from the forest and push to the coast. The Allies who were stacked on the Belgian border would be cut off from their communications with most of France to the south and be driven to the sea.

At first glance the German plan seemed irrational. The British and French together could send up superior air cover. The Dutch and Belgians were not quite paper tigers; together they had adequate arms and would be fighting on familiar terrain, perhaps on the flank of the Germans while the Wehrmacht's main force struggled through forests and crossing rivers. The vast majority of French territory to the south would be still untouched by war, its factories and manpower reserves free to send in newly equipped armies.

Yet after the Ardennes surprise, the French-British force collapsed in six weeks. In retrospect, the reasons for this stunning defeat seemed manifold: antiquated French tactics of static defense; the lack of a muscular and mobile central reserve; a failure of the British, French, Belgian, and

Dutch defenses to coordinate their efforts; inadequate communications and poor morale—all the wages of a decade of appeasement and more than eight months of sitting after the invasion of Poland, along with a fossilized high command of aged generals. Marc Bloch again summed up the collapse of Western Europe as a "strange defeat," given that the Wehrmacht invaded France with almost a million men fewer than the aggregate number of men under arms in the Netherlands, Belgium, France, and the British Expeditionary Force, as well as a shortfall of over four thousand artillery pieces and one thousand tanks. On the eve of the invasion, the French military had been steadily growing, while the Germans were still replacing equipment from the campaigns in Poland and Norway.

French author (and later resistance fighter) André Maurois remarked of the abrupt collapse:

> The myth of the enemy's invincibility spread rapidly and served as an excuse for all those who wanted to retreat. Terrifying reports preceded the motorized columns and prepared the ground for them. . . . the city was buzzing with rumors: 'The Germans are at Douai. . . . The Germans are at Cambrai.' . . . All this was to be true a little later; at the moment it was false; but a phrase murmured from shop to shop, from house to house, was enough to set thousands of men, women and children in motion, and even to startle military leaders into ordering their detachments to retire toward the coast, where as it turned out they were captured.

All this defeatism was a long way from Marshal Ferdinand Foch's famous defiance regarding his embattled French forces at the First Battle of the Marne, some twenty-six years earlier, "my center is giving way, my right is retreating, situation excellent, I am attacking."[5]

The Germans had planned an armored attack that had never been tried by an army on such a vast scale. The huge invading force, in characteristic German fashion, was divided into three groups (A, B, and C). And the senior army group commanders—Gerd von Rundstedt (45 divisions), Fedor von Bock (29 divisions), and Wilhelm Ritter von Leeb (18 divisions)—were the Wehrmacht's superstars. Von Rundstedt and von Bock had supposedly already changed the face of battle in Poland the prior autumn and now were charged with conducting large encirclements on an even grander scale. Group B was to rush into the Low Countries to tie down and push back the British and northern French Armies, with Group A barreling through the Ardennes to split the Allied armies in two. Group C planned to assault the Maginot Line while preventing counterattacks from the south on the Germans' northern flanking movements.

The French had believed that the legendary impenetrability of the Ardennes made it a natural extension of the Maginot Line, perhaps because they assumed all motorized divisions were as cumbersome as their own columns. In fact, the "mountainous" forest of the Ardennes (cf. Latin *arduus*, "steep") was mostly less than two thousand feet in elevation. It was not nearly as impassable as its reputation suggested. Generals Heinz Guderian, a Panzer group commander, and Erich von Manstein, a staff planner and corps commander, both felt that the Ardennes, in fact, offered an open doorway to the coast. The idea that the Germans would dare attack through both the mountains and against the Maginot Line would only enhance their reputation for audacity and contempt for conventional military wisdom. The realization that Germans were streaming in where they should not have, caused immediate panic. "The war," Marc Bloch later wrote while a prisoner of war, "was a constant succession of surprises. The effect of this on morale seems to have been very serious." A year later, a similar surprise three-part plan of attack under the same three army group commanders would mark the invasion into the Soviet Union.[6]

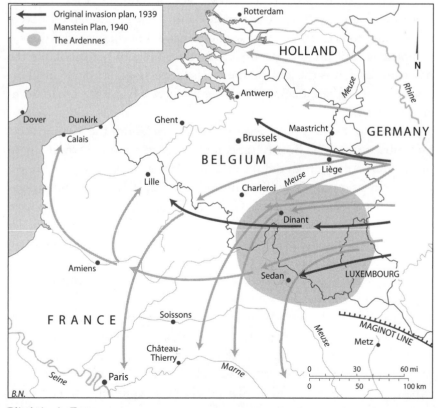

Blitzkrieg in France

The sudden surrender of a half million stunned French troops on June 22 all but ended the Battle of France. But there were still far more armed French troops in the center and south of the country, and almost as many potential partisans—the nucleus of a national resistance that might have turned rural France into what later followed in Yugoslavia under Josip Broz Tito or in central Russia. However, few French leaders called for a guerrilla war, or even for a concentrated retreat to a redoubt in the south. The better of the World War I French generals (Louis Franchet d'Espèrey, Ferdinand Foch, and Joseph Joffre) were dead, and the most innovative by French standards were too young or in 1940 lacked sufficient rank (Charles De Gaulle, Henri Giraud, Philippe François Leclerc, René-Henri Olry, Jean de Lattre de Tassigny). It was difficult to judge which of the commanding aged French generals—Maurice Gamelin (67), Alphonse Joseph Georges (64), Maxime Weygand (73)—proved the most defeatist. The French largely accepted the collaborationist visions of Marshal Philippe Pétain (84) rather than wishing to emulate the Finns. General Alan Brooke, veteran of World War I in France, an admirer of the French, and a British liaison officer with the French military in 1939, also despaired at the prewar French army's lack of morale: "Seldom have I seen anything more slovenly and more badly turned out. Men unshaven, horses ungroomed, clothes and saddlery that did not fit, vehicles dirty, a complete lack of pride in themselves or their units. What shook me the most, however, was the look on the men's faces, disgruntled and insubordinate looks, and although ordered to give 'eyes left' hardly a man bothered to do so."

Both the Western democracies (France, Belgium, the Netherlands, Luxembourg, and the British Expeditionary Force) and the Soviet Union fielded more troops than did the attacking Wehrmacht during its respective two invasions on May 10, 1940, and June 22, 1941. Both initially had as many planes and tanks as the Germans. In many cases their arms were of similar or superior quality to those of the Third Reich. Both the democracies and the Soviets were also similarly stunned by the German army's surprise attacks. And their generals were left demoralized and confused. What, then, was the key difference in their contradictory abilities to survive the first few weeks of blitzkrieg?

Whereas morale in the West imploded, it rebounded in the East. Historians ever since have argued over this strange disconnect, especially given the inverse experiences of World War I that had seen the democracies survive and Russia capitulate. They often correctly cite the vast expanse of the Soviet Union that allowed strategic retreat. The murderous authoritarianism of the Soviet state certainly made capitulation a capital crime. The harsh weather of Russia aided the defenders. And the chronic impoverished conditions of Russia created a desperation not found in France and the Low Countries during the post-Versailles 1920s and 1930s. Yet whatever the precise causes for such different resistance, the reactions to Hitler's early continental wars remind us that hackneyed military aphorisms of the superiority of the moral and spiritual to the physical and material are not so hackneyed.[7]

Yet victory posed problems for the Germans. The Third Reich was immediately entrusted with occupying about four hundred thousand square miles of additional territory in Western Europe, in addition to governing Belgium, Denmark, Norway, and Poland. Hitler never really fully appreciated that each serial conquest in Poland, Denmark, Norway, the Netherlands, Belgium, Luxembourg, France, Yugoslavia, and Greece required tens of thousands of occupation troops that otherwise might have served on his envisioned future front against the Soviet Union. Hitler also never comprehended German lessons of occupation after the Treaty of Brest-Litovsk of 1918, when German control of newly acquired vast swaths of Bolshevik Russia tied down a million German soldiers, ensuring that there were not enough German troops rushed westward to stem the flow of arriving Americans into France.

Hitler in the months after the fall of France toyed with plans to demobilize thousands from the army, so convinced was he that the shock over the destruction of the once-great French army would leave the Western world in utter despondency. In private he worried over the fact that an Allied naval blockade, and years of military buildup and now war were pushing the German economy to near financial insolvency. In any case, he assumed that the Munich generation of British diplomats would soon come again to Germany for terms. Without an end to the Allied maritime embargo, most thought it unlikely that Hitler would start yet another new war with the Soviet Union, which, after all, supplied almost a third of German oil.[8]

Although France fell in less than fifty days and suffered over 350,000 casualties, the German army itself took substantial losses, an often-forgotten fact of the supposed walkthrough. Nearly fifty thousand were killed, later died from wounds, or were declared missing; over a hundred thousand were wounded—a six-weeks' butcher's bill for victory comparable to the American losses in defeat after a decade of fighting in Vietnam. The relatively rapid conquest of all of continental Europe and the war at sea between September 1939 and June 1940 had still come at the cost of a hundred thousand German dead and over three times that number of wounded. The serial wars in Poland, Western Europe, Norway, and the

Battle of Britain—and more casualties to follow in spring 1941 in the Balkans—would cost the Luftwaffe over two thousand fighters and bombers, as well as hundreds of key transports.

Although undefeated in all these conflicts, the Wehrmacht was not necessarily in an improved strategic position even after the fall of France. The victory required a careful balancing act between outsourcing some occupation responsibilities to a supposedly autonomous turncoat Vichy government, at least until November 1942, and yet deploying enough soldiers (roughly 100,000) to keep resistance to a minimum. Soon the Italian army in North Africa was collapsing after a few months of fighting. Spain's autocratic leader, General Francisco Franco—now seduced, now rebuffed by Hitler—would not bring Spain into the war, ensuring that Gibraltar would still control the western Mediterranean's entry and exit. The Wehrmacht would learn that it could neither invade nor bomb Britain into submission. For all its successes, the frightening U-boat campaign had not cut off Britain from imported resources. In sum, there were enough worries for a depleted Wehrmacht, without attacking the Soviet Union, which now shared a border with the Third Reich—to say nothing of starting a war with the United States.

There was a final irony of the catastrophic fall of France. Within a year and a half of the French collapse, the long-term future of Europe would be more favorable to the defeated than to the victors. The free French people were to gain a generous ally in the United States, while Germany was to acquire a multifaceted enemy that it could not defeat in Russia. June 1940 was not quite the end of France; by the end of June 1945 there would be French soldiers in occupied Germany and no Germans left in France.[9]

THE TWO SUPERPOWERS on the Eastern Front in 1941 remained more alike than different: both were autocratic; both had no compunction about murdering millions of innocent civilians; both had made contingency plans to attack one another. Unfortunately, both de facto allies also shared a common border in occupied Poland after 1939. Germany and western Russia were the largest states in Europe. Each had huge armies and controlled a vast empire of occupied territories. Neither believed in the Western democratic notion of "rules" of modern warfare. So a land war like no other would follow on the Eastern Front.

The German army that invaded the Soviet Union on June 22, 1941, once again achieved complete initial surprise despite weeks of blatant overflights of Soviet territory, near exact Russian intelligence about the date of the impending surprise attack, serial warnings to Stalin from the British about Hitler's planned perfidy, and the obvious massing of German troops along the Russian border. This was the third occasion, after the assaults on Poland and France, on which well over a million German soldiers had staged a three-pronged attack without warning. The Axis army of nearly four million was not just the largest invasion force in history, but also the greatest European invading army that has *ever* been assembled anywhere—six times larger than Napoleon's force that took Moscow. The general plan (there was no sense of a master strategic blueprint that was sacrosanct) was to trisect the Soviet Union through vast Panzer sweeps that would encircle and destroy Western Russian armies before they could flee and regroup in the defense of Moscow and Leningrad. The army groups would enlist regional allies in their own particular geographical spheres of interest—Finns in the north, Hungarians and Romanians to the south—each spurred on by their own traditional border disputes with Russia and the possibility of recovering lost territory.[10]

Hitler thought the potential fruits of a victory over the Soviet Union were irresistible: the entire continental European war would now conclude in German victory, German chronic worries over food supplies and oil would fade, the position of an isolated Britain would prove nearly untenable, and Eastern European squabbles would be adjudicated by grants of Soviet borderlands. As it was, June 22 marked the beginning of the most horrific killing in the history of armed conflict, a date that began a cycle of mass death and destruction over the next four years at the rate of nearly twenty-five thousand fatalities per day until the end of the war.[11]

Hitler's fantasies were to shock and awe the Soviet government into paralysis, thereby freeing up eastern living space (*Lebensraum*) for planned arrivals of German settlers, thus obtaining natural wealth and food for the resource-hungry Third Reich that would make Germany immune from British and American sea-blockades of key materials. A continental superstate of some 180 million citizens would supposedly be at the mercy of an eighty-million-person Reich that was already stretched thin from northern Norway to the Atlas Mountains and from the English Channel to eastern Poland.

Hitler believed that his rapid progress across the Soviet Union would likely destroy Bolshevism, subjecting supposedly inferior peoples to either mass death or slavery, and turning the Soviet Union into German-controlled feudal estates at least to the Dnieper, Don, and Volga Rivers. The Third Reich could then build a veritable "living wall" of permanently based Wehrmacht soldiers further eastward at the historic dividing line between Europe and Asia at the foot of the Ural Mountains, and let what was left of eastern Russia starve. As early as summer 1940, Hitler even went so far as to believe that by attacking Russia, and no doubt knocking it out of the war, he would relieve the Japanese of worries in their eastern theaters and thereby assist them in neutralizing the American navy that was increasingly aiding the British. In Hitler's mind, his air force and navy had lost against Britain, but his army still remained undefeated and invincible.

Hitler also scapegoated the Soviets for supposedly falling short of their trade and commercial obligations to the Third Reich under terms of their nonaggression pact. He was especially irritated by Russian aggression in Eastern Europe, Finland, and the Baltic states, as if there should have been some honor among thieves. In early 1941, he whined to Admiral Raeder of Stalin's demand to take all the oil of the Persian Gulf rather than divide it with the Third Reich. He resented Stalin's apparent politicking in the Balkans with communist liberationist movements. Goering later claimed that after the Soviets' sudden invasion of Finland, the Nazis believed that Stalin might strike them at any time. For all Hitler's wild talk of needing resources, it nevertheless may have been true that the Wehrmacht's mobilization and near two years of warring were becoming unsustainable without new sources of food and oil. Ex post facto, these rationales all seem little more than fantasies, but in spring 1941 to an undefeated Wehrmacht, they seemed reasonable.[12]

The German High Command had a bad habit of prematurely assuming victory. In July 1941, the chief of the German Central Staff, General Franz Halder famously wrote in his diary just two weeks after the start of Operation Barbarossa that "on the whole, then, it may be said even now that the objective to shatter the bulk of the Russian army this side of the Dvina and Dnieper has been accomplished. I do not doubt the statement of the captured Russian Corps CG [commanding general] that east of the Dvina and Dnieper we would encounter nothing more. It is thus probably no overstatement to say that the Russian Campaign has been won in the space of two weeks."[13]

Halder would have been right *if* destroying large Soviet armies in western Russia and soon occupying perhaps 20 percent of total Soviet territory could be considered synonymous with the defeat of the entire Soviet Union. But the German theory of victory made sense only if one assumed that the Russians would, as expected, continue to fight as unimpressively as they had initially, or previously in Finland or Poland, or as the French had earlier—or if the German army maintained the same ratios of manpower and weaponry that it had enjoyed earlier in France. Yet there was no historical evidence that the Russian army had ever fought in lackluster fashion on its own soil as it so often did abroad. Nor were there many examples of Mother Russia ever running out of manpower to stop an invasion.

One of the chief architects of Operation Barbarossa, General Erich Marcks, had assumed in his planning that the occupation of industrialized European Russia would fatally cripple Soviet productive capacity. The sudden destruction of existing Soviet military forces would mean that replacement men and materiel would either come too late or in too small numbers to affect the outcome. German logic was that if Stalin's initial fears of potential German power had earlier persuaded him to seek the nonaggression pact with Hitler in August 1939, then he might sue for concessions once he experienced the reality of such force used to deadly effect against western Russia. In World War I, Hitler remembered, the communists, as ideologues rather than nationalists, had been eager in March 1918 to quit the war and with the Treaty of Brest-Litovsk accept almost any compromises demanded of them by the occupying Germans. Hitler entirely misread Stalinism, thinking it an incompetent globalist communist movement rather than a fanatically nationalist, and, in some sense, tsarist-like imperial project.

Despite Stalin's foolhardy initial refusals to trade space for time, Hitler again failed to appreciate historic Russian defense strategy based on ceding swaths of territory on the assurance that the sheer size of Russia would eventually exhaust the occupier while still allowing plenty of ground for retreating Russian forces to regroup. Tsar Alexander I had famously warned the French ambassador in 1811, a year before Napoleon invaded his country, "we have plenty of space . . . which means that we need never accept a dictated peace, no matter what reverses we may suffer."[14]

With the failure to take either Moscow or Leningrad by late 1941, or to destroy the Red Army and the Russian munitions industry, the Germans had already lost the war against the Soviet Union, making their defeat and occupation of European Russia an expendable lizard's tail that was shed without killing the once-attached body. Each day that the Wehrmacht went eastward as summer became autumn, it became ever more anxious to end the conflict outright. As late as October 1941, the General Staff still believed it could take Moscow and win the war before winter, especially given the huge encirclements and haul of prisoners at Vyazma and Bryansk. General Eduard Wagner of the Supreme Command of the Army on October 5 wrote, "operational goals are being set that earlier would have made our hair stand on end. Eastward of Moscow! Then I estimate that the war will be mostly over, and perhaps there really will be a collapse of the Soviet system. . . . I am constantly astounded at the Führer's military judgment. He intervenes in the course of operations, one could say decisively, and up until now he has always acted correctly." Wagner (eventually to commit suicide as a co-conspirator in the 1944 plot against Hitler) would change his rosy prognosis in less than three weeks and thereby reveal by his fickleness that the generals were just as foolhardy as their Führer: "In my opinion it is not possible to come to the end of this war this year; it will still last a while. The how? It is still unsolved." By November 7, 1941, Hitler himself was admitting to his generals that the original objectives of Operation Barbarossa—driving the Russians east of the Volga and capturing the oil fields of the Caucasus— would not be reached in 1941. The next day in a public address at Munich he disowned blitzkrieg, which he now dubbed an "idiotic word."[15]

The Eastern Front saw two general phases of fighting. The brief first interlude was the initial German offensive of June 22, 1941, which stalled on all fronts in mid-December 1941. It resumed in the south in spring 1942, and ended for good in the deadly cauldron at Kursk in July and August 1943, leaving outnumbered German troops on a vast thousand-mile front from Leningrad to the Caucasus inadequately supplied, outnumbered, and facing partisan resurgences to the rear.

When most initial German offensive operations ended, the Eastern Front then entered a second cycle of stubborn and sustained Russian offensive operations, punctuated by occasional German counterattacks. The slowness of the Russian recovery in 1942–1943 illustrated the skill of an outnumbered German army on the defensive, one that gave up the same, though less familiar, territory far more slowly than had the surprised Russians in summer 1941. By 1944 the Red Army—now nearly twice as large as the German army that in turn was for a while longer still larger than when it had entered Russia in June 1941—had advanced the Leningrad-Moscow-Stalingrad line to near the borders of East Prussia and was approaching Eastern Europe. By early 1945, most of the territory of the Eastern European allies of the Third Reich was either under Soviet occupation or their governments were joining the Red Army, as Stalin prepared for the final spring 1945 offensives into Germany and Austria proper.

Hitler's habit throughout the ground war against the USSR was to focus on Russian casualty figures rather than Russian replacements. Such adolescent thinking was characteristic of Hitler's entire anti-empirical appraisal of Soviet air, armor, and artillery strength. General Günther Blumentritt, deputy chief of the General Staff in January 1942, noted of Hitler's fantasies: "He did not believe that the Russians could increase their strength, and would not listen to evidence on this score. There was a 'battle of opinion' between Halder [chief of the German General Staff] and him. . . . When Halder told him of this [Russian numerical superiority], Hitler slammed the table and said it was impossible. He would not believe what he did not want to believe."[16]

By German logic, the Russians should have quit like all of Hitler's initial victims. Half of Russian tanks in 1941 were obsolete. Nearly 80 percent of Russian planes were outdated. But from the outset of the conflict the outcome did not hinge on initial German superiority but on whether Hitler's advantages were of such a magnitude as to offset the vast geography and the huge manpower and industrial reserves of the Soviet Union. Should the Wehrmacht not knock out the Red Army in weeks, the Germans would then find themselves in a war of attrition far from home, amid hostile populations and an enemy that had manpower reserves double those of the Third Reich. Prior to Operation Barbarossa the German army had not traveled on land much beyond two hundred miles in any of its prior campaigns, and had not fought a total war since 1918.[17]

Within six months of the invasion, Germany had occupied nearly one million square miles, the home of fifty to sixty million Russians—between one-quarter and one-third of the Soviet population—while killing or putting out of action over four million Russian soldiers and obtaining about half the food, coal, and ore sources of the Soviet Union. Hitler ranted about his invasion being a clash between Western cvilization and the racially inferior Slavic hordes of the East. There was a scintilla of truth to his idea of a vast multinational European anti-Bolshevik crusade, at least in the sense that, of the nearly four million Axis invaders, almost a million were Finns, Romanians, Slovakians, and eventually substantial numbers of Hungarians, Italians, and Spaniards, in addition to volunteers from all of occupied Western Europe, along with scavenged trucks, tanks, and artillery pieces from now-defunct European militaries.

By 1942 the Third Reich's eighty million people had been augmented by perhaps over a hundred million in Axis-occupied and-allied Europe, while an expanded Soviet Union's 180 million had been reduced below 150 million due to German occupation and losses. Yet the Soviets by 1943 usually fielded a frontline army on average of about six to seven million, nearly double the size of the Axis divisions on the Eastern Front, despite losing over four million in the first twelve months of the war. The anomaly was not explicable by the fact that the Germans drafted a smaller percentage of their population. Both militaries eventually conscripted somewhere between 13 percent and 16 percent of their available manpower pools. The Soviets were also able to put more of their wounded back at the front, while enlisting some two million women in combat units. One way of understanding Operation Barbarossa is Hitler's attempt to fight the Soviet Union on the cheap without sizable reserves of manpower and equipment—if the original invading army of four million Axis soldiers can ever be called inexpensive. He now owned the largest industrial base in the world and yet failed to fully mobilize the potential of all of Axis-occupied Europe, given that the German economy was parasitical and extracted from rather than invested in its occupied conquests.[18]

There were lots of other reasons why the German invasion failed. The original objective was never spelled out but was unspoken and assumed by OKW and OKH: Was it to be a direct assault on Moscow to force the protective mass of the Red Army to show its strength in one colossal battle and thus be destroyed between gigantic German pincer movements, then to ensure the capture of the iconic capital and nerve center of Soviet communism? No one knew, given that Hitler focused alternatively on the northern and southern flanks. As his generals in Clauswitzean fashion harangued that the focus of the front was Moscow where the Soviet army would swarm and thus could be surrounded and destroyed, Hitler answered with lectures on the northern industrial potential and the strategic location of Leningrad and the southern food and fuel riches of the Ukraine and Caucasus. "My generals understand nothing of the economics of war," Hitler screamed to General Heinz Guderian, who objected to the controversial August 1941 diversion of Army Group Center's Panzers away from Moscow to the Ukraine.

Hitler insisted that he had studied Napoleon's failure of 1812 and therefore was not obsessed with taking Moscow ("of no great importance"), whose capture had brought the French no strategic resolution. Still, he and his staff seemed ignorant of an entire host of history's great failed Asiatic invasions: Darius I's Scythian campaign, Alexander the Great's exhaustion at the Indus, the Roman Crassus's march into Parthia, and the Second through Fourth Crusades. The impressive initial strength of all these efforts had proved hollow, given the magnitude of the geography involved, the supplies needed, and war's ancient laws that invading forces weaken as they progress, sloughing off occupation troops, protecting always lengthening lines of supply, wearing out men and equipment as distances increase, and running out of time before autumn and winter arrive.[19]

Hitler's coalition army was perhaps sufficient to take Moscow and Stalingrad, but not to divide into three separate army groups along a 750-mile front that would expand even farther from the Baltic to near the Caspian Sea. The German generals, albeit mostly later in postwar interviews, had argued that a focus on just Leningrad or Moscow might have succeeded, but the long trajectory of Army Group South toward the Volga River both in 1941 and 1942 subverted all three efforts.[20]

Another flaw in Operation Barbarossa was the diversion of enormous German resources for nonmilitary objectives that made the conquest far more difficult, specifically the huge military resources devoted to the Final Solution. According to Nazi logic, the so-called Jewish Question could not be fully addressed unless Hitler moved into eastern Poland and western Russia, the historical home of the vast majority of European Jews. In addition, as German casualties climbed and the war with the USSR went into its second and third years, Hitler increasingly fell back upon the self-serving rationale that the invasion had been defensive and preemptive, a desperate act to hit Stalin before he would do the same to Nazi Germany—an allegation that only scanty postwar evidence might support. Yet for once Soviet Minister of Foreign Affairs Vyacheslav Molotov told the truth when apprised of the surprise attack in its first hours by the German ambassador in Moscow: "Surely, we have not deserved that." Yet in the end, the real reason for invading the Soviet Union may have been simply because Hitler thought that after conquering all of Western Europe and controlling most of Eastern Europe, he could do as he pleased, and do so rather easily.[21]

Hitler, always the captive of paradigms of World War I, found solace in the fact that Germany had defeated Russia in World War I, and with the Treaty of Brest-Litovsk had stripped the infant Soviet government of one million square miles and fifty-five million of its people. In Hitler's view, Stalin's communism would probably not marshal sufficient Russian manpower and willpower, given that at the outset of the Soviet state, Lenin had surrendered these large swaths of Russia to Germany and Turkey in March 1918.[22]

After the victory in Poland, Hitler, not his generals, had rightly insisted that the Army could next wage a successful preemptory war in the West when his cautious OKW worried about supply shortages and operational deficiencies. On every occasion, Hitler, not his commanders, proved prescient, at least in the short term. In addition, the Soviets had not fought particularly impressively in the divvying up of Poland in September 1939 or the Finnish war of 1939–1940. Little was known in Germany about Marshal Zhukov's decisive victories over the Japanese along the Mongolian border in the Battles of Khalkhin Gol, at least in comparison with Hitler's greater knowledge of the Russian disasters of 1904–1905 and 1918, and Stalin's mass purges of the Soviet military between 1937 and 1939 that had led to the deaths or imprisonment of half of all the officers of the Red Army. In short, overconfidence also allowed Operation Barbarossa to proceed without focusing on clear objectives.

There was a litany of unwise tactical decisions that might have been averted, well beyond the sudden redeployment of Army Group Center from its original Moscow route in August 1941 to join Army Group South in its encirclements of Kiev, and the lack of logistical preparation for operations beyond six months. Hitler ordered a siege rather than a direct assault on Leningrad, when it might have been possible earlier to have taken the city. He relieved either directly or through his senior commanders, at one time or another, the Wehrmacht's most successful officers—von Bock, Guderian, von Leeb, von Rundstedt, Manstein, as well as thirty-five corps and division commanders alone in December 1941—often for arguing over necessary tactical pauses or withdrawals. Had the Russian winter that typically favored the defender over the attacker been more typical (a month later in onset, and of less severity), or had Hitler not gone into the Balkans in April 1941 to put down an uprising in Yugoslavia and to salvage Mussolini's Greek misadventure, or had Hitler not declared war on the United States on December 11, or

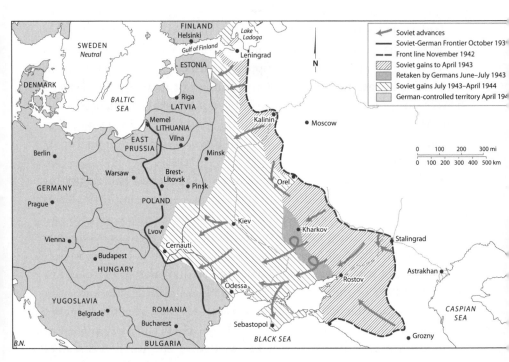

Soviet Advances on the Eastern Front, 1943–1944

had Hitler not again divided the forces of Army Group South in summer 1942 during the drive to the Caucasus (Case Blue), then there would have been an outside chance of at least short-term success.

All those "what ifs" cloud the reality that Germans were also a northern people who should have known as much about winter conditions as the Soviets. In the 1933 training manual of the German Army, officers were advised that "ears, cheeks, hands, and chins must be protected during cold weather." Besides additional warnings about proper clothing and supplies, the manual emphasized that "winter equipment requirements for men and horses must be planned well in advance." Nor was the Soviet Union an exotic Ethiopia or even a distant United States. Instead, it was a known commodity, a nation that had been more or less allied with Hitler since August 1939, and one that had enjoyed military cooperation dating back to the early 1930s. The idea that Hitler may have had no clue about the existence of the T-34 tanks is ipso facto an indictment of the entire mad idea of invading the Soviet Union without adequate intelligence. And the problem with Operation Barbarossa was not so much diversions and redirections of German armies, but the lack of sufficient manpower and equipment for such a vast enterprise in the first place.[23]

HITLER'S DECEMBER 11, 1941, declaration of war on the United States soon proved cataclysmic to German fortunes of the Eastern Front. The serious American strategic bombing that commenced in late 1942, along with Britain's ongoing effort, would eventually divert well over half the Luftwaffe's fighters from ground support in Russia to high-altitude bomber interceptors over Europe. Worse still for German ground troops, by 1943 German aircraft production had flipped, for the first time producing more fighters for the home front than ground-support bombers for the Wehrmacht on the Eastern Front. At least fifteen thousand superb field guns of various calibers likewise would be kept home outside German cities as flak defenses against Allied sorties, robbing the army of too many of its most effective weapons against Soviet tanks. Ten percent of the entire German war effort was devoted to producing anti-aircraft batteries and ammunition, and well over 80 percent of all such guns were deployed inside the Third Reich against British and American bombing attacks.[24]

One of the many reasons why the Luftwaffe could not supply the trapped Sixth Army at Stalingrad—aside from the weather, fuel shortages, and anti-aircraft batteries—was the inability to make up for the prior losses of transport planes during the invasion of Crete, and the later costly efforts at resupplying the Afrika Korps in Libya. For all Stalin's snarling attacks from 1941 to June 1944 on the British and Americans for failing to open a second front, the sudden rapidity with which the Red Army went on the offensive in 1943 was in part due to transfers of German resources from Russia back to the Mediterranean and the German homeland.[25]

An instructive way of understanding the historical role of Operation Barbarossa in determining the outcome of World War II is to consult General William Tecumseh Sherman. Even after the capture of Atlanta, he had forecast that the American Civil War would not end until the South's elite fighters were killed: "I fear the world will jump to the wrong conclusion that because I am in Atlanta the work is done. Far from it. We must kill those three hundred thousand I have told you of so often." What Sherman saw had to be done to the Confederate army was done to the Wehrmacht by the Red Army at the cost of well over eight million of its own soldiers between mid-1941 and early 1945. It neutralized what by all consensus was the best fighting force in the history of land warfare, albeit often unwisely and with unnecessary costs. At times the Soviet army committed nearly as many horrific atrocities as the Germans, and savagely raped and pillaged its way through Prussia. It reneged on almost all its assurances to the British and Americans made at the Yalta Conference (February 4–11, 1945) to allow liberated nations of Eastern Europe to form their own autonomous governments by free elections, once it crossed into Eastern Europe. But more than any other force, it destroyed the infantrymen and armor of the Wehrmacht.[26]

THE RUSSIAN FRONT not only fatally weakened the German army, but also revived the moribund Western theater. England had survived the Battle of Britain, and when Hitler's attention turned eastward, it took advantage of such a reprieve to reformulate its army, to send armies abroad, and with mixed success to attack the Axis powers where they were weakest. With the US entry into the war after Pearl Harbor, the Anglo-Americans would eventually return to France in June 1944 to fight in a way utterly different from the manner in which the French and British had fought four years earlier, ending at Dunkirk. Just as there had been two phases of Soviet retreat and advance on the Eastern Front, so too World War II would see two continental wars for Western Europe: the first ending badly in June 1940 and the second beginning well in June 1944.

In the next chapter, how the wars on the ground turned global after 1941 is explained through a variety of reasons. The Soviets in 1943 did not collapse, but retreated and regrouped in a way the Western Europeans had not in 1940. The Red Army went back on the offensive against Germany without the need of a substantial navy or vast air fleet, in a way that the armies of the Anglo-Americans, eventually to be based in Britain, could not.

A common theme developed in the various theaters in China, Burma, and the Pacific Islands, along with the fighting in North Africa, Sicily, and Italy. The newfound alliance of Britain and the United States as yet lacked armies large and experienced enough to invade either the German or Japanese homeland. That fact drew their ground forces to the circumference of the Third Reich in North Africa, Sicily, and Italy, and the Pacific islands and Burma at the edges of the Japanese Greater East Asia Co-Prosperity Sphere. By late 1943, the ascendant British and American armies had evolved into experienced, deadly forces, and saw their expeditionary fighting in the Mediterranean and Pacific as the necessary requisites for invading Germany and Japan in order to win the war decisively—and to win it on their terms.

# 13

# Armies Abroad

A S THE RUSSIANS slogged it out from mid-1941 to 1944, their British and American allies avoided direct pathways to Germany and Japan. Yet by fighting in North Africa, Sicily, and Italy, while their own homelands were largely untouched, the Anglo-American armies grew experienced, lethal, and well supplied. In the Pacific, the Red Army had ceased fighting the Japanese in 1939 and honored its nonaggression agreement of April 1941, putting the onus of an eventual Allied attack on Japan seemingly on the shoulders of the British and Americans. Unlike Germany, Japan was an island power with a formidable navy, making any landings on the Japanese home islands even more challenging than invading occupied France. Therefore, the British and Americans first sought to peel off rings of the Japanese land and maritime empire, mostly by using their amphibious ground forces to cut off supply lines to the homeland, and to secure naval and air bases critical to support the eventual ground invasion of Japan itself.

THE WEATHER OF the Mediterranean was warm and clear, and conducive to both air and armored operations. In contrast to the later Russian front, German generals felt that "Africa was paradise." Nor did terrain pose serious impediments. Unlike 1917–1918 when the British had sought to destroy the Ottoman colonial empire in the Middle East, Arab resident populations of North Africa were not much of a factor, without strong inclinations to support either side. Both sides fought on neutral ground; perceived victory or defeat hinged on their own actions rather than on external factors beyond their control.[1]

At least until the arrival of the Americans in November 1942, the ground war was fought mostly by expeditionary forces—British, French, German, and Italian—familiar with the North African littoral landscape. The theater fighting is often dubbed "desert warfare," and it was, for the most part—but in a desert corridor that was in many places populated and in sight of the Mediterranean. The armies did not yet possess mastery of armored or indeed mechanized mobile warfare typical by 1944. Nor was there the savagery that characterized the Eastern Front and later at times the Western, largely because the war was not over the home soil of any of the belligerents, and the Soviets were not involved. The Americans had not fought against any European army in nearly a quarter-century. Both the British and the Italians had only campaigned a few weeks in France before meeting up in Egypt. The French would eventually fight on both sides. In sum, North Africa was the first meeting of all the major European Axis and Allied armies, and proved the arena for a sorting-out process in which the supposed inexperienced forces evolved and the apparent veterans stagnated. Because it was the first great front involving most of the armies of the English-speaking world, North Africa is oddly better known than the far more important cauldron on the Eastern Front.[2]

After the declaration of war on the British by the Italians on June 10, 1940, the two were initially the only major belligerents with forces in North Africa. At that moment, the Axis seemed to have the most potential for controlling the African coast. The French navy was soon neutralized. The creation of Vichy France turned Algeria, Morocco, and Tunisia into veritable Axis ground. The Regia Marina enjoyed numerical parity with the Royal Navy on the Mediterranean. It posed a real challenge to British supremacy, given the latter's responsibilities to protect convoys in the North Atlantic. The few British troops in North Africa were far to the east, in Egypt, protecting the Suez Canal and the port at Alexandria.[3]

The North African war initially hinged on whether small, prewar constabulary British forces could survive and keep entries into the Mediterranean at Gibraltar and the Suez Canal open. Had Britain lost Suez, Malta, and Gibraltar in 1940, there never would have been an Allied landing in North Africa in November 1942, and the Mediterranean may well have become Mussolini's *Mare Nostrum*, spelling an end to a key British lifeline. On the other hand, maintaining troops abroad while Britain was being bombed at home was Churchill's risky proposition. General Alan Brooke, chief of the Imperial General Staff, had noted as late as summer 1941 of Britain's scarce resources, vast commitments, and endless debates concerning where to defend and where to withdraw: "These are all questions where a wrong answer may mean the end of life as we have known it in this country and the end of the British Empire!"[4]

With western North Africa under collaborationist France, the Italian Fifth and Tenth Armies—accompanied by auxiliary forces numbering nearly 250,000 troops in fourteen divisions—combined to head eastward from Libya against General Archibald Wavell's Middle Eastern Command of some forty thousand British imperial troops in Egypt. Wavell was a sober and steady commander, but he faced an unenviable situation without much chance of immediate reinforcements. A quarter-million Italian occupation troops to the south in Italian East Africa were static but still unconquered. Another enemy army of roughly the same size was advancing from the west, with the likelihood that some German reinforcements would show up at any time. After a brief war—and victory—against the British the prior month in Somaliland, the Italians had convinced themselves that because of their numbers, they would likely bury the British in Egypt and annex North Africa into the Italian empire.[5]

The huge size of the Italian army fooled few. It had no updated armored vehicles comparable to even the British lighter cruiser tanks. Its sole competent and charismatic commander, Air Marshal Italo Balbo, who served as commander in chief of Italian North Africa, was shot down by friendly fire over Tobruk on June 28, 1940. His loss resulted in centralizing the supreme command under the well-connected Marshal Rodolfo Graziani. But the hesitant and mediocre Graziani dallied for weeks until mid-September before invading Egypt. Without the machines or the supplies to match a British force a fraction of the size of his own army, Graziani privately predicted disaster. He soon got what he prophesied.[6]

Count Galeazzo Ciano, Italian foreign minister and son-in-law of Mussolini, glumly wrote in his diary of the Italian misadventure: "In Libya an Italian general has allowed himself to be taken prisoner. Mussolini is taking it out on the Italian people, 'It is the material that I lack. Even Michelangelo needed marble to make statues. If he had had only clay he would have been nothing more than a potter. A people who for sixteen centuries have been an anvil cannot become a hammer within a few years.'" Eight days after that entry, on June 29, Ciano commented on General Balbo's death: "A tragic mistake has brought about his end. . . . Balbo did not deserve to end up like this. . . . He did not desire war, and opposed it to the last. But once it had been decided, he spoke with me in the language of a faithful soldier, and if fate had not been against him, he was preparing to act with decision and daring."

By August, Ciano was adding even more pessimistic entries: "The water supply insufficient. We move toward a defeat, which, in the desert, must inevitably become a rapid and total disaster. . . . I reported this to the Duce, who was very unhappy about it because in his last conversation with Graziani he had understood that the offensive would start in a few days. Graziani did not set a date with me. He would rather not attack at all, or, at any rate, not for two or three months. Mussolini concluded that 'one should not give jobs to people who aren't looking for at least one promotion. Graziani has too many to lose.'" Italian air forces in North Africa—some three hundred bombers and fighters—on paper seemed impressive. In fact, fuel and parts shortages grounded much of the Regia Aeronautica. Meanwhile, the fuel-short Regia Marina was too worried about encountering the Royal Navy near the Egyptian coast to ferry supplies along the Italian route of advance.[7]

Outnumbered British forces were commanded well enough by Generals Wavell and Richard O'Connor. The British retreated as the huge Italian Tenth Army marched over sixty miles into Egypt in an amazingly short three days. But inexplicably Graziani then hunkered down at Sidi Barrani, waiting for further supplies from Tobruk to blunt the inevitable British counterattack. Rarely in military history had an advancing expeditionary army simply stopped in its own tracks of its own volition. Still, it took the mostly unprepared British almost three months to resupply and go on the offensive (Operation Compass). But in another three months, they drove the Italians back into central Libya, effectively destroying the Italian Tenth Army, taking somewhere between 110,000 and 140,000 prisoners, along with the army's entire supplies of mechanized vehicles, guns, and planes. The British then went on to chase the poorly supplied Italians beyond the port at Tobruk (which was to change hands four times within 18 months). The key Libyan port fell to the British on January 22, 1941. Of the Italian defeat at Bardia (January 5), Anthony Eden was later supposed to have said, "never has so much been surrendered, by so many, to so few."[8]

With air and naval superiority, and resupply through Tobruk, the giddy British pressed on to Benghazi and should have closed out the theater for good in victory. They arrived there in early February 1941, and then advanced further along the coast to El Agheila, well over six hundred miles beyond the original British launching point in Egypt. There were only some hundred thousand Italian troops left in Libya, and the British needed only to stop the resupply at Tripoli of the surviving Libyan Fifth Army.[9]

When combined with the successful evacuation from Dunkirk in June 1940, the inability of the Germany army to invade Britain, the ongoing resistance against the Luftwaffe during the Blitz, and the pushback against the U-boat campaign, the destruction of more than half of Italian forces in Italy reminded the world of the courage of the outnumbered

North African Campaigns

and often overstretched British military. But Churchill—with perhaps more pressure from generals like Wavell and others than he later would admit—reluctantly ordered the pursuit stopped at El Agheila, Libya, in order to transfer precious British veteran forces to the lost cause in Greece (Operation Lustre), on the admirable but unsound principle that Britain's only active ally, Greece, should not be abandoned. Nearly sixty thousand troops would be sent from Alexandria to Piraeus, the Greek port of Athens, in a doomed effort to stop the Wehrmacht's Hellenic invasion, which would reach Crete by April. Over twenty thousand British soldiers would be killed, captured, or wounded—a needless sacrifice that failed to stop the fall of the Balkans but ensured for a while longer the survival of the Italian army in North Africa along with the arrival of Erwin Rommel and the small forces of the newly formed German Afrika Korps.[10]

For the next year and a half, British and Axis forces in North Africa alternated in chasing the other, until the pursuer's lines lengthened and supplies waned, giving the pursued in turn the opportunity to commit the same errors of exuberance. As long as the German-Italian infantry forces equally matched the British, as long as neither side achieved naval or air superiority, and as long as outside theaters sapped equally the strength of both sides, North Africa was stalemated. Finally, two unforeseen events would settle the issue for good: the arrival of a huge force of Americans in November 1942, and the growing German quagmire at, and aftermath of, Stalingrad, which drew reinforcements to Russia that might have been sent to bolster Axis forces in Libya and Egypt.

To rescue the Italians, Hitler on February 12 had sent to Tripoli, Libya, Lieutenant General Erwin Rommel, an egocentric but unrelenting division commander during the fall of France. With a small force soon to grow to two divisions of the new Afrika Korps, Rommel was supposed to coordinate a joint Italian-German defense, stop the British advance in Cyrenaica—the coastal region of eastern Libya—and save what was left of Italian expeditionary forces.

The long North African front, eventually in the west to extend from Tunis, Tunisia, to El Alamein, Egypt, stretched roughly 1,600 miles, four hundred miles farther than the overland route from Berlin to Moscow. And Rommel was to have nothing comparable to the more than 150 German divisions that would soon invade the Soviet Union. Still, he arrived in North Africa at a time when the German army had never suffered a major defeat, and still believed that its quality trumped the quantity of resources of any enemy it faced. In a famous exchange, Rommel was supposed to have told a captured British general, "What difference does it make if you have two tanks to my one, when you spread them out and let me smash them in detail?" Rommel's more precise orders were to wait until May when a second division, the 15th Panzer, arrived. Then he was to tie down British troops while not diverting resources and attention from the impending Operation Barbarossa.

Almost immediately upon arrival with just one German and two Italian divisions Rommel went back on the offensive near El Agheila in March 1941. He was to sweep the heretofore victorious British—who were weakened by the transfer of four divisions to Greece—entirely out of Cyrenaica. North Africa was the swashbuckling Rommel's landscape: flat, clear, and ideal for Panzer operations—and distant from both the controlling Hitler and the yes-men of the German General Staff. Yet Rommel's supplies were inadequate, his tanks near obsolete.[11]

No matter. In just twelve days the Germans advanced 350 miles. By splitting his smaller forces—both to follow the coast and cut across the desert—Rommel caused panic among the British, in much the same way they had just done to the Italians. Within three weeks Benghazi had fallen, Tobruk was surrounded, and the British were back across the border into Egypt—even before the much-awaited April arrival of the German 15th Panzer Division.[12]

Rommel's complete turnaround of the North Africa war proved tactically brilliant and suggests he could have done the Wehrmacht even more

good on the Eastern Front, especially given his ability to work with underequipped and poorly trained allies. "The Italians," Rommel sighed,
"had acquired a very considerable inferiority complex, as was not surprising in the circumstances. Their infantry was practically without anti-tank
weapons and their artillery completely obsolete. Their training was also
a long way short of modern standards, so that we were continually being
faced by serious breakdowns. Many Italian officers had thought of war as
little more than a pleasant adventure and were, perforce, having to suffer
a bitter disillusionment."[13]

Rommel's reinvention of the Axis force was accomplished with just
the German light 5th Division and its Italian cohorts. His superiors
among the Supreme Command of the German Army were aghast. The
original mission had been to save a wrecked Italian army. The Axis aim
was not yet to open an entire new offensive on the eve of Operation Barbarossa, especially as there was no serious German strategic blueprint to
follow from even the most successful of Rommel's envisioned victories.
The generals at the Supreme Command of the Armed Forces in Berlin
could never quite figure out how to square the circle of Rommel's successes becoming too much of a good thing, somewhat in the manner that
George S. Patton's later brilliant August 1944 dash across France did not
fit SHAEF's (Supreme Headquarters Allied Expeditionary Force) pre-
conceived outline for a broad-front, Anglo-American advance toward the
Rhine.

One of Rommel's staff intelligence officers, the well-regarded Friedrich Wilhelm von Mellenthin, thought at one point Rommel might have
changed the complexion of the entire war:

> The German High Command, to which I was subordinate, still failed to
> see the importance of the African theatre. They did not realise that with
> relatively small means, we could have won victories in the Near East,
> which, in their strategic and economic value, would have far surpassed the
> conquest of the Don Bend [in Southern Russia]. Ahead of us lay territories
> containing an enormous wealth of raw materials; Africa, for example, and
> the Middle East—which would have freed us from all our anxieties about
> oil. A few more divisions for my Army, with supplies for them guaranteed,
> would have sufficed to bring about the complete defeat of the entire British
> forces in the Near East. But it was not to be.[14]

If he were supplied, and if his superiors in Berlin had a consistent
grand strategy to further German aims against Britain and a soon-to-be
enemy Russia, there was no reason why Rommel could not defeat the

retreating British in Egypt as he had in Libya. But his logistics first depended on capturing the besieged port of Tobruk, the ability of the Italian navy to remain on the offensive, and Hitler's willingness to send him more than just two divisions. Unfortunately, Generals Franz Halder and Friedrich Paulus of the German General Staff found Rommel a pain, full of "inordinate ambition" with "character defects" and a "brutality" that made him "extremely hard to get along with." The British military analyst B. H. Liddell Hart perhaps best summed up Rommel as "exasperating to his staff officers, he was worshipped by his fighting troops." Nonetheless, Rommel could not persuade Hitler that he had the ability to take Suez, cut off the British from Mideast oil, and turn the Mediterranean once again into an Axis lake. Or rather he was not able to make the argument to OKH that the Wehrmacht had sufficient supplies and the ability to get them to Rommel commensurate with the needs of such bold operations.[15]

By mid-June 1941, Rommel had beaten off all of General Wavell's series of sustained British attacks from the east designed to relieve British-held Tobruk—perhaps the first time in the war that Germany had fought a purely defensive battle. With the British exhausted, now all of Egypt to Suez was largely defenseless. Wavell's beaten forces retreated toward El Alamein, a rail stop just sixty-six miles west of Alexandria. Yet without the small port and fortress at Tobruk, no sustained German operations eastward were likely. So the war entered yet another phase of continued seesaw momentum. Only a third major British effort in November 1941 by the newly constituted Eighth Army under General Claude Auchinleck finally relieved Tobruk.[16]

British failures had lured Rommel to conduct a counteroffensive that faltered for lack of supplies. Now he was forced to give up taking Tobruk and began to undertake a long retreat all the way back to El Agheila, where he had started his original offensive the prior March. By New Year's 1942, Rommel's forces were smaller than when he had begun. And the British, despite their losses, had far more men, tanks, and planes than before the arrival of Rommel. Most generals would have resigned in desperation and written the entire past year off as an utter failure, as a prelude to a bitter retirement.

Not Rommel. With some modest resupply and a growing Luftwaffe presence under Field Marshal Albert Kesselring, he steadily reclaimed all that he had lost. Rommel soon enjoyed almost mystical status among his Africa Korps troops, bringing to mind Virgil's famous comment on improbable achievement: *"Possunt, quia posse videntur"* ("They can, because they think they can," *Aeneid* 5.231). Perhaps Rommel—the erstwhile battalion commander responsible for Hitler's personal safety—won for a time without adequate logistical support because he made his troops assume that they were not just invincible but also professional soldiers who were more a throwback to the German Imperial Army than Hitler's Wehrmacht.

Six months later on June 21, 1942, a returning Rommel finally took Tobruk in a single day, capturing thirty-three thousand British and Commonwealth prisoners. The port was full of supplies. Rommel believed at last that he could resume attacks eastward toward Alexandria. With an initially successful Case Blue—the 1942 renewed offensive into the Caucasus, and Army Group South on the advance to the Volga River—combined with the recent fall of both Singapore and the Philippines, the Axis in the operational sense seemed once again unstoppable. Unfortunately for now Field Marshal Rommel, his supply lines, never adequate, had deteriorated even more since the past summer. Germany had suffered over a million casualties on the Eastern Front, and faced an existential struggle in its drive to the Caucasus, with a rendezvous looming at Stalingrad. The Italian navy had lost its brief Mediterranean parity. America had entered the war and was already sending increased supplies to the British and soon to the Russians, with plans to invade both Algeria and Morocco. Because of transfers of men and air power to the East, the Luftwaffe was losing air supremacy in the Mediterranean.

Nonetheless Rommel sent the Axis troops for a third time into British-held Egypt. He had no assurance that his army could be supplied, and knew well the logistical failures of both prior Axis invasions of Egypt. But in the best—or most blinkered—traditions of the Imperial German Army of World War I, Rommel felt that his own leadership was an unquantifiable force multiplier and that ensuing operational success might create unforeseen strategic opportunities. More darkly, the alternative would be to have static forces wither on the vine and die. By the end of June, Rommel's forces approached El Alamein, just over seventy miles from Alexandria, and encamped in hopes of replenishing supplies from Tobruk. All the German fantasies of nearly reaching the end of the war (seeing the spires of the Kremlin, whittling down the RAF to the last reserve squadron, or climbing Mt. Elbrus in the Caucasus) reappeared: control of the Suez Canal, link-up in the oil-rich Caucasus with Army Group South, and an Axis Mediterranean. But Rommel's support base at Tobruk was still some 350 miles away. Some Axis supply ships could only be landed at Tripoli, 1,400 miles distant. Predictably by late September Rommel's lengthening supply train gave out. Eighty-five percent of his vehicles, in the tradition of German parasitism, were worn-out captured British models, and there were no reserves of gasoline left.

At the second battle of El Alamein, which began on October 23, the Afrika Korps faced off against newly appointed General Bernard Montgomery and his resupplied Eighth Army. Monty enjoyed vast advantages over Rommel in every category of manpower, fuel, artillery, planes, and tanks, including a fresh shipment of three hundred new American Shermans. (In autumn 1942, for a brief moment Shermans were still superior to almost all German armor in North Africa.) Monty was above all prudent, and not the commander to charge into Rommel's prepared defenses.[17]

Allied intelligence intercepts supplied Montgomery with accurate knowledge of Rommel's plans; the landscape of El Alamein favored the defensive preparations of the British. The German High Command on the eve of the battle was a mess. A sick Rommel himself was on medical leave when the fighting began; he could not return until its third day. His replacement, General Georg Stumme, died on the second day of the battle of an apparent heart attack. Hitler intervened, forbidding strategic retreats, repeating suicidal orders given on the Eastern Front. The fighting outside Stalingrad deflected almost all the attention of OKW to Russia.

In over two weeks of fighting (October 23–November 7), Montgomery steadily wore down Rommel's defenses. The problem with a German withdrawal was that the Afrika Korps had neither adequate supplies nor sufficient air cover to save the army. Without fuel supplies, Germans could not advance, yet they could not really retreat either. All that saved what was left of the Afrika Korps was the decision by Rommel, who had finally returned to the battlefield on October 25, to ignore Hitler's stand-fast orders. He would abandon most of Libya and scamper all the way back to near the Tunisian border, betting that the cautious Montgomery would not aggressively pursue and that the Americans would not yet land and march from the west at his rear. When Rommel finally disengaged from the running battlefield, his German and Italian forces had fewer than ten thousand combat-ready troops. The rest had been killed, wounded, captured, or were without any equipment. For all practical purposes, there was no Afrika Korps left in North Africa other than Rommel's remnants and a few Italian garrison troops in Libya. [18]

Rommel had gambled that his tiny forces could be supplied by drawing on relatively idle German occupation troops and assets in France and Norway, as well as taking Malta to ensure more supply convoys. Rather than redirecting supplies from the Eastern Front, Rommel may have thought he could open and win a new theater that might help relieve the troubled German efforts in Russia.[19]

Only a bold effort to hit Alexandria and cut off Suez justified a German presence in the North African backwater at all. Rommel knew that even in summer 1941 Germany still had the supplies to fuel his advance. Later Hitler confirmed his suspicion when he somehow sent considerable reinforcements under more trying conditions to Tunisia, much of them by air, to meet the Americans in November 1942 and early 1943. Rommel rightly believed that his supply dilemma had hinged on willpower, or perhaps on creating facts on the 'ground through spectacular victories that would force OKW to send help.[20]

The experience of all successful invading European captains in North Africa—whether Scipio Africanus's invasion of Carthage in 203 BC, Gaius's defeat of the Numidian king, Jugurtha (107–105 BC), or the Byzantine Belisarius's destruction of the Vandal Empire in AD 528—hinged on relatively small armies advancing with secure supply routes, usually ensured by sea from Europe. Rommel's unsuccessful experience proved no different. But whereas ancient armies knew what their objectives were in North Africa, Hitler's did not—other than not losing too quickly to superior Allied forces.[21]


AFTER PEARL HARBOR and the decision to concentrate on Europe first, General George Marshall, chief of staff of the US Army, understandably argued for an invasion of the French coast as soon as possible. In part, the Army staff was also guided by the American experience of World War I. The United States then had declared war on April 6, 1917, likewise with an army of less than two hundred thousand. Yet from June 26, 1917, to November 11, 1918, the United States had deployed over two million soldiers in France, finally arriving at the rate of ten thousand a day. The huge buildup led to the general collapse of the Imperial German Army. Even though all of continental Europe was now de facto under German control, and landing in 1942 would be quite different from 1917 (France no longer existed as an Allied state), the Americans still believed that at least an early 1943 invasion could replay World War I. After all, in 1918 they had beaten the predecessor of the German army that they were about to meet in battle. Some in the Army Air Force were still convinced that daylight unescorted bombing might render the Third Reich ill-prepared for the defense of Europe. When the US Army was finally persuaded by the British that the Western Allies had neither the numbers nor the requisite landing craft, armor and artillery, and air support to land in Western Europe in 1943, much less 1942, the compromise solution—on the specific order of President Franklin Roosevelt, who overrode his military advisors—sent the Americans into the fight on the periphery in North Africa. A landing somewhere in western North Africa would show the

American people that their ground troops were at last in the fight against Germany and Italy, and help to ensure safe shipping through the Mediterranean from Gibraltar through Suez.[22]

Several scheduled Anglo-American landings in Morocco and Algeria (Operation Torch) were designed to capture the key ports at Casablanca, Oran, and Algiers. Over a hundred thousand British and American troops—embarking from both the United States and Britain—would pressure Vichy French forces to join them. This display of vast Anglo-American power would help to convince Spain that it had been and should continue to be wise to remain neutral. The British and Americans would soon block the German and Italian forces in Tunisia, while squeezing the Germans between the advancing and vastly reinforced Eighth Army under Montgomery. The American Army saw all this as a warmup for a cross-Channel landing the next year—an opportunity to evaluate doctrine, equipment, and command personnel. But the British did not. They instead envisioned the conquest of North Africa as a stepping-stone to knocking Fascist Italy out of the war and advancing through the so-called soft underbelly of Europe into Austria. That thrust might preclude entirely a costly cross-Channel invasion of France and not put Britain in the position of functioning as a launching pad for an amphibious attack on the French Atlantic Coast that would probably fail.[23]

The fighting took six months because a belated but substantial German airlift to Tunis had brought in tons of supplies, tanks, artillery, and initially over a division of fresh soldiers. The sudden attention that Hitler paid to North Africa was an odd development, since during far better times a year earlier he had assured Rommel that there were no such forces to be spared for his Egyptian sideshow. But by the end of November 1942 the reconstituted "German-Italian Panzer Army" had altogether three new divisions to add to the existing Italian army in Libya and what was left of the original Afrika Korps. Rommel took command of what by early 1943 would be known as an enlarged "Army Group Afrika," and obtained some successes against the inexperienced Americans and their incompetent senior officers, especially in a series of battles culminating in their first major encounter at the Kasserine Pass (February 19–24, 1943), before turning the supreme command over to General Hans-Jürgen von Arnim in March 1943. But the Western Allies were pouring in men and supplies at a rate well beyond the Axis's ability to match. And the Americans, after suffering nearly 6,500 casualties and nearly two hundred tanks destroyed at Kasserine to the withering fire of German anti-tank guns, were retraining and determined never again to be humiliated in battle.

Rommel flew home in March, hoping either to obtain more reinforcements or a decision to evacuate. He achieved neither and never returned to North Africa. The Axis surrendered nearly a quarter-million men on May 13, 1943—a loss comparable to the destruction of the Sixth Army at Stalingrad—although propaganda minister Joseph Goebbels sighed that at least most of the Third Reich soldiers were captured by Western forces rather than sent to their certain deaths in Soviet camps, as was true after Stalingrad. For the duration of Rommel's life, he would receive forwarded letters of encouragement from his old veterans of the Afrika Korps—but from their imprisonment in the American South. In a famous anecdote reported in a contemporary issue of *Time* magazine, Italian prisoners on their way to prison camps in America replied to the jeers of one of their American captors, "All right laugh, but we're going to America. You're going to Italy."[24]

Tens of thousands of Germany's best veteran troops, along with their Italian allies, had needlessly been left to fend for themselves. Colonel Hans von Luck was sent by the Afrika Corps to Berlin, presumably as an authentic voice of the plight of the surrounded Axis armies, to beg Hitler to allow a withdrawal to Sicily. "Listen Luck," General Alfred Jodl, head of OKW, told Luck when he arrived in Berlin, "there is absolutely no question of evacuating elements of the African Army, or of considering a 'German Dunkirk', as you call it. The Fuehrer is not ready to think of retreat. We won't even let you see him personally. He would have a fit of rage and throw you out." Luck was then led to a campaign map of the Eastern Front, where Jodl pointed out to him the similar, but perhaps even greater recent catastrophe at Stalingrad. Between the twin disasters of Stalingrad and North Africa, the German army lost over half a million of their best soldiers and never recovered.[25]

The Mediterranean had suddenly become an Allied lake. Sicily was now endangered, and German-held Crete was soon to become largely irrelevant. Millions of tons of Allied shipping could without opposition reach Britain from the Indian Ocean through the shorter route via the Suez Canal with far less worry of German aircraft and U-boats. Vichy North Africa and the fence-sitting dictatorships of the Iberian Peninsula made the necessary political adjustments. The Western Allies' tactical air forces grew enormously. But at this juncture in the war, new German Tiger tanks were still rare, Panthers nonexistent, and early model Mark IIIs and IVs no better than the far more numerous new Shermans. Given their respective performances in North Africa, Generals Patton and Montgomery seemed comparable to the best of German generals, and the British and American armies still concentrated on a single front.

The Anglo-Americans had gained valuable experience with amphibious operations and trained the armies that were eventually to reach Germany. German strength had been weakened by the Mediterranean war; Allied power had been increased.

THE VICTORIOUS BRITISH and Americans next chose to invade not France but Italy. By starting in Sicily, they were following in the footsteps of history's prior African-based armies such as Belisarius's small Byzantine force in AD 535, given that the closest distance from Cape Boeo, Sicily, to Cape Bon, Tunisia, across the Mediterranean is only about seventy-five miles, a shorter distance of travel than from the western Sicilian city of Marsala to the Straits of Messina. The Roman historian Livy records the dramatic story of how the Elder Cato warned the Roman Senate of the dangers of an aggressive Carthage by dropping a fig from a fold in his toga, while admonishing the senators that it was still fresh, given that it had been picked just three days earlier, the aggregate direct travel time between Carthage and Rome.[26]

The British thought that while taking Sicily was ideal for invading southern Italy, history suggested that it hardly would be conducive as a starting point for an invasion into Austria. A better idea, they argued, might have been to attack Italy farther northward from the island of Sardinia or even Corsica. Occupation of either island would have far more easily facilitated a subsequent amphibious landing in northern Italy, cutting off German forces higher up on the peninsula. The Americans, however, saw Sicily not so much as a pathway into central Europe as a way to ensure an open Mediterranean to shipping and to use air bases in Sicily as an alternate method of bombing the southern and eastern regions of the Third Reich. More important, Sicily was the first amphibious operation in the European theater of an unequivocally hostile coast. The campaign was felt by the Americans in particular to be a needed warmup for the anticipated invasion of France in spring 1944.[27]

Three American divisions left from Tunisia, a fourth from Oran, Algeria. They all linked up as the Western Task Force under Major General George Patton's Seventh Army that landed on the southern corner of the island. Bernard Montgomery's British imperial force steamed from Suez, landing near Patton. The British and Americans envisioned launching attacks from a hundred-mile strip of beaches northward to Messina to prevent some quarter of a million Axis troops from escaping to Italy.

Operation Husky (July 9–August 17, 1943), however, was conceptually flawed from the beginning, or simply too sophisticated, given the level of Allied experience and training. Montgomery and Patton were rivals rather than partners. Airdrops—the first of a checkered pattern to follow—were plagued by high winds that scattered paratroopers well beyond their targets. The Western Allies did not send amphibious forces to Messina to block an early Axis escape to the Italian mainland. Omar Bradley and British generals deprecated George Patton's use of small amphibious operations to outflank German resistance, when they should have encouraged more of them and on a greater scale. After five weeks of hard fighting, the British and Americans linked up in Messina, but not before more than half the defending force, consisting of over a hundred thousand Italians and Germans, had crossed the straits safely into Italy. General Montgomery (as well as Omar Bradley) had shown a peculiar habit of winning campaigns while letting a defeated enemy flee to regroup: after El Alamein, here in Sicily, and soon at the Falaise Pocket in Normandy. Any time Hitler did not insist on a trapped army standing fast to the last man dead or captured, German armies had an uncanny ability to escape sure encirclements.[28]

Strategically, the invasion of Sicily at least had prompted the arrest of Mussolini on July 23 and the collapse of his fascist government. That exit forced Hitler to assume control over the Axis defenses, ensuring a civil war inside Italy—a scenario that the two Allies in some ways would have perhaps liked to avoid. Yet the Americans and British had Sicily as an air base to ensure bombing attacks on the Italian mainland. Both British and American units fought well against the more seasoned Germans, losing about as many casualties as they inflicted. Sicily bridged the British desire for a Mediterranean strategy and an American warmup for a cross-Channel invasion. Sicily for a brief time placated the nagging Stalin that his allies were determined to eventually open a major second front on the ground.

Yet the Americans and British still had not reached the European mainland. To do so would require a new series of amphibious landings along the southern and central Italian coast, to be followed by a plodding march upward through various fortified German defensive lines, rivers, and mountain ranges that would not end until the end of World War II itself. Italy had not been formally decided upon as the next Allied step before the invasion of Sicily. But it was apparently the logical follow-up, given the near proximity of large Allied forces and their growing confidence of routing the Axis.

Although it was close and an otherwise plausible target, the Italian mainland presented another degree of difficulty. Even Naples, in whose environs the American Fifth Army under General Mark Clark landed at Salerno on September 9, was over five hundred miles from Vienna,

Austria—more than the distance from the Normandy coast to the Rhine. Nor was it certain that the collapse of Mussolini's government and the new government's official alliance in September with the Western Allies meant all that much. The sudden surrender of hundreds of thousands of Italian troops and millions of dependents required that vast amounts of food and fuel be diverted. Liberated from Mussolini's fascism only to be subjected to Hitler's, Italy now experienced the war on its own ground with frightening new intensity. The Wehrmacht had little reason to respect the property and lives of its former hosts. Italian fascist diehards battled communist partisans, and as most Italians were neither, they got caught between outbreaks of civil strife and also between American, British, French, and German armor, artillery, and bombs.

In early August 1943 the mercurial and exhausted General Patton grew increasingly irate when told of a rising number of combat stress cases in his Seventh Army that required evacuation to hospitals. As a result, Patton slapped two US soldiers on separate visits to evacuation hospitals. Both men were suffering from more than battle fatigue: one from malaria, the other from dehydration and fever. The resulting media and public outcry over what appeared to be bullying ill combat soldiers, in a fashion antithetical to American values, forced General Eisenhower to insist on Patton's subsequent removal from a combat command for eleven months. Although Patton had not been scheduled to lead forces in Italy, he nonetheless sat idle in Sicily while the stalled American army was poorly led not far away in Italy and in great need of his service. The failure to utilize Patton's expertise and savvy both in Italy and in the initial planning and landings of Operation Overlord probably cost Allied lives, and raised difficult questions of military morality. Patton's misguided efforts to increase battlefield participation were at odds with the egalitarian and democratic nature of the American army; yet, sidelining the best combat general in the US Army at a time when competent commanders were in short supply caused deaths both in Italy and perhaps during the initial American immobility in Normandy.[29]

The bitter Allied experience in Italy would be plagued by almost continual command mistakes and catastrophes until the end of the war in 1945. General Matthew Ridgway wisely cancelled ill-considered initial airborne drops on Rome at the last minute. General Mark Clark's caution almost ruined the Allied amphibious effort at Salerno. The Allies had vastly underestimated the effect of winter and spring weather in going northward, as well as the rough terrain of the Apennine Mountains.

The Nazi zealot and Hitler favorite Field Marshal Albert Kesselring (later charged and convicted of war crimes) was underrated by General

Clark and would prove as skilled as the more famous generals Walter Model and Gotthard Heinrici when fighting on the defensive. In strict military terms, the fanatic Kesselring was the German version of the equally gifted but similarly underappreciated General William Slim, the British savior of Burma, perhaps because Slim likewise often fought in theaters that were less known and publicized. The Allies had little conception of the difficulty of breaching the network of winter obstacles incorporating the Gustav, Bernhardt, and Hitler lines, and were stymied both by entrenched Germans and rough weather for the remainder of 1943. They lost an initial opportunity for a breakout from the amphibious landing at Anzio (January 22, 1944) due to the sluggishness of Major General John P. Lucas, who allowed the initially stunned Germans to regroup, when they might have been entrapped by the more vigorous leadership of a Patton. The entire series of German defensive lines presaged the brilliant preparations that General Ridgway would later use in early 1951 to bleed advancing Chinese Red Army troops into South Korea, or perhaps was analogous in spirit to Robert E. Lee's inspired defense of Richmond that nearly destroyed the cohesion of the attacking Army of the Potomac for much of the late spring and summer of 1864.[30]

General Clark, as Field Marshal Kesselring had anticipated, ordered his forces when they finally broke out from Anzio in May to head to Rome to claim the ancient glories of the triumph. They entered Rome on June 4, two days before D-Day. The capture may have been symbolically rewarding, but in practical terms it probably allowed the German Tenth Army to escape encirclement, nullifying some of the original purpose of the Anzio landing. The earlier supposedly diversionary frontal assault across the Rapido River (January 20–22, 1944) had proved a veritable pathway into German minefields and artillery barrages, and reflected the vintage World War I ineptness of the Allies, more of whom would die after Anzio than prior to the landing, often in courageous though poorly thought-out assaults on prepared German positions.

The area bombing of the monastery at Monte Cassino (February 15, 1944) proved a military and cultural nightmare. The failure to bridge the Germans' carefully prepared Gothic Line spanning northern Italy in fall 1944 derailed Churchill's dream of a huge pincer heading up through Slovenia into Austria through the Ljubljana Gap, relieving pressure on the Allied armies in France and occupying at least some of Eastern Europe before the arrival of the Soviet Red Army. The survival of Mussolini's northern Italian fascist puppet government (*Repubblica Sociale Italiana*) led to more civil war among warring Italian factions. The withdrawal of thousands of American troops to western and southern France (as part of Operation Dragoon's expeditionary force of a half-million soldiers) and of the British to Greece reminded the Western Allies that they had far too few ground troops in Europe and likely contributed to the Allied inability to reach Austria before the end of the war.[31]

The 608-day effort to invade, occupy, and traverse Italy, as opposed to shifting attention elsewhere after Sicily, remains the most controversial Allied theater of the war. In terms of relative causalities—312,000 Allied versus 435,000 German—and results achieved, it is hard to justify the costs. The theater drew off resources from the planned Allied invasion of France as much as it weakened German defenses in Western Europe. The conquest of Sicily had already resulted in conditions that would doom Mussolini and sow political chaos among the Axis, but without having to enter the mainland quagmire of domestic factionalism and German retribution. New Allied air bases on the island more or less ensured air superiority over most of the Mediterranean, although bomber bases in southern Italy proved additionally useful in attacking eastern Germany. Most German forces in Italy would still have been kept in a defensive crunch in Italy, away from the Normandy invasion, without the messy fact of a major invasion.

The Italian theater had other drawbacks. British and American disagreements about a Mediterranean grand strategy for defeating Germany weakened their cooperation. To achieve a quick victory in 1943–1944 would have required an aggressive Allied supreme theater commander other than Mark Clark. The impending D-Day landings shorted supplies and manpower. The irony was manifold: Churchill grew depressed that his pet project was a costly failure, while Roosevelt, whose generals opposed the Italian invasion, remained upbeat that the attrition of German forces was worth the effort. Although the Americans had been right all along that the quickest way to end the war was instead to land in France and head eastward, the British had correctly warned that the Allies were not up to the task until mid-1944. In between those two irreconcilable positions lay the open wound in Italy. The crotchety and often hyperbolic J.F.C. Fuller, an insightful student of military history, may well have been mostly right to have concluded of the Italian effort that it was a "senseless campaign of destruction," one with "inadequate means; with no strategic goal and with no political bottom."[32]

By SPRING 1944 most Allied bomber strategists privately accepted that they were never going to end the war with air power, or at least negate the need for a second infantry Western Front in France. The only way both to fulfill the promise to the Soviets of fighting on the European continent and to reach Germany and play a decisive role in the surrender and occupation was to land—as envisioned at the beginning of the American entry into the war—on the western coast of France and to march eastward and cross the Rhine.

The D-Day invasion of Normandy (Operation Overlord) was the largest combined land and sea operation conducted since the invasion of Greece by King Xerxes of Persia in spring 480 BC. It dwarfed all of history's star-crossed beach landings from Marathon to Gallipoli (April 1915). Normandy would serve as a model for large subsequent American seaborne operations from Iwo Jima (February 1945) and Okinawa (April 1945) to Inchon (September 1950). It made all prior iconic cross-Channel invasions in either direction—Caesar's (55 BC), William the Conqueror's (1066), Henry V's (1415), or the 1809 British landing in Flanders—seem minor amphibious operations in comparison.

What made Operation Overlord feasible—aside from Allied air, naval, and materiel superiority and accumulated amphibious experience in North Africa, Sicily, and Italy—was that unlike many of their earlier seaborne operations in the Mediterranean, the Allies were based nearby in Great Britain. Even the most distant French beaches at Normandy were only about 140 miles away from Portsmouth and the British supply, embarkation points, and air fields. For weeks on end and all through the landings and breakout, the American and British air fleet easily pounded Normandy and, as a decoy, most of the northern French ports. And the result was that aside from shredding German communications and rail links, French citizens died in droves. Between the bombing, strafing, and artillery strikes once the Allies landed, and the five-month preparatory bombardment before D-Day, at least 35,000 French residents were killed, roughly equal to all the fatalities of American and British ground forces in the Normandy campaign (June 6–August 25). When added to civilian fatalities in bombing operations other than those connected with D-Day, the total number of French civilians killed by Allied firepower may have exceeded seventy thousand—a figure far greater than all British civilians killed in the Blitz and during the V-1 and V-2 attacks, and all French civilians killed by Germans after the 1940 occupation, and nearly equal to the number of French Jews rounded up and sent eastward to the extermination camps.[33]

Over 150,000 Allied troops landed the first day on five British, Canadian, and American assigned beaches, along with over twenty-five thousand airborne soldiers dropped behind German lines. Unlike possible spots in the Cotentin Peninsula or at Calais, the Allies believed that landings in Normandy would pose far more of a surprise, given the somewhat greater distance from Britain. More important, the expansive geography of the Normandy beaches would not box in the invading Allied armies on a confined peninsula or allow the Germans to focus on a narrow front. Unlike the prior landings in Sicily and Italy, Operation Overlord had been carefully planned for over a year, drawing on the lessons from the Allies' past amphibious problems at Dieppe, Sicily, Salerno, and Anzio. New inventions and weapons were crafted for the invasion, from portable "Mulberry" harbors to PLUTO ("pipelines under the ocean") fuel lines laid under the English Channel and to Sherman and Churchill tanks modified to uncover mines, cut barbed wire, provide pathways over the soft beaches, and bridge obstacles.[34]

Never had a larger, more powerful fleet (Operation Neptune) been assembled in the English Channel to transport, supply, and protect the invasion force. The British and Canadian navies provided over 80 percent of the armada of well over a thousand warships, accompanied by almost six thousand supply vessels and landing craft. The sailors—nearly two hundred thousand—were more numerous than the troops who landed the first day.

The days of the *Bismarck* and the *Prinz Eugen* on the high Atlantic seas, or of U-boats leaving their Channel concrete pens in wolf packs, were long gone. Although the Germans were now equipping their western forces with superb second-generation weapons—from Tiger and Panther tanks to Panzerfausts (single-shot, disposable anti-tank weapons) and Panzerschrecks (improved German versions of the American bazooka) and to the StG 42 assault rifle—Allied tactical air supremacy, especially Typhoon and Thunderbolt fighter-bombers, proved far more the force multiplier.[35]

The successful landings did not go as smoothly as planned, partly due to the rough seas and high winds that blew landing craft off course or submerged them. Partly the confusion was due to the sheer complexity of the operation and to the nature of the beaches, which were far less known than those at Calais. Partly, planners had underestimated the disadvantageous landscapes behind the beaches, especially in the case of Omaha. But perhaps most important, the Allied generals had misjudged the depth of German defenses at the American beaches and had failed to insist on a much longer and heavier naval bombardment, a lapse that probably cost hundreds of American lives. In fact, only two beaches of the five were linked up the first day. Few nearby towns, such as Bayeux, Carentan, and Saint-Lô, were immediately captured as envisioned. The major city of Caen would not be taken for six weeks. The Allies suffered ten thousand casualties on the beaches, including over four thousand dead.

The Germans—in the manner of the French over half a millennium earlier before the Battle of Agincourt (1415), who were unsure whether Henry V's English army would land at Normandy or Calais—were still more confused than the attackers and affected by their elaborate efforts at deception. The defenders were somewhat confident that the main enemy focus would either come far to the north at Pas de Calais or perhaps not be staged amid storms. The Allies quickly achieved a foothold that was secure enough over the next week to serve the huge push of men and materiel that followed pathways in part secured by airborne troops. Allied air power and naval gunfire helped to ward off some counterattacks on the beachheads. The Germans had never quite decided whether to adopt General Rommel's wiser advice to commit the Panzer reserves immediately against the beachheads (before the Allied logistical advantages became overwhelming), or—in the traditionalist view of General von Rundstedt and most others at OKH, especially General Guderian—to keep the armor back as a central reserve to cut off the invaders once they broke out.

In the end, the Germans did both and succeeded at neither. The counterassaults of the reserve Panzer units against the beaches were too fragmented and small, and under constant air attack. Within a week, there was a nearly hundred-mile contiguous beachhead. Within a month, a million Allied troops had landed and the vision of the original planners of the Supreme Headquarters Allied Expeditionary Force entering Germany was now becoming clearer. It no longer mattered whether Hitler's Panzer reserves were immediately deployed at the beachheads or sent in from the rear: Allied air superiority attacked them anywhere they moved, even down to the individual motorcyclist and foot soldier. The widespread appearance of both the American P-47 Thunderbolt—heavy, fast, with considerable firepower and a durable, air-cooled engine—and the British Hawker Typhoon, when used as ground-support fighter-bombers, was worth the equivalent of hundreds of tanks.[36]

The Allied efforts to reach Germany now had two main continental fronts, east and west, in addition to the stalled effort in Italy—and all their comparative rates of progress would become roughly interconnected and at times abrasively politicized. The Russians had complained since autumn 1941 that they were bearing most of the weight of the Wehrmacht. Stalin shamelessly ignored his own prior partnership with Hitler and hopes for a Nazi victory over Great Britain, as well as the huge shipments of British and American supplies to the Red Army. He kept silent about the previous North African, Sicilian, or Italian campaigns as valuable second fronts, given that the Germans had not substantially reduced their Eastern Front forces much below three million soldiers. Nor even by June 1944 had strategic bombing drawn off enough artillery and fighters from the Wehrmacht, at least in the eyes of the Red Army. At this time Stalin also had no interest or little ability in helping the Anglo-Americans against the Japanese in Asia and the Pacific by opening a second front, and most certainly did not wish to end his agreements with the Japanese, who were allowing Soviet-flagged American Lend-Lease merchant ships free entry into Vladivostok.

After the victory at Stalingrad (February 1943), Stalin had believed that the Wehrmacht was on the verge of collapse, prompting a series of unwise Soviet offensives that achieved almost nothing, especially given that Hitler had transferred twenty divisions from the West on the hunch that there would be no second front in 1943. Yet Stalin had regained his confidence after the key Battle of Kursk (July 4–August 23, 1943), and once again was becoming somewhat less insistent on an Allied cross-Channel invasion, a fact that might suggest that privately he understood the valuable role of both Allied bombing and fighting in the Mediterranean in drawing off German resources from the Eastern Front, or felt that the resurgent Red Army alone could overrun all of Germany and even liberate Western Europe to the postwar advantage of the Soviet Union.

Nonetheless, as the Russians neared the Polish border and set to commemorate the three-year anniversary of the German invasion, the Red Army was preparing a knockout blow against the German Army Group Center—Operation Bagration (June 22–August 19, 1944)—which would divert German attention to the east while the Allies were pinned in the hedgerows beyond the Normandy beaches. Bagration would prove the largest and most successful Soviet operation of the war. Over two million troops from the Soviet Baltic and Byelorussian armies—the most mobile of Soviet forces with over two hundred thousand mostly US-supplied trucks—in less than a month all but destroyed Army Group Center. That hole in the German front now offered a clear trajectory to Warsaw. And by July, the Red Army was about the same distance from Berlin as were the newly landed Allies in Normandy.

The veteran Russians were closer to the heartland of traditional German militarism in East Prussia, but the Allies in the West were also only about five hundred miles from the industrial Ruhr and the center of the German military-industrial complex. The paradox arose that the Allies could reach central Germany at about the same time as the Russians, even though they would have been only fighting in northern Europe less than a year in comparison to the Soviets' four in the East, and would kill a small percentage of the German soldiers compared to those who fell to the Red Army. Moreover, the Allies would retake Northern Europe's wealthiest ground; the Soviets, what had been its poorest, even before it was often plundered by the retreating German army. Stalin complained as well that the Allies' progress was only possible because of the Wehrmacht's decision to put up fiercer resistance to the East. In a way, that was true. As early as June 1944, the departing General Gerd von Rundstedt, who saw how the Western Front was draining German resources in the East, remarked to General Keitel at OKW of fighting in the West, "make peace, you fools."[37]

After a brilliant landing at Normandy, the Allied advance from the beaches, between June 6 and July 25 had become mostly static. Montgomery remained stalled outside Caen tying down the bulk of German Panzer forces, while the American First Army especially was bogged down in the thick hedges of the Normandy bocage. An anonymous US infantry officer summed up hedgerow fighting: "In a war like this everything was in such confusion that I never could see how either side ever got anywhere." The Allies may have known all of the minutiae surrounding the tides and sands of the Normandy Beaches, yet they apparently had forgotten that just a few miles behind the beaches, most prominently Omaha, ran miles of hedgerows whose thickets, sunken woods, berms, and narrow roads were ideal for German defense. That was an odd lapse, given that at least a few of the American planners should have been familiar with the French countryside after their deployments in World War I and somewhat knowledgeable of the peculiar landscapes near Omaha.[38]

The deadlock behind Omaha was partially ended by equipping American tanks with welded metal bumper teeth to break up the hedgerows. Soon armored "rhinos" were plowing through the berms, scooping up dirt to create passages cross-country and thereby avoiding the deadly narrow roads. Americans had unwisely initially rejected the full array of British general Percy Hobart's "funnies"—ingenious adaptations of Churchill and to a lesser extent Sherman tanks to meet German obstacles at D-Day. Apparently, ad hoc American ingenuity was less injurious to a sense of national pride than was adopting long-planned British modifications to Churchills and their own Shermans.

To break out of the difficult terrain and stubborn Germany resistance, the Americans eventually called on some 1,500 B-17 and B-24 heavy bombers to smash German fixed positions around St. Lô—on two occasions accidentally killing and wounding hundreds of American soldiers, among them Lieutenant General Lesley McNair. The air-assisted Operation Cobra (July 25–31) breakout opened up a wild month-long war of rapid advancement from August 1 to early September. Speed was now the objective to the Normandy campaign and would lead to vast encirclements of the German Seventh Army at the so-called Falaise Pocket, where much of the German resistance in the West offered by the German Army Group B was trapped and ripped apart by American and British pincers, until surviving remnants escaped across the Seine River. General George Patton's newly activated Third Army, for a brief period, advanced at rates of fifty miles per day—for a few days achieving a pace reminiscent of Sherman's "March to the Sea." The volatile American press hyped the contrast between Patton's audacity and Monty's supposed timidity, enshrining such an armored dash as an American trademark that might end the war outright in 1944.[39]

As British, Canadian, and American momentum quickened, it became clear SHAEF planners had never quite calibrated their planned tripartite eastward thrusts according to the nature of the respective generals who were commanding them and the strategic objectives for which they were intended. British and American differences soon crystallized over advancing on a broad versus narrow front. General Montgomery harped that his smaller forces should be given priority to thrust on a shorter choice route through Belgium and the Netherlands into the Ruhr, rather than having the Allies privilege the American Third Army's longer swing into Bavaria and Czechoslovakia that was to proceed simultaneously with a general advance all along the Allied line by General Courtney Hodges's First Army. Later German generals confessed that a concentrated thrust in late 1944 might have penetrated German defenses in a way that the broad approach never did before spring 1945.[40]

Still more paradoxes threatened Anglo-American unity in Normandy. General Montgomery was systematic and methodical, and was caricatured, only occasionally unfairly, as a plodder. His trademark was the careful and long-planned advance. Monty was determined to take few risks in order to lower casualties, while avoiding German encirclement. He was an unlikely thruster for the shorter assigned route into the Ruhr, much less for a complex operation like the later Operation Market-Garden attempt in September 1944 to take the various Dutch bridges near the mouth of the Rhine and hop into the Ruhr. Nor did it make much sense to stall Patton's ongoing blistering advance as he approached the Rhine in early September in order to focus supplies on Market-Garden. True, Patton's route was circuitous and ultimately headed onward to Czechoslovakia, and his thrust had never really been part of the original SHAEF playbook. Yet by late August, his frantic advance had left Germans confused and scarcely able to regroup to offer serious resistance.[41]

The D-Day planners also never had fully anticipated the impossibility of ever wresting control of the Atlantic ports from the Germans. When the British and Americans finally entered key French port cities, they found many ruined; as a result, supply shortages stalled them as early as mid-September 1944, less than three months after the start of operations, and led to acrimony over competing claims for scarce fuel. The more the Allies landed additional troops, and the longer they advanced from the coast, the more likely they ended up short of fuel, food, and parts, at least until the capture of the approaches to the key harbor at Antwerp.[42]

In short, the Western Allies' advance eastward into Germany after D-Day became erratic, characterized by two- or three-month cycles of both rapid advance and veritable immobility. Much of the slowdown was unavoidable, well beyond problems of supply. The coming of winter's shorter days and poorer weather would limit and hamper Allied air cover. Allied troops were more often camped outside in inclement autumn and winter weather, while retreating Germans were more often in familiar towns and cities. The Americans, British, and Canadians were short of ground combat troops, given the demands of their respective enormous air forces and navies and of ongoing infantry campaigns in Italy, Burma, and the Pacific Islands. Intra-Allied rivalries began to affect joint operations. But above all, the Germans remained superb fighters who became even more formidable as they sought to bar entry into their homeland.

With the close of the Normandy campaign in late August, perhaps a half-million German soldiers had been killed or captured, or were casualties. The vast majority of their armor and heavy weapons was lost. Yet the German army was scattered, not destroyed, and there were still over a million soldiers regrouping west of the Rhine to offer an autumn resistance. By mid-September 1944, the war in the West had stalled in yet a third cycle as rapid advances ceased and the Allies once again returned to their slow progress of the previous June and early July.

Bad weather and new Wehrmacht formations turned the Allies' mobile warfare into a depressing World War I scenario of fixed positions in the Hürtgen Forest, a small area near Aachen of densely wooded hills and ravines on the border between Belgium and Germany, as well as all across the larger Ardennes Forest and mountains to the southwest, slogs that would last for months, ensuring that the Red Army would be met in Germany, not in Eastern Europe, and that perhaps another million Jews and Russian and Eastern European prisoners would die in the Nazi death and work camps. By World War I standards, the Wehrmacht might now have sought an armistice. But the necessary Allied demand for unconditional surrender of the criminal Third Reich, along with Hitler's directives,

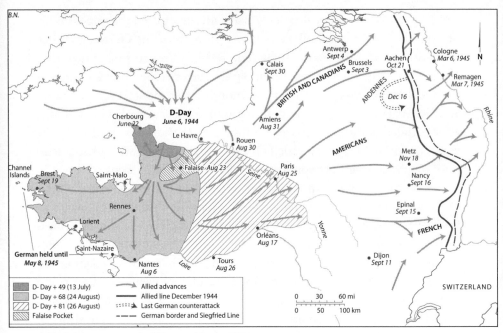

Allied Advances on the Western Front, 1944

required the utter collapse of German resistance to end the war. Oddly, when the British and Americans had announced their demand for unconditional surrender at the Casablanca Conference in January 1943, the German General Staff had seemed indifferent to the assurance of an existential war to the end. General Warlimont remarked of the reaction at OKW to news of the Allied demand: "As far as I remember I noticed hardly any notice was taken of it at German Supreme Headquarters."[43]

By February 1945, German reserves were once again—and for the final time—depleted after Hitler's foolhardy and failed "Watch on the Rhine" offensive in the Ardennes. Then, a fourth and fluid stage of the Western theater saw the Allies in March cross the Rhine and race forward in all directions, often on the German autobahns. In early April, mobile Allied divisions sliced across the Third Reich, capturing hundreds of thousands of prisoners in vast encirclements, and meeting the Russians at the Elbe. Especially later, at the height of the Cold War, debate would grow over General Eisenhower's decision, as supreme commander of all British, Canadian, and American ground forces, not to send his armies to take Berlin, but instead to abide by the letter of the preliminary agreements with the Soviets on spheres of influence in the postwar occupation of Germany and to avoid assumed tens of thousands of needless British and American casualties by operating in the planned Russian zone. Yet it was never quite determined whether German armies would have offered the Western Allies less resistance, had they driven into Berlin, than the fierce defenses that met the Russians in Germany.[44]


IT IS EASY to critique a series of Allied blunders that spiked infantry casualties and lengthened the war, some of them concerning the failure to exploit properly the talents of the unpredictable and occasionally obnoxious General Patton, the most talented of the senior Allied field generals. Generals Bradley and Montgomery were largely responsible for the delay in closing the Falaise Pocket (August 8–21), thereby allowing thousands of trapped Germans to escape, some of whom from the II SS Panzer Corps were eventually refitted and made their way to the Netherlands and an unfortunate rendezvous in a few weeks with British and American paratroopers during the Market-Garden debacle.

Distracted by his Market-Garden plans to leap over the Rhine River, General Montgomery in early September failed to secure the estuary approaches to the major Belgian port at Antwerp. The ensuing so-called Battle of the Scheldt cost the British and Canadians over twelve thousand casualties; the Allies would not have full use of Europe's largest port until the end of November, ensuring a continued supply shortage that would stall all Allied advances west of the Rhine. Another sixty-five thousand soldiers of the German Fifteenth Army also escaped Montgomery's assault on the estuaries around Antwerp, and would join the Normandy remnants under Field Marshal Walter Model, who had assumed supreme command of German forces in the West, to stymie the British attempt less than a month later at the "too far" Arnhem Bridge over the Rhine.

In fact, Montgomery's Market-Garden operation to leap the Rhine at the border of the Netherlands into Germany (September 17–25, 1944) proved an unfortunate waste of resources, and ensured that the war would go on into 1945. It was flawed from the outset: bad or warped intelligence, poor weather forecasting, and poor planning to send an armored column on a narrow exposed road over at least six major enemy bridges, assumed to be secured in advance only by lightly armed airborne troops, many of whom had been dropped far too distant from their objectives. The resources allotted to the failed operation not only led to the delays in acquiring the free use of Antwerp, but also probably took away supplies from more mobile American armies and helped to stall the progress of the Third Army—another reason why the war would not end in 1944. Things became no better after the Allied disasters in the Netherlands and the Hürtgen Forest (September 19, 1944–February 10, 1945). At the

Battle of the Bulge (December 16, 1944–January 25, 1945), the Americans, despite some warnings, were completely and needlessly surprised. The Germans focused nearly a quarter million of Hitler's last reserves in the West on the green 99th and 106th Divisions and the veteran but exhausted 28th, and blew them apart.

More depressing still, the eventual American counterattack on the exposed German salient might have far better cut off its base rather than push it back mostly from the nose. The slow and methodical German retreat out of the Bulge would make it the single costliest American battle of the war (over 100,000 casualties), at a time when the German army was wrongly surmised to be fatally weakened and incapable of such damage. In war, the victor's penultimate casualties are always the most grievously felt—from the Union Army's 1864 summer catastrophes in Virginia to the deadly German spring offensive of 1918 to the disaster on Okinawa— as if there could have been better ways to finish off a cornered and beaten enemy than to sacrifice infantry divisions in head-on confrontations. By the end of 1944, the Allies enjoyed Ultra intercepts (the British-supplied intelligence gathered by breaking German military codes) and virtual air superiority, had sizable intelligence units on the front lines, and were aided by thousands of resistance fighters in occupied Belgium and France. And yet they failed to anticipate right under their noses the largest single mustering of German troops in the West since the invasion of France in 1940.

Among the other miscalculations that stalled the Anglo-American drive into Germany, the American First Army should never have entered the fifty square miles of the Hürtgen Forest, where for five months the confined rough landscape stalled its motorized advance and cost thirty-three thousand dead, wounded, and missing. General Hodges certainly should have been upbraided at best and at worst relieved for such an unnecessary theater—and he might have been, had not the outbreak of the far larger Battle of the Bulge diverted attention from the ongoing nightmare. Once they entered the Hürtgen, the Americans gave up all their hard-won advantages. The forest made air support difficult. The trees and terrain nullified the edge of Allied air and mechanized mobility, as well as numerical superiority and superb artillery. Field Marshal Model may have been outnumbered five to one, but he was a defensive artist known as an expert in stalling enemy advances and he had found a perfect canvas for his greatest defensive masterpiece. Most of these difficulties could easily have been anticipated before the Americans were worn down in the longest continuous battle in US history. When the Americans finally prevailed in the Hürtgen in February 1945, it was only because of the sheer preponderance of supply and numerical superiority.[45]

Better weather and German exhaustion facilitated the crossing of the Rhine in mid-March and empowered Allied armored thrusts into Germany. Despite the Allied blunders, the crossing of the Rhine just nine months after the Normandy landing remained an astounding, if still controversial, achievement. For just a brief moment in late August 1944 it had seemed possible, with some imagination and improvisation, for the Third Army to have bounded over the Rhine into Germany despite its longer trajectory into Germany and the uncertainty of whether such a narrow salient would have trapped German forces on the Rhine or instead would have eventually been itself trapped on the German side of the river. Yet despite that disappointment, the veritable destruction of all German resistance in the West in just eleven months still exceeded most realistic pre-invasion predictions. In the American tradition of intense self-criticism, somehow doing better than expected did not excuse the missed opportunity of doing *far* better than expected.

Historians cannot agree on the relative contributions of the respective Allied armies in defeating German ground forces. The huge Red Army since June 21, 1941, had always faced far greater German resistance than had the British and Americans in terms of numbers of ground troops, aggregate tanks, and artillery; it may have killed three to four times as many German soldiers. But that said, the less-experienced and far-smaller

The Fall of Germany, 1945

armies of the British and Americans had managed to travel from the Normandy beaches to the German interior (75 percent of the distance from Moscow to Berlin) in eleven months, not the four years that it took the Red Army to reach the German capital. And the Western Allies did so at *5 percent* of the Soviet cost in infantry fatalities. Along their long advance, they had dispelled the specter of World War I that had haunted them with nightmares of another multiyear slog in France and Belgium against superior German infantry on the defensive and supplied by interior lines. World War II in the Anglo-American mind has now often crystallized into the iconic eleven months from D-Day to the motorized race through Germany in April and May 1945. Such chauvinism is often ridiculed, given that the terrible cost on the ground of destroying the German army in World War II was largely the story of Armageddon on the Eastern Front. True, but no other army on either side of the war other than that of the British and Americans had the ability to conduct such a huge amphibious landing and to supply and equip such a large army at such great distances from its embarkation. The primary achievement on the Western European battlefield of 1944–1945 was not the British, Canadians', and Americans' outright victory there or that they were responsible for the collapse of the German Army, but rather that they were even able to land, fight, and prevail at all—and at such relatively tolerable costs.

A FINAL EXPEDITIONARY theater was the Allied effort in the Pacific and Asia, where American and British forces, as a requisite for either invading Japan or bombing it into submission, sent large expeditionary forces to cut off Japanese forces in order to liberate Allied territory and to gain air and naval bases to disrupt imports to the Japanese home islands. Fighting Japan was a war in and of itself, sometimes more analogous to the far earlier American campaign in the Philippines (1899–1913) than to the contemporary conventional armored and mechanized collisions in North Africa, Western Europe, and the Soviet Union. In other words, there was a conventional ground campaign in the Pacific and Asia, but given the geography, the Japanese way of war, and the manner in which the combatants fought in the vast Pacific, it staggers the imagination to believe it was even part of the same war as the multiple infantry drives against the Third Reich.

Other than some hard fighting in securing Malaya (February 1942) and the Philippines (April 1942), the Japanese army pressed its offensive war against the Anglo-Americans after Pearl Harbor against little initial opposition. Indigenous troops often fled from the Japanese. There were few British or American ground forces outside the Philippines, Malaya, and Burma. By January 1942, Japanese expeditionary armies had successfully invaded Guam, Wake Island, the Dutch East Indies, New Guinea, the Solomon Islands, Kuala Lumpur, and Rabaul—while conducting major offensives in Burma and at times in China. In February, the Japanese conquered Bali and Timor as they neared Australia and bombed Darwin. Japanese forces cut the Burma Road in April and May 1942, isolating Chinese Nationalists from easy resupply from British and American forces.

The Japanese aim was to secure supplies of food, oil, and strategic minerals in crafting a new Pacific empire, often by easily appropriating prior American, British, Dutch, and French infrastructure. Britain was to be severed from both India and Suez, and the Americans corralled east of Pearl Harbor, as a series of concentric rings of bases grew around Japan that both supplied and protected the homeland. In less than two years, and mostly in the first six months of the Pacific war, the Japanese had occupied the coast of mainland Asia from northern Manchuria to Indochina, and the Pacific from northern New Guinea to Wake Island and the Aleutians. It would take the British and Americans nearly four years to reclaim what Japan had grabbed in just a few months.[46]

Still, unquestioned Japanese military superiority did not last all that long. After the naval battles of the Coral Sea (May 1942), Midway (June 1942), and off Guadalcanal (August–November 1942), with new American carriers and fast battleships already under construction and most scheduled to arrive in 1943, the Japanese gradually lost the ability to land troops where they wished. Soon they could not easily supply their own recent occupations. Ideally, the quickest way for the British and Americans to end the Pacific war would have been to attack the Japanese mainland in 1942–1943 and destroy the seventy-million-person nerve center of the vast Japanese Empire, leaving its two-million-man expeditionary force to wither in China and on the Pacific Islands. Yet that strategy—analogous to the fantasies of landing in France in 1942 or 1943—was impossible for three reasons. First, the British and Americans would not enjoy the air and naval superiority required to attack the Japanese mainland until early 1944. The vast Pacific was a far better defensive barrier than the Rhine or the Oder-Neisse line, a sometime eastern boundary of Germany. Second, the Allies probably would not have the requisite number of ground troops to invade Japan until the war was over in Europe. And third, the ability to bomb or blockade the industry of Japan required possession of bases within reasonable air range of the mainland, and the production of far more bombers and training of more crews, as well as a sizable increase in Allied air, surface, and submarine fleets.

Instead, the initial American strategy was to wage a series of naval battles and air campaigns to regain free transit on the Pacific. Then the United States would insidiously peel off layer after layer from the Japanese Empire, to a point where new multi-engine bombers and naval air forces could mine the sea routes, support leapfrogging amphibious operations, and directly bomb the industrial centers of Japan. All the while, submarines and surface ships would chip away at merchant shipping and blockade Japan's recently acquired islands.

Still, there were a number of intrinsic problems that would hamper these Allied strategic agendas. First, even before Pearl Harbor, British and American planners had loosely agreed on a Europe-first policy that governed the allotment of men and materiel. The survival of Britain was considered more pressing than that of China, and the liberation of France more important than that of the Philippines, which in strictly strategic terms was as much a burden as an asset in the prewar wars. What Allied planners had not anticipated was that the enormous productivity of British and US industry, as well as the huge scope of the American mobilization, meant that even in a secondary theater Allied forces would become rapidly far better supplied than Japanese forces. While sharp disagreement initially arose between the irascible and brilliant Admiral Ernest King, chief of US Naval Operations and commander in chief of the United States Fleet, who hammered for more resources for the Pacific, and General Henry "Hap" Arnold, the commanding general of all US Army Air Forces, who insisted on Mediterranean priority for aircraft allotments, by 1943 their divide would fade as Allied military production increasingly fueled two fronts.[47]

Second, Anglo-American cooperation characteristic of the European theater was looser in the Pacific, largely because of British colonial interests and the American sense of greater proximity to hostilities. The British army and Royal Navy largely concerned themselves with protecting the Indian Ocean approaches to the Suez Canal (critical for the supply of British troops in Egypt before the destruction of the Italian fleet and German air power in 1943), and their surviving colonies in India and Malaya. Despite the veneer of Allied cooperation and infusions of large numbers of US troops, especially air forces, into their theaters of command, British and Commonwealth sea, air, and land forces—which would eventually reach one million men deployed to Burma under Supreme Allied Commander Admiral Lord Louis Mountbatten and ground commander General William Slim—would not be directly joined with the Americans on their island drive toward Japan itself until the final months of the war.[48]

Third, the Americans themselves were even further divided on how best to reach Japan. The disagreement sometimes pitted the army against the navy, the iconic General Douglas MacArthur, supreme commander of Allied Forces in the Southwest Pacific Area, versus Admirals Ernest King and Chester Nimitz, commander in chief, United States Pacific Fleet—and thus a dispute over following a more westerly approach through the Philippines or a northern route from Guadalcanal up through various archipelagos to Okinawa. At the root of the disagreement was whether the United States needed at all to retake the huge Philippine Island group—fulfilling MacArthur's pledge that he would return to Manila—to reach the Japanese mainland, or could instead bypass its three-hundred-thousand-man Japanese garrison. In retrospect, the Philippines might well have been skipped, especially given the terrible losses to Americans and Filipino civilians incurred by storming Manila and the lax measures to combat illness and disease, albeit while inflicting serious casualties on the Japanese. In sum, there was little strategic wisdom in dividing American forces into two rival advances.[49]

Finally, after late 1942, in hundreds of garrisons from New Guinea to Okinawa, the Japanese army had months to prepare fortified bunkers and stockpile supplies. In light of the Japanese army's warrior code that almost eliminated the option of surrender, US ground forces would have to dig out and kill hundreds of thousands of Japanese defenders, a gruesome task that Tokyo believed might take years, would soon tire out the Americans, and might prompt eventual requests for an armistice. Dispersing Japanese soldiers all over the Pacific and Asia made their resupply almost impossible, but also often made American counterstrategy seem unfocused and incoherent. American soldiers—in most cases the US Marines and over twenty Army divisions—were forced to fight a type of war unlike those on all other fronts, including perhaps even the savage Eastern Front, where millions of Germans and Russians were at least willing *in extremis* to surrender.

The trick in American island hopping through the Pacific was in determining when and where to invade (or not to), and to acknowledge that the more valuable targets were usually the best defended and their conquest might be the costliest. Sometimes as in the case of parts of Borneo or the northern Philippines, enemy bases were taken that were better off bypassed, especially since by 1943 it was proving difficult for Japan to use any of its bypassed fortresses, such as those at Rabaul or Truk, to aid the motherland. One irony characterized all the island hopping from its beginning at Guadalcanal (August 1942–February 1943) to its end at Okinawa (April–June 1945): the Americans radically improved their art of amphibious operation over its three-year lifespan, but so did the Japanese commensurately ratchet up their defensive and increasingly nihilistic capabilities. After the carnage at Tarawa (November 20–23, 1943; 1,700 Americans killed, 2,000 wounded), the Americans refined their technique with closer air and naval support and wiser tactics on landing. Yet their final assault on Okinawa—combining the lessons of seventeen months of further amphibious operations—proved the costliest (12,000 dead, 38,000 wounded) of the entire Pacific war. If simply killing Americans had been the proper barometer of the Pacific war, then the Japanese seemed to have been improving faster than the Americans could defend themselves.

After leaving Guadalcanal and the Solomon Islands, Admiral Nimitz's leapfrogging began from Tarawa, Makin, and Apamama in the Gilbert Islands (in November 1943). Then the fleet and Marines and Army units headed northward to Kwajalein Atoll, Majuro, and Enewetak of the Marshall Islands (January–February 1944). The key Marianas taken in

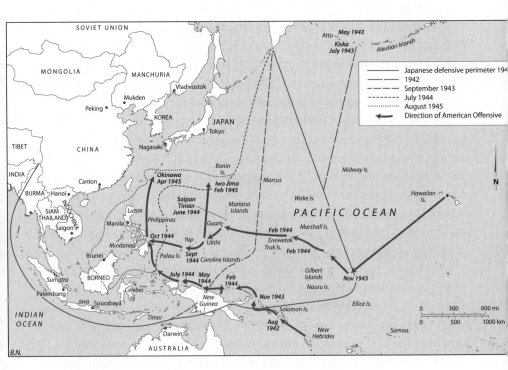

Allied Advances in the Pacific Theater

June–August 1944 were perhaps the most important of all the island acquisitions for future American air strikes against the Japanese mainland,
given their suitability as long-range B-29 bomber bases. The Americans
headed north through the Bonin Islands at Iwo Jima (February–March
1945) and finished at Okinawa in the Ryukyu Islands, about four hundred
miles from the Japanese coast.

Meanwhile, Douglas MacArthur's simultaneous Operation Cart-
wheel, after the Solomons campaign, headed eastward along the north
coast of New Guinea (June 1943), through the neighboring Bismarck
and Admiralty Archipelagoes (December 1943), detoured to Peleliu (September 1944), and then onward to the prize of the Philippines (October
1944). Such steady, incremental advances were critical to ensure US lines
of supply until air and naval bases could be established close enough to
Japan to either bomb it into submission or conduct landings on the Japanese mainland. That said, just the two campaigns on the Philippines
and Okinawa cost American and Allied air and land forces over 150,000
American casualties, but neither island group then factored into the air
campaigns that eventually ended the war.[50]

The US Marines alone had over a hundred thousand casualties spear-
heading island hopping. The Army lost around two hundred thousand
killed, wounded, and missing. In addition, the Army Air Force suffered
twenty-four thousand total casualties in the Pacific, in partnership with
the Navy's own efforts to destroy the Imperial Japanese Fleet, while
achieving campaign kill ratios ranging from three-to-one to ten-to-one
against Japanese island defenders. Both Army and Marine commanders
under MacArthur and Nimitz soon discovered a disconnect about these
operations: unparalleled naval barrages and constant bombing softened
up the islands, but did not always materially weaken the Japanese ability to resist attack, at least immediately. And precisely because the Marines and amphibious army units proved such effective soldiers, and the
US Navy a superb supporting force, expectations for always quicker, less
costly, and more frequent campaigns followed each impressive victory,
especially in light of the fact that by mid-1943 there was little chance of
ultimate Japanese success.

The final outcome in the Pacific was largely foreordained by American manpower and materiel superiority. There was little chance that the
United States would run out of either supplies or men, and none that it
would lose heart and call off its amphibious campaign. Nor was there
much mystery, from late 1942 to summer 1945, over how many Japanese
would die. The death toll could be accurately approximated by the total
number of soldiers stationed on all those island garrisons that were not

bypassed. The final paradox of the island hopping strategy was that it alone provided the necessary air bases for atomic attacks on the Japanese mainland, which in turn precluded the climax of island hopping itself: a frontal amphibious assault on the Japanese home islands.

Two themes characterized the expeditionary campaigns of World War II that were waged simultaneously with the Soviet-Axis bloodbath on the Eastern Front. The Western Allies, which were not contiguous by land to their enemies, had neither the immediate willingness nor the initial amphibious ability to invade the homelands of Germany and Japan, given the anticipated ferocity of respective Axis militaries fighting on home soil. Instead, the British and Americans first chose to weaken their opponents by landing troops in the Mediterranean, the Pacific, and Asia on the periphery of the two major Axis powers, in order both to whittle down enemy manpower and cut off supplies to Germany and Japan. Despite serious losses and quagmires in Italy and the Philippines and on Okinawa, Allied expeditionary ground forces won all their campaigns, largely because of superior naval and air forces. The Axis powers belatedly recognized that they had spread their own troops far too widely and thinly to fight a global war, especially against the world's two largest navies and strategic bomber fleets.

A second fact aided the Allies: their division of global responsibilities was not matched by the three Axis nations. Whereas the German army was bled white by the Red Army in Russia, and the Japanese were bogged down in China, neither the British nor the Americans, at least after mid-1940 and before mid-1944, were engaged in continental wars. As a result, during those four years, Britain and America were usually freer than Germany and Japan to bring more troops and supplies to a series of overseas fronts. Moreover, the Axis expeditionary ground forces were almost always fighting on the defensive. The multidimensional skills acquired by mobile fighting in North Africa, Sicily, and Italy, especially the use of close ground support and naval supply, gave the Western Allies enormous advantages when they did meet the German army in France, specifically their increasing expertise at moving, protecting, and supplying armies. Moreover, once Axis air and naval support was neutralized abroad, German, Italian, and Japanese ground troops were usually trapped, either to be wiped out on islands like the Marianas and Iwo Jima or forced to surrender en masse as in Tunisia.

In sum, the expeditionary wars ended in quite opposite fashion for the respective belligerents. The Western Allies won battles, gained experience, and honed their skills, as they moved always closer to their enemies' homelands, and without much interest in annexing and exploiting the lands that they fought on and conquered. In contrast, the Axis powers, which had sent their ground forces abroad early in the war—often with tenuous supplies and support, with the assumption that they would be fighting against weaker or inexperienced opponents, and with the idea of acquiring overseas territories—suffered disaster. Few of the many sent abroad came home.

Apart from the great continental wars and the expeditionary campaigns, there was a third and most ancient sort of ground fighting in World War II: the besieging of cities and strongholds discussed in the next chapter. While many sieges were more iconic than transformational, a few were not—and they changed the course of the entire war.

# 14

# Sieges

I LIVED FOR a time in the late 1970s on Mikras Asias Street in the Zographou section of Athens. The neighbors sometimes talked of "Black Tuesday." They were referring to Tuesday, May 29, 1453, when Constantinople fell. I gathered from residents that it was likely that an angel had rescued the emperor, Constantine XI Dragases Palaiologos, minutes before he supposedly charged to his death against the Islamic hordes. Constantine had been delivered and turned to stone, or perhaps he was still suspended in marbleized animation. One day he would once again wake up, become flesh, and lead Orthodox Greek-speaking Christians on a crusade to take back their millennium-old capital of Hellenism from the Turks, with Constantinople the center of a Greek Aegean lake.

Many elderly in the neighborhood had arrived in Zographou as refugees from Ionia after 1922, a half-century earlier, having fled a burning Smyrna ahead of a new Turkish army. They often went on to amplify Edward Gibbon's account of the fall of Constantinople, with folk tales of the desperate survivors waiting inside beneath the dome of the Cathedral of Holy Wisdom for the arrival of an archangel who would save them before the Ottoman Janissaries burst through the great doors.

A half millennium had passed since the capture of Constantinople by the Ottomans, but my district of Athens, and much of Greece of the 1970s, still equated the siege of Byzantium with not just the collapse of Hellenism—the ancient idea of a Greek-speaking Mediterranean from Asia Minor to Egypt—but of civilization itself. Sieges against people resonate tragedy like no other manifestation of battle. The Fall of Constantinople or the Sieges of Vienna are more than battles. They become iconic of the fate of culture—history's flashpoints or perhaps metaphors of conflict itself. The sieges of World War II were not much different, and took place in the Pacific, Asia, Russia, North Africa, and Europe.[1]

IT IS EASY to calibrate in strategic terms and geographical diversity the importance of siegecraft in World War II. Hitler finally saw sieges as the only way of slowing down the Allied advances in 1944–1945. At various times declaring that Warsaw, Budapest, Kohlberg, Königsberg, Küstrin, Danzig, and Breslau had become *Festungen* ("fortresses"; sing. *Festung*) meant that the advancing Red Army might be bled white as it periodically bogged down in block-by-block fighting—a reverse Stalingrad many times over. By late 1944, Hitler the nihilist cared little whether the resulting collateral damage inordinately killed Poles, Czechs, Hungarians, or even Germans. In like manner, Hitler's Atlantic port fortresses in the West, such as Brest, Calais, Dieppe, Dunkirk, Le Havre, and Saint-Malo, were never in mid-1944 expected to see ships again, or indeed even to survive, but only to disrupt Allied advances.

The civilian body count was often a savage reminder of the importance of siegecraft in the war. More than one million died at Leningrad amid mass starvation, epidemics, cannibalism, and daily barrages—a greater toll than any siege in history. There were over two hundred thousand Russians and Germans killed in the final siege of Berlin. More German women were likely raped there than during any siege of the past.[2]

The fighting inside a besieged Stalingrad proved to be the most costly single battle of World War II. At least 1.5 million Russians and Germans died over months of contesting the city's rubble, comparable only to the World War I German attack on the fortress complex at Verdun. Indeed, the deadliest front of the war, the Eastern, ultimately hinged on taking just three cities: Leningrad, Moscow, and Stalingrad. That the triad survived may have explained the larger failure of Operation Barbarossa. The European war itself ended when Berlin was successfully captured—or rather besieged, bombed, and shelled into ruin. We remember names of less existential encounters, like the otherwise obscure strongholds at Corregidor and Tobruk, largely because sieges are always the stuff of mass surrender or heroic resistance, and can demoralize or inspire an entire people well beyond their strategic importance.

The mass death at Leningrad or the relentless destruction that rained down on Monte Cassino (January 17–May 18, 1944) might be explained by the spiking anger of the besiegers over their inability to capture or even bypass their targets. Although World War II attackers did not, in sixteenth-century fashion, catapult the heads of prisoners inside the walls of Sevastopol, they could fire, as the Germans did at Sevastopol, a huge 31-inch rail gun ("Gustav") that blew apart far more flesh and bone with its fourteen-thousand-pound shells than any devilry that Demetrius I

("The Besieger") or Mehmed II ("The Conqueror") could conjure up. The horrors of Leningrad, from pestilence to cannibalism, were medieval.

Of Hitler's Festung siege defenses, three were especially brutal: Budapest (December 29, 1944–February 13, 1945), Breslau (February 15–May 6, 1945), and Berlin (April 16–May 2, 1945). In all three, the retreating German armies vainly sought to create their own Leningrad or Stalingrad that might exhaust the Red Army amid the rubble and lead to better terms of surrender. Or the besieged thought that the Red Army could be slowed down enough to allow other Germans, both civilians and military, to reach British and American lines.

Furious German resistance was also predicated on nothing other than the fact that there were no other options, and surrender to the Soviet forces was felt to offer no better choice than fighting to the death. Somewhere around one million Soviet and Axis troops were killed, wounded, or missing in the fighting in and around Budapest, Breslau, and Berlin, with the Soviet victors losing more aggregate casualties (600,000?) than the besieged and defeated Germans (500,000?). German-occupied cities now fell in a way that Soviet ones earlier had not, largely because the Russian besiegers enjoyed not numerical parity, as had the Wehrmacht in 1941–1942, but rather overwhelming superiority at rates exceeding five to one.

The combination of *siege* and *World War II* immediately invokes two horrific names: Leningrad and Stalingrad. New force multipliers made the old agendas of previous invaders of Russia—whether the 1708 attack by Charles XII of Sweden or the grand failure of Napoleon in 1812—far more deadly for all involved. Totalitarian ideologies framed the struggle in Manichean terms unlike anything seen in the rivalries of the past. Hitler planned a war of Nazi extermination to either kill off or enslave the supposedly inferior race of Slavic *Untermenschen* of Russia and liquidate millions of Jews in his eastward path.

In turn, Russian resistance was couched in terms of communism's existential defense against fascism. Lives were not spared when it was a question of the very survival of the state *apparat*. Both civilians and prisoners were considered fair game. Both states mobilized a level of forces against the enemy, and employed a degree of coercion against their own citizens on a scale unseen before: the Nazis intended to level their besieged targets, buildings as well as people. The Soviets in turn preferred to see their own entrapped citizens perish if the Wehrmacht might be delayed or stymied than declare a Leningrad or Stalingrad an open city, or systematically evacuate urban residents.

Before he faltered, Hitler had promised to wipe Leningrad off the map and implied the same for Moscow ("Moscow . . . must disappear from the earth's surface") and Stalingrad. Stalingrad only survived in the sense that the Russians won the rubble that was left of the city. Berlin was captured and all but destroyed. Germans in Berlin saw their impending defeat as a mirror of what they had wished to do to Leningrad, and expected commensurate vengeance from the Russians.

A failed effort to storm a stronghold often left the exhausted and depleted attackers in almost as dire circumstances as those in a captured city. Army Group North never quite recovered its momentum once Leningrad did not fall. By late 1941 the would-be besiegers of Moscow were for a time in danger of becoming the besieged. In a matter of weeks, the German Sixth Army went from virtually conquering Stalingrad to being virtually destroyed by the very attempt.[3]

The capture of a stronghold or city was often iconic quite aside from the cost to the doomed defenders. Britain suffered its two greatest psychological defeats in its long military history with the nearly inexplicable surrenders of Singapore and Tobruk, both the result of utter incompetence of the commanders in charge. Both Hitler and Churchill accepted that encircling cities could convey a sense of defeat in a way disproportionate to the cities' actual strategic importance, and conversely that withstanding the siege could encourage a sense of salvation. Of the dozens of great and minor sieges in World War II, however, only two might have changed the outcome of the war. Had Leningrad quickly fallen by August 1941, or had Stalingrad on the arrival of the German Sixth Army promptly succumbed a year later, the Russian front would have looked quite different by late 1942.

Otherwise, even the dramatic fall of a Tobruk did not necessarily alter the ultimate course of the war. The capture of a Berlin or Breslau in 1945 was never really in doubt. Even the defeats at Singapore and Corregidor, as psychologically damaging as they were to the British and the Americans, did not much change the eventual outcome in the Pacific. That many German-controlled Atlantic ports survived until the war's end, or that Sevastopol fell in 1942, ultimately did not alter the verdict of either the Western or the Eastern Front.

In the past, the collapse of entire civilizations—Carthaginian (146 BC), Jewish (AD 70), the Abbasid Caliphate (1258), Byzantine (1453), Al-Andalus (1492), and Aztec (1521)—often followed the capitulation of their capital or largest cities. It is understandable that even in the twentieth century the fate of a Leningrad, London, Malta, Moscow, or

Stalingrad marked at least a temporary shift in the direction of the war. In most theaters of World War II, armies headed for capitals: the Nazis thought the fall of Paris doomed France just as the Allies did when they later bartered over who would storm Berlin. Operation Barbarossa aimed at taking Leningrad, Moscow, and Kiev.[4]

The majority of the major sieges of World War II proved successful— Berlin, Breslau, Budapest, Corregidor, Sevastopol, Singapore, and To- bruk. Yet the most decisive and lethal sieges, either by land or air, at Leningrad, Stalingrad, and Malta—replete with constant bombing—all failed. As a general rule, Axis sieges (e.g., Singapore, Corregidor, or To- bruk) were effective before mid-1942, when Germany, Italy, and Japan had air or naval superiority or at least rough military parity with their enemies. After that turning point, the Axis usually failed and the Allies took most of the strongholds they targeted or themselves survived when besieged, given the growing reversal in relative logistics and air power.

In all the changing landscapes of war—from submarines beneath the sea to bombers above twenty thousand feet—successful operations hinged on advantages in supply, logistics, aggregate experience, man- power, technology, morale, and generalship. At exception were the final redoubts of the Japanese and Germans when faced with overwhelming odds. The Allies assumed that their Axis enemies ensconced by 1944 in Singapore, Corregidor, and the Atlantic fortified ports would not surren- der as they themselves had earlier when surrounded in these exact same fortresses. As a result, they often decided that they would not suffer much strategic disadvantage by simply delaying assaults until later in the war (e.g., Corregidor) or bypassing such fortresses (Singapore), many of which surrendered only at the end of the conflict.

While the widespread use of rebar and other forms of reinforced con- crete helped the besieged, defenders also had recourse to their own artil- lery and air assets to neutralize air attack—flak, anti-aircraft guns, and fighter planes. Besieged populations could sometimes be resupplied by air or sea, or at least by ground or naval forces protected by air cover. As was frequent in the long history of siegecraft, better defense prompted an improved offensive response.[5]

There were plenty of sieges in World War I, but none where air power proved significant. Yet just two decades later, for the first time in history, fixed citadels and cities were subject not just to distant artillery, but also to regular and heavy aerial bombing. The Soviets, for example, would fire over a million shells into Berlin, but mostly after the city had almost been reduced to rubble by Allied bombers. Even if aircraft could not obliterate a city without sustained air superiority, planes could at least provide cover for the attacks of the besiegers and prevent relief columns from reaching the trapped garrison.[6]

Indeed, one reason why there were not even more sieges in World War II's vast intercontinental arena of conflict was the preference for aerial destruction, a nihilistic siege by bombers without the costly use of ground troops. Hitler, who never invested in heavy bombers, talked of razing entire cities of the Soviet Union, but lacked the resources to wipe away Leningrad and Moscow in the manner that the Allies bombed the urban cores of Hamburg, Dresden, and Tokyo into rubble. There were numerous destructive "sieges" of this sort conducted against Cologne, Dresden, Hamburg, London, and most of the major Japanese cities, with a motive of destroying or terrorizing rather than capturing the urban core. Yet even among the debris of a bombed-out city, what little was left was not captured until infantry caught up with the planes and physically occupied the rubble.

The armies of World War II sometimes besieged the same cities that, given the timeless referents of history and geography, had always been strategic linchpins in past wars. Replace the Ottoman Janissaries with the Luftwaffe and the Regia Aeronautica, and some four centuries later the walls of Malta once more were battered by the invader. Hitler may have been encouraged, and at times confused, by the successful Napoleonic assault on Moscow, and perhaps by the earlier conflagration set by the Crimean Tatars in 1571 that engulfed the city. Sevastopol had never been bombed before the arrival of the Germans, but it had been besieged, shelled, and captured by Western Europeans in 1855.[7]

The German encirclement of Leningrad was the longest and most lethal siege in history at 872 days. When it began on September 8, 1941, Leningrad was the largest city—at 2.5 million inhabitants—ever to endure complete envelopment. Yet amid Nazi bombing, artillery strikes, starvation, disease, the cold, and the desperate effort to evacuate the blockaded city, Leningrad nevertheless was among the first major sieges of the twentieth century to fail.[8]

Nearly four million Russian soldiers were killed, wounded, went missing, or were captured in the fighting in and around Leningrad and on the nearby Baltic front during the siege. Indeed, the Red Army suffered 14 percent of all its World War II casualties defending the single city and key port on the Gulf of Finland. Russian dead in and around

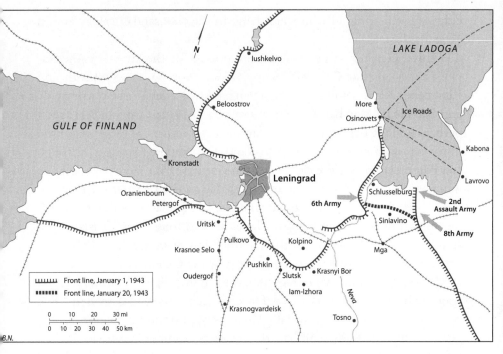

The Siege of Leningrad

Leningrad were *four times greater* than the death toll of *all* Americans lost in World War II.[9]

Leningrad—known as St. Petersburg before 1914 and then Petrograd between 1914 and 1924—also may have been the first major attempt of attackers, since the final days of Tenochtitlán (1521), to extinguish rather than to seize a city, although Hernán Cortés, unlike Hitler, originally had not planned to kill its inhabitants altogether. "The Fuehrer has decided to erase the city of Petersburg from the face of the earth," read a Nazi directive. "We propose to closely blockade the city and erase it from the earth by means of artillery fire of all caliber and continuous bombardment from the air."[10]

Even the Romans who had leveled Carthage and the Ottomans who sacked Constantinople did not envision killing *all* the besieged as Hitler planned at Leningrad ("I have no interest in the further existence of this large population point after the defeat of Soviet Russia"). In the end the opposite occurred, and Leningrad ground down Hitler's Army Group North into a shell of its former self even as Pearl Harbor, the Japanese ascendency in the Pacific, the Stalingrad nightmare, Kursk, and the Italian campaign all took world attention away from besiegers and the trapped citizenry at Leningrad who were dying in the thousands per day and in obscurity.[11]

Three German army groups were poised for the attack on the Soviet Union on June 22, 1941. Army Group North—the Sixteenth and Eighteenth Armies and the Fourth Panzer Army—led by the purportedly anti-Nazi Field Marshal Wilhelm Ritter von Leeb, was the smallest. Yet it perhaps had the best chance of obtaining its objectives. Some twenty-nine divisions of about 655,000 infantry and air personnel stormed through the Baltic states and the northwestern border of the Soviet Union. Simultaneously, the Finns—the most capable of the Germans' European allies—approached southward toward Leningrad with perhaps a quarter million of their own troops. The latter had fought the Russians to a standstill in 1939, and yet in the continuation of that war in 1941 were never given adequate military equipment by the Germans.

Colonel General F. I. Kuznetsov's "Baltic Special Military District," whose charge was the defense of Leningrad, was inadequately equipped and poorly led. Initially Kuznetsov (soon to be relieved in August) commanded less than half the invaders' number, or about 370,000 total troops. The Russians, however, enjoyed the advantage of fighting on familiar ground. For a while, they drew on the vast manpower and munitions industries of Leningrad itself. The defenders began the battle with an impressive number of tanks, artillery pieces, and planes. That said, General von Leeb in the days preceding his arrival before the city, assumed that the Luftwaffe would have at least softened up Leningrad. That may have been an odd conjecture, given that Luftwaffe bombers, despite enjoying air superiority, had never really broken the will of any Russian city. For example, German air forces would conduct ninety major raids on Moscow and drop over fifty thousand incendiaries in achieving almost no strategic results.[12]

The five-hundred-mile route of advance of Army Group North, from staging areas around Königsberg in East Prussia to the suburbs of Leningrad, was somewhat shorter than the Wehrmacht's central axis to Moscow or the southern path to Kiev and on to the distant Caucasus. The pathway was well known to Germans who had reached within a hundred miles of Petrograd (St. Petersburg) in March 1918. Unlike Hitler's other two Army Groups, Central and South, Group North's divisions passed much of their way on sympathetic ground. The people of the recently Russian-occupied Baltic states saw von Leeb's troops as liberators. Lithuanians, Latvians, and Estonians anticipated the German arrival by staging insurrections against Soviet occupiers, as if new foreign authoritarians might be better than old totalitarians.

The Finnish national army had proved itself against the Russians and was the most knowledgeable of Hitler's allies of the Soviet way of war, and yet also abided by the Finnish unwritten understanding with Stalin that after 1940 neither the Finns nor the Russians would enter into the heartland of each other. Finnish General Carl Gustaf Emil Mannerheim's sixteen divisions were to approach Leningrad from the north to occupy the shore of Lake Ladoga—the immense body of fresh water on the city's northeastern border and the largest lake in Europe—and to stop both escape from and supply to the city. In a historic decision, the Finns would not directly besiege Leningrad but rather sought to reclaim only surrounding territory lost to the Russians in the 1939 border war.[13]

Leningrad was a major port. The Russian Baltic fleet would be routed and destroyed, and thus the city's imported supplies cut off. Army Group North, in turn, could, and would in part, be supplied through the Gulf of Finland by maritime transport far more easily than could the other German army groups to the south by rail or road. The greatest naval defeat of the European theater was the panicked Soviet naval evacuation from nearby Tallinn, Estonia, between August 27 and 30, 1941. German—and to a lesser extent Finnish—bombing, coastal artillery barrages, surface attacks, and mines killed over twelve thousand Russian seamen and evacuees. The Germans and Finns sank sixteen warships and about sixty transport vessels, and completely shut off Leningrad's access to the sea. The two main ports on the Gulf of Finland, Helsinki and Tallinn, remained Axis-held for nearly the entire siege of Leningrad.[14]

Lake Ladoga became Leningrad's only remaining lifeline by autumn 1941. But just as Hernán Cortés finally turned Lake Tenochtitlán against the besieged Aztec capital, so too the Germans believed that they could use Lake Ladoga as a barrier and so make their blockade that much tighter. Such thinking, however, was predicated on taking the city before the lake froze over. When that did not happen, the lake became a land bridge from Russian lines to the city limits.[15]

Von Leeb's original plan had assumed that Group North would race through Estonia and hit nearby Leningrad on the run. The armored assault led by the Fourth Panzer Army would surprise the city in the way Warsaw, Copenhagen, Amsterdam, Brussels, Paris, Belgrade, and Athens had all been shocked into capitulation. In Hitler's mind, German control of the shores of the Baltic ensured iron ore imports from Sweden, which were essential to German industry. Army Group North, and the Finns on their own ground, would need only to station residual forces to oversee the quick starvation of Leningrad's population, as shelling and bombing reduced the city to rubble. Hitler's initial directives to Army Group

North were clear that Leningrad had to be captured; the Baltic coast had to be secured; Soviet naval power had to be destroyed; and Kronstadt had to be leveled—all before the final assault on Moscow.[16]

As Operation Barbarossa began, Army Group North moved at the rate of more than twenty miles a day through the Soviet-occupied Baltic states, covering the first 280 miles in just two weeks. Von Leeb finally slowed in mid-July. Yet German progress never ceased entirely. By early August, the Germans were only sixty or so miles from Leningrad. Despite worn-out equipment, exhausted and dead horses, mounting losses, and unexpectedly stiff Soviet defenses, at the beginning of September some Panzers were camped just thirty miles outside of Leningrad, days away from taking the city. In adopting a strategy of "active defense," Mannerheim's Finnish forces then dug in, waiting to hook up with Army Group North on the shores of Lake Ladoga, about twenty miles north of the city.[17]

By mid-September only seven miles separated the German front to the south from the city limits. Given the unexpectedly ferocious resistance, a baffled Hitler now began to have second thoughts and ordered Army Group North to adopt static siege positions around Leningrad. Perhaps the daily bombing, shelling, and starvation would destroy Leningrad without a frontal assault, and save German troops for the impending attack on Moscow. Hitler's armies were so far unbeaten. He had no intention of sending them into street-by-street fighting, given that almost every other targeted enemy city had surrendered or capitulated almost as soon as the Panzers appeared at the city limits. At Leningrad, Hitler would avoid inducing the quagmire that he would endure a year later at Stalingrad.

Nazi logisticians figured that they might still be on the way to Moscow by mid-October, as if their worn-out forces could mount another major offensive as autumn wore on. But, along with his later diversions of elements of Army Group Center to the Kiev front, the sudden cancellation of a direct assault on Leningrad would become one of Hitler's additional miscalculations. Bombing and shelling civilians, as well as ensuring starvation and disease, was not the same thing as entering and occupying a city.

The ensuing siege of Leningrad would soon turn premodern. By February 1942, on some days ten thousand city residents perished from exposure, starvation, and infection. Sporadic cannibalism broke out. Plagues spread. Corpses remained unburied. In a diary entry dated December 23, 1941, Valery Sukhov lamented: "Papa barely walks. Mama staggers. We're hoping for January. In the evening I sat down to draw. I forgot about everything. A week ago I began to study German. We cooked soup from carpenter's glue and ate all of the starch. . . . Papa is prepared to eat the corpses of those killed in the bombardment. Mama refuses."

Power, water, and sewage services failed. Due to prior evacuation, military enlistments, and death, the city shrank to a fourth of its prewar population. Hitler congratulated himself on not wasting German soldiers in running street battles. The truth was that he was squandering forces that were never designed for static siege operations and running out of time as the cold weather worsened. In November 1941 both the Fourth Panzer and recently added Third Panzer Armies were pulled out and sent southeastward for the planned final assault on Moscow. That transfer was confirmation that Operation Barbarossa had essentially failed. According to the plans of the frustrated German High Command, the fate of Leningrad would now have to wait until 1942, although it was still confident of the final outcome: "Early next year we enter the city (if the Finns do it first we do not object), lead those still alive into inner Russia or into captivity, wipe Leningrad from the face of the earth through demolitions, and hand the area north of the Neva to the Finns."[18]

Hitler, for all his fantasy talk about a superior race of *Übermenschen,* miracle weapons, and the role of willpower, ironically had no idea of the mettle of the Russian people, who had suffered enormously before the war from Stalin's purges, state-induced famines, and brutal industrialization, and could withstand hardship in a way that perhaps only the Japanese could match. Nor did he appreciate the talent of the residents of Leningrad itself, which in terms of civic achievement, scientific excellence, university life, and cosmopolitan culture was the equal of any European city.[19]

While the conditions inside Leningrad were horrific, the besiegers also by November 1941 were suffering terribly from the fierce cold and lack of shelter. The swamps, marshes, lakes, and rivers around Leningrad in summertime had seemed to aid the Germans' lines of circumvallation. But by winter they froze and offered porous holes in the besiegers' defenses, especially when bad weather often grounded the Luftwaffe. Skilled Soviet engineers were able to craft an ice road ("The Road of Life") across Lake Ladoga, sending in tons of supplies from eastern Russia during the winter months and bringing out over one million half-starved city residents. Finally, Hitler never developed any comprehensive strategy about whether it was wiser to storm, blockade, or bypass Soviet centers of resistance. Because Germans started and then interrupted sieges in ad hoc fashion, transferring armies northward and southward while firing generals, Leningrad, Moscow, and Stalingrad all survived.[20]

Resistance at Leningrad doomed over one million Russians. But Stalin accepted that human catastrophe as part of the cost of saving the greater Soviet state, itself nearly fatally exposed to German aggression as a result of Stalin's own nonaggression pact with Hitler. Had Stalin declared Leningrad an open city, as the Allies had Athens, Brussels, and Paris, he would have abetted the German drive on Moscow, and Leningrad's citizens likely would have been slaughtered with little chance of fraternization with the occupiers. As long as Leningrad was besieged, a fourth of German forces were for all practical purposes tied down far from the pivotal fronts around Moscow, and later in the Crimea and at Stalingrad, where the war would be won or lost. The suffering and survival of Leningrad, a city famous for both its St. Petersburg tsarist heritage and its later eponymous communist vanguard status, served as a powerful global symbol of resistance to fascism.

In the immediate aftermath of the war, rumors mounted that Stalin had diabolically seen some strategic advantage in not making sacrifices to save or completely evacuate the city. As a result, the architects of Leningrad's miraculous survival grew in stature even within the Communist Party. Stalin struck back. Many of those whose brilliance had saved Leningrad from Hitler were either executed or exiled in the so-called Leningrad Affair, a bitter footnote to the resistance.[21]

The Germans for their part never disengaged from the Baltic front. After the siege began, German forces, despite haphazard reinforcements, insidiously shrank. The Red Army always grew. Army Group North had occupied the least amount of Mother Russia's territory of all Hitler's pincer groups. It eventually was to be besieged itself by an enemy that became better equipped and better led, even as it endured far more dead and wounded. For the Russians, Leningrad was both a victory and a holocaust; for the Germans, it was another fork on the highway to oblivion.[22]

THE NAME *STALINGRAD* still invokes horror. Yet when Operation Barbarossa began in June 1941, few in the German army had ever heard of the city. Certainly it was not a major strategic objective as were Kiev, Leningrad, and Moscow. Today Stalingrad is renamed Volgograd ("Volga City"), a provincial city of about a million people, largely unknown outside of Russia.

The attack on Stalingrad (also formerly known as Tsaritsyn) was never a conventional siege. Or rather it soon became two sieges. The first was the German near-encirclement of the Russian city between August 19 and November 22, 1942, by a huge army from the northern wing of

Army Group South, led by General, and eventually Field Marshal, Friedrich Paulus. In early August, his army with surprising speed and economy reached the key Volga River as part of a larger plan to capture or destroy—or both—the riverside industrial city of Stalingrad. That way, Paulus, as part of the more northern wing of Army Group B, could next pivot southward along the banks of the Volga, clean up pockets of resistance, and protect the flank of Army Group A of Army Group South.

Under the general outlines of Hitler's Case Blue plan, laid out in a Führer Directive of April 1942, the two recombined armies, after cutting off the Volga River, would then advance in tandem to expropriate Soviet oil supplies from the Caucasus and Caspian Sea fields. Supposedly, the Russians, bewildered that the main German thrust of 1942 had not focused on their sizable but stalled armies around Leningrad and Moscow, would lose the major source of their fuel. Yet the Germans persisted in the same flawed assumption that large Russian cities could be rapidly stormed or forced to surrender, releasing the besiegers to move on to rejoin the general envelopment of trapped Soviet armies.

What doomed Case Blue was not just the stubbornness of the Stalingrad defense. First was the foolhardiness of Hitler's dividing the limited forces of Army Group South roughly in half, as if Germans by 1942 had the resources all at once to take the city, cut the Volga River, and capture and exploit the oil of the Caucasus before reaching the Caspian Sea. Expanding and thinning the front, while battle still raged along a now 1,500-mile Russian axis, as well as in North Africa, and over the skies of Germany itself, would prove strategic lunacy.

Second, that error of splitting German forces was compounded by fighting for weeks amid the rubble of Stalingrad, when for all practical purposes the aims of General Paulus's Sixth Army had already largely been met: much of the traffic on the Volga had been disrupted, and Stalingrad was rendered mostly uninhabitable and unproductive. Paulus could have redirected his army southward to rejoin Army Group South or to have established a defensive shoulder, well before it was encircled. Hitler's orders to take Stalingrad at all costs seemed to have contradicted his original strategic objectives "to finally destroy the active fighting strength remaining to the Soviets and to take away as far as possible their most important resources of war." That required the Wehrmacht to "unite all available forces in the southern sector, with the objective of annihilating the enemy forward of the Don, and then gain the oil fields in the Caucasus region and the passage over the Caucasus itself."[23]

By late 1942, Hitler finally had begun to worry about America's involvement in the Allied cause and was eager to make additional American logistical capability irrelevant, in the way the German High Command had tried in early 1918. Hitler sought to gain the resources of the Soviet Union, knock it out of the war, and hold a defensive line along the Volga before the industry of the United States revived both Britain and Russia. Joseph Goebbels noted in his diary on March 20, 1942, on the eve of the Case Blue offensive, that Hitler "is determined under all circumstances to end the campaign at the beginning of next October and to go into winter quarters early. He intends possibly to construct a gigantic line of defense and to let the eastern campaign rest there. . . . Our position toward what remains of Russia would then be like that of England toward India." Goebbels apparently failed to note that Britain for centuries had governed the huge population of India with a modest constabulary, in part because of clever statecraft of the sort that would have disgusted the Nazis.[24]

Stalingrad, however, soon became emblematic of the conditions that had previously stalled all German armies in the East. For a second time, the Wehrmacht, birthed in a wintry climate, did not prepare well for the Russian cold. German generals complained constantly of the poor Russian roads, even as their plans hinged on relying on the worst of them in the south. When German armies ground to a halt, Hitler, a captive of maps, intervened directly, ordering impossible offensives and no retreats, while diverting tens of thousands of soldiers in sudden new directions, without any knowledge of the living hell that his soldiers faced. He seemed to think that the nightmare of winter 1941 was long over, its lessons learned and never to be repeated, especially far to the south of Moscow.[25]

The besiegers of Stalingrad soon became the besieged in late November. Two huge Soviet pincers (dubbed the Stalingrad and Don fronts) targeted the Sixth Army's northern and southern flanks, which were poorly guarded by the ill-equipped subordinate Romanian Third and Fourth Armies. The ensuing Operation Uranus was a vast Soviet effort to spring the trap far to the German rear, near the city of Kalach. Unlike the earlier and incomplete German efforts of the Sixth Army to cut off Stalingrad at the Volga River, the Russian ring soon formed a 360-degree encirclement. The Sixth Army became separated from its supplies and was soon pulverized by massive artillery barrages in subzero weather that made reliable air support impossible. Equally important, Hungarian, Italian, and Romanian allied forces along the Don River were threatened, collapsed, and suffered catastrophic losses that were to lead to political repercussions back home.

The Sixth Army was surrounded from November 23, 1942, to its final surrender on February 2, 1943. The combination of cold, hunger, and disease—typhus most prominently—proved as lethal as the Russians. If the Sixth Army was one of Hitler's premier armies, its workmanlike administrator Friedrich Paulus was not one of Hitler's more imaginative field generals. In fact, by any definition Paulus was not a field general at all. He was a respected staff officer who had never held a major battle command in his life. By summer 1942, those far more gifted had either been killed, captured, fired, forcibly sent into retirement, bought off, or were stationed far from the strategic nexus of the war. Paulus perhaps combined the worst two traits for dealing with the mercurial Hitler. He whined in private about Hitler's erratic behavior, yet he took no action to nullify it and salvage his army—in the manner, for example, of General Paul von Kleist, commander of Army Group A, who would ignore Hitler's orders, save the surrounded German Eighth Army in March 1944, and thereby would be relieved, or of General Erwin Jaenecke, who would be dismissed and put on trial for refusing to sacrifice the trapped Seventeenth Army in the Crimea. Paulus was not liked by his staff and was later blamed by his officers for failing to use the brief window of possible escape from the pocket.[26]

The Soviet commander at Stalingrad, General Vasilii Chuikov, was a brawler who bivouacked with his men. While Paulus lamented that his once-mobile divisions were mired in a rat's war (*Rattenkrieg*), General Georgy Zhukov, the ultimate architect of the Soviet counteroffensive, stood up to Stalin to ensure his plans for Operation Uranus were carried out as he envisioned. In terms of imagination and daring, Operation Uranus, conceived in haste and desperation, was far more logical an operation than the complex and carefully planned Case Blue. Hitler's greedy authorship of multiple agendas, in trademark fashion, had ensured that a huge army either could have taken Stalingrad and cut off the key Volga supply route, or could have reached the Caspian Sea and deprived Stalin of much of his oil, but it could not quite do both. By attempting both, it could do neither. In terms of Hitlerian nihilism, it would have made far more sense in September to focus on bombing the Soviet oil hubs of Grozny and Baku than to keep hitting the rubble of Stalingrad.[27]

Even without accurate intelligence about the Soviet buildup, General Paulus had at least warned Hitler of such a nightmare scenario as early as September, as his own siege of the city stalled and the Sixth Army's supply lines lengthened. Hitler was so close to winning a key siege that in his exuberance he completely forgot that the Sixth Army was soon to be outnumbered by the defenders, and without reliable supplies with winter approaching. Most of his generals seemed to have lacked all historical perspective that a failed siege often meant not the withdrawal but the ruin of the attacker.

By late December 1942, efforts of General Erich von Manstein's Army Group Don (Operation Winter Storm) to reach the entrapped Sixth Army ended. His failure was due to Hitler's continued interference in day-to-day operations, as well as bad weather that hampered air supplies. The inexperienced Paulus also did not initiate a simultaneous breakout from his entrapment. And even the highly regarded "fireman" Manstein apparently did not fully grasp the difficulty of advancing to Stalingrad at a time of growing Russian strength. Either Paulus feared to act independently of Hitler's edicts, or he was too paralyzed in depression over his own self-induced predicament. Like most forlorn German generals, he blamed the Luftwaffe: "What should I say, as supreme commander of an army, when a man comes to me, begging: 'Herr Generaloberst, a crust of bread?' Why did the Luftwaffe say that it could carry out the supply mission? Who is the man responsible for mentioning the possibility? If someone had told me that it was not possible, I would not have reproached the Luftwaffe. I would have broken out." But it was hardly difficult for a German general to doubt Hermann Goering's ludicrous bombast that he could supply the Sixth Army completely by air even given bad weather, Soviet air defenses, and too few planes.[28]

Hitler may have talked grandly of Stalingrad as a Festung, but, in fact, as one veteran put it, "one could not speak of a 'fortification' anywhere. The term 'Fortress Stalingrad' . . . must have sounded like pure irony, if not bloody sarcasm, to the encircled troops." On February 2, 1943, between ninety and a hundred thousand near-starving besieged besiegers surrendered—all that was left of Germany's once grand three-hundred-thousand-man Sixth Army. Thousands of stragglers were found amid the ruins for weeks thereafter and Soviet and German recordkeeping in any case was not always complete. The few left who went into Soviet captivity were famished and cold, many were sick, and nearly nine out of ten soon died.[29]

All but six thousand German prisoners perished in Russian camps. The survivors were only returned to Germany in September 1955, following an embassy from West German Chancellor Konrad Adenauer. Aside from those who surrendered, Stalingrad had cost the Axis coalition another 150,000 to 200,000 dead and missing, including tens of thousands of lost Hungarians, Italians, and Romanians. When the failed Case Blue offensive essentially ended in November 1942, Army Group South's various divisions of Group A had in addition suffered yet another three hundred thousand casualties. The Soviets, as customary before 1944, suffered even greater losses, perhaps all told over a million killed, wounded, missing, or taken prisoner.

In terms of disasters, fewer surviving Germans surrendered at Stalingrad than would give up within six months in Tunisia (perhaps over 230,000 Italians and Germans) to the British and Americans. Moreover, the surrender of the survivors at Stalingrad per se was not comparable to the horrendous encirclements that the Soviets suffered in 1941, such as the Kiev cauldron (665,000 Russians captured) or the Vyazma and Bryansk pockets (650,000). Immediately prior to Stalingrad the Soviets in July and August alone had lost another six hundred thousand prisoners, seven thousand tanks, and six thousand artillery pieces to the encirclements of Army Group South.[30]

Yet the unique melodramatics of Stalingrad made it far worse than all prior or subsequent mass surrenders on the Eastern Front, and in fact the worst military moment in Germany's history. Unlike Stalin, who was on the defensive while forming massive new armies, Hitler was waging an offensive without reserves. All that could be said for Case Blue was that the strategic aims were so ambitious that even Stalin—who as a Marxist-Leninist materialist supposedly would have anticipated an offensive to steal resources and end the Soviet means of production—was initially surprised that the 1942 offensive had not targeted either Moscow or Leningrad.

In the context of historic German defeats, the German disaster at Stalingrad was reminiscent of, but far worse than, Napoleon's rout of the Prussians at the Battle of Jena-Auerstedt in 1806. Before Stalingrad, the German Army had stalled but had not suffered outright defeat. After Stalingrad it never conducted a clear-cut, sustainable offensive campaign again. As Joachim Wieder, a survivor of the battle put it: "Drifting through the snowstorm, this was the wreck of Sixth Army that had advanced to the Volga during the summer, so confident of victory! Men from all over Germany, doomed to destruction in a far-off land, mutely enduring their suffering, tottered in pitiful droves through the murderous eastern winter. They were the same soldiers who had formerly marched through large parts of Europe as proud conquerors."[31]

Before Stalingrad, German morale had recovered from the disaster of late autumn 1941 when blitzkrieg had stalled at Leningrad and Moscow. After February 1943, however, survival, not victory, was the only hope on the Eastern Front. Stalingrad entered the realm of the surreal—a distant Soviet outpost some sixteen hundred miles by land from Berlin, little known to the public back home, where a huge German army had not been just mauled or been forced to retreat or suffered terrible casualties but had simply been swallowed whole.

The captured General Paulus and other high officers offered the Soviets a propaganda coup, and were soon to broadcast defeatist warnings on Soviet radio. Even the Soviets could not initially grasp the magnitude of their destruction of the Sixth Army. Yet the Red Army after Stalingrad eventually earned a reputation for invincibility that lasted for most of the war. "You cannot stop an army which had done Stalingrad," became a common Russian refrain. In contrast, for the German veterans of Stalingrad, the defeat became accepted as "the turning-point of the war."[32]

When the second year of the Russian offensive began in spring 1942, Hitler had faced a reckoning. His armies had suffered enormous losses in 1941: over 1.1 million casualties, with 35 percent of the original army that entered Russia in June 1941 now gone. Such attrition was not fully replaced by mid-1942. German forces were now half a million men fewer in number than the force that began Operation Barbarossa. In the first six months of Barbarossa, the Germans only added a hundred thousand troops to the army on the Eastern Front; the Soviets in contrast increased their military by well over three million. The German army at times was capable of killing Red Army soldiers at unimaginable rates of seven or eight—but not thirty—to one.[33]

By early 1943, much of the Germans' cobbled-together motor transport had been destroyed or worn out and the majority of its horses were dead, at a time when the Allies were beginning to rush shipments of thousands of trucks to motorize the Red Army. The once-backwater Italian effort in North Africa had grown into an open German sore that siphoned off vital resources from Russia to the Afrika Korps, in a doomed effort to prevent the loss of North Africa. As the disaster of Stalingrad ended, Soviet munitions production increased, even as diversions of German air power from the Eastern Front spiked to protect the homeland. Yet while the Sixth Army stalled to the north at Stalingrad, an orphaned Army Group B of some fifty divisions, led by General Maximilian von Weichs, reached the Volga. Its twin, Army Group A under Field Marshal Wilhelm List, got close to Grozny, some of its soldiers on August 21, 1942, climbing Mt. Elbrus, the highest peak in the Caucasus. By October 1942 the Luftwaffe was sporadically bombing some of the oil fields around Grozny—a strategy that had it begun earlier might have done far more damage to Soviet oil production. The subsequent campaign at Stalingrad doomed all that effort. In sum, blitzkrieg, dying at Stalingrad in 1942, would soon be entombed in 1943.[34]

Both Goering and Propaganda Minister Joseph Goebbels in their postsurrender broadcasts tried immediately to invoke history's glorious last stands to romanticize the catastrophe, as if Stalingrad, as an official Nazi communique put it, was "one of the most treasured possessions in German history." General Manstein's invocation of the last stand of the

Spartan defenders at the pass of Thermopylae in 480 BC was pathetic and mendacious, as if the Sixth Army was battling for freedom and consensual government on its home ground rather than for National Socialism abroad. But in the end, the proper classical allusion is Thucydidean. Indeed, Stalingrad proved to be Germany's fatal wound in the manner of the Athenian Empire's disastrous defeat in far-off Sicily (415 BC), so famously summed up in *The Peloponnesian War*: "At once most glorious to the victors, and most calamitous to the conquered. They were beaten at all points and altogether; all that they suffered was great; they were destroyed, as the saying is, with a total destruction, their fleet, their army, everything was destroyed, and few out of many returned home."[35]

THE FORTIFIED EASTERN Libyan harbor of Tobruk changed hands four times during the war. Before 1940 and after 1943 the port was little known and of no real strategic importance, as it is a backwater today for the occasional visitor to war-torn Libya. But for a brief two and a half years, Tobruk became renowned as the center of fierce Allied-Axis fighting along the Libyan-Egyptian border.

The Italians initially surrendered Tobruk to the British on January 22, 1940. The British and Dominion forces then held it heroically against attacks, as the port served as a key British base of operations for seventeen months until June 21, 1942, when a German and Italian army under Colonel-General Erwin Rommel stormed the city. But just five months after Rommel's feat, the Germans themselves abandoned Tobruk on November 12, 1942, as Rommel's forces fled westward in hasty retreat after their defeat at the second battle of El Alamein.[36]

Tobruk's value was that it was almost exactly halfway in the vast 650-mile mostly empty seaside expanse between the British port of Alexandria to the east and the Italian harbor at Benghazi to the west. Each side saw its alternating possession of Tobruk as proof that it had reached a point halfway to its destination, whether British-held Alexandria or Axis-occupied Benghazi. Along the huge Libyan and Egyptian coastal battlefront, it offered the only developed harbor where sizable ships could unload.[37]

For the Axis, Tobruk was also at the end of a near-perfect north-south vertical line across the Mediterranean, from German-held Athens through Crete to North Africa. Nothing much had changed from antiquity, when Tobruk was known as Antipyrgos—directly "opposite from Pyrgos," the key ancient Greek port in southern Crete. For the British as well, Tobruk marked an equally straight but quite different latitudinal supply route from Alexandria to Malta. The war in a desolate eastern North Africa hinged on supplying fuel, food, and ammunition along these two antithetical lines, given that there was little support to be had from either indigenous towns or the desert.

After the Germans' capture of Tobruk on June 21, 1942—one of the last great victories of the Axis—Rommel dreamed of using the port and its captured stocks to supply his smaller army in a reenergized race eastward. For a brief moment in midsummer 1942, Germany saw second-chance glimpses of grand victory. The old fantasy of grabbing the British naval base at Alexandria, Egypt, and cutting off entirely the British in Cairo now seemed to seduce the Germans. From there, Rommel thought that he might even storm the Suez Canal and cut off Britain from its direct routes to its Middle East oil supplies. And Rommel dreamed even more grandly that his tiny Afrika Korps then could continue eastward to join a victorious Army Group South descending from the Black Sea and the Caucasus. If the German armies met in the oil-rich Middle East, then both Russia and Britain would be denied almost all their Persian Gulf or Caspian Sea oil. Or so Rommel imagined after his brilliant capture of Tobruk with its ample supplies, without much serious reckoning that his wild dreams were largely dependent on the continuous captures of such Allied stocks, while the Allies assumed that they could replace far more than they lost.[38]

The initial Italian surrender at Tobruk in 1940 and the final British recapture of the port in November 1942 are today little remembered. Even the heroic British and Commonwealth resistance to Rommel's early failed efforts to storm the port is often forgotten. Instead, Tobruk is most famous for its second fall, the dramatic but rapid surrender to a returning Rommel on June 21, 1942. The British collapse riveted the world, largely because the unthinkable suddenly had become the inevitable.

Despite the odds and problems of supply, Rommel in late May 1942 had risked another battle against the defensive line extending south from Gazala, west of Tobruk, on the Mediterranean coast, to draw out the British Eighth Army under General Neil Ritchie. Rommel maneuvered his armor next to enemy minefields, dubbed "the Cauldron." With his flank protected, he waited for Ritchie's counterattack and then blew apart most of the British armor with the Afrika Korps' veteran anti-tank gun batteries. The beaten British backed off from their fortified Gazala line. After the Luftwaffe and artillery had blasted a hole in Tobruk's defenses, Rommel poked right through and captured the port on June 21 from the bewildered South African General Hendrik Klopper.

The effect of Rommel's sudden victory was stunning. Churchill was in Washington planning grand strategy with his new wartime American ally, only to be humiliated by the shock of Tobruk. The disaster was too reminiscent of the disgrace of the fall of Singapore (February 15, 1942), in sharp contrast to the grim (and ultimately successful) resistance of the civilians and soldiers of a defiant Russian Leningrad, even as they suffered hundreds of thousands of deaths. The news would cause Churchill to return home to a motion of censure from Parliament. Although the resolution was easily defeated, the debate was a sign of popular outrage that once again a sizable Commonwealth force had quit rather than fight to the death.[39]

Until the fall of Tobruk, the Allies had dreamed that the tide of war might be already turning. The Battle of Midway (June 4–6, 1942) had checked the advance of the Japanese fleet. The Germans had split their forces and the northern contingents were nearing Stalingrad but were meeting stiff resistance from the Red Army. The Italians and the Germans had failed in their first assault on Tobruk and had retreated back to El Agheila.[40]

Rommel should not have been able to take the city. Although he commanded about eighty thousand German and Italian troops, total respective British and Axis forces in the theater were about equal at around 120,000 men. The British also had nearly twice as many tanks and armored vehicles and over two hundred more aircraft, and the Luftwaffe was insidiously losing air superiority. While most of Rommel's supplies and reinforcements were running low, Tobruk was stocked full of food, fuel, and ammunition. By mid-1942, supporting naval gunfire along the coast was more often British than Italian. Malta still held out. The British had received new American Grant medium tanks with 75 mm guns that were superior to any of Rommel's early-model Panzers. The Americans promised much more, and there was already talk of a late autumn Anglo-American landing to the west in Algeria and Morocco. All that said, the British remained in awe of Rommel and often praised him as a "splendid military gambler." Churchill gushed, "we have a very daring and skillful opponent against us, and, may I say across the havoc of war, a great general." The Afrika Korps fought with an élan lacking among the defenders of Tobruk. And it did not help the British cause that their various Dominion troops often served under commanders who were not their own.[41]

Churchill was not shy of what might follow Tobruk in his bleak assessment to the House of Commons:

Rommel has advanced nearly four hundred miles through the desert, and is now approaching the fertile Delta of the Nile. The evil effects of these events, in Turkey, in Spain, in France, and in French North Africa, cannot yet be measured. We are at this moment in the presence of a recession of our hopes and prospects in the Middle East and in the Mediterranean unequalled since the fall of France. If there are any would-be profiteers of disaster who feel able to paint the picture in darker colours they are certainly at liberty to do so. A painful feature of this melancholy scene was its suddenness.[42]

Yet in terms of casualties or strategic ramifications, the fall of Tobruk was hardly like the sieges of Leningrad or Stalingrad. There were few civilians in the city and almost none were either British or German. Collateral damage was limited. More important, Rommel failed in North Africa, even after his capture of Tobruk. The effects of the port's capture were instead again psychological. The heroic and successful resistance in 1941 and 1942 was merely a prelude to tragedy. Tobruk also raised the specter that the disaster at Singapore five months earlier might not have been a fluke but symptomatic of a British—or indeed Western democratic—propensity to give up rather than fight on. That Tobruk also shortly followed the American surrender at Corregidor on May 6, 1942, shook the entire alliance.

These worries about innate British and American equivocation would vanish a little more than four months later, 350 miles to the east in Egypt at the second battle of El Alamein. There the British army, far better equipped and under newly assigned General Bernard Montgomery, stopped an ill-supplied Rommel for good. The Afrika Korps had taken their key port at Tobruk. But the victory won little more than a cratered harbor without ships and just enough supplies to reach El Alamein and defeat.

UNLIKE TOBRUK, THE formidable Soviet naval base at the tip of the Crimean Peninsula at Sevastopol may have been the most impressive fortified citadel in the world by the outbreak of World War II. The stronghold, made famous during the nineteenth-century Crimean War, had once taken the British, French, and Turks a year to storm it despite the allies' unquestioned naval superiority on the Black Sea and well before its twentieth-century massive concrete and steel fortifications.[43]

Sevastopol was protected by the Soviet Black Sea fleet, not large by blue-water standards and often poorly maintained, but preeminent within the confines of a quasi-inland sea. Even if the paltry Axis naval forces had controlled the Black Sea approaches, it was nearly impossible to stage amphibious landings. Steep cliffs bristling with casements loomed above the harbor. Unlike at Singapore and Corregidor, the large-caliber artillery batteries of Sevastopol easily could be aimed out to sea as well as inland. The permanent arsenal was beefed up with over four hundred mobile artillery pieces and still more mortars and anti-aircraft guns.

The landward routes of attack were mined, fortified with artillery and bunkers, and bordered by dense forests and uneven terrain. The Soviet Independent Coastal Army under Major General Ivan Petrov had over one hundred thousand Soviet troops burrowed into the fortifications. The besieging Axis forces of General Erich von Manstein—given the preparations for the impending dual offensives aimed at the Volga and the Caspian Sea—enjoyed only a two-to-one numerical superiority over the entrenched defenders. Manstein was under pressure to take the city quickly and join the German drive to the south. Yet Manstein's numerical edge was due only to the presence of Romanian allies under Major General Gheorghe Manoliu. Time was on the side of the defenders—and it was not clear in a strategic sense whether the fortress was even worth the cost of taking it.

An exasperated Army Group South had wisely considered bypassing Sevastopol in the initial invasion of the Soviet Union in 1941, after attempting and then failing to surprise and storm the base. By November, Sevastopol was cut off by land. For the next eight months it remained isolated, except for occasional supply by sea. The city posed no threat to the German advance except for a few Soviet bombers that the Germans feared might disrupt the planned assault on the Caucasus oil fields to the east.

Even as Army Group North remained static far to the north at Leningrad, Hitler in early 1942 demanded Sevastopol's immediate capture, given his obsessions with preserving and expanding his oil supplies and the resistance of iconic enemy cities. After the failures to take Leningrad and Moscow in 1941, Hitler was also adamant that the Wehrmacht should now successfully storm any enemy city that it approached or surrounded. To isolate the garrison by sea, Manstein had only a motley collection of Italian boats and small submarines that were of little aid to some light German craft. If he could not cut off the city's maritime lifelines, he instead relied on air power that at least might hamper convoys to the city and ensure that Russia's Black Sea fleet could not shell the besiegers. The lack of simultaneous land and sea operations cost the Germans dearly in blood and time.

Sevastopol and indeed the entire Black Sea were not critical to the strategic calculus of World War II. The base offered few long-term advantages in advancing Germany's aims in 1942. Given British control of the eastern Mediterranean, there was little chance of supplying the Wehrmacht through the Black Sea (which Hitler had dismissed as "merely a frog pond"). The Crimean Peninsula itself was a dead end, well off the track of Army Group South's main supply routes from Eastern Europe to the Caucasus. Sevastopol was a relatively small city without much industrial importance. The Soviet defenders had crafted the far better strategy of drawing in and tying down nearly two hundred thousand Axis troops for over a year. In the fashion of the nonsensical Norway garrisoning, the Germans remained sidetracked. They eroded their strength in Crimean fighting that offered no hope of achieving the favored German goals of either destroying huge Soviet armies by encirclement or securing Germany's oil needs.[44]

That said, after nearly a year of Russian resistance, somehow General Manstein's German Eleventh Army, along with his Romanian and some Italian allies, surrounded Sevastopol and stormed the impregnable fortress in a mere month without much help from the sea. Manstein had two initial advantages. He at first enjoyed easy air superiority. The Luftwaffe's Fliegerkorps VIII was in good shape after recovering from its losses of 1941. Stukas and medium bombers, in round-the-clock preparatory assaults, had within days sunk or damaged most Soviet ships. They destroyed almost all power and water services inside the garrison. Whereas the Germans had adequate rail supplies from their Romanian supply depots, the Russians in the very first two weeks of the siege lost the ability to bring in adequate supplies and reinforcements by sea or land. The besieged could only hope that the Luftwaffe itself might run short on fuel and ordnance, or that the Case Blue campaign might eventually force Hitler to transfer planes away from Sevastopol.

Manstein also thought he had secret weapons of a sort: huge artillery guns designed to destroy even the thickest Russian concrete bunkers. To complement his arsenal of over eight hundred Axis artillery pieces, the Germans had the largest artillery batteries in the world: six GAMMA mortars (420 mm), three Karl-Gerät mortars (600 mm), along with the surreal 800 mm "Gustav" cannon that could fire shells in some cases heavier than seven tons—an explosive payload more than three times larger than those carried on the later V-2 guided missiles. The Germans also had twelve large but more quickly firing and less awkward 280 mm coastal howitzers and an additional twelve 14-inch howitzers.[45]

Yet once again German gigantism—the huge mortars and rail guns required thousands of man-hours of labor to assemble the platforms and fire shells—still could not substitute for a messy ground assault. The final victory would eventually cost the Germans over twenty-five thousand casualties, and a month's delay for the Eleventh Army in participating in Case Blue. No accurate records exist of how many Soviet defenders were killed or taken prisoner when the city fell on July 4. Of the more than a hundred thousand Russian soldiers garrisoning the stronghold, only a few, mostly officers, escaped. The bastion and indeed the city itself were left in rubble, hit by more than thirty thousand tons of artillery shells, the largest German bombardment of the war.[46]

The Germans never fully benefited from Sevastopol as either a major supply or naval base. The prolonged absence of Manstein's army from the Case Blue offensive was sorely felt by autumn. Sevastopol played no real role in the later German offensives of 1942 or during the Wehrmacht's retreats of 1943–1944. About two years after its capture, in May 1944, surrounded German and Romanian forces hastily abandoned Sevastopol by sea and air.[47]

One of the most brutal and impressively conducted sieges of World War II resulted in almost no strategic advantage for the victors.[48]

UNTIL 1940, GERMANY had never enjoyed direct access to the Atlantic Ocean. As a result, its wartime strategies in both World War I and II were obsessed with the capture and defense of such major and well-protected harbors on the western coasts of France and Belgium as La Rochelle, Saint-Nazaire, Lorient, Brest, Saint-Malo, Cherbourg, Le Havre, and Antwerp. The notorious 1914 German *Septemberprogramm* memo of the philosopher Kurt Riezler, which had floated possible terms to be imposed on Western Europeans in anticipation that they would lose World War I, had included provisions for German annexation of northern French coastal territory, an apparently ingrained strategic desire of the later German Reich.[49]

After the June 1940 defeat of France, Admiral Karl Doenitz began to redeploy most of his U-boat fleet in what would soon be fortified pens at Brest, Lorient, Saint-Nazaire, La Pallice (La Rochelle), and Bordeaux. German submarines were freed from the bottleneck in the North and Baltic Seas, with easy access to the convoy routes of the Atlantic and Mediterranean. The reinforced concrete U-boat shelters at Lorient were huge, self-contained, and immune from almost any imagined Allied attack.[50]

As the later 1944 Allied invasion of Western Europe loomed, Hitler was intent on denying the British and Americans use of these key deep-water ports. As early as March 23, 1942, in fear that the recent entry of the United States into the war might lead to an early Allied landing in France, Hitler had ordered all the key harbors on the Atlantic to serve as the linchpins of a new Atlantic Wall. None was ever to be surrendered: "Fortified areas and strongpoints will be defended to the last man. They must never be forced to surrender from lack of ammunition, rations, or water." The Calais area—given its proximity to Great Britain, the most likely focus of any Allied amphibious invasion—was so heavily fortified that early on British planners looked for alternative landing sites, while deluding the Germans into constantly investing even further sums and manpower in its defense.[51]

The rationale of the German Atlantic Wall strategy was not necessarily that thousands of fortifications built on the beaches and cliffs would repel invaders at the shore. Rather, if the Allies survived the beaches and moved inland, the French coastal ports were to be turned into self-contained killing traps. Continuing the work of the French before the war, the Germans invested the harbor fortresses with reinforced concrete bunkers, coastal artillery, and underground supply depots, and surrounded them with vast mine fields on land and at sea. Their capture would become so costly that the Allies simply would either avoid besieging them, or, if they succeeded in taking the harbors, the invaders would find them ruined to the point of being useless. Either way, the Allied expeditionary armies would then die on the vine for want of supplies.[52]

For the most part, the Germans were both successful in denying the Allies use of these harbors and unsuccessful in stopping the Allied advance. In the initial weeks after the D-Day invasion, few ports supplemented the two Allied Mulberry piers (the American-designated Mulberry A was destroyed in a June 19 storm) that were towed to Normandy and erected three days after the landings in expectation of initial fierce German defense of the French and Belgian ports. Until the November 1944 opening of Antwerp, logistics plagued the Allies and caused a marked slowdown in the British and American advances.[53]

Sieges of the Atlantic ports fell into two broad categories: the few harbors that the Allies attempted to storm in 1944 (and in every case eventually succeeded in capturing), and the rest that they bypassed, given that taking a likely ruined port was soon discovered not to be worth the effort. Cherbourg, in the Cotentin Peninsula (along with Le Havre) was the largest deepwater harbor nearest the Normandy landings. Invasion planners naturally deemed Cherbourg's docks critical to fuel the post-invasion advance, even after the Americans showed brilliant ad hoc abilities in July to unload up to fifteen thousand tons per day directly onto Omaha Beach during low tides.

The Americans made rapid progress in advancing from the area around Utah Beach to surround Cherbourg. Indeed, the port surrendered on June 29, just three weeks after the D-Day landings. The victory immediately gave some hope that the other Atlantic ports might quickly follow suit. Yet the German navy commander at Cherbourg, Rear Admiral Walter Hennecke, had so wrecked the harbor infrastructure and docks—an action that earned him the Knight's Cross of the Iron Cross—that the port could not be used to bring in freight until mid-August, and then never in quantities that had been earlier envisioned.[54]

General Patton's Third Army, activated on August 1, 1944, almost two months after the Normandy landings, was originally assigned to capture the Brittany ports to the south and west, especially the key harbor at Brest. Yet after the unexpected Allied breakout during Operation Cobra and the chance of trapping an entire German Army Group at Falaise, Patton split his forces. Most of Third Army headed east, while VIII Corps was assigned the capture of Brest, in the opposite direction from Germany.

The rapidly advancing Americans thought that they might catch the Germans unawares and grab the more distant Brest within a week, and with it solve much of the growing Allied supply dilemma in a single bold swoop. But General Troy Middleton of VIII Corps soon discovered that the Germans predictably had already beefed up Brest's natural defenses, stockpiled vast amounts of ammunition, and were busy destroying the harbor facilities. The fighting soon degenerated into house-to-house skirmishing and a siege assault on the inner massive walls of the old city, as each side reverted to the role of medieval besiegers and besieged.

More than six weeks passed before over twenty-thousand surviving Germans surrendered Brest on September 19. But the Allied effort was largely for naught. The port facilities had been blasted into ruin. By the time the harbor was repaired, Brest had already been rendered largely irrelevant by the impending capture of the far larger and more strategically located port at Antwerp to the north and its growing distance from the advancing American front. It probably would have been far more effective for the Germans to have initially blown up the harbor, and then evacuated the garrison so it could join in the defense of Normandy.

After the dual debacles at Brest and Cherbourg, the Allies de facto conceded that the nihilistic strategy of the Germans made it hard to justify the costs of frontal assaults. As a result, they began skipping further sieges of many of the coastal ports. Until Antwerp was ready for shipping in November 1944, the Allies continued to bring in supplies at the sole British Mulberry, directly onto the Normandy beaches, and, after August, at Marseilles (an undeniable dividend of the Operation Dragoon invasion of southern France), but still continued to grow short of supplies. In ironic fashion, the Allies also figured that German strategy could be turned on its head: thousands of German troops could be bottled up defending port cities at precisely the time when Germany's fading resistance was in desperate need of such manpower.[55]

After the messy fighting in Brest, the next key port, La Rochelle, was cut off in early September and blockaded. But otherwise the diehard garrison was left alone until the German 265th Division surrendered the city at war's end on May 8, 1945. Saint-Nazaire and Lorient followed the same "Atlantic Pocket" strategy of La Rochelle: both were surrounded by the Allies by mid-August 1944, but never stormed. Saint-Nazaire, in fact, was the last German-held French city to capitulate at the war's end.

The strategically important ports at Saint-Malo and Le Havre were belatedly besieged in September 1944. Both were among the most formidable strongpoints in the Germans' Atlantic Wall, and their defenses had been vastly upgraded to the point of making them nearly invulnerable to the effects of naval gunfire, land artillery, and aerial bombing. Nevertheless, the Allies now tried the tactic of burying the citadels under massive bombardments, in hopes that they could avoid the losses incurred at Cherbourg and Brest, and still rebuild the harbor facilities out of the rubble. The first hope came to fruition; the second did not. Saint-Malo was attacked in early August 1944 and immediately proved unassailable, prompting a horrendous incendiary bombing that ruined the city. When the Americans entered the harbor on August 17, the historic old port was little more than rubble.

Le Havre was likewise literally reduced to ruins. Its surviving garrison of twelve thousand Germans was captured in just three days after the final assault (September 10–12). Although the British losses were light, the port was left in shambles and of little value in supplying the last ten months of the war effort. General Montgomery considered the northernmost French Channel ports at Boulogne, Calais, and Dunkirk critical to supply the advance of the British army and far easier to besiege. Yet in the end, they too mostly followed the prior frustrating paradox of either being bypassed until the war's end (Dunkirk, September 15, 1944–May 9, 1945) or subjected to so much firepower as to be rendered useless. Even those few ports that were captured in September 1944 and taken with only moderate losses (e.g., Boulogne, September 17–22, and Calais, September 22–October 1) brought little advantage to the Allies, given the wreckage of their harbors.

Much of the Allied confusion over whether to storm or bypass the French ports resulted from the uncertain status of Antwerp, less than two hundred miles as the crow flies from central London. Along with Rotterdam (not liberated until May 5, 1945), it had traditionally served as one of the two great European harbors on the Atlantic. At first, it seemed that with the capture of both Antwerp proper and Brussels in August 1944 the Allies now had less need for the French ports. Antwerp was intact. Its huge size and proximity to the industrially rich German Ruhr (little over 120 miles distant) offered hopes that the Allies might still reach Germany before winter 1944. But General Montgomery had failed to secure the Scheldt estuaries in early September. And without control of these long approaches to the harbor, ships could not in safety reach the otherwise secure docks at Antwerp. A costly and tragically unnecessary battle then ensued from October 2 to November 8 to free up the estuaries and gain unfettered access to the Belgian port. Only after November 12 were the majority of Allied supplies able to pass through Antwerp, largely due to the heroism of the Canadian attackers. With the full use of Antwerp, and the invaluable harbor at Marseilles on the Mediterranean, the once-pressing need either to storm French harbors to the south or to ensure the rapid repair of those already in Allied hands mostly passed.[56]

All the German coastal garrisons—at one point encompassing over four hundred thousand troops—were trapped. And all would eventually surrender. But key questions were never answered about the wisdom of besieging them: how quickly, at what cost, and to whose profit? The Allied besiegers, in efforts to gain the ports without massive losses, were faced with dilemmas, whether immediately and at great risk to assault the harbor fortresses, or to bomb them first into rubble, or to blockade these strongpoints and bypass them altogether.

The proper answer hinged on intangibles, and again was never properly addressed, explaining why the single surviving artificial Mulberry harbor remained in service for eight months until early 1945. If the harbors were rendered useless to the Allies, their garrisons were in turn rendered useless to the eventual defense of the German homeland. General Rundstedt was on record that he thought Hitler's stand-and-die orders doomed tens of thousands of German soldiers in the ports who otherwise might have offered key manpower in defense of the Reich, "We subsequently lost 120,000 in these concrete posts. When we withdrew from France I always considered this to be a tragic waste of useful manpower. As for the Atlantic Wall, it had to be seen to be believed. It had no depth and little surface. It was sheer humbug." According to the wartime Berlin diaries of the White Russian aristocrat Marie Vassiltchikov, the sham fortifications apparently had been sold to the German public as a viable obstacle to the Allies. On June 6, 1944, she noted, "The long-awaited

D-Day! The Allies have landed in Normandy. We had been told so much about the famous *Atlantikwall* and its supposedly impregnable defences; now we shall see!"[57]

ISLAND CITADELS OFTEN required the attacker to undertake amphibious operations or to build a land bridge from the mainland, as Alexander the Great had done to capture the island city of Tyre (332 BC). Yet the fate of these fortresses usually hinged not so much on the nature of the fortifications and the size of the garrison, as on the relative strategic situation at the time and the nature of the defenders: trapped Axis and Russian forces rarely ever gave up, British and Americans often did. The degree of naval and air superiority in the vicinity made resupply either reliable or impossible, and so the redoubt became either a fortress or a tomb.

Tiny Malta (just 100 square miles in size, with 250,000 people in 1940) should never have survived, just as it should never have withstood the overwhelming forces of the Ottoman sultan Suleiman the Magnificent that failed to capture the Christian stronghold in 1565. On June 10, 1940, modern Malta was first attacked by Mussolini's air forces not long after Italy opportunistically declared war on the Allies. Over three thousand Italian and German bombing missions were to follow against what Il Duce called *"Malta nostra."* Within a year, a bombed-out Malta was reduced to a lonely, isolated Allied island in an Axis lake. The northern Mediterranean coast—Spain, France, Italy, Yugoslavia, Greece, and Turkey—was either in Axis hands or nominally neutral but pro-German. In mid-1942, Rommel was forcing the British out of Libya and back to Egypt. The African shoreline was still mostly either in German or Italian hands, or left to the collaborationist Vichy French.[58]

The other historical stepping-stones of invasion from Europe to Africa and vice versa—Crete and Sicily—were likewise Axis held. So were Corsica and Sardinia. After the collapse of France in June 1940, and the extinction of the French Mediterranean fleet, Malta was without secure sea-lanes. In terms of relative size, the Italian fleet now outnumbered vulnerable British Mediterranean naval forces that lacked air superiority any time they dared to steam between Gibraltar and Alexandria. Even before the French collapse, the British and French had pondered abandoning Malta altogether. Britain already had lost almost all hope, given that Malta's air force of three obsolete biplane Gloster Gladiators—dubbed *Faith*, *Hope*, and *Charity*—provided no deterrent. Almost every major event of the Mediterranean war between 1940 and 1942—the loss of the French fleet; the control of Morocco, Algeria, and Tunisia by Vichy France; the entrance of Italy into the war; the Axis invasions of North Africa; the establishment of enemy bases in Sicily and Crete; the appearance of German U-boats in the Mediterranean—made things seem even more hopeless for Malta.[59]

The island's formidable ramparts had always required an invader to obtain regional naval supremacy, and to have adequate supplies to ensure an amphibious landing, blockade, and occupation. That was difficult in any age, as the Ottomans in 1565 had learned after their failed efforts against the outnumbered defenses of the Knights Hospitaller. Even modern air and naval power did not really change that age-old calculus. While the Germans and Italians nearly destroyed the air forces of Malta, regular British aircraft resupply by carriers ensured that the Luftwaffe never quite achieved aerial supremacy. The Axis never landed any troops on the island. For all his braggadocio, Mussolini had no serious plans of invasion after his dramatic declaration of war.[60]

There were two air sieges of Malta. The first was Italian led, framed around Mussolini's efforts in 1940 to secure Libya. Despite the initial inability of the British to supply the island with modern warplanes or to base capital ships safely at Valletta, the Italians failed utterly in all their half-hearted efforts between June and December 1940. Their naval, air, and land forces lacked sufficient fuel, supplies, and expertise systematically to bomb the city into submission, defeat the British fleet, or land forces on the island. The Italian navy had neither independent air capability nor expertise at night operations; despite some heroic efforts, it would not win any of its three early major encounters with the British fleet at Taranto, Calabria, and Cape Matapan. As long as British-held Gibraltar and Suez governed both the entry and exit of the Mediterranean Sea, it was nearly impossible for either Germany or Japan to send sizable forces to join the Italian war effort in the Mediterranean.[61]

Malta's brief reprieve from Mussolini mostly ended in February 1941 when Erwin Rommel started operations in Libya with his Afrika Korps to save the stalled Italians. German bases in Sicily (just 90 miles from Malta) and, by June 1942, in Tripoli (220 miles distant) meant that succor for Malta from the west was nearly cut off, while German-held Crete interdicted aid from the endangered British in Egypt.

Malta was saved by unforeseen events. The successful airborne conquest of Crete (May 20–June 1, 1941) proved so costly (nearly 7,000 German casualties) that Hitler was reluctant ever again to stage a Mediterranean parachute assault. Nonetheless it seemed inexplicable that the

Führer, who by the end of 1941 had sent hundreds of thousands to their deaths in a foolhardy invasion of Russia, would not dare to risk a fraction of such forces in a much more likely victory at Malta, which had far fewer defenders, was far smaller than Crete, and was far more strategically important in terms of transporting supplies southward by rail from northern Europe and on by ship to North Africa.

The Germans lacked not only aircraft carriers but also any major surface ships in the Mediterranean, and were not eager to send U-boats near Gibraltar. After the Allies' invasion of Sicily (July 1943) and even before the Operation Dragoon landings in southern France (August 1944), U-boat activity sputtered and then ceased almost entirely. While nearly half a million tons of Allied merchant shipping were lost to U-boats in the Mediterranean, including twenty-four Royal Navy ships, Allied east-west sea-lanes in the Mediterranean between Alexandria and Gibraltar were never completely cut off, even though they were far longer and more tenuous than the north-south Axis traffic between southern Europe and North Africa.[62]

Finally, the arrival of the new US ally meant that Allied naval and amphibious forces would be in North Africa by November 2, 1942, just eleven months after both Germany and Italy had declared war on America. Growing Allied power would finally end Malta's isolation and eventually doom U-boat operations and the occasional breakout of the Italian fleet. The US carrier *Wasp* had already helped bring additional Spitfire fighter aircraft to Malta on two occasions in spring 1942. One of the reasons why the Axis failed in North Africa was their control of only two (Crete and Sicily) of the five modern Mediterranean choke points (the remaining being the more strategically positioned Gibraltar, Malta, and Suez) that were critical for supply between Europe and North Africa. Had Hitler taken Gibraltar, Malta would have been doomed.

Malta-based ships and planes eventually took a heavy toll on Axis convoys. As the war changed with the entry of the Soviet Union and then the United States into the conflict, the logistics of the Mediterranean also radically shifted. By late 1942 over a quarter of all Axis supplies to North Africa were being destroyed by Malta-based planes and ships. In the fighting over and around Malta, over five hundred Axis planes were lost. More than two thousand Axis merchant ships were sunk, and over seventeen thousand sailors and airmen were killed.

The British also paid a high price to keep and strengthen Malta: two carriers, one battleship, two cruisers, nineteen destroyers, and almost forty submarines. Controversy still exists over whether it was Malta-based

forces, or the coming of the Americans and the huge Allied fleet in November 1942, or the continued German drain on the Eastern Front that
explained the disintegration of Axis supply lines. But without Malta, the
Allies would have had little reliable air deterrent in the central Mediterranean. The Axis generals were right that the survival of Malta helped
finish their efforts in North Africa. The bombed-out ruins of Malta were
once again more proof that in the landscape of twentieth-century siegecraft, air power could level a city without guaranteeing either its capture
or extinction.[63]

SINGAPORE, THE BRITISH island bastion at the tip of the Malay Peninsula, was often dubbed the Gibraltar of the Pacific. But it was hardly that,
either in terms of strategic importance or impregnability. Although the
base was praised as a showcase British port fortress, and likewise autonomous from the surrounding Malaysian mainland, Singapore was no strategic choke point. To enter the Mediterranean from the west, every ship
had to pass within about eight miles of Gibraltar's defenses. In contrast,
there were ways of navigating between the Australian and Asian continents, and the Pacific and Indian Oceans, without entering the straits
near Singapore. After the Japanese capture, the Allies simply bypassed the
fortress for the entire duration of the war, apparently finding the Japanese
bases there no obstacle to dismantling the Japanese overseas empire.[64]

As was the case with many pre–World War II island fortresses, Singapore reflected the age of the battleship. Its five huge 15-inch naval guns,
armed with large stocks of armor-piercing shells to be aimed at incoming
capital ships, were designed to face seaward, into an increasingly empty
ocean. The huge batteries could bar the approach of battleships like the
*Yamato* or *Musashi* that never came. But they could not so easily stop a
more likely landward attack from the mainland or naval air attacks from
distant carriers or fighters based in Southeast Asia. Its fighter forces, like
those at Malta, were both out of date and too few. Depression-era Britain
had apparently determined that it could only protect its home waters and
have a respectable presence in the Mediterranean if it mostly shorted its
Pacific bases, and Singapore in particular.[65]

All that said, Singapore need not have fallen, at least not as quickly
as it did in February 1942. Initially, it was resupplied with some relatively
modern Hawker Hurricane fighter planes by British carrier forces. The
overall commander of the fortress's defenses, Lieutenant General Arthur Percival, a decorated veteran of World War I with notable interwar

service, had at least a hundred thousand Dominion defenders, almost a third of them British and Australians.

In contrast, Japanese general Tomoyuki Yamashita—who would be executed by Allied courts for war crimes after the war—headed down the Malay Peninsula with only thirty-five thousand Japanese attackers, slogging the arduous 650-mile trek from Thailand at the rate of ten miles per day. By the time they neared the island fortress, they had been worn out by the jungle and harassing attacks. Yamashita's forces approached the city with only a fourth of the numbers of the defenders, who were still relatively battle ready. In the history of siegecraft, such numerically inferior attackers almost never successfully stormed a fortress city. Those who tried, from the Athenians at Syracuse to the Germans at Moscow, usually met with disaster. Yet Yamashita prevailed.

Morale explains much of his success. For most of December 1941 and February 1942, Yamashita insidiously beat British forces back to Singapore, a bewildering experience for the once confident Dominion troops, who had come to fear the jungle (and had bizarrely assumed that the largely urban Japanese were better equipped, as Asians, to navigate through it). The appearance of Japanese air forces, especially Mitsubishi fighters and two-engine bombers, added to British insecurities. The Japanese pilots usually bested the dwindling number of British Hawker Hurricanes that had been flown in as reinforcements, more than two years after these planes had played such a prominent role in saving Britain from the German Luftwaffe. In short order and despite heroics, the fortress's obsolete original fleet of Swordfish and Wildebeeste bombers and Brewster Buffalo fighters all proved veritable "flying coffins." The British were stunned that they had already matched the supposedly indomitable Luftwaffe, and yet with two additional years of experience were ill-prepared for the supposedly less-sophisticated Japanese.[66]

Inexplicably, on the eve of the outbreak of the Pacific war, the British—who had staged a brilliant naval air assault on Italian battleships at Taranto over a year earlier, and had just sunk the *Bismarck* in late May 1941 in part due to carrier aircraft slowing down the German battleship's escape—had sent to Singapore two frontline ships (Force Z) without air cover. The almost new battleship HMS *Prince of Wales* and the old but still powerful battle cruiser HMS *Repulse*, along with four destroyers, might have proved formidable with 14- and 15-inch batteries against Japanese capital ships in a classical engagement like the Battle of Jutland.

Yet three days after Pearl Harbor, both ships were blasted apart about a hundred miles north of Singapore by at least eighty-two

Indochina-based Japanese torpedo and dive bombers—a horror that led
to subsequent British despair in holding the base itself. Much of Singapore's defenses rested on fantasies that the British were innately superior to the Japanese, and that their ships and planes were better built and
manned. In fact, just the opposite was true, given superb first-generation
Zero pilots and the fact that by February 1942 Japan had the largest aircraft carrier fleet in the world. The British, who had invented the aircraft
carrier in 1912, had forgotten their own axiom that battleships without air
cover were negligible assets. It proved tragic irony that Admiral Sir Tom
Phillips, one of the few British high officers who had not appreciated the
vulnerability of capital ships to air power, was killed by Japanese bombers
and torpedo planes. Singapore was quickly exposed as a sad paradox: a
huge naval base without a single major warship.[67]

Japanese soldiers suddenly went from backward Asiatics to Pacific supermen. Lieutenant General Percival came to believe that his forces simply could not stop the advance of the implacable Japanese on land, in the
air, or by sea, and that there was not much point in fighting further once
he ran out of space to retreat. In truth, by the time Yamashita had isolated
the island of Singapore from the mainland and crossed over on February
8, his army was nearly exhausted by the jungle and sick. Yet once the Japanese easily made their way over the narrow channel and landed on the
island city-state, it took only a week to force a British collapse. When Percival surrendered, British-led forces had suffered only five thousand killed
or wounded in the defense of the island. Over one hundred thousand
soldiers of various sorts were still able-bodied, equipped with over seven
hundred artillery pieces, and field guns.

A distant and disheartened Winston Churchill found all this disgrace-
ful. Although he had unwisely allowed Force Z to proceed to Singapore
without the aircraft carrier HMS *Illustrious* (disabled in the Caribbean),
and foolishly sought to defend Singapore by sending only piecemeal reinforcements, he nevertheless later wrote that the loss of his favorite ships
depressed him as few other events of the war: "In the war I never received a more direct shock. . . . As I turned over and twisted in bed the
full horror of the news sank in upon me."

Churchill famously remarked of the surrender that it was "the worst
disaster and largest capitulation in British history." In truth, it was not
quite the worst British military catastrophe (here one can think of a long
litany, such as Yorktown, New Orleans, Passchendaele, Gallipoli, the
Somme, or Dunkirk), but rather the most humiliating surrender. Apparently, Churchill had reckoned that the British at Singapore might fight

like the heroic besieged in Russia, where, for example at Leningrad, over twenty times more Russian civilians and soldiers would die in saving their city than those at Singapore did in losing it.[68]

In Percival's defense, Singapore was a colonial metropolis that had grown with refugees to at least half a million residents, and whose food and water supplies were finite. He apparently believed that continued resistance was not only futile, but threatened the survival of thousands of civilians. If not Yamashita's force today, a greater Japanese expeditionary force would arrive in the near future, given that the chances of a British or American rescue fleet on the horizon were nil.

The British might not have surrendered so readily had they been suspicious of the far worse specter of Japanese savagery to follow for both civilians and their own prisoners. Well over fifty thousand Chinese were subsequently executed by the secret police of the victorious Japanese, especially during the infamous Sook Ching Massacres. Few Europeans or Americans this early in the war quite fathomed that their own capitulation to the Japanese ensured the slaughter of thousands of Asians, who were condemned by their friendship to the enemies of the so-called Greater East Asia Co-Prosperity Sphere.[69]

Percival—pale, thin, bucktoothed, non-photogenic—may have been easily caricatured after his ignominious surrender as a deer-in-the-headlights fossil, but there was also truth to his image as a British colonial apparatchik with no clue of the ferocity or modern resources of his enemy, and bewildered that his race and nationality no longer conferred any inherent deference. He seemed to have thought that relative power in the East had ossified around 1920, and had no clue of what the Japanese had achieved in air power and naval power twenty years later. As for the siege itself, Percival had not in any serious fashion fortified the island's coastline. He had misjudged the location of the main thrust of the enemy attack, stubbornly convinced the Japanese would land on Singapore's northeastern shore. Nor did he have much idea of the symbolic importance of Singapore's survival in steadying British forces in the Pacific during the dark days of early 1942.[70]

To be fair to Percival, it is also difficult to imagine a British-held Singapore surviving much longer than did Corregidor. If the American stronghold in the Philippines was more isolated, it was also a more defensible fortress, and characterized by better leadership, higher troop morale, and far more effective integration of native troops. Yet it also fell just three months later.

Britain's "Singapore Strategy" of predicating forward British Pacific defense on the great naval base was inherently flawed, given the paucity of the actual forces at its disposal. Preliminary prewar discussions between the Americans and the British concerning forward basing some US ships at Singapore failed due to mutual suspicions and shared ill-preparedness. But even had Singapore hosted a greater Allied surface fleet, the idea that one or two British and American carriers would have defeated the finest and largest carrier fleet in the world in the first days of World War II in the Pacific was unlikely.[71]

At the time of Singapore's fall, there were only four major active Allied capital ships—three American carriers and one battleship—operating in the eastern Pacific. By late 1942 only one surviving American carrier was left operational. All available Allied fighters were mostly inferior in number and quality to the Japanese. Tactical blunders and strategic obtuseness had doomed Singapore; yet there was truth to Percival's complaint, when a prisoner of the Japanese: "I lost because I never had a chance." Singapore could have been saved for a while in 1942, but it is hard to see how it could have survived for long, given the dominance of the Imperial Japanese Navy.[72]

Ironically, for the duration of the war, the Japanese found little strategic advantage in holding Singapore other than its propaganda value. There were closer bases for staging operations against India and Burma, and far better ones for defending Japan. Other than serving as an Axis submarine base, and its chief strategic importance as a depot for invaluable Malayan tin and rubber (then 60 percent of the world's supply), Singapore proved a Japanese Norway, tying down thousands of occupation troops in an increasing backwater of the war. The advancing Americans and British in 1944–1945 bypassed it altogether to focus on islands closer to the Japanese mainland. Singapore, in the manner of the French Atlantic ports, did not surrender until September 1945. The British found it much as they had left it in February 1942, albeit without tens of thousands of civilians who had been executed during the brutal Japanese occupation.[73]

IN CONTRAST TO Singapore, the Philippines were closer to both China and Japan. Manila was just seven hundred miles from Hong Kong, and nineteen hundred miles distant from Tokyo itself. The islands were key to the Japanese naval supply routes of its envisioned new Pacific Empire. For the Japanese in early 1942, capturing a huge American base was strategically and even psychologically far more critical than acquiring British Singapore.

Corregidor (Fort Mills) was the largest and most important of the four small islands that the Americans had fortified (along with Forts

Drum, Hughes, and Frank) to guard the entrance to the vast Manila Bay and to ensure veritable administrative control of the entire Philippine archipelago. On the eve of the Pearl Harbor attacks, the American general in charge of the Philippines, the legendary Douglas MacArthur, had marshaled about seventy thousand troops, including some twenty-five thousand Americans. The bulk of his forces were stationed on the island of Luzon, ringed around the Philippine capital at Manila. Unlike Malaya, the Philippines had already been granted a transition to independence and the Americans had little experience as a colonial power. The result was a closer relationship between native forces and foreign occupiers.

Unlike Singapore's defenses, MacArthur's air arm was more formidable, with some 107 newer model P-40 fighters and thirty-five B-17 bombers, as well as additional but admittedly obsolete aircraft. But MacArthur also assumed that his more forward forces might be hit in any future war well before the American fleet at Pearl Harbor was endangered, and thus could be resupplied from Hawaii. The brilliance of the Japanese Pearl Harbor attack was in first striking the supposedly safest of American Pacific bases, and the nerve and supply center for the more exposed outposts of US naval and land power.

On the first day of the war, Major General Lewis Brereton's air forces in the Philippines were caught on the ground. Eighteen B-17s (51 percent of his force) and sixty-three P-40s (59 percent) were destroyed, nearly wrecking American air effectiveness before the siege had even begun. By mid-December 1941, due to constant aerial combat and evacuations of the remaining bombers to Australia, the Americans had little else but antiquated P-35 fighters. The same story proved true of the Philippines' naval forces. Japanese bombing quickly took out most of the supplies and (often defective) torpedoes essential for the effectiveness of the islands' twenty-nine submarines, which were quickly redeployed to Australia.[74]

After the initial Japanese landing on December 22, north of Manila, the forty-three-thousand-man army of General Masaharu Homma (executed by firing squad for war crimes after the war rather than hanged, as was General Yamashita, the conqueror of Singapore) quickly captured Manila. In such a worst-case scenario, the Americans had counted on a rugged fighting retreat through the Bataan Peninsula and the denial of all entry into Manila Bay. In the unfortunate words of an initially overconfident General MacArthur that would haunt him later, "Homma may have the bottle, but I have the cork." In fact, MacArthur was inside the bottle, and Homma had the stopper.[75]

For a short siege, Corregidor ("The Rock") was almost invincible. Its mere 1,735 acres bristled with fifty-six heavy artillery weapons, anchored by two 12-inch guns that could hit approaching ships at a seventeen-mile distance with nine-hundred-pound projectiles. Even more impressive were 12-inch mortars in sunken pits that had greater utility against enemies on the mainland. The other smaller island fortresses were likewise protected by massive reinforced concrete bunkers—and, in the case of Fort Drum, even larger 14-inch guns. Such ossified weapons, however, were hardly effective in a new age of air power, mechanized assault, and mobile batteries. Instead, as was true of Singapore, the American big guns reflected the defensive and often colonial mentality of a distant and bygone age. The usual turn-of-the-century threats to colonial outposts were the dreadnoughts of other Western fleets, and not overland attacks by Asian ground troops.[76]

Even before evacuations from Bataan, there were over five thousand troops manning the fortress. Corregidor was a veritable fortress with a sixty-mile labyrinth of underground tunnels and an array of interconnected passages, and roads, and even a twenty-mile electric trolley line. Lateral passages were stocked with food, ammunition, and gasoline. But like the British defenses at Singapore that had fallen just weeks earlier, the nature and deployment of Corregidor's four-decade-old batteries were ill suited against shelling and bombing, or against invasion launched from its rear on the Philippine mainland.

There were other problems also similar to Singapore's. While the larger batteries were ample, most of their ammunition was armor-piercing shells intended to shred warships, not dug-in infantry. And the typically flatter trajectories of many of the bigger guns were not as suitable for hitting nearby land targets. Corregidor had never been fully fortified and armed in anticipation of air attack. The two largest guns, for example, were still exposed on concrete pads and appeared from the air as veritable shooting targets. Corregidor was the land version of hugely impressive but largely irrelevant battleships such as the *Bismarck*, *Tirpitz*, *Musashi*, and *Yamato*.

Unlike conditions at Malta, there were not to be friendly fleets, much less convoys, anywhere in the surrounding Philippine seas to resupply the bastion for an extended defense. Any rare attempts at supplying Corregidor by sea usually failed to pierce the Japanese naval blockade. Pearl Harbor was over five thousand miles distant, and still in shock from the December 7 attacks. By January 1942 the Japanese enjoyed de facto air and naval superiority over most of the Pacific west of Hawaii.[77]

Inflicting some twenty thousand Japanese casualties after four months of fighting may have justified the Americans' dogged defense. Yet had Corregidor survived longer, there was still no immediate likelihood that American naval, air, and land forces would have broken through to save the islands. That task would require three more years of American preparation and overwhelming air and naval supremacy.

The Philippines were so deeply embedded in the American psyche— partly from the habit of playing the neocolonial occupier after the post-Spanish-American insurrection, partly due to a costly put down of Philippine insurrections, partly in self-congratulatory pride from shepherding the Philippines to its promised independence—that both its defense and later liberation transcended strict military logic. At the beginning of the war, Dwight Eisenhower, who had served as an assistant military liaison to the Philippines under General Douglas MacArthur, remarked of the US obligations to the Philippines: "In spite of difficulties, risks, and fierce competition for every asset we had, a great nation such as ours, no matter how unprepared for war, could not afford coldbloodedly to turn its back upon our Filipino wards, and the many thousand Americans, troops and civilians in the Filipino Archipelago. We had to do whatever was remotely possible for the hapless islands, particularly by air support and by providing vital supplies."[78]

Once Bataan fell, Corregidor's population swelled from nine thousand to over fourteen thousand. It was almost impossible to feed the large number of noncombatant civilians. The fortress's tiny earthen runway was too small and exposed for reliable airlifts, even if there had been relief from the nearby Philippine islands not yet occupied by the Japanese. When the fortress fell on May 4–5, 1942, after a veritable four-month siege, over eleven thousand captives were dispersed to Japanese prison camps all over Asia and to the Japanese mainland. Somewhere around a thousand of the defenders were killed, and another thousand wounded.

CORREGIDOR, LIKE SINGAPORE, accurately reflected the larger truth about the sieges of World War II. British, American, and Italian forces more often surrendered their positions rather than face annihilation. In contrast, Japanese and Russian defenders, often Germans as well, were more likely to resist to the end. No side had a reputation for a particular mastery of siegecraft in the manner of the Athenians during the age of Pericles, the imperial Romans, or the Ottomans. Instead, brute force, not art, determined whether a fortress held out or fell, and the side with the most bombs, shells, guns, and soldiers—and the will to use them without worry over civilian casualties—usually won.[79]

Sieges, like all other modes of war, were also mirrors of the ebb and flow of the World War II battlefield. After 1943 the Axis did not conduct a single major successful siege, in contrast to a prior record of successes at Corregidor, Singapore, Sevastopol, and Tobruk. Why Singapore and Corregidor fell, while Malta survived, is not explained entirely by the prewar neglect of these fortresses' defenses, given that Malta was poorly garrisoned through much of 1939 and 1940. That said, its greater proximity to Britain allowed eventual reinforcements impossible in the Pacific, where the Japanese fleet posed a far greater comparative threat than the Italian in the Mediterranean. When the Axis or Allies were ascendant, they were more likely to win sieges, and when the war seemed to go poorly, then both were more likely to lose them.

Completing full encirclement also increased the chances of a successful siege. Leningrad survived largely because of the open pathway through Lake Ladoga. The Russian presence on the eastern bank of the Volga made it difficult for the Germans to completely surround Stalingrad. The Germans never reached the eastward perimeter of Moscow. Equally important were the differences in morale, expertise, and willpower. For example, all things being equal, the Japanese probably would have taken Malta, while the Italians could have taken neither Singapore nor Corregidor.[80]

The democracies rarely talked of defending a city or garrison "to the last man." When Churchill hinted of such sacrifice for those trapped at Singapore or Tobruk, no one took him too seriously, as they did similar orders from Hitler, Stalin, and the Japanese militarists. No Russian supreme commander perhaps would have been ordered out of an iconic Leningrad or Stalingrad with his family in the manner MacArthur was directed to leave Corregidor.[81]

Selecting the proper target counted a great deal. Deft German diplomacy and concessions might have won the Spanish over to a joint attack on Gibraltar at least before November 1942. Had the Japanese bypassed Singapore and the Philippines and used those assets first to take Pearl Harbor, they would have done far more damage to the American Pacific Fleet and allowed a breathing space to consolidate occupation and exploitation of resource-rich islands. Moscow, not Stalingrad, was the better prize. Who occupied Tobruk was not nearly as important as who occupied Malta, Gibraltar, Alexandria, and Suez.

Why we speak of a siege of Malta or Leningrad, but not commonly of a siege of Metz or Aachen, may depend on intangibles, such as the target's relative emblematic status, its special relationship to the battlefield, the tactical and strategic consequences of a siege, when the fighting occurred, and who were the combatants. The war was in the balance at Malta, not so much at Aachen by October 21, 1944, whose fate was predetermined when the Americans neared the city. The world knew of the iconic cities of Leningrad and Moscow, less so of Metz.

The canard in World War II that permanent, fixed, and linear defenses rarely could withstand attack proved largely true. Despite the formidable reputation of the great barrier walls, all of them were breached, sometimes easily so. The Maginot Line (1940), the Atlantic Wall (1944), and the Siegfried Line (1945) were parachuted over, bypassed, outflanked, or simply plowed through. Had Hitler invested as much thought and expense in taking Stalingrad or Leningrad as he had in building the Atlantic and West Walls, or had the French spent as much on investments in their armored armies as on the Maginot Line, the early course of the war might have turned out somewhat differently.[82]

Following World War II, there was once again the expectation in the age of guided missiles and motorized armies that besiegers would no longer attempt to batter their way into strongholds and cities. Yet both successful and failed blockades remained as common as ever, from a surrounded Berlin (1948–1949) that survived and Dien Bien Phu (1954) that did not, to the unconquerable defenders at Khe Sanh (1968), Dubrovnik (1991–1992), and Sarajevo (1992–1996).

The sieges of World War II remind us that while the technologies of the attackers and the attacked had changed from antiquity, their respective aims have always remained the same. Because most government, industry, commerce, military hubs, and transportation are urban enterprises, major cities—especially on the Eastern Front where there were no intervening seas—were natural targets in World War II.[83]

Had the Allies captured the major French Atlantic ports intact in June 1944, their armies might have crossed the Rhine by December. Had the Allies held Singapore and Corregidor, the Pacific war would have proceeded differently. The survival of the Soviet cities of Leningrad and Stalingrad, and the British garrison on Malta, changed the course of the war.

PRIOR TO THE twentieth century, artillery was mostly stationary, given its size and weight, and the absence of internal combustion engines. Only at sea could ships move large-caliber guns with any speed, largely to be used against other ships. Even after the advent of combat aircraft in World War I, high-explosive weapons were limited to bombs and rockets, given that the weight of shells and barrels, and the recoil of artillery larger than calibers of .40 mm were too great for most fighter and bomber airframes.

The armies of World War I, however, had marked a revolution by adapting gasoline engines to chassis with wheels or tracks to move large guns, often cross-country apart from major roads. In the past history of warfare, artillery had been static and with difficulty sought to target mobile infantry; now guns were moved at speeds as fast or faster than that of foot soldiers. As is noted in Part Five, because artillery by 1939 fired more rapidly with deadlier shells, the combination of a new mobility and deadliness made big guns the most effective weapons of the war. Equally ominous for infantry, improved shelling was not just confined to larger, more mobile guns; at the other end of the spectrum, a new generation of light mortars, with ever-larger-caliber shells, meant that there often was no divide between artillery and small-arms fire. The World War II foot soldier could become a shooter of both small bullets and large shells.

Big guns killed the greatest number of ground troops in a war that was supposed to be mobile and fluid, thereby liberating foot soldiers from the previous nightmares of the trenches and the likely death sentence of constant shelling. Given that reality, it was no surprise that of all the major weapons systems of the war, from ships to airplanes, the belligerents produced more artillery, mortars, and tanks than all other weapons combined.

## PART FIVE

# FIRE

The deadliest guns

*The alchemists in their search for gold discovered
many other things of greater value.*

—Arthur Schopenhauer[1]

# 15

# Tanks and Artillery

FROM THE BEGINNING of civilized warfare, advancing infantry—especially when outnumbered—has dreamed of finding collective protection from missile attacks, so that the fewer brave were not slain by the more numerous mediocre. Foot soldiers and horsemen thought it somehow unfair that they might perish beneath anonymous barrages of arrows, bolts, or catapult projectiles fired from afar by their military inferiors.

The fourth-century BC Spartan king Archidamus III summed up the ancient heroic lament upon first seeing a catapult: "By Herakles, the valor of an individual no longer matters." He anticipated General George S. Patton's moan in Tunisia in March 1943. The general looked from his trench at advancing but unprotected German grenadiers, caught in the crossfire of American artillery, and lamented, "my God, it seems a crime to murder good infantry like that."[1]

Prior to the industrial age there were few methods to protect men in the field collectively against the haphazard onslaught of missiles. Heavy chariots were never popular in the wars of the Greek city-states. The terrain of the southern Balkans was too rough. Pasturing ponies in an arid Mediterranean climate often proved too expensive. Usually no more than two combatants could fit in a war chariot anyway. After Alexander the Great, some of his successors' armies fielded dozens of elephants. They sometimes advanced like living tanks to batter infantry, scatter cavalry, and offer a mobile platform for bowmen. But elephants were costly to import and maintain. They were also difficult to train. Their skins were thick but not quite impenetrable, and their vulnerable orifices and feet were favorite targets. In panic, elephants could wreak as much havoc on their own troops as on the enemy.[2]

Roman legionaries were terrified of mass barrages of missiles, especially when they fought on their eastern fronts against Parthian horse archers. In response to all these challenges, they had long mastered the tactic of the *testudo* ("tortoise"), a sort of human tank. When archers appeared, legionaries abruptly formed a veritable shell. A roof and walls of their locked rectangular shields deflected most aerial attacks. Yet the *testudo*, while occasionally mobile, was mostly a static and temporary defensive mechanism, one hardly analogous to offensive armor.[3]

The growing use of gunpowder in the fourteenth century changed the balance between offense and defense. Projectiles were no longer defined by the limits of muscular strength. Both their size and velocity steadily increased, shattering stone walls in a way even catapults could not. Harquebuses and later musket fire usually could penetrate body armor. Mobile armor—traditional barriers of wood or hides or even metal on wheels—that might be sufficiently strong to stand up to missiles was simply too heavy to be powered by either humans or animals.[4]

The science fiction novelist H. G. Wells wrote a 1903 short story about steam-powered armored vehicles, "The Land Ironclads." Wells's massive tanks were to lumber across the battlefield protecting riflemen encased in their armored cabins, from which they would be able to pick off the enemy with impunity.[5]

Three breakthroughs brought the tank out of the world of fantasy into the cauldron of World War I. By the latter nineteenth century, both the machine gun and shrapnel artillery shells gave new advantages to the offense. Just a few trained gunners could in minutes now slaughter hundreds of unprotected soldiers. That newfound danger led to renewed demands for new ideas of infantry defense.

Second, relatively small, light, gasoline-powered internal combustion engines made possible self-powered armor. Gas and diesel engines were an enormous improvement on steam power and at last allowed land vehicles the same mobility as ships at sea. A third and less appreciated invention was the continuous track. In lieu of wheels, tracks better redistributed the great weight of iron and steel armored vehicles throughout the entire chassis. Caterpillar tracks opened up otherwise impassable terrain that had punctured tires and clogged axles. Suddenly self-propelled armored units might follow, or even lead, almost anywhere that infantry tread.

In September 1916 the British first used gasoline-powered primitive tanks at the Battle of the Somme. Despite the general failure of these unreliable prototypes, the tanks administered a shock to the static world of trench warfare. A handful of the strange vehicles made some inroads through German lines in a way previously impossible. Over a year later at the First Battle of Cambrai, waves of nearly four hundred British Mark IV combat tanks broke through German lines on November 20, 1917, before faltering a few days later due to mechanical breakdowns and enemy artillery fire.

In the last two years of World War I, the Allies built thousands of tanks; the British and the French alone produced almost eight thousand of them, as fighting at last sometimes was unleashed from the trenches. The Germans and Austrians deployed almost none. But armored vehicles were still too mechanically unreliable and slow to change the dynamics of trench war. For the most part, their offensive armament was not commensurate in lethality with artillery, and their armor was not thick enough to deflect most shells.[6]

Between the world wars, debate raged over the proper use of the new armor, as tactical theory raced ahead of the technological limitations of tanks. Traditional supporters of infantry wanted tanks, in the fashion of armored cars, to stay with foot soldiers as support vehicles. They could offer movable shields and mobile machine gun platforms when integrated within the ground advance. In turn, accompanying soldiers could spot land mines and anti-tank ambushes and thereby save the huge investments in armored vehicles.

Or perhaps tank men might instead become the ultimate manifestation of romantic mailed knights, autonomously charging through the enemy while safely encased in body armor, but now fueled by gas rather than hay. The cavalry lobby resisted independent motorized armor, just as the wooden and wind-powered warship interests had scoffed at steam-powered ironclads. Nonetheless in Europe by the 1920s, once any major land power went "tank," others had to follow to ensure parity and deterrence, and calls went out to subject armored forces to the same arms limitations sought for ships. The result was that by the eve of World War II every major power either had armored forces or was scrambling to acquire them.[7]

Prophets of independent armor formations fell sharply into diverse camps, in the manner of the simultaneous fights in the 1930s over air power and strategic bombing. The new armored visionaries—Generals J.F.C. Fuller, Jean-Baptiste Estienne, Charles de Gaulle, and Heinz Guderian, and Captain B. H. Liddell Hart—envisioned armor replacing heavy cavalry as an independent shock corps. Fast-moving armored divisions in the next war would range far ahead of slower-moving infantry, as bullets bounced off their steel hides in a way they most surely did not the flanks of horses. Tanks would blast holes in enemy lines. Then they would race through or around the enemy's rear. Panic would ensue. Such vast envelopments of enemy armies would lead to moral collapse. Supporting infantry would follow and mop up stunned and surrounded enemies.

Armor would not just protect gunners inside as they killed infantry with near impunity. It would instead win entire wars, by creating psychological havoc behind the lines to collapse armies through fear and shock—doing to infantry on the battlefield what the contemporary bombers would supposedly do to civilians at home. Tanks would cut through barbed wire, run over foxholes, and with their main guns blast fortifications, as their machines guns and cannon swept the battlefield. As with bombers, the tank would always get through.[8]

By the early 1930s tank theorists no longer sounded so unworldly, given the reality that armored vehicles were steadily becoming bigger, faster, and far more reliable than their plodding World War I counterparts. With the advent of the modern fighter plane, the advanced submarine, and the aircraft carrier, the world of Western warfare seemed to have been turned upside down, in a way unseen since the fourteenth-century spread of gunpowder.

The post–World War I tank was envisioned as an anti-Verdun, anti-Somme weapon. As Patton put it in 1939, "the shorter the battle the fewer men will be killed and hence the greater their self-confidence and enthusiasm. To produce a short battle, tanks must advance rapidly but not hastily." The prewar dreams of military strategists in the 1930s hinged on mobile warfare anchored by fleets of fast-moving armored vehicles: battles would be short, mobile, and decisive, no longer static, fixed, and endless. Smoky, dirty, shell- and bullet-spewing machines were romanticized as a way to deter or at least shorten wars of the future.[9]

By the end of World War II, the effectiveness of tanks hinged not just on the quality of the machine or crew training but also on sheer numbers. Just as far-larger cavalry forces usually defeated smaller ones—even with less hardy horses and less effective cavalrymen—so too tanks became a decisive force on the World War II battlefield, especially when one side had far more serviceable armored vehicles than did its enemy. Without "armor superiority," battle simply was transferred to more expensive, and often inconclusive, duels between tanks. Thus the value of tanks was not necessarily their armor per se, or prowess against other tanks, but the ability to be freed against armies that did not field a comparable armored force.

Many weapons could stop a rapidly advancing tank: other tanks, fighter-bombers, artillery, hand-held anti-tank rockets, or mine fields. But ostensibly the easiest way was for another tank to blow up its counterpart. And when that did not or could not happen, panic among tank crews often ensued. In summer 1941, an invading Panzer regiment became

terrified that none of their accustomed weaponry could stop the onslaught of strange new T-34 and KV-1 Soviet tanks. An official German
army report chronicled their plight: "The heavy tanks cannot be beaten
by our weaponry. . . . The men have almost no ammunition left and are
being run down by Russian tanks." The fright of the Panzer crewmen
was akin to fears of lesser predators that a lion or tiger was roaming their
jungle.[10]

On rare occasions superior tanks simply wiped out their armored
enemies without respite. On June 13, 1944, legendary Waffen SS Panzer
captain Michael Wittmann a week after D-Day—in perhaps the most celebrated, and often mythicized, single tank charge in armored history—
slammed his small formation of Tiger tanks into units of the British 7th
Armoured Division at the battle of Villers-Bocage. While details of the
engagement remain in dispute, apparently when Wittmann's crew and
accompanying tanks were through firing the 88 mm guns of their Panzerkampfwagen Mark VI Tigers, they may well have destroyed fourteen
tanks, fifteen other armored vehicles, and a few anti-tank guns. (Few
standard tanks other than the Sherman "Firefly" in the American and
British armored arsenal of mid-1944 could stop a Tiger tank commanded
by a skilled veteran of the Eastern Front.) Yet for all Wittmann's audacity,
for all the marked advantages of his huge Tiger and the élan of German
armored units, his daring led nowhere. He soon retreated in the face of
Allied reinforcements and air superiority, leaving behind damaged Tigers
and without materially altering the pulse of the larger battle. Wittmann,
it turned out, had too few tanks. He had brought along too few accompanying soldiers. And there were too few planes of the Luftwaffe overhead
and too few supply trucks to ensure him fuel and ammunition.[11]

Wittmann was purportedly responsible for an astonishing 138 tank
"kills" before being blown up himself, probably by a Canadian Sherman
"Firefly" on August 8, 1944. Yet the larger lesson from his virtuoso action was that in armored warfare the seemingly mundane mattered as
much as overt battle élan. When tanks were well supplied with fuel and
replacement parts, easily serviceable, present in large numbers, protected
by air cover, accompanied by skilled infantry, and supported by covering
artillery or anti-tank weapons, then the actual specifications of a tank's
armor protection and offensive capability, within parameters, played a
lesser role. German Panzers, the war's most seasoned armored forces,
eventually equipped with the most feared tanks, were nonetheless unable to change the course of *any* major campaign after 1942. Tanks, like
ancient elephants or modern battleships, were formidable weapons, and

the stuff of deadly romance. But their achievement ultimately rested more with routine considerations than the impenetrability of their armor, the power of their guns, and the heroics of their crews.

WHEN WORLD WAR II started in 1939 no one quite knew what defined a tank. Peacetime tank field trials, as well as the experience of the Germans, Italians, and Russians in the Spanish Civil War, raised operational controversies well beyond the proper tactics of armored warfare. Such confusion would never really be resolved until nearly the last two years of the war.[12]

The variables of tank design appeared almost endless. Unfortunately, usually one asset came at the expense of another in a zero-sum trade-off. The thickness and quality of armor were important requisites to ensure that the tank was immune from ground fire, bombing, mines, artillery, or other tanks. But if so, the thick-skinned, huge, weighty, costly but underpowered and unreliable German Tigers should have been the war's most effective tanks.[13]

Tanks were also evaluated by their own offensive power. But there were lots of ways to calibrate the optimum tank gun beyond the diameter of the barrel. Just as important were the barrel length, the quality of its high-grade steel construction, the amount of propellant in the shell, the nature of the projectile (e.g., HEAT [high-explosive anti-tank] or APDS [armor-piercing discarding sabot] rounds available late in the war along with other variants), the gun's recoil and sighting systems, the speed of loading, and shell-carrying capacity. The problem for gun designers was that the war came upon them so suddenly and without much of a tradition of technological experience that no one quite understood the complex relationship between projectiles, armor, and internal combustion engines.[14]

A tank's speed (20–35 mph) and mobility—perhaps epitomized by the well-rounded Russian T-34—were essential to armored success, to entrap the enemy or to escape other tanks. At first designers were unsure whether tanks should have machine guns and one gun or, like the French Char and American Lee/Grant, two. There was no consensus whether the most effective tank engines were the more common gas-powered power plants. Such engines were certainly more familiar to American mechanics. They usually started more easily in cold weather and traditionally they had run on a fuel more plentifully refined (though at greater cost) per barrel of oil. In contrast, diesel engines—standard in the T-34 and a few models of the American Sherman—offered more torque per horsepower. Diesel engines were usually also more reliable and longer lasting, and were not beset with the problems of ignition or gas-engine carburetors that so often plagued German tanks. They were somewhat less flammable (although 25 percent of diesel T-34s on the Eastern Front caught fire after being hit), and more fuel-efficient. In this regard, the rate of fuel consumption and the range of the tank (60–150 miles) before the need to refuel were key.

As important was less-glamorous mechanical reliability, as expressed by the ratio between the hours of tank maintenance needed per hour of actual deployment on the battlefield. In that regard, the much-criticized American Sherman was perhaps the most easily maintained and repaired of all tanks, enjoying an extraordinary high percentage of deployed units staying operational. The far-fewer-produced Panthers or Tigers were more often under repair or out of fuel, diminishing the importance that they could outduel the ubiquitous Shermans. Per unit cost affected all the above criteria, and thus fielding lots of mass-produced good tanks, such as Shermans and T-34s, proved more advantageous than relying on fewer but finely crafted and superb Panthers. Clearly, a single tank could not meet all the desiderata. Yet at the outbreak of the war it was still debatable whether it was wiser to produce different models for different tasks— such as light, medium, and heavy tanks—or to focus on a generic mul-titask tank and produce it in the thousands with standardized parts and maintenance regimes.[15]

Ironically, Germany's war against its mostly ill-prepared European neighbors had started with the simple premise of quantity over quality: lots of light, vulnerable tanks such as Panzer Mark Is and IIs were apparently preferable to having a few with superior characteristics comparable, for example, to the heavy French Char B1. But as the war progressed beyond Denmark, Norway, Poland, and France, and as the Third Reich met the Russians and British, the pace of the evolution of armored fighting vehicles was soon taking on a life of its own.

The German Mark I tankettes 9 (less than 6 tons, 2 light machine guns, and less than an inch of armor) that rolled into Poland in September 1939 bore little resemblance to the so-called Tiger IIs ("King Tiger"), the huge monstrosities that appeared just four years later (70 tons, an 88 mm cannon, and up to 7 inches of armor). In between the two models were hundreds of thousands of dead tankers and their victims, from whose fatal lessons would finally emerge a rough consensus at war's end as to the properly designed tank. If the war had broken out with little affinity among French, British, German, Russian, or American tanks—some with cannon, some not; some with small guns, others with large; some with one, multiple, or no turrets; some with wide, some with narrow treads; some gas powered, some diesel—by the end of the war everyone's ideal tank oddly looked about the same. The Americans, who reviewed the shortcomings of their ubiquitous Sherman, thought they knew exactly what was needed in an improved tank by 1945. As the commander of the 2nd Armored Division, Major General Ernest H. Harmon, put it in 1945: "First: gun power; Second: battlefield maneuverability; Third: as much armor protection as can be had after meeting the first two requirements, still staying within a weight that can be gotten across obstacles with our bridge equipment."[16]

That archetypal tank by 1945 was expressed in various ways by the upgraded Russian T-34, the German Panther, the American Pershing, and the British Comet. The apparent common minimum denominators were weights over thirty tons but less than fifty; a long-barrel, high-velocity cannon of between 76 mm and 90 mm; relatively low silhouettes and cast turrets; wide tracks, and sloped armor of about 100 mm thickness or over. Indeed, seventy years after World War II, and despite revolutions in armor and armament, a twenty-first-century T-90 Russian tank or an American M1 Abrams does not look all that much different from a German Panther, while, in contrast, a 1945-vintage P-51 Mustang bears little resemblance to a twenty-first-century F-22 Raptor.[17]

Once the war began, universal tank design soon reflected two realities. One, for both Allied and Axis designers it was hard to discover and quickly collate common experiences in various theaters from outside Moscow to Libya to find an optimum consensus. The Americans, for example, had little idea that their new and much heralded Shermans that often reigned supreme in autumn 1942 in North Africa (largely due to the fact that many German Panzers before mid-1942 were still not yet up-gunned beyond 50 mm) were already outdated, given the knowledge learned from the Russian front. Two, long-held practices and national attitudes about industrial production and technological design sometimes warped practical empirical decisions: Germans sought craftsmanship and size, Americans reliability and practicality, Russians mass production, and the British specialization. Consequently, distillation of diverse lessons from the battlefield, especially on the Eastern Front in late 1941 and 1942, took about two years.

Armor designers unfortunately often ignored the uncomfortable conditions of battle inside a tank. None were more uncomfortable than the superb Russian T-34. Yet a cramped and poorly designed interior, along with accompanying operator fatigue, were intangibles that could affect overall armor efficiency. Tanks were, after all, designed to protect soldiers from machine guns and artillery shells while spitting out both to devastate unprotected infantry. If they were too crowded (e.g., too many soldiers in the turret posed problems in early American tanks), their interior air noxious (particularly in early tank designs), the interior quarters poorly laid out, the engines unreliable (designs from the 1930s had insufficient horsepower), the tracks prone to premature wear, and the fuel consumption excessive, then crew performance suffered to the point of rendering good armor and offensive punch less relevant. It proved almost impossible to square the circle of ensuring crew safety and comfort when trapped in a riveted or welded steel shell of stored gasoline, high-explosive shells and machine gun bullets, sparking engine plugs, and incoming projectiles.

TANK FLEETS WERE not always worth the enormous investment in strategic materials and production costs that often came at the expense of ship, plane, and small-arms output. Artillery and armor brought little advantage to the battlefield if these weapons were easily neutralized by cheaper hand-held anti-tank guns, mines, tank-destroying artillery, fighter-bombers, or even other—and especially more cheaply produced—tanks. The key, as in the use of air and sea power, was to ensure that armor was liberated to collapse or destroy vulnerable infantry and fixed positions. The Germans had proved that fact in their serial border wars between 1939 and 1940, when even poorly designed early Panzers were not seriously checked by either opposing tanks or artillery, and therefore rolled over enemy resistance. "Armor superiority" determined the cost-to-benefit worth of tanks, and even a tankette could win a battle if unopposed by enemy armor.

Given poor French morale, it brought the French little advantage that their advanced heavy Char B1 tanks on paper were superior to any armored vehicle that the Germans brought into France in May and June 1940. In addition, the French were reluctant to form independent offensive armored formations and did not coordinate their fuel-hungry French tanks with fleets of refueling trucks. French tanks, like French fighter planes, might be better than their German counterparts, but French armored forces, again like French air forces, were usually worse, given their organizational, operational, and morale problems.

The German blitzkrieg of September 1939 and the invasion of France (May–June 1940) were proved the antitheses to the later static tank duels on the Eastern Front from 1943 to 1945, where German and Russian tanks ground one another down without being unleashed on infantry. The key was mobility and the ability to hit exposed infantry. Or as General Rommel put it about the great armored thrusts of the North African campaigns: "Against a motorised and armoured enemy, non-motorised infantry divisions are of value only in prepared positions. Once such positions have been pierced or outflanked and they are forced to retreat from them, they become helpless victims of the motorised enemy. In extreme cases they can do no more than hold on in their positions to the last round." In contrast, when tanks blasted apart tanks or were destroyed by foot soldiers before attacking infantry, or found themselves mired in impassable terrain, manpower and capital devoted to armor simply proved a lost expense.[18]

At the epic tank battle of Kursk (Operation Citadel, July 5–16, 1943), both the Russians and Germans deployed quality tanks to prevent their enemy from slicing through infantry. But given that superior Russian numbers were matched by German marginal quality and training advantages, the two armored forces neutralized each other without either side achieving a breakout. The Russians suffered three times as many casualties and seven to ten times the number of tank losses. Yet they still ensured both a tactical and strategic German defeat, a fact that might suggest numbers rather than the quality of Russian tanks and the training of the crews were pivotal. Of the masses of Russian infantry and armor at Kursk, a despairing Panzer crewman thought Russian tanks were scurrying "like rats" all over the battlefield.[19]

General Erhard Raus saw the armored stalemate at Kursk as the turning point of the entire Eastern Front: "Victory was once again in the offing, but it turned out to be a Russian one. Our eleven panzer divisions—reconstituted during a lull lasting three months—could not come to grips with the Red Army's reserves to annihilate them because Hitler threw all of the German armor into Operation Citadel in July 1943 and bled it white upon running into a fortified system of hitherto unknown strength and depth. Hitler thereby fulfilled Stalin's keenest hopes and presented him with the palm of victory." Kursk proved to be Germany's Pyrrhic battle of Heraclea (280 BC) or Asculum (279 BC), when Greek invaders won battles in Italy only by suffering losses and erosion of morale that would preclude ultimate strategic victory. Generals Model and Manstein, to paraphrase Pyrrhus's lament of Asculum's strategic consequences, might have sighed, "if we prove victorious in one more such battle with the Russians, we shall be utterly ruined."[20]

THERE WAS NOTHING in the immediate German past to suggest that the Nazi government would produce the most lethal tanks by the end of World War II, at least as narrowly defined by their superiority in tank-on-tank battles. Germany had produced just a handful of its clumsy A7V tanks in World War I. In 1939–1940 German tankers startled the world with blitzkrieg victories, due not to superior tanks but to their better training, unit cohesion, officer corps, and morale. On the Eastern Front, their inferior German tanks achieved impressive kill ratios over clearly more lethal Russian T-34s, and continued to do against the late and vastly improved Russian models of 1944–1945.[21]

However well-trained the crews, however visionary the officers, however great the global reputation of blitzkrieg, the vast majority of early German (and Czech) tanks before 1942 nonetheless were no better and often worse than Russian, American, and British designs. The thinly armored PzKpfw I (approximately 1,500 built) tankette had no main battle gun and was originally designed as a trainer. Its replacement, the PzKpfw II (approximately 1,900 built), was initially outfitted with only a light 20 mm gun of the sort used for anti-aircraft duty. Even the prewar American M2 light tank, obsolete when the war began, was outfitted with a much larger 37 mm main gun. The envisioned successor to the PzKpfw II, the PzKpfw III, was slated to become the backbone of the new armored corps (some 5,700 built). But even its updated gun—a longer-barrel, high-velocity 50 mm that replaced the original 37 mm—did not ensure superiority over most Allied tanks of the time. There was no valid reason by late 1941 to believe German armor should have proven the terror of the European continent.[22]

Blitzkrieg played on the myth of German technological superiority and industrial dominance. But the successes of early Panzer divisions were instead predicated on the poor preparation and morale of Germany's enemies. The PzKpfw Is and IIs, Stuka dive bombers, and horse-drawn artillery and transport were formidable only against European border enemies whose militaries were not battle ready, such as those of Poland, Denmark, Norway, Belgium, Luxembourg, France, Yugoslavia, and Greece. Some of the German generals were aware of their Panzer mirage. As early as mid-1940, veterans of armored encounters were warning Hitler's staff that the Wehrmacht was in no shape to invade any country that possessed tanks comparable to their Panzers and air support.[23]

One of the most inexplicable facts of World War II was the chronic poor quality of German tanks that entered Russia in 1941, almost twenty-two months after the war had begun. Not only were the Panzers (over 50 percent of them obsolete Mark Is and IIs and Czech models) little better than most of their Russian counterparts, and often quite inferior to growing numbers of T-34s and KV-Is, but they also were outnumbered. This lapse, and the utter German failure to acknowledge it prior to the invasion, was astonishing, given that the success of Operation Barbarossa was predicated on rapid armored assaults achieving a "shock and awe" victory within a few weeks, in the fashion of those earlier triumphs of 1939–1940. German tank inferiority in 1941–1942 did not necessarily mean that the largest armored invasion in history was doomed. But it did ensure that there would be no quick collapse of Russia.[24]

Hitler reportedly understood the Wehrmacht's dilemma. He supposedly remarked to General Heinz Guderian at Army Group Headquarters on August 4, 1941, "if I had known that the figures for Russian tank strength which you gave in your book were in fact the true ones, I would not—I believe—ever have started this war." It was a stunning admission that the single issue of tanks had altered the entire course of World War II. Hitler had just sent almost four million Axis troops against a former ally in hopes of a quick victory spearheaded by tanks, but without any appreciation of the quantity, quality, or production capacity of his new enemy's armored forces—information that was known to his generals as early as 1937. Guderian, infamous for his ex post facto, self-serving revisionism, nonetheless may be right that he had "estimated Russian tank strength at that time as 10,000; both the Chief of the Army General Staff, Beck, and the censor had disagreed with this statement. It had cost me a lot of trouble to get that figure printed; but I had been able to show that intelligence reports at the time spoke of 17,000 Russian tanks and that my estimate was therefore, if anything, a very conservative one."[25]

Only with the updated later models of the PzKpfw IV did Germany first produce a good tank in respectable numbers (approximately 9,000). With sloping armor and a reliable engine, the PzKpfw IV would eventually become the most widely produced German tank of the war, a workhorse continually updated with increased armor and a more powerful gun. Yet when even a few of the improved PzKpfw IVs entered Russia in the first German waves of Operation Barbarossa, their crews were still astounded at how an otherwise poorly organized and deployed enemy matched up evenly, and how hard it was for Germans to knock out even the small numbers of new T-34s with the PzKpfw IV's still underpowered gun.

One veteran anti-tank battery crewman's recollection of first meeting a T-34 proved surreal: "Half a dozen anti-tank gun shells fire at him which sound like a drum roll. But he drives staunchly through our line like an impregnable prehistoric monster." In a December 1941 shootout with T-34s, a German tanker said of the effect of his 50 mm gun on Russian tanks: "But there was no visible effect. Damned peashooter!" The fright of German Panzer crews at unaccustomed Russian weapons was a trope throughout the history of warfare. It was felt just as much by Philip V's confident Macedonian cavalry, who on first encountering the lethal swordplay of Roman horsemen, were shocked at the carnage that a Spanish *gladius* might inflict on supposedly invincible troops such as themselves: "For men who had seen the wounds dealt by javelins and arrows and occasionally by lances, since they were used to fighting with the Greeks and Illyrians, when they had seen bodies chopped to pieces by the Spanish sword, arms torn away, shoulders and all, or heads separated from bodies, with the necks completely severed, or vitals laid open, and the other fearful wounds, realized in a general panic with what weapons and what men they had to fight."[26]

Official reports from the Russian front as early as a few weeks into the invasion suggested similar widespread panic on the part of German crews when confronted by superior Russian tanks: "Time and again our tanks have been split right open by hits from the front, and the commander's cupolas on the Type III and IV tanks have been completely blown off. . . . The former pace and spirit of the attack will die down and will be replaced by a feeling of inferiority, since the crews know that they can be knocked out by enemy tanks while they are still a great distance away." Note again that Type III and IV tanks (Mark IIIs and Mark IVs) were the *best* models of German tanks that entered Russia; over half the Panzer fleet was far worse.[27]

As a result, many German officers by late 1941 hoped that German industry might in desperation quickly reverse engineer or outright copy T-34s to produce them in similar numbers. But the obstacles to duplicating the T-34 were not only German pride in engineering. Guderian, an original German architect of Panzer doctrine and later inspector-general of armoured troops, claimed, probably correctly, that by 1942–1943 Germany lacked enough strategic materials (especially bauxite) to copy the T-34 aluminum diesel engine and high-quality steel armor. It may be a damning concession that in the very first months of Operation Barbarossa—a gamble predicated on armor dashes—the Third Reich's tanks were not only inferior to Russian T-34s, but that German industry did not have the wherewithal to copy superior enemy models in sufficient numbers.[28]

A tank race followed that ultimately reached absurd lengths. The shock of the T-34 also suggested that there might be further Russian surprises on the horizon. Russian armored production also now brought into doubt the entire ideological premises for invading Russia in the first place: to take Russian territory from inferior and backward peoples and to give it to those more technologically sophisticated, who, by their intellectual superiority, deserved it. Hitler failed to grasp that the antidotes to the T-34 (and to the heavier Russian KV-I) were not just to be found in thicker armor and bigger guns, although he would eventually accomplish both those traits with the deployment of the Tiger, the so-called King Tiger, and the more versatile Panther. To thwart Russian armor, prototypes of improved German heavy tanks were suddenly rushed into production, most famously the Panzerkampfwagen VI Tiger. A few of the so-called Tiger Is appeared in August 1942. They usually handled with ease the offensive and defensive challenges of the early models of the T-34. Equipped with a seven-hundred-horsepower engine, a vastly superior 88 mm main gun, and up to five inches of sloped armor, the early Tiger models had good odds of destroying Russian tanks at ranges of well over a mile. And at that distance it was largely immune from penetrating counterfire. But the Tiger's record weight (almost 60 tons), size (20 feet long and over 12 feet wide), and cost (over twice that of an updated PzKpfw IV) often nullified what advantages it offered over the T-34.

In contrast, the T-34's success came from the Russian ability to produce it in enormous numbers, while ensuring that it remained mostly reliable and continually upgraded. As a general rule, then, the answer to strapped German industry by late 1942 was not to produce a few good weapons, but plentiful adequate ones.[29]

Gigantism—the psychological disorder that ever bigger is always better—had been historically a bane of military technology, from Demetrius the Besieger's outlandish *Heliopolis* siege engine to the Japanese super-battleships *Yamato* and *Musashi* that likewise led to a colossal waste of men and material, and yet were scheduled to be superseded by a "super-*Yamato*" of ninety thousand tons with 20-inch guns. Hitler suffered especially from the disease that seems to infect autocrats with a special vengeance. Tigers were too large for many bridges and roads, and wore out their tracks and transmissions quickly. They were expensive to transport. They gulped fuel at record rates. They were costly and time-consuming to produce, built to exacting specifications, required extensive training to operate and maintain, and ultimately were produced in too few numbers (1,350) to make much difference on the Eastern Front, despite their feared reputation among enemy tank crews. Most important, they took over ten times as many man-hours of labor to produce as American or Russian medium tanks.[30]

Nonetheless, German gigantism continued with the upgraded Tiger II, or so-called King or Royal Tiger—an impractical monstrosity, ten tons heavier than its predecessor, four feet longer, and with two inches of additional armor. Yet if Tiger IIs were the deadliest tanks in World

War II, they were also rare on the battlefield, given that fewer than five hundred were produced. The fetishes of German tank design with regard to firepower and armor led to even more absurdities. Prototypes of the so-called Maus tank (PzKpfw VIII) were to reach thirty-three feet long and two hundred tons in weight, armed with a 128 mm cannon, and protected by over ten inches of armor in places. They were similar in spirit to the huge Krupp rail guns and V-weapons that might have been technologically impressive but otherwise proved a poor investment in terms of cost-benefit ratios of delivering effective explosives to the enemy.[31]

The Panther was a far better answer to the T-34 than the huge Tigers. The Panther was heavier (45 tons) than the T-34, and better armed (a lethal, long-barreled, high-velocity 75 mm gun) and armored (over 4 inches, on average). Its reengineered transmission finally proved far more reliable. The quality of its steel construction was superior. Yet the Panther was not as unwieldy, underpowered, or inordinately expensive as the Tiger, which is not to say it was ever reliable or as easily maintained as the American Sherman. Still, its sudden appearance in summer 1943 raised the question of why the Nazi hierarchy had not rushed something like it into production by mid-1941 to coincide with a vast invasion predicated on superior armor.

Initial reliability problems led Hitler at first to compare the Panther to the innovative but problem-plagued Heinkel 177 heavy bomber ("the Panther is the crawling Heinkel"), but the Panthers in the last two years of the war were considered by armored commanders on both fronts as the best all-around tank. Perhaps had Hitler waited to invade the Soviet Union until 1943 (and had he not been under Allied bombing attack) with the final combined production numbers of seventeen thousand PzKpfw IVs, Tigers, and Panthers, then his own strategic blunders might not have so quickly nullified the excellence of his soldiers and officers.[32]

Germany was faced with an enemy alliance that was capable of producing nearly a quarter-million tanks in American, British, and Russian factories: five times the eventual total German output. Russia was able to move much of its entire tank industry eastward; the Third Reich was never fully able to exploit operating tank factories in France and Czechoslovakia in occupied Europe to maximize German output.

The solution to that problem on a multitude of fronts was perhaps not six thousand Panthers, but in theaters from Anzio and Normandy to the Crimea either to field fifty thousand Panthers and PzKpfw IVs, or a corresponding enormous production of 88 mm anti-tank guns and fighter-bombers. What best illustrated the ultimate fate of the German Panzers was that by 1944 there were no longer proper Panzer divisions at all, with each division having only one or two tank battalions of well fewer than ninety tanks each, while American armored divisions typically deployed three battalions of anywhere from two hundred to three hundred tanks each.[33]

After the war the Nazi production minister Albert Speer claimed that he had sought both to simplify and expand tank production to match the Allies. For all his later mythmaking and contradictory recollections, he probably did cut out duplication, end waste, and focus on fewer models of weaponry, so much so that even after the bombing of 1944–1945, by war's end Speer was producing four times the number of weapons from each ton of raw steel that Germany had managed in 1941. Nonetheless, by 1944 even Speer's efforts were too late, given shortages of strategic materials, Hitler's ingrained interference in industrial policy, labor shortages, damage from Allied bombing, and fuel disruptions. Germany ended the war with a relatively small number of excellent tanks after beginning it with a relatively large number of mediocre ones. The one constant to German Panzer forces over forty-four continual months of fighting was not quality tanks, but superior crews, who achieved astounding kill ratios over the tanks of all their enemies—an impressive, but in the end, irrelevant achievement.[34]

A MYSTIQUE ABOUT Russian tanks inspired awe on the Germans, who were forced to confront them, and among the Russians themselves, who rightly equated tanks with their national salvation. Some Russian couples wrote to officials offering to use their own money to buy a tank, so that they could operate it in tandem. Indeed, one Russian patriot Alexandra Koitos commanded a huge forty-five-ton IS-2 Stalin tank, with her husband serving as mechanic and they fought through the Baltic states all the way to Berlin.[35]

It was not just Soviet propaganda that made claims that Russian heavy tanks were vastly superior to German models. Until 1943, German officers had wholeheartedly agreed. From Hitler on down there was praise from the German High Command for the T-34. First Panzer Army General Paul von Kleist summed up the early T-34s that he had encountered with the simple declaration, "it should be clear to us that the infantry, at this time, runs away from every Russian tank because they have no defence against them."[36]

Part of the problem in initially assessing the T-34 was that Western powers—both Allies and Axis—knew very little about Stalin's military capabilities. Most of what was written about Soviet industry in general proved to be untrue, emblemized perhaps by the writings of the Pulitzer Prize–winning journalist for the *New York Times*, Walter Duranty, who falsely reported about the successes of the Soviet state in the 1930s. But along with misinformation about the starvations, show trials, and purges, Westerners and the Japanese also vastly underappreciated the extent of the Russian prewar arms buildup. Even if they were to grant that Soviet factories could turn out lots of munitions, they could not yet conceive that the finished products were comparable to Western quality.[37]

The initial and problem-plagued models of the T-34s nevertheless shocked the Germans, not unlike the manner in which unfamiliar Parthian mounted archers flummoxed supposedly superior Roman Republican legions in the East, or the massed ranks of longbowmen stunned the French crossbowers at the Battle of Crécy (1346), or improvised explosive devices had stymied Americans in Iraq when such mines began shredding thin-skinned Humvee transport vehicles. General Guderian best summed up German confusion: "We believed that at the beginning of the new war we could reckon on our tanks being technically better than all known Russian types; we thought this would more or less cancel out the Russians' vast numerical superiority." Such arrogance was bolstered by successes of German armor so far, despite the demonstrable inferiority of Panzer Mark Is, IIs, and IIIs. German armored divisions had lost only 1–2 percent of their crews to enemy action, and seen only 2–3 percent of their early-model light tanks destroyed in the conquest of Poland (in addition to numerous damaged and worn-out tanks), and later, despite heavier losses in the West, had easily found ways to counter some of the heavier, better-armed and better-armored French tanks. The lesson from France was that superior morale and training allowed German tankers to ignore the quality of enemy armor. But, in fact, the Russians had at least as much experience in tank battle as had the Germans prior to Operation Barbarossa. The Soviet border fighting with Japan (1938–1939) and against Finland (1939–1940)—fought in diverse landscapes and climates—had taught the Russians more about the limitations of undergunned and underarmored light tanks than the Germans had learned in the relatively rapid and easy blitzkrieg victories over Poland and Western Europe.[38]

The new Russian T-34 tank that reached widespread production by late 1942 reflected a decade of adapting imported German, British, and American suspensions, engines, and armament technology, and was constructed on American principles of mass production, using simple designs that were of moderate cost, easy to operate, and simple to maintain. After only a few weeks in Russia, German tank crews were already meeting some of the nearly one thousand newly produced T-34s, and the experience made them almost immediately shed all the confidence gained against mostly outnumbered and inadequate European tanks in 1939–1940. One Panzer regimental commander, Hermann Bix, noted in an October entry in his diary, "and then we saw something that we heretofore would not have considered possible: We saw our tanks pull back by the company, turn around and then make haste to disappear over the high ground."[39]

The T-34's strengths were manifest in a variety of characteristics. Its lighter aluminum diesel engine was often less likely to ignite when hit than the otherwise dependable gasoline engine in the German PzKpfw IV tank. It offered a good degree of power for its weight. A high-velocity 76.2 mm gun was better than the PzKpfw IV's 50 mm cannon, and, in fact, perhaps superior to almost any 75 mm or 76 mm tank gun in the world in 1941–1942. The Russian tank's sloped armor and wider tracks meant that it was both less vulnerable and more mobile than the Mark-series German tanks that entered Russia's decrepit road system in June 1941—if not also more cramped and sometimes dangerous for crews.[40]

Most important, by focusing on just a few models, and eventually moving most tank production out of harm's way beyond the Ural Mountains, by the end of 1942 the Soviet Union was exceeding German tank production, and yet was deploying tanks, at least until the arrival of Tigers and Panthers, of comparable and often superior quality. Despite poor tactics and inexperience, Russian armored forces were able to hold off German Panzer forces by early 1943 at Stalingrad, and began to grind them down six months later at Kursk.

For all its clumsiness, limited production, and inexperienced crews, the even-heavier KV-I (Kliment Voroshilov) tank (45 tons, 90 mm of armor, a 76 mm main gun, and a 550 hp engine) outclassed any heavy German tank until the appearance of the Tiger in late 1942. A Panzer brigade commander, Heinrich Eberbach, summed up the typical German reaction at meeting a few KV-Is in January 1942: "Our tanks encountered a Russian tank brigade, which was exclusively outfitted with heavy tanks—T-34's and KV-I's. The steel giants were overwhelmingly superior to our Panzer III's and Panzer IV's. . . . I had to give my soldiers, who were accustomed to victory, the order to pull back twice in order to avoid being destroyed."[41]

On average, the Germans destroyed somewhere between three and seven T-34s for each German tank lost. Yet the successful deployment of armor forces rarely rests on the premise of tank-versus-tank battles, or Panzer "aces," however dramatic and deadly particular tank crews could be. If such principles won armored battles, the Germans would have knocked out Soviet armor by the third year of the war. Indeed, in any given one-on-one tank battle by mid-1943, the initial models of the T-34 proved mostly inferior to both the Tiger and Panther, and perhaps no better than the late model and updated PzKpfw IV (or for that matter latter models of the American Sherman, especially the ingeniously adapted "Firefly"). Its optics were mediocre and accuracy questionable. The 76 mm gun itself was large enough with good velocity, but was surpassed in size by the Tiger and in quality by the Panther. The two-man turret of the T-34 ensured slowness in aiming and firing. Most early models lacked reliable radios. The advanced design of the sloped armor also meant reduced space for crews and poor visibility. Early T-34 engines were powerful for their weight but had a short life, and were plagued by poor air filters.

Despite the parity of late-model T-34s and the superiority of heavy Stalin IS-2s, German Panther tank crews on average tended to be more highly trained and skilled even late into the war. In March 1945 in a not-unusual tank battle, two Panthers near Danzig wiped out an entire column of Russian heavy tanks. During the three days of fighting, twenty-one heavy and super-heavy enemy tanks were destroyed by German Panzers without a single loss. By late 1942, T-34s were more vulnerable to updated German wheeled and hand-held anti-tank guns than were German tanks to Russian counterparts, especially because German hand-held Panzerfausts and Panzerschrecks were the most effective hand-held anti-tank recoilless rifles and rocket launchers of the war.[42]

The Soviets deployed an astonishing four hundred thousand tank crewmen in World War II. Perhaps three hundred thousand perished— an eerie testament to German skilled air, artillery, and tank crews. Yet Russian tank forces grew each year of the war, analogous to the increase of the US merchant marine fleet, which expanded in size even in the depressing months of 1942 as U-boat kills reached all-time highs.

Accept two paradoxes and then the controversies over the American M4 Sherman tank's effectiveness become somewhat irrelevant—or rather emblematic of the entire American approach to total war. First, when Shermans initially appeared in 1942 and early 1943 in North Africa and Sicily, they were perhaps the best tanks in the West. Yet by the time Shermans were deployed in the thousands in 1944 and 1945 in Italy and Western Europe, they were clearly inferior to most German models, with traumatic psychological effects on the entire American armor corps. Typical was the experience of Sherman tanker Corporal Patrick Hennessy, who watched his tank round bounce off a Tiger tank: "I thought: 'To hell with this!' and pulled back." Another Sherman tanker noted: "The Sherman was a very effective workhorse, but as a fighting tank it was a disaster."[43]

Second, Shermans in American rather than British sectors did not often encounter superior German Tiger and Panther models in tank-to-tank battles, and they outnumbered German medium and heavy tanks in Western Europe by ratios of about ten-to-one by late 1944. Later accounts of British and American analysts found that the great killers of Sherman tanks were not German Panzers but rather anti-tank guns and the Panzerfausts. If the reputation of a tank rests on its ability to support infantry rather than overcoming enemy tanks, then the Sherman proved invaluable—a fact that was never fully appreciated during and only rarely after the war.[44]

Americans should have entered the war with well-armored vehicles. After all, despite not producing tanks in World War I, the United States had invented the idea of assembly production of tractors and automobiles. No country was more familiar with the internal combustion engine than America. When the war broke out in September 1939, the still-neutral Americans had over two years to learn from the strengths and weaknesses of blitzkrieg. American strategists noted that French tanks were well armed and well protected but lacked cohesive tactics, radios, mobility, and reliability, while the German PzKpfw I-III tanks were wanting in the former and yet formidable in the latter characteristics.[45]

The Americans fulfilled their hope of at least entering the fighting with tank superiority, an impressive achievement given that in 1940 there had been only 440 obsolete tanks in the entire country and a mere 330 new tanks produced that year. In just two years, the Americans would build tanks at the rate of more than twenty thousand per year, and go on to produce more tanks and general armored vehicles than any other nation. In addition, the new M4 Sherman that appeared in late 1942 at the second battle of El Alamein was felt to have easily matched the undergunned, underarmored, and unreliable German PzKpfw I-III models, in a way that the British Churchill, Matilda, and Valentine models had not. And the Sherman was a vast improvement over early American light M3 Stuarts, medium M3 Lees, and Grants.[46]

The Sherman's 75 mm short-barrel gun was a practical dual-purpose cannon. It had long barrel life, proved ideal for high-explosive rounds against infantry, and with anti-armor rounds was superior to the existing 50 mm gun of both the upgraded PzKpfw III and the PzKpfw IV. At a little over thirty tons, the Sherman was heavier than the early model PzKpfw IV, with roughly about the same amount of armored protection. The heavier Sherman was as fast and mobile as early German tanks, with a larger, more powerful and durable engine. More important, the Sherman was more dependable mechanically and easier to maintain and repair than any of the German tanks. In many categories—radios, crew comfort, and ease of maintenance—it was superior to the Russian T-34. Unfortunately, such advantages did not always impress crews on the battlefield. The popular perception was that by 1944 Shermans when hit by most German tank guns had a tendency to burn up like "Ronson lighters," albeit due more to earlier poor ammunition-storage systems than to intrinsically inadequate armor or poorly designed gasoline engines. Yet of all tanks, the survivability ratio inside Shermans when hit by anti-tank fire was not inordinately low. Of the more than six thousand Sherman tanks in the European theater of operations that were knocked out, on average one of the five crewmen was killed, one wounded, and the other three (60 percent) were unscathed. Later applications of ad hoc armor and improved escape hatches likely increased survivability.[47]

Whereas the PzKpfw IV would shortly be upgraded with more armor and a much improved 75 mm gun, the more versatile Sherman for 1942 and 1943 remained largely static, as if it had met armor requirements and could rest on its laurels. In most cases, the classical German 75 mm tank gun (mostly known as the 7.5 cm KwK 42 L/70)—with a longer barrel and a more powerful shell—could usually penetrate thick armor at long distances in a way that the Sherman's 75 mm could not.

Yet other American strategic and tactical principles would explain why Shermans could survive against German upgraded PzKpfw IVs, Tigers, and Panthers after the Allies landed in Normandy in June 1944. Even if a superior German tank might encounter a Sherman, the Americans assumed they could rely on excellent support from heavy artillery (often in direct FM radio contact with Sherman crews), fighter-bombers, and a nearby fleet of roaming "tank destroyers." The latter were lightly armored but fast-moving gun platforms that supposedly were on call to race to the front to meet enemy tank advances, fire their more lethal shells, and then scramble out of harm's way. In fact, tank destroyer doctrine only made some sense by autumn 1944 with the haphazard introduction of the late-model M36 "Jackson," (1,400 built), which replaced the lighter M10 "Wolverine" and fast M18 "Hellcat" with their underpowered 76.2 mm barrels. The M36's 90 mm high-velocity gun and new anti-tank shells could penetrate most German tanks at great distances. Yet far earlier (and far more effectively), the Germans had mastered the idea of using their more numerous 88 mm flak artillery as anti-tank weapons. Later, when motorized as "tank destroyers" (*Jagdpanzers*), they proved even deadlier than the ubiquitous 75 mm *Sturmgeschütze* III assault guns. By 1945 the heavier armed *Jagdpanzers* were superior to most models of tank destroyers, due to larger gun calibers and superior shells, far better frontal armor, better training (at least initially), and mostly because they were seen as supplements to rather than replacements for tank-to-tank dueling.[48]

Soldiers and civilians wondered in late 1944: Where was the American tank equivalent of the P-51, the M1 carbine, or the Pacific aircraft carriers that were not just produced in great numbers, but proved qualitatively as good or better than individual enemy models? The fear that American tank crews were literally roasted alive in their rare encounters with Tigers and Panthers spread a sense of depression among tankers. Outrage followed back home that was not necessarily predicated on strategic realities. Upgraded and "jumbo" Shermans (the M4A3E2 and later M4A3E8 models) proved only stopgap measures that on occasion offered tank parity.

An American tank's best chance by summer 1944 in a tank duel with German armor was to catch a Panther or Tiger by surprise and then floorboard ahead to fire quick volleys at point-blank range at the sides and rear—a rare but not impossible scenario. General Patton once related such a Sherman victory: "Our tank had been coming down the road, hugging a high bank, and suddenly saw slightly ahead, in a hollow to its right, two Panther tanks at a range of about two hundred and fifty yards. These it engaged and put out of action; then, apparently, charged to finish them, and by so doing, uncovered three more tanks, which it engaged at a range of not more than forty yards. All the German tanks were put out and so was ours."[49]

Patton may have been right about how Americans might find ways to knock out Panthers and Tigers, but usually in these rare tank-to-tank battles the cost was far higher than Patton suggested, especially in France in summer 1944:

> During the First Army breakthrough battles in July and August, the 2d Armored Division tankers had learned how to fight German Panther and Tiger tanks with their M4 Shermans. They knew that the ammunition of the 75-mm. gun with which most of the M4's were armed [a low-velocity shell about 13 inches long, as compared with the 28- to 30-inch high-velocity 75 mm shell of the Panthers] would not penetrate at any range the thick frontal armor of the Panthers and Tigers, but could damage the sides and rear. Therefore, the tankers had used wide encircling movements, engaging the enemy's attention with one platoon of tanks while another platoon attacked from the rear. They had suffered appalling losses: between 26 July and 12 August, for example, one of 2d Armored Division's tank battalions had lost

to German tanks and assault guns 51 percent of its combat personnel killed or wounded and 70 percent of its tanks destroyed or evacuated for fourth echelon repair.[50]

The "Sherman" became an abstraction as the world's first modular tank, given that its sound foundation offered limitless opportunities for experimentation and variation, from "rhinos" that ploughed through the hedgerows to "funnies" that swam and exploded mines. Sherman models were eventually upgraded with both a 76 mm higher-velocity gun and, more famously, the British "17 pounder" (76.2 mm/3-inch barrel), whose muzzle velocity and large payload could at last match the feared German 88 mm gun of the Tiger I and Tiger II or the high-performance 75 mm Panther barrel.

The American armor tragedy was the failure by the June 1944 Normandy landings either to have an up-gunned model or to have fielded an additional heavier tank to supplement the Sherman and match the Tiger or Panther—and to have done so in far greater numbers. The United States could have produced at least a few hundred of the heavy M26 Pershing tanks by mid-1944 had General Lesley McNair and other advocates of tank destroyers and light tanks not opposed the idea. As a consequence of this lapse, Sherman tank crews were reminded to avoid tank-to-tank duels. Most by late 1944 needed no such admonition, given that they considered Shermans with even the 76 mm gun a "deathtrap." A certain paranoia about meeting a rare Panther or Tiger set in among American crews, prompting many to stack sandbags to add protection to their inadequate armor, a habit that infuriated General Patton: "I noticed that all the tanks were covered with sandbags. This was very stupid. In the first place, it made the soldiers think that the tanks could be hurt; in the second place, it overloaded the machinery; and in the third place, it added no additional protection. I ordered their removal at once." Barring the mass production of a new heavier tank, there should have been more of an effort to replace the Sherman's main 75 mm or 76 mm gun with either a longer, higher-velocity barrel, or a 90 mm gun, an idea that was raised and then quickly dropped. As in the case of Britain, but quite unlike the Russian or German experience, all American tanks had to be transported by sea to the front, making shipping weight, handling, and offloading important criteria.[51]

All these problems notwithstanding, American armored forces in North Africa, Sicily, Italy, and Western Europe ultimately defeated enemy tank and infantry forces. The United States prevailed in Europe because of ubiquitous and reliable Shermans that more often fought Axis infantry rather than enemy armored units. And when they met superior German

tanks, Shermans could often rely on close air and artillery support. It prevailed in the Pacific, where armored thrusts were not a part of island and
amphibious warfare to the same degree as in the European theater. Shermans proved superior to all Japanese tank models, and provided invaluable support in the major landings from Tarawa to Okinawa.

Still, the rare but horrific encounters with German heavy tanks were
such a searing experience for US armored units that the Americans vowed
never again to put their crews into a tank that could not easily outfight all
enemy armor. That conundrum was not perhaps solved until the early
1980s with the emergence of the Abrams tank, which would prove clearly
superior to its rivals for over three decades. During the First Gulf War,
US Abrams M1A1 tanks, in the last major tank-to-tank duels of the twentieth century, helped to destroy well over 160 Iraqi Russian-built tanks in
a series of engagements on February 26–27, 1991, without losing a single
American tank to enemy tank fire. It was as if the Americans had finally
married the reliability of the Sherman with the lethality of the Tiger.[52]

THE BRITISH INVENTED the tank. Their prewar theorists were among
the most sophisticated advocates of armored tactics and independent
tank units. Before the D-Day landings, the British, guided by Major General Percy Hobart, adapted the Churchill, and to a lesser extent the American Sherman tank (as a mine flayer and amphibious tank), to a variety
of ancillary duties, from bridging ravines and streams to flamethrowing
and clearing barbed wire. When the American Sherman tanks in summer 1944 proved undergunned against German counterparts, it was the
British who brilliantly reengineered the lethal 17-pounder gun into a
Sherman turret, creating the deadly "Firefly" and allowing an otherwise
inadequate Allied tank force emerging from Normandy to obtain some
parity with German Tigers and Panthers.[53]

Given such technical genius and experience, it was surprising that
the British entered the war with mediocre tanks and did not build first-
rate models until the end of the conflict. Part of the reason was that, like
the Americans with their flawed concept of "tank destroyers," so too the
British clung to their own tactical fallacies, especially a dual-use system of
tanks that complicated design and production. So-called infantry tanks—
plodding, well-armored tanks within infantry formations that would
blow holes through enemy lines—would be reinforced by faster and less
protected "cruiser tanks," which in independently operating units would
rush in to exploit breaches and achieve encirclements. All this was too
clever by half, and analogous to the flawed British naval idea of large,

fast, and vulnerable battle "cruisers" like the HMS *Hood* and HMS *Repulse* partnering with better-protected battleships. In fact, even British cruiser tanks were often slower than their German counterparts, and their infantry tanks even less protected. Such bifurcation likewise retarded the idea of a single versatile tank being integrated with air support, artillery, and infantry to break through enemy lines.[54]

By dispersing British talent and industrial resources on a variety of designs—Centurions, Challengers, Churchills, Comets, Cromwells, Cruisers, Crusaders, Matildas, Valentines, and a host of others—the British failed to incorporate lessons from the battlefield into one standard model. It was not that British industry was incapable of turning out thousands of good tanks. At war's end, Britain's total tank production had reached nearly thirty thousand, quantitatively comparable with that of Germany's Panzer output. There were other considerations that hampered initial British efforts to produce by 1943 a basic tank comparable to the Sherman, the T-34, or Panther. Like the Americans, the British fought not only the Germans but also the Japanese, who never produced an adequate tank. As a result, there was less pressure on the British to upgrade their tanks, given that their earlier models were still superior to the Japanese light types that the British met in Burma. And, of course, as in the case of the island Japanese and the North Americans, British military doctrine in general was not predicated on ground combat across borders, but rather on expeditionary forces whose transportation challenges favored lighter armor designs.[55]

Finally, after mid-1942, continuous battles on the Eastern Front had begun to sap German Panzers. British and American strategic planning was beginning to be envisioned as a specialized zero-sum game: the huge Soviet tank force, with its tens of thousands of T-34s, ensured that the majority of first-rate upgraded PzKpfw IVs, Tigers, and Panthers would never be used in full force on the Anglo-American fronts. Assuming that by 1944 there would be a British battle tank appearing in quantities and quality comparable to the T-34 was analogous to expecting the Soviets to deploy thousands of four-engine bombers. In a way, for the British, the superb Lancaster heavy bomber was their version of the T-34 tank; by late 1944 they did to German cities and industry by air what the Russians did on the ground to German infantry and armored forces. In fact, British strategic bombing of German plants—particularly the near destruction of Kassel—probably did as much to reduce the presence and operability of German Tigers as did T-34 Russian tanks.

The initial British infantry tanks—the Matilda Is and IIs—despite their satisfactory armor, were equipped only with light machine guns or small turret guns. They were barely adequate against infantry. German 88 mm artillery could easily blow apart the Matilda IIs at over a mile distant. By the time of the second battle of El Alamein in October–November 1942, most Matildas had been destroyed or worn out during the prior year of fighting.[56]

Faster Cruiser Mark I and Mark II tanks (A9 and A10) also had little luck fighting German Panzers and were built only in limited numbers. The hope for the newer Valentine tank was to restore British parity with the Germans. Although over eight thousand Valentines were produced—an impressive achievement that exceeded all German Panther tank production—and proved mostly reliable, they weighed only half of what the Shermans did. Their 40 mm and 57 mm guns were inadequate, and their armor remained insufficient.

Improved Cromwell cruiser tanks (4,000 built) soon followed. For the first time they seemed to offer the British an excellent all-purpose medium tank. Although they were slightly lighter than Shermans, Cromwells at least enjoyed a lower profile and more frontal armor than did early Sherman models. Cromwells were extremely fast and mobile. Their new Rolls-Royce Meteor engines were reliable. Yet even with increased armor and a 75 mm gun they did not marginally supersede the American tank.

Heavy Churchill tanks (7,300 built) were rushed into deployment in late 1942. The Churchill's weight (39 tons), substantial armor (up to 4 inches), and excellent suspension made it comparable to German later model tanks. But constantly upgraded Churchills soon proved underpowered. They were not as reliable or as easily maintained as Shermans. Their armor was not sloped, and even their improved main gun (75 mm) was not effective against Panthers and Tigers.

The British finally reached parity with the best German models in late 1944 with the Comet (A34). It fired the same caliber projectile as the Sherman 76.2 mm gun but was vastly upgraded with improved shells and velocity. The Comet's improved armor and Rolls-Royce Meteor engines made it in some ways superior to all models of the Sherman. The Comet, however, came too late, with only about 1,100 tanks produced by war's end. And when the British finally mastered the idea of a standard universal tank with the superb Centurion, the first British tank that was clearly superior to both Panthers and T-34s, the war was over.

The fact that the British received and deployed over twenty thousand American Stuarts, Lees, Grants, and Shermans—a sum almost greater than all British front line tanks produced during the war—was a reflection of its own inability for the first five years of the war to produce an adequate tank in large enough numbers to equip British armored divisions.

But that fact perhaps was an understandable lapse given Britain's insistence on fighting in all the wars of World War II—on and below the seas, in the skies, and across Asia, Europe, and North Africa—often in places where tanks were irrelevant.[57]

ONE PARADOX OF armored warfare during World War II was that a vehicle designed to protect its crew from shells and bullets often became the focus of such overwhelming concentrations of fire that it proved as much an incinerator as a refuge. Seventy-five percent of Soviet tank crews did not survive the war. Over 80 percent of all T-34s, possibly the best all-around tank of the war, were destroyed or disabled.

It is easy to see why tanks proved to be deathtraps. Tanks had limited visibility. They were neither especially fast nor particularly mobile. They were relatively easy to spot, and were targeted by lots of other tanks, anti-tank ground and shoulder-fired weapons, fighter-bombers, mines, and artillery. They were hard to climb into and even harder to escape from. Early riveted models encouraged "spalling," in which interior rivets dislodged to become lethal projectiles under the pressure of incoming enemy rounds. But the worst threat was the presence of stored high-explosive and armor-piercing shells and large-caliber machine gun ammunition inches away from an internal combustion engine.

There were lots of ways to stop a tank: blow it apart with another tank or artillery gun, destroy it from the air with bombs or rockets, have individual soldiers attack it with anti-tank projectiles or crude incendiary devices, lay mines and obstacles to block its passage, or simply deny it fuel. As a general rule, on all fronts by mid-1943 German tanks were not effectively stopped by Allied shoulder-mounted infantry weapons (unless the infantry was using captured German stocks), or even often by other tanks unless they were updated Russian T-34s and Stalins. Neutralizing Panzers instead required close air support, artillery, or disruption in German fuel supplies and deliveries—or occasionally by mid-1944, British up-gunned Sherman tanks.

The reason that the Russians lost most of the T-34s produced was not because of Soviet fuel shortages or mechanical difficulties, but rather because Luftwaffe fighter and dive bombers, Tigers and Panthers, Panzerfausts and Panzerschrecks, and 88 mm mobile artillery all were especially effective against even excellent Russian armor. In contrast, the British and Americans relied mostly on tactical air superiority and a clear numerical advantage in artillery to meet the threat of German tanks. Modified Sherman "Firefly" tanks were produced in greater numbers than were the

Tiger I and Tiger II combined (over 2,000 Fireflies were sent to France), and offered parity in rare tank-to-tank encounters on the Western Front. The Sherman "Firefly" proved a far more efficient investment in delivering a lethal shell to a heavy tank than were the huge Tigers.[58]

Amid the triumphalism of blitzkrieg, few remembered that it almost always was predicated on air dominance and superior numbers but otherwise was only possible for brief periods without reliable supply lines. Breakthroughs also usually required blunders on the part of the enemy to preclude timely retreat, or at least to mass on a narrow front with exposed and vulnerable flanks. Implicit to the success of armored encirclements was also finite area. Pity the poor enemy without the space to retreat before German armored advances, in hopes that the Panzers would outrun their supply lines.[59]

Rare armored dashes nonetheless might advance at rates of thirty miles per day and thereby through shock collapse entire enemy fronts. In their initial armor sweeps of summer 1941, for instance, the Germans altogether probably destroyed about five thousand Soviet tanks. They may well have captured or killed three million Soviet soldiers, and perhaps occupied territory responsible for about 40–50 percent of Soviet industrial production. In summer 1942 German armored forces of Army Groups A and B of Army Group South advanced over five hundred miles, and nearly reached the Caspian Sea—only to find their spearheads too far from supply lines and offering the Russians attractive salients for counterattacks. The German armored advances were almost always spearheaded by updated PzKpfw III and PzKpfw IV tanks, but also assumed absolute Luftwaffe superiority, plentiful mobile artillery, adequate fuel supplies, better tank crews, and superior numbers. Yet note that the two longest and most successful armored thrusts in history—in southern Russia and North Africa—did not lead to strategic victory.

Blitzkrieg ended in 1943 with the surrender at Stalingrad and later stasis at Kursk, not so much due to considerable German losses in both battles per se, as to the appearance of hundreds of new T-34 tanks each month, the end of Luftwaffe dominance, and the sheer number of new Soviet infantry divisions and artillery units. By latter 1942, the Eastern Front was costing the Third Reich a hundred thousand dead each month. In that year alone, the Germans lost 5,500 tanks, eight thousand guns, and a quarter-million vehicles.[60]

On a lesser scale, Rommel and his Afrika Korps were to meet the same fate, at about the same time as the 1942 German blitzkrieg stalled at Stalingrad. The causes of these failures were hauntingly familiar, despite the vast difference in ability of the two respective senior commanders.

Rommel, like Paulus, was forced to assume that German experience and expertise might still trump enemy numbers and material advantages, or that success in individual tank battles translated to strategic momentum. Instead, both German advances were again far from sources of supply. Neither had ever quite calculated how to be adequately provisioned with fuel, replacements, and food, even had they won respectively the landmark battles at El Alamein and Stalingrad.

On the Eastern Front, armored vehicles often returned to their late World War I role of accompanying and protecting infantry advances or slowing enemy assaults. As both the Germans and Soviets continued to deploy better tanks to the front and were terrified of being trapped by mobile pincer movements, all the more did armored warfare descend into a war of attrition. Still, a few of the most dramatic Allied armored advances of the war occurred in its last full year, when Axis air power nearly vanished from close ground-support roles and Hitler's serial orders of no retreat to trapped armies gave the Allies new opportunities. The late July 1944 breakout of the US First Army in Normandy (Operation Cobra) was predicated on massive bombing of the German front by the Eighth Air Force. A hole was blasted in German defenses on two back-to-back bombing missions by three thousand aircraft, marked by waves of 1,500 American B-17 and B-24 strategic bombers used for the first time on a large scale as tactical aircraft, with help from over a thousand medium American B-25 and B-26 bombers, and assorted fighter-bombers.[61]

A second breakthrough occurred after the collapse of German forces at the Falaise Pocket and the cumulative destruction of some forty divisions in the two-month battle for Normandy, followed by the mad dash toward the German border of Patton's Third Army for much of August 1944. Patton's unexpected breakout shared the same characteristics of Germany's early armor advances. Later, Hermann Goering, in his Nuremberg interviews, had that dash to the German border in mind when he stated that Patton was the most effective of the Allied commanders ("your most outstanding general"), and the breakout at Avranches the Americans' greatest achievement in the West. General Fritz Bayerlein, a Panzer division commander in Normandy, in grandiose language summed up Patton's armored thrust:

Not even the battles of annihilation of the 1940 Blitzkrieg in France or in 1941 in Russia, can approach the battle of annihilation in France in 1944 in the magnitude of their planning, the logic of their execution, the collaboration of sea, air and ground forces, the size of the theater, the strength of the combatants, the bulk of the booty, or the hordes of prisoners. Its greatest importance, however, consists in its strategic effects, that is, that it laid the foundation for the subsequent final and complete annihilation of the greatest military state on earth.

The German breakout phase of the so-called Battle of the Bulge (December 16, 1944–January 25, 1945) worked for just ten days (December 16–26), given that it was predicated on achieving initial surprise, on the superiority of a thin line of Tigers and Panthers on a limited front initially aimed at green troops, on bad weather that would ground Allied fighters, and on obtaining captured fuel. After a few days, all that proved too many ifs. Understandably the German offensive quickly lost steam once the weather cleared and Allied fighters returned, fuel shortages slowed the Panzers, and the Allies got over the shock of surprise and systematically brought to bear their advantages of manpower and equipment. After the war, General Gerd von Rundstedt, still bothered by the fact that Hitler's hare-brained scheme ("Watch on the Rhine") had been popularly labeled the Rundstedt Offensive, supposedly was reported to have scoffed, "Moltke would turn in his grave at Hitler's military tactics, particularly his tactics in the so-called Rundstedt Offensive, which Rundstedt said should be known as the Hitler Offensive."[62]

Nonetheless, rare massed tank assaults against infantry that were not supported by comparable tanks, or air and artillery, remained an almost mythical combat experience, analogous to the rare unleashing of heavy lancers against retreating nineteenth-century foot soldiers. During the Polish campaign, German officers observed that "numerically superior German tanks had such a demoralizing effect on enemy tank crews that they often jumped out or showed the white flag."

Such a specter of unchecked armored blitzkrieg had collapsed not just Polish, Dutch, Belgian, and French armies, but also their entire war efforts. The battles that involved the greatest number of captured soldiers almost always followed from armored encirclement or an unchecked armored advance: the Battle of Bialystok-Minsk (June 22–July 3, 1941), the Smolensk encirclement (July 6–August 5, 1941), the Battle of Uman (July 15–August 8, 1941), the First Battle of Kiev (August 23–September 26, 1941), Vyazma-Bryansk (October 2–21, 1941), Operation Uranus and the destruction of Axis forces near Stalingrad (November 19–23, 1942), the Falaise Pocket (August 12–21, 1944), and the destruction of two US divisions during the first days of the Battle of the Bulge (December 16–20, 1944).[63]

Every great tank breakout at some point ran out of fuel. Partly this was because World War II militaries put far more emphasis on a tank's defensive and offensive capability than on its fuel consumption, range, and logistical transport. During the battle for France, German Panzers often found themselves out of fuel and stalled waiting for tankers to catch up. The same was true after the first two weeks of Operation Barbarossa, and of Rommel in his race across Libya into Egypt. During Patton's August 1944 drive through France, his Third Army had outrun its supply lines and his Sherman tanks ground to a halt. Patton's army alone consumed 350,000 gallons of gasoline per day; collectively, the Allied armies in summer 1944 in France were burning eight hundred thousand gallons per day. The entire German strategy in the Battle of the Bulge was predicated on capturing Allied fuel supplies, a gambit that only half succeeded and was not enough to keep the gasoline-starved Panzers going. It was striking how both the Allies and the Axis accepted the dependence of tanks on steady fuel supplies and yet how often both sides found their offensives sputtering to a halt due to gasoline shortages.[64]

TANKS HAD HELPED to radically change the course of a conflict in only a few of the many theaters of World War II: in North Africa (1940–1943), and in Eastern (1939–1940) and Western Europe (1944–1945). In the first case, the coastal deserts, unobstructed terrain, clear weather, and sparse population proved ideal for armored operations between evenly matched British and Axis forces in periods when one side had not yet achieved air superiority. In the second, the good roads of Western Europe, rich infrastructure, and the short distances from border to border meant that it was less challenging to supply tanks with fuel and air support, and their crews with water and food. In contrast, the vast expanse of the Soviet Union, its primitive roads, and general impoverishment often meant that even huge armored encirclements did not always lead to enemy collapse, while the availability or shortage of fuel, food, and spare parts—not just armor and arms—spelled victory or defeat. Other than the British pursuit of the Italians in North Africa in late 1940, and the subsequent chase of Rommel in 1942, or the American breakout from Normandy in early August 1944, it is hard to cite the use of British and American tanks—in contrast to motorized infantry, artillery, or tactical and strategic air power—as the chief causes for the Allied success.[65]

Blowing a tank track off a T-34 with a Panzerfaust—a weapon that an American tank officer dubbed the "most concentrated mass of destruction in this war"—was a far better investment than building and deploying a seventy-ton Tiger II to outduel a Russian tank. By war's end, heavy tanks were increasingly risky investments of capital and labor; the

Americans and the Russians best squared the cost-benefit circle of the expense of tanks versus results achieved in enhancing infantry by focusing on just one or two simple designs, mass-producing them and at relatively cheap cost, and ensuring that they were reliable and easy to maintain.[66]

The great bloodbath on the Axis battlefields came in 1944–1945, when the Allies achieved tactical air superiority and were free at last to attack ground forces as they pleased. Germans suffered more military deaths just in 1944 than they had between 1939 and 1943, when the Luftwaffe had near parity with the Allied tactical air forces. Also, as important as the quality of tanks was the number of truck transports, fixed and mobile artillery pieces, the availability of machine guns, anti-tank weapons, mortars, and land mines, and effective radio contact with artillery batteries.

DESPITE THE MOBILE nature of combat in World War II and the romance of armor assaults, the great killer of Axis and Allied soldiers remained artillery. The exact percentages depended on the year and theater of operations, but at least half of the combat dead of World War II probably fell to artillery and mortar fire. The paradox of both greater mobility and also greater numbers of men killed by semi-stationary artillery is probably explained by the sheer number of shells fired in World War II: well over eight million field guns and mortar weapons were produced during the conflict. With the death of blitzkrieg at Stalingrad, much of the fighting from early 1943 onward on the Eastern Front—the great incinerator of Axis and Red Army soldiers—turned more static in the fashion of World War I in the West, and often regressed to artillery, rocket, and mortar barrages aimed at fixed infantry positions. In some sense, the trajectory of World War II hinged on the side that placed the greatest number of artillery pieces on the field of battle. Each of the three major Allied belligerents produced more large guns than did Germany, Italy, and Japan combined. The most significant statistic of the war was the ten-to-one advantage in aggregate artillery production (in total over a million large guns) enjoyed by the British Empire, the Soviet Union, and the United States over the three Axis powers.[67]

Over one billion artillery shells were produced in the United States alone. In addition, there was far more variety and specialization in artillery than just two decades earlier. Rates of fire increased along with greater accuracy and range. A plethora of smaller and more mobile projectiles made the life of the foot soldier ever more hazardous even as he himself became ever more lethal. New technology also put into his hands the ability to take out tanks and artillery platforms themselves. If the infantryman was buffeted by howitzer, mortar, and rocket attack, in turn he sometimes had the means to destroy artillery, tanks, and other armored vehicles with shoulder-fired artillery, in effect through a single cheap shot cancelling out hundreds of man-hours of labor invested in armor and artillery production and training.

The Germans produced both too many types of large artillery and in aggregate not nearly enough to fight on multiple fronts against the Allies. As was characteristic in World War I, Germany still pursued the evolutionary dead end of constructing huge, immobile Krupp rail guns: capable of firing five- to seven-ton projectiles, with a range of twenty-four to thirty miles. As we have seen at the siege of Sevastopol, such behemoth 800 mm (31-inch), 1,500-ton guns ("Gustav" and "Dora") proved largely wasted assets, given their slow rates of fire, immobility, enormous maintenance and transportation costs, and easy vulnerability to motorized infantry, tanks, and air power.

Yet all that said, the Germans nevertheless produced the most practical and lethal artillery pieces of the entire war: some twenty-thousand 88 mm flak guns of numerous varieties. The Allies may have produced anti-aircraft guns with greater ranges than the twenty-five-thousand-feet effective killing range of the German 88 mm, and anti-tank guns with larger and more lethal calibers. But no gun in World War II was as versatile as the German 88 mm. It could be set up in minutes, fire rapidly (15–20 rounds per minute), had superb accuracy and easy sighting, and in theory could with adjustments alternate between targeting bombers or tanks. For the two years of Operation Barbarossa, the long and high-quality barrel of the 88 mm offered about the only consistent German means for taking out Russian T-34 tanks. For just the cost of constructing two mostly irrelevant battleships, the *Bismarck* and *Tirpitz*, Hitler might have instead produced about 7,500 additional 88 mm guns, well over half the number that were transferred from the Eastern Front to protect the German homeland from Allied bombers.[68]

Toward the end of the war, the Germans began installing great numbers of high-velocity, long-barrel, rapid-firing, and high-powered fixed 75 mm assault guns on supposedly obsolete Mark III tank chassis. The resulting turret-less but up-armored *Sturmgeschütze* IIIs were highly mobile, low-profile, and easily maintained anti-tank guns that survived on average seven times longer on the Eastern Front than did late-model German tanks. Over ten thousand were built at costs far cheaper per unit than tanks.[69]

Even more impressive than the unique 88 mm gun, the Germans finally saw the wisdom of mass-produced, cheap weapons as they turned out some six million Panzerfausts ("tank fists"). At close distances, these cheap, single-shot, disposable anti-tank weapons in their final incarnations proved deadly to most Allied tanks on either the Western or Eastern Fronts. And when taken together with another three hundred thousand Panzerschrecks ("tank frighteners")—a German up-engineered copy of the American bazooka—single German soldiers often had the ability with an inexpensive weapon to knock out thirty- to forty-ton tanks. German foot soldiers with such weapons probably took out 10 percent of all enemy tanks that were lost in the war, despite the late entrance (1943) of the Panzerfaust in the war. The simple, reliable, cheap, and deadly Panzerfaust and Panzerschreck were the forerunners of the later rocket-propelled grenade (RPG) that likewise tended to level the playing field between sophisticated armor forces and poorly equipped foot soldiers.[70]

By 1943 the Wehrmacht's armor was outnumbered on every front, but its infantry's superior hand-held anti-tank weapons and mines mitigated some of the consequences of that numerical imbalance. General Erhard Raus related how desperate German soldiers, on the retreat in winter 1945, often could disable or destroy Russian T-34 tank columns with simple disposable Panzerfausts: "The NCO knocked out the last tank with one *Panzerfaust*, whereupon the second tank turned toward the group of houses, firing as it moved toward the spot from which the tank commander presumed the resistance had come from. But using bushes as cover, the NCO had already crept up to the tank and from only a short distance knocked it out as well, using his second and last *Panzerfaust*." Russian infantrymen sometimes could likewise take out early-model German tanks through use of their own anti-tank weapons. At Stalingrad a Soviet major in a Russian rifle regiment related how one of his subordinates, a single shooter, Igor Mirokhin, destroyed in succession four German tanks before being decapitated by a German tank shell.[71]

The Russians focused on the most effective infantry support weapons that they could build well and in great numbers, producing more artillery pieces and mortars than any other nation during World War II, perhaps four or five times as many as Germany alone. At the beginning of Operation Barbarossa, the Soviet Union (approximately 33,000 guns) already had over four times as many artillery units as the German invasion forces. And by war's end, the Soviets often enjoyed artillery superiority of seven-to-one, which mitigated the frequent loss in quality of Red Army replacement infantry units during the last two years of the war. Indeed, by 1945 it was not uncommon for particular Soviet offensives to muster over forty thousand artillery and mortar tubes, such as in January assaults on Silesia and East Prussia, and the final April assault on Berlin. Artillery was the sole category of weapon in World War II in which the Soviet economy roughly doubled the production of each of its other two major allies, Britain and the United States.[72]

Yet perhaps the most innovative artillery platform of the war was not even a barreled gun, but rather multiple, self-propelled rockets, or Katyushas (also known as "Stalin organs"). They were usually mounted in groups of fourteen to forty-eight launchers, on either trucks or tracked vehicles. Their advantages over artillery were chiefly ease and cost of production, given that there was no need for the precision craftsmanship required in making artillery barrels and shells. Even more important, the multiple and simultaneous launches of rockets resulted in a larger payload delivery with far less need for expertise and training in comparison to artillery, even if the Katyushas lacked the accuracy of traditional howitzers and large guns. The truck-mounted Katyushas could fire and leave from the launching site far more quickly than could even the most mobile artillery. Over ten thousand Russian Katyusha platforms were produced during the war, in calibers most commonly ranging from 82 mm to 300 mm.

As in the case of the T-34 tank, the Germans were shocked that the supposedly less sophisticated Russians had deployed a completely new but effective weapon that was cheap, simple, and easy to use. As a general rule, emulation proved the best indication of weapon efficacy. Just as Germans, British, and Americans eventually sought to copy many of the characteristics of the T-34 tank, so too the other belligerents rushed into production their own rocket batteries.[73]

As was also true of US plane and tank production, the Americans soon produced standardized artillery platforms in enormous numbers. Perhaps the best were the light M2A 105 mm and the longer-range M1 155 mm howitzers. Both were mobile, accurate, and easily towed by trucks, or in the case of the 105 mm, were occasionally self-propelled. In many ways, the motorized 105 mm howitzer was the most versatile all-around infantry-support gun of the entire war. But the real American contribution to artillery lethality was not to be found in artillery pieces per se, but rather in shells and a sophisticated system of targeting. Quite surprisingly for an isolationist nation that had assumed air and naval power would project power abroad, the United States entered the war with the best system of synchronized artillery fire in the world, eventually to be known as a time-on-target (TOT) methodology that allowed different batteries in varied locales to concentrate their fire on shared targets, resulting in near instantaneous arrivals of a variety of different type shells from multifarious distances, thus catching enemy infantrymen unexpectedly and out in the open in the first vulnerable seconds of a huge barrage. Fire Direction Centers immediately behind the front coordinated radio requests from infantry (and tanks) for artillery support, and then allotted requisite artillery pieces, while reviewing accuracy by forward spotters and light observation planes. Thus America entered the war prepared to ensure that its greener soldiers were usually covered by artillery barrages more accurate and numerous than those of their enemies—and as effective as the far larger arsenals of the Soviet Red Army.

By late 1944, most prominently at the Battle of the Bulge, US forces were allowed to begin using top-secret new proximity fuze shells— theretofore limited largely to bombs, anti-aircraft shells, and artillery in the Pacific—that could be reliably programmed to burst at predetermined heights above enemy targets, making it extremely difficult for troops to find safety from shrapnel in foxholes or field fortifications. These innovative radar-directed fuzes had earlier proved particularly useful for American anti-aircraft batteries against kamikaze attacks in the Pacific, given that radio transmitters set off the explosives in the shell when they sensed a target roughly within a general preprogrammed distance. When used against land forces in Europe the new proximity fuze shells showered shrapnel downward and shredded German troops in the way that even older, preset proximity fuzes had not.[74]

American artillery proved critical to the success of the GI. He entered the European and Pacific theaters with the least amount of military experience in comparison to the German, Italian, British, and Japanese soldier. And yet he was to be deployed in the most diverse theaters and at the greatest distances from his homeland of any combatant of World War II. The United States, also unlike Germany and Japan, did not have enough prior wartime experience to discover which of its prewar assumptions about tactics and weaponry were valid, but instead sent its green troops head-to-head with those who drew on years of hardened campaigning from Poland to the Soviet Union to Manchuria. Without superior armor or air support in the early going, Americans relied on their artillery; it proved a great equalizer for American soldiers, until they acquired greater expertise and reliable air cover.

Japan was not known for either tank or artillery innovation. While the Japanese may not have designed the best mortars of the war and in comparison to the Allies produced them in limited numbers, they focused on types that were ideal for close-in fighting during the Pacific island campaigns and in Burma. The Japanese Type 89 grenade launcher, also known as the "knee mortar" (although it was never to be fired from the knee), was a cheap substitute for artillery support and could fire a variety of generic Japanese grenades. Its light weight (about 10 pounds) and easy assembly made it an ideal weapon for the dense brush, heavy rains, and fluid fronts of Pacific island fighting, where even light artillery proved cumbersome and difficult to deploy. Quite different was the strange but more frightening 320 mm Type 98 "spigot" mortar. It weighed about 675 pounds and its barrels wore out quickly. But at a fraction of the cost of large artillery, it gave Japanese troops singular heavy artillery support in the same difficult terrain and weather.[75]

Historians understandably focus on landmark innovations in air and sea power, and armor: the B-29 Superfortress bomber, the *Essex*-class carrier, or the T-34 or Tiger tanks. Less-dramatic breakthroughs in time-tested technologies such as artillery and rifles were not so romantic or heralded. Yet most soldiers were killed or wounded by either artillery in all its frightening manifestations or by small-arms fire. In both categories, the Allies, and especially the Russians and the Americans, found almost immediate parity with, if not superiority over, their Axis enemies, despite the latter's terrifying all-purpose 88 mm artillery piece, MG 42 machine gun, or the landmark StG 44 assault rifle. The huge imbalance between Axis and Allied artillery production in large measure explains why the vaunted German army could never compensate for its inferiority in air ground support and vehicle production.

MACHINES WERE NOT automatons; they had to be built, produced, and used by people, who had a myriad of choices concerning their creation and application. The reason why the United States produced superb aircraft carriers and Germany did not reflected quite different policies enacted by Franklin Delano Roosevelt and Adolf Hitler and their respective advisors. Why the United States won the Battle of Midway was not just due to superior intelligence or luck but is also explained by the respective admiralship of Admiral Raymond Spruance and Chuichi Nagumo. That British prime minister Winston Churchill did not order something as comparably foolish as the Axis surprise attacks on the Soviet Union and Pearl Harbor ultimately ensured that the Allied forces, not the Germans or Japanese, would win the war. The American worker could build a four-engine heavy bomber far more rapidly than a German or Japanese assembler could produce a medium two-engine bomber. The nature of leaders and the manner in which they mobilized their followers was every bit as important as scientific discovery and technological advance.

The following four chapters of Part Six return to the human themes of Part One that concerned the ideas of leaders, elites, and the masses that prompted and shaped the conduct of the war. People as supreme leaders, warlords, and factory workers determined how their fellow citizens were armed, equipped, and led on the field of battle—decisions that in turn explained why and where sixty million died in World War II.

By 1941 the family munitions firm Friedrich Krupp AG was building the famous 88 mm cannon in plants expropriated throughout occupied Europe. Here a wartime French factory turns out anti-aircraft models of the famous gun. *World War II Pictorial Collection, Envelope CP, Hoover Institution Archives*

Despite their dramatic appearance, Germany's huge K-5 rail guns never justified the time, manpower, and expense involved in their deployment. The battery pictured here was integrated into the Atlantic Wall defenses in France by 1944. *World War II Pictorial Collection, Envelope FF, Hoover Institution Archives*

Contrary to general belief, German tanks—like this medium Panzer Mark III—
that entered France in May 1940 were mostly inferior to their heavy French
counterparts, with only 2 inches of armor and a small 37 mm main gun. The
Mark III was constantly upgunned and reinforced with heavier armor, but
largely proved obsolete by late 1942. *World War II Pictorial Collection, Box 1, Hoover
Institution Archives*

The tractor plant at Chelyabinsk ("tank city"), relocated safely beyond the Urals and out of reach of the Luftwaffe, turned out thousands of Soviet tanks and mobile artillery, such as these huge SU-152 "Beast Killer" self-propelled artillery platforms, equipped with 152 mm guns and used in infantry support and as tank destroyers. *Russian Pictorial Collection, Box fBW, Hoover Institution Archives*

Tank soviétique arrêté par les grenades anti-tank allemandes.

The Soviets fielded huge self-propelled howitzers, such as SU-152 tank destroyers, designed to knock out heavy German Tiger tanks and fortifications. Yet small, hand-held German Panzerfausts and Panzerschrecks could take out such monsters—such as this crippled and abandoned SU-152 that Germans on the Eastern Front are analyzing. *World War II Pictorial Collection, Envelope CP, Hoover Institution Archives*

"Winston Is Back" was a slogan of relief when Winston Churchill returned to government as First Sea Lord of the Admiralty just hours after the war had begun. Here Churchill arrives at the Admiralty door on September 4, 1939—to the same office he had last used in 1915. *World War II Pictorial Collection, Envelope FP, Hoover Institution Archives*

General Erwin Rommel, commander of the Afrika Korps, consults with his staff in Libya on June 16, 1942, just five days before his capture of British-held Tobruk. *World War II Pictorial Collection, Envelope F, Hoover Institution Archives*

As head of the SS and a chief architect of the Holocaust, Heinrich Himmler (posing here in early 1935) was perhaps the most feared Nazi Party officer of the Third Reich. Yet prior to joining the Nazi hierarchy, Himmler had failed as a fertilizer salesman and poultry farmer. *German Pictorial Collection, Box 10, Hoover Institution Archives*

At a private Christmas dinner, Joseph Goebbels, chief Nazi propagandist, banters with Adolf Hitler. *Thomas J. Day Photograph Collection, Envelope A, Hoover Institution Archives*

After the first month of Operation Barbarossa, Hitler and his confident commanders emerge on July 25, 1941, from a strategy session at Hitler's Wolf's Lair headquarters. *Left to right*: Field Marshal Wilhelm Keitel (chief of OKW), Colonel Werner Mölders (Germany's leading fighter ace, who would die as a passenger in a plane accident four months later), General Karl Bodenshatz (liaison officer of Hermann Goering), the Führer Adolf Hitler, Major Nicolaus von Below (Hitler's long-time military adjutant), and Reichsmarschall Hermann Goering (head of the Luftwaffe). *World War II Pictorial Collection, Envelope FP, Hoover Institution Archives*

Benito Mussolini pins medals on young Fascist Party members shortly before he was dismissed on July 24, 1943, by the Grand Council of Fascism. *World War II Pictorial Collection, Envelope BH, Hoover Institution Archives*

Benito Mussolini's rescue from his northern Italian jail on September 12, 1943, was spearheaded by German commandos flown in on gliders and commanded by the legendary SS Hauptsturmführer Otto Skorzeny. Here two German airborne troopers pose for pictures, about ten days after the raid. *World War II Pictorial Collection, Envelope BH, Hoover Institution Archives*

During the so-called Sextant Conference in Cairo, Egypt (November 22–26, 1943), US president Franklin D. Roosevelt and British prime minister Winston Churchill confer with Turkish president İsmet İnönü, who, after the litany of Axis disasters in 1943, was moving his country from its former neutrality closer to the ascendant Allies. *World War II Pictorial Collection, Envelope CL, Hoover Institution Archives*

During the dark hours of the Ardennes campaign, General Dwight D. Eisenhower *(left)* and Lieutenant Generals Omar Bradley *(center)* and George S. Patton *(right)*—the American Big Three—are interviewed by *Stars and Stripes* correspondent Jules Grad *(foreground)*. *World War II Pictorial Collection, Envelope CN, Hoover Institution Archives*

Prior to the formal opening of the Potsdam Conference (July 17–August 2, 1945), Marshal Joseph Stalin of the Soviet Union *(left)*, American president Harry Truman *(center)*, and British prime minister Winston Churchill *(right)* informally confer with their respective advisors. Truman had been president for only three months, following the sudden death of Franklin D. Roosevelt in April. During the conference Churchill would be voted out of office and his seat at the conference taken by the newly elected prime minister, Clement Attlee. *World War II Pictorial Collection, Envelope CL, Hoover Institution Archives*

Lieutenant General Tomoyuki Yamashita, accused of allowing atrocities under his command following the capture of Singapore and during the defense of Manila, was convicted of war crimes and hanged on February 23, 1946. *World War II Pictorial Collection, Envelope EP, Hoover Institution Archives*

When American soldiers liberated the Dachau concentration camp in April 1945, the sheer numbers of corpses had overwhelmed the capacity of the crematoria—their doors eerily stamped with name *Topf*, the manufacturer. GIs sent hundreds of pictures like these home and they were quickly published worldwide. *Robert T. Frederick Papers, Album fA (p. 25), Hoover Institution Archives*

The German invasion of Greece in April 1941 focused on bombing Greek port cities into rubble and trapping evacuating British units. Here three generations of Greek women sit in shock among the ruins. *World War II Pictorial Collection, Envelope DF, Hoover Institution Archives*

# PART SIX

# PEOPLE

Leaders and followers, the living and the dead

*Men are the city-state, and not walls nor ships empty of men.*

—Thucydides[1]

# 16

# Supreme Command

OVER FIFTEEN MILLION Russians and German soldiers perished on the Eastern Front because of Adolf Hitler's insistence on attacking the Soviet Union and Joseph Stalin's naiveté about the Molotov-Ribbentrop Pact and his own initial paralysis in June and July of 1941. Without Hitler's manic commitment to go eastward, perhaps even die-hard Nazi generals would not have been able to convince their colleagues of the wisdom of Operation Barbarossa. And without Stalin's well-known paranoia, the Soviet General Staff might have believed credible reports of Nazi deployments near the borders of Russia all through the spring of 1941 and made the necessary defensive adjustments.

A single supreme mind in war, whether good or evil, can lead to millions of deaths incurred or avoided, in a way unrivaled by scores of subordinate generals and admirals. Italy and Great Britain were roughly similar in population in 1940. But had a Winston Churchill led Italy and a Benito Mussolini Great Britain, the wartime fates of both countries might have been quite different. The decisions of Neville Chamberlain and Édouard Daladier not to confront Hitler over the *Anschluss* or Czechoslovakia made more likely a European war in 1939 that would eventually lead to the deaths of sixty million over the next six years.

President Harry Truman's determination to use the atomic bomb probably precluded the need for a far more costly invasion of Japan, and by abruptly ending the Pacific war limited somewhat Stalin's ambitions in postwar Asia. Mussolini himself was responsible for the deaths of hundreds of thousands of Italians, Ethiopians, and Libyans in his fantasy attempts to create a new Roman Empire in North Africa with entirely inadequate forces. It is hard to imagine either Italian royalty or the General Staff deploying and supplying almost a million Italian soldiers in the Balkans and North Africa in 1940–1941.

Before the twentieth century, the great captains like Alexander the Great, Julius Caesar, Frederick the Great, or Napoleon doubled as heads of state and senior commanders in the field. But with greater complexity in military affairs after the nineteenth century, even in dictatorial societies like Nazi Germany or Soviet Russia, rarely did supreme military commanders, albeit sporting gold-braided hats and chests of medals, lead their troops into battle. Technological progress, especially the phone, telegraph, and radio, made it unnecessary that Hitler, in the leadership style of Frederick the Great on a horse, would invade Poland atop a Panzerkampfwagen Mark II scanning the front. Nor would Mussolini, who otherwise liked to ride horses, like a modern-day Caesar trot through the snows of Albania. A head of state wearing a uniform in World War II did not translate into leading from the front, or knowing much of anything about tactics and strategy—or even earning all the gaudy medals on his chest.[1]

Sometimes wartime leaders are judged as beneficiaries of their political systems in the manner that the Duke of Wellington gained advantage by answering to a parliamentary government and Napoleon did not. Yet often an Epaminondas the Theban, Saladin, or Kemal Ataturk succeeded or failed on his own exceptional merits and trumped the system that created him. Material and strategic resources often determine the fate of leaders. Give Hitler the industrial infrastructure of 1942 Detroit, or the raw manpower of the Soviet Union, and he might have fared better. For all of Hannibal's genius, Carthage drew on fewer assets than did the military of Republican Rome, which in the Second Punic War could survive the blunders of its many incompetent generals, such as Flaminius, Sempronius, and Varro.[2]

Collective and shared ideas, not the individual men who champion them per se, are supposed to matter more in democracies, which supposedly create strategies by group consensus. Churchill, however, saved Great Britain in 1940, when probably few other democratic leaders could have, only to be unceremoniously voted out of office in July 1945, well before the close of World War II in the Pacific. At that moment, however, a dozen or so politicians easily could have completed Britain's successful efforts against Japan. Apparently, *in extremis* a man like Churchill was irreplaceable, at better times not so much. In democratic societies, few wish to concede that in times of crises there are rare and irreplaceable leaders of the caliber of a Themistocles or Pericles who alone tower over committees and coalitions of anonymous experts and politicians that are still competent enough to preserve what the singular leader has bequeathed them. An everyman Truman could take the place of a Roosevelt after April 1945 without disruption in the long-held Allied plan of action. Yet Truman probably lacked the eloquence and political skills (and machinations) to have readied America for war in 1940. Had Hitler or Mussolini died in 1942, Germany and Italy might well have found a leader who sought—and obtained—a negotiated surrender.[3]

Since antiquity, democracies have at least had the advantage of incorporating a broader participation in decision-making that can aid even a dynamic leader. A Churchill or a Roosevelt knowingly accepted that they had to be more sensitive to the public perceptions of success or failure, and that they had to deal with a number of brilliant advisors and rivals who were not shy in pointing out their shortcomings. In other words, they had to earn political legitimacy and always faced the audit of a fairly free government and press—and a host of rivals who wanted their jobs. That reality meant that once controversial policies were announced—the primacy of the European front over the Pacific or the demand for the unconditional surrender of the Axis powers—it was hard for the people to complain later that their elected representatives acted without consent of the governed.

The upsides of keeping leaders honest and open to advice and criticism were sometimes offset by the downsides of a fickle majority, subject to demagoguery and sudden bursts of moblike exuberance or outrage. Such democratic volatility was first and best recorded by the historian Thucydides during the debates over Athenian intervention in Mytilene, Melos, and Syracuse. The aristocratic historian noted that before and during the first years of the Peloponnesian War, the Athenian Pericles almost alone had successfully managed the strategic decision-making of radically democratic Athens, precisely because his personal clout allowed him extraordinary latitude that was rare in most volatile democracies: "Whenever he saw them [the Athenian *dêmos*] unseasonably and insolently elated," Thucydides tells us, "he would with a word reduce them to alarm; on the other hand, if they fell victims to a panic, he could at once restore them to confidence. In short, what was nominally a democracy was becoming in his hands government by the first citizen." Perhaps Thucydides was right that during existential conflicts like World War II democracies run by a single, powerful, though legitimate leader become the most effective war-makers.

In a few hours after Pearl Harbor an American electorate that had resisted many of Roosevelt's efforts to mobilize for war was suddenly demanding almost instant operations against the Japanese—with little memory of their own prior equally fervent isolationism. In response, Roosevelt increasingly began to rule, even more so than when engineering the New Deal, as "first citizen," with a range of executive powers not normally associated with democracies but reminiscent of the extraordinary and occasionally extra-constitutional powers of President Abraham Lincoln during the American Civil War.[4]

From 1939 to 1940 non-democratic dictators like Adolf Hitler, Benito Mussolini, and Joseph Stalin—as well as Hideki Tojo from October 1941 to July 1944—posed as adept strategists without much need for subordinates to second-guess their genius. Their Machiavellian diplomacy and preemptive attacks—without regard to public audit or legislative veto—were judged only by their results and so were initially considered by Germans, Italians, Russians, and Japanese to have enhanced their respective national interests at little cost. Dictatorship was the apparent wave of the future. For short, surprise border wars against the weak, strongmen often did not need to mobilize their entire economies or to craft a long-term agenda to win huge sacrifices from a wartime public.

In contrast, the soon-to-be-extinct Western European democracies, the appeasing Great Britain, and the isolationist United States had all been confused and stymied by the rise of these single-minded dictators, Hitler in particular. The future Axis powers, as well as the Soviet Union, appeared resolute, determined, and calculating under the leadership of popular strongmen. Yet by early 1943, the very opposite had proven true. The dozens of bickering strategists who surrounded Winston Churchill and Franklin Roosevelt seemed essential. Even the relatively unrestrained media of wartime America and Britain, and the requirement to articulate war aims in public speeches to Congress and Parliament, helped to audit military practices. In matters of total war and mass mobilizations, the need to court voters seemed to have given the surviving democratic powers innate advantages over unstable and increasingly isolated Axis leaders cocooned in their bunkers and fortresses, and fearing the wrath of their own people as much as the enemy.[5]

Mussolini and Hitler, despite absolute rule, failed fully to mobilize the Italian and German wartime economies until late 1942 or even later; Churchill and Roosevelt, who operated under a system of checks and balances, quickly put their nations on a war footing. The authoritarians worried of the public consequences from shared sacrifice; the democrats assumed a blank check to demand them, confident in the self-initiative and individual self-reliance of democratic culture. Hitler understandably rarely spoke to the German people after Stalingrad. Of the six major World War II leaders, only the Axis heads of state Hitler, Mussolini, and Tojo faced wartime assassination plots, many of them originating from their own militaries. Field Marshal, and soon-to-be-relieved commander of Army Group South, Erich von Manstein summed up how isolated his Führer had become: "Hitler . . . thought he could see things much better from behind his desk than the commanders at the front. He ignored the fact that much of what was marked on his far-too-detailed situation maps was obviously out of date. From that distance, moreover, he could not possibly judge what would be the proper and necessary action to take on the spot."[6]

An unpopular Mussolini was deposed after the successful Allied invasion of Sicily. After the loss of Saipan, Tojo was forced to resign as prime minister in July 1944, with a number of officers contemplating his assassination. The age-old problem with dictatorships, aside from the limited input from advisors and experts, was that the public could always tacitly and implicitly withdraw its support as news from the front grew ominous. Even—or rather especially—under autocracies, the people never feel accountable for their prior ecstatic allegiance to dangerous strongmen. They are never on record as formally approving risky national policies through free and transparent elections of such extremists in the first place.

Even autocrat Joseph Stalin, in his forced flip-flop from Axis sympathizer to Big Three ally, discovered that the more military authority he delegated and the more flexible his command, the more the Red Army was likely to avoid the catastrophic disasters of the sort that had followed his top-down dictates between 1941 and 1942. The more successful he became in the eyes of his countrymen, so too might his failures be blamed on semi-autonomous subordinates. The stature of Marshal Georgy Zhukov rose with Stalin even as the reputations of Field Marshals Guderian, Manstein, and Rommel waned in Hitler's eyes.[7]

Democracies vent palace dissent. Adversaries sought to dethrone Churchill or Roosevelt by leaks to the press, votes of no confidence in Parliament, or attacks in Congress, or by running for office in 1944 or 1945. But to rid Germany of a dangerous Hitler or free Italy from Mussolini often seemed to require a gun or bomb—a fact well known to dictators.

Finally, the presence of two democracies allowed the Allied Big Three to function in a way the authoritarian nations of the Axis could not. Hitler's Germany and Stalin's Russia could partner for only twenty-two months between August 1939 and June 1941 because each side logically suspected that the other would renounce its prior agreements. For a disparate alliance to succeed, it is advantageous that at least some leaders within it have obtained government office legitimately and thus learned methods of holding power other than through brute force and prevarication. Stalin, for all his objections, privately accepted that he could trust Churchill and Roosevelt in a way that he, Mussolini, and Tojo never could Hitler. There really is no honor among unelected thieves.[8]

Fights were common among generals and planners, and they often included the Supreme Allied Command. Roosevelt and Churchill advanced hare-brained schemes, but they listened to the objections against them. In contrast to the bickering of Allied politicians and generals, the Germans, from the man in the street to the chiefs of the German Staff, never quite knew what nation Hitler would attack next or for what reason— only that it would be dangerous to second-guess even the most foolish of the Führer's directives. The same absence of discussion was almost as true of both Italy and Japan. In neither Rome nor Tokyo had there been clearly announced war aims to the public, not just because such states were closed societies, but also because almost all their military commanders themselves were not quite sure what Mussolini and Tojo and his advisors were intending, and usually dared not ask.[9]

Such praise of wartime consensual government is not to suggest that brilliant supreme leaders do not emerge from dictatorships, whether Alexander the Great or Napoleon. Philip II of Macedon exhibited brilliant military leadership lacking in the fickle and unprepared democratic Greek city-states. The ruthlessness and iron will of Joseph Stalin in large part explained the USSR's ability to surmount the difficulties in late 1942 of finishing the relocation of entire industries beyond the Urals, or to endure the losses at both Leningrad and Stalingrad without declaring either an open city, forsaking any further defensive efforts. And there were plenty of mediocre elected leaders such as Prime Minister Neville Chamberlain or former French prime minister and later head of the Vichy government Pierre Laval who brought their democracies to near ruin. Constitutional leadership does not guarantee victory—as the Czechs, Danes, Norwegians, Dutch, Belgians, and French learned in 1939–1940—much less does it ensure that a pedestrian parliamentarian can be expected to trump a brilliant autocrat.

Natural talent and the personal experience of a leader, regardless of particular political system, mattered as well. Adolf Hitler knew a great deal about the nature of infantry combat, as did Benito Mussolini and Winston Churchill; all three supreme commanders had fought in the front lines during World War I. For a while, Hitler's singular constitution bore up under responsibilities that would have killed most younger men. He clearly had uncanny psychological instincts about what drove men of power like himself and how to manipulate them accordingly. Yet Hitler, who possessed enormous powers of recall and concentration, lacked formal knowledge of or even a natural instinct for grand strategy. The similarly wounded noncommissioned veteran Mussolini was likewise ignorant of how to correlate Italy's strategic ends with its practical means. Churchill, Roosevelt, and Stalin in contrast, had also served in high administrative positions of government—as first lord of the Admiralty, assistant secretary of the Navy, and people's commissar for defence, respectively—and far better understood military strategy, financing and budgets, the politics behind defense appropriations, and how to create large staffs of advisors. It is often said that only veterans can wisely adjudicate war policy or possess the moral right to do so. But that notion is as accurate or inaccurate as assuming that only working farmers should be allowed to establish food policies, or that experienced Wall Street investors can be best trusted to set national fiscal agendas.[10]

Hitler and Mussolini could serially offer stirring patriotic speeches. But as absolutists they felt no need to offer detail or to explain ambiguity within their policies, and thus their success as communicators hinged entirely on the perceived positive pulse of the battlefield. Even the most eloquent propaganda cannot turn a disaster like Stalingrad into a heroic last stand to defend the homeland such as Thermopylae, or reinvent the bloodless Nazi walkthrough into Denmark into a Napoleonic masterpiece such as the French victory against the odds at Austerlitz. As the Wehrmacht steamrolled into Western Europe, Hitler's rants mesmerized millions. When the Russians and Anglo-Americans were closing in on Germany, the Führer simply gave up public speaking in a way Allied leaders never did during the dark days after the fall of Singapore and the Philippines. When in late 1944 a German private on leave saw his bombed-out Munich home, he wrote in his diary: "Who is to blame for all this? The English? The Americans? Or the Nazis? Had a Hitler not come, there would have been no war. If the Nazis had not talked so big, or put on such a show, or done so much saber-rattling, we would have peace with those who are our enemies today." Mussolini could never convincingly explain to Italians why he had declared war on the United States or invaded the Balkans. Perhaps he did not know himself.[11]

Except for a few weeks during the British Blitz and the initial German aerial attack on Moscow, Allied leaders were usually able to work and meet with their staff free of fear. In contrast, Hitler spent most of the war after 1941 underground or barricaded in bunkers at the *Wolfsschanze*, Berghof, and *Führerbunker* in Nuremberg, East Prussia, Bavaria, and Berlin, cut off from most of his civilian government and in virtual isolation, even when hundreds of miles separated him from the front. Historian Gerhard Weinberg noted: "Even the Hitler of 1943 is no longer the Hitler of 1940. He no longer fights easily with good fortune at his side, but now does battle only doggedly against his fate."

An Axis leader had good reason to fear his public. Mussolini was in danger of being bombed from early May 1943 onward; the Japanese leadership, from autumn 1944 and especially after March 1945. Assassination was a more immediate danger for Axis strongmen; it had been a staple of Japanese political life in the decade before the war. Mussolini survived several attempts; Hitler perhaps ten potentially serious plots in a decade in public life. Fear of assassination, the chance of being bombed, the approach of enemy armies—these were all threats that after 1941 faced the Axis leaders alone.[12]

By MID-1939, AT relatively little military, political, or economic cost, and without recourse to war, Hitler had succeeded in his original aim of returning Germany to its preeminent position of 1914. By June 1940, Nazi Germany had achieved most of the objectives once envisioned by the Kaiser's Germany, should it have won World War I, and yet more still. Even under the tenets of the supposed *Septemberprogramm* of defeating and occupying France and Belgium, the Kaiser had never quite dreamed of absorbing all of Western Europe, while assuming the remaining neutral nations were partisans of the German Reich. Imperial Germany before 1918 may have dreamed of incorporating all lands with sizable populations of German speakers. But Adolf Hitler, for all his cheap talk of avenging the injustices of Versailles, went further in envisioning German-speaking lands cleansed of their native inhabitants, and in annexing territories that had nothing to do with the postwar settlements of 1919–1920.[13]

Yet a year after winning Western Europe, with German popular opinion enthralled by his successful high-risk gambles, Hitler invaded the Soviet Union, with an unbeaten Great Britain still at his rear and a hostile arsenal of democracy in America beginning to rearm. Such foolhardiness after such skillful brinkmanship and war making would lead to the loss of all that his cunning and instincts had won prior to 1939. And even if the generals had genuinely opposed the invasion and vehemently advanced their counterarguments, their opposition would likely have been ignored. As General Warlimont noted of his colleagues at OKW: "The highest military circles—and this applies not merely to the senior officers of the Wehrmacht—apparently shared Hitler's view that the campaign against Russia would probably go quickly. This did not alter the fact that in basic strategic questions such as these the Operations Staff was in no position to express any different views since it had come to consider itself merely as the military working staff of Hitler."[14]

It is disturbing to think that eventually Hitler might have gotten away with holding on to his gains prior to September 1, 1939, or even possibly before June 1941, had he canceled Operation Barbarossa, avoided war with America, and made major concessions to Great Britain that even Churchill might not have been in a position to refuse. After all, Hitler had fooled a generation of European leaders and talked his way into achieving the rebuilding of the Wehrmacht ("the German people wants no war"), the plebiscite in the Saarland ("I have repeatedly assured the French that when once the Saar question is settled, no further territorial difference will exist between us"), the militarization of the Rhineland ("Germany has no further claims to make from France, nor will she make any"), the *Anschluss* with Austria ("a work of peace"), the destruction of Czechoslovakia ("the last territorial claim which I have to make in Europe"), and the nonaggression pact with the Soviet Union ("Germany never again to enter into conflict with Russia")—all without cost in blood and treasure. Had Hitler stopped there without invading Poland, the Allies might well have conceded to a huge German-speaking empire, one larger and more influential than at any time since the birth of the German state.[15]

Clearly, seizing power and creating a German dictatorship of Nazi yes-men did not offer the preparation and savvy essential to winning a global war, at least in comparison with the alternative experience of forming coalitions and alliances to win elected office. After Hitler began World War II in September 1939, he had no blueprint to end the war-making power of Britain, the Soviet Union, and the United States, whose defeats were in varying ways critical to his ideological agendas. The problem was not just that the Wehrmacht and the German economy at the outbreak of the war were without the resources to finalize Hitler's dreams in a global war. Hitler also could *never* achieve the material means for such grandiose ends, given that he lacked the shrewdness to coax or successfully coerce others, both allies and millions of Europeans under occupation, in helping him to complete them. In lieu of logic and realism, Hitler always ventured into fantasy, citing miracle weapons on the horizon, pontificating about *Lebensraum* without any sensible information on agricultural policy and production, weighing in on racial and cultural fault lines without any appreciation of Russian or American history and traditions, blinded by anti-Semitic hatred without appreciation of centuries of Jewish landmark contributions to European culture and science. Hitler's chief flaw as a strategist was that he used wild emotion to push his own daydreams, only to retreat to logic to refute sound objections to his policies, reminding us of Thucydides's ancient warning that "it is a habit of mankind to entrust to careless hope what they long for, and to use sovereign reason to thrust aside what they do not desire."[16]

After the heady victory in France, Nazi planners assumed that the war would be over shortly. As a result, they either alienated the Western Europeans under their control or began outright looting of the occupied countries. And if the Nazis sought to increase production of munitions from foreign resources it was often through the inefficient means of stealing infrastructure and shipping workers back into Germany, rather than by recalibrating and utilizing existing labor and factories in situ. Few European munitions plants were taken over and efficiently utilized for the Third Reich, even in the sometimes clumsy manner of appropriating the Czech Skoda Works. Hitler's obsession with the Jews was as militarily unsound as it was savage. His partnerships with neutrals like Sweden or Spain were predicated only on the degree to which he appeared formidable and dangerous. Napoleon's pessimism about so-called friends ("the Allies we gain by victory, will turn against us upon the bare whisper of our defeat") was relevant to Hitler's—and to all dictators'—dilemmas.[17]

All warlords commit mistakes. But not all of them err fatally as did Hitler, especially if they allow some audit and criticism. Even Alexander the Great assented to turn back from going farther into India. After the disaster in the Teutoburg Wald, Augustus finally agreed not to try to annex Germany and its environs north of the Rhine and Danube. A wily Franco was smart enough not to rush into war during the Axis euphoria of July 1940, or rather lucky enough that when he did plan on entering the war, Hitler's own greed and chauvinism dulled his enthusiasm.[18]

Hitler guessed rightly that the loser of World War I would be willing to run far more postwar risks than would the complacent winners. His bluster that national cohesion would turn around the hopeless conditions of 1918 resonated with the German people. Especially attractive to the public was Hitler's central thesis that Jews, the intelligentsia, and communists, not German greed in absorbing western Russia while shorting the Western Front—along with needlessly provoking an isolationist America—had forfeited the victory after the defeat of Tsarist Russia. These were cynical insights critical in obtaining power in Germany and carving off slices of borderlands for a Greater Germany, but they were of no value in waging a global war against enemies superior in manpower, resources, and leadership skills, and who did not care much for the intricacies of European politics and rivalries.[19]

Hitler's first—and in some ways, least appreciated—strategic miscalculation was the 1939 invasion of Poland. The problem was not that the

Wehrmacht could not easily divide up Poland with the late arrival of the Soviet Union, but that Hitler failed to grasp that his Polish War ensured a likely fight with the English-speaking Western democracies—and quite soon, with the British Royal Navy and Royal Air Force—that he had no way adequately to finance and to supply, and thus no way to end, as well as creating a common border with the Soviet Union. Yet after the stunning surrender of Paris on June 14, 1940, Hitler's strategically flawed ideas were seen as no more unsound than was the unorthodox attack through the Ardennes that had crushed France in less than two months. In these pre–Operation Barbarossa halcyon days, he was lauded by General Keitel, head of OKH, as "the greatest warlord of all time." Yet if Britain could not be invaded or coerced into submission, then any attack on the Soviet Union that did not result in near instant victory spelled an eventual two-front war against huge industrial powers of the sort Hitler had promised to avoid. For a leader who had vowed to learn from and rectify the verdict of World War I, an amnesiac Hitler instead seemed to be trumping the same errors that had ruined Imperial Germany.[20]

Without a moral sense, Hitler assumed that those weaker than himself were ethical only in word as a substitute for strength in deed. For someone who bragged about willpower and the unconquerable spirit, Hitler counted only on the power of things, not of ideas and human emotions. As his noted biographer Hugh Trevor-Roper once put it, "he was a complete and rigid materialist, without sympathy or even tolerance for those immaterial hopes or fear of imaginations or illusions which, however absurdly, cast a faint ennobling gleam on the actions of mankind."[21]

Hitler also suffered from the symptoms of the autodidact: superficial knowledge without depth or audit, energized by a forceful character dulled by a lack of subtlety. While his armies were stalling in Russia, Hitler's midday and evening table talk ranged from the quality of honey bees to the best depth of cement for autobahns, always punctuated by conspiratorial interjections of anti-Semitism, contempt for Slavic peoples, crackpot views on art, and obsessions with his own health. Oddly, on some scattered topics—the vulnerability of New York skyscrapers to aerial attacks, the nutritional value of uncooked vegetables, or the eventual popularity of what would become the Volkswagen Bug—Hitler was occasionally strangely prescient.[22]

In truth, Hitler knew little of war beyond blitzing weaker neighbors. Concerning Hitler's halting decisions in both North Africa and the Soviet Union, General Warlimont at OKW noted as early as mid-1942 that "he proved incapable of taking even the most urgent decisions in good time." Hitler, who had neither fought on the Eastern Front nor visited Russia,

completely misread the Eastern lessons of World War I: that even conquest and occupation sapped critical resources from German efforts elsewhere. After Hitler declared war on the United States on December 11,
1941, a shocked General Alfred Jodl called his subordinate Warlimont,
and in amazement announced, "you have heard that the Fuhrer has just
declared war on America?" Warlimont, equally befuddled, replied of the
staff's shock, "yes, and we could not be more surprised."[23]

Hitler's reasoning, such as it was, seemed aimed mostly at placating
Admirals Raeder and Doenitz of the Kriegsmarine who swore they could
starve Britain by wrecking US convoys as they left ports on the East
Coast—and then provided too few submarines and almost no surface
ships to do it. He should have remembered that a quarter century earlier
the Kaiser was likewise both flummoxed by US tacit support for France
and Britain, and Germany's inability to do much about it, leading to the
folly of the so-called Zimmerman Telegram in bizarre hopes of prompting some sort of formal Mexican attack across the US border.[24]

Hitler also figured that his newfound enemies would freelance and
treat each other as duplicitously as he had the other Axis powers. When
he announced to the Japanese ambassador General Hiroshi Oshima in
January 1942, right after Pearl Harbor and more than half a year after the
invasion of Russia, "never before in history have two such mighty military powers so far separated from each other—Japan and Germany—
stood together in war," he still had not yet invited the Japanese to attack
the Soviets in the East, ostensibly intent on hoarding his envisioned Russian spoils.[25]

Gaining Italy as an ally in 1940 while surrendering the Soviet Union
as a partner in 1941, and turning a neutral United States into an enemy
were poor trade-offs. Armchair strategists have offered all sorts of alternative scenarios to Operation Barbarossa that might have prolonged or
permanently deadlocked the war. The most sensible counterfactual would
have been a concentration of Hitler's four-million man, pan–European
Axis army either on an invasion of Great Britain, or, more feasibly, directing a huge expedition into North Africa and the Middle East that
might have cut off many of Britain's options, saved Mussolini's Italy,
made the Mediterranean an Axis lake, linked strategy with the Japanese
in the Indian Ocean—and initially avoided war with both the USSR and
the United States. Later both Nazi strategists and top-ranking generals
seemed to acknowledge such a lost opportunity.[26]

Operationally, Hitler habitually thought that as a rare rationalist he
alone detected some underappreciated economic advantage to be tapped
or, quite irrationally, a particular, though hidden to most, avenue of

revenge to be pursued that excused departure from sound strategic doctrine. Consequently, he serially turned setbacks into catastrophes, from Stalingrad to the Battle of the Bulge. The Battle of Britain was lost—to the degree that it was ever winnable—when the Luftwaffe quit concentrating on British airfields, radar stations, and aircraft factories and chose to firebomb London as supposed payback for the ineffective British attack on Berlin. The Ardennes offensive of late 1944 had no chance of strategic success, but it did ensure that there would be insufficient German reserves at the Rhine. The common theme in all of these disasters was again Hitler's unwillingness to look empirically at rapidly changing conditions on the ground, instead preferring to envision a perpetual world of 1940, in which ideologically driven Nazi soldiers were unstoppable.[27]

Hitler at moments seemed aware of his own failings, manifested in self-doubt. To Albert Speer, Hitler confessed shortly before his death that he had always known that Hermann Goering was a drug addict, corrupt, and a delusional sybarite, but apparently he had been too timid to confront Goering, given his earlier key service to the Nazi cause, even as the latter's buffoonery cost tens of thousands of Luftwaffe air crewmen their lives. At the height of the Wehrmacht's reputation in October 1940, and after marathon deliberations, Hitler could still neither cajole nor force a recalcitrant General Francisco Franco to enter the war or even to allow transit for German troops through Spanish territory.[28]

Hitler had largely been free of major maladies between September 1939 and July 1944, and up to that point was still hale enough. Close associates had seen no evidence of mental exhaustion or serious illness that should have been obvious even prior to mid-1944. A few months later Hitler certainly was a sick man, jaundiced, visibly suffering from coronary disease, plagued by an array of psychosomatic maladies as well as the possible onset of Parkinson's disease, surrounded by quack doctors, and searching for fantastic medical cures in the identical manner that he sought absurd nostrums for his ill-omened war. The failed assassination attempt of July 20, 1944, certainly marked a downturn. Goering claimed that Hitler after July "trembled on his left side, and his mind was not clear enough to understand the real situation of Germany."[29]

Germany's tragedy was that Hitler was not incapacitated far earlier in the 1930s. His ministers had long since been ignored; the General Staff was isolated. Finally, Hitler surrounded himself only with a group of mediocrities and sycophants—Goebbels, Bormann, Himmler, Goering, Jodl, Keitel, von Ribbentrop—whose rubber-stamped directives the military sought to ignore without gaining Hitler's ire. Typically, diehard pro-Nazi generals like Walter Model, Sepp Dietrich, and Ferdinand Schörner were not fired or executed. The most capable ones, such as Rommel, Manstein, and von Rundstedt were eventually bought off, sacked, or retired, and occasionally haphazardly reused, but never to their full potentials. Had OKW been staffed continuously by a Manstein or von Rundstedt, in conjunction with an OKH of von Bock, von Leeb, or Kesselring, with a supreme commander who followed their advice, Nazi Germany's military efforts might have lasted until 1946 or later.

Before the war, Hitler had never visited America, Britain, or Russia, the major countries he would declare war on. He had no direct knowledge of much of anything more than a few hundred miles from his birthplace. Smarting from a sense of class and cultural inferiority, he gleaned from self-directed study just enough ammunition to hate cosmopolitans such as aristocrats, scholars, the intelligentsia, and captains of industry, and so never really integrated enough of them into his strategic circle. In contrast, Churchill and Roosevelt—who felt comfortable and confident among the privileged classes, both in their admiration and suspicion of them—knew Europe firsthand. Both had traveled in Germany and had visited each other's country. Their knowledge of national character was based on experience and analysis rather than deduced from popular prejudices. In critical areas such as assessing operations in terms of geography, terrain, and climate and weather, they were reasonable. Hitler and Mussolini, in contrast, lived and died by their reliance on maps. Neither had seen an American factory or farm, a British industrial city—or a Russian road in spring or city in midwinter.[30]

MUSSOLINI WAS BY far the longest reigning of the three Axis leaders. He exercised the powers of prime minister for nearly twenty-three years, at first constitutionally and then within three years illegally. The simple fact that he seized power well before the Iberian dictators, the Japanese militarists, and the Nazis did, apparently won Mussolini inordinate prestige in the eyes of Hitler and of some Western elites. Hitler waxed on about Mussolini even as Italy neared collapse: "I hold the Duce in the highest esteem, because I regard him as an incomparable statesman. On the ruins of a ravished Italy he has succeeded in building a new State which is a rallying point for the whole of his people."[31]

The vast abyss between global fascism's aims and its means to achieve them are best illustrated in Mussolini's erratic wartime leadership. His grand talk of "*spazio vitale*" ("living space," or *Lebensraum*) for supposedly ethnically and culturally superior Italians throughout the central Mediterranean proved a disaster, lacking even the inclusive pretexts of the

Japanese Greater East Asia Co-Prosperity Sphere. Italian racialism precluded most attempts at winning hearts and minds in occupied territories. Enthused about neocolonial expansion, the weak Mussolini convinced himself that he had the force, manpower, and economic resources to resettle Italians on thousands of square miles of land from the Adriatic to the Horn of Africa, and to keep them safe in the face of indigenous opposition. His idea of an Italian Mediterranean was every bit as fantastical as the Greek irredentist *Megalê Idea* ("Great Idea") of a modern Aegean Hellenism spanning from Istanbul to Alexandria. On the eve of the war, Mussolini had declared that "Italy is therefore in truth a prisoner of the Mediterranean, and the more populous and prosperous Italy becomes, the more its imprisonment will gall. . . . The bars of this prison are Corsica, Tunis, Malta, Cyprus. The sentinels of this prison are Gibraltar and Suez. Corsica is a pistol pointed at the heart of Italy. Tunisia at Sicily; while Malta and Cyprus constitute a threat to all our positions in the eastern and western Mediterranean." But when Italy did go to war, it had no realistic plans of seizing the bars of Malta and Cyprus, much less the sentinels at Gibraltar and Suez.[32]

Italy's war abilities were at best narrowly confined to attacking weak and often preindustrial people—in Europe, those of the Balkans, and in Africa, Ethiopians, Somalis, and Libyans—with no assurance of being able to consistently defeat them or permanently control their territories. Mussolini's army was equipped like a pre–World War I military aimed at border defense, which explained why it enjoyed little success as an expeditionary force in France in 1940, in North Africa in 1940–1943, or on the Eastern Front in 1941–1945. The technologically impressive Italian fleet and air arms were Potemkin forces, not backed by adequate fuel reserves, and rarely upgraded or resupplied when they suffered wartime losses and maintenance shortcomings—facts known to Mussolini. Mussolini's parasitical war aims became grandiose immediately following the German defeat of France and the British destruction of the French Mediterranean fleet. He abruptly entered the war, assuming that the aerial mastery of Britain would be a mere footnote to the humiliation of France and Western Europe.[33]

Italy originally both welcomed and feared any German entry into the Middle East in force along a North African trajectory, anticipating dividing up spoils but fearing that there would be few left for the junior partner. Unfortunately for Italy, Britain survived, along with its four great Mediterranean bases at Gibraltar, Malta, Cyprus, and Alexandria. Then Germany invaded the Soviet Union and declared war on the United States, drawing off some of the Third Reich's potential strength from the Mediterranean. That Mussolini knew little if anything in advance about the invasion of the Soviet Union or the German declaration of war against the United States reflects the Oz-like world in which he lived.[34]

Mussolini never foresaw how vast numbers of tanks, ships, and planes were necessary for victory, or how economies would have to be fundamentally reordered to produce them. He did not fully mobilize the Italian economy for war, correctly believing that had he done so, only a constant stream of victories would have kept the strapped populace compliant. Instead he blustered about millions of Italian bayonets and how fascism was a force multiplier of war, while being completely dependent on the statecraft and resources of Adolf Hitler.

Mussolini almost always ignored the often-sound advice of his close advisors, most importantly his under secretary for war production, Carlo Favagrossa, who warned him that Italy would not be ready to fight a modern war until at least 1942 or beyond. Prewar Italy had produced less than 10 percent of the coal, oil, steel, and iron of Great Britain, the smallest economy of the three major Allied powers. Italy's large army was not motorized, had little air support, few quality tanks, and scant logistical sustainability. *Tankette* was an English diminutive largely in currency to describe Italian Panzer forces. Prewar Italy had the fewest vehicles per thousand people of any of the major European powers. The military was largely analogous to the small nineteenth-century British colonial army, but without the latter's skill, organization, discipline, and supporting fleet.[35]

To the degree that the Italian campaign of 1943–1945 tied down Allied forces, it was almost entirely due to the Wehrmacht's fighting on Italian soil. Largely because of Mussolini's strategic incompetence—most prominently, Italy's bungled invasion of Greece on October 28, 1940— Italy proved as much a liability to Germany in World War II as it once had been a valuable Allied power in World War I. Mussolini's ambitions soon hinged on hope that Franco's Spain would enter the war, that Russia would quit the war, and that the loss of the French fleet and Britain's responsibilities in the Pacific would give him an opening to bully the Mediterranean. The one possible Italian-inspired strategy—a joint attack in 1940 on British-held Egypt from both East Africa and Libya, in conjunction with the assault of the Regia Marina on the British fleet at Alexandria—was quickly tabled. Mussolini was the least qualified of all the major World War II leaders to conduct war, which was a tragedy for Italy, given that it had the fewest resources to wage it.[36]

For nearly two decades Mussolini had established a modus vivendi of sorts with Italy's former allies, the Western democracies, without directly prompting a war with any of them throughout a series of crises from Abyssinia to the Spanish Civil War. Yet all of his experience counted for nothing when Hitler whistled. The always prescient General Quirino Armellino saw through Mussolini's impulsive blunders the minute that he attacked France to draw Italy into the war: "An incredible, terrible situation, which could end by submerging us all entirely. If the history of this is ever done, our successors will see the card that we are playing and judge us harshly."[37]

Like Stalin and Hitler, but quite unlike Churchill and Roosevelt, Mussolini grew up among the resentments of the lower middle classes, envisioning national fascism, to the degree that it had any coherence, as a meritocratic means of allowing real talent to emerge. He was attracted to what he saw as the ideological absolutism of the seminary. Mussolini soon rebelled against familial efforts at (a largely free) in-depth Christian education, although, again like the autocrats Hitler and Stalin, he seriously considered a pathway to the priesthood.

Mussolini also similarly manifested his sense of social and cultural inferiority in harangues against the capitalists and elites, while erratically dabbling among various socialist movements and rubbing shoulders with the industrialists and plutocrats. His genius at domestic politics, again comparable to that of Hitler and Stalin, was in appreciating the power of propaganda, especially ideologically driven journalism, and the opportunities for mass manipulation, given the general social chaos unleashed by the aftermath of World War I and the economic downturn of the late 1920s and early 1930s. Truth and falsity were not the touchstones of the new journalism; mass dissemination and sensationalism were.[38]

Like Stalin and Hitler, as a veteran of war Mussolini saw raw violence not just as a necessary but also as a welcome tool of political advancement, both at home and abroad, although again to be applied against weak countries without anticipation that stronger ones might intervene. It was uncanny how, also like Stalin and Hitler, Mussolini believed his meteoric rise through the cauldron of revolutionary politics to become head of state meant that he had the commensurate ability to do the same on the world stage. But whereas Stalin was saved by huge reserves of manpower and industrial output, two strong and largely forgiving allies, and by mid-1942 his private recognition of the limitations of his own military insight, Mussolini had no such resources, foreign salvation, or inner introspection. And the result was that his own megalomania and naiveté about the world beyond Italy's borders ensured the destruction of his own country in his third decade of rule.[39]

GENERAL HIDEKI TOJO came to power in Japan in October 1941 after a long career in the Japanese army. He emerged as part of a centrist faction that had somewhat reluctantly concluded that war with the United States was preferable to either being harangued into negotiating away Japanese gains in China or renewing the once-failed 1939 war with the Soviet Union. Yet, the sometime bureaucratic clerk Tojo never alone wielded quite the same degree of absolute political and military control that Hitler or Mussolini enjoyed. Unlike his partners, he lacked the charisma or desire to forge an independent fascistic movement centered around his own person.

Equally important, the military in Japan was the impetus behind the government, rather than a parallel, co-opted, or subordinate force, or eventually even a countervailing influence as was sometimes true in the later years of Nazi Germany. There was almost no chance that any Japanese army officers would revolt or try to topple their own military leadership—Italian or German style—to end the war. Perhaps the very opposite was true: fanatics might assassinate even war-hardened fascists who considered peace when the war effort was doomed.

The zeal of Tojo's Japan trumped that even of Fascist Italy and Nazi Germany. The Japanese emperor also played a far more determinative role in the war effort than did either King George VI of Great Britain or King Victor Emmanuel III of Italy. Both of the latter monarchs may have been far more visible than Emperor Hirohito, but they did not pick the supreme commander in the fashion that Hirohito had exercised in appointing Tojo, and they did not sign off on major operations. Neither could have stopped Winston Churchill or Benito Mussolini from going to war in the way that Hirohito might have prevented Tojo.[40]

Tojo, previously a second-rate staff officer, offered bureaucratic and organizational dependability. He knew little of war outside the Japanese experience in China, and even there had had limited combat experience. Unlike top-ranking generals, admirals, and diplomats like Tadamichi Kuribayashi (who organized the dogged defense of Iwo Jima), Yosuke Matsuoka (prewar foreign minister), or Isoroku Yamamoto (commander of the Combined Fleet), he had never traveled to the West. As a traditional army man, Tojo was not familiar with the new potentialities of naval air operations or strategic bombing. His infantry instincts told him to stay focused on China, without a clue how to win or get out. He wanted to avoid further war with the much more powerful and better-equipped Soviet Union, loosely partner with Hitler and Mussolini, and hope that the United States would recant in its efforts to force Japan to give up colonial conquests and would cease its trade embargoes. When the latter hopes all failed and the Imperial Japanese Navy insisted that they could not absorb orphaned European colonies without attacking the Philippines, Malaya, and Hawaii, Tojo also advocated war with the United States and approved the navy's plan of a Pearl Harbor strike, hoping that a crippled and demoralized United States would focus on Europe and not fight a total war against a distant Asian foe.[41]

Tojo enjoyed the briefest tenure of all World War II supreme leaders at less than three years. Like Mussolini, he lost control (on July 18, 1944) amid military catastrophes—in the Marianas and Burma—and left supreme office well before the war ended. Unlike the case of Mussolini, his departure did not mean any commensurate loss of martial fervor on the part of the Japanese military. Tojo was a reflection of, not a catalyst for, fascist militarism.[42]

Tojo's sin was supposed incompetence in waging war, not support for starting it, an assessment that was still echoed six decades later by his granddaughter, the fringe fascist politician Yuko Tojo (e.g., "If there was one mistake, however, it was the fact that we [Imperial Japan] lost"). Aside from being executed for war crimes, Tojo is now often remembered for approving the second most ill-conceived attack of the twentieth century—the December 7, 1941, surprise bombing of Pearl Harbor—followed by almost immediate assaults on British Singapore and the American-held Philippines. That he had earlier opposed just such radical military adventures, was initially skeptical about war with the British and Americans, was doubtful of the grand claims of the Imperial Japanese Navy, and did not embrace Nazi hatred of the Jews are all mostly forgotten.

Tojo was apparently unaware or did not care that there was no historical record of any American administration either losing or quitting a war—not the War of 1812, the Mexican War, the Civil War, the Spanish American War, or World War I—much less one that Americans had not started. Pearl Harbor ensured Japan a two-front conflict. That fact in and of itself spelled failure in a fashion eerily analogous to the disastrous Nazi invasion of the Soviet Union just six months prior. The ongoing conflict in China meant that the Imperial Japanese Army would never marshal the resources to contest a recouped Anglo-American effort in the Pacific and Burma, even had it been assured of continual air and naval superiority. The Japanese might have thought they protected themselves with their nonaggression pacts (informally in September 1939, and formally by mid-April 1941) with the equally conniving Russians after being bruised by them in 1939, freeing the army to focus on China and the Pacific while turning the navy toward the West. Yet all the Russian deal accomplished was to preclude the specter of a three-front war while ensuring a two-front conflict.

Perhaps what prompted the folly of turning against America and Britain was that Japan's huge investment in naval power in general, and in carrier air forces in particular, had brought Japan little advantage thus far in a plodding land campaign in China against a variety of enemies. For better or worse, the Pacific was properly the theater for which the costly Japanese prewar investment in air and naval power (which had alone achieved parity with the West) was best suited.[43]

Pearl Harbor was also supposed to have bought time for the Japanese or to have shocked and awed the United States into negotiations or to have kept the Americans too distant from Japanese sea-lanes to disrupt their new maritime empire. But a paltry two waves of Japanese planes did no damage to the US carriers, Pacific fuel reserves, or the viability of Pearl Harbor port facilities; two days more of attacks with an additional five or six carrier air missions might have. Even the timing of Pearl Harbor was ill conceived, occurring just when the Wehrmacht was proving a spent force outside Moscow. It would have been far better for the Japanese had the Americans acted on their intelligence and sent out their old battleships to preempt the Japanese carrier fleet in the Pacific, and thus lost them in the high seas along with all their crews and officers. In another perverse counterfactual, the trauma of Pearl Harbor thrust the most gifted of American naval leaders, Admirals Ernest King and Chester Nimitz, into supreme naval command in a way that might not have happened without such a wound. Tojo seemed to have no real knowledge of either the tactical limitations of the Pearl Harbor operation or its long-term strategic ramifications.[44]

Like the American Confederacy, whose martial spirit and tactical know-how never translated into a coherent strategy for defeating a far larger and richer opponent, Japan's well-trained and well-led army could win an initial series of land battles from Malaysia to the Philippines. But Tojo's Japan could not find a way to injure the more formidable British and American economies, a lapse that contradicted all the classical rules of successful preemptive or preventative war of diminishing the likelihood of effective payback. When Tojo and others spoke grandly about racial superiority in classical fascist style, they did not quite appreciate that their racist chauvinism only made it easier for the Allies to focus their own publics' enmity, in both political and racial terms, against the Japanese. Again, that fury would manifest itself in catastrophic ways for the Japanese in the Pacific island campaigns, the firebombing of Japanese cities, and at Hiroshima and Nagasaki. If any of those retributions were fueled by reciprocal racism, it proved hard for abject racists to appeal for sympathy on the basis of suffering what they so often had inflicted on others.[45]

Tojo suffered from the same delusions of grandeur that would eventually doom Hitler and Mussolini. A superficially impressive military that had run roughshod over militarily backward neighbors—Chinese coastal provinces playing the same role for Japan as Poland, Denmark, and Abyssinia did for Germany and Italy—deluded the Japanese officers into thinking Imperial Japan was comparable to the forces of larger industrial democracies. Roosevelt had doubts about the survival of European colonialism in Asia after the end of Hitler. Had Tojo detoured around British and American Pacific territory, the onus would have been on Churchill and Roosevelt to start a Pacific war to reestablish Western colonialism at a time when both were focused on Europe. An expansive Greater East Asia Co-Prosperity Sphere that had left British and American possessions in Asia alone might have at least offered opportunities for years of haggling and horse-trading. To the degree he exercised the ability to implement policies contrary to the will of the emperor and other military advisors, apparently at no time did Tojo ponder that an American nation that had built bombers with a radius of almost a thousand miles as early as 1937 surely might be able to create even larger ones with commensurately larger payloads and ranges by 1944 or 1945.

It is hard to determine the degree of General Tojo's culpability for both starting and losing wars with the United States and Great Britain, given that before Pearl Harbor he was never as fervently prowar as some others in the Supreme War Council, among them the heads of the respective branches of the Imperial Japanese military and the foreign ministry. Tojo, who was hanged for war crimes by the Allies on November 12, 1948, certainly did not act in contradiction to Emperor Hirohito's wishes. Nor was it ever clear exactly what Tojo's original strategy was behind his war with Great Britain and the United States—to the extent that such a bureaucrat thought deeply about geostrategic issues—given that success hinged on circumstances beyond Japanese control. The weakness of the United States in 1941 was its small and ill-equipped army. Its strength was a powerful and growing navy, its war colleges and officer-training programs that could ensure a professional admiralty, and a strategic Army Air Force specializing in long-range bombing missions. Japan chose a war against America's strengths.

No SUPREME LEADER of World War II entered office with worse prospects than had Winston Churchill on May 10, 1940. Unlike Hitler,

Mussolini, Stalin, and Tojo who in 1939–1941 led ascendant nations in victory, or Franklin Roosevelt, whose homeland was never in existential danger, Churchill came into office as prime minister on the day Hitler invaded France and the Low Countries and amid the immediate specter of sustained area bombing of London. Also unlike Stalin, Roosevelt, Hitler, and Mussolini, Churchill inherited another leader's war that was not only begun but also nearly lost. And unlike Stalin, Roosevelt, and Hitler, Churchill would be removed from office by his own people before the war ended, leaving the prime ministry on July 26, 1945, while conflict still raged in the Pacific.

By June 22, 1940, Churchill's Britain was the only major power actively opposing Nazi Germany, Italy, and their de facto ally the Soviet Union, and it was soon targeted for incendiary attack. Britain's position was worse than that of the beleaguered Romans after Cannae or the Athenians on the eve of Salamis, as it was vastly outnumbered, with most of its allies vanquished, and few others willing to come into the fray. Many of the British elite—including the former king, Edward VIII, Duke of Windsor, and the defeatist former prime minister David Lloyd George (1916–1922)—were onetime closet admirers of Hitler ("the greatest living German" in Lloyd George's estimation), at least when he was on the ascendency, and they may have privately dreamed of the careerist advantages of accepting some version of Hitler's vague offers of armistice between the two nations.

Without a formal wartime alliance with the United States, and with his European partners all defeated, Churchill nevertheless insisted on continuing the war without negotiations with the Axis powers. On the eve of the Blitz, Megan Lloyd George, daughter of the prime minister of Britain during World War I, gave Churchill a backhanded compliment that illustrated the contempt of the British elite when she complained of him: "What always appealed to him most was war. He studied the wars of the past and contemplated the wars of the future. He always imagined himself a military leader, destroying armies, sweeping through Europe, overthrowing his enemies, or putting them to flight. Military terms were always on his lips, and his head was forever full of military plans and projects. I am sure that today he is wholly absorbed and intoxicated by the war."[46]

Well before Churchill became Britain's supreme leader, he had alone of almost all prominent British leaders believed in the possibility of stalemating Nazi Germany, even in the bleak initial months of the war. The most resolute group of British politicians and statesmen who, presciently and often quite alone, opposed appeasement of Hitler—Leo Amery,

Duff Cooper, Anthony Eden, Harold Macmillan, and a few others—was naturally drawn to and energized by Churchill. Upon becoming prime minister, he did not punish the appeasers such as Chamberlain, Attlee, and to an extent Halifax, but instead, to the degree he could during the war, sought to tap—or to appear to tap—their talents.

As prime minister, Churchill focused on the absolute defeat of the Axis powers and the preservation of the British Empire through the ordeal of war. He was aware of the limitations on his own power well apart from the nature of parliamentary government, arising in part from the lasting effects on the British psyche of the prior disasters of fighting in France in World War I, the eroding stature of the British Empire, and the dilemma that Britain had to fight a three-front war against the Germans, Italians, and Japanese, but without the resources of its partner-in-arms, the United States. Churchill also was sensitive to his own unpopularity among many in the British political class, of his unapologetic aristocratic heritage in an age of social welfare, and of the shadow that still hung over his advocacy for the Gallipoli campaign of World War I, in which a bold plan to knock Turkey out of the war ended in catastrophe and the loss of nearly two hundred thousand British, Australian and New Zealand Army Corps (ANZAC), and Allied casualties.

Churchill's policy after Pearl Harbor hinged on winning the wartime partnership of America to fight a full-fledged two-front war, waged by equals, despite their vast manpower and material asymmetries. Shortly after Pearl Harbor, Churchill reviewed his visions in almost mystical terms to the US Congress:

> Prodigious hammer-strokes have been needed to bring us together again, or, if you will allow me to use other language, I will say that he must indeed have a blind soul who cannot see that some great purpose and design is being worked out here below, of which we have the honour to be the faithful servants. It is not given to us to peer into the mysteries of the future. Still, I avow my hope and faith, sure and inviolate, that in the days to come the British and American peoples will for their own safety and for the good of all walk together side by side in majesty, in justice, and in peace.[47]

Churchill, under whom Britain and its essential empire reached staggering levels of military production, still lacked the wherewithal at the disposal of both Stalin and Roosevelt. Like the visionary emperor Justinian, who likewise sought to preserve his empire and thus dispatched small contingents of Byzantine expeditionary forces all over the Mediterranean world, Churchill sought to accomplish by alliances, finesse, and caginess what he might not with raw power. At one time or another he boldly ordered British forces into the Arctic Sea, East Africa, the Balkans, Crete, Greece, Malaysia, Burma, and much of North Africa, while landing troops in Italy and France. Being everywhere at once, in addition to understandably cautious generalship, explains why the overmatched British suffered occasionally humiliating defeats at Crete, Dunkirk, Singapore, and Tobruk. As unlikely as Churchill's aims might at one time have seemed to most of the British leadership, Churchill was confident in achieving them. Like the Athenian statesman Themistocles, he had rare foresight—*pronoia*—a realistic appraisal of how the assets of Germany and Britain would eventually match up in England's favor, especially given Britain's historic invulnerability to invasion and its air and naval reach.[48]

Churchill believed that the British, at least if invaded, would fight fiercely in a way the French and other Western Europeans had not. They were islanders accustomed to going it alone, and they had the benefit of seeing the dire consequences of German occupation on the continent. Churchill knew the sea was a far better barrier to blitzkrieg than had been the Ardennes. He was now under no illusions that, whatever Hitler's rhetoric, negotiations would mean little other than the end of Great Britain and her empire altogether. Churchill made clear to the British public that a faint-hearted defense was tantamount to suicide. Like French prime minister (1917–1920) Georges Clemenceau, from whose speeches Churchill seems to have been inspired, he kept his head when all around were losing theirs.[49]

Churchill was convinced that Britain could even help to prompt two radical changes in the complexion of the European war. British resoluteness might help force an exasperated Hitler to move eastward against his onetime ally the Soviet Union. Likewise, if Britain survived the Blitz and thwarted an invasion, at some point the United States, impressed by British resilience, was likely to enter either a European or Pacific war, or both, thus creating an Allied triad whose resources and manpower would in time destroy the Axis. In short, Churchill's British strategy was to take advantage of Axis inferiority in bombers and ships to survive until either Russia or America brought in the manpower to confront the German army head on. In most ways, the war largely unfolded as he dreamed.[50]

That Churchill, a conservative imperialist, flattered and miraculously won over Roosevelt, an anti-imperialist progressive, and Stalin, a genocidal totalitarian, is often underappreciated. Such efforts were also couched in irony, given that Churchill, the colonialist, knew best that his Soviet and American allies would increasingly nose Britain out, as their powers grew and the Axis threat waned. Yet for all his genius, Churchill never quite came to accept that the logic of the Atlantic Charter, the United Nations, and the alliance with Joseph Stalin in various ways would shortly dismantle the British Empire. The war had unleashed enormous pent-up populist passions and transnational ideological movements, and in its aftermath there would be little likelihood of the British Empire making an argument to retain at least some of its colonies on the basis of its supposed prewar civilizing mission.[51]

Britain's strategic and operational mistakes, in which Churchill played a leading role, were many. An advocate of naval air power, he nonetheless sent British capital ships to Singapore without their accustomed accompanying air support and despite the Royal Navy's own prior carrier success against Italian battleships. The losses of the *Repulse* and *Prince of Wales* near Singapore were due in part, despite warnings, to his own impulsiveness and misplaced confidence in Admiral Sir Tom Phillips, who did not believe in the lethality of naval air power and so pressed ahead when the new carrier HMS *Indomitable* was damaged in the Caribbean and could not join the flotilla.

Perhaps Churchill's two greatest blunders predictably involved the diversions of limited resources: first, not forcing Bomber Command to turn over more long-range bombers earlier to antisubmarine efforts; second, the diversion of forces from ongoing success in North Africa to the doomed cause in Greece (March 1941) at precisely the time when the British might have destroyed the entire Italian presence in North Africa and closed out the theater. He bought promises from Bomber Command of victory largely from the air until the last year of the war, and yet early on could not force upon it the use of longer-range Spitfires with drop tanks as escort fighters. He championed marginal operations in the eastern Aegean that even had they worked offered few strategic avenues to shortening the war. He signed off on the foolhardy Market-Garden gamble. He allowed Montgomery to offend almost every high-ranking American officer he came into contact with after June 1944, as well as many of his own high-ranking air and naval officers. His idea of a soft underbelly of Europe did not factor in Italian weather, geography, Allied inexperience, or General Mark Clark as the supreme American and then supreme Allied commander in Italy. Churchill allowed Stalin a free hand in most of Eastern Europe, ostensibly as the price of saving Greece and Turkey.[52]

Usually these lapses shared a common theme of trying to inflict peripheral damage on the Third Reich and Japan in too many places without incurring British losses, and with constant attention to the effect of operations on Britain's postwar empire. Such errors were not lasting in their consequences to the Allied cause, given the resources of Russia and

America—a fact perhaps well understood by Churchill. For all his fussiness with day-to-day operations, Churchill for the most part did not cross his generals. And he rarely sought to overrule his chiefs of staff—among them the likes of Admiral of the Fleet Sir Andrew Cunningham, Air Chief Marshal Charles Portal, and Admiral of the Fleet Sir Alfred Dudley Pound—especially after receiving candid advice from senior advisors like General John Dill, General Hastings Ismay, and South African general and statesman Jan Smuts. None of these capable advisors was a yes-man, at least of the sort that Hitler had surrounded himself with, and all had combat experience from either World War I or Britain's colonial wars. The early stunning transformation of the British economy to produce war materiel on par with the Third Reich was mostly due to Churchill's confidence in his ability to harmonize private entrepreneurs like Lord Beaverbrook with trade union bosses like Ernest Bevin.[53]

In the major Allied decisions of the war, Churchill was often prescient. He understood immediately the need to support the Soviet resistance to Operation Barbarossa, in the pragmatic sense that no other power other than the USSR might do so much harm to the four-million-man-strong Axis land forces. His controversial decisions, on the advice of his generals and admirals, to keep back a large reserve of RAF squadrons from France in June 1940 and to cripple the Vichy French fleet were necessary steps that most leaders would have avoided. He rightly convinced the Americans to concentrate on Europe, where they had not been attacked, and to place secondary emphasis in the Pacific, where they and Britain had been.

Churchill was wise to oppose the premature American idea of opening the so-called second front by a cross-Channel invasion in late 1942 or 1943, when the Allies were not ready for such a major amphibious operation. He rightly stood up to Stalin and argued that strategic bombing, and the invasions of North Africa, Sicily, Italy, the Battle of the Atlantic, and the Pacific theater were all "second fronts" that alleviated Wehrmacht pressure on the Russians. He may have been right to oppose Operation Anvil (later codenamed Operation Dragoon), the invasion of southern France in August 1944, that drew off resources from the Italian theater and made major amphibious landings in northern Italy unlikely. In the closing weeks of the war, Churchill, unlike the Americans, understood that the possession of territory, more than Stalin's assurances, would adjudicate the fate of Europe for the next half century.[54]

In other fundamental ways, Churchill proved the most effective wartime leader of both the Allied and Axis powers. Far better than Franklin Roosevelt, he understood the full ramifications of supporting the Soviets in their catastrophic war with Hitler on the Eastern Front, most notably that there would be a high postwar price to be paid for any partnership with Stalinist Russia. As opposed to FDR, when Churchill offered concessions, it was usually through a rational calculus of costs versus benefits in light of the growing power of the Red Army and what it might mean for the postwar world. As early as 1944, he had feared that the Soviets might pose the same threats to a free Europe that Germany had in the past. In all these areas, he was proven right.[55]

Churchill's oratory came to symbolize the entire Allied cause. Britain until May 11, 1940, had no resonant voice. Later Roosevelt proved an effective orator, aided by excellent writers, but his forte was domestic politics, and often his soaring rhetoric was laced with naiveté. In contrast, Churchill invoked concrete history, taught the world why Hitler was a singular evil unlike any in civilization's immediate past, and was able to place both victory and defeat in Periclean contexts that encouraged the Allies neither to be fooled that early impressive tactical victories equaled final victory nor to succumb to defeatism after terrible setbacks.[56]

Finally, Churchill possessed the greatest moral courage of any leader of World War II, especially in the rawest, most physical sense. He was the only Allied leader to have served in the trenches of World War I, after seeing service in Britain's colonial wars, and had gained practical experience of combat. Stalin rarely left Moscow. When he did, he insisted that summits were to be proximate to Russia, whether at Tehran or Yalta. Roosevelt by 1943 was increasingly incapacitated. Churchill usually visited Roosevelt, not vice versa. He went to Moscow, not Stalin to London. Whether sick with pneumonia or battling coronary disease, he insisted on visiting the front lines, often through contested air and sea space. In January 1943, Colonel Hans von Luck, who was leading Panzer units disengaging from Tripoli in the face of the British advance, noticed through his binoculars an odd figure on the battlefield:

> More sensationally, Churchill appeared to be with him [General Bernard Montgomery], wearing a safari helmet. I was too far to open fire with our weapons; 88 mm guns and artillery were not available. I, at once, sent a radio message to [General Alfred] Gause: "Churchill and Monty believed located at great distance, no action possible." ... Later, I heard that it could well have been Churchill, who, on his way to Casablanca, had stopped off to see Monty and his troops. However that may be, we never saw Hitler in this theater of war, or even senior officers of the High Command of the Wehrmacht [the OKW].[57]

Britain was to fight much longer than in World War I (roughly 70 versus 51 months) on two distant fronts against a much more formidable coalition of enemies. Yet it suffered far fewer deaths (approximately 450,000 versus nearly one million fatalities) in achieving a far more lasting victory than in 1918. This was an extraordinary achievement, given that Britain had a continental army far smaller than those of either Germany, Russia, or the United States. Although Churchill may have despaired frequently—after the fall of France when an inglorious defeat seemed likely, the ignominious surrenders at Singapore and Tobruk, and in negotiations about the postwar world with undemocratic Joseph Stalin creating facts on the ground throughout Eastern Europe—he was the first Allied leader to see a way to beat Hitler and the only one to fight him from the beginning to the end.

FRANKLIN ROOSEVELT, ON the other hand, approached the war as if it were another political contest to enter and win what, until December 1941, had been seen as someone else's distant conflict. He began mobilizing a mostly unarmed and skeptical United States, particularly its navy, long before the surprise attack at Pearl Harbor, when the public was against intervention abroad. That political feat allowed the rearming nation to go on the permanent offensive as early as late 1942, and through existing Lend-Lease programs to help ensure that both Great Britain and the Soviet Union continued the war. Roosevelt may also have understood that gearing up for war had provided the economic stimulus that he had so often been unable to create through the New Deal. In that way he began to promote military rearmament as vigorously as he had once opposed it, even as his advisors warned that assistance to Britain and France would deplete US war supplies, and that more forward deployment of still-weak prewar American air and naval forces in the Pacific would make scarce resources vulnerable to attack rather than creating deterrence against the Japanese.

Japan rightly feared that many of the capital ships that might soon doom it were already at berth in US shipyards when it attacked the existing Pacific Fleet on December 7, 1941. Oddly, that anxiety of an inevitably superior American fleet by the mid-1940s may have spurred Japan to act preemptively in 1941 rather than to negotiate from future weakness. Without Roosevelt, there would not have been modest military spending in a stubborn Depression. The Democratic Party, dating back to William Jennings Bryan, had its own isolationists. In the midst of the Depression they argued that money expended on military readiness abroad came at the expense of domestic investments at home. And a large military only encouraged unnecessary adventurism incompatible with the mostly non-colonial traditions of the United States.

Most of the Republican Party of the 1930s was even more unapologetically isolationist. After World War I it had argued against any more Wilsonian engagement. Most Republicans, who may have initially supported occupation of Imperial Germany after its defeat, were still convinced that interventions abroad had led to larger government at home. Then there were the inevitable deficits that would require higher taxes such as those in the recent past that had funded a war to end wars, but that had ultimately failed to ensure a European peace. Onetime interventionist Theodore Roosevelt had earlier summed up the Republican disgust of engagement with the post-Versailles world: "I do not believe in keeping our men on the other side to patrol the Rhine, or police Russia, or interfere in Central Europe or the Balkan Peninsula."[58]

FDR saw the challenge of maneuvering the country away from isolationism as comparable to his earlier selling of the New Deal to a skeptical political class and desperate Depression-era public. In a December 1943 press conference, Roosevelt in an ostensibly damning admission explained how he thought he had superseded the New Deal with a wartime economy: "Old Doctor New Deal didn't know 'nothing' about legs and arms. . . . So he got his partner, who was an orthopedic surgeon, Dr. Win-the-War, to take care of this fellow. . . . And the result is that the patient is back on his feet."

Roosevelt was good at politics, the more Machiavellian the better. He genuinely believed that an unprecedented third—and eventually fourth—presidential term was critical to the war, especially for maintaining the rapport that he had established with the leadership of Britain and the Soviet Union. Well before Pearl Harbor, Roosevelt sent a number of envoys—among them William "Wild Bill" Donovan ("Coordinator of Information"), Harry Hopkins (New Dealer and presidential advisor), and Sumner Welles (Undersecretary of State)—to reassure the British that the United States was gearing up for an inevitable rendezvous with the Axis. To forge political consensus, Roosevelt had also enlisted the support of internationalist Republicans such as Wendell Willkie to tour Britain, and then to explain the need for engagement to the American people, especially Roosevelt's natural opponents. He brought into his administration senior Republican politicos and wise men like Frank Knox (Secretary of the Navy, 1940–1944) and Henry Stimson (Secretary of War, 1940–1945) to avoid the charge that the Democratic Party was leading the country to war, or that during the conflict liberals were making strategic decisions on the basis of partisan considerations, while turning a blind eye to Soviet communist aggrandizement. Nonetheless, ever the politician, Roosevelt pressured the military for an early landing in North Africa, if not in time for the 1942 midterm elections, then at least in the first full year of the war to involve the American people in the European front, and to convince the Navy's leadership that its assets were needed in a Europe-first strategy.[59]

For all the big-government intrusion of the New Deal into the free market, Roosevelt still did not insist on a planned or command war economy. Instead, he outsourced military preparations and production to private enterprise in loose partnerships with government bureaucracies. The War Production Board may have appeared as a wartime version of another New Deal agency, but Roosevelt was canny enough to staff it with proven captains of industry—T. S. Fitch (Washington Steel), William Murphy (Campbell Soup), Donald Nelson (Sears, Roebuck), Faustin Solon (Owens-Illinois Glass), and Charles Wilson (General Electric)—to ensure it unleashed private enterprise. In choosing William S. Knudsen, former president of General Motors, as chairman of the Office of Production Management and, after January 1942, the director of production in the Office of the Under Secretary of War, Roosevelt selected one of the most gifted industrialists, planners—and capitalists—in American history.[60]

Roosevelt lacked the historical vision of Winston Churchill. But he possessed a superior political savvy in domestic matters. He had an uncanny intuition of what the American people would tolerate, and how to push programs and objectives through guile, deception, and stealth that they would not have otherwise embraced if fully apprised. Whereas Churchill was defeated and left office before the final victory over Japan, even an enfeebled Roosevelt won an unprecedented fourth term.[61]

Roosevelt did not make decisions in the unilateral fashion of Hitler or Mussolini. Nor was he as engaged as Churchill in altering the operational pulse of the battlefield. Instead, his style was to solicit advice, create commissions and boards, and brainstorm with advisors by teasing out contrary positions, playing devil's advocate, and at times misleading his own advisors about his ultimate decision that could overrule even the consensus of his Joint Chiefs.

New Dealer advisor Harry Hopkins, chronically ill and often incapacitated, moved into the White House to help frame strategic questions in terms of winning the war and being acceptable to the public. General George Marshall and Admiral William Leahy of the Joint Chiefs probably offered as much advice privately as they did officially. Many members of the New Deal "Brain Trust" continued their advisory roles during the war, such as Supreme Court Justice Felix Frankfurter, Secretary of the Interior Harold Ickes, as well as formal executives like James Byrnes (Office of War Mobilization), Cordell Hull (Secretary of State), and Henry Morgenthau (Secretary of the Treasury). None of these men was a great strategic thinker; all were loyal, intimate with the president, and good planners.

The most controversial American decisions in the war, both good and terrible—the allegiance to the so-called Plan Dog strategic aim of 1940 to concentrate on Europe first; the understandable choice not to attempt to reinforce the Philippines in 1942; the cruel but necessary effort to conduct a costly strategic bombing campaign in Europe and unrestricted fire raids against Japan; the insistence on a second front through an amphibious landing in western France; the necessary insistence on unconditional surrender of the Axis powers; as well as a host of unfortunate strategic moves and policies (the needless and unconstitutional move to intern Japanese resident nationals and Japanese-American citizens, the naive effort to become not just an ally but a full partner of Stalin's Russia, or the costly retaking of the Philippines)—were largely Roosevelt's own, but ostensibly either arrived at through general consensus of the War and State Departments, or at least supported by the majority of key wartime advisors in various departments and on committees.[62]

Roosevelt did not influence the appointments of generals in the field in the manner of any of the Axis leaders or perhaps even his own allies Churchill and Stalin. He outsourced most of the key operational decisions to his senior advisors, who crafted the first Joint Chiefs of Staff: Generals Arnold and Marshall, and Admirals King and Leahy. The four, nominally equally representative of air, land, and sea power under the auspices of Leahy, mostly on their own made such decisions about which generals were appointed, transferred, or fired, with notable exceptions such as Roosevelt's decision to save and keep manageable the politically connected General MacArthur as supreme Pacific commander (and thus out of domestic politics) or quite unfairly to have fired the prescient Admiral James O. Richardson, expert on the Japanese Navy, who had warned about moving the unprepared Pacific Fleet to an exposed Pearl Harbor berth.

Such delegation was largely more successful than the alternative practiced by both the Axis and other allies, and usually led to the selection of superb field commanders. When it did not—a holdover showboat commander like Lieutenant General Lloyd Fredendall or an incompetent Major General John Lucas—the lapse did not reflect on Roosevelt's leadership. More interestingly, Roosevelt delighted in audacious commanders whose temperament and language could hardly be termed liberal. He made the necessary allowances for the talented but crusty Chief of Naval Operations Ernest King and kept him on after retirement age, indirectly supported the retention of George S. Patton after the infamous slapping incidents, and liked to hear of the aggressiveness (and even occasional recklessness) of admirals like Bill Halsey.[63]

A more hands-on commander in chief, appointing and firing generals as Lincoln did in managing Union strategy in the Civil War, might have raised greater skepticism about the costs versus benefits of early daylight and unescorted strategic bombing. He could have cross-examined the conduct of the Italian campaign, the Arnhem effort, or the preliminary plans to invade Okinawa. Yet Roosevelt's strength was his early intuition that Europe's early border wars between September 1939 and May 1941 presaged an existential struggle between democracy and an evil European fascism of a sort not seen before. Even in the mid-1930s, he rightly assumed that compromise with Hitler was impossible, something universally obvious in hindsight but not so clear to most of Roosevelt's European and American contemporaries other than the realist Winston Churchill. Perhaps, the president's tragic lapse was that he did not bring the same degree of deep distrust to an equally murderous Soviet totalitarianism. In its postwar planning, the United States sometimes went well beyond the realpolitik of encouraging and enabling Soviet resistance to the Wehrmacht to a naive belief that "Uncle Joe" was a reasonable man and his style of Soviet communism a mere rough sort of socialism that might become a possible future compliant partner of the British and American democracies.[64]

Had Roosevelt been as suspicious of Stalin's murderous gulag and expansionary plans as he was sometimes of Churchill's effort to preserve Britain's colonial possessions, the United States might have been better prepared for the Cold War that was already beginning by 1944. It is hard to know the extent to which Roosevelt's naiveté imperiled the alliance or led to the foundations of the Cold War, but there is no doubt that he was not only naive but vain about what he thought was his ability to manipulate an even wilier Stalin. He once inanely wrote Churchill in early 1942: "I know you will not mind me being brutally frank when I tell you that I think I can personally handle Stalin better than either your Foreign Office or my State Department. Stalin hates the guts of all your top people. He thinks he likes me better, and I hope he will continue to do so."[65]

The bottom line for FDR as a wartime leader is unambiguous. Under him, American planners charted out two spheres of responsibility against Japan: the Pacific Islands and their trajectories to Tokyo would be the focus of the United States, while Burma and the Indian Ocean area would be the greater colonial concerns of Britain. If the two allies would seek parallel paths to defeating Japan, in Europe their planning would be nearly uniform. Roosevelt assured the jittery British that they would no longer face Hitler alone, while in the Pacific, America would seek its own pathways toward Tokyo and not quibble with the British over their imperial interests but on occasion supply them ample troops and air power to fight in Burma.[66]

If Roosevelt lacked the street-fighting ability and experience of the lower-class Hitler, Mussolini, and Stalin, he nonetheless knew what it was to suffer physically. He was politically ruthless without being immoral, amid a cataclysmic war in which both his enemies and his ally Joseph Stalin were politically ruthless and homicidal. When America's numerous wartime strategic, economic, and operational successes are weighed against its much rarer lapses, Franklin Delano Roosevelt deserves great credit as a force multiplier of American industry and its twelve-million-man armed forces.

IF A WARTIME leader is to be judged solely on the amoral basis of promoting his country's short-term national interests, such as surviving a surprise attack of four million Axis troops, Joseph Stalin stands above all the rest. For the first three years of World War II (1939–1942), however, Stalin was often the stereotypical paranoid, parochial, and bloodthirsty communist apparatchik. Although Stalin had tripled the size of the Red Army in just the four years between 1937 and 1941, it was shorted over sixty thousand high-ranking officers, given his savage purges of 1937–1939 that sent some of his best commanders to the firing squad and mostly exiled the rest. The newly enrolled four hundred thousand officers of the Red Army that first met the Germans in June 1941 were, for the most part, without much more than two years' experience.

Stalin had also foolishly pushed the Molotov-Ribbentrop nonaggression pact, apparently clueless that Hitler would break it at his convenience. His idea that capitalist states would exhaust themselves in endless wars in Western Europe to the benefit of the Soviet Union displayed a deep misunderstanding of the strength of the Royal Navy and Royal Air Force, and of the central message of *Mein Kampf*, best summed up by Hitler's adage that "German victory [was] incompatible with Russian ideology." Stalin's effort to annex slices of southern Finland almost ended in disaster. He was criminally negligent in ignoring intelligence warnings about the impending Operation Barbarossa, again failing to grasp that

Hitler's destructive ideology was ultimately pointed eastward. He seemed to have experienced some sort of incapacity for the first two weeks of the German invasion and did not appear to the public until July 3, 1941. For the first three months of the German invasion, his no-retreat orders doomed over two million Russians, who were taken prisoner in huge encirclements and, for the most part, never accounted for. After stunning defensive successes at Moscow in December 1941 and Stalingrad in February 1943, Stalin ordered precipitous counteroffensives that often proved near catastrophic.[67]

Stalin's self-interested duplicities needlessly ensured a falling out with his own allies before the war's conclusion. His shrill and disingenuous demands for a second front ignored the fact that the Soviet Union had been Hitler's de facto ally and that there existed a second front of British expeditionary forces trying to help France in 1940 and when Germany bombed a lonely Britain months later. Unlike Britain, Stalin had only joined the antifascist side of the war when his fascist partner double-crossed him. Stalin envisioned the Allied alliance as a war only against the invaders of the Soviet Union, and delegated effort against Italy and the Japanese to the British and Americans.

It is impossible to underestimate Stalin's ingratitude. He was an amnesiac to the fact that the new Soviet Union under the terms of the March 1918 Brest-Litovsk Treaty with victorious Imperial Germany had lost nearly a quarter of its territory, and won much of it back nearly nine months later due only to the Western Allies' victory and insistence at Versailles that German-occupied territory be restored to its owners. Stalin gave little credit to the Allied effort in North Africa, Sicily, and Italy; the strategic bombing of the Third Reich; the Anglo-American war against the Japanese; Lend-Lease; and the naval war against the Axis, all of which predated the second front that opened on June 6, 1944.

Stalin's pouts and accusations were serial, and he often begged off conferences with his two Allied partners. Because Stalin had occasionally dreamed of (and concluded) various separate accommodations with Hitler, he was inevitably accusing Churchill and Roosevelt of just such duplicity. The irony of his rule was that his own responsibility for the deaths of millions of Russians in the collectivizations and purges of the 1920s and 1930s had hardened him psychologically for the mass death visited upon his people by the Wehrmacht. No wonder the murderous Hitler admired him most of the Allied Big Three.[68]

Stalin was of little or no direct help to the Allied European and Pacific strategic bombing campaigns. He made it almost impossible to continue fueling Allied bombers on turnaround stops in the Ukraine, and interned B-29 crews downed in Soviet territory. Ostensibly, Stalin triangulated out of fears of breaking accords with the Japanese and thus losing his safe transit lines of Lend-Lease materiel across the Pacific from the American West Coast, and more pragmatically hoped to gain an edge in the postwar era, such as by reverse engineering detained B-29s. He ensured that the Russian people did not know the full extent of British and American help to Russia and their contributions to winning the war. The Soviet massacre of over twenty thousand Polish officers in the Katyn Forest was Hitlerian; so was Stalin's contrived delay before Warsaw to allow the Wehrmacht to kill off his future Polish anticommunist rivals. His vision of a postwar communist Eastern Europe often trumped strategies for defeating the Wehrmacht in 1944–1945.[69]

All that said, it is hard to imagine any other wartime leader, with the possible exception of Churchill, who could have lost nearly 20–30 percent of his territory to enemy occupation, much of his industrial production, with over a quarter of his population destroyed or occupied, and yet in little over a year so reorganized his vastly reduced nation that it outproduced Nazi Germany in critical areas like tanks and planes. The wholesale transfer of Soviet industry far to the east of Moscow still staggers the imagination. So do the harsh conditions under which Soviet workers vastly outproduced their pan-European counterparts—a continuation of the increase in Soviet war production centered in the Urals that was already under way in the late 1930s.

When the Third Reich peaked and then ebbed in early 1943, there was no possibility of recovery analogous to the Russian rebound after the disasters of 1941–1942. Stalin's tenacity convinced even some of the German General Staff that the loss of European Russia and the chief cities of the Soviet Union would not de facto mean the end of the Soviet ability to wage war.[70]

More mysterious, the Soviet command economy produced not only vast amounts of munitions and weaponry, but also high-quality tanks, artillery, rockets, and fighter-bombers. Capitalism encouraged individual genius to produce unmatched technology in a way impossible in authoritarian societies and command economies. But during World War II, Stalin's Russia had so borrowed, stolen, or invented new weapons and processes of industrial production that its later armies were often the best equipped of the war.[71]

At war's end in September 1945, Churchill had been humiliated by being voted out of office. Roosevelt, Hitler, and Mussolini were dead; Tojo, discredited, bereft of supreme power, and fated to meet the gallows. In contrast to them all, the old dictator Stalin, perhaps the greatest mass murderer in recorded history, was thriving and would live on another eight years to threaten the two allies that had helped save him.

The Soviets would carve out a buffer zone in Eastern Europe before occupying their share of conquered Germany. Stalin rightly figured that the Allies would value the Russian destruction of the German army far more than they would worry about his own past genocides, his opportunistic armistice with Japan, or his apparent unwillingness to abide by promises of free elections in lands that the Red Army occupied. If Stalin's strategy was by needs one-dimensional, it also proved apt, relying on Allied material aid, various second fronts opening in the West, and an exclusive Anglo-American effort against the Japanese.

CHURCHILL, ROOSEVELT, AND Stalin were sophisticated strategic thinkers who knew why they went to war, where to fight it, and how to end it. In contrast, Hitler, Mussolini, and Tojo started wars without a realistic appreciation of the resources of their enemies, or of how they might impair the Allied ability to produce material and raise manpower—much less of how they were to close out such theaters to their own advantage. Basic questions of ensuring ample means for vaulted strategic ends were ignored by an Axis command blinded by ideology and impatient with the details of what it took to create effective militaries to fight on a global scale. Given Axis material inferiority on land, at sea, and in the air, Allied leaders needed only to be competent rather than inspired. That most Allied leaders—and, as discussed in the next chapter, generals and admirals as well—proved as good as or better than their German, Italian, and Japanese counterparts meant that a war largely predetermined by production and manpower could be won even more rapidly by skill and insight.

# 17

# The Warlords

CLASSICAL AUTHORS OFFER instructive biographies of foolish and wise generals such as the portraits of Nicias, Germanicus, and Pompey found in Thucydides, Tacitus, and Plutarch. How-to-do guides give point-by-point advice on organization, deployment, logistics, tactics, and strategy, especially the handbooks of Xenophon, Onasander, Aeneas Tacticus, Vegetius, and Maurice, and later interpolated by Machiavelli, Valturius, and other Renaissance humanists.

In this vast corpus of received military thought, common themes emerge. The commander in the field should be young, preferably under fifty, if not forty-five. J.F.C. Fuller once listed those he thought were the hundred greatest generals from antiquity through World War I, to prove that the best were under forty. Fuller made his point, but also failed to note that an advocate of experience and maturity might equally have made up a comparable list of winners who scored impressive victories in their fifties and sixties, including stars whom Fuller ignored, such as the Hellenistic general Antigonus Monophthalmus, the Spartan king Agesilaus, Justinian's right-hand firemen generals Belisarius and Narses, the German duo of Hindenburg and Ludendorff, the British colonial fighter Frederick Roberts, or the Athenian strategist Pericles. In sum, generalship is more like any other profession in which the advantages of youthful vigor clash with mature experience. In the context of World War II, Patton ended the war at sixty years of age; Nimitz was fifty-nine in 1945, MacArthur sixty-five—suggesting that in most cases thirty-five-year-olds are still too green, and most over seventy too tired.

Whatever his exalted station, the proverbial general also should have some firsthand experience of the front lines, and so be seen by his men in action. Supposed chateau generalship at the head of armies during World War I was widely criticized both during and after the war as a bureaucratic rejection of wise military counsel of some twenty-five hundred years that it was important to be seen with the army in battle. George Marshall's mythical "little black book" contained the names of dozens of vigorous colonels and youngish lieutenant colonels, whom Marshall (himself sixty at the time of Pearl Harbor) considered would be likely future generals in any upcoming war and a better investment than their peacetime senior officers.[1]

Health mattered, both physical energy and robustness of mind. Perhaps vigor proved more advantageous than even experience and sobriety—thus again Marshall's prewar preference for youth over age. Yet by World War II, at the dawn of the revolution in health and medicine, being fifty or fifty-five perhaps was not quite the same as it had been in 1814, especially given that generals, rather than riding or walking at the head of their armies, were driven, and ate food and drank water less likely to sicken them.

Past combat experience was almost essential. So was formal military education, not just in tactical arrangement, but also in strategic and operational arts learned by the study of history and memoirs of the great captains of the past. Individualism, even idiosyncrasy, was prized more than caricatured: showiness in dress, appearance, as well as comportment, and eccentricity in speech and behavior. The great general needed to prove why he was one with, but also different from, his men.

For Alexander, it was his trademark ram-horn helmet, for Pompey a blue rather than the more normal red cloak, for Patton his twin ivory-handled revolvers, for MacArthur his contrived corncob pipe and aviator sunglasses, for Ridgway in Korea a grenade and first-aid kit plastered on his chest ("old iron tits"). Grant and Sherman drew attention by appearing almost shabbier than their men, which by the bleak summer of 1864 might have had the same effect in boosting morale as did George B. McClellan's earlier occasional ostentatiousness.

These were only ideals and allowed latitude for notable exceptions, such as General Gebhard von Blücher, who saved Waterloo when seventy-two. General Dwight D. Eisenhower appeared a consummate bureaucrat and undistinguished in uniform, never speaking with much panache or turn of phrase. Omar Bradley or Courtney Hodges in uniform appeared naturally commonplace rather than commonplace by volition; neither was an orator (nor a great captain). The architects of earlier German victories in World War II, such as Generals von Bock, von Leeb, von Rundstedt, and Manstein, looked like ordinary bureaucrats.[2]

Generalship was sometimes not as important as supreme command, manpower, logistics, or equipment. At least, there was also an understanding that in modern industrial war the general could not overcome the impossible. The North African battlefield that faced the dashing Rommel in 1942 was different from the one in Normandy of 1944 that seemed to overwhelm the often tired and sick veteran general. It was easier for Manstein to shine in 1940 than in 1943. Bradley had a less-demanding task as an army commander in 1944 than did Georgy Zhukov in 1941. Defeat in the Battle of France is in part attributed to the blinkered and tired generalship of Generals Maurice Gamelin, Alphonse Joseph Georges, and Maxime Weygand, yet they were mere tesserae of a larger French mosaic of poor morale, social discord, and collective prewar weariness. The notable French battle generals of World War II instead emerged later, such as the vigorous Generals Henri Giraud, Jacques-Philippe Leclerc, and Jean de Lattre de Tassigny, but only when working in tandem with the British and Americans, and provided with plentiful equipment, to help a winning cause reclaim their homeland.

In other words, there was neither a master template for generalship across time and space nor any certainty that battlefield genius could trump the larger landscape of the war. We are left with a banality of a golden mean between youth and experience, education and pragmatism, knowledge and natural brilliance, and audacity and circumspection, along with the caveat that, other factors being roughly equal, a genius always beats a fool—and a captain with lots of money, weapons, manpower, and supplies at his back more often wins.

Perhaps the only constant in assessing great generalship is the rare ability occasionally to win battles despite the odds. In World War II, such savior generals were uncommon, with exceptions of the best like Hugh Dowding, George Patton, Erwin Rommel, William Slim, Raymond Spruance, Erich von Manstein, and Georgy Zhukov. More often, the American First Army was successful despite General Hodges, in the inverse way that no Italian general could have reached Alexandria, and even Erich von Manstein on his best day may have had no real chance to save Field Marshal Friedrich Paulus's trapped army at Stalingrad. Without General Curtis LeMay the B-29 program might have floundered for additional months; without the B-29 even LeMay could not have bombed Japan until July 1945.

ERICH VON MANSTEIN is ranked as the most brilliant of Hitler's generals. Yet his career in World War II serves as an illustration of both the genius and limitations of German generalship, and he serves as a model of why Germany's technocratic generals scored early tactical victories and yet found themselves so often in a strategic blind alley. Manstein's revisionary plan, with input from Heinz Guderian, to invade France in 1940 through the Ardennes turned a probable eventual German victory into a swift Gallic catastrophe; his madcap Panzer drive to Leningrad reflected the realization that the war had to be won in months. Yet Manstein's most impressive victory was the so-called Third Battle of Kharkov (February 19–March 15, 1943), when, after the disaster at Stalingrad in early 1943, Manstein, against all odds, cut apart a reckless Soviet pursuit, trapped over fifty Russian divisions, retook Kharkov, and bought six months respite for soon-to-be vastly outnumbered forces on the Russian front. Only a handful of World War II generals could have matched such a feat. Manstein proved absolutely unshakeable when threatened with a general collapse, and saw how careful defense could wound the Red Army far more than had even blitzkrieg.

Yet otherwise, Hitler's best general did not make all that much of a difference after the border wars ended in 1940, aside from his post-Stalingrad rebound. He eventually was part of the failed effort to salvage a draw at Stalingrad and win the Caucasus. Manstein captured Sevastopol in an operationally brilliant, but costly and strategically negligible campaign, and never seemed to appreciate how the time and costs of taking Sevastopol affected Case Blue. He did not conduct well the admittedly hopeless effort to free the trapped at Stalingrad, either administratively or operationally. Despite his often wise cautionary warnings, Manstein was nonetheless one of the driving forces behind the ultimately wrongheaded battle at Kursk—a needless head-on crash on the part of the outnumbered underdog akin to General Robert E. Lee's ordering of Pickett's Charge at Gettysburg or the blunt French final effort at Waterloo. For all his later denials and his military professionalism, Manstein nevertheless did nothing to object to the Nazification of the Wehrmacht, and ended up being its willing agent. Despite his written apologies, he had no insight on how to win over occupied peoples or even to deal with Hitler's insanities other than following standard Nazi Party directives. He was emblematic of the entire German contradiction of tactical brilliance for the sake of tactical brilliance, without moral compunction or strategic discernment.[3]

Consequently, problems arise when evaluating even Germany's best generals, well aside from the divide between strategists to the rear and field marshals at the front. Germany fought two diverse wars between 1939 and 1945. The first one—dauntingly successful between 1939 and 1942—was waged against mostly weaker contiguous or nearby weaker countries: Belgium, Denmark, Greece, Luxembourg, the Netherlands, Norway, Yugoslavia, and, to a different degree, France. Most of these defeated nearby nations either were surprised or lacked material parity, and usually both. Their fate seemed doomed by the collective skills of staff planners like General Franz Halder and General Walther von Brauchitsch, professional Army Group leaders such as Generals Gerd von Rundstedt, Fedor von Bock, Wilhelm Ritter von Leeb, and Günther von Kluge, and practitioners of blitzkrieg in the days before Stalingrad, such as Generals Heinz Guderian, Erwin Rommel, and Erich von Manstein.[4]

Soon, however, the Wehrmacht simultaneously battled American, British, and Russian armies, in addition to Allied air and naval power, usually without surprise or technological and material superiority, and often far beyond its own borders. Facing odds quite different from the glory days of 1939–1942, the elite of the German officer corps was nearly wiped out between 1943 and 1945. By war's end about 136 German generals who served as commanders of divisions, corps, and armies (rank of or above *Generalmajor*) had been killed in action, committed suicide, or were missing, a figure that does not include deaths from natural causes, incapacity due to illness, or forced retirement on Hitler's orders.[5]

Assessing the German generals is made most difficult by the omnipotent presence of Hitler and his National Socialist operatives. By 1940 true independence of thought was mostly impossible for German generals. Hitler eventually relieved most who dissented from his often bizarre orders. All German officers fought for a cause that ultimately furthered the enslavement of once-free nations and for the Final Solution, however much they claimed (usually falsely) not to know at least the outlines of the Holocaust. The fact that a general eventually espoused anti-Nazi views (albeit usually either privately, *in extremis*, or in captivity)—as did the sympathetic Ludwig Beck, the occasionally principled Johannes Blaskowitz and Gotthard Heinrici, and the more opportunistic Günther von Kluge, Wilhelm Ritter von Thoma, and Erwin von Witzleben—or in contrast was obsequiously pro–National Socialist—such as Sepp Dietrich, Walter Model, or Ferdinand Schörner—cannot but influence our judgment of his military abilities. Aside from his strategic or tactical brilliance, a Wehrmacht general was confronted with two unique challenges: first, that he might have to risk his life or career to dissent from OKH and instead follow what he thought was a winning military strategy; and, second, his success meant the advance of Nazism's uniquely homicidal agendas that had nothing to do with the art of war.[6]

Given these constraints, the resurrected German General Staff and Prussian military aristocracy produced perhaps the war's largest group of tactically and operationally competent army generals. It is hard to find among senior German field commanders many abject mediocrities like Friedrich Paulus, or many who were as undistinguished as British General Arthur Percival or Bernard Freyberg, or American Lieutenant

General Lloyd Fredendall or Major General John P. Lucas; or a theater commander as unimpressive as General Mark Clark or perhaps even the iconic General Omar Bradley. But while the sheer number of highly gifted German army generals such as Hermann Balck, Heinz Guderian, Gotthard Heinrici, Albert Kesselring, Walter Model, Erwin Rommel, Fedor von Bock, Günther von Kluge, Wilhelm von Leeb, Erich von Manstein, or Gerd von Rundstedt was unmatched by any other army, their efforts were often diminished by both their cause and superiors. Critics continue to argue whether the members of the General Staff were even more unimaginative than Hitler was strategically imbecilic, or were simple Prussian yes-men whose independence was mostly the stuff of diary entries and postwar mythologizing.[7]

Other than blitzkrieg, the mastery of large-scale motorized encirclements, and the use of combined operations on offense and defense, there were few lasting strategic insights achieved by German generalship. After the fall of France in July 1940, the General Staff had no grand strategies for consolidating its victories and ending the war through the absolute defeat of Germany's enemies. Although the German army had pioneered airborne operations, it proved not as adept in large airdrops as the British or Americans. The same was true of amphibious assaults. Few German commanders had as good operational intelligence as his British or American counterpart. Nor did the German logistics corps approach the sorts of supply genius displayed by the Western Allies during and after the Normandy landings. Anglo-American tactical evolution during the Battle of the Atlantic was more impressive than that of Admiral Karl Doenitz and his subordinates. Hare-brained schemes and ossified protocols like monster tanks, colossal artillery pieces, and reliance on horse-powered divisions were not all Hitler's doing.

In addition, the Wehrmacht by late 1943 was insidiously becoming a one-dimensional land force that monopolized the military talent of the Third Reich. The Luftwaffe by the end of 1942 had become marginalized as an independent striking force, and soon was devoting well over half its resources to the defense of the Fatherland from Anglo-American bombing. At the same time, the U-boat and surface fleets were increasingly rendered irrelevant. Luftwaffe commander Reichsmarschall Hermann Goering was not a leader comparable to Hap Arnold, Hugh Dowding, Curtis LeMay, Charles Portal, Carl Spaatz, Arthur Tedder, or Arthur "Bomber" Harris. Neither Admirals Doenitz nor Erich Raeder was in the same league, as either a planner or fleet admiral, as their Anglo-American counterparts such as Andrew Cunningham, William Halsey, Ernest King, William Leahy, Chester Nimitz, Bertram Ramsay, or Raymond Spruance.[8]

German military genius was so often expressed in either brilliant defense that could lead to no lasting strategic advantage or an inspired offensive that lacked the sustained logistical wherewithal and strategic insight to win the war. Hitler's *Feuerwehrmann* ("fireman"), the diehard Nazi Walter Model, devised a clever way to draw in and cut apart advancing Soviet armies after 1941. Yet his mission was to prolong, not to win the war, and he did so in excellent fashion at a series of battles on both fronts—before Moscow and at Rzhev, Arnhem, and especially in the Hürtgen Forest. Model largely served Hitler's dictates and ended up shooting himself on April 21, 1945, surrounded in the Ruhr and aware that the end of Nazi rule was near.

Rommel is often praised as a great tactical army group leader, but rightly faulted as naive about grand strategy and logistics, given his unsupported thrusts on two occasions into Egypt. Yet perhaps he was the most impressive of the German field marshals—even if he more often operated in smaller theaters and never fought in the meat grinder of the Eastern Front. Rommel understood blitzkrieg as a psychological tool of combined arms to collapse enemy morale through mobility and surprise rather than the force of manpower and material per se. He did not have sufficient men or equipment to push Montgomery out of El Alamein. But the alternative to his desperate gamble to race through the British lines to capture Alexandria and reach Suez was slow strangulation, as the German and Italian supplies waned in direct proportion to the vast monthly increases in American and British convoys. By February 1943, an exasperated and often sick Rommel wrote to his wife in despair, "if only we could win a major victory here. I rack my brains night and day to find a way. Unfortunately, the conditions for it don't exist. Everything depends on supplies—and has done for years."

In the great 1944 Wehrmacht debate over how to resist the Allied invasion of France—whether to fight in strength immediately near the beaches or to bank a central Panzer strategic reserve to the rear—Rommel, a seasoned architect of mobile Panzer tactics, was proved right that overwhelming Allied air power made obsolete the more reliable and time-tested strategy of a central Panzer reserve. Better to gamble losing it in fixed battle on the shore than to have armored divisions pruned away miles from the front, and hand the Allies a beachhead that would lead to a victory in the battle of logistics. In sum, in a Reich with an irrational leader, murderous ideology, and toadyish General Staff, Rommel sought to find a way to win when there was no way to win, and more often than not kept some of his professionalism in the process. The once pro-Nazi Rommel lost his life plotting against Hitler in a way the Pomeranian and

Polish estate owners Manstein and Guderian—the two German blitz-krieg generals who were in his class—chose not to.[9]

Despite Hitler's wild strategic fantasies and erratic supreme command, German officers and soldiers were able to exact devastating losses on all three major Allied armies, inflicting casualties on British and American troops at a higher rate than the losses they incurred, and on the Eastern Front exacting over three times as many Russian fatalities for each German fatality incurred. Whether early or late in the war, on the defensive or offensive, either enjoying numerical superiority or outnumbered, the German army consistently killed more of the enemy than the enemy killed Germans. Such superiority often came despite Hitler's strategic lapses and often without technological and air superiority, and can be attributed mostly to the operational excellence of German training, high morale—and competent officers.[10]

Of the other two Axis powers, the Italian General Staff and field generals were the most inexperienced and incompetent. The career of General Marshal Rodolfo Graziani, commander in chief of the Italian General Staff, is emblematic. Graziani rose to prominence in the Italian army in the 1920s and 1930s in the way most generals did—by unwavering allegiance to Mussolini and through brutal conquest and occupation of Italy's East and North African colonies. When faced with modern enemies at the outbreak of World War II, such as the undermanned and ill-equipped British Western Desert Force of late 1940, Graziani illustrated the contradictions of Italian command. The dearth of mechanization and the feeble logistics meant that the army could not operate as a modern fighting force, and yet the dependence of commanders on the political patronage of Mussolini ensured that they must not only fight the British (and later the Americans), but also mount poorly prepared offensives in which there was the likelihood of obliteration rather than mere defeat. When Graziani could no longer use his backward forces to slaughter mostly unorganized and poorly armed Ethiopians and Libyans, he stalled, hoped for a draw against the British in September 1940, and counted on his fascist credentials for a reprieve from Mussolini—and an ultimate bailout from the Germans.

The few competent Italian generals, such as Giovanni Messe and the fascist firebrand Italo Balbo, were either underused or killed early on. Even had either of them grown into an Italian Rommel or Patton, the dearth of fuel, adequate munitions, and logistics would have nullified their genius. To the extent that Italy's generals were prepared to fight a modern army, it was to be a supposedly isolated and ill-supplied and small British expeditionary force in Africa—not against Greeks, much less later the well-equipped Red Army, and British and American soldiers in Africa, Sicily, and southern Russia.

JAPAN OFFERS THE contrast of far more experienced and capable commanders, backed by larger and more effective forces, yet sharing the same strategic blindness and thus the same destruction at the hands of the Allies. The iconic Admiral Isoroku Yamamoto illustrates best the mythologies and realities of Japanese imperial military leadership: a trust in military fanaticism and operational excellence without proper consideration of the material means necessary to achieve strategic ends. He deservedly was credited with building up Japanese naval forces before the war, especially its key carrier arm of more than five hundred superb naval pilots. He rightly opposed costly investment in iconic but otherwise anachronistic super-battleships. Yet it is hard to find evidence that Yamamoto or his fellow admirals displayed much strategic insight before Pearl Harbor or once the war broke out. The Japanese-Soviet Neutrality Pact (signed April 13, 1941), welcomed by Yamamoto, had ensured that Japan would never closely coordinate with its German partner in a possible joint attack on two fronts against the Soviet Union, and thus turned Japanese attention to naval warfare in the Pacific and against America in particular, with disastrous results.

Yamamoto is often seen today as a Hamlet-like tragic figure—self-critical, stoic, and accepting that even his inspired tactical victories would not lead to ultimate strategic advantage but instead to a Japanese apocalypse. Yet he was mostly responsible for the reckless decision to attack Pearl Harbor that is, arguably, along with Operation Barbarossa, one of the two most foolish operations of the war. For all its operational daring of reaching Pearl Harbor undetected in midwinter, the surprise attack was poorly conceived and not carried out well by the incompetent Admiral Chuichi Nagumo. The Japanese fleet ignored the real possibility that carriers might be missing, that the old battleships were being supplemented by more modern and superior versions in short order, that in such shallow waters it was difficult to either sink and permanently destroy ships at dock or to ensure that their trained crews were drowned, and that critical fuel supplies and dock works needed for a reconstituted American fleet had to be part of the pre-attack planning. How exactly Yamamoto envisioned the submerging of a few old battleships as part of a strategic blueprint for neutralizing America's war effort remains a mystery.

Of all the Japanese admirals, the English-speaking Yamamoto supposedly knew the most about the nature of their American enemies, and at least feared them more than he admired Japan's newfound German and Italian allies. Yet he usually drew wrong conclusions from his past residence in America, or vacillated by warning of the consequences of waking the sleeping American giant at the same time that he ignored his own premonitions and rabidly lobbied for the attack. As in the case of diplomat Yosuke Matsuoka or even General Tadamichi Kuribayashi, those Japanese leaders with the most firsthand knowledge of and experience in America were sometimes those most likely to embrace flawed ideas of American frivolity and inability to take casualties—perhaps their prior youthful experience with American racism clouded their empirical military assessments.[11]

Yamamoto and his admirals also insisted on attacking the Philippines in addition to Pearl Harbor, although some in the Japanese army had advised picking off orphan European colonies while sidestepping these American bases in hopes of preventing an all-out war with the United States. Yamamoto foolishly split up Japanese forces at the Battle of Midway; his complex plans to destroy the American fleet in retrospect seem crackpot. He needlessly allowed the Americans near parity in carrier forces at the battle's focus point off Midway Island. After the earlier draw at the Coral Sea, Yamamoto's admirals paused and did not exploit the near victory. Had Yamamoto instead ordered that the carrier *Shokaku* be immediately repaired and replacement crews raced to staff the depleted air wings of the *Zuikaku*—during the same time period that the more crippled *Yorktown* was refitted—the Japanese might have fought with six rather than four carriers at Midway, even after the foolhardy diversions of carrier strength to the Aleutians. Admiral Yamamoto, who displayed a level of humanity foreign to many of Japan's admirals and generals, may have been the most overrated commander of World War II. His tragedy was that had he survived the successful American assassination attack on his plane, his leadership would have made absolutely no difference in the ultimate outcome of the war that he had both warned against and insisted upon. Complexity in operations, surprise, stubborn defense, and fanaticism in a global war were no substitute for inspired grand strategy and sustained military production.[12]

Most Japanese admirals reflected these institutionalized paradoxes. They professed a commitment to bold aggressive action befitting their martial mentalities, but often proved hesitant in battle, given that they were cognizant that they lacked the industrial base to make up heavy losses in carriers and other capital ships. In other words, they grew too attached to their ships in fears of losing them. Admiral Gunichi Mikawa, after inflicting one of the worst defeats on the United States Navy in its history on the night of August 8–9, 1942, at the Battle of Savo Island, abruptly withdrew his victorious forces rather than finish off the crippled American fleet. In the same manner, had Admiral Takeo Kurita not given in to his fears and backed out of his successful attack off Samar during the Battle of Leyte Gulf, he might well have destroyed far more enemy ships, perhaps even interfering with or stopping the American landings at Leyte.[13]

Japanese generals such as Tomoyuki Yamashita, the victor of Singapore, often outfought their Allied counterparts without enjoying material superiority. In early 1942 his worn-out army of thirty thousand marched down the Malay Peninsula and forced Lieutenant General Percival to surrender Singapore's 120,000 British imperial troops. Yamashita's later dogged defense of the Philippines against General Douglas MacArthur was doomed by disparities in resources, but nonetheless cost the Americans and their Filipino allies a terrible price in blood and treasure (80,000 American casualties, and an untold number of Filipinos), and raised fundamental questions about why the island archipelago was not bypassed for a more direct route to Japan, perhaps through Formosa. Masaharu Homma—likewise executed for war crimes at war's end—conquered most of the Philippines in 1942, but without the full support of his superiors. Mitsuru Ushijima shocked the United States on Okinawa, mastering the tactics of Japanese island defense and turning what was expected to be a relatively rapid and certain victory into the worst American ground experience of the Pacific war.

Confined to fighting mostly on the defense in rough terrain, occasional jungles, and on islands, Japanese generals—the brilliant and multitalented defender of Iwo Jima, Tadamichi Kuribayashi, was perhaps the best example—inflicted severe losses on their often more numerous and better-supplied Anglo-American enemies. The absence of large open expanses in the Pacific—where mobile artillery, tanks, and late-model fighter-bombers were critical for advancement—favored the tactics of Japanese entrenched resistance, as did Japanese militarist doctrines that precluded either surrender en masse or arranged armistices.[14]

In sum, Japanese commanders had originally assumed the Western Allies' two-front war with Germany would mean fewer Anglo-American resources devoted to the Pacific. They failed to realize that Marines, carriers, and naval aircraft were not so sorely needed in Europe, and that a belligerent like the United States with twice the manpower and well over five times Japan's industrial capacity could easily fight a two-front war that nearly bankrupted Japan. Japanese naval commanders were pioneers in carrier operations and yet had no plan for the mass training of replacement naval aviators, much less matching American carrier production and fighter output.

For all Japan's impressive industrialization, too often its military defined martial courage in medieval terms, largely as face-of-battle prowess, whereas their enemies took a more holistic view of lethality through the marriage of man with machine. Lots of good pilots in Hellcats were far more deadly than a few excellent pilots in Zeros. The 1st Marine Division or the 7th Army Division, eventually to be backed by limitless supplies and coupled with air and naval superiority, were man-for-man far more deadly than the most seasoned Japanese infantry after years of combat in China. The leadership was to blame for these misconceptions. After wrongly assuming that the surprised Americans would eventually sue for terms after December 7, 1941, the generals and admirals compounded their error by concluding that the Allies would not expend the necessary blood and treasure required to force an unconditional surrender on Japan. Japanese commanders had no margin of error in World War II, and rather than making up for material disadvantages, only compounded them.

No BELLIGERENT ON either side suffered more lost generals than did the Soviet Union. Over 150 generals were killed in action, often caught in the huge encirclements of 1941–1942. Still another fifty of various rank may have been executed by the Soviet high command during the rapid German advance in the first six months of the war, and especially after the fall of Kiev and the battle for Moscow. A few were shot on Stalin's orders on the eve of the war as part of the final purges of Soviet officers, and a small number, among them the well-known Andrey Vlasov, for a time joined the German effort as part of the Russian Liberation Army (ROA) and various volunteer groups or *Hilfswilligen* units integrated into the Wehrmacht. Almost all anti-Soviet generals were either killed in battle or executed after the war.

Included in the death toll were not just obscure commanders but some of the finest generals of the prewar Soviet army, such as those who were killed early in the war like Generals V. B. Borisov, N. A. Dedaev, P. M. Filatov, and Mikhail Kirponos. Yet amid the wreckage of Soviet generalship—from prior purges, executions, and the dark days of summer 1941—emerged some of the most brilliant commanders of the entire war, especially the famous triad of Ivan Konev, Konstantin Rokossovsky, and the iconic Georgy Zhukov. The criticism of Russian military leadership during World War II was that it sought to bury the Wehrmacht through largely frontal, artillery-backed assaults on a broad front, on the theory that Germany would run out of reserves and supplies before the Soviet Union, and that the United States and Britain would bleed Germany from the air and in the Western and Mediterranean theaters far more than Japan and the Italians would erode the Americans and British. The reason that the Russians could endure such untold numbers of casualties and not suffer a general collapse in the face of the German juggernaut was precisely because the Red Army insidiously became a sophisticated mechanized and mobile force. The Soviet Union had embraced the tactics of mechanized warfare in the 1930s and undertaken substantial tank production. It was the recipient of hundreds of thousands of American trucks and jeeps, and focused on tactical air support of ground forces.[15]

German generals often reported that the Red Army predictably assembled massive artillery and rocket batteries, blasted enemy lines, sent in its superb T-34 tanks accompanied by hundreds of thousands of well-trained troops, disregarded casualties, and waited to exploit tears and gaps in German lines. That generalization is not wrong so much as incomplete, given that the Soviets refined *maskirovka*, an institutionalized art of deception and misinformation that sought to fool German armies as to the size and intent of their Soviet counterpart, and which helps to explain why seasoned German veterans were so often surprised. Some of the greatest encirclements and inspired generalship of the war—especially when the Red Army was on the defensive and felt to be on the verge of defeat or collapse—were the work of Soviet generals. The transfer of eighteen divisions from the Far East, which led to the creation of a critical fifty-two-division reserve by Generals Zhukov and Aleksandr Vasilevsky, surprised and stopped the Germans on the outskirts of Moscow. Operation Uranus (November 19–23, 1942)—the complete encirclement and destruction at Stalingrad of the German Sixth Army, the Third and Fourth Romanian armies, as well as large parts of the German Fourth Panzer Army—was also planned by Generals Zhukov and Vasilevsky. The various Soviet defenses of Sevastopol organized by General Petrov stymied General Manstein off and on for over six months and helped foul the timetable of the Case Blue 1942 offensive to the Caucasus. Generals Ivan Konev, Konstantin Rokossovsky, the brilliant Nikolai Vatutin, and Georgy Zhukov were far better prepared than their German counterparts at Kursk, with elaborate minefields, anti-tank ditches, and fortifications that made it nearly impossible before the battle had begun for German Panzers to cut off the salient.

For the first two years of the war, British generals were assigned missions in Norway, France, Greece, and North Africa without adequate supplies or manpower. In such peripheral theaters, to injure Germany required mostly air forces, while the navy was devoted to ensuring that convoys reached Britain and entered the Mediterranean to supply the North African theater. The nightmare of World War I and the Dunkirk retreat had ensured that almost no one was eager to return sizable armies to France. Until the arrival of General Rommel in North Africa in February 1942, British generalship did not have to be especially inspired to defeat Mussolini's forces.

All that said, Britain's field leadership was superb. Its forte was strategic thinking and a reliable core of army generals such as Bernard Montgomery and William Slim, sea lords like Andrew Cunningham, Bertram Ramsay, and James Somerville, and air marshals such as Hugh Dowding, Charles Portal, and Arthur Tedder. For all their occasional condescension toward the Americans, they nonetheless forged the British and later Allied strategy to win the war: first knock out Fascist Italy through a North African and eventual Sicilian campaign while keeping the Atlantic sealanes open and bombing Germany until the entrance of the Soviet Union or the United States into the war might provide the wealth and manpower to counter the German army on the continent.

The typical complaint against British generalship—exclusively on land rather than at sea and in the air, where the British enjoyed greater comparative material resources—was overcautiousness. The British entered the war underequipped and outmanned by the Axis, and essentially lost the army's materiel and cohesion at Dunkirk, shocks that continued to affect British command well after the material advantages were with the Allies. There are numerous examples of when more audacious British generalship might have stopped German advances and shortened the war: General Neil Ritchie's confused response to an advancing Rommel during May–June 1942 that led to the fall of Tobruk; General Bernard Montgomery's reluctance to pursue the enemy in haste after the victory at El Alamein or to take greater risks to break out in June 1944 in Normandy, or to close the Falaise Pocket, or to secure the approaches to Antwerp; and the lack of urgency on the part of the otherwise solid General Brian Horrocks during the Market-Garden campaign. Good leadership could have stopped, at least for a few additional months, the outnumbered Japanese attackers at Singapore. General Freyberg was hesitant and did not fight well on Crete. The island's British defenses also drew on thousands of Greek volunteers who might easily have held out against airborne assault.[16]

After autumn 1942, there were few British blunders. The insistence on a convoy system in the Atlantic, the destruction of the French fleet at Mers-el-Kébir in Algeria, the initial preference for night rather than day strategic bombing in the days before fighter escort, the postponement of a second front in 1942–1943, and the idea of invading North Africa and Sicily were all sound. If the task of the British military leadership was to craft and follow a strategy to avoid crippling army losses, to bomb Germany without prematurely meeting the main forces of the Wehrmacht on land, to knock Mussolini out of the war early on, to keep resistance to the Axis alive until the arrival of either the United States or the USSR, to secure Suez and Gibraltar, to save Burma, and to keep India safe, then it succeeded magnificently.[17]

Another achievement of the British military leadership was to exercise a near-equal strategic and operational voice with its American and Soviet allies, despite a growing inferiority in men and war materiel as it fought two concurrent wars with less than half the fatalities incurred in World War I. In part, such influence was due to unmatched British technological know-how, from its preeminence with the so-called Ultra intercepts to mastery of sonar and radar. In addition, the British learned from over two years' longer experience than the Americans in fighting the Wehrmacht, and earned moral stature by alone keeping resistance to the Third Reich alive before June 1941. If British generals sometimes seemed too conservative to both their Russian and American counterparts, they were usually right when they advised what not to do and thereby provided a critical sobriety to the Allied cause. And if generals like Montgomery seemed arrogant in a petty way, it was perhaps because they believed (rightly) that the relative small size of the British army, in comparison to the Russian and American, was not an accurate illustration of Britain's overall contribution to the Allied war effort.[18]

IF A DISPROPORTIONATELY high number of German officers arose out of the nineteenth-century Prussian Junker aristocracy, the nurseries of American World War II generals and admirals were largely the middle classes of the suburbs, small towns, and farms, often disproportionately from the American Midwest, South, and rural coastlands—places like Perry, Georgia (Courtney Hodges); Abilene, Kansas (Dwight D. Eisenhower); Clark, Missouri (Omar Bradley); Lorain, Ohio (Ernest King); Boyertown, Pennsylvania (Carl Spaatz); Uniontown, Pennsylvania (George Marshall); Chatfield, Texas (Lucian Truscott); Field Creek, Texas (Ira Eaker); and Fredericksburg, Texas (Chester Nimitz).

Still, there was a fault line among American flag officers. On the one hand, there were most famously the quintessential American organizers and conciliators—perhaps emblemized by Generals Bradley, Eisenhower, Hodges, and Marshall, or Admirals Nimitz and Spruance. All were thoroughly professional, both in temperament and behavior, and reflected the strengths of American common sense in their sober and workmanlike decisions. They rarely made mistakes and in steady fashion maximized the material advantages that soon accrued to their forces. At the other pole, however, were a minority of maverick firebrands at different levels of command—King, Halsey, LeMay, Patton—some with checkered personal lives, some with flamboyant personas and blunt and often salty language (e.g., the aphorism attributed to Admiral King, "When they get in trouble, they send for the sonsabitches"). These latter classical archetypes sought to suffuse their swashbuckling personalities among their soldiers, as if they could turn GI conscripts into professionals akin to Alexander the Great's Companions, Caesar's Tenth Legion, or Napoleon's Old Guard, who might match and trump even the élan of the Waffen SS or the Japanese veterans of a decade's fighting in China. They believed that by sheer force of willpower, American soldiers and sailors could defeat Axis forces without waiting for absolute naval, air, or materiel superiority.

The supreme warlords Hap Arnold, Ernest King, William Leahy, and George Marshall shared an uncanny genius for recognizing military need and then raising and allotting the required resources to various theaters. Leahy, perhaps the most underappreciated but important of the four, proved to be Roosevelt's eyes and ears, and successfully balanced competing claims from the respective land, air, and sea interests. He was the most trusted by the British, though perhaps because he most enjoyed the confidence and intimacy of Roosevelt. It was also to the credit of King and Arnold that they did not see the headline-grabbing virtuoso commanders—Patton, MacArthur, Halsey, and LeMay—as threats to be sidetracked, but as assets to be supported and promoted.[19]

The laundry list of American strategic and operational lapses is long, and includes technological, operational, tactical, and strategic misconceptions: not initially escorting convoys, fantasizing about opening a front in France in 1942–1943, persisting in unescorted daylight precision bombing over Europe, believing that "tank destroyers" obviated the need for a heavier battle tank, the assumptions of radically reducing Japanese island concrete bunkers through preliminary naval shelling and aerial bombing, inertia at Salerno and Anzio, not better coordinating the MacArthur and Nimitz parallel strategies in the Pacific, a focus on taking Rome rather than encircling German forces in Italy, the dispersion of forces through a landing in southern France, shorting naval bombardment at Normandy, surprise about the hedgerows behind Omaha Beach, greenlighting Operation Market-Garden, General Bradley's failure to use experience from the Pacific theater ("bush league") to refine amphibious operations at Normandy, the ambiguous and lackadaisical attitude about Patton's unexpected rapid advance eastward across France in August 1944, logistical collapse in eastern France in September 1944, the piecemeal method of replacing infantry losses, entry into and head-on slogging in the Hürtgen Forest, surprise before the Battle of the Bulge and a later unwillingness to cut the German salient off at its base, tactical predictability on Okinawa, and the inability to relieve or demote quickly generals in way over their heads, such as John Lucas, Lloyd Fredendall, and Lesley McNair.[20]

American commanders were indoctrinated in two tactical traditions. One was made famous by Ulysses S. Grant and later John J. Pershing, emphasizing finding the enemy, then confronting and destroying him through overwhelming firepower. However, even by 1944 American soldiers did not always possess either overwhelming firepower—superior machine guns, tanks, anti-tank weaponry—or the battle experience to smash through German entrenched forces, whether in the bocage beyond Omaha Beach, in the Hürtgen Forest, or against urban strongholds such as Metz. Attempts to do so could prove bloody and counterproductive.

There was also a complementary tradition of mobility, envelopment, and stripping an enemy's ability to make war by destroying his infrastructure and morale. It could be argued that General William T. Sherman's great marches through Georgia and the Carolinas in 1864–1865 had equally collapsed Southern morale in concert with Grant's head-on advances in the summer and fall of 1864. By April 1865, Sherman's huge mobile army had disrupted Confederate supply and communications, cost few Union lives, and helped to force General Robert E. Lee's surrender by the specter of an unconquered Army of the West approaching through the Carolinas. General Patton, for most of his career, was more emblematic of that second tradition, which its proselytizer the British military analyst B. H. Liddell Hart had canonized as "the indirect approach." Had the US Army fully utilized its singular motorized mobility and tactical air power in the manner that Patton's Third Army had used them to cover its flanks, and then adopted a similar Shermanesque attitude toward bypassing more resistance, and conducting encirclements, the war in theory might well have ended before 1945.[21]

Eventually, the American Joint Chiefs got most of the critical strategic decisions right, especially when the huge productive capacity of the United States at last kicked in by 1943 and made possible all the grandiose schemes of simultaneously zeroing in on Berlin and Tokyo. The high command would insist that America was to defeat Germany first, through an eventual landing on the continent. Carriers and island hopping would spearhead the American effort to cut off the Japanese homeland from its empire and render it defenseless to invasion. Massive aid would be given to both Britain and the Soviet Union. The Joint Chiefs would support the megalomaniac (and politically untouchable) Douglas MacArthur—who had at times possessed a natural talent of creating armies and knowing where to deploy them—without turning over too many strategic decisions to his often unsteady judgment. No general more often was surprised, and surprised others, than MacArthur. He also had a unique talent for deploring the precise strategic and operational lapses in others that were characteristic of his own command. He could lament the Navy's wastage from Tarawa to Okinawa without acknowledging his own questionable insistence on slogging it out at the costly battles for Peleliu and the Philippines. MacArthur was not relieved or even reprimanded for being both forewarned and surprised in the Philippines in the early morning of December 8, 1941. Consequently, it still seems strange that Admiral Husband E. Kimmel and Lieutenant General Walter C. Short, along with the Army Air Force commander at Pearl Harbor, Major General Frederick Martin, were all sacked for being caught off guard on December 7, but it was ultimately fortuitous, given the post–Pearl Harbor ascendance of admirals like King and Nimitz.

Another area where the Americans outshone all other land forces was their astonishing number of brilliant division, corps, and army commanders deployed in Europe—mostly one-, two-, and three-star generals who were more talented than the four-star generals such as Bradley, Clark, and Hodges who commanded them. There were no finer division or corps commanders than Terry de la Mesa Allen, J. Lawton Collins, Manton S. Eddy, Leonard T. Gerow, Wade Haislip, Troy Middleton, Matthew Ridgway, Lucian Truscott, and Walton Walker. The general excellence of the Army's infantry and armor commanders was partly due to the combat experience of many in World War I; partly to the excellent system of war colleges and continuing tactical and strategic education, especially at the Command and General Staff School at Fort Leavenworth, Kansas, during the 1930s; and partly to the sheer winnowing-out process of the Depression-era army that created motivation and competition for scarce resources and rare promotions.[22]

IT WAS THE ultimate contradiction of World War II that the Axis military regimes that had bragged of their greater military expertise fielded the less-capable supreme leaders, strategists, and warlords. Instead of military men narrowing the odds against their larger and more materially rich enemies, German, Italian, and Japanese generals and admirals often widened them.

The next chapters emphasize how the rank and file back home played as critical a role in the war as did their officers and fighting men and women. The Allies initially enjoyed access to far greater natural wealth—especially oil, iron ore, food, and strategic metals—than did the Axis powers. But such natural bounty did not automatically equate to greater material advantages in war, especially in the case of Britain, which was bombed, and the Soviet Union, which was invaded.

Instead, Allied planners and industrialists proved more savvy than their Italian, Japanese, and German counterparts in exploiting their natural wealth, as their factory workers and farmers became more efficient producers. The resulting plethora of supplies gave the Allies untold material advantages, particularly in compensating for both frequent deficiencies in the quality of their arms and the occasional operational shortcomings of their generals and strategists.

By early 1942 the Axis powers had occupied a geographical expanse equal to that of the Allied homelands—a greater Third Reich together with the Greater East Asia Co-Prosperity Sphere and its adjacent landscapes under Japanese control that stretched from the English Channel to the Mongolian border, albeit with the British blocking free transit through the Mediterranean. Add in Mussolini's African and Balkan territories, and a global map of World War II in mid-1942 reveals a sea of Axis-controlled land. But whereas Americans, British, and Russians worked fervently to win the war for the idea of their very survival, those under Axis occupation were never eager to fuel foreign fascist agendas, even had their overseers been competent in organizing them to work productively.

Germany was acknowledged as a prewar industrial powerhouse, whereas the Soviet Union was written off as an assumed collective and totalitarian failure. Yet as the war progressed, the Russians turned out far more weapons than did Germany—often with help from the British Empire and the United States—and made even greater sacrifices to do so than did the supposedly fanatic adherents of National Socialism. In sum, if millions of workers under Axis occupation were far less productive than the often bombed and invaded laborers in Britain and the Soviet Union, the American military economy remained in a special category all by itself—safe from attack and organized by industrial geniuses never seen before—or perhaps since.

# 18

# The Workers

WORLD WAR II was won by the greater natural wealth, production, and capital of the Allies. Yet these advantages were not foreordained. Three themes characterize the growing material edge of the Allies over the Axis powers. First, Allied workers were less often guest or coerced workers, but labored willingly with national resolve. Second, the Allies enjoyed greater naval and air power that allowed them to tap into global resources and transport them to the front lines from areas in Asia, Africa, and the Americas that were often untouched by war. Third, by early 1943 almost all American, British, and Russian factories, transportation, and fields were beyond the reach of German Panzers and bombers, even as Allied air power—soon to be augmented by ground forces—began pounding Axis production.

After September 1939, perhaps one billion of the world's roughly two billion population were soldiers, partisans, and producers engaged in trying to kill people. Victory hinged on whether the Axis or the Allies would continually put on the field of battle the most soldiers with the most plentiful weapons and sustenance, to a point where the relative quality of generals, soldiers, and arms became somewhat secondary.

When the global war commenced in full in late 1941, the majority of the world's population was either neutral or on the Allied side. Great Britain and its active Dominions, the United States, and the Soviet Union possessed a combined population of over four hundred million persons, more than double the manpower available to the three major Axis powers, without consideration of the huge populations of an allied China or a British-held India. The ensuing imbalance in the value of what people made for the war was even more staggering. Despite the Germans' vast occupation of Western and parts of Eastern Europe and European Russia, by 1943 the three Allies together were producing an aggregate gross domestic product over twice the totals for Germany, Italy, and Japan combined. Indeed, the United States eventually produced a gross domestic product of approximately $2.6 trillion (in 2016 dollars), almost the same as what the British, Germans, Italians, Japanese, and Soviets produced together ($3 trillion).[1]

Economic organization, hand-in-glove with industrial production methods and resources, was the key to the war. Throughout history, smaller populations and economies have for a time bested much larger adversaries. Tiny Greece stopped the huge armada of Xerxes in 480 BC. With a field army under forty thousand, Alexander the Great destroyed the huge forces of the Persian Empire of Darius III. Hernán Cortés's expeditionary army ended an Aztec Empire ruling over a federation of perhaps four million, with a combat force of Spanish and indigenous allies that was a fraction of that number. Turn-of-the-century Japan had a population (approximately 46 million) about a third that of Tsarist Russia (nearly 140 million), and yet largely outfought the latter in the 1904–1905 Russo-Japanese War. Napoleon had neither the resources nor the population of the serial coalitions of Austria, Britain, Prussia, and Russia that for over a decade could not defeat him.

Yet the verdicts in these asymmetrical wars were history's exceptions. Usually, defeated nations with larger populations and greater resources either did not fully mobilize their human and materiel resources, or were less developed industrially and technologically, or found it politically convenient to agree to terms rather than fight a war of annihilation. World War II proved that all other criteria (leadership, morale, quality of weaponry, etc.) being roughly equal, the side with the most people and the most things won.

The Allies accepted that it would be difficult immediately to train soldiers to Axis levels of operational competency, even if their far more experienced enemies might not continue to improve and upgrade their already fine weapons throughout the war. The obvious answer to the immediate dilemma, however, was to outproduce the Axis, both in terms of mobilizing manpower and materiel. For example, the Allies needed not necessarily to produce a tank superior to the superb German Mark V Panther (6,000 produced) or nearly unstoppable Mark VI Tiger (over 1,300). They had only to ensure that the number of effective T-34s (over 80,000 of all types produced) and less formidable M4 Sherman tanks (over 50,000 produced) were fielded in numbers that would engulf German armor.

By war's end the Axis powers often matched or exceeded their Allied counterparts in terms of individual-weapon quality or technological breakthroughs: smaller arms such as the *Sturmgewehr* 44 (assault rifle) or *Maschinengewehr* 42 (light machine gun); jet fighters; high-performance piston-driven fighters such as the German Fw 190 or Japanese Nakajima Ki-84 Hayate; ballistic and cruise missiles; the so-called Fritz X radio-guided anti-ship smart bomb; snorkel-equipped submarines; *Yamato*-class battleships; and the Japanese Type 93 torpedo. Yet such Axis weapons were either produced in too few numbers or used by too few soldiers ultimately to affect the course of the war, or simply were not mechanically reliable or economically feasible to employ. The snorkel, the designs of the Type XXI U-boat, and the hydrogen-peroxide gas turbine engine were all known to be practicable by the late 1930s, yet either did not translate into new weapons until 1943–1944 or were never implemented at all, given German inability to marry technological genius with rapid practical production. Sometimes Allied bombers derailed Axis breakthroughs—such as the serial massive British and American bombing raids on the Peenemünde testing and production site of V-2 ballistic missiles—in a way not matched by the German or Japanese air forces.[2]

Initially well-trained and well-armed Axis soldiers by 1944 were outnumbered by the Allies, not just by ratios of two- or three-to-one, but more likely four- or five-to-one, and even more in terms of planes, vehicles, guns, and ships. Military analysts, often citing quite specific quantitative data, have suggested that to overcome such numerical and material disadvantages, an armed force must perform at correspondingly far greater rates of qualitative effectiveness. Perhaps that canon explains why the Wehrmacht on Eastern Front battlefields may have killed three Red Army soldiers for each German it lost in battle, but nevertheless was crushed in less than four years.[3]

World War II was fought by coalitions. The respective Axis and Allied alliances reflected quite different industrialized economies. Unfortunately for the Axis, the German, Italian, and Japanese war industries were rarely complementary in the sense of either sharing key scientific and industrial expertise or sending direct material aid to one another— especially in comparison to the far more effectively integrated Allied war machine. There is also a tendency to measure military effectiveness by the quality and quantity of weapons per se, rather than to emphasize equally important supportive infrastructure. In critical areas such as transport planes, merchant ships, locomotives, food supplies, medicines, oil production, and metals production, the Allies not only outproduced the Axis powers but indeed swamped them. Trucks and felt-lined boots proved every bit as important to the war effort as did machine guns and hand grenades.

When the war began, the British and French Empires, along with the other Western European democracies—in terms of GDP, territory controlled, population, and natural resources—enjoyed rough parity with the three future major Axis powers, Germany, Japan, and Italy. As late as mid-1942, the Axis probably even enjoyed advantages despite the British blockade of Axis ports, the inability to coordinate Axis resources, and the fact that Germany had only recently reached World War I levels of most armament production. France had been knocked out of the war. The U-boat campaign had hampered British imports and cut commerce within the empire. Germany had occupied most of the European and Asian continental landmass from near the Volga River to the Atlantic Ocean. Most of North Africa was controlled by the Axis powers or sympathetic neutrals. Japan had swept the eastern Pacific clean of European colonial powers and the United States. Neither the USSR nor the United States was fully mobilized. Neutrals such as Portugal, Spain, Sweden, Switzerland, and Turkey were considered more in tune with the Axis than the Allies. Sweden and Switzerland found a number of ways of making a great deal of money from favorable trade and commerce with the Third Reich.[4]

Yet by late 1943 the pulse of the war had radically changed—or rather the control of the war's lifeblood, oil, had. The addition of the Soviet Union and the United States to the British cause immediately gave the new alliance absolute control over most of the world's oil supplies and sea-lanes, and the result was becoming manifest in better-trained pilots, far more mobility and range in naval operations, and greater use of motorized divisions. In circular fashion, the combined huge British and American navies ensured the three major Allies far greater access to natural resources from around the globe. Germany had no imperial overseas reservoirs of natural and human resources as the British enjoyed in Australia and Canada. It had far less access to the natural wealth of Africa or the Americas than did the British and Americans.[5]

Before the war, the majority of all global oil production came largely from four general sources: huge US domestic production (55–60 percent of world output), the Soviet Union (8–10 percent), Latin America (12–15 percent), and areas in or under control of the British Empire or other European powers (12–15 percent). After the war began, Italy had few means to access these sources. Germany could not meet its needs from its own meager local oil fields or even those in more oil-rich Romania. Coal-to-oil conversion plants only contributed a little more than 20 percent of German consumption, although it would soar to over 50 percent by 1944. The Wehrmacht by late 1942 had neared the oil fields of the Caucasus, with Army Group South occupying Maikop (19 million annual barrels) and not far from Grozny (32 million). Even Baku (170 million) was in reach, which alone produced almost three times Germany's prewar consumption.

Yet the Germans harvested relatively nothing from Maikop's torched fields after the Soviets fled. Perhaps because none of the Axis powers themselves were experienced global oil producers and enjoyed little domestic output, they lacked the engineering experience, skilled labor force, and wherewithal to quickly restore hundreds of sabotaged wells. It might have been wiser to have invested in upgrading the oil fields of Romania and Eastern Europe than assuming the oil of the Caucasus could be exploited during wartime and sent far back on Russian rails to European refineries. Japan, even with access to some oil in Taiwan, Korea, and Manchuria, produced less than 10 percent of its oil needs. In July 1941, the United States had embargoed petroleum exports to Japan that accounted for over 80 percent of its prewar oil consumption. Even with stored oil, along with a small amount of domestic production and alternate sources of importation, Japan began the war with only about a year and a half of reserves.

By 1941 the oil fields in Borneo, Java, and Sumatra produced about sixty-five million barrels, or about 4 percent of the world's annual output. In theory, the Dutch East Indies could satisfy all Japanese planned wartime consumption. Yet given that the Dutch blew up several hundred wells in the Dutch East Indies, Japan's grand plans to replace American oil with Asian supplies were only partially realized. At its best, Japan managed to tap only 35 percent of its annual consumption from those fields and refineries that had not been either fired by the Dutch or later bombed. The challenge was not so much restoring Royal Dutch Shell production as getting the oil through the American air and submarine blockade to the Japanese mainland. By 1944 only half of the oil and refined petroleum products from the Dutch East Indies ever arrived in Japan. And by 1945 most Japanese tankers were being torpedoed or bombed, and oil importation stopped altogether.[6]

The Third Reich produced a prodigious amount of coal—over 2.5 billion tons of it—sustaining its huge electrical and steel production and coal liquefaction. But in comparison, just Britain and the United States together exceeded that figure by one billion tons of annually mined coal. In terms of grains, fodder, and meat production, the asymmetries grew even wider. The inefficient Ukrainian collective farms would have likely been more productive than the Nazis' own crackpot ideas of importing German colonial farmers into the foreign Ukraine. Both Italian and Japanese agriculture were centered upon traditional peasant farming and lacked the mechanization and larger acreages customary in the Soviet Union and the United States. These food and fuel imbalances after 1942 grew even more profound. As the only major belligerent whose oil fields were entirely immune from enemy attack of any sort, the United States produced almost three times as much fuel of all sorts as all the other Allied and Axis nations *combined*. During the war, the United States produced 365 million barrels of aviation fuel, seven times the combined output of all the other major belligerents. The United States provided 90 percent of the Allies' aviation fuel requirements, ensuring that they were able to train far more pilots, build more planes, and fly more sorties.

THERE WERE QUITE astonishing imbalances in military production by 1944, even as the Third Reich went from devoting about 25 percent of its resources to the war effort in 1939 to committing 75 percent of a larger GDP by 1944. Yet even an improved German military economy still could not match the growing Allied advantages. The Soviet Union alone produced more tanks and artillery platforms than all three Axis powers combined. If Britain had once been considered outmanned and outclassed by Hitler's Third Reich, which had taken control over much of what we now know as the European Union, the British and their empire still produced more airplanes of all categories (177,000) and artillery pieces (226,000) than did Germany (133,000 and 73,000). In terms of shipbuilding, Great Britain and its Dominions far outpaced the combined German production of surface ships and submarines. Even the British prewar economy of 1939, at least in terms of per capita GDP, had been more productive than Germany's, and it had begun to rival the Third Reich in actual GDP. In fact, many scholars believe that while prewar German and British manufacturing might have been roughly equal in terms of productivity, the hugely inefficient German farming sector meant that overall the British economy was far more efficient.

Great Britain also could more easily import food from distant Australia, Canada, and the United States than Germany could extract produce from its proximate occupied territories. Even without American direct military intervention, and with the Soviet Union supplying the Third Reich until June 1941, Great Britain nevertheless had proved indefatigable in the face of both the Blitz and a planned German amphibious invasion.[7]

In such matters of food production, the story is again one of unprecedented growth. Britain, supposedly the most vulnerable of the Allies to food shortages, nearly cut off by German U-boats from North America and the empire, and shut out from traditional European sources of imported food, in fact vastly increased domestic wheat and potato production, even as the tonnage of imported meats and dairy products soared. The United States, the greatest food supplier of the war, was somehow able to keep civilian consumption of calories at about prewar levels, while actually increasing protein consumption—again the result of a concentrated effort to increase, mechanize, and modernize agriculture.[8]

Indeed, the Allied-Axis productive asymmetry is quite astonishing in every category of military production: tanks, airplanes, artillery, and rifles.

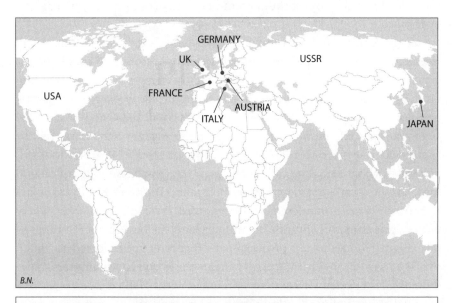

| Wartime GDP of the Great Powers, 1938–1945, in International Dollars and 1990 Prices (Billions) | | | | | | | | |
|---|---|---|---|---|---|---|---|---|
|  | 1938 | 1939 | 1940 | 1941 | 1942 | 1943 | 1944 | 1945 |
| *Allied powers* | | | | | | | | |
| USA | 800 | 869 | 943 | 1,094 | 1,235 | 1,399 | 1,499 | 1,474 |
| UK | 284 | 287 | 316 | 344 | 353 | 361 | 346 | 331 |
| France | 186 | 199 | 82 | — | — | — | — | 101 |
| Italy | — | — | — | — | — | — | 117 | 92 |
| USSR | 359 | 366 | 417 | 359 | 318 | 464 | 495 | 396 |
| Allied total | 1,629 | 1,721 | 1,758 | 1,797 | 1,906 | 2,224 | 2,457 | 2,394 |
| *Axis powers* | | | | | | | | |
| Germany | 351 | 384 | 387 | 412 | 417 | 426 | 437 | 310 |
| France | — | — | 82 | 130 | 116 | 110 | 93 | — |
| Austria | 24 | 27 | 27 | 29 | 27 | 28 | 29 | 12 |
| Italy | 141 | 151 | 147 | 144 | 145 | 137 | — | — |
| Japan | 169 | 184 | 192 | 196 | 197 | 194 | 189 | 144 |
| Axis total | 685 | 746 | 835 | 911 | 902 | 895 | 748 | 466 |
| Allied/Axis | 2.4 | 2.3 | 2.1 | 2.0 | 2.1 | 2.5 | 3.3 | 5.1 |
| USSR/Germany | 1.0 | 1.0 | 1.1 | 0.9 | 0.8 | 1.1 | 1.1 | 1.3 |

*Source:* Harrison, *The Economics of World War II*

The Relative GDP of the Major Allied and Axis Powers, 1938–1945

The unprecedented expansion of the total US economy—it increased 55 percent between 1939 and 1944 as military expenditures went from 1.4 percent of GDP to 45 percent—was such that even civilian outlays in real terms were almost as large in 1944 as they were in 1939. Whereas all the other economies of the war saw budgeting as a rivalry between guns and butter, in the United States the economy grew so vast that there was room for both the largest military and civilian economies in the nation's history.

Such American hyperefficiency was largely a result of bringing women and the unemployed into the workforce in record numbers, increasing work hours, improving techniques of mass production, building far larger and more modern factories, stepping up worker productivity, tapping into vast domestic supplies of cheap fossil fuels, and raising and freeing up untold amounts of capital. In contrast, Germany imported far less-productive slave workers to factories that after 1942 were bombed, and was without safe rails and highways or dependable supplies of oil and minerals. Incompetent *Obergruppenführers* and *Gruppenführers* in occupied territories looted, plundered, and organized the Holocaust. Nazi Party bribery was epidemic in both the military and the bureaucracy, and helps to explain why so-called professional officers never objected to much that they saw wrong in their midst. After the war, Hans Lammers, chief of staff at the Reich Chancellery, provided to his Allied interrogators a sample list of "bonuses"—huge cash awards and expropriated estates— he paid out to Nazi kingpins and Wehrmacht officers such as Generals Guderian (estate at Warthegau, Poland), von Kleist (estate in Silesia), von Leeb (estate in Bavaria), Heydrich (property in Jungfrau, Breschau), and von Rundstedt (estate in Silesia and 250,000 Reichmarks). According to postwar popular myths, conservative aristocratic officers had become completely ostracized by Hitler; in truth, they were recipients of lavish birthday presents, gifts, severance packages, and de facto hush money that was the lubricant of the Nazi regime. On the Allied side, the closest thing to prize money awarded generals were the large bank transfers from the Philippines' government accorded General Douglas MacArthur and some of his staff in February 1942 as signs of appreciation for their continued defense of the likely doomed archipelago.[9]

Germany by 1940 was cut off from most sea imports so necessary to its economy, with the exception of some vital resources from nearby Scandinavia, the Soviet Union, Eastern Europe, and the Iberian Peninsula. Without easy access to Russian and Eastern European fuels and ores, the Third Reich could not continue the war. Yet in June 1941 Hitler attacked the Soviet Union, which in the prior eighteen months had delivered, under favorable terms of credit and transport, 1.5 million tons of grain, 2 million tons of petroleum products, 140,000 tons of manganese, and 26,000 tons of chromium.[10]

A number of flawed assumptions explain the disastrous Axis strategic decisions. Japan and Germany, despite often quoted boasts of familiarity with America, knew very little about the United States. They assumed that the US economy had not produced adequate war goods in 1917–1918, given that the US Army often relied on European tanks, planes, and artillery. Yet in just a year and a half of that war, America had raised, equipped, and sent to Europe an expeditionary army of two million men, as well as financed and supplied critical food and fuels to the ailing British and French economies. At the end of World War I, the American production of shells, bullets, and gunpowder exceeded that of all its allies combined. After an initial year of confusion, the American economy ended the war by spending in just eighteen months over half of what France and Britain combined had spent on war production and mobilization in over four years.[11]

The United States, in comparative terms, had ostensibly not weathered the Great Depression as well as Germany or Japan. Over seven million Americans were out of work in 1940, and a quarter of American industrial capacity still remained idle. Germans estimated that the United States could not gear up its industry until the mid- or late 1940s, by which time the war would be won and over. No Axis power anticipated that over twenty million Americans would be added to the workforce after 1941, which would itself expand in size by over 50 percent. Apparently, neither the Japanese nor the Germans appreciated that before the Depression, the huge American economy had produced over 40 percent of the world's manufacturing output and could easily reboot, if not drastically expand, its idle factories and labor force.[12]

The Germans perhaps had some grounds to think that the United States would not enter the war, or if they did, would do so reluctantly and without full economic and military mobilization. Even eight months after the start of the war in Europe, the Americans seemed to think that there was still a chance that they could avoid war and that Hitler and his enemies could reach an armistice. Anthony Eden relates, in a brilliant touch of understatement, a strange March 1940 London conversation with the American diplomat Sumner Welles and the ambassador to Great Britain, Joseph Kennedy. Welles, Eden related, apparently wanted to see whether the war could still be rescinded, if perhaps an international consortium could oversee mutual disarmament, even after the end of both Czechoslovakia and Poland, and months of German hostilities. "Hitler, he [Welles] explained, had spoken to him at length about disarmament and alleged that he had several times made proposals which had been turned down, in particular one 'for a mutual pooling of armaments by Britain, France and the United States.' Had I any recollection of this scheme? I replied that I had none and that to the best of my belief no such suggestion had ever been made. It was in conflict with the general trend of Hitler's sentiments, which were antagonistic to international collaboration."[13]

Chronic appeasement in Britain also apparently had confused the Third Reich. Few in Germany had imagined that by the later 1930s the much smaller population of Great Britain had equaled Axis military vehicle and artillery output. Indeed, in every year of the war Britain exceeded German aircraft production in terms of the aggregate weight of planes produced. In total numbers of planes built, Britain also outpaced the Luftwaffe in every full year of the war save 1944. Hitler had a bad habit of assuming that because his enemies had not fully mobilized in 1939, the reason was because they could not, rather than that they had preferred not to.[14]

Even more astonishing, the British fleet—the largest in the world in 1939—saw more surface and merchant ships added during the war, including battleships and carriers, than the entire naval production of the three major Axis powers. Hitler never appreciated the fact that the British Navy ensured that the huge natural resources of the empire—especially from Australia and Canada, and the oil of the Middle East—were integrated with British production, albeit with the important qualifier that such sources of British supplies were largely immune from German bombs and rockets.

Japan—which was not much damaged by American bombing until March 1945—built an incredible sixteen aircraft carriers (of all sizes and categories, from fleet to escort and light) during the war. That was an amazing achievement until compared with more than the 150 light, escort, and fleet carriers that the United States deployed during the same period. More impressive was the constant improvement in Allied maritime production. With new methods of prefabrication of parts and assembly-line production, industrialist Henry Kaiser's shipyards were able to cut the construction time of ten-thousand-ton Liberty merchant ships from about 230 days to 24. Over 2,700 Liberty and over five hundred larger, better-designed, and faster Victory ships were built, ensuring that the US merchant fleet grew at a far greater rate than German U-boats could diminish it.

In 1942, it took about 54,800 man-hours to build a B-17, a bomber that had been in production since 1937. But just two years later, only

18,600 man-hours were required. A similarly astonishing decrease in labor was true for the gargantuan and complex B-29 bomber. The thousandth bomber to roll off the production line required half the man-hours to build as the four hundredth. No Axis power came close to such stepped-up productivity—all the more wondrous given that between 1941 and 1944 US labor earnings had increased 50 percent even as labor costs dived by two-thirds.[15]

Because the Third Reich mobilized almost as many combatants (at least 10 million in active service by 1944) as did the United States (and a far larger percentage of its population than was true of either America or the Soviet Union), and because it was some fifty-five million persons smaller, Germany quickly found itself short of laborers. Almost immediately after entering Russia, the Third Reich was forced to conscript workers from occupied Western Europe and slave laborers from the Eastern Front to make up for vast new drafts into the military of able-bodied German factory workers. Companies like Daimler-Benz and BMW vastly expanded their workforces, replacing skilled German laborers who were drafted into the army with conscripted foreign workers, until eventually foreigners made up about half their workforce, which was ironic, given that the war had turned topsy-turvy the Third Reich's loud agenda of cleansing so-called non-Aryan *Untermenschen* from German soil. None of these efforts matched Allied levels of productivity, however.[16]

Once the war started, the Axis did not create secure factories akin to the huge Russian tank industries across the Urals or the enormous 3.5-million-square-foot Willow Run B-24 plant in Michigan. In January 1939, the United States had about 9.5 million square feet of industrial plant space devoted to aircraft production; by the end of 1944, that figure had skyrocketed to 165 million square feet, an eighteenfold increase. In contrast, even during the disastrous first eighteen months of the war, when huge Soviet tank factories at Kharkov and Stalingrad were either destroyed or dismantled, the Soviet factories across the Urals produced considerably more tanks, aircraft, and rifles than did the Germans, and of comparable or often better quality. The Stalin Ural Tank Factory No. 183, relocated to and expanded at Nizhny Tagil, Russia, proved the largest producer of tanks in the world.[17]

One reason why the Axis powers failed to put their industries on a war footing between 1939 and 1941 was the easy (and often parasitic) nature of their conquests. Not only were the initial European enemies of the Axis unorganized and unable to draw out the war, they often were also rich in mostly prewar-produced arms and munitions. The flotsam and jetsam of defeat was scavenged and incorporated into the German military. After the absorption of Czechoslovakia, and the defeat of Poland, Holland, Belgium, France, and the British at Dunkirk, the Third Reich inherited tens of thousands of military vehicles and artillery pieces. The British alone at Dunkirk left behind 2,472 of their artillery platforms (90 percent of what they had arrived in France with), along with 63,879 motor vehicles (95 percent of what they had landed with). The next year, when the German army invaded the Soviet Union on June 22, it was only partially equipped by German industry but otherwise outfitted haphazardly with the confiscated war spoils of Europe. Scavenging diverse equipment, much of it nearing obsolescence, may have seemed cheaper in the short term than producing uniform material, but in the long run parasitism proved a maintenance nightmare, impeded technological advance, and induced complacency.[18]

Bombing attacks on Russian and British industrial centers were largely over by 1943, with the exception of the V-1 and V-2 blitzes and occasional German conventional raids that had almost no effect on British production. By the first quarter of 1944, British munitions production was 552 percent greater than when the war had begun. In contrast, by late 1944 Italy was out of the war and German industry was bombed daily; the majority of Japan's urban centers would be largely flattened by July 1945.[19]

By war's end, the United States had supplied about 20 percent of Britain's strategic requirements, largely as a result of massive shipments of fuel, food, Liberty ships, DC-3/C-47 transport planes, and naval aircraft. After 1943, Russia was able to supply a constant frontline army of seven million that would break the back of the Wehrmacht, but only if it were backed with material aid such as two thousand American locomotives, eleven thousand railcars, and half a million wheeled and tracked vehicles. Likewise, Americans and British exchanged their expertise, as for example the American production of the excellent British-designed and British-engineered Rolls-Royce Merlin aircraft engine that saved the P-51 fighter program, or the British "Firefly" modification of the Sherman tank that upgraded its gun with a high-velocity 17-pounder (76.2 mm). At war's end the United States had devoted between 15 percent and 20 percent of its own war production to military aid to Britain and the Soviet Union, in addition to staggering amounts of foodstuffs.[20]

Perhaps the key difference in the wartime economies of the major powers was the uncanny American insight into producing military infrastructure. While Hitler talked of "miracle weapons," or Mussolini bragged of his fast battleships, or the Imperial Japanese Navy boasted that its two super-battleships were the most powerful in the world, the United States focused on less ostentatious assets like fuel production, military trucks, heavy equipment, machine tools, Jeeps, landing craft, transport planes, locomotives, Liberty ships, radios, rations, and military clothing and gear. What is astounding is not just that the United States produced seven times more trucks than did the Third Reich, or that the British built over a hundred thousand more than the Germans (480,000 to 345,000), but also that Canada more than doubled Germany's military vehicle output (815,729).[21]

There were few counterparts in Germany, Japan, or Italy to American private industrialists like the Americans Henry Kaiser (of Kaiser Aluminum and Kaiser Steel), William Knudsen (of General Motors), or Charles Sorensen (of Ford Motor Company). An entire cadre of successful captains of industry created huge factories, focused on a few models of ships and bombers, and mass-produced them on assembly-line principles—and constantly demanded that extraordinary rates of production be further increased. Such magnates ensured that in just four years American private enterprise had produced nearly ninety thousand tanks of all types, over a quarter-million artillery pieces, 2.4 million trucks, 2.4 million machine guns, and over forty billion rounds of ammunition—along with 807 cruisers, destroyers, and destroyer escorts, 203 submarines, 151 carriers (of all categories), eight battleships, and over fifty million tons of merchant shipping, as well as three hundred thousand aircraft.[22]

Nazi Germany, Italy, and Japan declared war on the largest economy in the world, one that had the greatest supply of skilled labor, the most abundant fuels and metals, the largest capital reserves, and the most innovative entrepreneurial class—and that had been buoyed by a collective outrage after Pearl Harbor to punish the Axis for attacking the United States and declaring war on a neutral nation. The Third Reich assumed Soviet industrial production would be nullified by the occupation of European Russia, while Britain, if it survived, would lag behind Germany in the 1940s as it had in the 1930s; in truth, both nations soon outproduced both Germany and Japan in most categories of munitions.

In sum, victory in World War II was a morality tale of production besting killing: those who made more stuff beat those who killed more people.

# 19

# The Dead

THE NOUN AND adjectives *World War II* are synonymous with mass death as never before envisioned. The six years and one day of World War II (September 1, 1939–September 2, 1945) witnessed somewhere between fifty and eighty-five million deaths. Perhaps a figure of sixty to sixty-five million killed is the most likely guess. Or to put it another way, about 3 percent of the estimated two billion people alive in 1939 would die by force by 1945.

During the combined three centuries of conflict between 1700 and 1988, roughly one hundred million are estimated to have died in some 471 wars. Well over half that number perished in just the six years of World War II. The toll may have been even greater, given that the exact number of fatalities cannot be known due to poor wartime recordkeeping, especially in the former Soviet Union and China, the locales of over half the war's fatalities.[1]

Plenty of disagreement arises over the methodology of counting the war's losses, given the exact relationships between the war and famines, massive displacements, deportations, and disease. If a man died in 1946 from a war wound incurred in 1944, or if one first contracted tuberculosis at Dachau and succumbed in 1947, he was usually not counted as a direct fatality of World War II. The only constant in counting the human cost of the war is that over the last seventy years of scholarship, the number of fatalities attributed to World War II seems always to have been revised upward. The war dwarfed even the unprecedented horrors of World War I. Until 1939, the Great War had accounted for the greatest number of dead (15–20 million) of any conflict in history. Yet World War II resulted in at least three times that toll.

World War II was also the worst human-caused disaster in civilization's history—more deadly than the Mongol invasions, the forced collectivization of farmland and reordering of rural life ordered by Joseph Stalin between 1930 and 1932, and perhaps even more catastrophic than the later mass starvations caused by the various internal revolutions spawned by Mao Zedong. On the other hand, at war's end the armies of the victorious Allies had never been larger, better equipped, and more lavishly supplied, almost as if the more death and destruction that ensued, the more the military grew and the life of the soldier improved. The three major winners alone fielded forces in aggregate of nearly thirty million combatants. Despite the far greater carnage between 1939 and 1945, seventy years later historians rarely write of the political or strategic futility of the Second World War as they so often do of the First. Apparently, losing sixty million for a subsequent general seventy-year peace and the end of nightmarish ideologies was defensible, while losing fifteen to twenty million for a twenty-one-year hiatus was sometimes not.

The staggering twenty million who perished from the flu pandemic of 1918 were probably less than wartime losses inside the Soviet Union alone between June 1941 and spring 1945. The great Chinese drought of 1876–1879 (approximately 10 million dead) proved less deadly than the violence unleashed by the Japanese in China between 1931 and 1945. Even the horrific bubonic plague—the worst natural catastrophe in human history, which may have killed two-thirds (40 to 50 million) of Europe's population between 1346 and 1353—probably did not match the death toll of World War II.[2]

IN ADDITION TO the reasons noted in the prior chapters for the singular deadliness of the war, other considerations help to explain how a perfect six-year storm of death was unleashed by an otherwise brief German invasion of its neighbor Poland in 1939.

First, by the mid-twentieth century, the world had an estimated population of two billion. More people died in World War II than ever before because there simply were more people to fight and die. Armies were larger. Major belligerent countries such as Britain, China, France, Germany, Japan, the Soviet Union, and the United States had never been so populous or so urbanized. In no past era in history was an infantry force such as the Soviet Red Army of more than five hundred active ground divisions even conceivable. There had never been a navy such as the American fleet of nearly seven thousand warships. Some estimates put combined Axis and Allied mobilized military manpower at its peak at an aggregate seventy million people during six years of war.[3]

Second, like many of history's greatest conflicts, the war started in and spread from Europe. It was largely fought by Western or Westernized powers that were the most industrially advanced and technologically sophisticated nations in the world, and at the apogee of their scientific development. A South American border war, a continent-wide conflict in Africa, or even a battle engulfing all of Southeast Asia would not have involved the use of Zyklon B, napalm, B-29 bombers, atomic weapons, proximity fuze shells, land mines, millions of sophisticated tanks and artillery pieces, and ubiquitous semi-automatic weapons.

The Thirty Years' War (1618–1648) was fought in the heart of Europe and lasted five times longer than World War II. It was bloodier than any war of the seventeenth century outside of Europe, given the population size and degree of scientific advancement of the continent. Yet that savagery was a pre–Industrial Revolution conflict in which matchlock muskets fired at best at rates of one shot every two minutes, and were hardly accurate beyond a hundred yards. Such small-arms fire was light years away from the five hundred to six hundred rounds per minute capability of a World War II light machine gun or semi-automatic pre-assault weapon such as the *Sturmgewehr* 44, much less the much more terrifying *Maschinengewehr* 42 that spewed out bullets at a rate of 1,200 rounds per minute. One Wehrmacht soldier represented the firepower of a few hundred harquebusiers and could kill easily at three or four times the distance. In short, two developments—the emergence of rapid-firing rifles with cheap cartridges, and mass-produced artillery and shrapnel shells— changed the complexion of land warfare in the twentieth century. For the first time in military history, the percentage of losses between the victor and defeated evened out. In fact, in many battles the victorious side suffered far more than the losers. The number of weapons produced by all the nations of World War II was staggering: 440,000 military aircraft, five million military vehicles, over eighty billion bullets and mortar and artillery shells, and fifty million small firearms and artillery pieces. The previous notion of husbanding bullets because of their rarity and expense simply did not apply to most battles of World War II, at least in comparison to past conflicts.[4]

Third, global transportation and communications—the telephone, the radio, sophisticated internal combustion engines, and rapid and cheap air and oceanic travel—allowed the war to expand well beyond the confines of Europe. The world had shrunk. The fighting reached Asian, African, and Oceanic locales that otherwise had been largely immune from past internecine European conflicts. Napoleon had spread his war to Egypt. There were Middle Eastern and African theaters during World War I. Yet never before had so many combatants fought so violently so far apart over such vast expanses of territory—whether near the Arctic Circle or the Sahara Desert, from the Volga River to the waters off Miami, and in the

Aleutian Islands and across the Indian Ocean. Exotic places like Tarawa or far off cities such as Kursk became everyday referents to millions of European and Asian citizens in a way they never were before or since.

The use of radio guidance and radar allowed ships to travel in zero visibility and planes to bomb amid heavy cloud cover. The idea that a bomber such as a B-29 could fly 1,600 miles over the ocean to drop ten tons of incendiaries would have been considered absurd in 1939. But the notion was passé by September 1945 after months of lethal fire raids on Japan as the radius of war grew as never before.

Large oil-fired ocean-going transports and warships, processed foods and improved storage and packaging methods, along with air transports, allowed soldiers to reach the enemy in great numbers and be supplied almost anywhere on the globe. It would again have been beyond the power of the World War I American military to have conducted large-scale amphibious operations in the Pacific or to have landed consecutively in North Africa, Sicily, Italy, Normandy, and southern France. Italy in 1914 would not have been able to send a half-million men to eastern and northern Africa and support them. The German army of 1918 could not have parachuted troops into Crete and captured the island.

Fourth, World War II was an ideological war waged in the new age of secular modernism. There had been centuries of conflicts fueled by religious ideas, revolutionary fervor, and ethnic chauvinism in the West— from the Crusades to the Thirty Years' War to the Napoleonic Wars—that transcended traditional disputes over personalities, succession, territory, resources, or politics. But totalitarian ideologies of World War II, often claiming pedigrees from Darwin and Nietzsche to Marx and Engels, re-energized theories of racial superiority, state power, mass participation of civilians, technological determinism, and national destinies as never quite seen in the 2,500 years of Western history. Modernism had helped to re-invent morality in relativist terms. The 1930s championed the statist idea that the interests of the strong collective trumped the supposed selfishness of the weaker individual, as dying and killing were easily justified as necessary means to achieve utopian ends. One of the many reasons why the Eastern Front turned so horrific was the similarly totalitarian nature and morality of the Soviet and Nazi military leadership. Both the Red Army and the Wehrmacht censored all news from the battlefield. Both tolerated no dissenting voices and executed their own in vast numbers— in the case of the Germans, over twenty-five thousand through military courts-martial; for the Red Army, well over a hundred thousand. They conceded that surrender was usually tantamount to death and recklessly suffered enormous losses to protect the hierarchy of the state.

By the start of World War II, scientific development, especially in Nazi Germany, was also considered synonymous with ethical advancement, despite the fact that technologies were often used to enhance the mechanics of mass death. Science almost seemed to excuse or at least offer a veneer to barbarity. The quite contrary idea of material progress ensuring moral regress—a warning in classical literature from the early Greek poet Hesiod and classical tragedian Sophocles to the Roman imperial novelist Petronius and historian Tacitus—was never more evident. The great myth of the war was that ethics had evolved at the same pace as engineering, or that the diminution of edged hand-held weapons meant less barbarism and cruelty. No warlike premodern empire—not those of the Vandals, Mongols, Aztecs, Zulus, or Ottomans—systematically and deliberately killed as many civilians during a conflict as did the Third Reich.

The Nazis capitalized on breakthroughs in German engineering and chemical production at places like Auschwitz and Treblinka to ratchet up the death tolls to surreal levels. Topf & Sons was proud of its cutting-edge incinerators that facilitated the cremation of hundreds of thousands of gassed inmates at Auschwitz, understanding quite correctly that the bottleneck in the Final Solution was not just rail transportation to the East or insufficient gas chambers, but rather the inability to dispose of tens of thousands of corpses each day. The firm wanted its brand name prominently stamped on the doors to the Apocalypse.

Without German custom-built crematoria, the death camps would never have reached daily kill rates approaching eight to ten thousand in May and June 1944. Crematoria II and III at Auschwitz operated with clockwork efficiency:

> The basements of the crematoriums built on two levels included a hall for the handling of the corpses [for the pulling out of gold teeth, cutting women's hair, detaching prosthetic limbs, collecting any valuables such as wedding rings, glasses, and the like] by the Jewish *Sonderkommando* members [death camp workers] after they had dragged the bodies out of the gas chamber. Then elevators carried the corpses to the ground floor, where several ovens reduced them to ashes. After the grinding of bones in special mills, the ashes were used as fertilizer in the nearby fields, dumped in local forests, or tossed into the river nearby. As for the members of the *Sonderkommandos*, they were periodically killed and replaced by a new batch.[5]

The preindustrial Greeks and Romans executed prisoners and destroyed towns and cities, but not on such a huge scale or as a matter of national ideology as was true of the Wehrmacht. Hundreds of thousands of civilians can be killed with edged weapons rather quickly: over a million in Rwanda may have perished in just one hundred days in mid-1994, many of them by tens of thousands of killers armed with hand-held machetes. But such a nightmare could not reach the ghastly numbers targeted by Nazi Germany without the industry and technology of the modern dictatorial state.[6]

The Wehrmacht conceded that most Soviet prisoners taken between June 1941 and April 1945 would not survive German captivity. Only 40 percent did. The Soviet Union likewise did not worry about the approximately one million German prisoners who perished in Russian hands. Fascism, Nazism, and communism—and the determined responses of the democracies to them—created zones of war without quarter at a barbarous level never seen before. The Allies took for granted that in cities like Dresden and Tokyo tens of thousands of civilians who were not directly engaged in war production would nevertheless be incinerated along with those who were. They tolerated their deaths as an aberration from their own professed code of ethics in such an existential war against the modern barbarism of the Axis.

World War II was an anomaly in two respects: the number of dead was astronomical at over sixty million, and the victors suffered anywhere from five to seven times more dead than did the defeated. Both those paradoxes were entirely attributable to the horror of some forty million Russian and Chinese fatalities—well over thirty times the combined British and American losses. The respective populations of the Soviet Union and China were slaughtered as never before in the long history of warfare by ideological zealots who nonetheless lost the war. Taken separately, the Russian-German war in the East (27 million dead) marks the second most deadly conflict in the history of warfare after the combined other theaters of World War II.[7]

There was yet a fifth and unprecedented multiplier of death in World War II. In the age-old tension between technological challenge and response, the 1930s and 1940s had shifted the cycle to the clear advantage of the offense over the defense. World War II was a military world away from the defensive era of ancient Greek hoplite battle, when bronze body armor could turn away most arrows and spears and thus keep fatalities to an aggregate of about 10 percent of opposing hoplite armies, despite the horror of the head-on collisions of phalanxes. Nor was the war similar to combat during the twelfth century, when plate armor could protect heavy cavalrymen from most hand-held weapons and many projectiles. The era of World War II was not even the Medieval Age of castellation that shielded towns from pre–gunpowder catapult assault.[8]

World War II also lacked the protective options of later twenty-first-century warfare. There was as yet no effective body armor to deflect bullets from automatic weapons or shrapnel from mortars and artillery—as ceramic and Kevlar body armor in Afghanistan and Iraq would prevent body wounds entirely or diminish the rates of mortality from serious injuries.[9]

World War II anti-aircraft guns, without sophisticated computer systems, as a rule were not able to stop fleets of strafing fighter-bombers. There were no shoulder-fired guided missiles to stop tactical air attacks. German defensive planners accepted that it took an average of well over three thousand rounds from even their heralded medium-range 88 mm flak guns to down a single Allied bomber, and perhaps more when all calibers of flak guns were averaged together. Offensive considerations more often trumped defensive responses. To solve the cost-benefit dilemmas of B-29s, General Curtis LeMay did not put more guns and armor on the behemoth planes and keep them at higher altitudes, but rather reduced their weight and altitude to ensure heavier bomb loads in the anticipated effort to risk more lives to destroy more of Japan and win the war—and thus to curtail total bombing missions.[10]

Sixth, World War II went on longer than any other major war since the Industrial Revolution. From the invasion of Poland to the formal Japanese surrender marked a longer span than the American Civil War, the Franco-Prussian War, or the four-year horror of World War I. Six years of escalating violence led to unprecedented casualties. Key here is to remember that World War II started out as a series of declared wars from September 1939 through 1945, unlike the prior Axis interventions in China, Ethiopia, and Spain during the 1930s that, at least initially, began without declarations. Formally declared wars more quickly lead to demands for immediate and absolute victory in a way that police actions and interventions sometimes do not, which in turn become arguments for earlier mass mobilizations and retooling of industry.

Seventh, World War II, as mentioned earlier, was the first major war in which civilian fatalities far outnumbered military deaths, despite improved medical facilities and advances in food storage and preservation. The old nineteenth-century divide between soldier and civilian—obscured, but not ended in World War I—was completely obliterated in World War II. Or rather, the targeting of civilians was considered a legitimate strategy of both diminishing enemy military capability and exterminating ideological and racial enemies under the cloak of war. When Hitler bragged of the collective *Volk* or Stalin of the masses, enemies apparently took their boasts at face value and agreed that their militaries were indistinguishable from their populations.[11]

Finally, the rapid German and Japanese absorption of territory, followed by their equally abrupt forced withdrawals from their conquests
in 1944–1945, led to vast transfers of civilian populations. These were
not uncontested exoduses. Most of the long marches occurred in harsh
climates. They were concurrent to fighting, often arising from the fury
of ideological extremism and righteous revenge, amid severe shortages of
food and lack of shelter. East Prussia, for example, was erased from the
map entirely, never to reappear. Fascist ideologies early in the war had
been used to justify brutality in the evacuation and movement of conquered peoples. That barbarity empowered a proper notion of vengeance
in 1944–1945 against German and, to a lesser extent, Japanese civilians
who were forced to withdraw from what they had conquered or areas
where, in some cases, they had lived for centuries.[12]

MOST OF WORLD War II's sixty million victims died off the battlefield,
well apart from both bombs and camps. Perhaps all told, over twenty
million starved to death or were weakened by hunger and perished from
treatable illnesses and diseases. Yet improved food and water storage and
health care—vaccination, medicines, sanitation, hospitalization—should
have saved more combatants and civilians from hunger, disease, and exposure in the field. Nonetheless, there were still massive numbers of civilian deaths due to starvation and infection, largely due to the German
and Japanese occupations in the Soviet Union and China, respectively.
In addition, the capitulations of trapped armies in the Soviet Union and
China sent perhaps ten million into prisoner-of-war camps where over
half the detainees perished.[13]

Thousands of Western and central Europeans died from hunger, especially during the first six months of 1945 when Germans retreating
from Belgium, France, Italy, and the Netherlands stripped food stocks
or destroyed what they could not carry, as farms became battlefields and
some civilians like the Dutch ate tulip bulbs. There were also far greater,
though lesser-known, abattoirs of mass starvation: Eastern Europe, India, the large archipelagoes of the Pacific, and Southeast Asia.[14]

The causes of hunger varied from the general to the specific. The vast
diversion of manpower from farms to factories and to the army in war
zones often left fields unattended. Food was often not stockpiled in occupied countries but plundered and shipped to the Japanese and German
fronts. Thousands of civilians starved to death in occupied Greece to
supply Army Group South with foodstuffs on its advances to the Caucasus. Indochinese rice fueled the Japanese army. The wartime destruction

of transportation and infrastructure meant that produce rotted and never reached population centers. Disruptions in irrigation systems and shortages and diversions of petrochemicals ensured that what farmland was brought into production saw vastly reduced harvests. World War II occurred when nearly half the populations of the belligerents had moved to cities and required daily importation of food by rail or truck.

Even in peacetime, China was always on the cusp of starvation. Under Japanese occupation, perhaps five to six million Chinese starved to death or died from disease, a toll comparable to the European Holocaust. The Japanese were fighting somewhere in China for some fourteen years (1931–1945), the longest of any occupation associated at least in part with World War II. At the peak of the occupation, the Japanese military controlled, indirectly, some two hundred million Chinese, over a third of the country's population. Japanese-occupied China comprised a country larger in population than any nation in the world at the time except India. In the case of almost every famine of World War II, the death toll was predicated on the length of the Axis occupation, the geographical extent of the occupation, and the size of the occupation force. Life under a Japanese or German proconsul was synonymous with hunger.[15]

It is impossible to sort out the rough ratios of Russian civilian deaths from starvation, disease, and exposure, or a combination of all three. The best collective estimates range from five to ten million dead from such causes, largely during the flight before the Nazi offensives of 1941–1942, the siege of Leningrad, the great encirclements around Kiev, Minsk, Smolensk, and Uman, and the deliberate Nazi policies during the occupation of some one million square miles until 1944. Although the Soviet Union was self-sufficient in grain by 1941, its huge collective farms were not only inefficient but also far more vulnerable to disruptions in fuel, supplies, and transportation than had been true of the prior decentralized regimen of farm-owning kulaks, peasants, and small agrarians.

When the German army entered Ukraine, the collective Soviet system of food production simply collapsed. It was a deliberate policy of the invading Germans (the so-called *Hungerplan* of Nazi technocrat Herbert Backe) to strip the Soviet Union of all its available food. By starving to death millions of Russians, the Third Reich thought that it could feed the Wehrmacht from local stocks, send food surpluses back to the German homeland, and diminish Slavic populations to pave the way for eventual German resettlement. And while the *Hungerplan* was never fully implemented in its ghastly entirety, Stalin's scorched-earth policy in the retreats of summer 1941, the Russian counteroffensives after Stalingrad, and the German withholding of food from occupied populations all help to explain why millions of Russians starved to death. Hitler entertained lunatic visions of a new Germanized Russia, in which at best the population would be reduced to helotage:

> The German colonist ought to live on handsome, spacious farms. The German services will be lodged in marvelous buildings, the governors in palaces. Beneath the shelter of the administrative services, we shall gradually organise all that is indispensable to the maintenance of a certain standard of living. Around the city, to a depth of thirty to forty kilometres, we shall have a belt of handsome villages connected by the best roads. What exists beyond that will be another world, in which we mean to let the Russians live as they like. It is merely necessary that we should rule them. In the event of a revolution, we shall only have to drop a few bombs on their cities, and the affair will be liquidated. Once a year we shall lead a troop of Kirghizes through the capital of the Reich, in order to strike their imaginations with the size of our monuments.

On the eve of Operation Barbarossa, the future of occupied Russia was spelled out starkly in the Third Reich's official "Economic Policy Guidelines for Economic Organization East." Russian grain—Ukraine provided 40 percent of Soviet supplies—would be siphoned off to feed the Wehrmacht, easing shortages inside the Third Reich: "Many tens of millions of people in this territory will become superfluous and will have to die or migrate to Siberia. Attempts to rescue the population there from death through starvation by obtaining surpluses from the black earth zone can only be at the expense of the provisioning of Europe. They prevent the possibility of Germany holding out until the end of the war; they prevent Germany and Europe from resisting the blockade."[16]

Aside from the combined ten to fifteen million who starved to death or died from disease in China and Russia, there were the mostly forgotten eight to ten million civilians who perished in Burma, the Dutch East Indies, French Indochina, India, and the Philippines. Perhaps three million starved on Java alone. Here the common denominator was not just war. Allied forces, for example, had mostly skipped over the Dutch East Indies and for most of the war fought few battles along the borders of India proper or in French Indochina. Instead, Japanese occupation was again the culprit. The occupied were forced to give up food to supply the Imperial Japanese Army and starved as a consequence. The accessory killer of Asians was endemic poverty. The entrance of Japanese forces into such fragile human landscapes as the Pacific and Southeast Asia, largely to extract natural resources and critical manpower, proved a brutal force multiplier of death.

Outside the Eastern and Asia-Pacific fronts, perhaps another two to three million civilians starved or suffered fatal illnesses inside the respective Axis empires. Both Allied bombing and food shortages due to rationing, transportation disruptions, and expropriations resulted in widescale famine within both Germany and Japan. Over one million starved to death in the German-controlled Baltic states, the Netherlands, Poland, the Balkans, and Eastern Europe—countries that were either occupied after 1940–1941 or joined the Third Reich and later became battlefields between advancing Allies and retreating Germans in 1944–1945. If a country was not self-sufficient in food production before the war, and if it was felt to harbor a serious resistance movement, then it was especially vulnerable to harsh German requisitions. Accordingly, the Netherlands (16,000–20,000 dead) and Greece (estimates of 100,000–400,000 dead) were especially singled out.[17]

Well over four thousand divisions, in addition to auxiliaries, were raised during World War II. Such an unprecedented mobilization took seventy million able-bodied men away from peacetime work, and often from farms and agriculture-related industries. Vast amounts of global capital were also diverted to munitions from food production, chemicals, fertilizers, farm machinery, and infrastructure. Natural disasters did not take a holiday during the war. Disease was enhanced by deprivation. Over a quarter-billion Russians and Chinese were displaced refugees or remained under enemy occupation. Perhaps three hundred million in Europe at some point suffered a similar fate of leaving their homes.

THE BEST ESTIMATES—DESPITE inexact recordkeeping and frequent Soviet distortions—suggest that about twenty to twenty-five million died in combat during the war, with the Eastern Front being the meat grinder of the conflict, costing the lives of fifteen million German and Russian soldiers, among them perhaps four to four-and-a-half million Russian and German POWs. Ostensibly, most Germans died in the long westward retreats after 1943, while most Russians perished in the first two years of Operation Barbarossa. Huge numbers of Germans and Russians were killed every month after June 1941, well apart from the notorious slaughterhouses at Kursk, Leningrad, Stalingrad, and Warsaw. In fact, losses on both sides spiked in late 1943 through summer 1944, more than two years after the commencement of Operation Barbarossa, as both sides rushed more lethal artillery and the war's most potent armored vehicles to the front.[18]

Japan perhaps lost over one million soldiers in combat inside China. In turn, the Chinese suffered three to four million battle deaths in some fourteen years of on-off war. As on the Eastern Front, the majority of Chinese and Japanese battle fatalities in the Chinese War were in the army. Another one million Japanese died fighting Allied soldiers, largely in the Pacific and Burma, among them over four hundred thousand from the Imperial Navy, who suffered grievously from American submarines and carrier-based aircraft. Air and ground action between the Allies and Axis in Western Europe, Italy, and the Mediterranean added at least another one to two million dead. In addition, there were so many forgotten theaters both prior to and associated with World War II—the Italian invasion of Abyssinia in 1935, the Soviet-Japanese War of 1939, the Finnish War of 1939, or the Japanese invasion of Indochina in 1940—that no exact number of combat dead can ever be ascertained. Two general rules governed military fatalities in World War II. First, the smaller and less effective a nation's naval and air forces were, the greater its combined military's fatalities became, mostly as a result of slow-moving and poorly supported ground fighting. Second, democracies suffered far fewer military deaths than did autocracies, perhaps in part because they were often more concerned about incurring rather than inflicting losses.

OTHER BARBARITIES EXPLAINED an additional fifteen million lost civilians. The greatest causes of death were the mass executions—both in camps and ad hoc—associated with the Holocaust. They focused mostly on the grotesque effort to wipe out European Jewry, although the Roma, communists, homosexuals, and the disabled were all targeted at times for mass exterminations. Again, it is hard to distinguish the exact number of victims who perished between 1939 and 1945 in extermination, labor, or detention camps, as well as those who were murdered by special extermination squads or executed gratuitously by roaming individuals and packs. But educated guesses indicate that about six million Jews were slaughtered by the operatives of the Third Reich, in death camps, through open-air shootings, and through destructions of Jewish ghettoes.

Perhaps five million of those dead were Polish- and Russian-Jewish citizens, with another one million Western, Eastern, and southern European Jews. Somewhere between one to two million Slavs were also targeted for death, including those starved or worked to death in camps and those killed through open-air shootings ("mobile killing operations"), along with hundreds of thousands of mostly Eastern Europeans, Roma, Freemasons, homosexuals, disabled, and communists. Before Hitler went into Russia, he had warned his subordinates that they should use all methods necessary to fulfill his envisioned killing agenda: "All necessary measures—shooting, resettlement and so on."[19]

No other deliberate mass killings in history, before or since, whether systematic, loosely organized, or spontaneous, have approached the magnitude of the Holocaust—not the Armenian genocide, the Cambodian "killing fields," or the Rwandan tribal bloodletting. For all the efforts to locate the Holocaust in a historical framework, it remains savagely unique, unlike any other event of the past.[20]

The origins and catalysts of the Holocaust are complex and can only briefly be examined here. There were centuries of European persecution of the Jews deriving from ingrained popular anti-Semitism, religiously inspired hatred, envy of material and professional success, and the greedy desire to confiscate and loot Jewish property and capital. But none of these experiences prepared the world for such incomprehensible numbers of the murdered.

Poland and Russia were perhaps more anti-Semitic than Germany as late as 1930. Yet neither they nor any other country had embarked on such a systematic state-sponsored propaganda against Jews, leading millions of Germans by 1939 to manifest anti-Semitism or at least to feel that they themselves were victims of various Jewish machinations. Anti-Semitism soon became a wise career move under the Third Reich. After the war, the British secretly taped two mid-level bureaucrats from the industry of the Holocaust—Eugen Horak, a guard at Auschwitz, and Ernst von Gottstein, a functionary in the forced-labor program. After small talk about the admitted savagery of their colleagues, von Gottstein shrugged, "the only really good thing about the whole affair is that a few million Jews no longer exist." Horak agreed, but lamented the fate of the Holocaust planners: "But those who are responsible are now in the soup." In that regard, there were few, if any, instances of German soldiers after 1939 who faced serious punishments for declining to participate directly in the killing of Jews, a fact that makes the apologies of "just following orders" more difficult to sustain.[21]

One additional element made the unique Nazi brew of Jew hatred especially toxic: after Hitler's ascension to power, the general German abhorrence of Bolshevism was conflated with anti-Semitism. According to Nazi propagandists like the venomous Alfred Rosenberg, Jews such as Karl Marx and Leon Trotsky had invented communism and forced it upon the Soviet Union, and sought to do the same to Germany. Jews composed only a tiny fraction of the Soviet elite, but German propaganda had long insisted that Jewish Bolshevism invented and controlled the Soviet Union and wished dearly to absorb Eastern Europe and the German fatherland.[22]

The invasion of the Soviet Union ensured that millions of additional Jews would be now within the reach of Nazis. More important, the increasingly barbaric nature of the fighting, the Third Reich's first experience with military setbacks on the ground, and soaring fatalities were all translated by German propagandists into a new sense of national victimhood. The communist Bolshevik Jews and their henchmen were supposedly slaughtering German prisoners. For the German public, Jews were now not just to be slandered as conspiratorial and greedy but as murderers of German youth.[23]

The ultimate font of the extermination camps was, of course, Hitler himself. His singular ruthlessness in pursuing the Final Solution permeated the entire Third Reich and often trumped military priorities. Most members of the Nazi elite shared his hatred of the Jews—well beyond Heinrich Himmler, Hermann Goering, Reinhard Heydrich, Martin Bormann, and Adolf Eichmann. Nazi doctrine fed off the lower middle class's scapegoating for the humiliation of defeat in World War I and the economic downturn of the Depression. But no top Nazi other than Hitler was able to contextualize Jew hatred within a spellbinding public oratory that made Jewish perfidy an all-purpose explanation for the purported persecutions that Germany suffered after World War I. No politician of his age possessed such a savvy understanding of how to tap and so manipulate the deep-seated resentments and sense of shame within German-speaking Europe of the 1920s and 1930s.[24]

For Hitler, the one common denominator among capitalism, communism, and socialism was the subordination of nationalism to global Jewish manipulators who had allegiance to no country. Even more perniciously, Hitler's concept of *Das Volk* defined Germanness as entailing, in addition to shared citizenship, customs, tradition, residency, and language, a national destiny as well. Yet his idea of a German *Volk* was not really linguistic or even territorial, but racial, a supposed Aryan German tribe that since Roman times had remained pristine, unconquered, and unassimilated, safe from contamination beyond the Rhine and Danube—a conflation of race and nationality that energized Franco's and Mussolini's notion of *raza/razza*. Hitler's later wartime evening table talk was mostly consumed by thinly veiled promises to wipe out Jews: "The discovery of the Jewish virus is one of the greatest revolutions that have taken place in the world. The battle in which we are engaged today is of the same sort as the battle waged, during the last century, by Pasteur and Koch. How many diseases have their origin in the Jewish virus! . . . We shall regain our health only by eliminating the Jew."[25]

Hitler initially approached the planned exterminations with a degree of caution because of his fear that the German people, while supportive of his racialist ideology, might draw the line at the industrial killing of millions even under cover of existential war. Thus, his agents by 1943 played down news of the acceleration of the Final Solution. Perhaps they feared that the atrocities, when combined with catastrophic losses at the front and in bombing damage, might weaken public support for the National Socialist cause, especially by scaring Germans with the specter of their enemies having righteous causes for an impending terrible payback. Killing Jews may or may not have been wise, the Nazis seemed to shrug, but not finishing them off would earn vengeance from survivors, even as they feared that Allied bombers were incinerating Germans for their supposed crimes against the Jews. At the same time, the Nazi hierarchy sought to welcome hundreds of thousands, if not millions, in the actual mechanics of mass death, from doctors like Josef Mengele to industrialists who designed the crematoria. Such mass participation might ensure that Germans in general would be so invested in culpability for such unspeakable crimes that they would have no choice but to continue their killing to the bitter end.[26]

Most Germans and many Europeans under occupation seemed indifferent to the fact that Jews by 1943 were out of sight and of mind, without being bothered by the gory details of exactly how their disappearance had been carried out. Almost by magic, Jews had simply gone away to somewhere else, leaving their often valuable property behind. How and where they had gone were not the concern of their neighbors. Admiral Doenitz, who ended the war as Hitler's named successor, represented the official attitude of willful blindness when he claimed, "How, we asked ourselves, could such horrors have occurred in the middle of Germany without our having known?" What the Nazi architects required from the German and European publics was not just scapegoating of Jews, but something more appalling: general indifference to their ultimate fate.[27]

It was certainly true that German efficiency, from train door to crematorium ash, ensured a conveyor belt of death nearly impossible to impede by spontaneous riot or organized resistance, although on occasion both occurred. Subterfuge and illusion were integral parts of the death camps' operation, as inmates were told to pack for relocation, ready themselves for work on arrival, follow regulations to ensure their safety, shower and clean themselves—good German rituals developed to ensure that they would walk to, rather than run from, their deaths.

Genocide was choreographed, antiseptic, and scientific. As Hans Frank, the governor-general of Nazi-controlled Poland, in a December 1939 entry in his diary concluded, "we cannot shoot 2,500,000 Jews. Neither can we poison them. We shall have to take steps, however, designed to extirpate them in some way—and this will be done." The call for the IG Farben chemical conglomerate to supply its insecticide and fumigant Zyklon B for the death camps, or for Topf & Sons to offer new models of mass crematoria, was seen by industry as no different from a requisition for Mark V tank armor or shells for an 88 mm flak gun. Just as important, the Third Reich found it rather easy to recruit thousands of lawyers, professors, churchmen, bureaucrats, and doctors to use their expertise in pursuit of the goals of the Holocaust. The limitations of muscular labor and the problem of the disposal of the dead had always provided a check on history's mass murderers; Hitlerian science and state organization solved both age-old roadblocks to a holocaust.[28]

The daily death toll of the Final Solution spiked in the last two years of the war as it became clear that Germany would likely suffer a defeat, well after the infamous Wannsee Conference of January 20, 1942, that had outlined the organization and capital needed to exterminate the Jews. By March 1942, perhaps 75 percent of the eventual victims of the Holocaust may have been still alive. Initial ideas had considered deporting millions of Jews to foreign countries like Madagascar, or to the East in occupied Russia, or herding them into ghettoes to be starved, or allowing special mobile details to conduct mass executions, or even to hold them as hostages to be bartered for cash and supplies. However, all had been rejected by late 1941 as insufficient to liquidate the millions necessary to eradicate European Jewry.[29]

Besides the roles of Hitler, industry, technology, and the Nazi state, the fog of war obscured Nazi atrocity. Without the din of battle, the sounds of the industry of mass death would have been difficult to muzzle. In wartime it was not so difficult to censor detailed information surrounding the slaughter. The Jewish extermination still went on all through 1944–1945, when even the Nazi hierarchy, at least privately, assumed the war could not be won. In that existential context, eliminating the Jews became one of the few Nazi goals of the war that was still felt to have been obtainable, and that might justify renewed sacrifices amid general failure at the front.[30]

Of course, there is no guarantee that the Allies would have intervened to stop the bloodletting in the mid-1930s had Hitler begun to slaughter millions rather than thousands of Jews before the war. Hitler was not completely ostracized by the West even after the Nuremberg Race Laws of 1935 that excluded German Jews from German citizenship and forbid them from marrying non-Jewish Germans, as well as defining Jewishness by race, not by religion. The Allies did not boycott the Berlin Olympic Games of 1936; in fact, US Olympic Committee president Avery Brundage, for example, had dubbed the efforts to stop participation a "Jewish-Communist conspiracy."[31]

Before the advent of hostilities in 1938, Germany's neighbors were objecting loudly to the forced transfer of German Jews into their own territories. French foreign minister Georges-Étienne Bonnet reportedly asked German foreign minister Joachim von Ribbentrop to stop the shipments of Jews into France because the French "did not want to receive any more Jews from Germany." That plea prompted Ribbentrop to record that he had replied, "we all wanted to get rid of our Jews but that the difficulties lay in the fact that no country wished to receive them." During the Molotov-Ribbentrop Pact, Stalin turned down the Nazi request to accept Jews who were forcibly removed from the Third Reich.[32]

Even after the war began, ultimately it remained impossible to convince Britain and the United States to divert their own war resources to thwart the Holocaust, or even to systematically publicize the details of the Nazi death industry. It took months to smuggle out detailed descriptions of the everyday savagery at Auschwitz, such as the barbaric experiments of Joseph Mengele:

> Two, perhaps three days later the SS man brought them (two children, aged about four) back in a frightening condition. They had been sewn together like Siamese twins. The hunchbacked child was tied to the second one on the back and wrists. Mengele had sewn their veins together. The wounds were filthy and they festered. There was a powerful stench of gangrene. The children screamed all night long. Somehow their mother managed to get hold of morphine and put an end to their suffering.

By 1943 there were enough firsthand accounts of the death camps circulating in the US State Department, and by 1944 the possibility of at least bombing some of the camps (Auschwitz-Birkenau especially), that the failure of America, on the one hand, to take in hundreds of thousands of Jewish refugees and, on the other hand, to destroy many of the extermination camps was increasingly becoming indefensible. Americans at the highest levels of the Roosevelt administration were anxious about admitting what might become millions of Eastern European Jews into the United States, or diverting large military resources on what they feared would be a permanent project to save the Jews. Luminaries like wartime

Assistant Secretary of State Breckinridge Long and Assistant Secretary of War John J. McCloy were especially culpable, both in either downplaying the evidence of the death camps or incorrectly asserting that heavy bombers either could not reach camps like Auschwitz or could not be diverted from more important missions.[33]

There were endlessly tragic paradoxes about the destruction of European Jewry. The Jews in and out of Europe at the war's outbreak looked to Britain to defeat Hitler. Yet they accepted that British efforts to curtail immigration to Palestine reduced chances of escape for tens of thousands of those marked for death in Europe. Jews saw Western democracy as the enlightened antidote to the engines of the Holocaust, and the Red Army as the nearest means to end the death camps in the East, even as Britain, the United States, and the Soviet Union did not let in sufficient numbers of Jewish refugees, whom Hitler had cynically but presciently assumed would not find sanctuary among his enemies. American Jews lobbied for increased Jewish immigration and yet sometimes did not press their case out of fears that large influxes might spike wartime anti-Semitism.[34]

There was a final factor integral in the German algebra of death: wartime geography. As many as eight million Jews were in relatively easy reach of the Third Reich in both Eastern Europe—the Baltic states, Czechoslovakia, Hungary, Poland, and Romania—and western Russia. The ability of the Nazi government to forge alliances with Eastern European nations with large Jewish populations and to devote the vast majority of its military resources to the East—before June 1941 in Poland and the Balkans, afterwards in the Soviet Union—spelled the near doom of European Jewry. Certainly, the Nazis went after Western European Jews and built various detention, labor, and transit camps in the West by which hundreds of thousands of Jews perished or were shipped to the East, but such roundups were always more difficult. Western European Jews were less numerous. They were more dispersed through the population, more assimilated within Western European society, closer to neutral sanctuaries, and often more affluent and with greater financial means to flee. Governments in the West before the war were more democratic, and there was a clearer account of the persecutions of the prewar Third Reich, which gave Jews earlier warnings of the need, first, to flee Germany and, second, to leave the entire Western European continent.

In contrast, Jews in the East were far more numerous, mostly poorer, often concentrated in ghettoes, more apt to be orthodox and thus easily identifiable, and historically more subject to local pogroms. One of the ironies of the German requirement for Jews inside the Third Reich and its Western European occupied territories to wear yellow cloth badges at all times was the need at all to require any identification for a people who, according to Nazi ideology, were supposedly easily identifiable as *Untermenschen*. Even supporters of the yellow stars noted the disconnect. The fascist and anti-Semitic French novelist Lucien Rebatet approved of the odious requirement but noted about the supposed racial enemies being indistinguishable from Europeans: "The yellow star rectifies this strange situation in which one human group that is radically opposed to the people of white blood and which for eternity is unassimilable to this blood, cannot be identified at first glance."[35]

The Nazi authorities were able to kill more Jews within their first two months of the Russian invasion than they had during the previous eight years of Nazi rule and yearlong wartime occupation of Western Europe. A parade of Nazis for the first time in their lives visited Eastern Europe and western Russia between 1939 and 1941. They remarked on the quite contrasting status and appearance of Eastern from Western Jews, as if the difference made their own task of extermination somehow easier. After Joseph Goebbels returned from newly occupied Poland, he wrote to Hitler confirming their shared view that the conditions of Eastern European Jewry made their extermination more likely. Then he recorded in his diary, "The Jew is a waste product. It is a clinical issue more than a social one."[36]

In this regard, the June 22, 1941, invasion of the Soviet Union was the most critical turning point in the history of the Jewish people since the destruction of Jerusalem and the Second Temple in AD 70. Had Hitler not invaded the Soviet Union and not headed further eastward—absorbing all of eastern Poland, the Baltic states, and western Russia—it would have been impossible to carry out the full agenda of the Holocaust. The transport of Jews "to the East" was cloaked in disinformation. Had the death camps inside Poland been scattered throughout occupied France, for instance, the Holocaust would have been a nightmare far more difficult to disguise.[37]

ALL OF THE major powers of World War II built prisoner-of-war camps. But what distinguished the Soviet Union, the Third Reich, and Japan (which ran well over 250 major internment camps in Borneo, Burma, China, the Dutch East Indies, Formosa, Korea, Japan, Malaysia, the Philippines, and smaller centers almost everywhere else under Japanese occupation) was that, in addition to captured soldiers, these powers interned, mistreated, and often killed an entire array of dissidents and ethnicities. Hundreds more camps were established exclusively for civilian prisoners throughout the Japanese Empire.[38]

Death rates varied among prisoners, depending on the type and status of the enemy. Japan imprisoned fewer civilians than Germany. The Japanese were far more brutal to captured enemy soldiers than was Germany outside of the Eastern Front. About a third of all who were interned in camps by the Japanese perished. The worst survival rates of the war were among Soviet prisoners of the Germans (almost 60 percent, or over 3 million deaths), as well as Germans held by the Soviets (up to 1 million). American and British prisoners in German hands rarely died (3–5 percent). Nor did Germans and Japanese fare poorly under the Western Allies (1–2 percent death rates). It was hard to sort out the logic of Axis captors: few warring powers were more successful in keeping prisoners alive than were the Germans with their British and American captives; yet no country was as murderous as were the Germans to captured Russians in the East or Jews in their midst. Brutal Japanese prisoner-of-war camps wiped out nearly a third of the Allied soldiers who fell into them, with even higher death rates for Asian prisoners.[39]

Bombing may have directly accounted for well over 5 percent of the war's civilian dead. Most European capitals and major cities, except those of neutral nations (Dublin, Istanbul, Lisbon, Madrid, Stockholm, Zurich, etc.) at one time or another were bombed. In addition to at least some attacks on Amsterdam, Antwerp, Athens, Berlin, Brussels, London, Paris, Prague, Rome, Rotterdam, and Warsaw, Allied and Axis bombers hit as well cities far to the east, such as Chongqing, Darwin, Manila, Moscow, Leningrad, Shanghai, Singapore, Stalingrad, and Tokyo. It is almost impossible to know exactly how many of the roughly forty million civilians who perished in World War II died as a direct result of bombing. Even in the most deadly and infamous cases—Belgrade, Berlin, Cologne, Coventry, Dresden, Hamburg, Hiroshima, London, Nagasaki, and Tokyo— death tolls to this day remain disputed. Nonetheless, rough estimates suggest that in six years of combined Axis and Allied bombing, at least two million civilians perished.[40]

The size and efficiency of the attacking bombing force were crucial. The 828 B-29s with 186 fighter escorts that flew on the last day of major hostilities of World War II (August 14, 1945) carried an aggregate of over eight thousand tons of bombs—far larger even than the payload of 1,046 tons of the "thousand bomber" British raid over Cologne in February 1942, given that many of the earlier Cologne bombers were two-engine medium aircraft. There were great varieties in delivery capacity even among heavy four-engine bombers: the 339 B-29s that flew the devastating first fire raid against Tokyo on March 10, 1945—theretofore the greatest force of B-29s to fly on a single mission—carried bomb tonnage equivalent to the capacity of over a thousand B-17s.[41]

The nature of a fleet's bomb load (explosive or incendiary) also mattered. Firebombing took far more lives than high explosives and was largely used in area rather than precision attacks. The degree to which a bomber fleet was accompanied by fighter escorts was important but not always decisive. The quality of anti-aircraft defenses (barrage balloons, flak, radar, etc.) also determined how many died on the ground. Equally important were the nature of civilian and industrial construction at the target site (e.g., wood, stone, cement), the density of population (e.g., single-family dwellings, apartment blocks, urban, suburban), the effectiveness of firefighting responses, the presence of bomb shelters, and the efficiency of forward warning stations (e.g., border spotters, radio, radar) and evacuation plans. By late 1944 and 1945 all these considerations favored the attacking bomber in a way that had been largely untrue between 1939 and 1943.[42]

Between 1939 and 1941, most successful bombing attacks were conducted by the Axis. Yet despite the absence of effective Allied defenses, and despite systematic indifference to civilian attacks, they were never as lethal as what followed from the Allies. The Axis air forces had neither the number nor the quality of bombers or fighter escorts, nor the duration of air superiority that the Allied air fleets enjoyed after 1942. Still, German strategic and tactical attacks in Poland, the Balkans, Britain during the Blitz, and the Soviet Union in the initial eighteen months of Operation Barbarossa may have accounted for three hundred thousand deaths. No one knows how many Chinese civilians perished in fourteen years from Japanese bombing—perhaps over a hundred thousand—but the toll was limited not by Chinese defenses or Japanese intent but only by a lack of Japanese capability and resources. Axis bombing of cities in East and North Africa and against targets such as Malta might have upped the Axis tally by several thousands.

With the exceptions of the V-1 and V-2 attacks on London and Antwerp, and the ill-fated "Baby Blitz" over London (Operation Steinbock, January–June 1944), the Axis powers after 1943 were mostly unable to bomb Allied civilian centers effectively. Fuel shortages, the lack of long-range heavy bombers, insufficient fighter escorts, poor aircrew training, confused strategies, and loss of air superiority all conspired to make major missions no longer possible. At the same time that the Axis air offensive effort waned, the ability to stop incoming raids over occupied Europe and Germany likewise diminished. Allied air supremacy was achieved by the appearance of long-range, late-model fighter aircraft with drop tanks. No country during the war inflicted so many deaths through strategic bombing and suffered so few in return as the United States, a fact not lost to strategic planners for the next seven decades. Hitler himself after declaring war on America quickly grasped that he had no idea how to conquer the United States, and admitted to the Japanese ambassador that the problem could only be addressed "in the next generation."[43]

FAR MORE MILLIONS perished during and after World War II due to forced expulsions of civilians that mirrored the ebb and flow of the war. Two phases marked these massive transfers: an initial flight of Allied and neutral populations before Axis armies of occupation between 1939 and 1942, and a second displacement of civilians, this time of German, Italian, and Japanese civilians, after the collapse of their respective occupation armies. During 1944–1945, millions of Japanese civilians fled from Korea, Manchuria, and most of the Japanese-occupied Pacific. No one knows how many died in efforts to reach Japan, but it is generally considered a fraction of the many millions of Chinese who were forced out of their homes by the occupying Japanese between 1931 and 1945.[44]

Brutal forced transfers of ethnic German speakers from the East in 1945–1946, especially from Poland, East Prussia, and Eastern Europe, brought even more mass death home to Germany than did Allied bombers. Many of those fleeing had left eastern communities that dated from medieval times. In all, some twelve to fourteen million Germans were forced out of the eastern Third Reich, occupied Eastern Europe, and the western Soviet Union. They fled ahead of the advancing Red Army, or were exiled thereafter by Eastern European governments after liberation from German occupation or in the settling-up period of the first five years of the postwar era.

Exposure, disease, hunger, collateral damage from concurrent ground fighting, and bombing conspired to take the lives of somewhere between half a million to two million Germans fleeing the East—as great a toll as the Mongols' late thirteenth-century slaughter and devastation in Persia. The mass death of German refugees remains little publicized even today, and is not reckoned as infamous as the Armenian or Rwandan genocides that resulted in probably fewer deaths. The lack of sympathy for this vast human tragedy was summed up best by an East Prussian refugee: "It was our holocaust, but nobody cares." Anti-German sentiment peaked right after the war. Most in the East felt that most German civilians received what they had deserved. In any case, they suffered far fewer fatalities than what their military had inflicted on others. Most of the descriptions of German refugees after 1944 mirror-imaged those of Eastern Europeans and Russians in 1939–1942 who fled ahead of the German army or were removed by the German occupation.

Operation Hannibal, the huge German sea-lift to evacuate roughly nine hundred thousand German citizens and 350,000 Wehrmacht personnel trapped by the Red Army in East Prussia, proved more than three times larger than the Dunkirk operation. Yet such mostly unknown seaborne evacuations rescued less than 10 percent of the total of German refugees fleeing the East, even as Germany lost one-quarter of its prewar territory and 15 percent of its resident population. Americans and British, more concerned with polarizing the Soviet Union than in checking the abuses of the Red Army, looked the other way as the mass cleansing continued.[45]

Collateral damage during ground fighting also claimed the lives of millions of civilians caught in war zones: among the most deadly incidents were the massacres in and attacks on Nanking (200,000 dead), the siege of Budapest (40,000), the 125,000 German civilians who died in Berlin during the Soviet assault, the hundred thousand Filipinos lost in the American retaking of Manila, and the hundreds of thousands of Russians who were killed by shells and bullets when trapped in places like Kiev, Leningrad, and Stalingrad. From the first twenty-five thousand dead in the September 1939 attack on Warsaw to the nearly hundred thousand civilians caught up in Okinawa in April–July 1945, thousands of civilians died each day near or on the battlefield due to associated damage and through deliberate targeting. Those who "were in the way" accounted for a large percentage of the some eighteen to twenty-three thousand civilians who on average died each day of World War II—almost four times the number of dead at the Battle of Gettysburg.[46]


WORLD WAR II was a Russian catastrophe. The Soviet Union suffered the greatest number of losses of the war, somewhere between twenty and twenty-seven million military and civilian dead. Less than half that total was due to combat-related operations. A number of reasons explain the almost inexplicable number of Soviet fatalities. Except for China, nowhere was the war fought longer inside a single country, roughly from June 22, 1941, to March 1945. Britain and Japan were bombed but not invaded. Both Italy and Germany were likewise bombed, but Italy was only invaded and fought over for less than two years, Germany for less than eight months. The US mainland was untouched by enemy bombers, and never reached by Axis ground troops.

The Russians most often fought the Germany army, the most deadly of the Axis militaries, and on a front that would consume 75–80 percent of the Wehrmacht's resources. While Operation Barbarossa had included nearly a million Eastern European allies and pan-European volunteers, the war usually pitted Germans against Russians. The Eastern Front saw collisions between the greatest combined number of artillery pieces, armored vehicles, aircraft, and infantry in history, on a scale that dwarfed all other theaters. The armed conflicts were handmaidens to deliberate famines and mass executions.[47]

In the fighting itself in Russia, there were several cycles of mass death. The first came during the initial Nazi offensives between June 1941 and September 1942. In just over a year, the ascendant Wehrmacht killed over four million Soviet soldiers and an untold number of civilians. In these first fourteen months of the war, two considerations had upped the Russian death toll. The Germans enjoyed both surprise and air superiority. They possessed better artillery and initially for a few months often superior armor. Soldiers of the Wehrmacht, mostly veterans of the defeat of Poland and the fall of France, were more experienced and better supplied and organized. Hitler also ordered the army to exterminate hundreds of thousands of particular classes of captured enemies, especially partisans, commissars, and Jews.

Stalin in his early incarnation as supreme wartime leader opposed strategic retreats. His initial stand-or-die plans of resistance only added to the destruction of the Red Army through enabling vast Nazi encirclements such as those at Kiev (nearly 670,000 trapped) or Vyazma-Bryansk (666,000). Being captured in 1941–1942 as a result of strategically imbecilic orders most likely meant death in a German prisoner-of-war camp; survival assured lifelong suspicion and possible death upon repatriation. Between June 1941 and July 1943, over five million Red Army soldiers were swept up in German encirclements—catastrophes nearly as much Stalin's making as Hitler's.[48]

Second, as the German army advanced, it razed considerable infrastructure that it found without immediate military advantage, all within an occupied area perhaps soon to cover a million square miles in which the prewar Soviet economy had produced half its food, nearly two-thirds of its coal and ferrous metals, and 60 percent of its aluminum. The Nazi notion of *Lebensraum* meant that Soviet civilian deaths were not just useful in the short term for eliminating resistance, but also in the long term for making German colonization and usurpation all that much easier, at least until labor shortages inside the Third Reich meant that by 1943 it was more economical to work occupied peoples to death rather than to kill them outright.[49]

Third, as the Red Army initially retreated nearly a thousand miles in 1941 and 1942, it destroyed and uprooted its own infrastructure and industry, thereby ensuring misery and death for those Russians who could not escape or relocate. No other German enemy—not the Poles in 1939 or the French in 1940—had yet embraced such a deliberate policy of destroying its own assets. Only a totalitarian government such as Stalin's could wield enough state power to ensure that Russian subjects destroyed their own livelihood. Stalin's desolation was as effective as Tsar Alexander I's similar torching of the Russian motherland to rob Napoleon's Grand Army of much of its planned sustenance. The scorched-earth policies, along with partisan attacks in occupied Russia, explain in part why Germany was never able to plunder as much food in war as it had purchased from the Soviets in friendship.[50]

THERE ARE NO accurate figures for the staggering number of Chinese dead. Rough estimates suggest anywhere between ten and twenty million Chinese were lost, with a consensus that most likely fifteen to sixteen million perished during the more than a decade-long Japanese war and occupation. A number of factors explain China's gargantuan losses.

China was the most populated country in the world—about 660 million in 1931—and thus could suffer human losses that would have unwound almost all other nations, without necessarily collapsing. In such a populous landscape the sheer scale of Japanese barbarity was often underappreciated. Overpopulation, natural catastrophes, and stagnant agricultural practices had made food reserves rare even in times of peace.

Manchuria had turned into a battleground nearly a decade before the "official" outbreak of the Pacific war. The Chinese military was the least adept of the major allies. Racial animus and historical hatred between Chinese and Japanese only exacerbated the conflict. China, in fact, fought three wars simultaneously: a foreign one against Japanese occupiers, a civil war between Chiang Kai-shek's nationalists and Mao Zedong's communists, and the latter two factions' sometime alliance against the Japanese-sponsored collaborationists of Wang Jingwei.

If less systematic in their barbarity than the Nazis, the Japanese likewise envisioned war as inclusive of soldier and civilian. They had no reservations about murdering millions of Chinese civilians as part of their general aims to colonize parts of China and extract its national wealth.

In their so-called *Sankō Sakusen* ("Three Alls Campaign"), Japanese pro-tocol was to "kill all, burn all, and pillage all"—and may well have been sanctioned by the emperor himself. The Chinese front proved uncannily similar to the Russian: a vast landscape that drew in an outnumbered in-vader who battled the elements, enemy soldiers, and civilian onlookers, with no quarter given and none received—with race and ideology as force multipliers to the savagery.[51]

Despite methodical records, we still have no exact idea of how many German soldiers and civilians perished. That lacuna is largely due to the slaughterhouse of the Eastern Front in 1945 and the simultaneous expul-sion of well over twelve million German speakers from Eastern Europe. It is unclear how many German civilians reported as missing actually perished—or in fact survived, but disappeared from official records. Postwar political controversies often saw German historians insisting on greater fatalities, while their American, British, and Russian counterparts argued for fewer. The Cold War division between East and West Ger-many further politicized analyses of the German wartime dead. The col-lective German guilt from the Holocaust also played a more subtle role, as some German historians sought to envision bombing losses, POW deaths in the Soviet Union, and the expulsions from the East as the Allies' own versions of multifarious holocausts, perhaps less planned, but nonetheless accounting for millions of civilian dead.[52]

All that said, Greater Germany, including all German-speakers in the Third Reich, lost perhaps six to seven million soldiers and civilians, the third-greatest number of fatalities behind the Soviet Union and China. The ratio of far fewer civilian (approximately 2 million) than military dead (approximately 5 million) was unusual for the fighting of World War II that was waged in the heart of central and Eastern Europe for five and a half years. But neither Germany nor Austria was occupied in its western regions until March 1945. Unlike the Soviet Union, China, or Italy, Germany—aside from strategic bombing—was fought over for a matter of weeks, not years.[53]

A variety of causes accounts for over two million German civilian deaths. The Nazi regime over a decade itself probably killed two hundred thousand ethnic German dissidents, the disabled, communists, homo-sexuals, and others deemed undesirable, among them those convicted of military desertion and other political crimes. At least another two hundred thousand German and Austrian Jews perished in the extermi-nation camps. Yet another fifty to a hundred thousand noncombatants died in the 1945 two-front Allied advance and occupation of the Third Reich. British and American bombing, particularly after mid-1944, accounted for another four hundred to six hundred thousand dead, the vast majority civilians. But the largest toll was from the Russian-led ethnic cleansing of German speakers during the panicked 1945 retreat before the Red Army—a visitation that exacted a terrible retribution on any German who stayed behind in addition to those who died in the flight westward.

Germany's huge military losses and its civilian toll were mostly products of the last twelve months of the war. The Scandinavian, Belgian, French, Balkan, North African, Blitz, and U-boat campaigns before June 1941 had cost the Wehrmacht probably less than two hundred thousand military dead, which, although an enormous figure, is small in comparison to what would follow in the Soviet Union. Aside from naval and air operations, the military was relatively static from June 1940 until its April 1941 entry into Yugoslavia. Indeed, the German armed forces may well have suffered nearly as many casualties in the single month of January 1945 (451,742) as it had during the entire fighting of 1939, 1940, and 1941 combined (459,000).[54]


THE GERMAN INVASION of Poland on September 1, 1939, formally began World War II. Ostensibly, Poland should not have suffered any more fatalities than France or other Western European countries that were subsequently quickly overrun by the Wehrmacht. Poland capitulated (though never signed a formal surrender) to both the Third Reich and the Soviet Union in little over a month. The country was divided by its two conquerors on October 6 after enduring about sixty-six thousand fatalities. Yet by war's end, Poland would suffer between 5.6 and 5.8 million dead, the highest percentage of fatalities (over 16 percent) of a prewar population of any participant of World War II.

- The Polish people's curse had always been their location, sandwiched between Europe's strongest nations, Germany and western Russia, neither of which had enjoyed a long tradition of constitutional republican government. Poland's population was less than half of Germany's and a quarter of Russia's, and its unfortunate location often prompted twentieth-century realist alliances with distant France and Britain, which were geographically on the other side of Germany. Nothing can prove more dangerous than a sympathetic and powerful, though distant ally. In World War II Poland would fight both Germany and the Soviet Union, and suffer casualties through occupation by both.[55]

Poland was the laboratory of Nazi barbarity, given that it was the site of over 450 German extermination, concentration, labor, and prisoner-of-war camps. It was both the first country attacked by Hitler and the first to have its citizens—both Jews and Slavs—targeted for mass extinction. In the words of Reinhard Heydrich—the later infamous Deputy Reich Protector of the Protectorate of Bohemia and Moravia and a chief architect of the Holocaust—the conquest of Poland was planned as "a cleanup once and for all." The Holocaust accounted for the greatest number of Polish deaths, given that the prewar Jewish community of Poland—10 percent of the population—was the largest in the world at somewhere around 3.5 million persons. Scarcely over a hundred thousand Polish Jews survived the German extermination efforts. The six most infamous extermination camps of the Holocaust—Auschwitz, Belzec, Chelmno, Majdanek, Sobibór, and Treblinka—were all in Poland.[56]

It is unknown how many Poles perished in Soviet camps after the 1939 Eastern occupation, or were simply executed by the Russians. But the death toll of Polish intellectuals, officers, and supposed counterrevolutionaries, including those at the infamous Katyn massacre, numbered well over fifty thousand. After the June 1941 invasion of the Soviet Union, hundreds of thousands of Poles were released from Soviet prisoner-of-war camps or gathered up to form anti-Nazi units and died fighting the Germans. In addition, Polish refugees who had fled westward after the 1939 Nazi occupation numbered in the hundreds of thousands and joined Allied units and died in some of the most ferocious battles of World War II, from Monte Cassino to the hinges of the Falaise Pocket to the airdrops of Operation Market-Garden.[57]

Polish resistance fighters usually fought the Nazi occupation in a far more muscular fashion than their Western European counterparts, provoking a commensurately fearsome German response. For the historian, it is a near impossible task to ascertain how and where the non-Jewish Polish population perished. Many of the war's worst catastrophes were so often Polish: the Warsaw uprising and other insurgencies (250,000 Polish dead?), the Polish internment and work camps (800,000?), Polish civilians killed as collateral damage or direct targets of bombing during the war (250,000?), Poles shipped into the oblivion of captivity in the Soviet Union both in 1939 and 1945 (300,000?), Polish workers starved or worked to death inside the Third Reich (200,000–300,000?), and Polish military losses inside Poland in 1939 and during 1944–1945 in alliance with the Americans and Soviets (100,000–150,000?).

Poland alone lost more of its citizens than *all* the Western European nations, Britain, and the United States combined. It fought from the first day of the war through to the end of combat in the European theater of operations, and had the unfortunate fate to have been defeated and occupied by both Nazi Germany and the Soviet Union. It shared the Eastern European misfortune in World War II of losing its freedom in the defeat of 1939 and then again in the victory of 1945. The fate of Poland was emblematic of the entire tragedy of World War II.[58]

OF JAPAN'S PREWAR population of a little over seventy million, somewhere between 2.6 and 3.1 million died due to armed conflict (roughly 3–3.5 percent of the population), a ghastly figure that includes some six hundred to eight hundred thousand civilians. Although Japan formally entered World War II in December 1941 more than two years after Germany, it had warred far longer in China (off and on since 1931), and in a brief but bitter 1939 war against the Soviet Union along the Mongolian border (40,000–45,000 fatalities) that ended just three weeks after the outbreak of World War II. Japan's population was not that much smaller than that of Greater Germany (approximately 80 million). But both on a percentage and absolute basis, Japan suffered fewer losses than did the Third Reich. That fact is often overlooked, given the horrific nature of incendiary and atomic bombing of the Japanese mainland and the customary unwillingness of Japanese soldiers in the Pacific to surrender. Due to the collapses in China, Burma, and the Pacific, and the bombing of the mainland, Japan suffered more dead during the last year of the war than in all previous years since 1941 combined. A number of paradoxes explain the peculiar nature of Japanese casualties.[59]

First, Japan's war in China was protracted—the first phase in 1931–1937 and the second in 1937–1945. Eventually somewhere between half a million and one million Japanese soldiers died in battle. A comparable number were declared missing or casualties to famine and disease. And perhaps a third to a half of all Japanese army losses in China occurred outside of battle, due to starvation and illness.

Second, although bombed, Japan (unlike China, Germany, Italy, and the Soviet Union) was never invaded. Had it been in late 1945 or early 1946, the Japanese might have easily suffered fatalities comparable to Germany's. The Japanese declaration of war on Great Britain and the United States, given the asymmetry of relative industrial output and population, nevertheless did not lead to huge continental ground battles analogous to those on the Western Front. When large conventional engagements did occur—such as the American reconquest of the Philippines (well over 300,000 Japanese dead), the British slog in Burma (150,000 Japanese killed), or on Okinawa (approximately 110,000 Japanese fatalities)—Japanese losses soared. Britain finally deployed, for example, one million military personnel in Burma, and the size of the invasion force at Okinawa—ships, planes, and troops—was initially comparable to that at Normandy on D-Day.

The battles of Leyte Gulf, the Marianas, and Iwo Jima were savage, as was the near-complete destruction of the Imperial Japanese Navy and the Navy and Army Air Services in 1944–1945. Yet the geography of the Pacific resulted mostly in a succession of naval and amphibious battles where ground fighting was fierce but of short duration, not always sustained over several months, and involving far fewer troops than the collisions on the Eastern Front. Moreover these battlegrounds were sometimes sparsely settled islands and far distant from mainland Japanese cities. In contrast, the Japanese Imperial Navy in the Pacific over nearly four years of fighting lost perhaps over four hundred thousand dead, well over twice the number of naval fatalities of any other navy of the major belligerents, and almost a quarter of all Japanese military dead.

Third, the sustained American firebombing of the Japanese homeland and the two atomic attacks at Hiroshima and Nagasaki radically spiked Japanese losses (perhaps 600,000 civilians lost in all bombing attacks). It was Japan's misfortune that three of the most effective new weapons of the American arsenal—napalm, B-29 heavy bombers, and atomic weapons—appeared late in the war and were unleashed exclusively on its cities, which were more often built of flammable materials than was true of European structures. The surrender of Japan not only curtailed an American ground assault but also meant an end to the incineration of Japanese cities and casualties that had already exceeded even those inflicted on the civilians of the Third Reich.[60]

Many of the some eight hundred thousand Japanese missing in action were army troops marooned in the Pacific and China when the war ended, where they either starved or were dispatched by partisan forces. Yet of all the major belligerents of the war, Japan suffered the fewest number of lost prisoners. About seventy-five thousand Japanese died in Western captivity, whereas perhaps seven times that number perished while in Soviet hands—a testament to the reality both that Japanese soldiers rarely surrendered to their victors, and that if they did, until the last weeks of the war they most often fell into the hands of the British and Americans rather than the Chinese and Soviets. Perhaps another three hundred thousand Japanese were lost or unaccounted for during the nearly decade-and-a-half-long war in China.

In terms of killing versus being killed, the Japanese probably achieved the highest ratio of inflicting death versus receiving it, largely because of the Japanese Imperial Army's nightmarish killing of Chinese civilians. Suffering a ground invasion of the homeland was the most lethal experience of World War II, as was true of most wars of the past in general. Japan, as well as Britain and the United States, avoided such a fate, explaining why all three experienced the most lopsided ratios between fatalities inflicted and suffered.

ITALY SUFFERED NEARLY five hundred thousand fatalities, a hundred thousand of them civilians. Half a million dead is a shockingly large figure, inasmuch as Italy had not entered the war until June 10, 1940, and formally exited early on September 8, 1943, after less than three years of actual fighting. Yet these figures on the loss of life are tragically understandable, given the unusual nature of Italy's role in the war. In reckless fashion, Benito Mussolini had entered the fighting without even minimal preparation in terms of oil supplies, food, transportation, ammunition, armor, and air power. Worse, Mussolini chose to fight ambitious regional wars simultaneously in the Balkans, East Africa, and North Africa, whose various fronts Italy had no ability to sustain and in which medical care and easy supply were wanting.[61]

Italy's innate weakness drew the attention of the newly formed Anglo-American alliance and brought it, after victory in Tunisia in mid-1943, to Sicily and the Italian peninsula as the envisioned first steps of reconquering the European mainland. The early exit from the war, however, did not much lessen Italian casualties. German furor at supposed betrayal turned Italy into a battleground for two more years. What benefit Italy received from the Allies for its change in allegiance in 1943 was more than offset by the new hostility of Germany, whose troops far longer controlled a much larger percentage of Italian territory than did the Americans and British. Hundreds of thousands of indentured Italian soldiers and civilians were sent northward into the gulags of the Third Reich as forced laborers—perhaps as many as 650,000 soldiers alone. Few other people during the war became the targets of both the Allies and Axis, often simultaneously.[62]

Yet the human toll could have been far worse still if not for two unforeseen factors. First, Italy initially fought less-equipped and poorly prepared enemies such as the Albanians, Ethiopians, and Greeks, and British troops prior to 1942, who were often outnumbered in Africa. None of

Italy's initial adversaries, except Britain, had the industrial might to bring sustained air, artillery, or armor against the Italian army.[63]

Second, when the Italians were defeated by the British and Americans (as early as autumn 1941 in the case of the former), they usually surrendered en masse and into the hands of victors who, by the cruel standards of World War II, were rather humane in their treatment of prisoners. Prisoner-of-war status for an Italian soldier—unless he had surrendered to his former German allies in 1943–1945 or to the Soviets—was not synonymous with death, as it proved so often for both Germans and Soviets on the Eastern Front. Mussolini's fascism did not galvanize Italians with the same suicidal zealotry and indoctrination that the Germans and Japanese had, and Italians were therefore likely to be among the first to surrender and thereby avoid nightmares like the defeats at Stalingrad or Okinawa. In defeat, the Italian military did not incur the justified hatred that was so prevalent on the Russian, Chinese, or Pacific fronts and that led to existential wars of annihilation. Italy suffered terribly in the war, and had usually started its regional wars by surprise attacks, but as the weakest and most vulnerable member of a defeated Axis triad, it ironically escaped with far fewer human losses than did either the Germans or Japanese.[64]

THE WAR COST the United States over four hundred thousand lives, or about 0.3 percent of its prewar population, the *lowest* percentage of any nation of the major Axis and Allied powers. About 110,000 fatalities were due to noncombat causes, whether accidents or illnesses. Some twelve thousand dead were civilians on service abroad or on the seas in war zones, the smallest number of noncombatant fatalities of all the major belligerents.

Geography, for all the difficulties it posed in transportation and communications, was an American godsend. Unlike Germany, Italy, and the Soviet Union, the American homeland was never invaded. In fact, unlike Britain, Germany, Italy, Japan, and the Soviet Union, the forty-eight states of America were never even systematically bombed. Three-quarters of the civilian dead were some nine thousand sailors of the merchant marine who were in frontline convoys for most of 1942–1943 during the apex of the Battle of the Atlantic between German U-boats and Allied antisubmarine forces. Unlike the experiences of its enemies and allies, one of the safest places to be in during World War II was a US munitions plant.[65]

It is nearly inexplicable that the United States fought for over forty-five months, mostly on two widely separated and distant fronts, with a military that grew to twelve million, seven million of whom were at any given time stationed abroad—yet lost far fewer civilians and soldiers than, for example, the total lost to France (600,000), whose main forces fought only for six weeks in May and June 1940, and then as Allied auxiliaries in 1944–1945. The causes of massive French fatalities—being fought over both in 1940 and 1944–1945, being bombed by both Germans and Allies, retaliations against resistance fighters and then collaborators, the rounding up of Jews, and food shortages—all did not apply to the United States.

The seas provided security for America in the way they also made invasion of the island empires of Britain and Japan difficult. No country was so quickly or more fully mobilized for industrial production than was the United States. The amazing transformation of the vast US economy ensured that American forces had more motorized vehicles, ships, and planes, as well as food and medicine, than did any other military. Machines in World War II took but also saved lives. While military planners complained that only a fraction of US armed forces saw combat, the huge resources devoted to logistical and mechanical support ensured that not only were a small percentage of American soldiers exposed to combat, but also that they suffered far fewer losses once in battle.

In addition, no other nation fielded larger air and naval forces. The US Army Air Force numbered some 2.4 million, with an active fleet of over eighty thousand planes. While air losses were considerable (88,119 deaths from all causes), they represented less than 5 percent of the air force's aggregate strength, about half the relative percentage of army losses. At such a cost, the Army Air Force destroyed over forty thousand enemy planes, an untold number of enemy combat troops, and probably killed well over one million German, Japanese, and Italian civilians, many of them workers central to Axis industrial production, transportation, and logistical support. The result of such enormous investments in air power was that American infantry forces of World War II—often criticized by military historians for being too small, too reliant on artillery and air support, and too poorly led—proved continually successful without suffering high losses.[66]

The same was true of US naval power. By early 1944, the Navy had grown larger than the combined fleets of all the existing major powers of World War II. Except for subsequent kamikazes and occasional submarine attacks, its nearly seven thousand warships were largely immune from serious assaults by Axis capital ships. The American Navy provided infantry forces support when they disembarked at unprecedented levels and allowed the wounded, especially in the Pacific, to be evacuated in a manner unknown elsewhere during World War II. By war's end, the Navy had grown to 3.3 million men and women, and yet suffered only sixty-six thousand fatalities or missing in action, or a little over 15 percent of the dead incurred by the much smaller Imperial Japanese Navy.

After 1943 it was rare for any American force on land, at sea, or in the air to fight in a theater while outnumbered or outsupplied. Even at its most costly infantry battles—the Battle of the Bulge, Guadalcanal, the Hürtgen Forest, Iwo Jima, Okinawa, the Philippines—the United States enjoyed eventual numerical superiority, usually with at least parity in the quality and superiority in the quantity of its weapons.

There were no American strategic and tactical follies of the sort that Mussolini committed by trying to fight simultaneously in North Africa, Russia, and the Balkans, or the stand-or-die edicts that Hitler issued to German troops in the Soviet Union from late 1942 onward. The American army was never encircled in the fashion of the Sixth Army at Stalingrad, the Soviets in summer 1941 at Kiev, or the Italians and Germans in Tunisia. Nor did the Americans after Corregidor surrender in numbers and en masse as the British had at Tobruk. If critics faulted American generals for being too conservative, they at least conceded that the United States *in extremis* lost divisions, not whole corps and armies, as had most other World War II militaries.

In the final two deadly years of World War II, US sailors, airmen, and GIs were better trained and more fit than their Axis counterparts (over 5 million American males were rejected for military service on account of relatively minor physical deficiencies), whose huge losses had required wholesale levies of younger, older, and inexperienced troops who were shorted training. Due to manpower and fuel shortages, German pilots had trained for scarcely over a hundred hours of flight time before entering combat, compared to American and British pilots who had amassed nearly 350 hours. Japanese pilots had even fewer hours of schooling, given even greater fuel shortages. The formula for keeping a young man alive in World War II was lengthy precombat training, access to top-rate weapons and machines, and plenty of food, fuel, and medical care. In all three areas, the US military usually far outpaced its rivals, as demonstrated by suffering far fewer combat casualties.[67]

ABOUT FOUR HUNDRED thousand subjects of Great Britain died in World War II, including over sixty thousand civilians lost during the various Blitzes and subsequent V-1 and V-2 attacks on British cities. Britain fought the longest of any major belligerent of World War II, for just over six years. As in the case of the United States, Britain had invested heavily in its air forces and navy. The Royal Air Force suffered around seventy thousand dead, the Royal Navy over sixty thousand, but both had somewhat fewer losses than their respective American counterparts.

Among the major powers of World War II, three conditions resulted in high battle casualties, and Britain often was able to avoid most of them: fighting alone on a European ground front against the German army prior to 1944; fighting mostly static battles of annihilation on the ground such as at Kursk or the Battle of the Bulge; and fighting under harsh winter weather conditions of the sort that characterized the Eastern Front or near the German border in late 1944 and early 1945.

Nearly eighty thousand British soldiers were lost in the Burma campaign, but the British had deployed in toto about one million there in the nearly four-year-long successful effort. The fact that Britain was not invaded, that it did not itself have to bomb or invade Japan to ensure its defeat, and that in 1944 it invaded France only in concert with the United States and its Dominion allies likewise reduced fatalities. After Dunkirk, Britain waged war on the European continent—the cauldron of World War II—for less than a year in northern Europe and about two years in Italy. In the history of Western warfare, fighting on the ground of the European continent usually proved the most lethal of all theaters.

Perhaps just as important, British military and civilian leadership in World War II was both more adroit than in World War I and certainly keener to avoid the catastrophic losses of trench warfare. British army planners like Generals Harold Alexander, Alan Brooke, and Bernard Montgomery were competent. Montgomery's "set-piece" battles, whether at El Alamein or the crossing of the Rhine, were designed to minimize fatalities, and often did so, at least in the short term. After Dunkirk, Singapore, and Tobruk, generals were careful not to expose the British Army to encirclement or sieges, as the navy systematically cleared the seas of Axis war and support ships, and Bomber Command helped to wear down German fuel supplies and transportation capability.

British technology, such as General Percy Hobart's modified armored vehicles ("funnies"), the continual evolution of British radar and sonar, or the use of armored flight decks on aircraft carriers, often aimed at reducing casualties as much as inflicting them. The victorious British Army suffered about the same number of fatalities over six years of fighting from Norway to Burma as it had lost during the two nightmarish battles of Passchendaele and the Somme alone in World War I. It was again a credit to the political, diplomatic, and military leadership of Great Britain that it was able to protect its homeland and wage offensive war abroad to achieve victory against far more formidable enemies than in the past, yet at the cost of fewer combat casualties than any of the other five major belligerents.[68]

SEVERAL COUNTRIES THAT were not original members of the Allied or Axis alliances suffered more dead than did many of the major six or seven belligerents. Yugoslavia, for example, lost well over one million dead. The initial Axis invasion of April 6, 1941, saw Germany, Italy, and Hungary converge on Yugoslavia to punish the country for a perceived about-face from the Axis. The initial German-led invasion led to a collapse of the central government, and the resulting chaos was magnified by longstanding ethnic, religious, and political conflicts as the country dissolved into a myriad of factions: Serbs, Croatians, Bosnians, Kosovars, Macedonians, Montenegrins, and Albanians, as well as Muslims, Orthodox and Roman Catholic Christians, fascists, nationalists, and royalists, Chetniks, Ustashas, and partisan communists. Germans considered Serbs as one of many categories of Slavic subhumans and were particularly indifferent to civilians and vicious in their reprisals against partisans as well as in the initial bombing of Belgrade. Disease, harsh weather, and epidemics were the usual force multipliers that explain why 7–10 percent of the prewar Yugoslav population perished.

The Dutch East Indies and modern Indonesia (3–4 million dead) as well as the Philippines (500,000 to 1 million dead) suffered more than most European belligerents. All such theaters had large populations, but they had experienced quite different wars. The Dutch East Indies, after an initial Japanese invasion, was never liberated by the Allies. While the occupation was brutal, there was not mass death until 1944–1945, when the population suffered widescale famine due largely to Japanese expropriation of foodstuffs and the disruptions of traditional agriculture.

Perhaps one million Filipinos perished to famine, battle, and mass killings, and as captives and forced laborers. There was a familiar Pacific sequence to the slaughter: the initial resistance of American and Filipino forces against the Japanese in spring 1942, followed by a savage occupation (May 1942–March 1945), culminating in a brutal American reconquest (spring 1945). Unlike the case of the Dutch East Indies, where many Indonesians had initially welcomed the Japanese as liberators, most Filipinos in some manner resisted the Japanese from the beginning of the war. Over half the territory of the islands was never subdued by the invaders. Guerrillas continued partisan attacks on retreating Japanese occupiers until the end of the war in September 1945. Few in the West appreciate that far more civilians and combatants died on the Allied side in the reclamation of the Philippines than during the Battle of the Bulge, or that starvation in Indochina alone may have caused well over fifty times more deaths than in the Netherlands.


THE THREE MAJOR Axis powers directly or indirectly caused about 80 percent of the total World War II dead, while suffering somewhere around 20 percent—the majority of their losses incurred in their last six months of respective fighting. Rarely in any war of the past had the defeated inflicted so much carnage, in such lopsided fashion, on the victorious, largely as the result of the savagery unleashed against the Russian, Chinese, Polish, and Yugoslav people.

In sum, World War II by 1942 became a predictable story of Japanese and German soldiers butchering or starving millions of Chinese and Russian civilians while being increasingly defeated on the field of battle by Allied soldiers. The question of whether the ends of ridding the world of murderous ideologies and widespread extermination camps justified the means of losing sixty million lives is discussed in the final chapter.

# PART SEVEN

# ENDS

## Winners, losers, neither, and both

*A victory described in detail is indistinguishable from a defeat.*
—Jean-Paul Sartre[1]

# 20

# Why and What Did
# the Allies Win?

THE ALLIES WON World War II because in almost all aspects of battle they proved superior. In the air war, they produced the only successful heavy bombers of the conflict and deployed them in vast numbers. British and American fighters were as good as the best of those of Germany and Japan, but were built in far greater numbers. In key areas of pilot training, the production of aviation fuels, navigational aids, and transport aircraft, the Axis powers lagged so far behind their opponents that their occasionally superior—or surprise—weapons of the air, such as cruise missiles, rockets, jets, and kamikaze suicide planes brought no lasting advantage.

The same sort of paradoxes arose at sea. The Axis navies wasted scarce resources by building huge battleships, and yet unlike the Allies found no way to use such powerful gun platforms to support amphibious landings, the chief and perhaps only remaining justification for costly warships in World War II. Carrier war was the future of naval battle; yet Japan was the only one of the three Axis powers to even build an aircraft carrier fleet. It then squandered its prewar advantages in carrier strength by not taking seriously naval pilot training, in part because of chronic fuel shortages that limited both flight time and the range of warships, and in part because of a fossilized admiralty that equated naval power with aggregate battleship tonnage. The Japanese and Germans believed before the war that naval superiority was predicated on summative naval tonnage put to sea, without proper appreciation that it was not just the size and number of ships that mattered, but rather the type of war vessels that went to sea and the nature of the men who commanded them. In all these regards, the British and the Americans began the war with the world's two largest and most versatile fleets, and only further widened those respective advantages both by battle and by the efficiency of their naval yards and service academies.

German field ground forces may have demonstrated the most effective fighting power in the war, but they were vastly outnumbered by the armies of Britain, the Soviet Union, and the United States, and they were sent far abroad to fulfill strategic objectives impossible to achieve, given their finite numbers and shortages of equipment and supplies. In contrast, Allied ground forces were symphonic: the huge Red Army worked in concert with the highly mobile expeditionary forces of the Western Allies, in the former case to grind down, and in the latter to cut off and isolate, the strength and breadth of Axis ground forces.

Under the traditional calculus of siegecraft, Germany's huge artillery guns, its professional envelopments, and the expertise of its Prussian generals should have led to the capture of key Allied cities and fortresses. Instead, the survival of Leningrad, Moscow, Stalingrad, and Malta doomed the Axis cause. Germans could certainly capture strongholds like Sevastopol and Tobruk that ultimately did not affect the course of the war, but they could not storm those cites whose capture would have mattered.

Germany revolutionized armored warfare, yet Russia built the most and best tanks while the British and Americans deployed the most effective ground-support fighter-bombers. So great were the Allied material advantages in armor and artillery that the superiority of German tank crews and Panzer generals ultimately was for naught.

The Axis powers had surmised that the poor fighting ability of Allied military forces and the inexperience of their leaders would nullify the indisputable power of their factories. How strange then that they lost the war because their own enfeebled industries and blinkered masters and commanders nullified the spirit and competence of their fighting men.

WORLD WAR II finished with little ambiguity. Unlike World War I, there has never been any doubt as to who caused, won, and lost World War II. Rarely in the history of a major war had such formidable belligerents been so utterly and quickly defeated as were Germany, Japan, and Italy, nor so uniformly blamed for the global destruction that had transpired. All had their homelands ravaged by air or land or both, and occupied. Their bombed and shelled civilian populations paid dearly in blood and treasure for their prior support of their fascist governments. Their political systems were destroyed. Occupying Allied proconsuls determined their futures.[1]

Many of the principal German and Japanese leaders and generals who survived the war and did not commit suicide were put on trial for war crimes. Some were imprisoned, shot, or hanged. The terms of unconditional surrender made the prior Versailles Treaty seem innocuous in comparison. Germany, in another defeat, was now to face the fate of Carthage after the Third rather than the Second Punic War. Whereas the victors a generation earlier soon had second thoughts about Versailles, this time around no one believed that the far harsher terms forced on the Axis were at all unfair.[2]

For all the resources of the belligerents and the terrible costs of the war, the course of World War II was rapid; and for the defeated, obliteration not just capitulation was the result. The former Axis militaries were rendered impotent for well over a half century to follow. The destruction of the Axis states was accomplished in less than five and a half years in the case of Germany. Italy collapsed in little over three years; Japan did not last four after Pearl Harbor. Perhaps the destruction of the Axis is comparable to the end of the Vandals in North Africa or the Aztecs of central Mexico. Both those latter cultures were annihilated and their politics and ideologies mostly extinguished and replaced by those of their victors. The word *Prussian*, for example, has almost receded into history as a generic rather than a proper adjective, in much the same way as the noun *vandal* and the adjective *Byzantine* acquired nonexclusive connotations after both original cultures had vanished. As Fredrich von Mellenthin wrote after the war in homage to his brother, a full general in the Third Reich: "The old Prussians, of whom von Mellenthin was a typical example, are no more. Hardly anyone mentions Prussia these days." Berlin and Tokyo literally had ceased to exist as viable cities by late 1945.[3]

The world of 1939 had become scarcely recognizable by 1945. The frenzied research and development of World War II had ushered in a thorough revolution in arms with immediate and lasting consequences. War after 1945 would now have the potential to become far more lethal, even if conflicts remained more localized and never quite again global. Like many of the initial and subsequent belligerents, Germany went to war in 1939 with horse-powered infantry divisions, bolt-action rifles, and piston-driven propeller planes armed with traditional high-explosive bombs. Six years later, along with the Third Reich, Imperial Japan, the last of the Axis, went down to defeat in September 1945 in a brave new world of motorized transport, assault guns, jets, napalm, cruise and ballistic missiles, and nuclear weapons, along with suicide bombers and extermination camps. And because the two greatest wartime producers of military technology and weaponry, the Soviet Union and the United States, almost immediately entered a nearly half-century-long Cold War, their proxy conflicts saw previously relatively unarmed peoples now equipped with a plethora of high-quality arms unimaginable in the past. World War II had not just seen the introduction of radar, sonar, and sophisticated navigation, but also the production of millions of cheap and lethal arms such as stamped-out Sten submachine guns, assault weapons, simple land mines, and Panzerfausts (the precursors of rocket-propelled grenades) that flooded the world, along with the idea that everyone was now fair game in war. The victors believed that they had at least destroyed totalitarian ideologies that had married their absolutist doctrines to new technologies to kill millions. The Allies certainly had accomplished that goal with the defeat of Germany, Italy, and Japan, but the price was the empowerment of the Soviet Union that spread the fruits of its huge wartime arms industries among national liberation movements the world over.

Because the three major Allies accomplished such a rapid and complete victory, it is easy to forget that the prewar policies of Britain, the United States, and the Soviet Union toward the Third Reich—respective mollification, nonintervention, and active cooperation—had earned their own terrible ordeal to follow. Of course, in terms of resources, the combined manpower and industrial output of the United States, the Soviet Union, and the British Empire rapidly grew far greater than that of the three Axis powers. But their collective advantages accrued also because of the stupidity of the Axis: the surprise attacks on the Soviet Union and then the United States, together with the German and Italian declarations of war against America, and the Japanese invasion and occupation of mainland China, mark the five greatest strategic blunders of the war— and perhaps of any major war in history. The Axis, not the Allies, radically redefined the relative resources of the belligerents of 1939–1941, and in doing so ensured that the Axis powers would have no chance of strategic resolution.[4]

Could the Axis powers then have won the global war they blundered into? After 1941, only a few unlikely scenarios might have nullified the inherent material and demographic advantages of bringing Russia and America in on the side of Britain, at least once the USSR and the United States began their industrial and manpower mobilizations. The Axis had to win the war before the full potential of their Allied enemies was realized. As late as May 1942 that hope seemed briefly possible. With the fall of Singapore and the Philippines, the defeats of the Anglo-Americans in Burma, the stabilization of the Chinese front, and the destruction of many of the capital ships of the Allied Pacific fleet, Japan seemed to have some chance of successfully invading Midway, destroying the remaining American carrier fleet, and achieving a draw in the Pacific war, while cutting off Australia by militarizing the Solomon Islands.

Nazi Germany for a moment was also in sight of its ambitious goals, despite the sputtering Russian counteroffensives of late 1941. By July 1942

Hitler controlled much of what is now the European Union. Nearly one million square miles of the Soviet Union's most populated and richest land were under German occupation. Hitler's armies were still poised at the doorsteps of Leningrad and Moscow. Army Group South was barreling forward, seemingly unstoppable on its way to the oil fields of the Caucasus, with few enemies ahead—and fewer supplies behind. Rommel's advances in North Africa and the fall of Tobruk raised the specter of Afrika Korps Panzers in Egypt and perhaps eventually beyond Suez. In terms of manpower and territory under its rule, the Third Reich, now greater than Rome, stretched from the Arctic to the Sahara and from the Atlantic to two thousand miles east of Berlin on the Volga River. The majority of the key neutral European powers by mid-1942—Portugal, Spain, Sweden, Switzerland, Turkey, and colonial France—remained either anti-British, or pro-Axis, or were stealthily facilitating the war aims of Germany. Many of the major prewar Allied cities—Amsterdam, Athens, Belgrade, Brussels, Copenhagen, Kiev, Oslo, Paris, Warsaw—were firmly in Axis hands. The few that were not, like Leningrad, London, or Moscow, were either besieged, had been bombed, or remained in dire peril. In contrast, Europe's other great cultural or industrial metropolises such as Berlin, Bucharest, Budapest, Frankfurt, Hamburg, Istanbul, Lisbon, Madrid, Milan, Munich, Naples, Prague, Rome, Stockholm, Vienna, and Zurich were largely untouched and were either part of the Axis or neutral but often sympathetic to Nazism.

For all of Italy's failures, the central Mediterranean still remained an Axis lake by mid-1942. Tobruk would fall on June 21. When, not if, Malta was to be invaded was the chief mystery of 1941–1942. The northern and southern coasts of the Mediterranean were in Axis or pro-Axis hands; in Platonic terms, Axis frogs were croaking around a fascist pond. Europe as it had been known since the Napoleonic era no longer existed. Even the Ottomans had never controlled almost all the shores of the Mediterranean.

Then the Axis chimaera abruptly vanished. Just months later, by late autumn 1942, during and after the fighting at the landmark battles of El Alamein, Midway, Stalingrad, and Guadalcanal, the pulse of the battlefield had irrevocably changed. Almost overnight, Axis powers soon found themselves checked, if not outmanned and outgunned, and entering a new conflict in which their terrifying preemption and audacity would not matter as much as steady supply and manpower. The era of surprise German and Japanese attacks was over for good, and those Axis powers quite clearly lacked the air, land, and sea diversity and mobility so necessary to win the Second World Wars that they had prompted across the globe. When an exhausted Wehrmacht neared the Caucasus by late 1942, it still controlled only about one-sixth to one-fifth of the vast landmass of the Soviet Union. After nine months of war, Japan had not taken Midway Island, much less Pearl Harbor, and had lost as many capital ships as it had sunk after Pearl Harbor. Italy was rendered impotent in North Africa without constant succor from the Third Reich; neither power could stop Anglo-American landings in French North Africa in early November 1942.

Was such a rapid and dramatic turning point in the war preordained? Although the Axis powers could not win the war outright by late 1942, there were still ways to nullify escalating Allied advantages in industrial output and manpower and thus maintain some hope for a negotiated armistice. Indeed, for a moment, such salvation seemed possible. Operation Barbarossa had crippled some Russian factory production by early 1942. Over five million Red Army soldiers were either killed or captured. The U-boat campaign had cut off Britain from a great deal of maritime sources of supply. The loss of much of Burma made it difficult to supply China. The new ally, the United States, still inexperienced and not fully mobilized, faced enormous obstacles to delivering its growing human and material assets to the distant Pacific and Atlantic fronts, given German U-boats, the Japanese navy, and frequent Axis superiority in the air. By late 1942 there was only a single US carrier—the damaged *Enterprise*—operating in the Pacific. Germany under industrial minister Albert Speer was beginning to increase and prioritize its munitions production. Anglo-American bombers had suffered growing losses without yet systematically inflicting damage on the German homeland that might shatter production.

Yet by May 1943, the Axis goal of cutting off Allied supplies once more had proven an illusory episode. The pulse of the Battle of the Atlantic had shifted yet again, and this time permanently in favor of the British. The latter's productive capacity continued to grow and had not been much affected by the Blitz or the U-boats—or the V-rockets to come. Russia successfully completed the move of its industrial base eastward, thereby making it immune from further German attack—even as the front lines had moved back over one hundred miles westward from Germany's farthest advances of 1941–1942. The American fleet in a series of battles at the Coral Sea and Midway, and slugfests around Guadalcanal, kept the Pacific sea-lanes of supply open, and fought the Japanese navy to at least a draw. Already by 1943 there were unprecedented expansions in Allied production and the size of their armies and navies.

Still, could the Axis powers have incorporated their winnings, dug in, and made the counterattacks of the ascendant Allies too costly to achieve their ambitious strategic goals of unconditional surrender? In theory, given the resources and populations still under Axis control by mid-1942, there was no intrinsic reason why Hitler, in the Soviet style of 1941, could not have immediately reorganized Axis-controlled Europe from the Atlantic to Moscow to ensure greater industrial production and conscripted armies as large as those of the Soviet Union. The Japanese-held Pacific and occupied Asia, from northern China to Burma and from the Aleutians to Guadalcanal, offered nearly as many natural resources and recruits as were available in North America and the British Dominions.

Several obvious reasons explained why the Axis powers failed to mobilize the assets under their occupation and control—all largely innate to the prewar cultures of Germany, Italy, and Japan themselves. As noted earlier, the craft-based factories of the fascist powers did not quickly enough appreciate basic principles of industrial production, especially the importance of settling on a few practical designs of tanks, planes, trucks, and guns, and then fabricating them in mass and at little cost. Early victories of the Axis countries likewise created a sense of complacency, a "victory disease" that worked against full mobilization of their economies. Not only had Allied bombing hampered German, Italian, and Japanese production, but private industrial fiefdoms, endemic corruption, and bureaucratic infighting and suspicion had as well, all characteristic of nontransparent autocracies. At issue was not whether a B-17, B-24, Avro Lancaster, or B-29 was vulnerable to German and Japanese flak and fighters, and thus was often shot down in great numbers, but whether the Axis powers could stop the production of over forty thousand of these four-engine heavy behemoths that lit up their homelands—or could themselves send comparable air fleets to do the same to the Allied homeland factories. They clearly could do neither.

Between 1943 and 1945 victory hinged on air power, navies, armor and artillery, leadership, and industrial production. And the Allies had established superiority in all these areas by late 1943. Air and naval superiority, with special emphasis on merchant ships and transport planes, gave the Allies mobility to move armies and supplies around the globe. The ability of the Americans and British to devote huge percentages of their military budgets to air and naval power permitted them a global reach unthinkable to the Axis militaries. America could send supplies to Guadalcanal much more easily than Japan could import oil from the Dutch East Indies; Britain could dispatch convoys with a better chance of reaching distant Russia than Italy could across the Mediterranean to Libya. Hitler could reach America or eastern Russia only in his fantasies about an "Amerika" or "Ural" intercontinental or transcontinental bomber. Japan resorted to launching balloons and fantasizing about landing tens of thousands of Japanese "pirates" on the West Coast.[5]

The totalitarian systems of the Axis nations were cruel and unpopular abroad. But there was more than just savagery that hurt the Axis cause—after all, the prewar Soviet Union had been more murderous than Germany and Japan combined. The Axis brands of racist and nationalist ideologies made appeals to the hearts and minds of other Europeans and Asians difficult. Cooperation was predicated only on power and perceptions of success, not professed ideals. When the Axis powers rose, they had reluctant friends and when they receded, they had easily earned obdurate enemies. Hitler's racial hatreds transcended the Jews:

> No sooner do we land in a colony than we install children's crèches, hospitals for the natives. All that fills me with rage. White women degrading themselves in the service of the blacks. . . . Instead of making the natives love us, all that inappropriate care makes them hate us. . . . The Russians don't grow old. They scarcely get beyond fifty or sixty. What a ridiculous idea to vaccinate them. . . . No vaccination for the Russians, and no soap to get the dirt off them. But let them have all the spirits and tobacco they want.[6]

Ideology, of course, clouded military judgment. Tens of millions of man-hours were invested in the perpetration of the Holocaust and "reordering" of the East. To the degree that these operations had direct military consequences, the result was only to liquidate some of the brightest minds living within the confines of the Third Reich; many who had fled the specter of the Final Solution put their geniuses in service of the Anglo-Americans. The slave and extermination camps diminished the free European workforce, alienated neutrals, increased hatred of Germany, and drew down manpower and machines from the fighting on the Russian front. Killing sympathetic civilians in the Ukraine, in service of crackpot ideas about an inferior Slavic race, ensured that there was far less chance of tapping into mass popular discontent with Stalinism.[7]

Slave and coerced labor from occupied Europe and Russia illustrated that the workforce of the Third Reich was never as productive as its counterparts in Britain and the United States. From the Nanking to the Manila massacres, the Japanese may well have murdered outright well over fifteen million Chinese, Filipinos, Indochinese, Indonesians, and Koreans—a macabre effort that likewise diverted resources from frontline military fighting, fueled local revolts, and ensured indigenous support for the British and Americans. Asian hatred of the Japanese and their endemic cruelty ensured that a billion Asians favored the non-Asian Allied cause. The Bataan Death March and other early Japanese atrocities shaped the American mindset in a way that logically led to the napalming of Tokyo in March 1945.

The island British were able to make a better argument to win over continental Europeans than were fellow continental Germans and Italians. For all the crude Allied propaganda about the Kraut and Jap, there was never a counterpart to the Nazi *Rassenkampf,* or race war, that transcended all other considerations. By August 1941, Britain and the United States had already issued the propaganda of the Atlantic Charter, assuring the world that the United Nations sought no territory of their own, and that there would be freedom of self-determination for all after the defeat of the Axis.[8]

When the Allies incinerated masses of civilians at Dresden, Hamburg, Tokyo, or Hiroshima, the Allies at least did so on the argument—in some cases persuasive, in others dubious—that they were shortening the war by disrupting enemy military production. Even Dresden—where on February 13–14, 1945, British heavy bombers created a firestorm that devoured the historic old city—had some military value as a manufacturing site, communications center, and transportation nexus.[9]

Consequently, it was not just the Axis powers' strategic blunders, parochialism, ill-preparedness, and cruelty that lost them the worldwide war that followed 1941. The Allies had a vote too, and did almost everything right after 1942 in the manner that they had done almost everything wrong before then. They far more persuasively argued that those noncombatants whom they did kill were more likely to be embedded within the enemy war effort, while the Axis slaughtered far more gratuitously and for reasons irrelevant to combat operations. That fact was not lost on the hundreds of millions of people whose lands often became the battlegrounds between the Axis and Allies.

Another cause of the miraculously rapid Allied victory was close coordination in the alliance, and a de facto specialization of tasks. Mussolini, Hitler, and Tojo rarely consulted in the fashion of the Big Three, although ostensibly it was no more intrinsically difficult for them, as the older and more ideologically akin alliance, to do so than it was for the Allies. Yet as fascist dictatorships, the Axis powers had their own selfish and mutually suspicious aims. They were as likely to mistrust as to confer with their partners—sharing a way of doing business reflective of their own rise and hold on power within their own populations. The result was not just a series of Axis strategic lapses, but also of outright harm done to others of the alliance.

Both Germany and Japan fought and made pacts with Russia. And they did so at different times, without coordination, and often to the advantage of the Soviet Union. That opportunism was in sharp contrast to the simultaneous Allied pincers that by late 1944 were squeezing Germany from both east and west and at sea and in the air—with a firm understanding that *none* of the Big Three was to conduct a separate peace treaty with the Axis powers. Since antiquity, the dilemma of a two-front war has been not two theaters per se, but whether belligerents coordinated and synchronized their attacks for maximum effect against a common enemy.[10]

Allied leaders also more readily corrected their earlier flawed thinking; their Axis counterparts largely doubled down on their major blunders. Churchill's idea of focusing solely on invading Europe through Italy was overridden. He stopped sending battle cruisers and battleships without air cover out to sea under Axis-controlled skies and gave up on a major Aegean front. Even Stalin relented on his suicidal orders of no retreats under any circumstances that had led to the loss of entire Russian armies in 1941. His about-face was not due to the fact that the Soviet Union was any less totalitarian or savage than the Third Reich, but largely because he did not quite live in the same world of fantasy that an increasingly delusional Hitler routinely did by 1942. General Zhukov gained influence in strategic decision-making with Stalin; generals like Manstein or von Rundstedt, who were close to Zhukov's equal, steadily lost their earlier sway with Hitler.

The onetime assistant secretary of the Navy Franklin Roosevelt and the former first sea lord Winston Churchill proved more open to compromise with their military advisors than did the erstwhile corporal Adolf Hitler with the German General Staff, or the former corporal Mussolini with the Chiefs of Staff of the Italian military. It is hard to see how the Allies, in the strange manner of Hitler, might have deployed nearly four hundred thousand needed troops to garrison duty in places like Norway, when the Third Reich was so short of soldiers on the front lines in Europe. No wonder the Prussian aristocrat Field Marshal von Rundstedt scoffed once of Hitler's military ideas as fit for "a corporal's war." Certainly, the Allies avoided anything like the two great quagmires of the war—the invasions of Russia and China—where the German and Japanese armies were worn down for the course of the conflict and found that occupation of vast swaths of territory proved more costly than profitable.[11]

Finally, in the historical military tension between the moral and the material, Allied soldiers in the field quickly reached near battlefield parity with more experienced Axis fighters, while German and Japanese industrial production fell ever further behind burgeoning American, British, and Soviet factory output. The Allies learned to fight like the Axis; the Axis never learned to produce like Allies. By 1943 the American 1st Marine Division was every bit as ferocious as any Japanese veteran force, while once-superior Japanese aircraft mostly fell further behind in quantity and quality to American fighters and bombers. Russian soldiers at Kursk may not have been as well trained, equipped, and led as German infantry and Panzer divisions. Nonetheless, they were just as courageous and deadly, and their second-generation tanks, fighters, and rockets were often roughly equal and always more numerous. After 1943, it is hard to find instances where Allied troops lost any major battle due to a lack of martial courage or spirit, at least in the manner of the numerically superior French in 1940.

EARLY ON, THE astute Allies certainly foresaw the means necessary to win World War II. But as victors they could hardly predict how both their idealism and cynicism would lead to a postwar world quite different from what they had anticipated from the defeat of the Axis nations. Indeed, wartime cooperation among the Allies ended before the war itself, as the destruction of large swaths of Europe and Asia raised questions not just about the ideologies that caused the ruin, but also about those that had not prevented it. Entire cities by 1945 were little more than names— Berlin, Cologne, Hamburg, Leningrad, Sevastopol, Stalingrad, Tokyo, Yokohama, or Warsaw. Amid some of the wreckage, eighteenth-century ideologies like British imperialism vanished as global communism spread.

The United States never envisioned that it would inherit the unenviable responsibility for protecting postwar and unpopular Germany, Italy, and Japan from its former ally, the Soviet Union. Nor did it foresee that its long-term cherished partner, China, would be both communist and at war with America within five years, and soon would inaugurate genocidal policies whose eventual butcher's bill would probably exceed the toll of World War II itself. America was tainted by the task of rehabilitating fascists, while the Soviets boasted that the war for national liberation continued after 1945 spearheaded by the people's Red Army. Washington had hoped for a peaceful world overseen by the benevolent United Nations, under its own paternal aegis. By 1946 most of the world was more likely to condemn the bombing of Hiroshima and Nagasaki that ended the war than the nonaggression pacts that the Soviet Union had signed with both fascist Germany and Japan that had ensured World War II would go global.

Few foresaw the United Nations evolving into an often anti-American organization, its impotence alone mitigating the consequences of its antipathy to the United States. For all Franklin Roosevelt's inspired leadership, in his last enfeebled months he never quite grasped that his decisions about grand strategy made in 1944–1945 (drawing down US troops in China, not occupying Prague, not entering accessible German territory, inviting the Russians into the war against the Japanese, little worry about a future Russian presence in Korea) would soon have not only postwar implications but consequences that were antithetical to Roosevelt's own often idealistic views of a postwar permanent peaceful order.[12]

The Borders of Germany in 1937 and 1945

Early in the war Britain had sensed that its eroding empire was doomed, and that its world position was being eclipsed by both the Soviet Union and the United States. But the British never quite anticipated that their postwar economy would soon grow weaker than those of both defeated (though more populous) Germany and Japan, or that some of its former colonies would metamorphose so quickly from independent nations to pro-Soviet belligerents. The Soviet Union had hoped to eliminate a common vulnerable border with Germany, but never quite dreamed that it would do so rather easily by creating an entire belt of client states of the so-called Warsaw Pact.

GIVEN SUCH PARADOXES, were any of the prewar goals of the respective belligerents attained? Certainly not those of the defeated. Germany went to war to expand its borders, create a pure racial state to the Volga River, exterminate the Jews, destroy Bolshevism, reclaim its national confidence, and position Germany as the arbiter of European culture and civilization in the twentieth century. As a result of that megalomania, it shrank to its smallest size since its nineteenth-century birth. The war had guaranteed that between 1943 and 1945 Germany was to be the home to more non-Germans—mostly imported workers and slave laborers—than at any time in its history. Hitler's destruction of roughly half the world's Jewish population helped to ensure the birth of the state of Israel, stained and warped German culture for the remainder of the twentieth century, and allowed the Russian liberators of the Eastern death camps their greatest moral capital since the Bolshevik revolution. Only the stigma of the war and the Holocaust guaranteed that Germany, quickly to be the strongest economic nation in Europe, would nonetheless remain non-nuclear and militarily the weakest of the major European powers in the twenty-first century, at times still plagued by self-doubt and guilt about its distant Nazi past.

A defeated Germany was divided first into four parts, then in 1949 reconsolidated into two opposing and antithetical capitalist and communist states, demarcating an entire European fault line between East and West for the next half century of the Cold War. A quarter to a third of the Third Reich's territory of 1940 was lost to its neighbors.[13]

At least eleven million Germans were ethnically cleansed from German-speaking regions in 1945 by the Soviet Red Army and Eastern European satellite communist governments. None were accorded international refugee status in the fashion of simultaneously displaced peoples after the war. All were incorporated into either West or East Germany.

There was not much consideration that their centuries-long ancestral residence in East Prussia, Silesia, Poland, Pomerania, and Czechoslovakia should accord them victim status or reparations for lost properties. There were no permanent refugee camps in Germany analogous to those in the Middle East; and no one expected that there should have been.[14]

All that said, Germany did not suffer the fate of its initial defeated victims, such as Poland, which had ceased to exist by 1940 and had its population slaughtered and starved. Under the auspices of the Potsdam Agreement arranged by Great Britain, the Soviet Union, and the United States (July 17–August 2, 1945), the Western Allied occupation of Germany would prove comparatively mild compared to the recent German occupations of other nations' territory, especially for a country that had killed five to six times more soldiers and civilians than it had lost. The harsher so-called Morgenthau Plan—a trial balloon memorandum of 1944 floated by the American secretary of the treasury, Henry Morgenthau Jr.—called for deindustrializing Germany and was eventually shelved. Western capital and troops poured into the American, British, and French zones of occupation both to help rebuild the cities and to protect the new West Germany from Soviet absorption.

Compliant German postwar behavior was ensured by the Allied destruction of Nazi ideology. West Germany was to be a Western-style democracy, closely monitored by occupying Allied troops. By 1949 it had been brought into the larger fold of Western European nations as the Federal Republic of Germany and by 1955 as a member of the NATO alliance. The permanent loss of large chunks of German-speaking territory, and nearly half a century of partitioning Germany were seen as insurance that Germany would not be at the heart of a new European war for a fourth time.

The West German government paid sizable reparations to many Nazi-occupied nations, this time without deliberately inflating its currency. Still more strategies facilitated that goal, such as a new national German spirit of not yoking economic dynamism to military power, and the postwar anomaly of both an economically weaker France and Britain that stockpiled nuclear weapons while a stronger Germany stayed strategically disarmed. The result was that if Germany was only two-thirds as large as its earlier borders, eighty million German-speakers—roughly the same size as its World War II population—now no longer spoke of the need for more *Lebensraum*. For the first time in over a century, there were to be almost no blocs of German-speakers in postwar Europe that did not live inside German or Austrian borders—and no German minorities agitating for any sort of *Anschluss* with the Fatherland.

The Nuremberg war crimes trials had begun well by bringing to justice scores of Nazi criminals. But throughout the late 1940s and early 1950s many of the convicted had their sentences reduced or set aside or simply were never really hunted down. France, for example, handed out more death sentences to its own citizens for collaboration with the Nazis than the Western Allies did to high Nazi officials. So frequent were the charges of working with the Nazis that *Time* magazine reported a new French definition of collaboration: "Anybody who collaborated more than you did." None of the Allies quite knew what to do with most high-ranking German officers, given that most denied knowing of the Final Solution and, when clearly culpable of ordering executions, claiming they were only obeying Hitler's orders. By the late 1940s and early 1950s, many ex-Wehrmacht generals were seen as essential to rebuilding West German defenses and of some value to American and British strategists in analyzing the results of World War II.[15]

In the new millennium of a politically united Europe, the German financial powerhouse has dominated a weak European Union (whose own future is problematic), especially in reference to feeble indebted Mediterranean economies. Berlin often set unpopular European Union immigration policy. An underfunded NATO is increasingly marginalized. Germany is united and its military future is uncertain. It seems at times increasingly skeptical of US leadership, advancing all sorts of legitimate and dubious reasons for its growing estrangement from Washington. By 2015, Germany was polling the most anti-American (less than 51 percent approval) of all major European nations. Occasional German historical revisionism plays upon lingering bitterness over either losing the war or, when it was deemed lost, still suffering needless devastation and cruelty at the hands of Anglo-American bombers and the Red Army.[16]

JAPAN HAD GONE to war to ratify and expand its new hegemony in the Pacific and Asia, hoping to replace European colonial powers with an empire of its own. But by starting a brutal war against most of Asia and the United States, Tokyo ensured that it would become hated by its neighbors for over a half century, disarmed, pacifist, and completely dependent on America for its security.

Japan had fought the Red Army for only a few months between July 1938 and August 1945. Its ground forces did not suffer quite the fatal consequences comparable to that of the Wehrmacht. The long Japanese occupation of China was mostly a one-sided affair, and the vast majority of deaths were Chinese. Postwar Japan's growth was even more spectacular than was Germany's; it was never divided into separate nations or in the months after the war threatened by immediate communist invasion. If Japan had a smaller prewar population than did the Greater German Third Reich by 1939 (roughly 73 million versus 80 million), it vastly outgrew postwar Germany and by 2015 was nearly fifty million people larger, with an annual gross national product $1 trillion greater.[17]

In World War II, Japan did to China what Germany had done to Russia in invading and waging a nihilistic war fueled by racial animosity, although it suffered only less than half the casualties of the Wehrmacht on the Eastern Front. Again, given its island geography, postwar Japan forfeited much less of what it believed was its native territory than did Germany. The United States was also more likely to hand back Okinawa than liberated Poland or Czechoslovakia were willing to return their German borderlands.

In the last year of the war a great many Imperial Japanese forces in the Pacific were bypassed by the Americans and British. Installations with hundreds of thousands of Japanese soldiers in Malaya, Korea, China, and Formosa surrendered largely intact at war's end. All that said, Japan suffered enormous casualties—the fifth greatest toll in the war after Russia, China, Poland, and Germany. The firestorms from area bombing became routine in almost all the major Japanese cities, whose urban cores went up in flames from the incendiaries of the B-29s. Racism and righteous payback—and Japanese fanatical resistance—all explained why napalming Japanese cities did not earn the immediate moral outrage among the Allies that had followed the firebombing of Hamburg and Dresden. Of all the Axis powers, Japan remained the only one to suffer the devastation of nuclear weapons. Yet it was also the sole Axis nation whose central homeland was not invaded and fought over on the ground. That paradox may have explained why Japan, despite Hiroshima and Nagasaki, suffered fewer civilian casualties than did war-torn Poland and Yugoslavia, and why Japan did not as unequivocally as Germany renounce its wartime fascist past. In the Western world far less was known of the extent of Japanese savagery in China than of Germany's exterminations in the East.

Japan forfeited the south Kuril Islands, Sakhalin archipelago, and neighboring smaller islands to Russia, and lost some Pacific islands awarded from Germany after World War I. But not all these losses were considered traditional sacred Japanese ground. Nor was Taiwan, Manchuria, or Korea (Okinawa was, but by 1971 had been returned to Japan by the United States). Japan was occupied by the Americans and to a lesser extent by the British, but again, unlike Germany, never formally partitioned. Its former major enemies—China, Indonesia, Korea, and

Malaya—had far less clout in postwar negotiations with the victorious Anglo-Americans than did Germany's conquered or occupied neighbors. That fact too may explain greater Japanese reluctance to atone for its war-time sins.

Some of the most capable and infamous of Japanese field generals, such as Masaharu Homma, Iwane Matsui, and Tomoyuki Yamashita, were tried by various Allied courts and either hanged or shot, along with another nine hundred Japanese officers and government officials. There were a few other similarities with the reconstruction in postwar Germany. The Allied occupation forced land and voting reform, and a new constitution promoted Japanese commerce and forbade offensive military operations and a large military. Japan likewise channeled its national energy from its armed forces to economic prowess and soon its fiscal power became to the Pacific what Germany's had to Europe. Just as the world had grown to accept that Hitler's "People's Car" was now the lovable hippie's Volkswagen Bug, so too Mitsubishi came to be associated not with the deadly Zero fighter but with affordable and reliable compact automobiles; few seemed worried that in 2015 Japan's second new helicopter carrier was named *Kaga*, after one of Admiral Chuichi Nagumo's flattops at Pearl Harbor that was sunk six months later at Midway.[18]

The communist takeover of China and North Korea placed Japan in as vulnerable a geographic position as Germany had found itself with the Soviet Union. Security was found only under the nuclear defense umbrella of the United States. After the victory of the communists in the Chinese civil war and in North Korea, an economically powerful and friendly Japan was felt critical to the Western effort to stop the spread of communist aggression, in the same manner that occupied Western Germany had been enlisted as a military and economic buffer to the Soviet Union. That realist calculus was yet another reason why Japan did not confront its imperial past—a fact that in the twenty-first century still poses more paradoxes for its Asian allies.

BENITO MUSSOLINI DREAMED of a new Mediterranean Roman Empire. The war, however, ensured that there would never again be any Italian presence outside Italy itself. Indeed, Mussolini's Italy survived only three years of war and was the first of the Axis powers to fall. After huge losses and humiliation in North Africa and in the Balkans, the Grand Council of Fascism and King Victor Emmanuel III deposed the bewildered Il Duce in July 1943, even as the Allies overran Sicily. A new government sought to ingratiate itself with the occupying Allies, as if Italy could go from a being member of the Axis to part of the Allies overnight. In reality, thousands of pro- and anti-fascist partisans roamed the Italian countryside for the next two years, presaging the political tensions and factions that would characterize Italy's postwar governments for the next half century.[19]

Italy on its own in World War II won just one small war against the British in Somaliland in August 1940—and the verdict was overturned in months. The peculiar circumstances of both Mussolini's brand of incompetent fascism and his downfall, and the subsequent continuation of the war in Italy largely against German forces, led to a quite different and relatively less harsh postwar environment.[20]

By deposing Mussolini before the official end of the war, the Italians—fairly or not—could better advance claims that they, too, had been his victims. Citizens of none of the other Axis powers would kill their own dictator. Italians were supportive by late 1943 of American and British forces in their stalled drives against successive German lines of resistance. German reprisals and gratuitous barbarity against Italian civilians in Italy, Greece, and Germany likewise helped cement the image that Italy had been more likely victimized by Mussolini than systematically and inherently evil in the manner of the Germans. The Italians pointed to massacres of their soldiers by Nazi troops in 1943–1945 as proof that they now stood apart from the Axis that Mussolini forced them to join.[21]

Despite Mussolini's racism and cobbled-together fantasy talk of *razza* and *spazio vitale*, Italy never quite developed the savage racist ideology that had led to the Holocaust or Japan's widescale atrocities against the Chinese. For all its mythopoeic talk of twentieth-century modernism, Mussolini's ideology was reactionary, harkening back to reviving the grandeur of Rome as much as promoting a new racially superior civilization, as was the case for Germany and Japan.

Although Italy waged a brutal and inhumane war in Africa—with more than one million poorly equipped Ethiopian, Somali, and Libyan soldiers and civilians killed—the Eurocentric Allies were less likely to equate Italian savagery against Ethiopians and Somalis with the German crime of slaughtering European civilians. Sizable Italian minorities in the United States also were more influential politically than the earlier and mostly assimilated nineteenth-century German immigrants and, as Europeans, did not suffer quite to the same degree the racial prejudices accorded the West Coast Japanese. The wartime Vatican had remained the center of Catholicism, and it was soon easier for many Allies to equate Italianism with the Pope than with Mussolini. Jews usually fared better in Italy and its occupied areas than was true under the Third Reich.

Italy, moreover, was an entirely Anglo-American theater. The Russians did not enter the Italian Peninsula even belatedly, as in the case of the war against Japan. The British and Americans were free to adjudicate the fate of Italy as they saw best. Strangely, the Soviets only halfheartedly advanced the argument that the Italians, despite their surprisingly large presence on the Eastern Front (over 80,000 of their soldiers would never come home), had ever really been at war against the USSR.

Finally, the Italian homeland, bombed constantly, was also fought over far longer than was true of Germany: two years on the ground in comparison to less than four months. It took the Americans over three years to reach the German frontiers, but about half that time to land in Italy. The destruction to Italy wrought by American, British, and German armies—and Italian partisans—was substantial, even as Italy entered a quasi–civil war between fascist diehards and communists eager for reckoning. As a result, Italy was felt to have suffered enormously without the need for subsequent partitioning, especially given its maritime and Austrian buffers from the Red Army. The complete loss of its vast overseas empire in the Adriatic, Africa, the Aegean, and the Balkans was apparently considered punishment enough without additional territorial concessions.

IN SUM, DESPITE paradoxes that followed the war, the Allies certainly achieved at least some of their collective prewar aims. All the conquered territory absorbed by the Axis between 1939 and 1944 was liberated from German, Italian, and Japanese control, albeit with large chunks absorbed by the Soviet Union and its new satellite clients. The complete destruction of European Jewry was stopped, but only after over half of the murderous agenda of Hitler was already completed. Nazism, fascism, and Japanese militarism were not just destroyed as ideologies, but their most influential adherents were humiliated and hunted down as well. None exists as a viable movement today. Despite reprieves, commutations, and pardons, many of those most responsible for starting the war and committing crimes against humanity were put on trial and punished, in a way unique in some 2,500 years of Western military history.

The fear of such a postwar accounting led many like Adolf Hitler, Joseph Goebbels, and Heinrich Himmler to commit suicide rather than face postwar reckoning and hanging. The Axis Big Three—Hitler, Tojo, and Mussolini—all died violently as a result of their defeat. Allied leaders passed away peacefully of old age and infirmity. Successful democracies replaced Axis dictatorships. Germany, Japan, and Italy became model global citizens. Central Europe and the South China Sea for over a half century were no longer to be the powder kegs of war. Another world war was averted.

More long-term, utopian goals were only half realized. Nuclear weapons, the NATO alliance, and the fear of mutually assured destruction during the Cold War more likely prevented World War III than did the moral censure of the war-born United Nations. The totalitarian absorption of Eastern Europe that had proved a catalyst for World War II was institutionalized by 1945—albeit with Stalinist puppet governments replacing their earlier Nazi-dominated counterparts, an outcome that was not overturned until 1989 and afterward.[22]

In the ensuing decades perhaps some sixty to seventy million were eventually to perish from Mao Zedong's unending paranoid revolutions, a far greater death toll in relative peacetime than inflicted by the wartime Japanese. The immediate American postwar dream of a like-minded world governance of free-market democracies proved no more lasting than the British notion of an evolving empire turned into a close-knit commonwealth organized by enlightened British military and economic leadership.[23]

Of all the six major belligerents of World War II, the Soviet Union, despite suffering the worst losses of the war, best succeeded in its war aims: the defeat of the Axis powers, the reincorporation into the Soviet Empire of the Baltic states and occupied eastern Poland, followed by the establishment of huge buffer zones on the borders of the Soviet Union, all characterized by Eastern European communist dictatorships in fealty to Moscow. Most of what Stalin had stolen through his partnership with Hitler, he had retained by the time of the latter's death. The communist takeover of all of Eastern Europe, China, and much of mainland Asia realized Stalin's wartime visions. Finland and Austria were neutralized.

The embrace of and help to the Soviet Union after June 1941 by the United States and Britain explain many of these anomalies. Yet the partnering with such an odious ally, while morally repugnant, was militarily defensible. Helping Stalin was probably preferable to standing aloof and simply allowing tens of millions of Russian and Eastern European civilians to be wiped out or to commit millions of additional British and American infantry forces to neuter another two hundred of Hitler's divisions.[24]

Still, the necessary partnership with Russia blurred the focus on the prior mass murders by Stalin and the enslavements of Eastern Europeans to follow. The millions exterminated by Stalin before the war were overshadowed by the over twenty-seven million Russian war dead, who heroically perished to destroy National Socialism and helped to stop the final completion of the Holocaust. The postwar world seemed to have forgotten that Stalin had killed almost as many of his own Russians as did Hitler.

Meanwhile, the Soviets, erstwhile abettors of Hitler and partners in a nonaggression pact with the Imperial Japanese, broadcast that they continued to be "democratic" and thus the true liberators, now freeing colonial peoples from the fascist yoke in the fashion they had during the war. The Roosevelt administration's naiveté that Stalin might be a fellow anti-imperialist (and thus would share an American distrust of the British Empire) was perhaps the most embarrassing of all the American assumptions about the war, given that the Soviet Union's aggrandizement was ongoing, brutal, and always predictable.[25]

It was tragically ironic that shortly after the Yalta Conference of February 1945—when the Soviet Union at last conceded to British and American entreaties to enter the Pacific war against Japan within ninety days of the defeat of Hitler—the Allies would learn that Russia was mostly unneeded in the Pacific. Indeed, the Soviets' opportunistic entry into the Pacific war could only have deleterious effects on postwar China, Korea, Indochina, and Japan. Stalin had grown increasingly convinced after the Normandy landings and bombing campaigns that the democracies, in fact, were adept in war making and were winning back as much Axis territory as the Soviets, but at far less cost. Yet had Yalta perhaps taken place months later, when the full effect of the American fire raids on Japan of March 1945 were calibrated, when it was almost certain that an atomic bomb could be successfully tested by July 1945, when Harry Truman was president, and when the Allies had more evidence of Stalin's perfidy as he entered Eastern Europe, the Soviets might not have been lobbied to join in against Japan and thus might have had less postwar Asian influence in areas that would plague the West for the next half century.[26]

AT HOME, THE Allied wartime propaganda of fighting for the freedom of the individual was a chit that had to be redeemed, if only superficially, when hostilities ended. The ensuing movements for civil rights for African-Americans and other minorities, and for greater equality for women, began not just from vast changes in the wartime social and commercial fabric of America—among them a growing economy—but also from the arguments that a victorious American democracy had advanced in justifying its cause.

The war led to a new American engagement abroad. The United States spearheaded NATO and its lesser Pacific imitations, and began to intervene routinely around the world to shore up anticommunist and sometimes authoritarian regimes, as if engagement in the 1950s would not repeat the mistakes of what followed from the isolationism in the 1920s and 1930s. If stopping the Axis had saved the world, so too halting Stalinist communism was seen as crucial to rebuilding it. American isolationism of the prewar era was a victim of victory. So too was chronic worry about the resurgence of economic depression. Much of the world after 1945 lay in ruins. All the old industrial powers of France, Germany, Japan, and Russia had been bombed, looted, or occupied. The new economic Tigers of the twenty-first century—China, South Korea, and Taiwan—did not yet exist. America's only major competitor, Great Britain, turned inward, nationalizing much of its economy at home and dismantling its presence abroad. In such a commercial and security void, the United States for two decades after the war supplied the world with food, material and industrial goods, capital, and new products, and thus grew economically as never before. From 1945 to 1970, the United States usually ran a surplus balance of payments, but almost never after that.

The claims of the high-minded success of World War II were often juxtaposed to the complexity of the Cold War. The hardships of a Depression-era and war-fighting generation often were forgotten or underappreciated amid the postwar affluence and leisure of its progeny, an incongruity of outlooks labeled a "Generation Gap" in the decades following the war. To a more-affluent generation, that America had once fought the good fight seemed to suggest that it somehow could and should have waged the perfect fight in World War II.

In the end, Americans, who could not settle on much else, agreed that in World War II its greatest generation of leaders—Franklin D. Roosevelt, George Marshall, Dwight Eisenhower, Henry Stimson, Omar Bradley, George Patton, Chester Nimitz, Douglas MacArthur, and others—saved the country and perhaps civilization as well from the Axis, and created democracy in the political systems of Germany, Japan, and Italy, the countries that had once set the world on fire.


GREAT BRITAIN'S GREATEST contributions to the Allied effort were moral as well as material. Without its successful solitary resistance against Germany and Italy from June 25, 1940, until June 22, 1941, the war would have either been lost or not waged at all. Alone of all six belligerents, it fought the war from its very beginning in September 1939 to its final end in September 1945. That said, the various blitzes and German rocket attacks that hit the homeland killed over fifty thousand British subjects as the earlier violence of the trenches had not. The United States bore the greater financial and material cost in the struggle against Germany, Italy, and Japan. Yet in key areas—cryptography, radar, antisubmarine tactics, strategic bombing, and grand strategy—Britain's earlier experience in the war saved the Americans thousands of lives. Winston Churchill's refusal to deal with Hitler—when the Third Reich ruled Europe, allied itself with the Soviet Union, and was not at war with America—kept resistance to Nazism alive. Great Britain's defiance would eventually turn Hitler eastward to commit the greatest blunder of the war.

For a variety of reasons, wartime British industry, which had so often outproduced both German and Japanese munitions, in the postwar era gradually lagged behind both rebuilt economies, not always out of necessity but also due to poor economic policy. Countries of the old Axis found advantages in restarting their postwar economies ex nihilo. Britain was stuck with the consequences of victory.[27]

During the 1944 and 1945 Allied summits, American diplomats, especially in the case of Roosevelt during the Yalta Conference, occasionally played Churchill off against Stalin to tweak the British. American generals resented being treated in condescending fashion by British political and military leaders, as if they were playing Roman centurions to their British would-be Athenian-robed philosophers.[28]

The State Department felt that astute British worries about Stalin's plans for Eastern Europe were mostly nineteenth-century Great Game melodramas. Roosevelt, for example, unlike Churchill, was determined to suppress the truth of the spring 1940 Soviet massacre of Polish officers in the Katyn Forest, worried that Polish-Americans might draw the incorrect conclusions about the wartime alliance with the USSR. He also assumed that there was a moral equivalence between British imperialism and Soviet communism, and perhaps even thought that the former was by design exploitive but the latter was an idealism gone wrong. The British ethos after the war was perhaps best summed up (oddly in the midst of the 1962 Cuban Missile Crisis) by the British ambassador to the United States, Sir David Ormsby-Gore: "In the end it may well be that Britain will be honored by the historians more for the way she deposed of an empire than for the way in which she acquired it."[29]

American postwar military and economic aid, while generous to both friends and former enemies, focused as much on the defeated in Europe and Asia as on the exhausted British ally. The postwar appraisal of Stalin's aggression lagged behind in the United States and needed Winston Churchill's landmark 1946 "Iron Curtain" speech in Fulton, Missouri, to begin to see the realities of the ideological struggles ahead. Perhaps not until the United States inherited the British responsibilities of a global watchdog in the late 1940s did America fully appreciate Britain's paradoxes as a former global power between keeping order and promoting justice.[30]

Soon the Americans, with the zealotry of converts, pushed Cold War containment far more vigorously than the less materially equipped British. World War I had ended the Austro-Hungarian, German, Ottoman, and Russian Empires. World War II finished Britain's and birthed new Soviet and American successors. For all its worries of preserving imperial majesty, Britain nonetheless fought World War II to destroy Hitler, Mussolini, and the Japanese militarists rather than to attempt to accommodate fascism with its own imperial agendas.

In terms of combined air, naval, land, and industrial power, the smallest of the three major Allies proved stronger than any of the Axis powers. If Britain lost its global role in the postwar years, this was as much due to social changes as to the consequences of blood and treasure lost in World War II.

THE SOVIET UNION was both the biggest loser and the greatest winner of the war. It suffered the most dead—somewhere near twenty-seven million lives—of any Axis or Allied power. Much of its land and many cities from occupied Poland to the Volga were ruined, even as the Soviet Union reached its apex after the war, with acquisitions in the Baltic states, in southern Finland, and its vast new protectorate in Eastern Europe.

Millions of postwar Russians were without basic housing and secure food supplies. Soviet industry remained warped by wartime exigencies. The Great Patriotic War saved the reputation of Stalinism for another generation, but with catastrophic consequences for the millions who survived the war and were forced to live under it. As a result of the Cold War and the odious nature of Stalinism, the Soviet war effort was often not given full credit in the anticommunist West for its near-virtuoso destruction of the German army. But on balance, the wartime alliance also tended to downplay the fact that the horrific waste of Russian manpower was often due to the savagery of Stalin's leadership or the incompetence in 1941 of his generals.

The war, then, left both the Russians and the world at large confused by the Soviet Union's record of both heroism and duplicity. Stalin had once been both Hitler's greatest asset and his worst enemy, the salvation of the West during war and its existential enemy in peace. No other country lost so many of its own to Germany or killed so many Germans. No nation's army fought so ineptly and so brilliantly, and sacrificed millions of its own to kill millions of Germans.

In the postwar world, the country that had produced Katyusha rockets and the T-34 tanks that bested the Wehrmacht's Tigers and Panthers could never create anything for its own consumers approaching the craftsmanship or quality of a Mercedes-Benz or BMW automobile, much less millions of quality GE refrigerators and ranges. The Allies had won the war in part because the industrial might of the Soviet Union equipped a vast army of millions with thousands of simple, durable, and superb tanks, artillery, and rockets. After the war, these munitions flooded Cold War battlegrounds from Korea to Budapest and ensured that they were as much a bane to the West as they had once been a boon.

The human paradoxes were even greater. Russia helped to save the Allied cause by its great sacrifices. Yet the Allied war effort to defeat Germany saved communism. The Soviet cities of Leningrad, Moscow, and Stalingrad—unlike Amsterdam, Athens, Brussels, Copenhagen, and Paris—were never taken by the Germans, but they suffered more death and destruction in their survival than all of those in the West had in their capture. All of these incongruities logically followed from the most profound irony: the war against fascism was won only with the help of the greatest totalitarian power of all. After 1945, attempting to reason with Stalin to allow national self-determination and autonomy made about as much sense as trying to convince Hitler to stop at the *Anschluss* or with Czechoslovakia.

WITH THE ATLANTIC Charter, the rationale of the Nuremberg and Tokyo war crimes trials, and the promise of a United Nations, the Allies had created exalted moral expectations. Yet keeping to the highest moral ground in World War II had proved impossible for at least two reasons— aside from the inclusion of the totalitarian Soviet Union on the Allied side—that have complicated most moral appraisals of the war for the last eight decades.

First, the demand for unconditional surrender—a historically rare objective of most wars—required a level of violence unforeseen in the modern era, given the zeal, resources, and combined population of over 200 million in Germany, Italy, and Japan. Area, incendiary, and atomic bombing largely killed civilians. Indeed, far more German and Japanese noncombatants died than their British or American civilian counterparts. The logical argument that a belligerent's civilian casualties were tied to the savagery of its own military resonated only during the war.

Later, self-critical, affluent, and leisured citizens of the democracies asked why their fathers had killed more German and Japanese civilians than the latter had killed noncombatant British and Americans. A new postmodern idea of "proportionality" arose in the West (but certainly not in China and Russia), suggesting that in war the defender should seek to pay back aggressors with no more lethal force than was originally used against it. The classical idea that invaders are only permanently stopped by military defeat, occupation, humiliation, and a forced change in their politics appeared Roman and at odds with the evolving ethical professions of the West. The old unapologetic classical defenses of disproportionality— "they started it; we finished it" or "we killed more of them, to save more of us and ours" or "they will never try that again"—seemed vacuous to generations that had not survived a torpedoed Liberty ship in the icy Atlantic, parachuted out from a flaming B-17 over Schweinfurt, seen the ovens at Buchenwald, or fought at Sugar Loaf Hill on Okinawa. Stranger still, in discussions of Allied bombing, few note that the losing Axis powers inflicted 80 percent of the fatalities of World War II—the vast majority of them unarmed civilians.

Second, the postwar Allies became captive of their own self-professed idealism. Britain fought as an imperial power that sought to liberate Nazi-occupied nations and give them free elections, a liberality it had not yet extended to its own restless colonies from India to Africa. The United States went to war to extinguish fascist racism and brutality unleashed against those not considered members of the various Axis master races. Yet, the US military itself was a semi-apartheid force, in which blacks could not serve as equals to their white fellow citizens—a reflection of the segregation that plagued much of contemporary America in the 1940s, most prominently in the Old South.

The Anglo-Americans did not present well the more nuanced argument that they were evolving democratic societies, whose natural postwar trajectories would lead to greater self-determination abroad and political equality at home. Such subtleties are difficult to articulate at any time and perhaps impossible in the middle of existential wars. But the resulting reticence to deal with these issues set up the victors as easy targets of national liberationist invective in the decades that followed 1945 and have still fueled constant revisionism about the moral foundations of World War II.

THE PROPER MORAL appraisal of World War II is not as nuanced as we sometimes are led to believe. Aggressive fascist powers began hostilities with unprovoked assaults during peace as the logical consequence of their own ideologies; the only common bond that held together the diverse

Allies was that almost all had been surprise attacked at some point by Axis powers. As a general rule, during the war the Axis were far more likely to commit genocide and institutionalized savagery and brutality than the Allies. All other things being equal, third parties by 1943 had preferred to be liberated by the Allies than to continue to be occupied by the Axis. The attacked Allies responded with terrible retribution masked in liberationist idealism, aimed at destroying, not defeating, fascism, without much worry what the likely consequences of their disparate alliance would mean for the postwar world. For the victors, the way the war was fought and ended was not perfect, but just good enough, given the alternative world of a horrifying Axis victory.

World War II was novel in its industrial barbarity and unprecedented lethal consequences, but it was also a traditional Western conflict in that it broke out when the Allies in the late 1930s and early 1940s lost a sense of the power of deterrence. The Axis then gambled that they had more to gain than to lose in an otherwise unwise aggressive war, and that they could defeat or intimidate into submission their stronger enemies before they could unite, rearm, and mobilize. The ensuing conflict could only end when the aggressors were beaten in every respect, occupied, and humiliated—and they were in fact so defeated due to brilliant Allied leadership, wise industrial policy, technological ingenuity, and the morale of righteously aggrieved peoples.

Peace of a sort returned, as it always had in the West, when the fog of death cleared. Deterrence, a balance of power, and alliances more or less kept the global postwar calm in a way that supranational bodies tragically could not. As General George Patton publicly lamented during the last days of the war in Europe in his desire to keep the US military well equipped, "nobody can prevent another war. There will be wars as long as our great-great-grandchildren live. The only thing we can do is to produce a longer peace phase between wars."[31]

The tragedy of World War II—a preventable conflict—was that sixty million people had perished to confirm that the United States, the Soviet Union, and Great Britain were far stronger than the fascist powers of Germany, Japan, and Italy after all—a fact that should have been self-evident and in no need of such a bloody laboratory, if not for prior British appeasement, American isolationism, and Russian collaboration.

# *Notes*

## Preface

1. Reflections on the lives of William F. and Victor Hanson Jr.: Hanson, *Ripples of Battle*, 1–10.
2. On differing ways of dividing up and envisioning World War II, see Hew Strachan, "Total War: The Conduct of War, 1939–1945," in Chickering, Förster, and Greiner, eds., *A World at Total War*, 33–35.
3. Reynolds (*From World War to Cold War*, 14–18) discusses both the inadequacy of *world war* to designate the conflict of 1939–1945 and the fact that nations in the war did not employ the term.

## Part One. Ideas

1. Lec, *Unkempt Thoughts*, 21.

### Chapter 1
### The War in a Classical Context

1. Doenitz, *Memoirs*, 307.
2. Raeder, *Grand Admiral*, 322–323; Overy, *Interrogations*, 340–341. Cf. Manstein, *Lost Victories*, 163–165 on the need to invade Great Britain. Blitzkrieg: Hew Strachan, "Total War: The Conduct of War, 1939–1945," in Chickering, Förster, and Greiner, eds., *A World at Total War*, 45–46. Raeder's advice against Operation Barbarossa: Raeder, *Grand Admiral*, 336–337. Operation Sea Lion: McKinstry, *Operation Sea Lion*. Cf. Prior, *When Britain Saved the West*, 156–159. Hitler's strategic fantasies: Weinberg, *World at Arms*, 28–47, 86–87.
3. For the Meinecke quote (in a letter to Siegfried A. Kaehler dated July, 4, 1940), see Winkler, *Age of Catastrophe*, 694.
4. Ellis, *Brute Force*, 29.
5. Germany's rapid conquest of Greece: Mazower, *Inside Hitler's Greece*, 1–8; Beevor, *Crete 1941*, 3–58. Gibraltar's strategic and military role during

WWII: Jackson, *Rock of the Gibraltarians*, 270–293; Harvey, *Gibraltar*, 137–156.

6. Butow, *Tojo and the Coming of the War*, 166–168; cf. 342–343. Cf. Toll, *Pacific Crucible*, 275–277. On Tojo's thinking, Browne, *Tojo: The Last Banzai*, 210–211.

7. The celebration of the end of the war in Italy—*Festa della Liberazione* (Liberation Day), April 25, 1945—remains a matter for political dispute: Belco, *War, Massacre, and Recovery*, 129–132.

8. Cf. Willard C. Frank, Jr, "The Spanish Civil War and the Coming of the Second World War," in Finney, ed., *Origins of the Second World War*, 381–402; Weinberg, *World at Arms*, 133–134; 177–178. Franco's relations with Hitler: Preston, "Spain: Betting on a Nazi Victory," in Bosworth and Maiolo, eds., *The Cambridge History of the Second World War*, Vol. II: *Politics and Ideology*, 327–329.

9. The notion of "world" wars: Weinberg, *World at Arms*, 3–7. Cf. Bell, *First Total War*, 302–309. On casualties: Gates, *Napoleonic Wars*, 271–272; Churchill, *A History of the English-Speaking Peoples*, Vol. III: *The Age of Revolution*, 123–134.

10. A "Thirty Years'" war, Winkler, *Age of Catastrophe*, i, 904–906.

11. Savile, *Complete Works*, 229.

12. "Koran": Churchill, *The Gathering Storm*, 55.

13. Hechler, *Goering and His Gang*, 125.

14. German rearmament: Churchill, *The Gathering Storm*, 51. Guderian, *Panzer Leader*, 190, remarked that even by 1941 German tanks were largely inferior to their Russian counterparts.

15. On the relative resources: Mark Harrison, "The Economics of World War II: An Overview," in Harrison, ed., *The Economics of World War II*, 2–5.


Chapter 2
Grievances, Agendas, and Methods


1. Moorhouse, *The Devils' Alliance*, xx.

2. Gorodetsky, ed., *Maisky Diaries*, 239 (November 15, 1939). Cameron and Stevens, eds., *Hitler's Table Talk*, 301 (February 6, 1942). The quote of Krishna Menon: *The New York Times*, October 18, 1960.

3. Churchill, *Gathering Storm*, 484; Cf. Burdick and Jacobsen, eds., *Halder War Diary*, 31 (August 22, 1939). See in general: Winkler, *Age of Catastrophe*, 676. Churchill on appeasement: James, ed., *Winston S. Churchill: His Complete Speeches, 1897–1963*, Vol. 7, 1943–1949, 7251.

4. Hitler's anti-Soviet usefulness to Western conservatism: Winkler, *Age of Catastrophe*, 913.

5. Neutrals: Keegan, *Battle for History*, 31. Wilsonian idealism that fed neutralism after Versailles: see Winkler, *Age of Catastrophe*, 907–909.

6. War as reflections of relative power: Blainey, *Causes of War*, 108–124, especially 112–114. Cf. also, Hanson, *Father of Us All*, 3–49.

7. Tooze, *Wages of Destruction*, 663–664. On the "blunter wits": Thucydides 3.83.3.

8. Shirer, *Berlin Diary*, 245 (November 7, 1939). Speer, *Inside the Third Reich*, 290, for Goering's delusional ranting. Cf. Murray, *Luftwaffe*, 60–61.

9. Western European and British appeasers, cf. Anthony Adamthwaite: "France and the Coming of War," in Finney, ed., *Origins of the Second World War*, 82–88. On perception of the Depression in Germany and the United States versus facts, cf. Tooze, *Wages of Destruction*, 65.

10. Eden quote: Gorodetsky, ed., *Maisky Dairies*, 298 (italics in the original quotation).

11. Luck, *Panzer Commander*, 187.

12. Bullock, *Hitler: A Study in Tyranny*, 316–317.

13. R. Gerwarth, "The Axis: Germany, Japan and Italy on the Road to War," in Bosworth and Maiolo, eds., *The Cambridge History of the Second World War*, Vol. II: *Politics and Ideology*, 29–30.

14. On the causes of war, cf. Kagan, *Origins of War*, 566–573; Blainey, *Causes of War*, 205–223. See Thucydides 1.76.2 (and cf. 6.15; 1.23.6) for his famous trinity of "fear, honor, and interest."

15. See Norman J. W. Goda, "The Diplomacy of the Axis, 1940–1945," in Bosworth and Maiolo, eds., *The Cambridge History of the Second World War*, Vol. II: *Politics and Ideology*, 287.

16. Weinberg, *World at Arms*, 70, 86–89. Hitler's fantasies about the United States: Burdick and Jacobsen, eds., *Halder War Diary*, 345 (March 30, 1941).

17. Winkler, *Age of Catastrophe*, 723. Deprecating America: Hechler, *Goering and His Gang*, 75. On America's unused capacity, see Bernd Greiner, "The Spirit of St. Louis: Mobilizing American Politics and Society, 1937–1945," in Chickering, Förster, and Greiner, eds., *A World at Total War*, especially 246–247.

18. Fermor, *A Time of Gifts*, 115–116.

19. Compare Churchill, *The Gathering Storm*, 85; Duhamel, *The French Position*, 107. Cf. Sowell, *Intellectuals and Society*, 310–333.

20. Wilson quote: Sidney Aster, "'Guilty Men': The Case of Neville Chamberlain," in Finney, ed., *Origins of the Second World War*, 70–71. For von Papen, see Kershaw, *Hitler, 1936–45: Nemesis*, 83. Impediments to Allied rearming: Taylor, *Origins of the Second World War*, 19–22, 116–117.

21. Churchill, *Gathering Storm*, 319. Pessimism of the European intelligentsia: Overy, *Twilight Years*, 9–49. Cf. Weinberg, *World at Arms*, 95–97, on the Nazi home front.

22. Freedman, *Strategy: A History*, 126–128.

23. Raeder, *Grand Admiral*, 281. Cf. Richard Overy, "Hitler's War Plans and the German Economy," in Boyce and Robertson, eds., *Paths to War*, 114. See also Steiner, *Triumph of the Dark*, 607.

24. French tanks superiority: Mosier, *Blitzkrieg Myth*, 54–58.

25. Maurois, *Tragedy in France*, 126–127.

26. Germany's whines: Stephen A. Schuker, "The End of Versailles," in Martel, ed., *The Origins of the Second World War Reconsidered*, 38–56. See Overy and Wheatcroft, *Road to War*, 139–141. Foch quote: MacMillan, *Paris 1919*, 459.

27. Eden, *Eden Memoirs: The Reckoning*, 11. Appeasement of the 1930s: Weinberg, *World at Arms*, 22–39; Thornton, *Wages of Appeasement*, 78–88. Overy, *Origins of the Second World War*, 2–3. On Versailles: Blainey, *Causes of War*, 15–16, 262–263; Steiner, *Triumph of the Dark*, 345. On the reactions to appeasement and dogged Allied determination that World War II would end differently from World War I, see Weinberg, *Visions of Victory*, 149–150, 178–180. Cf. also, O'Connor, *Diplomacy for Victory*, passim.

28. Cf. Fuller, *Second World War*, 18–27.

29. A.J. Liebling, "Paris Postscript," *The New Yorker Book of War Pieces*, 49 (August 3/10, 1940). Aeschylus quote (fragment no. 394 in Sommerstein, ed., *Aeschylus Fragments*, 328–329) preserved in Stobaeus, *Anthology* 3.27.2.

30. See August 22, 1939, in International Military Tribunal, *Nazi Conspiracy and Aggression*, Vol. 3, 582. Halifax: A. Roberts, *Holy Fox*, 406–408. Eden's anecdote: Eden, *Eden Memoirs: The Reckoning*, 37. Hitler's assurance: Baynes, ed., *Speeches of Adolf Hitler*, Vol. II, 1181.

31. Weinberg, *World at Arms*, 6–20; cf. 536–586. Cf. Taylor, *Origins of the Second World War*, 19–22; Kagan, *Origins of War*, 285–297.

32. Hitler's quote: Fuller, *Second World War*, 40–41.

33. Warlimont, *Inside Hitler's Headquarters*, 210–211. On Japan's strategic dilemmas: Butow, *Tojo and the Coming of the War*, 128–129. Raeder's comments: Murray and Millett, *A War to Be Won*, 236. Italians and Barbarossa: Ciano, *Diary*, 590 (December 23, 1943). German unawareness of the Italian invasion of the Balkans: Mellenthin, *German Generals*, 137.

34. Ismay quote, cf. David Reynolds, "Introduction," in Reynolds, ed., *The Origins of the Cold War in Europe*, 13. First Punic War: Zonaras, *Epitome Historian*, 8.17, 1.62.1–9, 3.27.2–6; Zonaras 8.17; Lazenby, *First Punic War*, 156–159, 171; Lazenby, *Hannibal's War*, 19; Goldsworthy, *Punic Wars*, 128–129, 149–150.

35. See Barnett, *Collapse of British Power*, 315–319.

36. Kagan, *Origins of War*, 252–256.

37. Reassessment of Versailles: MacMillan, *Paris 1919*, 493–494; Weinberg, *World at Arms*, 6–16; Thornton, *Wages of Appeasement*, 70–72; Kagan, *Origins of War*, 285–297. Cf. Taylor, *Origins of the Second World War*, 19–22, 48–50. Cf. Blainey, *Causes of War*, 17.

38. French defeatism: Winkler, *Age of Catastrophe*, 690; Jackson, *Fall of France*, 112–116. Fall of France: Manstein, *Lost Victories*, 149. 1918 versus 1945: Gerhard L. Weinberg, "German Strategy, 1939–1945," in Ferris and Mawdsley, eds., *The Cambridge History of The Second World War*, Vol. I: *Fighting the War*, 130–131. Cf. Williamson Murray: "British Grand Strategy, 1933–1942," in Murray, Sinnreich, and Lacey, eds., *The Shaping of Grand Strategy*, 157–158.

39. Doyle, *World War II in Numbers*, 206–209.

40. Racist Axis: Steiner, *Triumph of the Dark*, 570–571. Hitler and the Westwall: Kershaw, *Hitler, 1936–45: Nemesis*, 103. Mussolini and the need "to kick ass": Ciano, *Diary*, 341 (April 11, 1940).

41. Hitler's so-called euthanasia program: Kershaw, *Hitler, 1936–45: Nemesis*, 260–261. Causes of mass death: R. J. Rummel, "War Isn't This Century's Biggest Killer," *The Wall Street Journal*, July 7, 1986.

42. British and American investment in air power: Overy, *Bombing War*, 609–633.

43. Lord Curzon's quote: Raeder, *Grand Admiral*, 209–210.

44. Production figures of transport trucks: Hyde, *Arsenal of Democracy: The American Automobile Industry in World War II*, 152–160. Germany's reliance on horses: DiNardo, *Mechanized Juggernaut or Military Anachronism: Horses and the German Army of World War II*, 24–25, 45–46. Goebbels quote: Hitler, *Hitler and His Generals*, 737.

45. On Raeder: Murray, *Change in the European Balance of Power*, 45.

46. For late-war German desperation, see Overy, *Bombing War*, 122–124.

Chapter 3
Old, New, and Strange Alliances

1. Kershaw, *Hitler, 1936–45: Nemesis*, 614–615.

2. Invasion of Poland: Weinberg, *World at Arms*, 55–58.

3. Speer, *Spandau*, 45. Richard Overy, "Hitler's War Plans and the German Economy," in Boyce and Roberston, eds., *Paths to War*, 111. Cf. Overy, *1939*, 6–13. Fall of France: Reynolds, *From World War to Cold War*, 26–28, and the same author's "Fulcrum of the Twentieth Century," *International Affairs* 66.2 (1990), 325–350.

4. Japanese strategic confusion: Morton, *Strategy and Command*, 58–59. Cf. John Lukacs, "No Pearl Harbor? FDR Delays the War" in Cowley, ed., *What Ifs? of American History*, 179–188; also in the same volume, Antony Beevor, "If Eisenhower Had Gone to Berlin," 189–204. Conrad Black, "The Japanese Do Not Attack Pearl Harbor," in Roberts, ed., *What Might Have Been*, 153–165; also in the same volume, Simon Sebag Montefiore, "Stalin Flees Moscow in 1941," 134–152. Andrew Roberts, "Prime

Minister Halifax: Great Britain Makes Peace with Germany, 1940," in Cowley, ed., *What If?* 2, 279–290; also in the same volume, Caleb Carr, "VE Day—November 11, 1944: The Unleashing of Patton and Montgomery," 333–343; and Richard B. Frank, "No Bomb: No End: The Operation Olympic Disaster, Japan 1945," 366–381.

5. Taylor, *Origins of the Second World War,* 120–121.

6. "Unconditional responsibilities": Fuller, *Second World War,* 364. Aims of the various Allied and Axis powers: Rothwell, *War Aims in the Second World War,* passim; Germany: Weinberg, *World at Arms,* 43–47; Italy: Knox, *Common Destiny,* 61–72, *Mussolini Unleashed,* 102; Japan: Hane and Perez, *Modern Japan,* chapters 12 ("The Ascendancy of Militarism") and 13 ("The Road to War"), 257–328. Reactions to World War I: Eric Goldstein, Georges-Henri Soutou, Lawrence E. Gelfand, and the comment of Antony Lentin in Part Two ("The Peacemakers and Their Home Fronts") of Boemeke, Feldman, and Glaser, eds., *Treaty of Versailles.* On the problems with Versailles: MacMillan, *Paris 1919,* 478–483. On idea of waging a war of annihilation against Germany rather than one of exhaustion, see the classical dichotomy in the work of Hans Delbrück: Gordon A Craig, "Delbrück: The Military Historian," Chapter 12 of Paret, Craig, and Gilbert, eds., *Makers of Modern Strategy,* 326–354; *Niederwerfungsstrategie* (the strategy of annihilation) versus *Ermattungsstrategie* (the strategy of exhaustion), see ibid., 341–344.

7. A war "like no other": Thucydides 1.23.1; cf. 1.1.1. Hanson, *War Like No Other,* 10–12. Death tolls in China, Germany, and Russia are discussed in Chapter 19.

8. Megargee, *War of Annihilation,* 144–148.

9. Genocide: Naimark, *Stalin's Genocides,* 15–29. Cf. Calvocoressi, Wint, and Pritchard, *Total War,* 233–263, and bibliography, 1250–1251. Cf. Jonathan Rauch, "The Forgotten Millions: Communism Is the Deadliest Fantasy in Human History (But Does Anyone Care?)," *The Atlantic Monthly* (December 2003), (http://www.theatlantic.com/magazine/archive/2003/12/the-forgotten-millions/302849/).

10. On conservative ideas of allowing the Soviet Union and the Third Reich to destroy each other: West, *American Betrayal,* 111–115,-271. On sitting out World War II in Europe leading to an improved position of Britain and especially the United States: P. Buchanan, *Churchill, Hitler, and "The Unnecessary War": How Britain Lost Its Empire and the West Lost the World* (New York: Crown, 2009), especially 413–424. Diplomacy with Hitler: Teddy J. Uldricks, "Debating the Role of Russia in the Origins of the Second World War," in Martel, ed., *The Origins of the Second World War Reconsidered,* 146–149.

11. Raeder's warning: Raeder, *Grand Admiral,* 336. Soviet geography, weather, logistics, and manpower: Megargee, *War of Annihilation,* 29–31.

On German officer support for Operation Barbarossa, see Kershaw, *Hitler, 1936–45: Nemesis*, 83.

12. Finland: Calvocoressi, Wint, and Pritchard, *Total War*, 115–118. Russian strength before Barbarossa: Bruce W. Menning and Jonathan House, "Soviet strategy," in Ferris and Mawdsley, eds., *The Cambridge History of The Second World War*, Vol. I: *Fighting the War*, 222–223.

13. Bremer quote: Salisbury, *900 Days*, 61; Hitler's "sandbox" fantasy: Speer, *Inside the Third Reich*, 173. See also Kershaw, *Hitler, 1936–45: Nemesis*, 305.

14. Calvocoressi, Wint, and Pritchard, *Total War*, 99–100.

15. Stalin on Hitler: Roberts, *Stalin's Wars*, 182. Hitler quote: Berthon and Potts, *Warlords*, 166–167.

16. Jackson, *Fall of France*, 237. Molotov-Ribbentrop Pact: Weinberg, *World at Arms*, 34–36; cf. Moorhouse, *Devils' Alliance*, 185–186. Cf. Kershaw, *Hitler, 1936–45: Nemesis*, 33–36. Stalin had read *Mein Kampf*: Suvorov, *Chief Culprit*, 19–22, 105–110, 146–152. Soviets' claims: Gorodetsky, ed., *Maisky Diaries*, 229.

17. Tensions among Axis and Allies: Earl F. Ziemke, "Military Effectiveness in the Second World War," in Millett and Murray, eds., *Military Effectiveness*, Vol. 3, 280–282.

18. Japanese-Russian accord: Calvocoressi, Wint, and Pritchard, *Total War*, 917. Cf. Warlimont, *Inside Hitler's Headquarters*, 145; cf. Cameron and Stevens, eds., *Hitler's Table Talk*, 35.

19. Japanese-Soviet Neutrality Pact: Hane and Perez, *Modern Japan*, 311–312. Cf. Roberts, *Stalin's Wars*, 30–42. Keitel's "Long war": Overy, *Interrogations*, 344. Japanese and German calculations: Murray, "The Axis," in Mansoor and Murray, eds., *Grand Strategy and Military Alliances*, 334–336.

20. Churchill, *Gathering Storm*, 449.

21. Soviet Russia's fears, duplicity, and strategic ambitions: J. Erickson, "Threat Identification and Strategic Appraisal by the Soviet Union, 1930–1941," in Finney, ed., *Origins of the Second World War*, 334–351. Japanese-Soviet Neutrality Pact: Weinberg, *World at Arms*, 81, 249–250; Paine, *Wars for Asia*, 177–180. On Soviet reluctance to fight the Japanese: Eden, *Eden Memoirs: The Reckoning*, 303.

22. British government's assessments and strategies: Reynolds, *From World War to Cold War*, 75–98. Imperial resources: David French, "British military strategy," in Ferris and Mawdsley, eds., *The Cambridge History of The Second World War*, Vol. I: *Fighting the War*, 50; Ashley Jackson, "The British Empire, 1939–1945," in Bosworth and Maiolo, eds., *The Cambridge History of the Second World War*, Vol. II: *Politics and Ideology*, 564–566.

23. In general: Edgerton, *Britain's War Machine*. See Sidney Aster, "'Guilty Men': The Case of Neville Chamberlain," in Finney, ed., *Origins of the Second World War*, 62–78.

24. Churchill, *Gathering Storm*, 223–224. See Orwell and Angus, eds., *The Collected Essays, Journalism, and Letters of George Orwell*, Vol. 4, 317.

25. American prewar defense spending: see O'Brien, *How the War Was Won*, 98–100.

26. Feeble Japanese attacks on the US homeland: Horn, *The Second Attack on Pearl Harbor: Operation K and Other Japanese Attempts to Bomb America in World War II*; Webber, *Silent Siege: Japanese Attacks Against North America in World War II*; Mikesh, *Japan's World War II Balloon Bomb Attacks on North America*, 16–36; Weinberg, *World at Arms*, 650–651.

27. American defense spending: Millett, "The United States Armed Forces in the Second World War," in Millett and Murray, eds., *Military Effectiveness*, Vol. 3, 48–50.

28. America's first-generation warplanes: Earl F. Ziemke, "Military Effectiveness in the Second World War," in Millett and Murray, eds., *Military Effectiveness*, Vol. 3, 285–287. B-17s and B-24s: O'Brien, *How the War Was Won*, 274–275.

29. Hechler, *Goering and His Gang*, 78. Hitler on Roosevelt: Baynes, *Speeches of Adolf Hitler*, Vol. II, 1605ff. Ribbentrop's claims: Overy, *Interrogations*, 321–322.

30. Wilmot, *Struggle for Europe*, 130–131. Cf. Jackson, *Fall of France*, 142. American strategic aims: Thomas G. Mahnken, "US Grand Strategy, 1939–1945," in Ferris and Mawdsley, eds., *The Cambridge History of the Second World War*, Vol. I: *Fighting the War*, especially 207–212.

# Part Two. Air

1. Wells, *The War in the Air*, 164.

## Chapter 4
## The Air Power Revolution

1. For examples of the nature of casualties caused by strategic bombing in Germany: Kassel and Magdeburg: Arnold, *Allied Air War and Urban Memory*; Berlin: Read and Fisher, *Fall of Berlin*, 122–129; Dresden: De Bruhl, *Firestorm*, 210–213.

2. On civilian dead and its military effects: Miller, *Masters of the Air*, 484–485. Assessments and cost effectiveness of air power: Overy, *Bombing War*, 398–408; Earl F. Ziemke, "Military Effectiveness in the Second World War," in Millett and Murray, eds., *Military Effectiveness*, Vol. 3, 282.

3. See O'Brien, *How the War Was Won*, 17–66.

4. Importance of air power in World War I: John H. Morrow, Jr., "The

War in the Air," Chapter 20 in Strachan, ed., *Oxford Illustrated History of the First World War*, 265–277.

5. Mosier, *Blitzkrieg Myth*, 23–24. Cf. Douhet, *The Command of the Air* (*Il dominio dell'aria*), 23. Air power in World War I: Buckley, *Air Power*, 42–69, 74–77; Mitchell, *Winged Defense*, 3. On manned flight before the airplane: Holmes, *Falling Upwards*, 122–155.

6. Fighter and bomber performance in the late 1930s: Buckley, *Air Power*, 108–110; Overy, *Bombing War*, 26.

7. Stanley Baldwin's speech of November 10, 1932: Middlemas and Barnes, *Baldwin: A Biography*, 735–736; Kennett, *Strategic Bombing*, 68–69. Cf. Buckley, *Air Power*, 14; Overy, *Bombing War*, 27. On Baldwin and Chamberlain: Dobson, *Why Do the People Hate Me So?*, especially 285–297.

8. The prewar prophets: Kennett, *Strategic Bombing,* 39–57. For the complexity of determining the efficacy of American strategic bombing, see the discussion of the January 18, 1944, report entitled "Germany's War Potential, December 1943: An Appraisal" in Gentile, *How Effective Is Strategic Bombing?*, 26–31. Walther Wever: Murray, *Luftwaffe*, 9–10.

9. Wells, *Courage and Air Warfare*, 36–45.

10. De Seversky, *Victory Through Air Power*, 130–131; cf. also 24–27; Libbey, *Alexander P. de Seversky*, chapters 12 ("Prophet of Air Power," 178–192) and 13 ("Victory Through Air Power," 193–211). Overy, *Bombing War*, 609–633.

11. Apart from Sun Tzu's, *The Art of War*, cf. Whitehead, *Aineias the Tactician*; Milner, *Vegetius*; Dennis, *Maurice's Strategikon*; Howard and Paret, *Clausewitz, On War*; Mendell and Craighill, *The Art of War.*

12. Air accidents: Wells, *Courage and Air Warfare*, 31–33. On the proximity of most sea battles to the coasts: Keegan, *Price of Admiralty*, 6. For Salamis, see Hale, *Lords of the Sea*, 55–74; Strauss, *Battle of Salamis*, passim; for Lepanto: Capponi, *Victory of the West*, 219–286; for Navarino: Woodhouse, *Battle of Navarino*, passim.

13. On the air improvements between the wars: Van Creveld, *Age of Airpower*, 66–67; cf. Wells, *Courage and Air Warfare*, 29.

14. Johnson, *V1-V2*, 21–25.

15. Wells, *Courage and Air Warfare*, 27–59 (Chapter 2: "The Nature of Air Combat During the Combined Bomber Offensive").

16. Unfamiliarity with Spitfires: Galland, *First and Last*, 37, 11; Galland's own promotion to general, 97; condemnation of Goering for denying the realities of Allied production figures and capabilities, 159, 234–235; Goering's failure to grapple with mechanics of air combat, 217–218, 221–222; Goering's final acceptance of Galland's arguments concerning the Me 262: 354.

17. Hechler, *Goering and His Gang*, 203. Cf. Doubler, *Closing with the Enemy*, 75–76.

18. Quoted in Wells, *Courage and Air Warfare*, 30.

19. He who wages war from afar: Plato, *Laws*, 778d-779b.

20. See Murray, *Luftwaffe*, 227–231. And in particular concerning Luftwaffe crashes and losses: Williamson Murray, "Attrition and the Luftwaffe," *Air University Review* 34.3 (March–April 1983), 66–77.

21. Arthur, *Last of the Few*, 97. Jarrell, *Complete Poems*, 144. Wounded and fatality ratios: Miller, *Masters of the Air*, 205.

22. Memoir of B-29 tail-gunner: Doty, *Backwards into Battle*, 121–122. Cf. Wells, *Courage and Air Warfare*, 6–22.

23. Buckley, *Air Power*, 147–153; Doubler, *Closing with the Enemy*, 79–81.


Chapter 5
From Poland to the Pacific


1. For comparative fighter and bomber production: see Ellis, *World War II*, tables 92–94 (278–280); tables 17–46 (231–244); Angelucci, Matricardi, and Pinto, *Complete Book of World War II Combat Aircraft*, 414; Angelucci *The Rand McNally Encyclopedia of Military Aircraft, 1914–1980*, Plate 114 (251).

2. Alvin D. Coox, "The Effectiveness of the Japanese Military Establishment in the Second World War," in Millett and Murray, eds., *Military Effectiveness*, Vol. 3, 4–5. Exaggerated Luftwaffe power: Murray, *Luftwaffe*, 60–61.

3. Murray, *Luftwaffe*, 28–38. Germany's medium bombers: Murray, *Change in the European Balance of Power*, 44.

4. Yenne, *Hap Arnold*, 301–303 (Appendix 4: Charles Lindbergh Letter to Hap Arnold, 1938). Cf. also Lindbergh, *Autobiography of Values*, 180–182. See Olson, *Those Angry Days*, 14–18, 25–27; also Smith, *Berlin Alert*.

5. Re-creation of the Luftwaffe: Buckley, *Air Power*, 118–121; and see 126–128 on the air campaign in Poland.

6. Murray, *Luftwaffe*, 38–39.

7. Axis fantasy bombers: Horn, *The Second Attack on Pearl Harbor: Operation K and Other Japanese Attempts to Bomb America in World War II*; cf. Frenzel, "Operation Pastorius: Hitler's Unfulfilled Dream of a New York in Flames," *Der Spiegel*, September 16, 2010. Goering's frustrations with the Heinkel 177: Hechler, *Goering and His Gang*, 495.

8. Failed He-177 program: O'Brien, *How the War Was Won*, 28–29. For Hitler's dreams: Cameron and Stevens, eds., *Hitler's Table Talk*, 307 (February 9, 1942). Cf. Overy, *Interrogations*, 304–305. Condition of Luftwaffe planes: Murray, *War, Strategy, and Military Effectiveness*, 241. Disrupted German aircraft production: Cairncross, *Planning in Wartime*, 127–128. Goering: Overy, *Interrogations*, 300–301.

9. Murray, *Luftwaffe*, 39–43.

10. For controversies over German intent and the Rotterdam bombing: http://www.rafbombercommand.com/personals_1_earlydays.html #stories_earlydays.html (accessed: February 24, 2014). See Overy, *Bombing War*, 64–65; van den Doel, "Not a Bridge Too Far: The battle for the Moerdijk bridges, Dordrecht and Rotterdam," chapter 10 in Amersfoort and Kamphuis, eds., *May 1940: The Battle for the Netherlands*, 382–392.

11. Jackson, *Fall of France*, 77–78. British air losses: Calvocoressi, Wint, and Pritchard, *Total War*, 133–134. Cf. Murray, *Luftwaffe*, 42–43.

12. Sunderman, ed., *World War II in the Air: Europe*, 8–16. Prior, *When Britain Saved the West*, 140–141. Cf. F.R. Kirkland, "The French Air Force in 1940—Was It Defeated by the Luftwaffe or by Politics?" *Air University Review* 36.6 (September–October 1985), (http://www.airpower.maxwell .af.mil/airchronicles/aureview/1985/sep-oct/kirkland.html). Cf. Mosier, *Blitzkrieg Myth*, 136–138; 193–195.

13. Battle of Britain production figures: Overy, *Bombing War*, 66–82. Luftwaffe on the eve of Operation Barbarossa: Luther, *Barbarossa Unleashed*, 50–51. Cf. Murray, *Luftwaffe*; see especially 53–54. Strategic thinking that invading Russia would pressure Britain in a way the Battle of Britain had not: Overy, *Bombing War*, 73–74, 110–112. See Hechler, *Goering and His Gang*, 381.

14. Myth of British inferiority: O'Brien, *How the War Was Won*, 98–100, 122–124.

15. Marshal Dowding, see Ray, *Battle of Britain*, passim; Overy, *Bombing War*, 103–104; Prior, *When Britain Saved the West*, 246–249.

16. Goering: Overy, *Bombing War*, 75; cf. Guderian, *Panzer Leader*, 444.

17. Buckley, *Air Power*, 119–120. Failed German blitz: Murray, *Luftwaffe*, 601.

18. Roberts, *Storm of War*, 87–118.

19. German bombing of the Soviet Union: Overy, *Bombing War*, 197–234.

20. Soviet TB-3: Hardesty and Grinberg, *Red Phoenix Rising*, 46.

21. Overy, *Bombing War*, 234.

22. Eastern Front air losses: Van Creveld, *Age of Airpower*, 110–111. Cf. Murray, *Luftwaffe*, 84–91.

23. On Russian aircraft production: Buckley, *Air Power*, 144–147.

24. Transferred Luftwaffe units to the west: Murray, *Luftwaffe*, 214–215. Cf. O'Brien, *How the War Was Won*, 278–282.

25. Kennett, *Strategic Bombing*, 93–94, 117–120. Overy, *Bombing War*, 50–51. Bomber Command's failed offensive during the summer months of 1940: Overy, *Bombing War*, 251–254; cf. 86–88.

26. For Cologne, see Kennett, *Strategic Bombing*, 133–135; for Essen, ibid. 142–143. Hitler's cynicism: Speer, *Spandau*, 200.

27. Battle of the Ruhr: Tooze, *Wages of Destruction*, 596–601. And cf. Tami Davis Biddle, "Anglo-American Strategic Bombing, 1940–1945," in

Ferris and Mawdsley, eds., *The Cambridge History of the Second World War*, Vol. I: *Fighting the War*, 500–504. Cf. Harris, *Bomber Offensive*, 52. Cf. Evans, *Third Reich at War*, 438–439.

28. The 1943 Anglo-American raids: Kennett, *Strategic Bombing*, 146–149. American protestations: Miller, *Masters of the Air*, 336–337. The history of American bomb-sighting technology: McFarland, *America's Pursuit of Precision Bombing, 1910–1945*.

29. Chuikov, *Fall of Berlin*, 20.

30. Losses of the raid: Dugan and Stewart, *Ploesti*, 222–246. Misplaced optimism of Harris: Murray, *Luftwaffe*, 201–202.

31. Bendiner, *Fall of Fortresses*, 174.

32. Mythologies and misconceptions of the bomber campaign: Miller, *Masters of the Air*, 211–213, 481–482. Substantial damage to the two plants: O'Brien, *How the War Was Won*, 278–282.

33. Spitfire and escort fighter service: D. Stubbs, "A Blind Spot? The Royal Air Force (RAF) and Long-Range Fighters, 1936–44," *Journal of Military History* 78 (April 2014), 673–702.

34. O'Brien, *How the War Was Won*, 76–77. Loss of air parity over Germany: Murray, *Luftwaffe*, 286–295. See 262–263 for catastrophic Luftwaffe losses.

35. Ellis, *Brute Force*, 220–221. Cf. Allan R. Millett, "The United States Armed Forces in the Second World War," in Millett and Murray, eds., *Military Effectiveness*, Vol. 3, 61–62. Morality of the bombing: Tami Davis Biddle, "Anglo-American Strategic Bombing, 1940–1945," in Ferris and Mawdsley, eds., *The Cambridge History of the Second World War*, Vol. I: *Fighting the War*, 525–526.

36. Blumenson, *Patton Papers, 1940–1945*, 681 (Diary, April 7, 1945).

37. Murray quotes in *Luftwaffe*, 242, and *War, Strategy, and Military Effectiveness*, 254. American bombing strategy: Allan R. Millett, "The United States Armed Forces in the Second World War," in Millett and Murray, eds., *Military Effectiveness*, Vol. 3, 46–47. Luftwaffe attrition: Overy, *Bombing War*, 365–369; cf. 377–409. On losses, see also Buckley, *Air Power*, 158–162.

38. O'Brien, *How the War Was Won*, 226–228.

39. Craven and Cate, eds., *Army Air Forces*, Vol. II, 568–569.

40. Ehlers, *Mediterranean Air War*, 322–355; cf. 397–406.

41. The German aircraft carrier *Graf Zeppelin* was never completed; nor was the Italian *Aquila*. On Taranto and the new importance of naval air power, see the Royal Navy's Admiral Andrew Cunningham quote: https://www.gov.uk/government/news/navy-commemorates-70th -anniversary-of-battle-of-taranto.

42. Comparative carrier strength: See tables in US Strategy Bombing Survey: http://www.ibiblio.org/hyperwar/AAF/USSBS/JapansStruggle /index.html#A3; cf. the statistics in Ellis, *World War II*, 245–249 (Tables 47–50), 293–302 (Table 100).

43. Battleships versus carriers: Van Creveld, *Age of Airpower*, 77–78. Costs of building *Yamato*: Lengerer and Ahlberg, *Yamato Class*, 69–73.

44. Okumiya and Horikoshi, *Zero!*, 187. Cf. Alvin D. Coox, "The Effectiveness of the Japanese Military Establishment in the Second World War," in Millett and Murray, eds., *Military Effectiveness*, Vol. 3, 19.

45. On the enormous Japanese investment in top-flight ships and planes: O'Brien, *How the War Was Won*, 66.

46. Cf. O'Brien, *How the War Was Won*, 423.

47. *"Dieu n'est pas pour les plus gros bataillons, mais pour ceux qui tirent le mieux"*: Voltaire, *Complete Works*, 547 and cp. 647.


Chapter 6
New Terrors from Above


1. On the nature of Japanese air defenses and the aviation industry: O'Brien, *How the War Was Won*, 403–405.

2. The B-29 program: Pace, *Boeing B-29 Superfortress*, 19–74; Birdsall, *Saga of the Superfortress*; Kozak, *LeMay*, 170–172.

3. Kozak, *LeMay*, 174; cf. Dorr, *Mission to Tokyo*, 27–29. Cf. Jeffrey Fear, "War of the Factories," in Geyer and Tooze, eds., *The Cambridge History of the Second World War*, Vol. III: *Total War: Economy, Society and Culture*, 108.

4. B-29 losses: Anderton, *B-29 Superfortress at War*. Mechanical problems: LeMay and Kantor, *Mission with LeMay*, 321. Survivability rates of B-29 crews: http://ww2aircraft.net/forum/aviation/29-losses-4429.html; http://www.econseminars.com/6th_Bombardment_Group_Tinian/Risks.pdf.

5. Hitler's fear: Hitler, *Hitler and His Generals*, 610–614. Stalin's copying of the B-29: Gordon and Rigmant, *Tupolev Tu-4: Soviet Superfortress*, 24–68. Cf. Hardesty and Grinberg, *Red Phoenix Rising*, 348–354.

6. Japanese production figures: Alvin D. Coox, "The Effectiveness of the Japanese Military Establishment in the Second World War," in Millett and Murray, eds., *Military Effectiveness*, Vol. 3, 18–21. See Kozak, *LeMay*, 230.

7. LeMay's altering B-29 missions: LeMay and Kantor, *Mission with LeMay*, 345–351.

8. LeMay's own flights: LeMay and Kantor, *Mission with LeMay*, 329–331; LeMay's order from General Arnold as passed on by Brigadier General Lauris Norstad: ibid., 347. Urbanized Japanese vulnerable to fire attacks: Murray and Millett, *A War to Be Won*, 504–508.

9. Ethical controversies over the firebombing: Edgerton, *Warriors of the Rising Sun*, 316–317.

10. Quoted in Van der Vat, *Pacific Campaign*, 373. Cf. U.S. Strategic Bombing Survey (Number 96), 95.

11. LeMay's incendiary raids: Wheeler, *Bombers Over Japan*, 169–171. B-29 mining campaign: United States Strategic Bombing Survey, *The Campaigns of the Pacific War*, 382–387.

12. Combustibility of Tokyo: Toll, *Pacific Crucible*, 178. Kennett, *Strategic Bombing*, 164.

13. Leaflets and eroding Japanese civilian morale: Kozak, *LeMay*, 218–225. Cf. O'Brien, *How the War Was Won*, 472–474. "War criminal": Rhodes, *Dark Sun*, 20–21.

14. On Japanese observations of B-29 raids: Okumiya and Horikoshi, *Zero!*: 308–309, 334–335.

15. LeMay's assessment of the raids: LeMay and Kantor, *Mission with LeMay*, 388. Cf. "Air-Power Philosophers in the Modern Era," in Boyne, *Influence of Air Power*, 354–357.

16. German disillusionment with the effectiveness of V-weapons: Calvocoressi, Wint, and Pritchard, *Total War*, 673–674.

17. Widely different numbers about V-weapons productions and launchings, and the nature of the V-weapons' navigation: Overy, *Bombing War*, 121–125; Neufeld, *The Rocket and the Reich*, 273–274. The V-1 was also officially known as FZG (*Flakzielgerät* ["flak-aiming device"])-76 (Fieseler Fi 103), and the V-2 more loosely as *Aggregat* 4.

18. Gunston, *Rockets & Missiles*, 46–47. See Rosenau, *Special Operations Forces*, 29–34.

19. Allied efforts to destroy the V-weapons, and differences between the V-1 and V-2: in Sunderman, ed., *World War II in the Air: Europe*, 306–317.

20. On English fears of V-weapons: Campbell, *Target London*; Gunston, *Rockets & Missiles*, 48–49. For the quotation, see S.N. Behrman, "The Suspended Drawing Room," *The New Yorker Book of War Pieces*, 421.

21. V-weapons: Miller, *Masters of the Air*, 297–304, 481. V-2: Neufeld, *The Rocket and the Reich*, 267–280; Baker, *Rocket*, 37–64. Buckley, *Air Power*, 142–143, on the USSBS analysis of the costs of the V-weapons program for Germany. Morale at OKW: Warlimont, *Inside Hitler's Headquarters*, 403. Man-hours for various Reich weapons, especially V-2 versus Fw 190: O'Brien, *How the War Was Won*, 29.

22. Reischauer, *Japan*, 50–51.

23. The official Japanese name for kamikaze was "special attack unit" (*okubetsu Kōgekitai*).

24. Kamikaze sorties, losses, and hits on targets: Zaloga, *Kamikaze*, 12–13.

25. Zeros made up 79 percent of all kamikaze sorties: Okumiya and Horikoshi, *Zero!*, 276–277.

26. Roberts, *Storm of War*, 565.

27. Buckley, *Air Power*, 138–169, on the German air war. Mustang: Kennedy, *Engineers of Victory*, 118–125; O'Brien, *How the War Was Won*, 320–322. Overy, *Interrogations*, 349.

28. Van Creveld, *Age of Airpower*, 113–121.

29. Buckley, *Air Power*, 138–145, 181–186, on air power in the European and Japanese theaters. Cf. also, ibid. 19 and 189–191.

30. Misplaced investments in jet fighters and rockets: Wilmot, *Struggle for Europe*, 660–661.

31. Overy, *Bombing War*, 213–216.

32. C-47: Herman, *Freedom's Forge*, 20, 227, 203–205. Goering's crackpot ideas: Speer, *Inside the Third Reich*, 224–225.

33. Sea Eagles: Tillman, *Clash of the Carriers*, 111–112.

34. American fighter success: Allan R. Millett, "The United States Armed Forces in the Second World War," in Millett and Murray, eds., *Military Effectiveness*, Vol. 3, 80–83. Consequences of losing carrier pilots: Okumiya and Horikoshi, *Zero!*, 115–116.

35. See the comments of the veteran naval pilot Masatake Okumiya and the designer of the *Zero* Jiro Horikoshi: *Zero!*, 186. Health care and sanitation on Allied versus Axis air bases: 186–187. Overy, *Bombing War*, 96–97.

36. Mellenthin, *Panzer Battles*, 275; O'Brien, *How the War Was Won*, 88; Buckley, *Air Power*, 149–153.

37. Cf. United States Strategic Bombing Survey, *Summary Report (European War)*. Efficacy of Allied bombing: Overy, *Bombing War*, 398–409; 450–467. Cf. Murray, *Luftwaffe*, 276–277 and 282–284.

38. Cost effectiveness of bombing and air defense: Murray, *War, Strategy, and Military Effectiveness*, 231–264. Cf. Overy, *Bombing War*, 186–196. Conclusions of the strategic bombing survey of the Allied European campaign is accessed at http://www.anesi.com./ussbs02.htm (p. 17).

# Part Three. Water

1. Mahan, *The Influence of Sea Power Upon History, 1660–1783*, 3.

### Chapter 7
### Ships and Strategies

1. *Wilhelm Gustloff*: Prince, *Death in the Baltic*, 35–36; cf. Hastings, *Armageddon*, 285–288.

2. Ancient sea battles: Strauss, *Battle of Salamis*; G.K. Tipps, "The Battle of Ecnomus," *Historia: Zeitschrift für Alte Geschichte* 34 (1985), 432–465. Lepanto: Hanson, *Carnage and Culture*, 233–275. Fatalities listed by service: Ellis, *World War II*, 254 (Table 52). Casualty figures: see Chandler, *Campaigns of Napoleon*, 936; Glantz and House, *Armageddon in Stalingrad*, 714–718.

3. On the HMS *Hood*: Norman, *HMS* Hood, 129–141. Compare other single-ship losses during World War II: (*Taiho*) (http://www.combinedfleet .com/Taiho.htm); USS *Indianapolis* (CA-35) (http://www.ussindianapolis .org/crew.htm).

4. Evans and Peattie, *Kaigun*, 243–245.

5. Drury and Clavin, *Halsey's Typhoon,* 297–307. Halsey's occasional blunders: Murfett, *Naval Warfare 1919–1945*, 490. Cf. the Navy's report from the Bureau of Naval Personnel, Washington DC, April 18, 1947 (http://www.history.navy.mil/library/online/aviation_fatal.htm).

6. Tiger I's cost about 250,000 Reichmarks; the *Bismarck* about 200 million RM. Hitler's anger at naval costs: Cameron and Stevens, eds., *Hitler's Table Talk*, 27 (August 10–11, 1941, night).

7. Limitations of sea power: Kennedy, "The Influence and Limitations of Sea Power," *International History Review* 10 (1988), 2–17; and the same author's *Rise and Fall of British Naval Mastery*, 7–8, 18, 169, and (for World War II) 312. Cf. in general Corbett, *Some Principles of Maritime Strategy*, and Widen, *Theorist of Maritime Strategy*, 123–124. Rise of early Greek sea power: Casson, *The Ancient Mariners*, 33–43, 75–79. Sparta and Athens: see Hanson, *War Like No Other*, 271–287.

8. Venice serves as an example of a naturally poor state made rich by its maritime empire: Lane, *Venice: A Maritime Republic*, passim; Crowley, *City of Fortune*, 276–289.

9. Political utility of sea power (particularly the "theory of suasion"): Luttwak, *Political Uses of Sea Power*, 71–72; Walker, "Sea Power and the Law of the Sea: The Need for a Contextual Approach," *Ocean Development & International Law* 7 (1979), 299–326.

10. On US battleship policy: O'Connell, *Sacred Vessels*, 304–306. Genda's contempt: Prange, *At Dawn We Slept*, 24–25. See comments of Vice Admiral Inoue (quoted in Asada, *From Mahan to Pearl Harbor*, 184–185). Cf. Howarth, *Fighting Ships of the Rising Sun*, 211–219. Sinking of majestic battleships: Ireland, *Jane's Naval History of World War II*, 232–251. Again, Hitler's comments on battleships: Cameron and Stevens, eds., *Hitler's Table Talk*, 708 (June 19, 1943, at table). Japanese concept of building super-battleships: Evans and Peattie, *Kaigun*, 382–383. Oil: Alessio Patalano, "Feigning Grand Strategy: Japan, 1937–1945," in Ferris and Mawdsley, eds., *The Cambridge History of The Second World War*, Vol. I: *Fighting the War*, 179.

11. Venetian Arsenal: Lane, *Venice: A Maritime Republic*, 361–364. Athenian naval superiority: Thucydides 2.62.2; also Morrison, Coates, and Rankov, *The Athenian Trireme*, 62, 94–95, 114–118; Hale, *Lords of the Sea*, xxiv–xxv, 126–128.

12. Axis and Allied battleship construction: O'Connell, *Sacred Vessels*, 290–307; Rose, *Power at Sea*, Vol. 2, 26–30; Murfett, *Naval Warfare 1919–1945*, 27–34.

13. Hitler's naval arms race: Cameron and Stevens, eds., *Hitler's Table Talk*, 27 (August 10–11, 1941). Cf. Hinsley, *Hitler's Strategy*, 1–13, 61–62, 86–89.

14. Naval considerations and Hitler's decision to declare war on the United States: Doenitz, *Memoirs*, 195–224. Cf. Shirer, *Rise and Fall*, 757 (quoting Shulman, *Defeat in the West*, 50).

15. Germans had a smaller fleet in comparison to the British in 1939 than they did in 1914: Showell, *German Navy Handbook*, 10–15. Anglo-German Naval Agreement (May 18, 1935): Holger H. Herwig, "The Failure of German Sea Power," *International History Review* 10.1 (1988), 68–105.

16. Richard D. Fisher, Jr., "Reflections on China's Military Trajectory and the US Pivot," in Chow, ed., *US Strategic Pivot*, 207–225; cf. Laird, Timperlake, and Weitz, *Rebuilding American Military Power in the Pacific*.

17. German naval strategy at the beginning of the war: Keegan, *Price of Admiralty*, 220–221.

18. Napoleon's lack of naval prowess: Roberts, *Napoleon*, 57. A more favorable estimation of his strategy: Chandler, *Campaigns of Napoleon*, 324. Prewar pessimism of the German Navy: Murray, *Change in the European Balance of Power*, 45–47.

19. Weinberg, *World at Arms*, 70. German naval strategy, Z Plan, and the aim of Hitler's shipbuilding program: Blair, *Hitler's U-Boat War*, Vol. 1: *The Hunters 1939–1942*, 29–49; Miller, *War at Sea*, 29–34.

20. For details of the Battle of Tsushima: Pleshakov, *The Tsar's Last Armada*, 267–286.

21. Comparative Pacific fleets at the end of 1941: Evans and Peattie, *Kaigun*, 353–390, especially Fig. 10-1 (355) and Table 10-3 (365). Cf. Evans, ed., *Japanese Navy*, 5–6. Lack of American preparedness: Morton, *Strategy and Command*, 137–139. Praise of the genius of the Pearl Harbor attack: Calvocoressi, Wint, and Pritchard, *Total War*, 958–959.

22. Okumiya and Horikoshi, *Zero!*, 118–119. Japan's early achievement: Alessio Patalano, "Feigning Grand Strategy: Japan, 1937–1945," in Ferris and Mawdsley, eds., *The Cambridge History of the Second World War*, Vol. I: *Fighting the War*, 181. Paine, *The Wars for Asia*, 188.

23. Cf. Loxton and Coulthard-Clark, *The Shame of Savo*, 254–270.

24. Prewar fleet: Zimm, *Attack on Pearl Harbor*, 394–400 (which lists the ships in Pearl Harbor and vicinity on the day of the attack.); cf. also 33–35.

25. Japanese failure to exploit fully tactical victories: Evans and Peattie, *Kaigun*, 494–495. The *Zuikaku* had been replenished with planes from the *Shokaku*: Calvocoressi, Wint, and Pritchard, *Total War*, 1056.

26. Shortage of trained Japanese carrier pilots: Potter, *Yamamoto*, 163–164; Polmar, *Aircraft Carriers*, 506–507. For end-of-the-war comparisons

of relative American and Japanese naval strength: Evans and Peattie, *Kaigun*, Table 10-4 (366) and Fig. 10-2 (367).

27. Problems of Japan even reaching Pearl Harbor: Evans, ed., *Japanese Navy*, 8–10.

28. Prewar flawed Japanese strategic assumptions: Evans and Peattie, *Kaigun*, 447–486. The Long Lance: Dull, *Imperial Japanese Navy*, 60–61; Evans and Peattie, *Kaigun*, 266–272.

29. Italian naval inferiority in 1935–1936 in relation to the British Navy: Mallett, *Italian Navy and Fascist Expansionism*, 54–56. Mussolini and the Anglo-French back down over Abyssinia: Knox, *Mussolini Unleashed*, 33; Greene and Massignani, *Naval War in the Mediterranean*, 10–19. Mussolini's "wait and see" doctrine: John Gooch, "Mussolini's Strategy, 1939–1943," in Ferris and Mawdsley, eds., *The Cambridge History of the Second World War*, Vol. I: *Fighting the War*, 135–137.

30. Disparities between the Italians and British at sea: Boyne, *Clash of Titans*, 45–51.

31. Ship-to-ship British-Italian comparisons: Bragadin, *Italian Navy*, 8. (See also the statistics of ship losses for both belligerents on 359–364.)

32. Regia Marina's defensive strategies: Salerno, *Vital Crossroads*, 61–62, 66–67, 86–90, 132–134, 190–191, 209–210. And cf. Hattendorf, ed., *Naval Strategy and Policy in the Mediterranean*, 108–146.

33. See worries about America in Ciano, *Diary*, 515 (April 29, 30–May 1, 2, 1942).

34. End of Italian fleet as a combat force: Sadkovich, *Italian Navy in World War II*, 328–329.

35. For some statistics of British losses, see http://www.naval -history.net/WW2aBritishLosses10tables.htm. And on World War I: https://ia800502.us.archive.org/23/items/statisticsofmili00grea/statistics ofmili00grea.pdf.

Cf. American naval manpower losses: https://www.history.navy.mil /research/library/online-reading-room/title-list-alphabetically/u/us -navy-personnel-in-world-war-ii-service-and-casualty-statistics.html. If escort carriers are included in the aggregate carrier losses, then the Americans lost a total of more aircraft carriers. See also http://www.navsource .org/Naval/losses.htm#ca were greater.

36. British grand naval strategy at the war's outset: Gibbs, *Grand Strategy*, 420–436.

37. US Pacific Fleet and Germany-first policy: James Kurth, "The U.S. Navy in World War II," *Foreign Policy Research Institute FootNotes* Vol. 14, No. 24 (September 2009), and available at: http://www.fpri.org /articles/2009/09/us-navy-world-war-ii. Cf. Dennis Showalter, "Global Yet Not Total: The U.S. War Effort and Its Consequences," in Chickering, Förster, and Greiner, eds., *A World at Total War*, 110–111.

38. Synopses of US naval strategy and War Plan Orange: Miller, *War Plan Orange*, 347–370.

39. US Atlantic fleet's efforts against the U-boat threat: Morison, *History of United States Naval Operations*, Vol. 1: *The Battle of the Atlantic, September 1939–1943*, 400–409.

40. American insight in building carriers: O'Connell, *Sacred Vessels*, 308–309, Cf. Williamson Murray, "US Naval Strategy and Japan," in Murray and Sinnreich, eds., *Successful Strategies*, 296–297. And on the contribution of Carl Vinson, see Cook, *Carl Vinson: Patriarch of the Armed Forces*, 78–153; Jones, *WWII*, 102. American naval buildup: Thomas, *Sea of Thunder*, 108–110, 151–152. Stalin's view of Allied superior production: Shtemenko, *The Last Six Months*, 423–425.

41. Submarine construction and constant improvement during the war: Fontenoy, *Submarines*, 23–38.

42. Battleship and heavy cruiser support of amphibious landings: Barbara Brooks Tomblin, "Naval Gunfire Support in Operation Neptune: A Reexamination," Chapter Six in Piehler and Pash, eds., *The United States and the Second World War*, 150–215. Cf. On D-Day bombardments: Kennedy, *Engineers of Victory*, 253, 256, 264.

43. Strategies behind Soviet naval construction and strategy: Rohwer and Monakov, *Stalin's Ocean-Going Fleet*, 117–121. Cf. Mark Harrison, "The Volume of Soviet Munitions Output, 1937–1945: A Reevaluation," *Journal of Economic History* 50.3 (1990), 569–589.

44. See in general on the Soviet fleet, and the German view of naval strategy in the Baltic and Black Seas: Ruge, *Soviets as Naval Opponents*. Cf. Boyne, *Clash of Titans*, 349–351. Lend-Lease through Vladivostok: Weeks, *Russia's Life-Saver: Lend-Lease Aid to the U.S.S.R.*, 2–3.

45. Soviet prewar and wartime naval grand strategy: Rohwer and Monakov, *Stalin's Ocean-Going Fleet*, 20–24, 41–42, 43–45, 77–85, 117–119.

46. On battleship gunnery in general: Campbell, *Naval Weapons of World War Two*.

47. Battleship romance: O'Connell, *Sacred Vessels*, 277–316.

48. Italy never finished its two carriers *Aquila* and *Sparviero*: Bragadin, *Italian Navy*, 98–99 and 346. On July 12, 2006, the Cypriot research vessel *RV St. Barbara* discovered the wreck of *Graf Zeppelin* 55 kilometers off the northern coastline of Poland. On *Graf Zeppelin*: Showell, *German Navy Handbook 1939–1945*, 176.

49. Listing of the specifications and dimensions of individual battleships and carriers: Spilling, ed., *Weapons of War: Battleships and Aircraft Carriers*, passim. Relative costs of carriers vs. battleships: see the text of "The Staggering Burden of Armament," *A League of Nations* 4.2 (April 1921), 245, 251–253. Doenitz vs. Raeder: Speer, *Spandau*, 120.

50. Poirier, "Results of German and American Submarine Campaigns" (Appendix I). Crew losses on both sides and merchant marine deaths: White, *Bitter Ocean*, 2–6; cf. also 289–298.

51. US submarines against Japanese targets: Paine, *Wars for Asia*, 195–196. Cf. also, ibid., 218–219 for additional statistics related to shipping losses.

52. Classical definition of a destroyer by displacement and armament: Friedman, *U.S. Destroyers*, 22–24. Washington Naval Limitation Treaty and subsequent agreements in London: John H. Maurer, "Arms Control and the Washington Conference," in Goldstein and Maurer, eds., *The Washington Conference, 1921–22: Naval Rivalry, East Asian Stability and the Road to Pearl Harbor*, 267–292. Cf. Williamson Murray, "US Naval Strategy and Japan," in Murray and Sinnreich, eds., *Successful Strategies*, 289–291.

53. French destroyers of *Le Fantasque*–class: Whitley, *Destroyers of World War II*, 42–44. The destroyer's ultimate wartime incarnation was perhaps the American *Gearing* class that attained nearly 400 feet in length, with displacement of over 2,600 tons, and six 5-inch guns—but was now equipped with an assortment of anti-aircraft batteries, torpedo tubes, and depth-charge throwers. The biggest and most lethal of the war's destroyers—those of the Japanese *Akizuki*-class—were oversized at 2,700 tons displacement with eight 3.9-inch anti-aircraft guns in four power-operated turrets, along with four 24-inch torpedo tubes. On the American *Gearing* class, see Friedman, *U.S. Destroyers*, 129–130, 473–474; Whitley, *Destroyers of World War II*, 292–295. For the Japanese *Akizuki*-class destroyers, see Evans and Peattie, *Kaigun*, 386; Whitley, *Destroyers of World War II*, 204–205.

54. Destroyer losses: Tucker, ed., *World War II at Sea*, 233–234.

## Chapter 8
### From the Atlantic to the Mediterranean

1. German U-boats in World War I: Halpern, *A Naval History of World War I*, 287–380. Rivalry between Doenitz and Raeder and ramifications to German naval strategies: Bird, *Erich Raeder*, 199–201, 221–222.

2. On the relative size, nature, and advantages of the German and British fleets at the war's outset: Kennedy, *Rise and Fall of British Naval Mastery*, 299–303. On how the war quickly clarified British prewar advantages, see Murray, *Change in the European Balance of Power*, 46 (only 26 U-boats in September were ready for long patrols across the Atlantic).

3. Number of naval and merchant vessels produced respectively by the Axis and Allies from 1939 to 1945: Ellis, *World War II*, 280 (Table 95). The British and Americans out-built the Germans, Italians, and Japanese in every category of warship (36 fleet carriers vs. 16 carriers of all classes; 13 vs. 7 battleships; 80 vs. 17 cruisers; 589 vs. 115 destroyers)—except one.

The Germans deployed nearly twice the number of U-boats as did the British, Americans, and Soviets combined (over 1,100 vs. 568).

4. Cf. Blair, *Hitler's U-boat War,* Vol. I: *The Hunters,* 148–152.

5. Lack of naval coordination between the Axis powers: Calvocoressi, Wint, and Pritchard, *Total War,* 964. Cf. Gerhard L. Weinberg, "World War II," Chapter 16 in Chickering, Showalter, and Van de Ven, eds., *The Cambridge History of War,* Vol. IV: *War and the Modern World,* 379 (citing his entry "Axis Strategy and Co-operation," in Dear and Foot, eds., *The Oxford Companion to World War II,* 97–99). Cf. Issraeljan and Kutakov, *Diplomacy of Aggression,* 184–186, for the Soviet perspective. On World War II coalitions, see in general Greenhalgh, *Victory through Coalition.*

6. British ability to combat the U-boat fleet in 1939: Murfett, *Naval Warfare 1919–1945,* 52. Cf. Williamson, *Kriegsmarine U-boats 1939–45,* 6–35, for a survey of German submarine types.

7. On the destroyer deal: Black, *Roosevelt,* 605–606, 620–623.

8. U-boat numbers in 1939: Blair, *Hitler's U-boat War,* Vol. I: *The Hunters,* 43–47 (including on 43, Plate 4: The Prewar German U-boat Buildup June 1935-September 1939), and 101–104.

9. U-boat sinkings in the North Atlantic: Blair, *Hitler's U-boat War,* Vol. I: *The Hunters,* 709–725 (Appendix 2: U-boat Patrols to the North Pacific August 1939–August 1942).

10. On the number and nature of the new U-boat bases in France, and their effect on the volatile Battle of the Atlantic, see Showell, *Hitler's U-Boat Bases,* 85–126 and Bradham, *Hitler's U-Boat Fortresses,* 19–28. Total British tonnage sunk by German Condors: Pimlott, *Luftwaffe: The Illustrated History of the German Air Force,* 52.

11. U-boat losses versus tonnage sunk during the last months of "Happy Time": Boyne, *Clash of Titans,* 93–94.

12. *Bismarck*: Boyne, *Clash of Titans,* 52–61; Bercuson and Herwig, *Destruction of the Bismarck*; and cf. in general Rhys-Jones, *Loss of the Bismarck*; Shirer, *Sinking of the Bismarck.*

13. Enigma codes: Sebag-Montefiore, *Enigma: The Battle for the Code,* 132–146.

14. King and convoy escorts: Murfett, *Naval Warfare 1919–1945,* 51. Cf. Borneman, *The Admirals,* 26–40.

15. Operation Drumbeat (*Paukenschlag*): Gannon, *Operation Drumbeat*; Blair, *Hitler's U-Boat War,* Vol. 1: *The Hunters 1939–1942,* 440–442; 460–466. On the toll of 1942, see O'Brien, *How the War Was Won,* 231–232.

16. Deploying long-range four-engine bombers against U-boats: Boyne, *Clash of Titans,* 102–110; Kennedy, *Engineers of Victory,* 5–73.

17. O'Brien, *How the War Was Won,* 246–248.

18. Naval communications and the finds from U-boat 559: Kahn, *Seizing the Enigma,* 218–227. Admiral Horton's new tactics: Chalmers, *Max Horton and the Western Approaches,* 158ff.

19. Convoy ONS 5: see in general Seth, *Fiercest Battle*; Gannon, *Black May*, 115–240. US merchant ship construction: (accessed March 18, 2016): http://web.archive.org/web/20061023011524/http://www.colton company.com/shipbldg/ussbldrs/wwii/merchantsbldg.htm.

20. U-boat losses: Niestlé, *German U-Boat Losses*, 201–202 (Appendix 2: Tabular Monthly Overview on the Causes of U-boat Losses). Cost/benefit analyses of relative losses, cf. again, Poirier, "Results of German and American Submarine Campaigns" (Appendix I). For Doenitz's confessions of defeat, see Doenitz, *Memoirs*, 341.

21. Failed British Aegean campaign: Bell, *Churchill and Sea Power*, 59–75, 201–212. Cf. Howard, *Mediterranean Strategy in the Second World War*, 10–12.

22. Relative initial naval strength in the Mediterranean Sea: Sadkovich, *Italian Navy in World War II*, 1–44.

23. Battle of Taranto: Greene and Massignani, *Naval War in the Mediterranean*, 101–114.

24. Battles off Greek territory: Greene and Massignani, *Naval War in the Mediterranean*, 141–173.

25. Axis strategies to win the Mediterranean: Sadkovich, *Italian Navy in World War II*, 345–349. Cf. Cameron and Stevens, eds., *Hitler's Table Talk*, 479 (May 13, 1942). Franco and Gibraltar: Calvocoressi, Wint, and Pritchard, *Total War*, 165–166.

26. U-boat losses in the Mediterranean: Paterson, *U-Boats in the Mediterranean 1941–1944*, 19.

27. Mussolini's imperial dreams: Bosworth, *Mussolini*, 337–338.


Chapter 9
A Vast Ocean


1. Allied naval disaster at the first Battle of the Java Sea: Morison, *History of United States Naval Operations*, Vol. 3: *The Rising Sun in the Pacific, 1931–April 1942*, 292–380. Relative strength of the opposing navies on December 7, 1941: Morison, *History of United States Naval Operations*, Vol. 3: *The Rising Sun in the Pacific, 1931–April 1942*, 58.

2. Anglo-American rivalries and disagreements over naval operations in the Pacific: Bell, *Churchill and Sea Power*, 236–253.

3. Marines in Europe and North Africa: in general, Edwards, *A Different War*.

4. The huge American battleship fleet: Friedman, *U.S. Battleships*, 345–387.

5. Escort carriers: Y'Blood, *Little Giants*. Cf. Elliot, *Allied Escort Ships*, 451–479. See in general, Franklin, *Buckley-Class*; Cross, *Shepherds of the Sea*.

6. Respective losses of the Japanese first- and second-wave attacks ("29 aircraft with their crews, and five sunken midget submarines"), and

total US losses ("2,403 people dead or dying and another 1,178 wounded"): Zimm, *Attack on Pearl Harbor*, 151–172.

7. Admiral Nagumo cited various reasons why he did not order further attacks: Prange, *At Dawn We Slept*, 544–548. Japanese strategic thinking: Morison, *History of United States Naval Operations*, Vol. 3: *The Rising Sun in the Pacific, 1931–April 1942*, 48–79. Japanese content with the destruction of US battleships: O'Connell, *Sacred Vessels*, 315.

8. British and American naval losses, between the attack on Pearl Harbor and the Battle of the Coral Sea: Boyne, *Clash of Titans*, 143–169.

9. How the *Yorktown* was made ready for Midway, while the *Shokaku* and *Zuikaku*, with less damage, were not: Hanson, *Carnage and Culture*, 373–375; Frank and Harrington, *Rendezvous at Midway*, 135–137, 143–146.

10. For long descriptions of both the battles at Coral Sea and Midway: Morison, *History of United States Naval Operations*, Vol. 4: *Coral Sea, Midway and Submarine Actions, May 1942–August 1942*, 21–64, 69–159.

11. Lapses of Yamamoto at Midway: Dull, *Imperial Japanese Navy*, 166–167.

12. Japanese realizations after the defeat at Midway: Lord, *Incredible Victory*, 284–286; Fuchida and Okumiya, *Midway: The Battle That Doomed Japan*, 260–268.

13. Status of US carrier forces by the end of 1942 and early 1943: Polmar, *Aircraft Carriers*, 298–309, 355. Criticism of timidity in the use of fleet carriers during 1942–43: Morton, *Strategy and Command*, 354–356.

14. Cf. the summaries of Hornfischer, *Neptune's Inferno*, 409–430. Savo Island: Loxton and Coulthard-Clark, *The Shame of Savo*, 254–270.

15. Leyte: Thomas, *Sea of Thunder*, 151–322; cf. Morison, *History of United States Naval Operations*, Vol. 12: *Leyte, June 1944–January 1945*.

16. The toll from American subs: Beach, *Submarine!*, 21. US submarine cost-benefit ratios: Poirier, "Results of the American Pacific Submarine Campaign." Morison, *History of United States Naval Operations*, Vol. 12: *Leyte, June 1944–January 1945*, 398–414.

# Part 4. Earth

1. *On Infantry*, 167.

## Chapter 10
## The Primacy of Infantry

1. Classical views of infantry supremacy: Hanson, *Carnage and Culture*, 158–162; cf. Keegan, *History of Warfare*, 282–298.

2. Changing ideas of ground troops in modern warfare: Lt. Col. L. Freeman, "Can the Marines Survive?," *Foreign Policy*, March 26, 2013. Western public's trust in ground troops: "Obama's Request for Military Action against ISIS Receives Majority Support . . . Many Americans Say Boots on the Ground Are Needed" (accessed March 23, 2015), at http://maristpoll.marist.edu/wp-content/misc/usapolls/us150211 /Complete%20NBC%20News%20Marist%20Poll_National_February %202015.pdf. Cf. in general, Emile Simpson, *War From the Ground Up: Twenty-First Century Combat as Politics*. On ageless infantry superiority: Field-Marshal Viscount Wavell, "In Praise of Infantry," *The Times* (London, England), Thursday, April 19, 1945, p. 5.

3. Casualties at Midway: Lundstrom, *Black Shoe Carrier Admiral*, 296–297; Hone, ed., *Battle of Midway*, 192. Kursk: Glantz and House, *Battle of Kursk*, 336–346 (Appendix C: Comparative Strengths and Losses in the Battle of Kursk). Cf. Goralski, *World War II Almanac*, 424–428.

4. New weapons of World War II: Hogg, *Encyclopedia of Infantry Weapons*, 6. US divisions and firepower: Mansoor, *GI Offensive in Europe*, 38–39; 257–262, cf. 149. Patton's praise of the M1: Duff, *M1 Garand*, 107. Cf. Patton, *War As I Knew It*, 262; Kindsvatter, *American Soldiers*, 225. And on the Springfield: Coffman, *The Regulars*, 405. On 47 billion rounds: https://www .nraila.org/articles/20030520/the-great-arsenal-of-democracy.

5. Hand-held semi-automatic and machine guns: Hogg, *Encyclopedia of Infantry Weapons*. Cf. McNab, *German Automatic Rifles 1941–45*, 26–29, 53–62.

6. Armor versus infantryman's weapons: Weigley, *History of the United States Army*, 469–470. See also Walker, *Bracketing the Enemy*, 8–28.

7. On the loads of World War II infantry: Orr, "History of the Soldier's Load," *Australian Army Journal*, Vol. VII, No. 2 (2010), 67–88.

8. M-1 helmet (accompanied by excellent photographs): Oosterman, *M-1 Helmet*; and cf. Reynosa, *M-1 Helmet*.

9. Number of American divisions: Weigley, *History of United States Army*, 439.

10. The invasion of France versus Operation Barbarossa: Evans, *Third Reich at War*, 122–127 (France) and 160–166 (Soviet Union). Cf. Kershaw (cited by Evans, *op. cit.*, 160 n. 123), *Hitler, 1936–45: Nemesis*, 305. See also Ziemke and Bauer, *Moscow to Stalingrad*, 7–8.

11. Warlimont, *Inside Hitler's Headquarters*, 496.

12. Patriotism and the homeland: Viroli, *For Love of Country*, 44–51. Viroli quotes Lipsius's *De Constantia* (1584) for his discussion of death for the fatherland. In the classical Greek context, see Hanson, *Other Greeks*, 280–287.

13. Melos, 416 BC: Thucydides 5.84–116.

14. Prewar expectations about airborne troops: Stanley, *Evolution of Airborne Operations*, 8–33; and the German use of parachute drops: 34–60.

15. Initial German success and confidence in airborne units: Fuller, *Second World War*, 113–114.

16. British and German orders of battle on Crete: Appendix B of Beevor, *Crete 1941*, 354–359. The drop and ensuing chaotic battle: ibid., 104–120.

17. Allied airborne experience in Sicily: D'Este, *Bitter Victory*, 307–309, 378–379. American paratroopers' reputation, see Gavin, *On to Berlin*, 32.

18. Market-Garden disaster: in general Ryan, *A Bridge Too Far*; Middlebrook, *Arnhem 1944*, 436–444.

19. Operation Varsity and its controversy, Wright, *The Last Drop*, 287–329.


## Chapter 11
## Soldiers and Armies


1. Assessing infantry capability: Van Creveld, *Fighting Power*, 4–6.

2. Earl F. Ziemke, "Military Effectiveness in the Second World War," in Millett and Murray, eds., *Military Effectiveness*, Vol. 3, 286. American combat divisions: Doubler, *Closing with the Enemy*, 235–236. U.S. Army in Europe, see Weigley, *Eisenhower's Lieutenants*, 12–16, 727.

3. Doubler, *Closing with the Enemy*, 235–236, 243–251.

4. US army numbers: Weigley, *History of United States Army*, 568–569. Prewar US Army: see ibid., 419–421; cf. also 438–439. Similar size of the Italian and American armies: MacGregor Knox, "The Italian Armed Forces, 1940–3," in Millett and Murray, eds., *Military Effectiveness*, Vol. 3, 141–142.

5. June 6 operations: Goralski, *World War II Almanac*, 553–559.

6. "Combat fatigue" or "battle fatigue": Wilbur J. Scott, "PTSD in DSM-III: A Case in the Politics of Diagnosis and Disease," *Social Problems* 37.3 (1990), 296–297. Rommel's view: Liddell Hart, ed., *Rommel Papers*, 407.

7. Matheny, *Carrying the War to the Enemy*, 264.

8. Hastings, *Armageddon*, 68–9. German kill ratios in Russia: Dupuy, *A Genius for War*, 290–299; cf. 79–80.

9. Luttwak, *Grand Strategy of the Roman Empire*, 40–46. Cf. the discipline of Roman soldiers: Stephan G. Chrissanthos, "Keeping Military Discipline," in Campbell and Tritle, eds., *Oxford Handbook of Warfare in the Classical World*, 320–327.

10. Patton's colorful pre-battle speeches: D'Este, *Patton: A Genius for War*, 602–605, 622–624; Hanson, *Soul of Battle*, 351–366, 461 n. 105. Cf. Yellin, *Battle Exhortation*, 63–65.

11. American organizational genius: Cline, *Washington Command Post* (available online at: http://www.history.army.mil/html/books/001/1–2 /CMH_Pub_1–2.pdf).

12. American and Allied combined arms operations: O'Brien, *How the War Was Won*, 374–429. Cf. also Ehlers, *Mediterranean Air War*, 397–406. On FDR and a second front: Black, *Roosevelt*, 741–746. German weakness in logistics and intelligence: Condell and Zabecki, eds., *German Art of War*, 8–9.

13. Army participation in the Pacific: C. Kingseed, "The Pacific War: The U.S. Army's Forgotten Theater of World War II," *Army Magazine*, 63.4 (April 2013), 52–53.

14. Hew Strachan, "Total War: The Conduct of the War, 1939–1945," in Chickering, Förster, and Greiner, eds., *A World at Total War*, 50–52.

15. US military global reach: Leighton, *Global Logistics and Strategy, 1940–1943*. Cf. Shrader, *U.S. Military Logistics, 1607–1991*. Britain: Morton, *Strategy and Command*, 80–81. Admiral King's complaints on resource allotments: 383–385. Europe-first strategies: Eisenhower, *Crusade in Europe*, 27.

16. Quality of the American army's weapons: Allan R. Millett, "The United States Armed Forces in the Second World War," in Millett and Murray, eds., *Military Effectiveness*, Vol. 3, 60–62. The dearth of trucks in the German army: Cooper, *German Army*, 211–213.

17. American artillery: see Weigley, *History of United States Army*, 472–475. Americans' greater tendency to cut off offensive salients: Liddell Hart, *German Generals Talk*, 258. M1 rifle and the genius of John Garland: Ezell, *Great Rifle Controversy*, 33–40.

18. Effectiveness of German infantry: Dupuy, *A Genius for War*, 232–236; Van Creveld, *Fighting Power* 5–9; cf. 13–14. Mishaps in entering Austria, see Murray, *Change in the European Balance of Power*, 141–154, esp. 143–149; H-class, 329. American kill ratios of German aircraft: Allan R. Millett, "The United States Armed Forces in the Second World War," in Millett and Murray, eds., *Military Effectiveness*, Vol. 3, 80. American military education: Schifferle, *America's School for War*, especially 36–61. See the criticisms of Van Creveld, *Fighting Power*, 59–60.

19. Warlimont, *Inside Hitler's Headquarters*, 73.

20. Atrocities committed during World War II: Christopher J. M. Safferling, "War Crimes in Europe," in Zeiler and DuBois, eds., *A Companion to World War II*, 929–944. Japanese treatment of Allied prisoners: Tanaka, *Hidden Horrors*, 70–78. Eastern Front and the conduct of German and Soviet troops: Kenneth Slepyan, "Battle Fronts and Home Fronts: The War in the East from Stalingrad to Berlin," in Zeiler and DuBois, eds., *A Companion to World War II*, 314, 321; Mark Edele and Michael Geyer, "States of Exception: The Nazi-Soviet War as a System of Violence, 1939–1945," in Fitzpatrick and Geyer, eds., *Beyond Totalitarianism: Stalinism and Nazism Compared*, 345–395; Snyder, *Bloodlands*, 119–154.

21. American Army in World War II: Van Creveld, *Fighting Power*, 94–95, 100–101, 124–125, 154–155. Psychiatric problems of American soldiers: Kindsvatter, *American Soldiers*, 158–172. American shooting of

prisoners: D'Este, *Patton*, 509–510, 700. Voracious appetites of Allied armies in Europe: Van Creveld, *Supplying War*, 206–226.

22. Great Depression and the GI: Kindsvatter, *American Soldiers*, 12–13. See Manchester, *Goodbye, Darkness*, 119–158, for the Depression-era mentality of the US Marines. Cf. Patton, *War As I Knew It*, 281.

23. Growth, reserves, and losses of the Soviet army: Dunn, *Hitler's Nemesis*, 22–29, 38–39; cf. 48–50. Cf. Glantz and House, *When Titans Clashed*, 291–307.

24. Eisenhower, *Crusade in Europe*, 467–468.

25. Remembrances of Unteroffizier Fritz Huebner: Luther, *Barbarossa Unleashed*, 265.

26. Luther, *Barbarossa Unleashed*, 608.

27. Importance of Anglo-American Lend-Lease: Glantz and House, *When Titans Clashed*, 285.

28. For Soviet Union tanks, see the tables in Harrison, *Soviet Planning in Peace and War, 1938–1945*, especially 250. Luftwaffe on the eve of Operation Barbarossa: Luther, *Barbarossa Unleashed*, 145–146. Red Army small arms: Chant, *Small Arms of World War II*, 82–95. Soviet tank, truck, artillery, and aircraft numbers: Dunn, *Hitler's Nemesis*, xvi-xix, 132–133, 148–150, 168–170, 177–178; Harrison, *Soviet Planning in Peace and War, 1938–1945*, 249–250.

29. Luther, *Barbarossa Unleashed*, 628.

30. For Stalin's purges of Soviet generals, see Deutscher, *Stalin*, 372–385, 425–426; Glantz and House, *When Titans Clashed*, 9–11. Soviet wartime economy: Mark Harrison, "The USSR and Total War: Why Didn't the Soviet Economy Collapse in 1942?" in Chickering, Förster, and Greiner, eds., *A World at Total War*, especially 155–157. Cf. Jeffrey Fear, "War of the Factories," in Geyer and Tooze, eds., *The Cambridge History of the Second World War*, Vol. III: *Total War: Economy, Society and Culture*, 109–110. See Dunn, *Hitler's Nemesis*, 43–50, 150–153. Soviet production achievements: Dunn, *Stalin's Keys to Victory*, 1–61.

31. British army strategic dilemmas: Roberts, *Storm of War*, 602–603. Percentages of army troops of the major combatants' total military strength: Earl F. Ziemke, "Military Effectiveness in the Second World War," in Millett and Murray, eds., *Military Effectiveness*, Vol. 3, 286.

32. British losses until El Alamein: Gwyer, *Grand Strategy*, Vol. III, Part I, 339–340. Fall of Singapore, the threat to Malta, the loss of Burma, the war in the Atlantic, and the defeat in North Africa: Baron Moran, *Churchill Taken from the Diaries of Lord Moran: The Struggle for Survival, 1940–1965*, 78–79.

33. Combat losses in the British army: Mellor, *Casualties and Medical Statistics*, 834–839. Total casualties—incorporating statistics from the Royal Navy and Royal Air Force as well—come to 264,443 killed, 41,327 missing, 277,077 wounded, and 172,592 prisoners of war.

34. Conservatism of British officers and sometimes mediocre weapons: Williamson Murray, "British Military Effectiveness in the Second World War," in Millett and Murray, eds., *Military Effectiveness*, Vol. 3, 113–116.

35. Alanbrooke's worry that Monty had gone too far: *War Diaries*, 638.

36. British efforts to dissuade Americans on particular strategies: Reynolds, *From World War to Cold War*, 121–133 ("Churchill and Allied Grand Strategy in Europe, 1944–1945: The Erosion of Influence").

37. Prussian-inspired emphasis on the force-multiplying effects of German combat power: Condell and Zabecki, eds., *German Art of War*, 18.

38. German institutional shortcomings: Condell and Zabecki eds., *German Art of War*, 9; Kaiser Wilhelm II's quote of November 1914: Lloyd, *Hundred Days*, 72.

39. Cf. Matheny, *Carrying the War to the Enemy*, 201. German army superiority: Van Creveld, *Fighting Power*, 6.

40. German armor during the Polish campaign: Cooper, *German Army*, 171–176. Invasion of Poland: Murray, *Change in the European Balance of Power*, 323, 325–326. Inferiority of the Mark I-III German tanks: Mosier, *Blitzkrieg Myth*, 45–50. 2nd Panzer Army: cf. Steiger, *Armour Tactics*, 49. Looted German vehicles and horse dependency: Jürgen E. Förster, "The Dynamics of *Volksgemeinschaft*: The Effectiveness of the German Military Establishment in the Second World War," in Millett and Murray, eds., *Military Effectiveness*, Vol. 3, 202–203; Phillips Payson O'Brien, "Logistics by Land and Air," in Ferris and Mawdsley, eds., *The Cambridge History of the Second World War*, Vol. I: *Fighting the War*, 623.

41. German reliance on horses during Operation Barbarossa: Di-Nardo, *Mechanized Juggernaut*, 33–54. Horses versus motor vehicles: Weinberg, "Some Myths of World War II," 717–718. See too Condell and Zabecki, eds., *German Art of War*, 3–7; Zabecki, *German 1918 Offensives*, 62–63, for the origins of *Weisungsführung* and *Auftragstaktik*. Exaggerations surrounding Blitzkrieg: Cooper, *German Army*, 23–24, 1189.

42. Overy, *Interrogations*, 249.

43. Halder's observations of Hitler: Warlimont, *Inside Hitler's Headquarters*, 95. Dunkirk folly: Karl-Heinz Frieser, "The War in the West, 1939–1940: An Unplanned Blitzkrieg," in Ferris and Mawdsley, eds., *The Cambridge History of the Second World War*, Vol. I: *Fighting the War*, 309–312. Arms of a German division: Haskew, *The Wehrmacht, 1935–1945*, 61–70. Limitations of the German army: see Dunn, *Hitler's Nemesis*, 23–24. Hitler's unstable leadership: von Mellenthin, *German Generals*, 29, 59. Relationship between OKW and OKH: Warlimont, *Inside Hitler's Headquarters*, 56–60.

44. Army inability to meet Hitler's demands: Jürgen E. Förster, "The Dynamics of *Volksgemeinschaft*: The Effectiveness of the German Military

Establishment in the Second World War," in Millett and Murray, eds., *Military Effectiveness*, Vol. 3, 186–187.

45. Limitations—and corruption—of German military leaders: Weinberg, "Some Myths of World War II," 705–706.

46. German army expansion and erosion of quality: Cooper, *German Army*, 275.

47. On the MG 42: Myrvang, *MG-34–MG-42: German Universal Machine Guns*; for the StG 44, see Senich, *German Assault Rifle*, 79–102.

48. Weinberg, "Some Myths of World War II," 705–706. "Commissar Order": Jacobsen, "The *Kommissarbefehl* and Mass Executions of Soviet Russian Prisoners of War," in Krausnick, Buchheim, Broszat, and Jacobsen, eds., *Anatomy of the SS State*, 522.

49. Organization of the Imperial Japanese Army: Drea, *Japan's Imperial Army*. 190–221. Militarists in Japanese government: see Hane and Perez, *Modern Japan*, 271–283.

50. Alvin D. Coox, "The Effectiveness of the Japanese Military Establishment in the Second World War," in Millett and Murray, eds., *Military Effectiveness*, Vol. 3, 8–9. Khalkhin Gol: Edgerton, *Warriors of the Rising Sun*, 239–242; Glantz and House, *When Titans Clashed*, 13–15. Cf. Calvocoressi, Wint, and Pritchard, *Total War*, 878–879.

51. Japanese-Soviet hostilities: Issraeljan and Kutakov, *Diplomacy of Aggression*, 147–186.

52. Strategic confusion of the Japanese army: Drea, *Japan's Imperial Army*, 146–162, 222–231, 256–257.

53. Japan's field generals: General Yamashita (Kiamichi Tachikawa, "General Yamashita and His Style of Leadership") and Lieutenant-General Mutaguchi (Kenichi Arakawa, "Japanese War Leadership in the Burma Theatre"), both in Bond and Tachikawa, eds., *British and Japanese Military Leadership in the Far Eastern War, 1941–1945*, 75–87, 105–122. On General Homma, see Toland, *Rising Sun*, 317–320.

54. Zealotry of Japanese infantry: see Alvin D. Coox, "The Effectiveness of the Japanese Military Establishment in the Second World War," in Millett and Murray, eds., *Military Effectiveness*, Vol. 3, 34–35, 38–39. On fatality ratios, cf. http://www.japanww2.com/wt14.htm. Sato quote: Butow, *Tojo and the Coming of the War*, 19.

55. Japanese army munitions: Forty, *Japanese Army Handbook, 1939–1945*, 113–158.

56. Size of the Italian army: Knox, *Hitler's Italian Allies*, 54–55.

57. Italian economy: Vera Zamagni, "Italy: How to Lose the War and Win the Peace," in Harrison, ed., *The Economics of World War II*, 177–223. Italian foreign policy: Peter Jackson, "Europe: the Failure of Diplomacy, 1933–1940," in Bosworth and Maiolo, eds., *The Cambridge History of the Second World War*, Vol. II: *Politics and Ideology*, 227–232.

58. Italy's military agenda: Knox, *Hitler's Italian Allies*, 170–174. Germany vs. Italy: Cloutier, *Regio Esercito*, 38–39.

59. Inadequate Italian weapons and equipment: Macgregor Knox, "The Italian Armed Forces, 1940–1943," in Millett and Murray, eds., *Military Effectiveness*, Vol. 3, 140, 154, 159–160.

60. Italian disaster in the Balkans: Knox, *Mussolini Unleashed*, 231–285, and cf. Koliopoulos and Veremis, *Greece: The Modern Sequel*, 291–292.

61. Italian losses in Russia: Jowett, *Italian Army*, 9–11; Cloutier, *Regio Esercito*, 97–166. See John Gooch, "Mussolini's Strategy, 1939–1943" in Ferris and Mawdsley, eds., *The Cambridge History of the Second World War*, Vol. I: *Fighting the War*, 150–153.

62. Italian ambiguity about fighting the Allies: MacGregor Knox, "The Italian Armed Forces, 1940–3," in Millett and Murray, eds., *Military Effectiveness*, Vol. 3, 170–172. See John Gooch, "Mussolini's Strategy, 1939–1943," in Ferris and Mawdsley, eds., *The Cambridge History of the Second World War*, Vol. I: *Fighting the War*, 157.

Chapter 12
The Western and Eastern Wars for the Continent

1. Strange French defeat and consequences: Calvocoressi, Wint, and Pritchard, *Total War*, 144–145. French rearmament: Goutard, *Battle of France*, 19–44. Superiority of French weapons: Mosier, *Blitzkrieg Myth*, 130–148. Hitler's sometimes moody expectation of a long war: Liddell Hart, *German Generals Talk*, 114–115.

2. Perverse admiration of the Soviet Union: Moorhouse, *Devils' Alliance*, 30–31. For Goering's comment, see Goebbels, *Goebbels Diaries, 1942–1943*, 263.

3. Alanbrooke, *War Diaries*, 20.

4. Lack of coordination between British and French forces: John C. Cairns, "Great Britain and the Fall of France: A Study in Allied Disunity," *Journal of Modern History* 27.4 (1955), 365–409. Comparative number of troops and tanks: see Cooper, *German Army*, 209–215. General von Thoma's views: Liddell Hart, *German Generals Talk*, 13, 95–96. For the quotation, see Bloch, *Strange Defeat*, 37. Jackson, *Fall of France*, 112–116, 222–227.

5. Comparative tanks, artillery, and infantry: Cooper, *German Army*, 214–215; Maurois, *Tragedy in France*, 106. For Foch: Recouly, *Foch: Le Vainqueur de la Guerre*, 121 ("*Mon centre cède, ma droite recule, situation excéllente, j'attaque*"). French arms and manpower: Jackson, *Fall of France*, 12–20.

6. German plan of attack: Cooper, *German Army*, 205–206.

7. Reasons for the French collapse: Cooper, *German Army*, 240–242; Jackson, *France: The Dark Years*, 118–126. Cf. Bloch, *Strange Defeat*, 48.

German institutional aggressiveness: Condell and Zabecki, eds., *German Art of War*, 18. Alan Brooke's negative view: Jackson and Bramall, *The Chiefs*, 185.

8. Poor German production of heavy trucks: Cooper, *German Army*, 212–214. Hitler's enormous prestige after the fall of France: Cooper, *German Army*, 244–245, Kershaw, *Hitler, 1936–45: Nemesis*, 300. Oil anxieties: Murray and Millett, *A War to Be Won*, 327–328.

9. German High Command's supposed worries over invading Russia after the fall of France: Cooper, *German Army*, 257. On the French irony: Martin S. Alexander, "French Grand Strategy and Defence Preparations," in Ferris and Mawdsley, eds., *The Cambridge History of the Second World War*, Vol. I: *Fighting the War*, 106.

10. Prior Soviet military mediocrity: John E. Jessup, "The Soviet Armed Forces in the Great Patriotic War, 1941–5," in Millett and Murray, eds., *Military Effectiveness*, Vol. 3, 256–276, especially 273. Multilateral nature of Hitler's invading force: Wendy Lower, "Axis Collaboration, Operation Barbarossa, and the Holocaust in Ukraine," in Kay, Rutherford, and Stahel, eds., *Nazi Policy on the Eastern Front, 1941*, 186–219, esp. 188–189. Hitler's increasing influence: Cooper, *German Army*, 181.

11. Clear warnings of the attack: Read and Fisher, *Deadly Embrace*, 632–639.

12. Hitler's arguments for invading Russia: Luther, *Barbarossa Unleashed*, 53–54; Wilmot, *Struggle for Europe*, 71; cf. also, 56–57. Goering's view: Hechler, *Goering and His Gang*, 499. Dire economic straits of the Third Reich by May 1941: Tooze, *Wages of Destruction*, 430–434.

13. German strategic objectives, and Halder's famous diary entry: Burdick and Jacobsen, eds., *Halder War Diary*, 446 (July 3, 1941). False sense of Soviet weakness: Reynolds, *From World War to Cold War*, 34–38. See further premature claims of victory in Murray and Millett, *A War to Be Won*, 83–84.

14. Tsar Alexander I is quoted in Ziemke and Bauer, *Moscow to Stalingrad*, 515, drawing on the memoirs of the French ambassador General Armand de Caulaincourt. On French arrogance, see also Chandler, *Campaigns of Napoleon*, 746–747.

15. General Wagner's various prognoses: Megargee, *War of Annihilation*, 101–102, 107–108. "Idiotic word": see the discussion in Ziemke and Bauer, *Moscow to Stalingrad*, 43.

16. Hitler's unwillingness to accept the growth in the size of the Red Army: Liddell Hart, *German Generals Talk*, 195. General Marcks's original visions of Operation Barbarossa: Cooper, *German Army*, 260–261. Hitler's apparent realistic lowering of expectations is quoted in Ziemke and Bauer, *Moscow to Stalingrad*, 43.

17. Relatively small areas of prior operations in Poland: Cooper, *German Army*, 173. Comparative German and Soviet military expenditures in

the period 1939–1941: Ziemke and Bauer, *Moscow to Stalingrad*, 15. Cf. Luther, *Barbarossa Unleashed*, 61.

18. Russian ill-preparedness: Dunn, *Hitler's Nemesis*, 5–6. Relative demographic pools and conscription: Dunn, *Hitler's Nemesis*, 48–55. Goebbels in his many lamentations over failures in Russia notes the numerical disparity: *Goebbels Diaries, 1942–1943*, 185 (April 25, 1942).

19. German sense of foreboding in late 1941: Liddell Hart, *German Generals Talk*, 185. Cf. Cooper, *Germany Army*, 263–264.

20. German emphases on the flanks versus the center: Cooper, *German Army*, 290–291. Hitler's attack on Guderian: von Mellenthin, *German Generals*, 94.

21. Read and Fisher, *Deadly Embrace*, 640. Hitler's pretexts for invading the Soviet Union: Olaf Groehler, "Goals and Reason: Hitler and the German Military," in Wieczynski, ed., *Operation Barbarossa*, 48–61, esp. 59–61. Notion of a Soviet preemptory attack before Barbarossa: Bruce W. Menning and Jonathan House, "Soviet Strategy," in Ferris and Mawdsley, eds., *The Cambridge History of the Second World War*, Vol. I: *Fighting the War*, 226.

22. World War I German occupation of Russia: Herwig, *First World War*, 384–386; Freund, *Unholy Alliance*, 1–33.

23. "What-ifs" of Operation Barbarossa: Showalter and Deutsch, eds., *If the Allies Had Fallen*, 52–65. For mass firings of generals: Keegan, *Second World War*, 206–207. German army manual on cold weather: Condell and Zabecki, eds., *German Art of War*, 78–79. Case Blue as proof of failure: Weinberg, *World at Arms*, 269–270.

24. O'Brien, *How the War Was Won*, 24–26; cf. 292–295, 301, on the diversion of concrete and building materials to civil defense against bombing attacks. Drain on the Eastern Front due to Allied bombing in the West: Evans, *Third Reich at War*, 460–462.

25. Urals and Transcaucasia factories: Glantz and House, *When Titans Clashed*, 101–102. German air losses in the Mediterranean: ibid., 149–150. See also Murray, *Luftwaffe*, 144 (Table XXX) for German losses by theater January–November 1943. Cf. Air Ministry, *Rise and Fall of the German Air Force*, 219–220, 249–251, for an analysis of the Luftwaffe's position in the Mediterranean in 1942–1943.

26. Sherman quote: Hanson, *Soul of Battle*, 208–209. Cf. Glantz and House, *When Titans Clashed*, 286.


Chapter 13
Armies Abroad


1. Political explanations for Operation Torch: Reynolds, *From World War to Cold War*, 55–58. Cf. also, Howard, *Mediterranean Strategy in the Second*

*World War*, 69–71. Desirability of the African climate for Panzer operations: Liddell Hart, *German Generals Talk*, 98.

2. Conditions of battle in North Africa: Atkinson, *Army at Dawn*, 1–20.

3. Naval balance in the Mediterranean in 1940–1942: Salerno, *Vital Crossroads*, 213–220.

4. Alanbrooke, *War Diaries*, 174.

5. Numerical disparities facing Wavell's command: Butler, *Grand Strategy*, Vol. 3 [Part II], 297–312.

6. Change in Italian command: Knox, *Mussolini Unleashed*, 135–137.

7. Count Ciano's various diary entries: *Diary*, 367, 375. Italian air capability: Murray and Millett, *A War to Be Won*, 34.

8. Italian losses: Knox, *Mussolini Unleashed*, 251–256; Cloutier, *Regio Esercito*, 46. Anthony Eden's quote—a parody of Churchill's "Never in the field of human conflict was so much owed by so many to so few." (August 21, 1940): Churchill, *Grand Alliance*, 12–13; Liddell Hart, *History of the Second World War*, 117.

9. Remaining Italian forces after Operation Compass: Knox, *Mussolini Unleashed*, 280–282.

10. Criticisms of Operation Lustre: Lawlor, *Churchill and the Politics of War*, 165–259; Murfett, *Naval Warfare*, 103.

11. Rommel quote: Fuller, *Second World War*, 174. Rommel's original orders: Heckmann, *Rommel's War in Africa*, 21–36.

12. Rommel's so-called "First Offensive": Heckmann, *Rommel's War in Africa*, 37–47.

13. Liddell Hart, ed. *Rommel Papers*, 134.

14. Liddell Hart, ed., *Rommel Papers*, 191. Rommel's sudden strategic impulses: von Mellenthin, *German Generals*, 64.

15. Disparagement of Rommel by Generals Halder and Paulus, and Hitler's pipe dreams: Cooper, *German Army*, 357–359. Cf. also, Liddell Hart, *German Generals Talk*, 54.

16. Operation Battleaxe (June 15–17, 1941) and the subsequent replacement of Wavell: Butler, *Grand Strategy*, Vol. III (Part II), 525–532. Operation Crusader (November 18–December 30, 1941): Gwyer, *Grand Strategy*, Vol. III (Part I), 219–244.

17. Sherman tank shortcomings: Hastings, *Armageddon*, 86–87.

18. Afrika Korps after El Alamein: Cooper, *German Army*, 384–385.

19. Rommel's plans of logistical support, Cooper, *German Army*, 364–365.

20. See the balanced assessment of Rommel: von Mellenthin, *German Generals*, 69–70.

21. For Scipio Africanus: Scullard, *Scipio Africanus, Soldier and Politician*; John Briscoe, "The Second Punic War," in Astin, Walbank, Frederiksen,

and Ogilvie, eds., *CAH* 82 59–65, 73–74; for Marius: Sallust, *Bellum Iugurthinum* 84–114, and Syme, *Sallust*, 150; for Belisarius: Hanson, *Savior Generals*, 66–72.

22. American obsessions with entering Europe from the west: Harrison, *Cross-Channel Attack*, 13–35.

23. Operation Torch: Breuer, *Operation Torch*, 12–30.

24. Goebbels, *Goebbels Diaries, 1942–1943*, 376 (May 12, 1943). Cf. *Time*, May 10, 1943.

25. Von Luck, *Panzer Commander*, 121.

26. Plutarch, *Elder Cato*, 27.1.

27. Rationale of invading Sicily: Atkinson, *Day of Battle*, 5–9.

28. Operations on Sicily: Zaloga, *Sicily 1943: The Debut of Allied Joint Operations*, 89–91. Cf. D'Este, *Bitter Victory*, 552.

29. Slapping incidents and the fate of George Patton: D'Este, *Bitter Victory*, 483–491, 564–566.

30. General Lucas and the Anzio near disaster: Blumenson, *Anzio: The Gamble That Failed*, 197–208, especially on Lucas at 57–61. Cf. the brief synopsis in Laurie, *Anzio*, 12, 25–26. On the 1946 congressional hearings over the Rapido River disaster and some general remarks on the Monte Cassino mess: Atkinson, *Day of Battle*, 349–350, 586–587; 463–473.

31. Orphaning of the Italian front: Lamb, *War in Italy, 1943–1945*, 7–11.

32. Wisdom or folly of invading Sicily: Fuller, *Second World War*, 325. But cf. Peter R. Mansoor, "US Grand Strategy in the Second World War," in Murray and Sinnreich, eds., *Successful Strategies*, 341–345; Atkinson, *Day of Battle*, 582–583. Italy's casualties: Atkinson, *Day of Battle*, 581. On Italy, Churchill, and Roosevelt, see Hamilton, *The Mantle of Command*, 386–388; 330–332.

33. Allied damage to French infrastructure and the population: Beevor, *D-Day*, 519–520.

34. D-Day military innovations: Falconer, *D-Day: 'Neptune', 'Overlord' and the Battle of Normandy*.

35. Operation Neptune: Symonds, *Neptune*, 353–362.

36. Allied tactical air power after Normandy: A. Jacobs, "The Battle for France, 1944," in Cooling, ed., *Case Studies in the Development of Close Air Support*, especially 249–251. On the methodologies of counting the D-Day dead: http://fivethirtyeight.com/features/the -challenge-of-counting-d-days-dead/.

37. Wilmot, *Struggle for Europe*, 347.

38. Hedgerows: Doubler, *Closing with the Enemy*, 36–38; Lewis, ed., *D-Day As They Saw It*, 165–169.

39. Operation Cobra: D'Este, *Decision in Normandy*, 351 ff.

40. Stalin's political stalling outside Warsaw: Khlevniuk, *Stalin*, 244.

41. Broad versus narrow front: D'Este, *Patton*, 648–650. Cf. Eisenhower, *Crusade in Europe*, 291–320.

42. Allied demarcation lines: Weinberg, *World at Arms*, 792–798. General Jodl on a narrow Allied thrust: Hechler, *Goering and His Gang*, 779.

43. Warlimont, *Inside Hitler's Headquarters*, 316.

44. Allied slogging in the Ardennes and Hürtgen Forests: Beevor, *Ardennes 1944*, 56–79, 350–370. Backing off from Berlin: Eisenhower, *Crusade in Europe*, 399–403.

45. Hürtgen Forest campaign: Astor, *The Bloody Forest*, 356–366.

46. Wild Japanese expansion after Pearl Harbor: Toll, *Pacific Crucible*, 232–301.

47. Historical singularity of the Anglo-Americans' successful two-front war: Williamson Murray, "U.S. Strategy and Leadership in World War II: The Problem of a Two-Front Strategy," in Murray and Ishizu, eds., *Conflicting Currents: Japan and the United States in the Pacific*, 83.

48. Early bickering over "Europe First": Morton, *Strategy and Command*, 334–336.

49. Debate between the MacArthur route and Nimitz's preference: Murray and Millett, *A War to Be Won*, 362–364, 493–496; O'Brien, *How the War Was Won*, 412–429. On the Philippines, see Williamson Murray, "US Naval Strategy and Japan," in Murray and Sinnreich, eds., *Successful Strategies*, 288. Counterproductive effects of two simultaneous advances to Japan: O'Brien, *How the War Was Won*, 398–402.

50. Undue costs of the Philippines and Okinawa campaigns: Astor, *Crisis in the Pacific*, 600–624. See the assessments of Feifer, *Tennozan*, 376–409.

## Chapter 14
## Sieges

1. The Asia Minor catastrophe of 1922: Smith, *Ionian Vision: Greece in Asia Minor, 1919–1922*, 284–336. Fall of Constantinople: Ostrogorsky, *History of the Byzantine State*, 552–572; Treadgold, *A History of the Byzantine State and Society*, 797–803; Philippides and Hanak, *The Siege and the Fall of Constantinople in 1453: Historiography, Topography, and Military Studies*, passim. Gibbon's famous description of the siege and its immediate aftermath: *The Decline and Fall of the Roman Empire*, Vol. 6 (chapter 68), 489–514; Constantinople's last hours, 500–504. Vienna (September 27–October 15, 1529): Shaw, *History of the Ottoman Empire*, 93. Vienna (July–September, 1683): Stoye, *Siege of Vienna* and Barker, *Double Eagle and Crescent*. See also Davies, *God's Playground*, 481–487 for Polish sovereign Jan III Sobieski's role in defending Vienna; and Shaw, *History of the Ottoman Empire*,

213–215, and for the consequences to the Ottomans of the failure to take the Hapsburg capital, 218–219.

2. Rape of German women: Naimark, *Russians in Germany*, 69–140; fall of Berlin, see Ryan, *Last Battle*, 488–493.

3. Wiping out things Russian: Cameron and Stevens, eds., *Hitler's Table Talk*, 4–5 (night of July 5–6, 1941), 400–401 (April 5, 1942).

4. Carthage: Polybius 38.19–22; Jerusalem: Josephus, 6.1–10; Baghdad: Allsen, *Mongol Imperialism*, 1–7, 83–88; Morgan, *Mongols*, 132–133; Saunders, *History of the Mongol Conquests*, 109–111; Grenada: Constable, *Medieval Iberia*, 496–507; Fletcher, *Moorish Spain*; Hillgarth, *Spanish Kingdoms*, 366–393; O'Callaghan, *Reconquest and Crusade*, 213–214; Tenochtitlán: Hanson, *Carnage and Culture*, 170–232. Greek and Roman siegecraft: Kern, *Ancient Siege Warfare*, 135–162; Barry Strauss, "The Experience of Siege Warfare," in Chapter 7 of Sabin, van Wees, and Whitby, eds., *Cambridge History of Greek and Roman Warfare*, Vol. I, 243–247.

5. Watson, *Sieges*, 6.

6. On some World War I sieges: Przemyśl: Keegan, *First World War*, 171–172; Strachan, *First World War*, 30–31. Kut-al-Amara: Strachan, *First World War*, 120–124; Watson, *Sieges*, 83–105; Hammond, *Battle in Iraq*, 71–109. Cf. Braddon, *The Siege*, and Crowley, *Kut 1916*. On Verdun, see Keegan, *First World War*, 278–286; Strachan, *First World War*, 180–185.

7. Watson, *Sieges*, 57–81.

8. Morality of sieges: Walzer, *Just and Unjust Wars*, 165–170.

9. Losses at Leningrad: Glantz, *Battle for Leningrad*, 467–469, Appendices F ("Soviet Military Casualties"), 543–546, and G ("Estimated Civilian Losses in the Siege of Leningrad"), 547.

10. For Directive No. 1a 1601/41, "Concerning the Future Existence of the City of Leningrad," see Glantz, *Battle for Leningrad*, 85–86.

11. On the forgotten ordeal in Leningrad, cf. Reid, *Leningrad*, 313–315.

12. Glantz, *Battle for Leningrad*, 27–31, and Appendix E ("A Rough Comparison of Red Army and *Wehrmacht* Forces"), 537–542. See Roberts, *Storm of War*, 152–154. Planning for Operation Barbarossa: Olaf Groehler, "Goals and Reason: Hitler and the German Military," in Wieczynski, *Operation Barbarossa*, 48–61. Bombing Moscow: Hardesty and Grinberg, *Red Phoenix Rising*, 64–65.

13. Finnish support for Army Group North: Lunde, *Finland's War of Choice*, 183–212.

14. Russian naval disaster: Jones, *Leningrad: State of Siege*, 110–112. Maritime efforts to supply Army Group North: Askey, *Operation Barbarossa*, 319–330.

15. Destruction of Tenochtitlán: Hanson, *Carnage and Culture*, 185–193. Lake Ladoga: Glantz, *Battle for Leningrad*, 101, 139–145.

16. See Hitler's demands as paraphrased by Salisbury, *900 Days*, 94.

17. Limited strategies of the Finnish: Carrell, *Hitler Moves East*, 267.

18. Horrific conditions inside Leningrad: chapter 4 ("The Struggle to Survive: The Dying City") in Bidlack and Lomagin, *The Leningrad Blockade*, 262–328. The quotation is taken from Document 48, 267–268. The single entry for January 28, 1942, was, "Papa died." German plans: Murray and Millett, *A War to Be Won*, 130–136. Reid, *Leningrad*, 133. Cf. Buttar, *Battleground Prussia*, 18.

19. Prewar savagery in Stalin's Soviet Union: Calvocoressi, Wint, and Pritchard, *Total War*, 484–486.

20. Why Leningrad survived: Carrell, *Hitler Moves East*, 267–269.

21. Stalin's criminality and Leningrad: Kirschenbaum, *Legacy of the Siege*, 237–258.

22. Army Group North after withdrawing from Leningrad: Ziemke, *Stalingrad to Berlin*, 248–266.

23. Portions of the directives are quoted in Wieder, von Einsiedel, and Bogler, *Stalingrad: Memories and Reassessments*, 13.

24. Cf. Goebbels, *Goebbels Diaries, 1942–1943*, 136 (March 20, 1942). German perceptions of the United States in World War I: Strachan, *First World War*, 220–223, 285, and in World War II, see Roberts, *Storm of War*, 195–200.

25. Hitler on German ill-preparedness during the winter of 1941–1942: Cameron and Stevens, eds., *Hitler's Table Talk*, 339–340 (February 26–27, 1942).

26. Ellis, *Stalingrad Cauldron*, 58–60. Dislike of inept Paulus: Wieder, von Einsiedel, and Bogler, *Stalingrad: Memories and Reassessments*, 192–195. Blaming Hitler: Manstein, *Lost Victories*, 360.

27. Assessment of Field Marshal Paulus: Wieder, von Einsiedel, and Bogler, *Stalingrad: Memories and Reassessments*, 87; cf., 206–213. Russian views of Stalingrad: Rotundo, *Battle for Stalingrad*, especially 41–110.

28. See Hayward, *Stopped at Stalingrad*, 234, 251–310 (quote on 303).

29. "Fortress Stalingrad": Wieder, von Einsiedel, and Bogler, *Stalingrad: Memories and Reassessments*, 42, 79.

30. Russian losses before, and German losses after, 1941: Antill, *Stalingrad 1942*, 39, 87–88; Roberts, *Victory at Stalingrad*, 49. Cf. Beevor, *Stalingrad*, 430–431, for the final prisoner release of 1955; Glantz and House, *Armageddon in Stalingrad*, 714–718.

31. The Battle of Jena-Auerstedt: Chandler, *Campaigns of Napoleon*, 479–502. Worst defeat in German history: Beevor, *Stalingrad*, 398; and the final wretchedness: Wieder's quote in Wieder, von Einsiedel, and Bogler, *Stalingrad: Memories and Reassessments*, 95.

32. Soviet jubilation after Stalingrad: Beevor, *Stalingrad*, 404. General German view: see again Wieder, von Einsiedel, and Bogler, *Stalingrad: Memories and Reassessments*, 164. Cf. Galland, *The First and the Last*, 149.

33. Ellis, *Brute Force*, 77.

34. Blitzkrieg's epitaph: paraphrased from the assessment of Glantz and House, *When Titans Clashed*, 125. On Soviet industrial output increases, see Mark Harrison, "The Soviet Union: The Defeated Victor," in Harrison, ed., *The Economics of World War II*, 272–274, and more generally, the same author's *Accounting for War: Soviet Production, Employment, and the Defence Burden, 1940–1945*. Folly of dividing Army Group South: Roberts, *Victory at Stalingrad*, 73–74; 86–88 (Hitler's thinking in besieging Stalingrad); cf. Ziemke and Bauer, *Moscow to Stalingrad*, 358–361. Flanks at Stalingrad: Wieder, von Einsiedel, and Bogler, *Stalingrad: Memories and Reassessments*, 35–36. Cf. Roberts, *Victory at Stalingrad*, 78–80. Huge size and breakdown of Army Group South: Antill, *Stalingrad 1942*, 23–24.

35. On Goebbels, see Beevor, *Stalingrad*, 398–399. The Athenian disaster: Thucydides 7.87.6. German assessments of Thermopylae: Wieder, von Einsiedel, and Bogler, *Stalingrad: Memories and Reassessments*, 177–178.

36. On Tobruk: Seymour, *Great Sieges*, 257–277. A diary of events of the successful resistance to Rommel before June 1942: Bowen, *Back from Tobruk*, 93–134.

37. On the Italian garrison at Tobruk, see Seymour, *Great Sieges*, 258–259. I visited the site in 2006, and like most of Muammar Gaddafi's cities, it had extinguished most traces of its colonial past.

38. Dreams of Rommel after the fall of Tobruk: Liddell Hart, ed., *Rommel Papers*, 513–515; cf. also 191–192. On the German view, see also Fraser, *Knight's Cross*, 304–306.

39. See Jackson, *Battle for North Africa*, 237–238. Cf. Churchill, *Hinge of Fate*, 401–402.

40. Morale during the battle for Tobruk: Fennell, *Combat and Morale in the North African Campaign*, 214–215, 281–283.

41. Jackson, *Battle for North Africa*, 150–151. See Churchill on Rommel, *Grand Alliance*, 200.

42. Churchill, *Hinge of Fate*, 401–402. The breakdown of British losses: Mitcham, *Rommel's Greatest Victory*, 183–184.

43. German awe at Sevastopol's defenses: Carrell, *Hitler Moves East*, 464–466.

44. On "frog pond": Cameron and Stevens, eds., *Hitler's Table Talk*, 301. For the Crimea, see Weinberg, *World at Arms*, 408–413.

45. Flawed logic of the monster guns: Manstein, *Lost Victories*, 263. Cf. Ziemke and Bauer, *Moscow to Stalingrad*, 309–310; Weinberg, *World at Arms*, 537. See also Kaufmann and Kaufmann, *Fortress Third Reich*, 189–192.

46. Ziemke and Bauer, *Moscow to Stalingrad*, 321. In Manstein's account (*Verlorene Siege*, 282), he says "over 90,000" died.

47. On the record German bombardment of Sevastopol, see Melvin, *Manstein*, 263–264.

48. For the entire questionable Axis strategy of investing in Sevastopol, cf. Melvin, *Manstein*, 271–273.

49. An analysis, along with an English translation of Riezler's *Septemberprogramm* memo, is found in Fischer, *Germany's Aims in the First World War*, 98–113.

50. The huge submarine pen projects are discussed in Kaufmann and Kaufmann, *Fortress Third Reich*, 182–189.

51. Hitler's directive: Kaufmann and Kaufmann, *Fortress Third Reich*, 196.

52. See also Kaufmann, Kaufmann, and Idzikowski, *Fortress France*, 99–108.

53. On the German strategy for holding the ports and their long-term strategic aims, cf. Kaufmann and Jurga, *Fortress Europe*, 388–389.

54. Kaufmann and Kaufmann, *Fortress Third Reich*, 319. Cherbourg: Harrison, *Cross-Channel Attack*, 386–449; cf. 441–442.

55. German strategy and the Atlantic Wall: Zaloga, *Atlantic Wall*, 5–33.

56. Antwerp and the Canadian sacrifice at the Scheldt: Zuehlke, *Terrible Victory*, 442–460.

57. Von Runstedt: Delaforce, *Smashing the Atlantic Wall*, 112–113. Vassiltchikov, *Berlin Diaries*, 178–179.

58. Şahin, *Empire and Power in the Reign of Süleyman*, 149, and n. 66 (citing Setton, *Papacy and the Levant*, Vol. 4, 853–8580. For "the Ottoman apologetic narrative": İsmail Hami Danişmend, *İzahlı Osmanlı Tarihi Kronolojisi*, Vol. 2 M. 1513–1573, H. 919–981 [Istanbul: Türkiye Yayınevi, 1948], 330–340.

59. Disastrous strategic consequences for Malta following the fall of France: Perowne, *Siege Within the Walls*, 34–35.

60. Mussolini's ineptness: Perowne, *Siege Within the Walls*, 58–59.

61. Weaknesses of a superficially impressive Italian surface navy: Marc' Antonio Bragadin, *Italian Navy in World War II*, 324–325. See also Sadkovich, *Italian Navy in World War II*, 331–350; Roberts, *Storm of War*, 149, 284. Allied strategy in the Mediterranean: Howard, *Mediterranean Strategy*, 1–39.

62. Entry and record of U-boats around Malta: Paterson, *U-Boats in the Mediterranean 1941–1944*, 158–174.

63. Assessment of German and British military leaders: Shankland and Hunter, *Malta Convoy*, 34–36. Cf. Perowne, *Siege Within the Walls*, 54–55.

64. British surrender of Singapore to the Japanese in February 1942: Allen, *Singapore 1941–1942*, 175–184; Warren, *Singapore 1942*, 253–270. Humiliation and the exaggeration of the strategic consequences of losing Singapore: Morton, *Strategy and Command*, 174–175. Churchill's characterization of British disasters at both Singapore and Tobruk: *Hinge of Fate*, 81.

65. Singapore's naval guns: Hack and Blackburn, *Did Singapore Have to Fall?*, 102–131. Calvocoressi, Wint, and Pritchard, *Total War*, 839.

66. Allen, *Singapore 1941–1942*, 51–53; Hack and Blackburn, *Did Singapore Have to Fall?*, 65–66.

67. For Force Z, see Allen, *Singapore 1941–1942*, 136–145; Hough, *The Hunting of Force Z*; Middlebrook & Mahoney, *The Sinking of the Prince of Wales and the Repulse*, 283–314. Cf. Dull, *Imperial Japanese Navy*, 38–41.

68. British losses: Allen, *Singapore 1941–1942*, 270–271. Controversy over number (100,000–130,000?) who surrendered: A. Yoji, "General Yamashita Tomoyuki," in Farrell and Hunter, eds., *Sixty Years On*, 199–201. Churchill and Singapore: R. Callahan, "Churchill and Singapore," in Farrell and Hunter, eds., *Sixty Years On*, 156–169. On Churchill's often quoted reaction, see Warren, *Singapore 1942*, 77.

69. The massacres: Allen, *Singapore 1941–1942*, 35–36. General Yamashita and the massacres: A. Yoji, "General Yamashita Tomoyuki," in Farrell and Hunter, eds., *Sixty Years On*, 199–201.

70. Cf. Allen, *Singapore 1941–1942*, 186–187. Loss of British prestige: Warren, *Singapore 1942*, 137–146. Cf. the assessments of Adolf Hitler: Cameron and Stevens, eds., *Hitler's Table Talk*, 274–275 (February 2, 1942, midday). On Percival, cf. C. Kinvig, "General Percival and the Fall of Singapore," in Farrell and Hunter, eds., *Sixty Years On*, 241–261. Field Marshal Earl Wavell on the surrender of Singapore: Brian P. Farrell, "The Dice Were Rather Heavily Loaded: Wavell and the Fall of Singapore," in Farrell, ed., *Leadership and Responsibility*, 182–234.

71. Relative air power: John R. Ferris, "Student and Master: Airpower and the Fall of Singapore," in Farrell and Hunter, eds., *Sixty Years On*, 104.

72. Flaws of the so-called Singapore Strategy: Malcolm H. Murfett, "Reflections on an Enduring Theme: The 'Singapore Strategy' at Sixty," in Farrell and Hunter, eds., *Sixty Years On*, 16–22. Local Malaysian defenses: Allen, *Singapore 1941–1942*, 247–263. On Percival's quote, see C. Kinvig, "General Percival and the Fall of Singapore," in Farrell and Hunter, eds., *Sixty Years On*, 261.

73. Warren, *Singapore 1942*, 290. Churchill's policy toward Singapore: Hack and Blackburn, *Did Singapore Have to Fall?*, 186–187.

74. Air and naval defenses on the Philippines: Belote, *Corregidor*, 36–40.

75. MacArthur and War Plan Orange: Belote, *Corregidor*, 36–53; see again, Belote, *Corregidor*, 37–40.

76. Corregidor's defenses: Flanagan, *Corregidor*, 32–34. Strength and weakness of Corregidor's big guns: Belote, *Corregidor*, 12–13, 15–19.

77. Corregidor's prewar defenses: Flanagan, *Corregidor*, 26–33; Devlin, *Back to Corregidor*, 5–8; its isolation: Morris, *Corregidor*, 23. Cf. "Washington's Modification of the Military Strategy," in Masuda, *MacArthur in Asia*, 40–41.

78. Eisenhower, *Crusade in Europe*, 21.

79. Morris, *Corregidor*, 426–467.

80. Japan's ascendance: Belote, *Corregidor*, 32–35.

81. Morris, *Corregidor*, 426–467.

82. Malise Ruthven, "Hitler's Monumental Miscalculation," *New York Review of Books* (NYR Blog), June 5, 2014 (http://www.nybooks.com/blogs/nyrblog/2014/jun/05/hitlers-mighty-miscalculation/?insrc=hpss). Maginot Line, Atlantic Wall, and Siegfried Line: Kaufmann and Kaufmann, *Maginot Imitations*, 31–50; Kaufmann and Kaufmann, *Fortress Third Reich* 182–255; and in general, Kaufmann and Kaufmann, *Fortress France*.

83. Athens' walls during the Classical period: David L. Berkey, "Why Fortifications Endure: A Case Study of the Walls of Athens During the Classical Period," in Hanson, ed., *Makers of Ancient Strategy*, 58–92.

# Part 5. Fire

1. Schopenhauer, *Collected Works*, 8.

## Chapter 15
## Tanks and Artillery

1. King Archidamus's quote: Plutarch, *Moralia* 219a. Patton's observation: Atkinson, *Army at Dawn*, 442.

2. Elephants in classical antiquity: Scullard, *Elephant in the Greek and Roman World*; Kistler; *War Elephants*, 54–57; Philip Sabin, "Battle: A. Land Battle, I. Exotic Weapons," in Chapter 13 of Sabin, van Wees, and Whitby, eds., *Cambridge History of Greek and Roman Warfare*, Vol. I, 419–421.

3. The *testudo*: Cassius Dio (49.30). Cf. also Plutarch, *Antony* 45; Flor. 2.20.6–7. Cf. Reinhold, *From Republic to Principate*, 62; Catherine M. Gilliver, "Battle: II. Land Battle, 2. Combat Mechanics," in Chapter 4 of Sabin, van Wees, and Whitby, eds., *Cambridge History of Greek and Roman Warfare*, Vol. II, 130–131, 134. The scorpion and other movable Roman bolt and missile launchers: Gilliver, op. cit. 128 (II. Land Battle, 2. Deployment), 151 (V. Siege Warfare); Marsden, *Greek and Roman Artillery*, 188–190.

4. Heavy knights: Parker, *The Military Revolution*, 69–70; Bernard S. Bachrach ("The Myth of the Mounted Knight") in Parker, ed., *The Cambridge History of Warfare*, 82–83; Brauer and Van Tuyll, *Castles, Battles, & Bombs: How Economics Explains Military History*, 49, 63.

5. For fantasy tanks, see H. G. Wells, *Complete Short Stories*, 603–620, especially 610.

6. Development of the tank and its use in World War I: Wright, *Tank*, 23–80. Cambrai: Macksey, *Tank Versus Tank*, 30; cf. 38–39; Zabecki, *The German 1918 Offensives*, 59–60.

7. Cf. Steiner, *Lights That Failed*, 372–383.

8. Prewar armor theorists in Britain, France, and Germany: Macksey, *Tank Versus Tank*, 24, 60; Boot, *War Made New*, 216–224. Cf. Williamson Murray, "Armored Warfare: The British, French, and German Experiences," in Murray and Millett, eds., *Military Innovation in the Interwar Period*, 6–49. Cf. Wright, *Tank*, 70–71, 220–228.

9. Blumenson, *Patton Papers, 1940–1945*, 8.

10. Steiger, *Armour Tactics*, 80.

11. Michael Wittmann: Agte, *Michael Wittmann*, Vol. I, 265–284; II: 17–90. Cf. Hart, *Sherman Firefly vs. Tiger*, 52–69.

12. Prewar tank experiences and lessons: Habeck, *Storm of Steel*, 247–287.

13. Steiger, *Armour Tactics*, 72–73.

14. Tank gun performance: Macksey, *Tank Versus Tank*, 106–114.

15. Russian diesel engines: Carius, *Tigers in the Mud*, 23. Panther tank craftsmanship in comparison to T-34s: Forczyk, "T-34 vs. Panther," in Zaloga, ed., *Battleground*, 80–85. Forty, *World War Two Tanks*, 168–170.

16. Mayo, *Ordnance Department: On Beachhead and Battlefront*, 328.

17. On the specifications of the plethora of British, German, American, Soviet, French, Italian, and Japanese tanks, see Forty, *World War Two Tanks*, especially 64–107 (Germany) and 156–173 (the Soviet Union).

18. Pimlott, ed., *Rommel*, 147–148.

19. "Like rats": Strawson, *Hitler as Military Commander*, 177.

20. Theories of tanks as tank-destroyers: Roberts, *Storm of War*, 525 (citing Guderian, *Achtung! Panzer!*). Battle of Kursk: Glantz and House, *Battle of Kursk*, with figures of "Comparative Strengths and Losses" in Appendix C (336–346). See Raus, *Panzer Operations*, 347. Pyrrhus: Plutarch, *Pyrrhus* 21.9.

21. German reluctance to build tanks in World War I: Gudmundsson, *On Armor*, 66–67. Supposed superiority of German tank crews: Keegan, *Second World War*, 399.

22. German tank specifications: Forty, *World War Two Tanks*, 64–107.

23. Shortcomings of the Panzers during the 1939–1940 victories: von Mellenthin, *Panzer Battles*, 155 n. 3; Guderian, *Panzer Leader*, 138. Inadequacies of Luftwaffe's ground support: Luther, *Barbarossa Unleashed*, 80–82.

24. End of blitzkrieg in Russia: Steiger, *Armour Tactics*, 53.

25. Hitler's remarks: Guderian, *Panzer Leader*, 190; cf. Steiger, *Armour Tactics*, 78.

26. Livy's (31.34.3) description of the strange cavalry encounter before the battle of Cynoscephalae in Thessaly (197 BC). Unimpressive German tank force that entered the Soviet Union in June 1941: see Stahel, *Operation Barbarossa*, 110–114.

27. The Russian "monster": see Steiger, *Armour Tactics*, 79; and cf. 82. "Peashooter": Schäufler, *Panzer Warfare*, 54. German tank production figures: Guderian, *Panzer Leader*, 143. See also Roberts, *Storm of War*, 425.

28. On the impossibility of reverse engineering the T-34: Guderian, *Panzer Leader*, 276–277; Keegan, *Second World War*, 399–402. See Steiger, *Armour Tactics*, 83–85. On Guderian's appointment to inspector-general of armoured troops on March 1, 1943, see Guderian, *Panzer Leader*, 284–300.

29. Cf. von Mellenthin, *Panzer Battles*, 301. Standardization in military production: Cameron and Stevens, eds., *Hitler's Table Talk*, 415–416 (April 9, 1942, midday).

30. The Tiger: Carius, *Tigers in the Mud*, 26. Cf. Weinberg, *World at Arms*, 539. The envisioned super-*Yamato* battleship class: Lengerer and Ahlberg, *Yamato Class*, 553–555.

31. Three options that confronted the Germans in their efforts to match the T-34: Showalter, *Armor and Blood*, 46–47. Speer's assessment of the V-2: *Inside the Third Reich*, 366.

32. Mosier, *Blitzkrieg Myth*, 181.

33. Hitler's disgust with the initially unreliable Panther: Heiber and Glantz, *Hitler and His Generals*, 415.

34. Differing notions of industrial production: Milward, *War, Economy and Society, 1939–1945*, 186–188. The Maus tank: Guderian, *Panzer Leader*, 278; Forty, *World War Two Tanks*, 107; Senger und Etterlin, *German Tanks of World War II*, 75–77. Misplaced German munitions priorities: Murray and Millett, *A War to Be Won*, 333–335. Speer's abilities: Evans, *Third Reich at War*, 328–329.

35. Cf. Wright, *Tank*, 298.

36. Steiger, *Armour Tactics*, 83–86.

37. German hubris prior to the invasion of the Soviet Union: Roberts, *Storm of War*, 137–145. Underestimation of the strength of the Red Army: Stahel, *Operation Barbarossa*, 143–145; Raus, *Panzer Operations*, 1–2.

38. Burdick and Jacobsen, eds., *Halder War Diary*, 345. On Russian-German joint research on prewar tanks: Habeck, *Storm of Steel*, 71–124. British contributions: Gat, *British Armour Theory*, 43–67. Crécy: Ormrod, *Edward III*, 271–321; Curry, *Hundred Years' War*, 14–15; DeVries, *Infantry Warfare*, 155–175; Russell Mitchell, "The Longbow-Crossbow Shootout at Crécy (1346): Has the 'Rate of Fire Commonplace' Been Overrated?" in Villalon and Kagay, eds., *The Hundred Years War: A Wider Focus*, 233–257. Cf. Steiger, *Armour Tactics*, 4–6. Cf. Guderian, *Panzer Leader*, 143. Prewar Soviet armored experience against the Japanese at Lake Khasan (1938) and Khalkhin Gol (1939), and against the Finns: Habeck, *Storm of Steel*, 247, 277–279, 285–287, 289–291.

39. Schäufler, *Panzer Warfare*, 38. Cf. Steiger, *Armour Tactics*, 84–85. On more firsthand German experiences: Schäufler, *Panzer Warfare*, 68.

40. For the T-34's specifications, see Forty, *World War Two Tanks*, 168–170.

41. Kliment Voroshilov I tanks: Macksey, *Tank Versus Tank*, 85–87.

42. T-34 battle losses in Krivosheev, *Soviet Casualties and Combat Losses*, 253–254. Cf. Schäufler, *Panzer Warfare*, 69. For the figures from Kursk, see Showalter, *Armor and Blood*, 269–270. Cf. Raus, *Panzer Operations*, 212. German tanks and armored vehicles before and after Stalingrad: O'Brien, *How the War Was Won*, 308–310. For more German testimonies on the T-34's superiority, see Steiger, *Armour Tactics*, 82, 265–266; Raus, *Panzer Operations*, 32–33; Luther, *Barbarossa Unleashed*, 153.

43. See Hastings, *Armageddon*, 86.

44. Balanced final assessment of the Sherman: Zaloga, *Armored Thunderbolt*, 327–330. On the manner in which Shermans were destroyed: Zaloga, *Armored Thunderbolt*, 236–238.

45. American automobile industry mobilization for war production: Baime, *Arsenal of Democracy*, 65–85, and Arthur Herman's review in the *Wall Street Journal* (http://online.wsj.com/articles/book-review -the-arsenal-of-democracy-by-a-j-baime-1402693102).

46. Sherman superiority in 1942 and early 1943 in North Africa: Zaloga, *Armored Thunderbolt*, 49–54. Total tank production of the United States and the Soviet Union: Forty, *World War Two Tanks*, 108–173.

47. Shermans and burning: Zaloga, *Armored Thunderbolt*, 55–56; Forty, *World War Two Tanks*, 142. Survivability of Sherman crews: Zaloga, *Armored Thunderbolt*, 238.

48. The tank destroyer: Weigley, *Eisenhower's Lieutenants*, 10–11.

49. Patton, *War As I Knew It*, 138. Cf. Nicholas D. Molnar, "General George S. Patton and the War-Winning Sherman Tank Myth," in Piehler and Pash, eds., *The United States and the Second World War*, 129–149.

50. McAleer, *Dueling*, 12–23; Mayo, *Ordnance Department*, 322.

51. "Deathtrap": Mayo, *Ordnance Department*, 334; Patton, *War As I Knew It*, 243. See Showalter, *Hitler's Panzers*, 334–335. On various schemes to upgrade the Sherman, see Mayo, *Ordnance Department*, 329.

52. Tank fighting and the Abrams: Murray and Scales, *Iraq War*, 88–128.

53. British adaptations of the Sherman tanks, and General Hobart's "funnies": Forty, *World War Two Tanks*, 142–149.

54. Macksey, *Tank Force*, 79.

55. British tank production and models: Forty, *World War Two Tanks*, 9; cf. 8–56. Tank production was often lumped together with other armored vehicle output, which makes distinct statistics sometimes problematic.

56. Matildas: Forty, *World War Two Tanks*, 39–43.

57. Coombs, *British Tank Production*, 122–123.

58. Zaloga, "Tiger vs. Sherman Firefly" in Zaloga, ed., *Battleground*, 148–153. Percentages of Russian tank losses: Gudmundsson, *On Armor*, 130.

59. Blitzkrieg in France: Antoine de Saint-Exupéry, *Pilote de Guerre*, 94–95, quoted in Williamson Murray, "May 1940: Contingency and Fragility

of the German RMA," in Knox and Murray, eds., *Dynamics of Military Revolution*, 155: Cf. Steiger, *Armour Tactics*, 67, quoting Bauer, *Der Panzerkrieg*, 9.

60. German losses in 1942: Overmans, *Deutsche Militärische Verluste*, 276–284; Luftwaffe losses: Murray, *Luftwaffe*, 112–142; for tank losses: Showalter, *Armor and Blood*, 38.

61. Operation Cobra: Yenne, *Operation Cobra*, 36–71; especially 38–39; Zaloga, *Operation Cobra 1944*, 18–31; cf. 25–26.

62. Curtailment of German Blitzkrieg due to shortages of fuel, supplies, and spare parts: Steiger, *Armour Tactics*, 126–128. Von Rundstedt: Goldensohn, *Nuremberg Interviews*, 167.

63. On the fear instilled by Panzers: Steiger, *Armour Tactics*, 25.

64. Allied fuel consumption: D'Este, *Patton*, 649–650.

65. Comparative fuel consumption of Tigers and Shermans: Green, Anderson, and Schulz, *German Tanks*, 73–74; Zaloga, *Armored Thunderbolt*, 331–338, cf. 331. Russian roads: Luther, *Barbarossa Unleashed*, 322–323. Cf. von Mellenthin, *Panzer Battles*, 155. Hitler on roads: Cameron and Stevens, eds., *Hitler's Table Talk* (June 27, 1942, at dinner), 537–538.

66. Cf. Steiger, *Armour Tactics*, 13. Mayo, *Ordnance Department*, 333.

67. For tables of artillery production in World War II: http://ww2 -weapons.com/german-arms-production/; http://ww2-weapons.com/russian -arms-production/; http://www.nationalww2museum.org/learn/education /for-students/ww2-history/ww2-by-the-numbers/wartime-production .html; http://ww2-weapons.com/u-s-arms-production/.

68. US artillery shell production in World War II: "History of the Ammunition Industrial Base," (www.jmc.army.mil/Docs/History/Ammunition %20Industrial%20Base%20v2%20%202010%update.pdf), Joint Munitions Command, JMC History Office, ASMSJM-HI DSN: 793–0392, page 15; Cf. Hogg, *German Artillery*, 162–170. Inadequacy of German tanks in Russia: Steiger, *Armour Tactics*, 53. A *Bismarck* or *Tirpitz* probably cost around 250 million Reichsmarks, an 88 mm perhaps 33,600 RM.

69. Gudmundsson, *On Armor*, 122–124. Cf. Senger und Etterlin, *German Tanks of World War II*, 39–40.

70. See Gavin, *On to Berlin*, 205: Americans preferred captured Panzerfausts to their own bazookas.

71. Raus, *Panzer Operations*, 337. Hellbeck, *Stalingrad*, 159.

72. Murray and Millett, *A War to Be Won*, 472, 482; Olive, *Steel Thunder on the Eastern Front*, 137–155. Cf. Dunn, *Stalin's Keys to Victory*, 23–42; Luther, *Barbarossa Unleashed*, 148.

73. On rockets vs. artillery in World War II, and Katyushas and their copies, see Baker, *Rocket*, 81–83; Weinberg, *World at Arms*, 538. Gunston, *Rockets & Missiles*, 24, includes discussion of the Type 212 and 212A missiles, calling the later "potentially the most formidable tactical missile in the world prior to World War 2."

74. Cf. Baldwin, *Deadly Fuze*, 85–89, 302–304. Buderi, *The Invention That Changed the World*, 221–228. On technological questions, see in general: Johns Hopkins University Applied Physics Laboratory, *The World War II Proximity Fuze*.

75. Fear of Japanese mortars: Sledge, *With the Old Breed*, 72–74. Concept of "shell shock": Tracey Loughran, "Shell Shock, Trauma, and the First World War: The Making of a Diagnosis and Its Histories," *Journal of the History of Medicine and Allied Science* 67 (2012), 94–119; cf. also Kramer, *Dynamic of Destruction*, 258–259; Watson, *Enduring the Great War*, 25–37, 238–240.

# Part 6. People

1. Thucydides, *The Peloponnesian War*, 7.77.7.

## Chapter 16
## Supreme Command

1. Difference in the style of supreme leadership: Keegan, *Mask of Command*, 311–352. See Weinberg, "Reflections on Running a War: Hitler, Churchill, Stalin, Roosevelt, Tojo," in Weinberg, *Germany, Hitler, and World War II*, 287–306.

2. Qualities of the great generals and statesmen: Cohen, *Supreme Command*, 1–14, 208–224.

3. Generalship seen when the odds are unfavorable: Hanson, *Savior Generals*, 3–5.

4. Thucydides on Pericles: 2.65.9. Cf. Plutarch, *Pericles*, 15. See Kagan, *Pericles of Athens and the Birth of Democracy*, 62–64, and cf. 230–231. Democracies at war: Hanson, "Ferocious Warmakers: How Democracies Win Wars," *Claremont Review of Books*, 2.2 (2002). (http://www.claremontinstitute.org/crb/article/ferocious-warmakers-how-democracies-win-wars/). See Thucydides (8.1.4), for an assessment of democratic warfare and Sicily (415–413 BC).

5. United States enjoying the advantages of democracy during World War II: O'Neill, *A Democracy at War*, 429–434. Cf. also Reiter and Stam, *Democracies at War*, 193. Mussolini's "deep-seated distrust of his subordinates": Knox, *Mussolini Unleashed*, 7.

6. Manstein on Hitler: *Lost Victories*, 284 ff.

7. Stalin's move away from his earlier micromanaging of the war: Roberts, *Storm of War*, 601–602. For a contrasting view, cf. Deutscher, *Stalin*, 466–467; Roberts, *Stalin's Wars*, 159–162. Zhukov's brilliance: Hastings, *Armageddon*, 232.

8. Axis mistrust: Ciano's diary entry for July 20, 1941 (*Diary, 1937–1943*, 446) on the "treacherous" Germans.

9. Cf. the fierce criticisms of Roosevelt by General Alan Brooke, Chief of the Imperial General Staff: Alanbrooke, *War Diaries*, 272–273; 590. On plots against Hitler: Stone, *Shattered Genius*, 265–310; Weinberg, "July 20, 1944: The German Resistance to Hitler," in Weinberg, *Germany, Hitler, and World War II*, 245–253. See Megargee, *Inside Hitler's High Command*, 230–236, for a contrasting view on the complicity between Hitler and his generals. For opposition to Nazi rule: Hansen, *Disobeying Hitler*, 324–332.

10. For Churchill's unique prewar experiences: Gilbert, *Churchill: A Life*, Preface, xix.

11. Raeder's postwar doubts about Hitler: Raeder, *Grand Admiral*, 241–242. The Allied rhetoric of Churchill and Roosevelt: Reynolds, *From World War to Cold War*, 49–71. German discontent with Hitler: Hastings, *Armageddon*, 327.

12. Cf. Weinberg's introduction in Heiber and Glantz, *Hitler and His Generals*, xxxiii. Over forty (?) vague plans to kill Hitler of which twenty were more serious: Moorhouse, *Killing Hitler: The Plots, the Assassins, and the Dictator Who Cheated Death*, 2–3.

13. German war aims in World War I: Rothwell, *War Aims*, 9–12.

14. Warlimont, *Inside Hitler's Headquarters*, 145. See also Keegan, *First World War*, 341–343; Strachan, *First World War*, 261–262.

15. Hitler's false assurances: Baynes, *Speeches of Adolf Hitler, Volume II*, 1181, 1211, 1304, 1425, 1517. Cf. Williamson Murray, *Change in the European Balance of Power*, 359–360.

16. Heiber and Glantz, *Hitler and His Generals*, xxxii. Hitler's self-assessment of his strategic acumen: Strawson, *Hitler as Military Commander*, 50–54. Cf. Schramm, *Hitler*, 184–191. Thucydides's aphorism: 4.4.108.

17. Inefficient use of European industry under Nazi control: Murray, *Luftwaffe*, 99–100. Hitler's frequent panics and temporizing: Karl-Heinz Frieser, "The War in the West, 1939–1940: An Unplanned Blitzkrieg," in Ferris and Mawdsley, eds., *The Cambridge History of the Second World War*, Vol. I: *Fighting the War*, 306. Flaws in Hitler's grand strategy: Williamson Murray, "Thoughts on Grand Strategy," in Murray, Sinnreich, and Lacey, eds., *The Shaping of Grand Strategy*, 8–9 and n. 26. Napoleon quote: DeLiancourt, *Political Aphorisms, Moral and Philosophical Thoughts of the Emperor Napoleon*, 10.

18. Alexander's decision to halt his advance into India: see Arrian, *Anabasis* 5.26–29.1; Diodorus 17.93.3–94.5; Quintus Curtius 9.2.9–11; Plutarch, *Alexander* 62. Roman defeat at the Teutoburg Wald: Dio 56.19.1–22.2; Valleius Paterculus 2.119.1–5, Tacitus, *Annals* 1.61–62. Augustus's response to Varus's defeat: Suetonius, *Divus Augustus* 23. Cf. Goldsworthy, *Augustus*, 447–457.

19. Relationship between Hitler's strengths and weaknesses, and his conduct of the war: Bullock, *Hitler: A Study in Tyranny*, 372–410; Schramm, *Hitler*, passim; Strawson, *Hitler as Military Commander*, 222–246.

20. Hitler's triumphalism: Kershaw, *Hitler, 1936–45: Nemesis*, 300–301.

21. Hitler and the masses: Hugh Trevor-Roper in Cameron and Stevens, eds., *Hitler's Table Talk*, especially xxxix.

22. Bullock, *Hitler: A Study in Tyranny*, 35–36. Hitler's ramblings: see the survey by Hugh Trevor-Roper in Cameron and Stevens, eds., *Hitler's Table Talk*, especially xxxvi–ix.

23. Warlimont, *Inside Hitler's Headquarters*, 208–209.

24. Germany's proposals to Mexico in World War I: Boghardt, *Zimmermann Telegram*, 33–47.

25. Warlimont, *Inside Hitler's Headquarters*, 209. Decision to declare war on the United States: Roberts, *Storm of War*, 193–197. See Strawson, *Hitler as Military Commander*, 148.

26. Counterfactuals of a German Mediterranean strategy in place of Barbarossa: David M. Glantz, "What If the Germans Had Delayed Barbarossa Until After Dealing with Great Britain (in 1942 or 1943)?," in Showalter and Deutsch, eds., *If the Allies Had Fallen*, 52–53. Cf. Fuller, *Second World War*, 84–87. See also Howard, *Mediterranean Strategy in the Second World War*, 12–13.

27. Hitler's strategic disasters following 1942: Lewin, *Hitler's Mistakes*. Lübeck and the Baedeker Raids: Evans, *Third Reich at War*, 438–440. Hitler's strategic shortcomings: Murray and Millett, *A War to Be Won*, 84–85. Warning against Case Blue: Schramm, *Hitler*, 203.

28. Hitler's reversals of decisions: Strawson, *Hitler as Military Commander*, 92–93, 108–122. Hitler's palace: Speer, *Inside the Third Reich*, 156; cf. 483, on Hitler's admissions about Goering. Hitler's profits from the public purse: Speer, *Spandau*, 104–105. Cf. Stratigakos, *Hitler at Home*, 24–46. On Goering, see Murray, *Luftwaffe*, 13–14.

29. Hitler's poor health as exaggerated: Neumann and Eberle, *Was Hitler Ill?*, 186–190. Cf. Kershaw, *Hitler, 1936–45: Nemesis*, 638–639, and Hitler's downturn by September (726–727). See also Goering's assessment: Hechler, *Goering and His Gang*, 587. Hitler's self-pity: Bullock, *Hitler: A Study in Tyranny*, 756.

30. Hitler's parochialism, populism, and distrust of intellectuals: Evans, *Third Reich in Power*, 298–299, 498.

31. Hitler's esteem for Mussolini: Cameron and Stevens, eds., *Hitler's Table Talk*, 437 (April 23, 1942, at dinner).

32. Italy's colonial dreams: Knox, *Mussolini Unleashed*, 39–40.

33. Italy's dearth of capital and key natural resources: Vera Zamagni, "Italy: How to Lose the War and Win the Peace," in Harrison, ed., *The Economics of World War II*, 177–223, especially 178–189. Italian aims and means in the war are surveyed in Rothwell, *War Aims in the Second World War*, 52–58.

34. Mussolini's efforts to persuade Hitler to adopt a southern strategy: Ansel, *Hitler and the Middle Sea*, especially 33–39.

35. Mark Harrison, "The Economics of World War II: An Overview," in Harrison, ed., *The Economics of World War II*, 1–42; cf. Tables 1.6 and 1.7, 15–17. Italian shortage of vehicles: Knox, *Common Destiny*, 150–151.

36. See Knox, *Hitler's Italian Allies*, 89–91; 100–101. On Nazi Germany's furor at a crumbling Italy and what followed after 1943, see Roberts, *Storm of War*, 384. Using the province of Arezzo as a local example of a national phenomenon, Victoria C. Belco, *War, Massacre, and Recovery in Central Italy, 1943–1948*, examines German retribution against Italy and the challenges faced by the Italian people in response to Italy's change in alliance from Axis to Allies, and the subsequent battles for Italian territory.

37. General Armellino: Steinberg, *All or Nothing*, 16.

38. Mussolini's character and mood swings: Hibbert, *Mussolini*, especially 101–113; Mussolini's journalistic career: Ridley, *Mussolini*, 47–55. "Energetic without being industrious": Calvocoressi, Wint, and Pritchard, *Total War*, 133–134, 169.

39. Inadequacy of the Italian military to meet Mussolini's agendas: MacGregor Knox, "The Italian Armed Forces, 1940–3" in Millett and Murray, eds., *Military Effectiveness*, Vol. 3, 170–172.

40. Tojo's ascendance and the basis of his power: Weinberg, *Visions of Victory*, 59–62. Cf. Shillony, *Politics and Culture in Wartime Japan*, 29–43.

41. Alternate Japanese plans of focusing on China: Hane and Perez, *Modern Japan*, 312–327; Feis, *Road to Pearl Harbor*; Butow, *Tojo and the Coming of the War*; Lu, *From the Marco Polo Bridge to Pearl Harbor*, 188–190.

42. Tojo demoted: Toland, *Rising Sun*, 523–530; the nature of his successors: Craig, *Fall of Japan*, 27–29. Cf. Toll, *Conquering Tide*, 533–534.

43. U.S.-Japanese diplomatic negotiations prior to Pearl Harbor: Schroeder, *Axis Alliance*, 73–107, 168–199. Japanese shipbuilding: Alvin D. Coox, "The Effectiveness of the Japanese Military Establishment in the Second World War," in Millett and Murray, eds., *Military Effectiveness*, Vol. 3, 6–7. Yuko Tojo's praise of her grandfather: *The Japan Times*, July 4, 2007 (http://www.japantimes.co.jp/news/2007/07/04/national/candidate-tojo-seeks-resolution-against-a-bombings/#.VwsMwiQbCYV).

44. Japan's prewar investment for a Pacific War: Keegan, *History of Warfare*, 375. What the Japanese *might* have done at Pearl Harbor: Zimm, *Attack on Pearl Harbor*, especially "Appendix D: The Perfect Attack," 401–412. Cf. Williamson Murray, "US Naval Strategy and Japan," in Murray and Sinnreich, eds., *Successful Strategies*, 283.

45. Japanese militarism as an aberration from traditional Japanese history: Calvocoressi, Wint, and Pritchard, *Total War*, 768–794. Japanese racial propaganda: Dower, *War Without Mercy*, 203–233.

46. Rumors of conciliation between Hitler and British grandees after the fall of France: Black, *Roosevelt*, 576. On the miserable World War II years of Lloyd George, see Lukacs, *Five Days in London*, 128; Cross, ed., *Life With Lloyd George*, 281. Shortly after the German invasion of France,

Lloyd George also purportedly told Ivan Maisky, Soviet ambassador to Britain, "the Allies cannot win the war. The most we can think about now is how to hold the Germans back till autumn and then see" (Gorodetsky, ed., *Maisky Diaries*, 278). Megan Lloyd George's quote: 304. For British Tory acquiescence, see Reynolds, *From World War to Cold War*, 42–44; and cf. 80–83 for Churchill's occasional pessimism.

47. Churchill's speech before Congress on December 26, 1941, Churchill, *The Grand Alliance*, 671–672.

48. For Themistocles's *pronoia*, see Hanson, "The Strategic Thought of Themistocles," in Murray and Sinnreich, eds., *Successful Strategies*, 17. Cf. Alanbrooke, *War Diaries*, 209, on Churchill and US entry into the war.

49. Churchill's "Finest Hour" speech before Commons on June 18, 1940: http://www.winstonchurchill.org/resources/speeches/233–1940 -the-finest-hour/122-their-finest-hour.

50. See Roberts, *Masters and Commanders*, 215–216. Churchill's strategy: Reynolds, *From World War to Cold War*, 80–88.

51. Britain's diminished postwar international influence: "British Grand Strategy, 1933–1942," in Murray, Sinnreich, and Lacey, eds., *The Shaping of Grand Strategy*, 147–181, esp. 167–181. Cf. Talbot Imlay, "Western Allied Ideology, 1939–1945," in Bosworth and Maiolo, eds., *The Cambridge History of the Second World War*, Vol. II: *Politics and Ideology*, 47–48.

52. Roberts, *Masters and Commanders*, 468–471. Monty's feuding with Eisenhower: Weidner, *Eisenhower and Montgomery*, 370–376. Churchill and the Allies at Yalta: David Reynolds, "The Diplomacy of the Grand Alliance," in Bosworth and Maiolo, eds., *The Cambridge History of the Second World War*, Vol. II: *Politics and Ideology*, especially 319–322.

53. Mobilization of the economy and Churchill's input: Stephen Broadberry and Peter Howlett, "The United Kingdom: 'Victory at All Costs'," in Harrison, ed., *The Economics of World War II*, 43–80; Gilbert, *Churchill: A Life*, 645–648. British war strategists: O'Brien, *How the War Was Won*, 157–168.

54. Churchill's strategic acumen: Hastings, *Finest Years*, 178–179, 478–479. The German view: Hechler, *Goering and His Gang*, 493.

55. Churchill's suspicions of Stalinist Russia: Alanbrooke, *War Diaries*, 483–484 (on Tehran Conference, November 28, 1943).

56. Churchillian rhetoric: Cannadine, *In Churchill's Shadow*, 85–113.

57. Von Luck, *Panzer Commander*, 109. Churchill's health problems: Hastings, *Finest Years*, 352–355, 362–363. Churchill's personal risks during the war: Jablonsky, *Churchill and Hitler*, 40–41.

58. Roberts, *History of the English-Speaking Peoples*, 147. Isolationism of the 1930s: the website of the United States Department of State (https: //history.state.gov/milestones/1937–1945/american-isolationism); Herring, *From Colony to Superpower*, 484–537.

59. Roosevelt's bipartisan support for the war: Fullilove, *Rendezvous with Destiny*, 332–356.

60. Friedberg, *In the Shadow of the Garrison State*, 9–33, for the private-sector preponderance of the US war economy. Cf. Herman, *Freedom's Forge*, 335–336.

61. Roosevelt's toughness toward his wartime domestic opponents in his January 11, 1944, State of the Union address, delivered as a fireside chat (accessed at http://docs.fdrlibrary.marist.edu/011144.HTML).

62. Roosevelt's method of decision-making: James Lacey, "Toward a Strategy: Creating an American Strategy for Global War, 1940–1943," in Murray, Sinnreich, and Lacey, eds., *The Shaping of Grand Strategy*, 182–209, esp. 207–209. Roosevelt's keen strategic sense: Peter R. Mansoor, "US Grand Strategy in the Second World War," in Murray and Sinnreich, eds., *Successful Strategies*, 333–338.

63. Roosevelt and his generals: Black, *Roosevelt*, 1124–1126. Cf. Persico, *Roosevelt's Centurions*, especially 528–539.

64. Roosevelt's hyper-criticism of British help for the Soviets: Berthon and Potts, *Warlords*, 139, quoting from Blum, *Roosevelt and Morgenthau* (March 11, 1942).

65. Roosevelt's sometimes snubbing of Churchill and courting of Stalin: Kimball, *Churchill & Roosevelt*, Vol. 1, 421–422. See Black, *Franklin Delano Roosevelt*, 481–482, 864–865.

66. Roosevelt's assurances to the British on American complementary strategy: Roberts, *Masters and Commanders*, 124–125. Cf. Stoler, *Allies and Adversaries*, 84–102. "Europe first" as simplistic description: O'Brien, *How the War Was Won*, 206–207.

67. Stalin's disastrous first two weeks of silence: Ulam, *Stalin*, 538–543. Cf. Pleshakov, *Stalin's Folly*, especially 98–112, on Stalin's mismanagement at the outbreak of war. Hitler's quote: Murray and Millett, *A War to Be Won*, 114.

68. Stalin's disingenuousness at the Tehran Conference about a second front: Ulam, *Stalin*, 589–590. Hitler's admiration of Stalin: Kershaw, *Hitler, 1936–45: Nemesis*, 628, 844, and cf. 898.

69. Stalin's atrocities: Antonov-Ovseyenko, *The Time of Stalin*, 123–124 and passim.

70. The Soviet Union's productive losses after June 1941: Mark Harrison, "The Soviet Union: The Defeated Victor," in Harrison, ed., *The Economics of World War II*, 282–284. Soviet increased war production in 1939: Murray and Millett, *A War to Be Won*, 112–113; Soviet war industries in the Urals: ibid., 117–118.

71. Remarkable record of Soviet production after the Germans invaded in June 1941: Dunn, *Stalin's Keys to Victory*, 23–41.

Chapter 17
The Warlords

1. Cf. Cray, *General of the Army*, 90. The "little black book": Cole King-seed, "Marshall's Men," *Army Magazine* (December 2009), 52–55. Cf. Fuller, *Generalship*, 41–44.

2. Von Blücher's loyalty and dedication: Chandler, *Campaigns of Napoleon*, 1068–1069.

3. Genius and shortcomings of Manstein: Melvin, *Manstein*, 504–510.

4. Murray and Millett, *A War to Be Won*, 74–75.

5. Cf. Maclean, *German General Officer Casualties*, 5.

6. Moral dilemmas of German generals: Melvin, *Manstein*, 506; Hansen, *Disobeying Hitler*, 55–58 (on Rommel and von Kluge).

7. American successful and mediocre generals: Ricks, *The Generals*, 17–134.

8. Training of German officers: Dennis E. Showalter, "'No Officer Rather Than a Bad Officer': Officer Selection and Education in the Prussian/German Army, 1715–1945," in Kennedy and Neilson, *Military Education*, 53–56. German generals' special pleading about Operation Barbarossa: Williamson Murray, "British Military Effectiveness in the Second World War," in Millett and Murray, eds., *Military Effectiveness*, Vol. 3, 96–97.

9. Model and Rommel: Barnett, ed., *Hitler's Generals*, 293–317 (Martin Blumenson on Rommel), and 319–334 (Carlo D'Este on Model). Praise of Rommel: Calvocoressi, Wint, and Pritchard, *Total War*, 375. Letter of February 26, 1943: Liddell Hart, ed., *Rommel Papers*, 410–411. Hitler's plans following the envisioned victory in Russia: Weinberg, *World at Arms*, 266–268.

10. Dupuy, *A Genius for War*, 253–254.

11. American experiences of Yamamoto and Matsuoka: Potter, *Yamamoto*, 14–26; Lu, *Agony of Choice*, 6–16.

12. Yamamoto's simultaneous doubts and enthusiasm for war: Potter, *Yamamoto*, 312–313; Thomas, *Sea of Thunder*, 15–19. Cf. Weinberg, "Some Myths of World War II," 715–716. Yamamoto versus the generals: Murray and Millett, *A War to Be Won*, 172.

13. Battle of Savo Island (August 9, 1942): D'Albas, *Death of a Navy*, 161–170, esp. 169–170, note 5 (added by Rear Admiral Robert A. Theobald); Loxton and Coulthard-Clark, *The Shame of Savo*, 237–240; Warner and Warner, *Disaster in the Pacific*, 244–259; Toshikazu Ohmae, "The Battle of Savo Island," in O'Connor, ed. *The Japanese Navy in World War II*, 74–85; Dull, *Imperial Japanese Navy*, 187–194. Defense of the Japanese admirals: see again Dull, 193–194; cf. 322–323; D'Albas, *Death of a Navy*, 312–335, esp. 329–331, note 4 (added by Rear Admiral Robert A. Theobald); Tomiki Koyangi, "The Battle of Leyte Gulf," in O'Connor, ed., *The Japanese Navy in World War II*, 106–118, esp. 112.

14. Skill of Japanese generals between 1944 and 1945: Okinawa (Ushijima), Sloan, *The Ultimate Battle*, 14–18; Iwo Jima (Kuribayashi), Newcomb and Schmidt, *Iwo Jima*, 8–20; Manila (Yamashita), Connaughton, Pimlott, and Anderson, *Battle for Manila*, 66–70; and Singapore (Yamashita), Hack and Blackburn, *Did Singapore Have to Fall?*, 87–91.

15. Murray and Millett, *A War to Be Won*, 20, 25. Captured and killed Soviet generals: Maslov, *Captured Soviet Generals*; Maslov and Glantz, *Fallen Soviet Generals*, 245–269.

16. Dunkirk: Eisenhower, *Crusade in Europe*, 143–145.

17. Comparisons between British and American generals: Weigley, *Eisenhower's Lieutenants*, 33–38; Overy, *Why the Allies Won*, 268–274.

18. Supposed British English brains guiding American brawn: Reynolds, *From World War to Cold War*, 129–133.

19. Jackson and Bramall, *The Chiefs*, 224–228. King's quote and rambunctiousness nature of American commander: Williamson Murray, "U.S. Strategy and Leadership in World War II: The Problem of a Two-Front Strategy," in Murray and Ishizu, eds., *Conflicting Currents*, 89.

20. Bradley's dismissal of the Pacific ("bush league"): Williamson Murray, "U.S. Strategy and Leadership in World War II: The Problem of a Two-Front Strategy," in Murray and Ishizu, eds., *Conflicting Currents*, 94.

21. Criticism of American doctrine in Europe between 1944 and 1945: Weigley, *Eisenhower's Lieutenants*, 728–729. Various traditions of American generalship: Ricks, *The Generals*, 17–19.

22. Berlin, *U.S. Army World War II Corps Commanders*, especially 9–13; Mansoor, *The GI Offensive in Europe*, particularly 249–268.

Chapter 18
The Workers

1. Mark Harrison, "The Economics of World War II: An Overview," in Harrison, ed., *The Economics of World War II*, 7–10, Tables 1.2–3.

2. Holger H. Herwig, "Germany and the Battle of the Atlantic," in Chickering, Förster, and Greiner, eds., *A World at Total War*, 78–79. Attacks on V-2 facilities: Miller, *Masters of the Air*, 201–202, 418.

3. Relative air superiority based on aircraft quality and quantity: Van Creveld, *Age of Airpower*, 128–129.

4. Germany's failure to mass-produce munitions before 1943: Albert Speer, *Inside the Third Reich*, 212–213; cf. Weinberg, *World at Arms*, 76–78.

5. Changing nature of the respective assets and production of the Allies and Axis: Mark Harrison, "The Economics of World War II: An Overview," in Harrison, ed., *The Economics of World War II*, 6–27.

6. Edgerton, *Britain's War Machine*, 181–194. On the Third Reich's oil dilemmas, see Becker, "The Role of Synthetic Fuel in World War II

Germany," *Air University Review* (July–August 1981), (http://www.airpower
.maxwell.af.mil/airchronicles/aureview/1981/jul-aug/becker.htm). Cf.
Murray and Millett, *A War to Be Won*, 52. For the Dutch East Indies and
Japan, see O'Brien, *How the War Was Won*, 72–74.

7. Cf. Edgerton, *Britain's War Machine*, 12–13, 31–46. See especially
Tooze, *Wages of Destruction*, 140–141.

8. Edgerton, *Britain's War Machine*, 172–178; Stephen Broadberry and
Peter Howlett, "The United Kingdom: 'Victory at All Costs,'" in Harrison, ed., *The Economics of World War II*, 61–63. On British rationing,
see Calvocoressi, Wint, and Pritchard, *Total War*, 438–439. Aviation gas:
Carew, *Becoming the Arsenal*, 279–280.

9. Hugh Rockoff, "The United States: From Plowshares to Swords," in
Harrison, ed., *The Economics of World War II*, 81–121; cf. 23–24. Myth of large-
scale consumer sacrifices: Lacey, *Keep from All Thoughtful Men*, 49. Bribes:
Overy, *Interrogations*, 274–275. And cf. Evans, *Third Reich at War*, 493–495.
On MacArthur, see the allegations in Masuda, *MacArthur in Asia*, 83–85.

10. For Hitler's dependency on Soviet imports, cf. Roberts, *Stalin's
Wars*, 42–43.

11. America's economic involvement during World War I: Stephen
Broadberry and Mark Harrison, "The Economics of World War I," in
Broadberry and Harrison, eds., *Economics of World War I*, 5–13. Cf. also in
the same edited volume, Hugh Rockoff, "Until It's Over, Over There: The
US Economy in World War I," 310–343.

12. America's astounding productive gains: Koistinen, *Arsenal of World
War II*, 448–450.

13. Eden, *Eden Memoirs: The Reckoning*, 93.

14. British aircraft statistics: Millett and Murray, *A War to Be Won*,
535 (Table 2: Major Weapons Produced by Allies and Axis Powers,
1940–1945).

15. For Liberty ship construction, cf. Herman, *Freedom's Forge*, 176–
191. A detailed account of all aspects of the program—including design,
materials, and labor—is found in Lane, *Ships for Victory*. For the remarkable advances in American aviation production, see Cairncross, *Planning in
Wartime*, 178. On America's ability to have produced even more munitions,
see Koistinen, *Arsenal of World War II*, 500–501. On the radical decrease
in cost of the proximity fuze as an example of American productivity, cf.
Baldwin, *Deadly Fuze*, 217–220.

16. For the changing workforce in Germany between 1943 and 1945,
see Evans, *Third Reich at War*, 350–352.

17. See Cairncross, *Planning in Wartime*, 176–177; for German and Soviet comparisons, see Ziemke and Bauer, *Moscow to Stalingrad*, 514–515.

18. For the German use of Czech military equipment, especially tanks,
as well as confiscated French armor, see Green, Anderson, and Schulz,
*German Tanks of World War II*, 28–30; Mosier, *Blitzkrieg Myth*, 46–47.

19. Stephen Broadberry and Peter Howlett, "The United Kingdom: 'Victory at All Costs,'" in Harrison, ed., *The Economics of World War II,* 58.

20. Cf. Mark Harrison, "The Economics of World War II: An Overview," in Harrison, ed., *The Economics of World War II,* 22–23; Edgerton, *Britain's War Machine,* 12–13, 79–81; cf. 279–280. Lend-Lease to Russia: Weeks, *Russia's Life-Saver,* 115–127.

21. Hitler's technological follies: Cornwell, *Hitler's Scientists,* 21–37; Lewin, *Hitler's Mistakes,* 81–100. Cf. the contrast among Allied planners: Kennedy, *Engineers of Victory,* 5–74; see the review of Kennedy by Michael Beschloss in *The New York Times Book Review* (February 10, 2013), 15. Hitler's big talk: Hechler, *Goering and His Gang,* 57.

22. Herman, *Freedom's Forge,* 335–336. Brilliant British planners: Edgerton, *Britain's War Machine,* 86–112. Cf. Patterson, *Arming the Nation for War,* 46.

## Chapter 19
## The Dead

1. Aggregate dead: Clodfelter, *Warfare and Armed Conflicts,* Vol. I, xxxiii–iv; for the more conservative figure of 40 million, cf. Vol. II, 954.

2. Black Death: Rosen, *The Third Horseman,* 254–259. Parker, *Global Crisis,* explores the devastation brought on by climate changes during the seventeenth century.

3. Population reaching largest size on the eve of World War II, and for the number of mobilized soldiers: Clodfelter, *Warfare and Armed Conflicts,* Vol. II, 956.

4. Rate of fire and distance of matchlock musket: Parker, *The Military Revolution,* 17–19. Fatality ratios between winners and losers: Clodfelter, *Warfare and Armed Conflicts,* Vol. I, xxxi–xxxii.

5. Friedländer, *Years of Extermination,* 503.

6. Khan, *Shallow Graves of Rwanda,* 7, 9; cf. also, Odom, *Journey into Darkness: Genocide in Rwanda,* 75–77.

7. Mortality statistics including and excluding the Eastern Front: Clodfelter, *Warfare and Armed Conflicts,* Vol. II, 838.

8. Hoplite battle in Classical Greece: Hanson, *Western Way of War,* passim; protection offered by hoplite armor: ibid., 81–83; on 10 percent battle casualty rates, see ibid., 209. Advantages of castles: Brauer and van Tuyll, *Castles, Battles, & Bombs,* 59–66.

9. Hypotheses about body armor and the reduction of fatalities: Michael Vlahos, "Could Body Armor Have Saved Millions in World War I?," *The Atlantic* (April 30, 2013), online at: http://www.theatlantic .com/international/archive/2013/04/could-body-armor-have-saved -millions-in-world-war-i/275417/.

10. Approximating the average number of flak rounds needed to down an Allied aircraft: Westermann, *Flak: German Anti-Aircraft Defenses, 1914–1945*, 292–295.

11. Clodfelter, *Warfare and Armed Conflicts*, Vol. II, 952.

12. Russian vengeance when the Red Army entered Berlin: Ryan, *Last Battle*, 459–465.

13. Historical ratios between soldiers lost to disease versus combat, cf. Clodfelter, *Warfare and Armed Conflicts*, Vol. I, xxxii–xxxiii.

14. Dutch during the harsh winter of 1944–1945: Van der Zee, *The Hunger Winter*, 304–310.

15. Famine in China and the millions of its war dead: Mitter, *Forgotten Ally*, 178ff.

16. Cameron and Stevens, eds., *Hitler's Table Talk*, 23–24. How the Soviet Union coped with food shortages: Moskoff, *Bread of Affliction*, 42–69. German *Hungerplan*: Tooze, *Wages of Destruction*, 477–485, 513–551; Alex J. Kay, "'The Purpose of the Russian Campaign Is the Decimation of the Slavic Population by Thirty Million': The Radicalization of German Food Policy in Early 1941," Chapter 4 of Kay, Rutherford, and Stahel, eds., *Nazi Policy on the Eastern Front, 1941*, 101–129; and 110 for the "Economic Policy." Snyder, *Bloodlands*, 411; Gesine Gerhard, "Food and Genocide: Nazi Agrarian Politics in the Occupied Territories of the Soviet Union," *Contemporary European History* 18.1 (2009), 45–65, esp. 54ff. Anecdotes from German soldiers on treatment of Russians: Gerlach, *Kalkulierte Morde*, 53, quoted also in Collingham, *Taste of War*, 39.

17. For a brief review of Japanese atrocities and starvation of occupied peoples, see Russell A. Hart, "Asia and the Pacific: Japanese Occupation, 1931–1945," in Ciment, ed., *World Terrorism*, Vol. 1, 49–51. Starvation and deaths to disease in occupied Europe and during the Nazi invasions and retreats: Hitchcock, *Bitter Road to Freedom*, 121–122, 227–238; Hastings, *Armageddon*, 407–417. On Greece, see Hionidou, *Famine and Death in Occupied Greece, 1941–1944*, 158.

18. Monthly loss rates of the German and Soviet armies: http://www .feldgrau.com/stats.html; cf. Krivosheev, *Soviet Casualties and Combat Losses*, 85–97. For discussion of Soviet exaggerations of German losses and false information concerning Russian casualties, see Mosier, *Deathride*, 338–340; 421.

19. Nature of the German death squads: Browning, *Ordinary Men*, 159–189. Cf. Hilberg, *Destruction of the European Jews*, 97–153; Winkler, *Age of Catastrophe*, 715. Non-Germans' roles in the Holocaust: Jochen Böhler, "Race, Genocide, and Holocaust," Chapter 39 of Zeiler and DuBois, eds., *A Companion to World War II*, 669–673.

20. In general on the Armenian genocide: Kévorkian, *The Armenian Genocide: A Complete History*; Cambodian "killing fields": Kiernan, *The Pol*

*Pot Regime*; Etcheson, *After the Killing Fields*; Rwandan tribal bloodletting: Khan, *Shallow Graves of Rwanda*; Melvern, *Conspiracy to Murder.*

21. Differences between Western European and transatlantic notions of human rights and the German concept of the citizen: Winkler, *Age of Catastrophe*, 887–888. Cf. Browning, *Ordinary Men*, 170: "In the past forty-five years no defense attorney or defendant in any of the hundreds of post-war trials has been able to document a single case in which the refusal to obey an order to kill unarmed civilians resulted in the allegedly inevitable dire punishment." Desire for Jewish loot: Hilberg, *Perpetrators, Victims, Bystanders*, 212–224; Overy, *Interrogations*, 196–198.

22. Conflation of Bolshevism and anti-Semitism: Kershaw, *Hitler, 1936–45: Nemesis*, 389.

23. For the effect of Operation Barbarossa on the Final Solution, see Evans, *Third Reich at War*, 247–248.

24. Friedländer, *Years of Extermination*, 23–24. Wannsee Conference, where the Final Solution was finalized: C. Gerlach, "The Wannsee Conference, the Fate of German Jews, and Hitler's Decision in Principle to Exterminate All European Jews," in Bartov, ed., *The Holocaust: Origins, Implementation, Aftermath*, 106–161.

25. Hitler's influence on Franco, see in general Casanova, *The Spanish Republic and Civil War*; Payne, *Franco and Hitler*; and Whealey, *Hitler and Spain*. Hitler's anti-Semitism: Hitler, *Mein Kampf*, 640; Domarus, *Hitler, Speeches and Proclamations 1932–1945*, Vol. 3, 1449. "Jewish virus": Cameron and Stevens, eds., *Hitler's Table Talk*, 332 (February 22, 1942). Hitler's March 1921 essay is quoted in Wünschmann, *Before Auschwitz*, 76.

26. Nazi deceptions: Gilbert, *Auschwitz and the Allies*, 341. German public opinion: Kershaw, *Hitler, the Germans, and the Final Solution*, 186, cf. also, 120, 142. Cf. Mengele's dissertation, see Lifton, *Nazi Doctors*, 339; cf. also Helena Kubica, "The Crimes of Josef Mengele," in Gutman and Berenbaum, eds., *Anatomy of the Auschwitz Death Camp*, 318; Martin Klettner's patent application for crematoria: Jean-Claude Pressac with Robert-Jan van Pelt, "The Machinery of Mass Murder at Auschwitz," in the same edited volume, 240. Krupp: Buruma, *Year Zero*, 183.

27. Doenitz, *Memoirs*, 467. German public opinion: Kershaw, *Hitler, the Germans, and the Final Solution*, 186, cf. also, 142–148; Hitler's unique role, see 110–116, especially 111.

28. IG Farben: in general, Jeffreys, *Hell's Cartel*. Involvement of thugs and criminals: Hilberg, *Perpetrators, Victims, Bystanders*, 51–74. Cf. Hilberg, *Destruction of the European Jews*, 27–37, on the legal and administrative contortions necessary to define Jewishness under the Third Reich. Cf. 244–246 for the conveyor belts of death.

29. "Jewish Question": Kershaw, *Hitler, the Germans, and the Final Solution*, 62–64, and cf. 73–74. Death tolls: Browning, *Ordinary Men*, xv. Prewar

Nazi abuse and killing: Wünschmann, *Before Auschwitz*, 58–99. Transition from mass shootings to gassing: Jürgen Matthäus, "Nazi Genocides," in Bosworth and Maiolo, eds., *The Cambridge History of the Second World War*, Vol. II: *Politics and Ideology*, 177–178.

30. Holocaust seen by Nazis as one of their lasting achievements: Friedländer, *Years of Extermination*, 226–230, 658–660. German indifference during the war: Kershaw, *Hitler, the Germans, and the Final Solution*, 220–223. Hitler's decision about the Final Solution, cf. ibid., 262–265. Cf. Richard Bessel, "Murder Amidst Collapse: Explaining the Violence of the Last Months of the Third Reich," in Weise and Betts, eds., *Years of Persecution, Years of Extermination*, 255–268.

31. 1936 Olympic Games and Avery Brundage's anti-Semitism: Guttmann, *The Games Must Go On*, 62–95. Cf. Mandell, *The Nazi Olympics*, 233–249.

32. Quotes from Hilberg, *Destruction of the European Jews*, 159. Why did Jews not leave the Third Reich earlier?: Friedländer, *Years of Extermination*, 9–11.

33. Mengele's horror lab at Auschwitz: Kubica, "The Crimes of Josef Mengele," in Gutman and Berenbaum, eds., *Anatomy of the Auschwitz Death Camp*, 324. American indifference: Winik, *1944*, 466–476. On making the Holocaust possible: Browning, *Ordinary Men*, 186. Bombing and the Holocaust: Wyman, "Why Auschwitz Wasn't Bombed," in Gutman and Berenbaum, eds., *Anatomy of the Auschwitz Death Camp*, especially 579–583; Overy, *Bombing War*, 583–596; Gilbert, *Auschwitz and the Allies*, 307–341. See also Fleming, *Auschwitz, the Allies and Censorship*, 275.

34. Allies' obstacles to emigration from Third Reich: Friedländer, *Years of Extermination*, 88–95.

35. Rebatet quote and further reflections on the yellow star: Jacoby, *Bloodlust*, 101–102.

36. Five-week toll: Gilbert, *Holocaust*, 175. Cf. Goebbels, *Goebbels Diaries, 1939–1941*, 183 (November 2, 1940). Differences in Jewish life between Eastern and Western Europe and the Nazi stereotyped perception of such: Friedländer, *Years of Extermination*, 16–18, 84–86. Jews' greater prewar fears of Russia than Germany: Hilberg, *Destruction of the European Jews*, 123, and De Bruhl, *Firestorm*, 140–144.

37. Difference in rounding up Jews in the West in comparison to the East, and the mystery of the East: Gilbert, *Auschwitz and the Allies*, 81–87.

38. Waterford, *Prisoners of the Japanese*, 171–185. Nazi nihilism: Bullock, *Hitler: A Study in Tyranny*, 806–807.

39. Number of those subject to Japanese control by mid-1942: Waterford, *Prisoners of the Japanese*, 31–32.

40. British casualties as a result of bombing raids in World War I: Overy, *Bombing War*, 20–23 (1,239 dead). Cf. also Arnold, *Allied Air War and Urban Memory*, 72–73. On World War II dead from bombing on both

sides, see Overy, *Bombers and the Bombed*, 306–307. Keegan, *Second World War*, 432–433; Evans, *Third Reich at War*, 42–43. For Japan, Frank, *Downfall*, 334; cf. USSBS's Morale Division's report of 900,000 killed and 1.3 million injured.

41. Cf. Kozak, *LeMay*, 220; Coffey, *Iron Eagle*, 146–165. LeMay's decision to launch incendiary raids against Japan: Maj. Gene Gurney, "The Giant Pays Its Way," in Sunderman, ed., *World War II in the Air: The Pacific*, 247–265. US official casualty estimates from the firebombing of Tokyo and the two nuclear attacks: United States Strategic Bombing Survey, *Summary Report (Pacific War)*, 16. For revised estimates, see Mark Selden, "A Forgotten Holocaust: US Bombing Strategy, the Destruction of Japanese Cities and the American Way of War from World War II to Iraq," *The Asia Pacific Journal: Japan Focus*, (http://www.japanfocus.org/-Mark-Selden/2414/article.html) posted May 2, 2007; cf. also Clodfelter, *Warfare and Armed Conflicts*, Vol. II, 952–953.

42. Trade-offs in bomber design and use: Mosier, *Blitzkrieg Myth*: 196–200.

43. Ian Krshaw, "Nazi Foreign Policy: Hitler's 'Programme' or 'Expansion Without Object'?," in Finney, ed., *Origins of the Second World War*, 140–142.

44. Expulsions of Japanese: Watt, *When Empire Comes Home*, 19–55, and for statistics, see 39 (Table 1: Estimates of Japanese Nationals Abroad at the End of World War II). Japanese ordeal in Manchuria: in general, Maruyama, *Escape from Manchuria*. Experiences of soldiers returning to Japan from former empire: Mariko Asano Tamanoi, "Soldier's Home: War, Migration, and Delayed Return in Postwar Japan," Chapter 2 of Biao, Yeoh, and Toyota, eds., *Return: Nationalizing Transnational Mobility in Asia*, 39–62.

45. German expulsion from the East: Ahonen, *After the Expulsion*, 15–24; Hitchcock, *Bitter Road to Freedom*, 164–169. Mass dislocations of Germans in the East: de Zayas, *Terrible Revenge*, 82, and cf. 152, where he conjectures that there were over 14 million German-speaking refugees, and 2 million deaths. Operation Hannibal (and "nobody cares"): Hastings, *Armageddon*, 285, 294, 497.

46. Civilians caught in war zones, see Hastings, *Armageddon*, 478, cf. 477–495. Chuikov, *Fall of Berlin*, 40–42. If 40 million civilians perished, the daily death rate was somewhere around 18,000; if 50 million, perhaps 23,000.

47. Earlier famines of 1921–1922: Kotkin, *Stalin*, 447–449. Hunger of 1931–1933: Khlevniuk, *Stalin*, 117–122. Famine struck again in 1936: Khlevniuk, *Stalin*, 124. On the so-called Great Terror of 1937–1938: Khlevniuk, *Stalin*, 150–182. In general, see Rutherford, *Combat and Genocide on the Eastern Front*. Veterans of all fronts conceded the singular brutality of the Eastern theater: Bartov, *Eastern Front*, 106–141.

48. German POWs on the Eastern Front: Overmans, *Deutsche militärische Verluste im Zweiten Weltkrieg*, 286–289. On the encirclements: Megargee, *War of Annihilation*, 82–83, 100–101.

49. Scorched-earth policies of the Red Army and the Wehrmacht: Rutherford, *Combat and Genocide on the Eastern Front*, 357–373. Soviet productive capacity under Nazi control: Keegan, *Second World War*, 222.

50. Tsar Alexander's scorched-earth tactics during Napoleon's 1812 campaign: Chandler, *Campaigns of Napoleon*, 757–758, 855–856. See the remarks of Tsar Alexander to Narbonne in May 1812: ibid., 765. Cf. Roberts, *Napoleon*, 584–585.

51. Second Sino-Japanese War, Japanese occupation of China, and the ongoing Chinese civil wars: Paine, *Wars for Asia*, 122–169: 95 million Chinese citizens became refugees (133), and the Three Alls Campaign as the Three Prohibitions Campaign, "admonishing the Chinese not to burn, commit crimes, or kill" (155).

52. Controversies over German losses: Müller and Ueberschär, *Hitler's War in the East, 1941–1945*, 345–376. German losses in Eastern Europe: Murray and Millett, *A War to Be Won*, 555. On little sympathy for vast German relocations in 1945–1946: Weinberg, *World at Arms*, 895.

53. Red Army's offensive into East Prussia: Hastings, *Armageddon*, 261–297.

54. Monthly losses of the Wehrmacht: Overmans, *Deutsche militärische Verluste im Zweiten Weltkrieg*, 237–240.

55. Role of geography in Polish history: Davies, *God's Playground*, 23–60.

56. Holocaust in Poland, and Nazi views of Poland: Hilberg, *Destruction of the European Jews*, 64–96; for Heydrich: 65.

57. Keegan, *Six Armies in Normandy*, 262–282. On the Polish underground movement: in general, Ney-Krwawicz, *Polish Resistance Home Army*.

58. Breakdown of the Polish dead: Dear and Foot (*Oxford Companion to World War II*, 290 [Demography, Table 1]) cite as total war-related deaths 123,000 military and 4,000,000 civilian losses.

59. Japanese population: Dear and Foot, eds., *Oxford Companion to World War II*, 605. Losses: Paine, *Wars for Asia*, 214.

60. Japanese losses: Toland, *Rising Sun*, 726. Paine, *Wars for Asia*, 216. On Japanese naval losses, and comparisons to both Japan's allies and enemies: Ellis, *World War II*, 254 (Table 52).

61. Italy's World War II losses: Dear and Foot, eds., *Oxford Companion to World War II*, 290 (Demography, Table 1). Cf. Walker, *Iron Hulls, Iron Hearts: Mussolini's Elite Armoured Divisions in North Africa*, 26.

62. Germany's treatment of Italians: Evans, *Third Reich at War*, 471.

63. Harsh reprisals against Italians by the Germans: Lamb, *War in Italy, 1943–1945*, 129–135; Agarossi, *A Nation Collapses*, 115. Cf. also Belco,

*War, Massacre, and Recovery in Central Italy*, 57–79. And see Evans, *Third Reich at War*, 471.

64. Italian forced laborers in the Third Reich: Dear and Foot, eds., *Oxford Companion to World War II*, 384 (Forced labour, Table 2).

65. Browning, *United States Merchant Marine Casualties of World War II*, for all US Merchant Marine casualties from 1940 to 1946.

66. Losses suffered and inflicted by the Army Air Forces: Correll, "The US Army Air Forces at War: a Statistical Portrait of USAAF in World War II," *Air Force Magazine*, 78.6 (June 1995), 33–36. Command and General Staff College (Fort Leavenworth, Kansas), "Battle Casualties by Type of Casualty and Disposition, and Duty Branch: 7 December 1941–31 December 1946," *Army Battle Casualties and Non-battle Deaths in World War II: Final Report*, 73–77 (http://cgsc.cdmhost.com/utils/getfile/collection /p4013coll8/id/128/filename/117).

67. Allan R. Millett, "The United States Armed Forces in the Second World War," in Millett and Murray, eds., *Military Effectiveness*, Vol. 3, 52–53.

68. Hobart's "funnies": Delaforce, *Churchill's Secret Weapons*, 49–82. Numbers and nature of the British war dead: Mellor, *Casualties and Medical Statistics*, 834–839. On the advantages and disadvantages of British armored flight decks: S. Slade and R. Worth, "Were Armored Flight Decks on British Carriers Worthwhile?," http://www.navweaps.com/index _tech/tech-030.htm (June 14, 2002).

# Part 7. Ends

1. Sartre, *The Devil & the Good Lord*, 4. "*Une victoire racontée en détail, on ne sait plus ce qui la distingue d'une défaite.*" *Le Diable et le Bon Dieu* (Act I, Scene I) (Paris: Éditions Gaillimard, 1951).

Chapter 20
Why and What Did the Allies Win?

1. Lord, *Proconsuls*, 91–108, 109–132.

2. Walzer, *Just and Unjust Wars*, 111–117; cf. 289–296, 319–322.

3. Prussians: von Mellenthin, *German Generals*, 145.

4. Ellis, *Brute Force*, 538; cf. 349.

5. O'Brien, *How the War Was Won*, 479–488. General Kojiro Sato's fantasies ("My idea is that if bands of such death-daring men should be thrown in upon San Francisco it would be very interesting indeed"): Butow, *Tojo and the Coming of the War*, 19.

6. Cameron and Stevens, eds., *Hitler's Table Talk*, 319.

7. Pasher, *Holocaust versus Wehrmacht*, 275–290. Transportation to the camps: R. Hilberg, "German Railroads/Jewish Souls," *Society* 14.1 (1976), 60–74. Effects of the Holocaust later in Russia: D. Acemoglu, T. Hassan, and J. Robinson, "Social Structure and Development: A Legacy of the Holocaust in Russia," *The Quarterly Journal of Economics*, 126.2 (2011), 895–946. On the increase in American scientific patents granted to Jewish emigres, see Petra Mosher, Alessandra Voena, and Fabian Waldinger, "German-Jewish Emigrés and U.S. Invention," (December 21, 2013), available at SSRN: https://ssrn.com/abstract=1910247 or http://dx.doi.org/10.2139/ssrn.1910247.

8. "The Atlantic Charter" (August 14, 1941): http://www.nato.int/cps/en/natolive/official_texts_16912.htm.

9. De Bruhl, *Firestorm*, 180–181, 212–213, 280–282.

10. German ignorance of Pearl Harbor: Weinberg, "Pearl Harbor: The German Perspective," in Weinberg, *Germany, Hitler, and World War II*, 194–204. Cf. Roberts, *Masters and Commanders*, 71–73.

11. von Mellenthin, *German Generals*, 235.

12. American postwar confidence in the United Nations: Dennis Showalter, "Global Yet Not Total: The U.S. War Effort and Its Consequences," in Chickering, Förster, and Greiner, eds., *A World at Total War*, 132–133. Roosevelt's confusion over American postwar objectives: James Lacey, "Toward a Strategy: Creating an American Strategy for Global War, 1940–1943," in Murray, Sinnreich, and Lacey, eds., *The Shaping of Grand Strategy*, 208–209.

13. Naimark, *Russians in Germany*, 1–9. Loss of West Prussia, Posen, and Upper Silesia to Poland, Hultschiner Ländchen to Czechoslovakia, Memel to Lithuania, North Schleswig to Denmark, Malmedy-Eupen to Belgium, and Alsace-Lorraine to France; fate of East Prussia: Egremont, *Forgotten Land*, 316–322.

14. Doyle, *World War II in Numbers*, 206–208. On total losses: Germany—4,450,000 military, 1,050,000 civilian; Austria—260,000 military, 120,000 civilian; ethnic Germans—600,000 military, 50,000 civilian. As a percentage of the population, Germany lost 7.9 percent, Austria 5.7 percent, and ethnic Germans suffered losses of 9.7 percent.

15. *Time* (January 29, 1945). War crime trials, and the defense of German military officials: Hébert, *Hitler's Generals on Trial*, especially 8–36, 57–98, 99–128. Cf. edited volume of Mettraux, ed., *Perspectives on the Nuremberg Trial*, beginning with R. Jackson, "The Challenge of International Lawlessness," 5–12.

16. Pew poll at http://www.pewglobal.org/2015/06/23/1-americas-global-image/ International Poll. For an example of German revisionist history, see Friedrich, *The Fire: The Bombing of Germany, 1940–1945*.

17. Paine, *Wars for Asia*, 171–221. On 2015/16 world GDP see the figures of the International Monetary Fund accessed from http://www.imf.org/external/index.htm.

18. On the new *Kaga*: Sam LaGrone, "Japan Launches Latest Helicopter Carrier," *USNI News* (August, 27, 2015) accessed at https://news.usni.org/2015/08/27/japan-launches-second-helicopter-carrier; for Japan's withdrawal from abroad to mainland after defeat in 1945: Watt, *When Empire Comes Home*, 2–7, 190–210.

19. Anticipated aims and real ends of the war: Rothwell, *War Aims in the Second World War*, 221–226.

20. Greek victories against the Italian army: Carr, *Defence and Fall of Greece*, 100–138. Cf. Mazower, *Inside Hitler's Greece*, 219–234.

21. Lamb, *War in Italy, 1943–1945: A Brutal Story*, 56–79. Germans committing 165 murders a day against Italians: http://www.spiegel.de/international/europe/war-crimes-report-explores-world-war-ii-nazi-brutality-in-italy-a-874024.html.

22. Postwar ambitions of the Soviet Union and China: Naimark and Gibianskii, eds., *Establishment of Communist Regimes*; 1–17; B. McLoughlin and K. McDermott, "Rethinking Stalinist Terror," in McDermott and Stibbe, eds., *Stalinist Terror in Eastern Europe*, 1–18. Cf. Gatrell and Baron, eds., *Warlands*, 1–22.

23. On the controversies over Mao's body count (45–70 million dead?) as a result of his various failed policies, see the account of Jung Chang and Jon Halliday, *Mao: The Unknown Story* (New York: Knopf, 2005), 3: "responsible for well over 70 million deaths in peacetime"—and, in general, the reactions of the academic community to such staggering death tolls, collected and edited in Benton and Chun, eds., *Was Mao Really a Monster?*

24. Hitler on the Allies' problematic triad: Cameron and Stevens, eds., *Hitler's Table Talk*, 538–539 (June 27, 1942).

25. Winkler, *Age of Catastrophe*, 913–915; Orwell: "Revenge is sour," *Tribune* (November 9, 1945); cf. Bloom, ed., *George Orwell, Updated Edition*, 115. American criticism of British imperialism: Hamilton, *The Mantle of Command*, 244–245.

26. Stalin, Yalta, and the Allied agendas: David Reynolds, "The Diplomacy of the Grand Alliance," in Bosworth and Maiolo, eds., *The Cambridge History of the Second World War*, Vol. II: *Politics and Ideology*, 319–322.

27. Collapse of the Churchill government and the conservatives: Butler, *Britain and Empire*; 28–62. British withdrawals from overseas: Childs, *Britain Since 1945*, 28–53. Promotion of social equity and greater government spending: C. Pierson, "Social Policy," in Marquand and Seldon, eds., *The Ideas That Shaped Post-War Britain*, 139–164.

28. For George Marshall's flexibility on the timing of the cross-Channel invasion, see James Lacey, "Toward a Strategy: Creating an

American Strategy for Global War, 1940–1943," in Murray, Sinnreich, and Lacey, eds., *The Shaping of Grand Strategy*, 201–204.

29. Marshall Plan aid: see Sanford, "The Marshall Plan: Origins and Implementation," 11–14; Mee, *Marshall Plan*, 246–263; Gerard Bossuat, "The Marshall Plan: History and Legacy," Chapter 1 in Sorel and Padoan, eds., *The Marshall Plan: Lessons Learned for the 21st Century*, 13–23; Imanuel Wexler, "The Marshall Plan in Economic Perspective: Goals and Accomplishments," Chapter 7 in Schain, ed., *The Marshall Plan: Fifty Years After*, 147–152; Hogan, *Marshall Plan*, 54–87. Relationship between Churchill and Roosevelt: Reynolds, *From World War to Cold War*, 99–120. Ormsby-Gore's comment: cf. *The New York Times*, October 28, 1962. Lend-Lease to Britain: Adam Tooze and Jamie Martin, "The Economics of the War with Nazi Germany," in Geyer and Tooze, eds., *The Cambridge History of the Second World War*, Vol. III: *Total War: Economy, Society and Culture*, 42. Katyn Forest: Gorodetsky, ed., *Maisky Diaries*, 507–511. Allied duplicity in hushing up the Soviet murdering in the Katyn Forest: Sanford, *Katyn and the Soviet Massacre of 1940*, 1–2, 144, 158–165. Roosevelt's suspicions of British designs: Hamilton, *The Mantle of Command*, 236–237, 242–245. Show trials: see Jo Fox, "The Propaganda War," in Bosworth and Maiolo, eds., *The Cambridge History of the Second World War*, Vol. II: *Politics and Ideology*, 108–109. French censoring of the Nazis: Weber, *Hollow Years*, 126.

30. Churchill's influence on America's hardening attitudes toward the Soviet Union: Harbutt, *The Iron Curtain*, 117–150.

31. Blumenson, *Patton Papers, 1940–1945*, 544 (September 7, 1944).

# Works Cited

Acemoglu, D., T. Hassan, and J. Robinson. "Social Structure and Development: A Legacy of the Holocaust in Russia," *The Quarterly Journal of Economics*, 126.2 (2011), 895–946.

Agarossi, Elena. *A Nation Collapses: The Italian Surrender of September 1943* [Harvey Fergusson II, tr.] (Cambridge: Cambridge University Press, 2000).

Agte, Patrick. *Michael Wittmann and the Waffen SS Tiger Commanders of the Leibstandarte in WWII*, Vol. 1 (Harrisburg, PA: Stackpole Books, 2006).

Ahonen, Pertti. *After the Expulsion: West Germany and Eastern Europe, 1945–1990* (Oxford; New York: Oxford University Press, 2003).

Air Ministry (Great Britain). *The Rise and Fall of the German Air Force: 1933–1945* (New York: St. Martin's Press, 1983).

Alanbrooke, Field Marshal Lord. *War Diaries, 1939–1945: Field Marshal Lord Alanbrooke* [Alex Danchev and Daniel Todman, eds.] (London: Weidenfeld & Nicolson, 2001).

Allen, Louis. *Singapore 1941–1942* (London: Davis-Poynter, 1977).

Allsen, Thomas T. *Mongol Imperialism: The Policies of the Grand Qan Möngke in China, Russia, and the Islamic Lands, 1251–1259* (Berkeley: University of California Press, 1987).

Amersfoort, Herman, and Piet Kamphuis, eds. *May 1940: The Battle for the Netherlands* (Leiden: Brill, 2010).

Anderton, David A. *B-29 Superfortress at War* (New York: Scribner, 1978).

Angelucci, Enzo. *The Rand McNally Encyclopedia of Military Aircraft, 1914–1980* (Chicago: Rand McNally, 1981).

Angelucci, Enzo, Paolo Matricardi, and Pierluigi Pinto. *Complete Book of World War II Combat Aircraft* (rev. ed.) (Vercelli, Italy: White Star Publishers, 2007).

Ansel, Walter. *Hitler and the Middle Sea* (Durham, NC: Duke University Press, 1972).

Antill, Peter. *Stalingrad 1942* (Oxford: Osprey Publishing, 2007).

Antonov-Ovseyenko, Anton. *The Time of Stalin: Portrait of a Tyranny* (New York: Harper & Row, 1981).

*Army Battle Casualties and Non-battle Deaths in World War II, Final Report, 7 December 1941–31 December 1946* (Prepared by Statistical and Accounting Branch, Office of the Adjutant General, Under Direction of Program Review and Analysis Division Office of the Comptroller of the Army, OCS).

Arnold, Jörg. *The Allied Air War and Urban Memory: The Legacy of Strategic Bombing in Germany* (Cambridge: Cambridge University Press, 2011).

Arthur, Max. *Last of the Few: The Battle of Britain in the Words of the Pilots Who Won It* (New York: Skyhorse Publishing, 2011).

Asada, Sadao. *From Mahan to Pearl Harbor: The Imperial Japanese Navy and the United States* (Annapolis, MD: Naval Institute Press, 2006).

Askey, Nigel. *Operation Barbarossa: The Complete Organisational and Statistical Analysis, and Military Simulation*, Vol. IIB: *The German Forces, Mobilisation and War Economy: June to December 1941* (Raleigh, NC: Lulu Press, 2014).

Astin, A. E., F. W. Walbank, M. W. Frederiksen, and R. M. Ogilvie, eds. *The Cambridge Ancient History*, Vol. VIII: *Rome and the Mediterranean to 133 B.C.* (2nd ed.). (Cambridge: Cambridge University Press, 1989) [= *CAH* 8²].

Astor, Gerald. *Crisis in the Pacific* (New York: Donald I. Fine Books, 1996).

———. *The Bloody Forest: Battle for the Huertgen, September 1944–January 1945* (Novato, CA: Presidio Press, 2000).

Atkinson, Rick. *An Army at Dawn: The War in North Africa, 1942–1943* (New York: Henry Holt & Co., 2002).

———. *The Day of Battle: The War in Sicily and Italy, 1943–1944* (New York: Henry Holt & Co., 2007).

Baime, A. J. *The Arsenal of Democracy: FDR, Detroit, and Their Epic Quest to Arm an America at War* (Boston and New York: Houghton Mifflin Harcourt, 2014).

Baker, David. *The Rocket: The History and Development of Rocket & Missile Technology* (New York: Crown, 1978).

Baldwin, Ralph Belknap. *Deadly Fuze: The Secret Weapons of World War II* (San Rafael, CA: Presidio Press, 1980).

Barker, Thomas M. *Double Eagle and Crescent: Vienna's Second Turkish Siege and Its Historical Setting* (Albany: State University of New York Press, 1967).

Barnett, Correlli. *The Collapse of British Power* (New York: Morrow, 1972).

———, ed. *Hitler's Generals* (London: Weidenfeld & Nicolson, 1989).

Bartov, Omer. *The Eastern Front, 1941–1945, German Troops and the Barbarisation of Warfare* (2nd ed.) (Houndsmills, Basingstoke, Hampshire: Palgrave, 2001).

———. *The Holocaust: Origins, Implementation, Aftermath* (London; New York: Routledge, 2000).

Baynes, Norman H., ed. and tr. *The Speeches of Adolf Hitler, April 1922–August 1939* (2 vols.) (New York: Oxford University Press, 1942).

Beach, Edward L. *Submarine! The Classic Account of Undersea Combat in World War II* (New York: Pocket Books, 2004).

Beevor, Antony. *Ardennes 1944: Hitler's Last Gamble* (London: Viking, 2015).

————. *Crete 1941: The Battle and the Resistance* (New York: Penguin Books, 2014).

————. *D-Day: The Battle for Normandy* (New York: Viking, 2009).

————. *Stalingrad* (New York: Viking, 1998).

Belco, Victoria C. *War, Massacre, and Recovery in Central Italy, 1943–1948* (Toronto: University of Toronto Press, 2010).

Bell, Christopher M. *Churchill and Sea Power* (Oxford: Oxford University Press, 2013).

Bell, David A. *The First Total War: Napoleon's Europe and the Birth of Warfare as We Know It* (Boston: Houghton Mifflin Co., 2007).

Belote, James H., and William M. Belote. *Corregidor: The Saga of a Fortress* (New York: Harper & Row, 1967).

Bendiner, Elmer. *The Fall of Fortresses: A Personal Account of the Most Daring, and Deadly, American Air Battles of World War II* (New York: G. P. Putnam, 1980).

Benton, Gregor, and Lin Chun, eds., *Was Mao Really a Monster?: The Academic Response to Chang and Halliday's* Mao: The Unknown Story (London: Routledge, 2009).

Bercuson, David J., and Holger H. Herwig. *The Destruction of the Bismarck* (Woodstock, NY: Overlook Press, 2001).

Berlin, Robert H. *U.S. Army World War II Corps Commanders: A Composite Biography* (Fort Leavenworth, KS: US Army Command and General Staff College, Combat Studies Institute, 1989).

Berthon, Simon, and Joanna Potts. *Warlords: An Extraordinary Re-creation of World War II Through the Eyes and Minds of Hitler, Churchill, Roosevelt, and Stalin* (Cambridge, MA: Da Capo Press, 2006).

Biao, Xiang, Brenda S. A. Yeoh, and Mika Toyota, eds. *Return: Nationalizing Transnational Mobility in Asia* (Durham, NC: Duke University Press, 2013).

Bidlack, Richard, and Nikita Lomagin. *The Leningrad Blockade, 1941–1944: A New Documentary Archive from the Soviet Archives* (New Haven: Yale University Press, 2012).

Bird, Keith W. *Erich Raeder, Admiral of the Third Reich* (Annapolis, MD: Naval Institute Press, 2006).

Birdsall, Steve. *Saga of the Superfortress: The Dramatic Story of the B-29 and the Twentieth Air Force* (Garden City, NY: Doubleday, 1980).

Black, Conrad. *Franklin Delano Roosevelt: Champion of Freedom* (New York: PublicAffairs, 2003).

Blainey, Geoffrey. *The Causes of War* (3rd ed.) (London: Macmillan Press, 1988).

Blair, Clay. *Hitler's U-Boat War.* Vol. 1: *The Hunters, 1939–1942* (New York: Random House, 1996).

Bloch, Marc. *Strange Defeat: A Statement of Evidence Written in 1940* [Gerard Hopkins, tr.] (New York: Norton, 1968).

Bloom, Harold, ed. *George Orwell, Updated Edition* (New York: Chelsea House, 2007).

Blum, John Morton. *Roosevelt and Morgenthau: A Revision and Condensation of From the Morgenthau Diaries* (Boston: Houghton Mifflin Company, 1970).

Blumenson, Martin. *Anzio: The Gamble That Failed* (New York: Cooper Square Press, 2001).

———. *The Patton Papers: 1940–1945* (Boston: Houghton Mifflin, 1974).

Boemeke, Manfred F., Gerald D. Feldman, and Elisabeth Glaser. *The Treaty of Versailles: A Reassessment After 75 Years* (Cambridge: Cambridge University Press, 1998).

Boghardt, Thomas. *The Zimmermann Telegram: Intelligence, Diplomacy, and America's Entry into World War I* (Annapolis, MD: Naval Institute Press, 2012).

Bond, Brian, and Kyoichi Tachikawa, eds. *British and Japanese Military Leadership in the Far Eastern War, 1941–1945* (London; New York: Frank Cass, 2004).

Boot, Max. *War Made New: Technology, Warfare, and the Course of History, 1500 to Today* (New York: Gotham Books, 2006).

Borneman, Walter R. *The Admirals: Nimitz, Halsey, Leahy, and King—The Five-Star Admirals Who Won the War at Sea* (New York: Little, Brown and Co., 2012).

Bosworth, R.J.B. *Mussolini* (New York: Oxford University Press, 2002).

Bosworth, Richard, and Joseph Maiolo, eds. *The Cambridge History of the Second World War*, Vol. II: *Politics and Ideology* (Cambridge: Cambridge University Press, 2015).

Bowen, Crosswell. *Back from Tobruk* (Sterling, VA: Potomac Books, 2012).

Boyce, Robert W. D., and Esmonde M. Robertson, eds. *Paths to War: New Essays on the Origins of the Second World War* (New York: St. Martin's Press, 1989).

Boyne, Walter J. *Clash of Titans: World War II at Sea* (New York: Simon & Schuster, 1995).

———. *The Influence of Air Power upon History* (Gretna, LA: Pelican Publishing Company, 2003).

Braddon, Russell. *The Siege* (New York: The Viking Press, 1969).

Bradham, Randolph. *Hitler's U-Boat Fortresses* (Westport, CT: Praeger, 2003).

Bragadin, Marc' Antonio. *The Italian Navy in World War II* [Gale Hoffman, tr.] (Annapolis, MD: Naval Institute Press, 1957).

Brauer, Jurgen, and Hubert Van Tuyll. *Castles, Battles, & Bombs: How Economics Explains Military History* (Chicago: The University of Chicago Press, 2008).

Breuer, William B. *Operation Torch: The Allied Gamble to Invade North Africa* (New York: St. Martin's Press, 1986).

Broadberry, Stephen, and Mark Harrison, eds. *The Economics of World War I* (Cambridge: Cambridge University Press, 2005).

Browne, Courtney. *Tojo: The Last Banzai* (New York: Holt, Rinehart and Winston, 1967).

Browning, Christopher R. *Ordinary Men: Reserve Police Battalion 101 and the Final Solution in Poland* (New York: Harper Perennial, 1998).

Browning, Robert M. *United States Merchant Marine Casualties of World War II* (rev. ed.) (Jefferson, NC: McFarland & Co., 2011).

Buckley, John. *Air Power in the Age of Total War* (Bloomington: Indiana University Press, 1999; London: UCL Press, 1999).

Buderi, Robert. *The Invention That Changed the World: How a Small Group of Radar Pioneers Won the Second World War and Launched a Technological Revolution* (New York: Simon & Schuster, 1996).

Bullock, Alan. *Hitler: A Study in Tyranny* (rev. ed.) (New York: Harper & Row, 1962).

Burdick, Charles, and Hans-Adolf Jacobsen, eds. *The Halder War Diary 1939–1942* (Novato, CA: Presidio, 1988).

Buruma, Ian. *Year Zero: A History of 1945* (New York: Penguin Press, 2013).

Butler, J.R.M. *Grand Strategy*, Vol. 3: *June 1941–August 1942* [Part II] (London: H. M. Stationary Office, 1964).

Butler, L. J. *Britain and Empire: Adjusting to a Post-Imperial World* (London: I. B. Tauris, 2002).

Butow, Robert J. C. *Tojo and the Coming of the War* (Princeton: Princeton University Press, 1961).

Buttar, Prit. *Battleground Prussia: The Assault on Germany's Eastern Front, 1944–45* (Oxford: Osprey Publishing, 2010).

Cairncross, Alec. *Planning in Wartime: Aircraft Production in Britain, Germany, and the USA* (New York: St. Martin's Press, 1991).

Cairns, John C. "Great Britain and the Fall of France: A Study in Allied Disunity," *Journal of Modern History*, Vol. 27, No. 4 (December 1955), 365–409.

Calvocoressi, Peter, Guy Wint, and John Pritchard. *Total War: The Causes and Courses of the Second World War* (rev. 2nd ed.) (New York: Viking, 1989).

Cameron, Norman, and R. H. Stevens, eds. *Hitler's Table Talk, 1941–1944: His Private Conversations* (3rd ed.) (New York: Enigma Books, 2000).

Campbell, Brian, and Lawrence A. Tritle, eds. *The Oxford Handbook of Warfare in the Classical World* (Oxford: Oxford University Press, 2013).

Campbell, Christy. *Target London: Under Attack from the V-Weapons During WWII* (London: Little, Brown, 2012).

Campbell, John. *Naval Weapons of World War Two* (London: Conway Maritime Press, 1985).

Cannadine, David. *In Churchill's Shadow: Confronting the Past in Modern Britain* (Oxford, New York: Oxford University Press, 2004).

Capponi, Niccolò. *Victory of the West: The Story of the Battle of Lepanto* (New York: Macmillan, 2006).

Carell, Paul. *Hitler Moves East, 1941–1943* [translated from the German *Unternehmen Barbarossa* by Ewald Osers, 1963] (Boston: Little, Brown and Company, 1964).

Carew, Michael G. *Becoming the Arsenal: The American Industrial Mobilization for World War II, 1938–1942* (Lanham, MD: University Press of America, 2010).

Carius, Otto. *Tigers in the Mud: The Combat Career of German Panzer Commander Otto Carius* (Harrisburg, PA: Stackpole Books, 2003).

Carr, John C. *The Defence and Fall of Greece 1940–1941* (Barnsley, UK: Pen & Sword Military, 2013).

Casanova, Julián. *The Spanish Republic and Civil War* (Cambridge: Cambridge University Press, 2010).

Casson, Lionel. *The Ancient Mariners: Seafarers and Sea Fighters of the Mediterranean in Ancient Times* (2nd ed.) (Princeton: Princeton University Press, 1991).

Chalmers, William Scott. *Max Horton and the Western Approaches: A Biography of Admiral Sir Max Kennedy Horton* (London: Hodder and Stoughton, 1954).

Chandler, David G. *The Campaigns of Napoleon: The Mind and Method of History's Greatest Soldier* (New York: Macmillan, 1966).

Chant, Chris. *Small Arms of World War II* (Minneapolis: Zenith Press, 2001).

Chickering, Roger, Stig Förster, and Bernd Greiner, eds. *A World at Total War: Global Conflict and the Politics of Destruction, 1937–1945* (Washington, DC: German Historical Institute; Cambridge: Cambridge University Press, 2005).

Chickering, Roger, Dennis Showalter, and Hans Van de Ven, eds., *The Cambridge History of War*, Vol. IV: *War and the Modern World* (Cambridge: Cambridge University Press, 2012).

Childs, David. *Britain Since 1945: A Political History* (London and New York: Routledge, 2001).

Chow, Peter C. Y., ed. *The US Strategic Pivot to Asia and Cross-Strait Relations: Economic and Security Dynamics* (New York: Palgrave Macmillan, 2014).

Chuikov, Vasilii I. *The Fall of Berlin* [Ruth Kirsch, tr.] (New York: Holt, Rinehart and Winston, 1967).

Churchill, Winston S. *A History of the English-Speaking Peoples*, Vol. III: *The Age of Revolution* (London: Cassell and Co., 1957).

Ibid. *The Second World War*, Vol. 1: *The Gathering Storm;* Vol. 3: *The Grand Alliance;* Vol. 4: *The Hinge of Fate* (Cambridge, MA: The Riverside Press [Houghton Mifflin Company], 1948, 1950, 1950).

Ciano, Galeazzo, Conte. *Diary, 1937–1943* (various contributors) (New York: Enigma Books, 2002).

Ciment, James, ed. *World Terrorism: An Encyclopedia of Political Violence from Ancient Times to the Post-9/11 Era*, 3 Vols. (2nd ed.) (Armonk, NY: M.E. Sharpe, 2011).

Cline, Ray S. *Washington Command Post: The Operations Division* (Washington, DC: Center of Military History, US Army, 2003).

Clodfelter, Michael. *Warfare and Armed Conflicts: A Statistical Encyclopedia of Casualty and Other Figures, 1494–2007* (2 vols.) (Jefferson, NC: McFarland & Co., 2008).

Cloutier, Patrick. *Regio Esercito: The Italian Royal Army in Mussolini's Wars, 1935–1943* (Lulu.com, 2013).

Coffey, Thomas M. *Iron Eagle: The Turbulent Life of General Curtis LeMay* (New York: Crown Publishers, 1986).

Coffman, Edward M. *The Regulars: The American Army, 1898–1941* (London: Belknap Press, 2007).

Cohen, Eliot A. *Supreme Command: Soldiers, Statesmen, and Leadership in Wartime* (New York: Free Press, 2002).

Collingham, E. M. *The Taste of War: World War Two and the Battle for Food* (London: Allen Lane, 2011).

Condell, Bruce, and David T. Zabecki, eds. *On the German Art of War: German Army Manual for Unit Command in World War II* (Harrisburg, PA: Stackpole Books, 2008).

Connaughton, R. M., John Pimlott, and Duncan Anderson. *The Battle for Manila* (Novato, CA: Presidio, 1995).

Constable, Olivia Remie, ed. *Medieval Iberia: Readings from Christian, Muslim, and Jewish Sources* (2nd ed.) (Philadelphia: University of Pennsylvania Press, 2012).

Cook, James F. *Carl Vinson: Patriarch of the Armed Forces* (Macon, GA: Mercer University Press, 2004).

Cooling, Benjamin Franklin III, ed. *Case Studies in the Development of Close Air Support* (Washington, DC: Office of Air Force History, US Air Force, 1990).

Coombs, Benjamin. *British Tank Production and the War Economy, 1934–1945* (London: Bloomsbury, 2013).

Cooper, Matthew. *The German Army, 1933–1945: Its Political and Military Failure* (New York: Stein and Day, 1978).

Corbett, Julian S. *Some Principles of Maritime Strategy* (introduction and notes by Eric J. Grove) (Annapolis, MD: Naval Institute Press, 1988).

Cornwell, John. *Hitler's Scientists: Science, War and the Devil's Pact* (London: Viking, 2003).

Correll, John T. "The US Army Air Forces at War: A Statistical Portrait of USAAF in World War 2," *Air Force Magazine*, 78.6 (June 1995), 33–36.

Cowley, Robert, ed. *What If? 2: Eminent Historians Imagine What Might Have Been* (New York: G. P. Putnam, 2001).

————, ed. *What Ifs? of American History: Eminent Historians Imagine What Might Have Been* (New York: G. P. Putnam, 2003).

Craig, William. *The Fall of Japan* (New York: Dial Press, 1967).

Craven, Wesley Frank, and James Lea Cate, eds. *The Army Air Forces in World War II*, Vol. II: *Europe, Torch to Pointblank, August 1942 to December 1943,* Vol. VI: *Men and Planes* (Washington, DC: Office of Air Force History, 1949, 1976).

Cray, Ed. *General of the Army: George C. Marshall, Soldier and Statesman* (New York: W.W. Norton, 1990).

Cross, Colin, ed. *Life with Lloyd George: The Diary of A. J. Sylvester, 1931–45* (London: Macmillan, 1975).

Cross, Robert F. *Shepherds of the Sea: Destroyer Escorts in World War II* (Annapolis, MD: Naval Institute Press, 2010).

Crowley, Patrick. *Kut 1916: Courage and Failure in Iraq* (Stroud, UK: Spellmount, 2009).

Crowley, Roger. *City of Fortune: How Venice Won and Lost a Naval Empire* (London: Faber & Faber, 2011).

Curry, Anne. *The Hundred Years' War: 1337–1453* (Oxford: Osprey Publishing, 2002).

D'Albas, Andrieu. *Death of a Navy: Japanese Naval Action in World War II* [Anthony Rippon, tr.] (New York: Devin-Adair Company, 1957).

Danişmend, İsmail Hami. *İzahlı Osmanlı Tarihi Kronolojisi,* Vol. 2 (Istanbul: Dogu Kutuphanesi, 2011).

Davies, Norman. *God's Playground: A History of Poland,* Vol. I: *The Origins to 1795* (New York: Columbia University Press, 1982).

Dear, I.C.B., and M.R.D. Foot, eds. *The Oxford Companion to World War II* (Oxford: Oxford University Press, 1995).

De Bruhl, Marshall. *Firestorm: Allied Airpower and the Destruction of Dresden* (New York: Random House, 2006).

DeLiancourt, G. *Political Aphorisms, Moral and Philosophical Thought of the Emperor Napoleon* [James A. Manning, ed.] (London: T.C. Newby, 1848).

Delaforce, Patrick. *Churchill's Secret Weapons: The Story of Hobart's Funnies* (London: Robert Hale, 1998).

————. *Smashing the Atlantic Wall: The Destruction of Hitler's Coastal Fortresses* (London: Cassell, 2001).

Dennis, George T., tr. *Maurice's Strategikon: Handbook of Byzantine Military Strategy* (Philadelphia: University of Pennsylvania Press, 1984).

De Seversky, Alexander P. *Victory Through Air Power* (New York: Simon and Schuster, 1942).

D'Este, Carlo. *Bitter Victory* (Milan: Mondadori, 1990).

————. *Decision in Normandy* (New York: Dutton, 1983).

————. *Patton: A Genius for War* (New York: HarperCollins, 1995).

Deutscher, Issac. *Stalin: A Political Biography* (New York: Oxford University Press, 1967).

Devlin, Gerald M. *Back to Corregidor: America Retakes the Rock* (New York: St. Martin's Press, 1992).

DeVries, Kelly. *Infantry Warfare in the Early Fourteenth Century: Discipline, Tactics, and Technology* (Woodbridge, Suffolk: The Boydell Press, 1996).

De Zayas, Alfred M. *A Terrible Revenge: The "Ethnic Cleansing" of East European Germans, 1944–1950* (New York: St. Martin's Press, 1994).

DiNardo, R. L. *Mechanized Juggernaut or Military Anachronism: Horses and the German Army of World War II* (New York: Greenwood Press, 1991).

Dobson, Jeremy. *Why Do the People Hate Me So?: The Strange Interlude Between the Two Great Wars in the Britain of Stanley Baldwin* (Leicester, UK: Matador, 2009).

Doenitz, Karl. *Memoirs: Ten Years and Twenty Days* [R. H. Stevens, tr.] (Westport, CT: Greenwood Press, 1959).

Domarus, Max. *Hitler: Speeches and Proclamations, 1932–1945* (London: I. B. Tauris, 1990).

Dorr, Robert F. *Mission to Tokyo: The American Airmen Who Took the War to the Heart of Japan* (Minneapolis: Zenith Press/MBI Publishing, 2012).

Doty, Andy. *Backwards into Battle: A Tail Gunner's Journey in World War II* (Palo Alto, CA: Tall Tree Press, 1995).

Doubler, Michael D. *Closing with the Enemy: How GIs Fought the War in Europe, 1944–1945* (Lawrence: University Press of Kansas, 1994).

Douhet, Guilio. *The Command of the Air* [Dino Ferrari, tr.] (Tuscaloosa: University of Alabama Press, 2009) [New York: Coward-McCann, 1924; Washington, DC: Office of Air Force History, 1983]).

Dower, John W. *War Without Mercy: Race and Power in the Pacific War* (New York: Pantheon Books, 1986).

Doyle, Peter. *World War II in Numbers: An Infographic Guide to the Conflict, Its Conduct, and Its Casualties* (Buffalo, NY: Firefly Books, 2013).

Drea, Edward J. *Japan's Imperial Army: Its Rise and Fall, 1853–1945* (Lawrence: University Press of Kansas, 2009).

Drury, Bob, and Tom Clavin. *Halsey's Typhoon: The True Story of a Fighting Admiral, an Epic Storm, and an Untold Rescue* (New York: Atlantic Monthly Press, 2007).

Duff, Scott. *The M1 Garand, World War II: History of Development and Production, 1900 Through 2 September 1945* (Greensburg, 1993).

Dugan, James, and Carroll Stewart. *Ploesti: The Great Ground-Air Battle of 1 August 1943* (rev. ed.) (Washington, DC: Brassey's, 2002).

Duhamel, Georges. *The French Position* (London: Dent, 1940).

Dull, Paul S. *A Battle History of the Imperial Japanese Navy (1941–1945)* (Annapolis, MD: Naval Institute Press, 1978).

Dunn, Walter S. *Hitler's Nemesis: The Red Army, 1930–1945* (Westport, CT: Praeger, 1994).

———. *Stalin's Keys to Victory: The Rebirth of the Red Army* (Westport, CT: Praeger Security International, 2006).

Dupuy, T. N. *A Genius for War: The German Army, 1807–1945* (Englewood Cliffs, NJ: Prentice-Hall, 1977).

Eden, Sir Anthony. *The Eden Memoirs: The Reckoning* (London: Cassell, 1965).

Edgerton, David. *Britain's War Machine: Weapons, Resources and Experts in the Second World War* (London/New York: Penguin, 2012).

Edgerton, Robert B. *Warriors of the Rising Sun: A History of the Japanese Military* (New York: Norton, 1997).

Edwards, Harry W. *A Different War: Marines in Europe and North Africa* (Washington, DC: History and Museums Division, Headquarters, US Marine Corps, 1994).

Egremont, Max. *Forgotten Land: Journeys Among the Ghosts of East Prussia* (London: Picador, 2011).

Ehlers, Robert. *The Mediterranean Air War: Airpower and Allied Victory in World War II* (Lawrence: University Press of Kansas, 2015).

Eisenhower, Dwight D. *Crusade in Europe* (Baltimore: Johns Hopkins University Press, 1997).

Elliot, Peter. *Allied Escort Ships of World War II: A Complete Survey* (Annapolis, MD: Naval Institute Press, 1977).

Ellis, Frank. *The Stalingrad Cauldron: Inside the Encirclement and Destruction of the 6th Army* (Lawrence: University Press of Kansas, 2013).

Ellis, John. *Brute Force: Allied Strategy and Tactics in the Second World War* (New York: Viking, 1990).

———. *World War II: A Statistical Survey: The Essential Facts and Figures for All the Combatants* (New York: Facts on File, 1993).

English, John A., and Bruce I. Gudmundsson. *On Infantry* (Westport, CT: Praeger, 1994).

Etcheson, Craig. *After the Killing Fields: Lessons from the Cambodian Genocide* (Westport, CT: Praeger, 2005).

Evans, David C., ed. *The Japanese Navy in World War II: In the Words of Former Japanese Naval Officers* (Annapolis, MD: Naval Institute Press, 1986).

Evans, David C., and Mark R. Peattie. *Kaigun: Strategy, Tactics, and Technology in the Imperial Japanese Navy* (Annapolis, MD: Naval Institute Press, 1997).

Evans, Richard J. *The Third Reich at War, 1939–1945* (London: Allen Lane, 2008).

———. *The Third Reich in Power, 1933–1939* (New York: Penguin Press, 2005).

Ezell, Edward Clinton. *The Great Rifle Controversy: Search for the Ultimate Infantry Weapon from World War II Through Vietnam and Beyond* (Harrisburg, PA: Stackpole Books, 1984).

Falconer, Jonathan. *D-Day: 'Neptune', 'Overlord' and the Battle of Normandy: Operations Manual: Insights into How Science, Technology and Engineering*

*Made the Normandy Invasion Possible* (Sparkford, Yeovil, Somerset, UK: Haynes Publishing, 2013).

Farrell, Brian P., ed. *Leadership and Responsibility in the Second World War: Essays in Honour of Robert Vogel* (Montreal & Kingston: McGill-Queen's University Press, 2004).

Farrell, Brian, and Sandy Hunter. *Sixty Years On: The Fall of Singapore Revisited* (Singapore: Eastern Universities Press, 2002).

Feifer, George. *Tennozan: The Battle of Okinawa and the Atomic Bomb* (New York: Ticknor & Fields, 1992).

Feis, Herbert. *The Road to Pearl Harbor: The Coming of War Between the United States and Japan* (Princeton: Princeton University Press, 1950).

Fennell, Jonathan. *Combat and Morale in the North African Campaign: The Eighth Army and the Path to El Alamein* (Cambridge: Cambridge University Press, 2011).

Fermor, Patrick Leigh. *A Time of Gifts* (New York: Harper & Row, 1977).

Ferris, John, and Evan Mawdsley, eds. *The Cambridge History of the Second World War*, Vol. I: *Fighting the War* (Cambridge: Cambridge University Press, 2015).

Finney, Patrick, ed. *The Origins of the Second World War* (London: Arnold, 1997).

Fischer, Fritz. *Germany's Aims in the First World War* (Chatto & Windus, 1967).

Fitzpatrick, Sheila, and Michael Geyer, eds. *Beyond Totalitarianism: Stalinism and Nazism Compared* (Cambridge: Cambridge University Press, 2009).

Flanagan, Jr., E. M. (Lt. Gen.). *Corregidor: The Rock Force Assault, 1945* (Novato, CA: Presidio Press, 1988).

Fleming, Michael. *Auschwitz, the Allies and Censorship of the Holocaust* (Cambridge: Cambridge University Press, 2014).

Fletcher, Richard A. *Moorish Spain* (Berkeley: University of California Press, 1992).

Fontenoy, Paul E. *Submarines: An Illustrated History of Their Impact* (Santa Barbara, CA: ABC-CLIO, 2007).

Forty, George. *Japanese Army Handbook 1939–1945* (Gloucestershire, UK: Sutton Publishing, 1999).

———. *World War Two Tanks* (Oxford: Osprey Publishing, 1995).

Frank, Pat, and Joseph D. Harrington. *Rendezvous at Midway: U.S.S. Yorktown and the Japanese Carrier Fleet* (New York: John Day, 1967).

Frank, Richard B. *Downfall: The End of the Imperial Japanese Empire* (New York: Random House, 1999).

Franklin, Bruce Hampton. *The Buckley-Class Destroyer Escorts* (Annapolis, MD: Naval Institute Press, 1999).

Fraser, David. *Knight's Cross: A Life of Field Marshal Erwin Rommel* (New York: HarperCollins, 1993).

Freedman, Lawrence. *Strategy: A History* (Oxford and New York: Oxford University Press, 2013).

Freeman, Lloyd, Lt. Col. "Can the Marines Survive?" *Foreign Policy*, March 26, 2013.

Freund, Gerald. *Unholy Alliance: Russian-German Relations from the Treaty of Brest-Litovsk to the Treaty of Berlin* (New York: Harcourt Brace, 1957).

Friedberg, Aaron L. *In the Shadow of the Garrison State: America's Anti-Statism and Its Cold War Grand Strategy* (Princeton: Princeton University Press, 2000).

Friedländer, Saul. *The Years of Extermination: Nazi Germany and the Jews, 1939–1945* (New York: HarperCollins, 2007).

Friedman, Norman. *U.S. Battleships: An Illustrated Design History* (Annapolis, MD: Naval Institute Press, 1985).

———. *U.S. Destroyers: An Illustrated Design History* (rev. ed.) (Annapolis, MD: Naval Institute Press, 2004).

Friedrich, Jörg. *The Fire: The Bombing of Germany, 1940–1945* [Allison Brown, tr.] (New York: Columbia University Press, 2006).

Fuchida, Mitsuo, and Masatake Okumiya. *Midway: The Battle That Doomed Japan, the Japanese Navy's Story* (Annapolis, MD: Naval Institute Press, 2001).

Fuller, J.F.C. *Generalship, Its Diseases and Their Cure: A Study of the Personal Factor in Command* (Harrisburg, PA: Military Service Publishing Co., 1936).

———. *The Second World War, 1939–45: A Strategical and Tactical History* (London: Eyre and Spottiswoode, 1948).

Fullilove, Michael. *Rendezvous with Destiny: How Franklin D. Roosevelt and Five Extraordinary Men Took America into the War and into the World* (New York: Penguin Press, 2013).

Galland, Adolf. *The First and the Last: The Rise and Fall of the German Fighter Forces, 1938–1945* [Mervyn Savill, tr.] (New York: Henry Holt and Company, Inc., 1954).

Gannon, Michael. *Black May* (New York: HarperCollins, 1998).

———. *Operation Drumbeat: The Dramatic True Story of Germany's First U-Boat Attacks Along the American Coast in World War II* (New York: Harper & Row, 1990).

Gat, Azar. *British Armour Theory and the Rise of the Panzer Arm: Revising the Revisionists* (Houndmills, Basingstoke, Hampshire: Macmillan, 2000).

Gates, David. *The Napoleonic Wars, 1803–1815* (London and New York: Arnold, 1997).

Gatrell, Peter, and Nick Baron, eds. *Warlands: Population Resettlement and State Reconstruction in the Soviet-East European Borderlands, 1945–50* (Houndmills, Basingstoke, Hampshire; New York: Palgrave Macmillan, 2009).

Gavin, James M. *On to Berlin: Battles of an Airborne Commander 1943–1946* (New York: Viking Press, 1978).

Gentile, Gian P. *How Effective Is Strategic Bombing?: Lessons Learned from World War II to Kosovo* (New York: New York University Press, 2001).

Gerhard, Gesine. "Food and Genocide: Nazi Agrarian Politics in the Occupied Territories of the Soviet Union," *Journal of Contemporary European History*, Vol. 18, Issue 01 (February 2009).

Gerlach, Christian. *Kalkulierte Morde: Die Deutsche Wirtschafts und Vernichtungspolitik in Weissrussland 1941 bis 1944* (Hamburg: Hamburger Edition, 1999).

Geyer, Michael, and Adam Tooze, eds. *The Cambridge History of the Second World War*, Vol. III: *Total War: Economy, Society and Culture* (Cambridge: Cambridge University Press, 2015).

Gibbon, Edward. *The Decline and Fall of the Roman Empire*, Vol. 6 (London: D. Campbell, 1993–1994).

Gibbs, N. H. *Grand Strategy*, Vol. 1: *Rearmament Policy* (London: H. M. Stationary Office, 1976).

Gilbert, Martin. *Auschwitz and the Allies* (London: M. Joseph Rainbird, 1981).

———. *Churchill: A Life* (London: Heinemann, 1991).

———. *The Holocaust* (New York: Holt, Rinehart and Winston, 1985).

Glantz, David M. *The Battle for Leningrad: 1941–1944* (Lawrence: University Press of Kansas, 2002).

Glantz, David M., and Jonathan M. House. *Armageddon in Stalingrad: September–November 1942* (Lawrence: University Press of Kansas, 2009).

Glantz, David M. with Jonathan M. House. *Battle of Kursk* (Lawrence: University Press of Kansas, 1999).

———. *When Titans Clashed: How the Red Army Stopped Hitler* (Lawrence: University Press of Kansas, 1995).

Goebbels, Joseph. *The Goebbels Diaries, 1939–1941* [Fred Taylor, ed. and tr.; foreword by John Keegan] (New York: Penguin Books, 1984).

———. *The Goebbels Diaries, 1942–1943* [Louis P. Lochner, ed. and tr.] (Garden City, NY: Doubleday, 1948).

Goldensohn, Leon. *The Nuremberg Interviews* (New York: Alfred A. Knopf, 2004).

Goldstein, Erik, and John H. Maurer, eds. *The Washington Conference, 1921–22: Naval Rivalry, East Asian Stability and the Road to Pearl Harbor* (Ilford, Essex, UK; Portland, OR: Frank Cass, 1994).

Goldsworthy, Adrian. *Augustus: First Emperor of Rome* (New Haven: Yale University Press, 2014).

———. *The Punic Wars* (London: Cassell, 2001).

Goralski, Robert. *World War II Almanac 1931–1945: A Political and Military Record* (New York: Putnam Adult, 1981).

Gordon, Yefim, and Vladimir Rigmant. *Tupolev Tu-4: Soviet Superfortress* (Hinckley, UK: Midland Publishing, 2002).

Gorodetsky, Gabriel, ed. *The Maisky Diaries: Red Ambassador to the Court of St. James's, 1932–1943* (New Haven: Yale University Press, 2015).

Goutard, A., Col. *The Battle of France, 1940* [A. R. P. Burgess, tr.] (London: Frederick Muller Ltd., 1958).

Green, Michael, Thomas Anderson, and Frank Schulz. *German Tanks of World War II in Color* (MBI, 2000).

Greene, Jack, and Alessandro Massignani. *The Naval War in the Mediterranean 1940–1943* (London: Chatham Publishing, 1998).

Greenhalgh, Elizabeth. *Victory Through Coalition: Britain and France During the First World War* (Cambridge: Cambridge University Press, 2005).

Guderian, Heinz. *Achtung—Panzer!* (London: Orion, 2012).

———. *Panzer Leader* (London: M. Joseph, 1952).

Gudmundsson, Bruce I. *On Armor* (Westport, CT: Praeger, 2004).

Gunston, Bill. *The Illustrated Encyclopedia of the World's Rockets & Missiles: A Comprehensive Technical Directory and History of the Military Guided Missile Systems of the 20th Century* (New York: Crescent Books, 1979).

Gutman, Israel, and Michael Berenbaum, eds. *Anatomy of the Auschwitz Death Camp* (Bloomington: Indiana University Press, 1994).

Guttmann, Allen. *The Games Must Go On: Avery Brundage and the Olympic Movement* (New York: Columbia University Press, 1984).

Gwyer, J.M.A. *Grand Strategy*, Vol. III: *June 1941–August 1942* [Part I] (London: Her Majesty's Stationary Office, 1964).

Habeck, Mary R. *Storm of Steel: The Development of Armor Doctrine in Germany and the Soviet Union, 1919–1939* (Ithaca: Cornell University Press, 2003).

Hack, Karl, and Kevin Blackburn. *Did Singapore Have to Fall?: Churchill and the Impregnable Fortress* (London: RoutledgeCurzon, 2004).

Hale, John R. *Lords of the Sea: The Epic Story of the Athenian Navy and the Birth of Democracy* (New York: Viking, 2009).

Halpern, Paul G. *A Naval History of World War I* (Annapolis, MD: Naval Institute Press, 1994).

Hamilton, Nigel. *The Mantle of Command: FDR at War, 1941–1942* (Boston: Houghton Mifflin Harcourt, 2014).

Hammond, J. M. *Battle in Iraq: Letters and Diaries of the First World War* (London: The Radcliffe Press, 2009).

Hane, Mikiso, and Louis G. Perez. *Modern Japan: A Historical Survey* (4th ed.) (Boulder, CO: Westview Press, 2009).

Hansen, Randall. *Disobeying Hitler: German Resistance in the Last Year of WWII* (London: Faber & Faber, 2014).

Hanson, Victor Davis. *Carnage and Culture: Landmark Battles in the Rise of Western Power* (New York: Anchor Books, 2001).

———. *The Father of Us All: War and History, Ancient and Modern* (New York: Bloomsbury Press, 2010).

————. "Ferocious Warmakers: How Democracies Win Wars," *Claremont Review of Books*, Vol. II, No. 2 (Winter 2002).

————, ed. *Makers of Ancient Strategy: From the Persian Wars to the Fall of Rome* (Princeton, Princeton University Press, 2010).

————. *The Other Greeks: The Family Farm and the Agrarian Roots of Western Civilization* (New York: Free Press, 1995).

————. *Ripples of Battle: How the Wars of the Past Still Determine How We Fight, How We Live, and How We Think* (New York: Doubleday, 2003).

————. *The Savior Generals: How Five Great Commanders Saved Wars That Were Lost—From Ancient Greece to Iraq* (New York: Bloomsbury Press, 2013).

————. *The Soul of Battle: From Ancient Times to the Present Day, How Three Great Liberators Vanquished Tyranny* (New York: Free Press, 1999).

————. *A War Like No Other: How the Athenians and Spartans Fought the Peloponnesian War* (New York: Random House, 2005).

————. *The Western Way of War: Infantry Battle in Classical Greece* (2nd ed.) (Berkeley: University of California Press, 2009).

Harbutt, Fraser. *The Iron Curtain: Churchill, America, and the Origins of the Cold War* (Oxford, Oxford University Press, 1986).

Hardesty, Von, and Ilya Grinberg. *Red Phoenix Rising: The Soviet Air Force in World War II* (Lawrence: University Press of Kansas, 2012).

Harris, Arthur, Sir. *Bomber Offensive* (London: Greenhill Books; Mechanicsburg, PA: Stackpole Books, 1998).

Harrison, Gordon A. *Cross-Channel Attack: U.S. Army in World War II: The European Theater of Operations* (Washington, DC: Center of Military History, US Army, 2002).

Harrison, Mark, *Accounting for War: Soviet Production, Employment, and the Defence Burden, 1940–1945* (Cambridge Russian, Soviet and Post-Soviet Studies [Book 99], Cambridge: Cambridge University Press, 1996).

————. *Soviet Planning in Peace and War, 1938–1945* (Cambridge: Cambridge University Press, 1985).

————. "The Volume of Soviet Munitions Output, 1937–1945: A Reevaluation," *Journal of Economic History* 50.3 (1990), 569–589.

————, ed. *The Economics of World War II: Six Great Powers in International Comparison* (Cambridge: Cambridge University Press, 1998).

Hart, Stephen. *Sherman Firefly vs. Tiger: Normandy 1944* (Oxford: Osprey Publishing, 2007).

Harvey, Maurice. *Gibraltar* (Staplehurst, UK: Spellmount, 1996).

Haskew, Michael E. *The Wehrmacht 1935–1945: The Essential Facts and Figures for Hitler's Germany* (London: Amber Books, 2011).

Hastings, Max. *Armageddon: The Battle for Germany, 1944–1945* (New York: Alfred A. Knopf, 2004).

————. *Finest Years: Churchill as Warlord, 1940–45* (London: Harper Press, 2009).

Hattendorf, John B., ed. *Naval Strategy and Policy in the Mediterranean* (London; Portland, OR: Frank Cass, 2000).

Hayward, Joel S.A. *Stopped at Stalingrad: The Luftwaffe and Hitler's Defeat in the East, 1942–1943* (Lawrence: University Press of Kansas, 1998).

Hébert, Valerie. *Hitler's Generals on Trial: The Last War Crimes Tribunal at Nuremberg* (Lawrence: University Press of Kansas, 2010).

Hechler, Ken. *Goering and His Gang: My Interrogation of Nazi Germany's Top Officials* (Missoula, MT: Pictorial Histories Publishing Company, 2011).

Heckmann, Wolf. *Rommel's War in Africa* [Stephen Seago, tr.] (Garden City, NY: Doubleday, 1981).

Heiber, Helmut, and David Glantz. *Hitler and His Generals: Military Conferences 1942–1945* (Enigma Books, 2002).

Hellbeck, Jochen S. *Stalingrad: The City That Defeated the Third Reich* (New York: PublicAffairs, 2015).

Herman, Arthur. *Freedom's Forge: How American Business Produced Victory in World War II* (New York: Random House, 2012).

Herring, George C. *From Colony to Superpower: U.S. Foreign Relations Since 1776* (New York: Oxford University Press, 2008).

Herwig, Holger H. "The Failure of German Sea Power, 1914–1945: Mahan, Tirpitz, and Raeder Reconsidered," *International History Review* 10.1 (1988), 68–105.

———. *The First World War: Germany and Austria, 1914–1918* (London and New York: Arnold, distributed exclusively in the US by St. Martin's Press, 1997).

Hibbert, Christopher. *Benito Mussolini: The Rise and Fall of Il Duce* (rev. ed.) (Harmondsworth, Middlesex, England: Penguin Books, 1965, c1962).

Hilberg, Raul. *The Destruction of the European Jews* (Chicago: Quadrangle Books, 1967).

———. "German Railroads/Jewish Souls," *Society*, Vol. 14, Issue 1 (1976), 60–74.

———. *Perpetrators, Victims, Bystanders: The Jewish Catastrophe, 1933–1945* (New York: Aaron Asher Books, 1992).

Hillgarth, J. N. *The Spanish Kingdoms, 1250–1516,* Vol. II: *1410–1516, Castilian Hegemony* (Oxford: Clarendon Press, 1978).

Hinsley, F. H. *Hitler's Strategy* (Cambridge: Cambridge University Press, 1951).

Hionidou, Violetta. *Famine and Death in Occupied Greece, 1941–1944* (Cambridge: Cambridge University Press, 2006).

Hitchcock, William I. *The Bitter Road to Freedom: A New History of the Liberation of Europe* (New York: Free Press, 2008).

Hitler, Adolf. *Hitler and His Generals: Military Conferences 1942–1945: The First Complete Stenographic Record of the Military Situation Conferences from Stalingrad to Berlin* (London: Greenhill, 2002).

———. *Mein Kampf* [Ralph Manheim, tr.] (New York: Houghton Mifflin, 1943).

Hogan, Michael J. *The Marshall Plan: America, Britain, and the Reconstruction of Western Europe, 1947–1952* (New York: Cambridge University Press, 1987).

Hogg, Ian V. *The Encyclopedia of Infantry Weapons of World War II* (New York: Thomas Y. Crowell Company, 1977).

———. *German Artillery of World War Two* (Barnsley: Frontline, 2013) (paperback ed., 2013).

Holmes, Richard. *Falling Upwards: How We Took to the Air* (London: William Collins, 2013).

Hone, Thomas C., ed. *The Battle of Midway: The Naval Institute's Guide to the U.S. Navy's Greatest Victory* (Annapolis, MD: Naval Institute Press, 2013).

Horn, Steve. *The Second Attack on Pearl Harbor: Operation K and Other Japanese Attempts to Bomb America in World War II* (Annapolis, MD: Naval Institute Press, 2005).

Hornfischer, James D. *Neptune's Inferno: The U.S. Navy at Guadalcanal* (New York: Bantam Books, 2011).

Hough, Richard. *The Hunting of Force Z: The Brief Controversial Life of the Modern Battleship and Its Tragic Close with the Destruction of the 'Prince of Wales' and 'Repulse'* (London: White Lion, 1974).

Howard, Michael. *The Mediterranean Strategy in the Second World War* (London: Weidenfeld and Nicolson, 1968).

Howard, Michael, and Peter Paret, trs. *Carl von Clausewitz, On War* (Princeton: Princeton University Press, 1984).

Howarth, Stephen. *The Fighting Ships of the Rising Sun: The Drama of the Imperial Japanese Navy, 1895–1945* (New York: Atheneum, 1983).

Hyde, Charles K. *Arsenal of Democracy: The American Automobile Industry in World War II* (Detroit: Wayne State University Press, 2013).

International Military Tribunal. *Nazi Conspiracy and Aggression*, Vol. 3 (Washington, DC: US Government Printing Office, 1947).

Ireland, Bernard. *Jane's Naval History of World War II* (London: HarperCollins Publishers, Inc., 1998).

Issraeljan, V., and L. Kutakov. *Diplomacy of Aggression: Berlin-Rome-Tokyo Axis, Its Rise and Fall* (Moscow: Progress Publishers, 1970).

Jablonsky, David. *Churchill and Hitler: Essays on the Political-Military Direction of Total War* (Portland, OR: Frank Cass, 1994).

Jackson, Julian. *The Fall of France: The Nazi Invasion of 1940* (Oxford: Oxford University Press, 2003).

———. *France: The Dark Years, 1940–1945* (Oxford and New York: Oxford University Press, 2001).

Jackson, W.G.F. *The Battle for North Africa 1940–43* (New York: Mason/Charter, 1975).

Jackson, William G. F. *The Rock of the Gibraltarians: A History of Gibraltar* (Rutherford: Farleigh Dickinson University Press, 1987; London and Toronto: Associated University Presses, 1987).

Jackson, William, and Field Marshal Lord Bramall. *The Chiefs: The Story of the United Kingdom Chiefs of Staff* (London: Brassey's, 1992).

Jacoby, Russell. *Bloodlust: On the Roots of Violence from Cain and Abel to the Present* (New York: Free Press, 2011).

James, Robert Rhodes, ed. *Winston S. Churchill: His Complete Speeches, 1897–1963* (Vol. 7: 1942–1949) (New York: Chelsea House, 1974).

Jarrell, Randall. *The Complete Poems* (New York: Farrar, Straus & Giroux, 1969).

Jeffreys, Diarmuid. *Hell's Cartel: IG Farben and the Making of Hitler's War Machine* (New York: Metropolitan Books, 2008).

The Johns Hopkins University Applied Physics Laboratory. *The World War II Proximity Fuze: A Compilation of Naval Ordnance Reports* (Silver Spring, MD: The Laboratory, 1950).

Johnson, David. *V1-V2: Hitler's Vengeance on London* (New York: Stein and Day, 1981).

Jones, James. *WWII: A Chronicle of Soldiering* (Chicago: University of Chicago Press, 2014).

Jones, Michael. *Leningrad: State of Siege* (London: John Murray, 2008).

Jowett, Philip. *The Italian Army 1940–45,* Vol. 3: *Italy 1943–45* (Oxford: Osprey Publishing, 2001).

Kagan, Donald. *On the Origins of War and the Preservation of Peace* (New York: Doubleday, 1995).

———. *Pericles of Athens and the Birth of Democracy* (New York: Free Press, 1991).

Kahn, David. *Seizing the Enigma: The Race to Break the German U-Boat Codes, 1939–1945* (rev. ed.) (Annapolis, MD: Naval Institute Press, 2012).

Kaufmann, J. E., and Robert M. Jurga. *Fortress Europe: European Fortifications of World War II* (Conshohocken, PA: Combined Books, 1999).

Kaufmann, J. E., and H. W. Kaufmann. *Fortress Third Reich: German Fortifications & Defense Systems in World War II* (New York: De Capo Press, 2003).

———. *Maginot Imitations: Major Fortifications of Germany and Neighboring Countries* (Westport, CT: Praeger, 1997).

Kaufmann, J. E., H. W. Kaufmann, and Tomasz Idzikowski. *Fortress France: The Maginot Line and French Defenses in World War II* (Mechanicsburg, PA: Stackpole Books, 2007).

Kay, Alex J., Jeff Rutherford, and David Stahel, eds. *Nazi Policy on the Eastern Front, 1941: Total War, Genocide and Radicalization* (Rochester, NY: University of Rochester Press, 2012).

Keegan, John. *The Battle for History: Re-Fighting World War Two* (New York: Vintage, 1996).

———. *The First World War* (New York: Alfred A. Knopf, 1999).

———. *A History of Warfare* (London: Hutchinson, 1993).

———. *The Mask of Command* (London: Jonathan Cape, 1987).

————. *The Price of Admiralty: The Evolution of Naval Warfare* (New York: Viking, 1988).

————. *The Second World War* (London: Hutchinson, 1989).

————. *Six Armies in Normandy: From D-Day to the Liberation of Paris, June 6th–August 25th, 1944* (London: Jonathan Cape, 1982).

Kennedy, Greg, and Keith Neilson. *Military Education: Past, Present, and Future* (Westport, CT: Praeger, 2002).

Kennedy, Paul. *Engineers of Victory: The Problem Solvers Who Turned the Tide in the Second World War* (New York: Random House, 2013).

————. "The Influence and Limitations of Sea Power," *International History Review* 10 (1988), 2–17.

————. *The Rise and Fall of British Naval Mastery* (New York: Charles Scribner, 1976).

Kennett, Lee. *A History of Strategic Bombing* (New York: Charles Scribner, 1982).

Kern, Paul Bentley. *Ancient Siege Warfare* (Bloomington: Indiana University Press, 1999).

Kershaw, Ian. *Hitler, 1936–45: Nemesis* (New York: W. W. Norton, 2000).

————. *Hitler, the Germans, and the Final Solution* (Jerusalem: International Institute for Holocaust Research, Yad Vashem; New Haven: Yale University, 2008).

Kévorkian, Raymond H. *The Armenian Genocide: A Complete History* (London and New York: I. B. Tauris, 2011).

Khan, Shaharyar M. *The Shallow Graves of Rwanda* (London: I. B. Tauris, 2000).

Khlevniuk, O. V. *Stalin: A New Biography of a Dictator* (New Haven: Yale University Press, 2015).

Kiernan, Ben. *The Pol Pot Regime: Race, Power, and Genocide in Cambodia Under the Khmer Rouge, 1975–79* (New Haven: Yale University Press, 1996).

Kimball, Warren F. *Churchill & Roosevelt: The Complete Correspondence* (3 vols.) (Princeton: Princeton University Press, 1984).

Kindsvatter, Peter S. *American Soldiers: Ground Combat in the World Wars, Korea and Vietnam* (Lawrence: University Press of Kansas, 2003).

Kingseed, Cole C., Col. "Marshall's Men," *Army Magazine* (December 2009), 51–59.

————. "The Pacific War: The US Army's Forgotten Theater of World War II," *Army Magazine*, Vol. 63, No. 4 (April 2013), 50–56.

Kirkland, F.R. "The French Air Force in 1940—Was It Defeated by the Luftwaffe or by Politics?" *Air University Review* 36.6 (September–October 1985), (http://www.airpower.maxwell.af.mil/airchronicles /aureview/1985/sep-oct/kirkland.html).

Kirschenbaum, Lisa A. *The Legacy of the Siege of Leningrad, 1941–1995: Myth, Memories, and Monuments* (New York: Cambridge University Press, 2006).

Kistler, John M. *War Elephants* (Westport, CT: Praeger, 2006).

Knox, MacGregor. *Common Destiny: Dictatorship, Foreign Policy, and War in Fascist Italy and Nazi Germany* (Cambridge: Cambridge University Press, 2000).

———. *Hitler's Italian Allies: Royal Armed Forces, Fascist Regime, and the War of 1940–43* (Cambridge and New York: Cambridge University Press, 2000).

———. *Mussolini Unleashed, 1939–1941: Politics and Strategy in Fascist Italy's Last War* (Cambridge: Cambridge University Press, 1982).

Knox, MacGregor, and Williamson Murray, eds. *The Dynamics of Military Revolution, 1300–2050* (Cambridge: Cambridge University Press, 2001).

Koistinen, Paul A. C. *Arsenal of World War II: The Political Economy of American Warfare, 1940–1945* (Lawrence: University Press of Kansas, 2004).

Koliopoulos, Giannes, and Thanos Veremis. *Greece: The Modern Sequel, From 1831 to the Present* (New York: NYU Press, 2002).

Kotkin, Stephen. *Stalin,* Vol. 1: *Paradoxes of Power, 1878–1928* (New York: Penguin Press, 2014).

Kozak, Warren. *LeMay: The Life and Wars of General Curtis LeMay* (Washington, DC: Regnery, 2009).

Kramer, Alan. *Dynamic of Destruction: Culture and Mass Killing in the First World War* (Oxford: Oxford University Press, 2007).

Krausnick, Helmut, et al., eds. *Anatomy of the SS State* (New York: Collins, 1968).

Krivosheev, G. F. *Soviet Casualties and Combat Losses in the Twentieth Century* (London: Greenhill Books; Harrisburg, PA: Stackpole Books, 1997).

Kurth, James. "The U.S. Navy in World War II," *Foreign Policy Research Institute FootNotes* Vol. 14, No. 24 (September 2009).

Lacey, Jim. *Keep from All Thoughtful Men: How U.S. Economists Won World War II* (Annapolis, MD: Naval Institute Press, 2011).

Laird, Robbin F., Edward Timperlake, and Richard Weitz. *Rebuilding American Military Power in the Pacific: A 21st-Century Strategy* (Santa Barbara, CA: Praeger, 2013).

Lamb, Richard. *War in Italy, 1943–1945: A Brutal Story* (London: John Murray, 1993).

Lane, Frederick C. *Ships for Victory: A History of Shipbuilding Under the United States Maritime Commission in World War II* (Baltimore: Johns Hopkins University Press, 1951).

———. *Venice, A Maritime Republic* (Baltimore: Johns Hopkins University Press, 1973).

Laurie, Clayton D. *Anzio* (Washington DC: US Army Center of Military History, 1994).

Lawlor, Sheila. *Churchill and the Politics of War, 1940–1941* (Cambridge and New York: Cambridge University Press, 1994).

Lazenby, J. F. *The First Punic War: A Military History* (Stanford: Stanford University Press, 1996).

————. *Hannibal's War: A Military History of the Second Punic War* (Warminster, UK: Aris & Phillips, 1978).

Lec, Stanisław Jerzy. *Unkempt Thoughts* [Jacek Galazka, tr.] (New York: St. Martin's Press, 1962).

Leighton, Richard M. *Global Logistics and Strategy, 1940–1943* (Washington, DC: Center of Military History, US Army, 1995).

LeMay, Curtis E., and MacKinlay Kantor. *Mission with LeMay: My Story* (Garden City, NY: Doubleday, 1965).

Lengerer, Hans, and Lars Ahlberg. *Capital Ship of the Imperial Japanese Navy 1868–1945,* Vol. III: *The* Yamato *Class and Subsequent Planning* (Ann Arbor, MI: Nimble Books LLC, 2014).

Lewin, Ronald. *Hitler's Mistakes* (London: Leo Cooper, 1984).

Lewis, Jon E., ed. *D-Day As They Saw It* (rev. ed.) (New York: Carroll & Graf Publishers, 2004).

Libbey, James K. *Alexander P. de Seversky and the Quest for Air Power* (Washington, DC: Potomac Books, 2013).

Liddell Hart, Basil Henry, Sir. *The German Generals Talk* (New York: William Morrow, 1948).

————. *History of the Second World War* (London: Cassell, 1970).

————, ed. *The Rommel Papers* (New York: Harcourt Brace, 1953).

Lifton, Robert Jay. *The Nazi Doctors: Medical Killing and the Psychology of Genocide* (New York: Basic Books, 1986).

Lindbergh, Charles A. *Autobiography of Values* (William Jovanovich and Judith A. Schiff, eds.) (New York: Harcourt Brace Jovanovich, 1978).

Lloyd, Nick. *Hundred Days: The End of the Great War* (London: Viking, 2013).

Lord, Carnes. *Proconsuls: Delegated Political-Military Leadership from Rome to America Today* (Cambridge: Cambridge University Press, 2012).

Lord, Walter. *Incredible Victory* (New York: Harper & Row, 1967).

Loughran, Tracey. "Shell Shock, Trauma, and the First World War: The Making of a Diagnosis and Its Histories," *Journal of the History of Medicine and Allied Science* 67 1 (2012), 94–119.

Loxton, Bruce, and Chris Coulthard-Clark. *The Shame of Savo: Anatomy of a Naval Disaster* (Annapolis: Naval Institute Press, 1994).

Lu, David J. *Agony of Choice: Matsuoka Yōsuke and the Rise and Fall of the Japanese Empire, 1880–1946* (Lanham, MD: Lexington Books, 2002).

————. *From the Marco Polo Bridge to Pearl Harbor: Japan's Entry into World War II* (Washington, DC: Public Affairs Press, 1961).

Luck, Hans von. *Panzer Commander: The Memoirs of Colonel Hans von Luck* (New York: Praeger, 1989).

Lukacs, John. *Five Days in London, May 1940* (New Haven: Yale University Press, 1999).

Lunde, Henrik O. *Finland's War of Choice: The Troubled German-Finnish Coalition in WWII* (Philadelphia: Casemate, 2011).

Lundstrom, John B. *Black Shoe Carrier Admiral: Frank Jack Fletcher at Coral Sea, Midway and Guadalcanal* (Annapolis, MD: Naval Institute Press, 2006).

Luther, Craig W. H. *Barbarossa Unleashed: The German Blitzkrieg Through Central Russia to the Gates of Moscow, June–December 1941* (Atglen, PA: Schiffer Publishing Ltd., 2013).

Luttwak, Edward N. *The Grand Strategy of the Roman Empire: From the First Century A.D. to the Third* (Baltimore: Johns Hopkins University Press, 1976).

———. *The Political Uses of Sea Power* (Baltimore: Johns Hopkins University Press, 1974).

Macksey, Kenneth. *Tank Versus Tank: The Illustrated Story of Armored Battlefield Conflict in the Twentieth Century* (New York: Crescent Books, 1991).

———. *Tank Force: Allied Armor in World War II* (New York: Ballantine Books, 1970).

Maclean, French L. *German General Officer Casualties in World War II—Harbinger for U.S. Army General Officer Casualties in Airland Battle* (Fort Leavenworth, Kansas: School of Advanced Military Studies, 1988).

MacMillan, Margaret. *Paris 1919: Six Months That Changed the World* (New York: Random House Trade Paperbacks, 2003).

Mahan, A. T. *The Influence of Sea Power Upon History, 1660–1783* (New York: Dover Publications, 1987).

Mallett, Robert. *The Italian Navy and Fascist Expansionism, 1935–40* (London: Frank Cass, 1998).

Manchester, William. *Goodbye, Darkness: A Memoir of the Pacific War* (Boston: Little, Brown, 1980).

Mandell, Richard D. *The Nazi Olympics* (New York: Macmillan, 1971).

Mansoor, Peter R. *The GI Offensive in Europe: The Triumph of American Infantry Divisions, 1941–1945* (Lawrence: University Press of Kansas, 1999).

Mansoor, Peter R., and Williamson Murray, eds. *Grand Strategy and Military Alliances* (Cambridge: Cambridge University Press, 2016).

Manstein, Erich von. *Lost Victories* [Anthony G. Powell, ed. and tr.] (Chicago: Henry Regnery, 1958).

———. *Verlorene Siege* (Bonn: Athenaum-Verlag, 1959).

Marquand, David, and Anthony Seldon. *The Ideas That Shaped Post-War Britain* (London: Fontana Press, 1996).

Marsden, Eric William. *Greek and Roman Artillery: Technical Treatises* (Oxford: Clarendon, 1971).

Martel, Gordon, ed. *The Origins of the Second World War Reconsidered: A. J. P. Taylor and the Historians* (2nd ed.) (London and New York: Routledge, 1999).

Maruyama, Paul K. *Escape from Manchuria: The Rescue of 1.7 Million Japanese Civilians Trapped in Soviet-Occupied Manchuria Following the End of World War II* (Mustang, OK: Tate Publishing and Enterprises LLC, 2014).

Maslov, Aleksander A. *Captured Soviet Generals: The Fate of Soviet Generals Captured by the Germans, 1941–1945* (London and Portland, OR: F. Cass, 2001).

Maslov, Aleksander A., and David M. Glantz. *Fallen Soviet Generals: Soviet General Officers Killed in Battle, 1941–1945* (Portland, OR, and London: Frank Cass, 1998).

Masuda, Hiroshi. *MacArthur in Asia: The General and His Staff in the Philippines, Japan, and Korea* (Ithaca: Cornell University Press, 2012).

Matheny, Michael R. *Carrying the War to the Enemy: American Operational Art to 1945* (Norman: University of Oklahoma Press, 2011).

Maurois, André. *Tragedy in France* (New York: Harper, 1940).

Mayo, Lida. *The Ordnance Department: On Beachhead and Battlefront: United States Army in World War II, The Technical Services* (Office of the Chief of Military History, US Army, 1969).

Mazower, Mark. *Inside Hitler's Greece: The Experience of Occupation, 1941–44* (New Haven: Yale University Press, 1993).

McAleer, Kevin. *Dueling: The Cult of Honor in Fin-de-Siècle Germany* (Princeton: Princeton University Press, 1994).

McDermott, Kevin, and Matthew Stibbe. *Stalinist Terror in Eastern Europe: Elite Purges and Mass Repression* (New York: Palgrave Macmillan, 2010).

McFarland, Stephen L. *America's Pursuit of Precision Bombing, 1910–1945* (Washington, DC: Smithsonian Institution Press, 1995).

McKinstry, Leo. *Operation Sea Lion: How Britain Crushed the German War Machine's Dreams of Invasion in 1940* (London: John Murray, 2014).

McNab, Chris. *German Automatic Rifles 1941–45* (Oxford: Osprey Publishing, 2013).

Mee, Jr., Charles L. *The Marshall Plan: The Launching of the Pax Americana* (New York: Simon and Schuster, 1984).

Megargee, Geoffrey P. *Inside Hitler's High Command* (Lawrence: University Press of Kansas, 2000).

———. *War of Annihilation: Combat and Genocide on the Eastern Front, 1941* (Lanham, MD: Rowman & Littlefield, 2006).

Mellenthin, F. W. von. *German Generals of World War II: As I Saw Them* (Norman: University of Oklahoma Press, 1977).

———. *Panzer Battles: A Study of the Employment of Armor in the Second World War* [H. Betzler, tr.] (Norman: University of Oklahoma Press, 1956).

Mellor, W. Franklin. *History of the Second World War: Casualties and Medical Statistics* (London: H.M.S.O., 1972).

Melvern, Linda. *Conspiracy to Murder: The Rwandan Genocide* (London and New York: Verso, 2006).

Melvin, Mungo. *Manstein: Hitler's Greatest General* (London: Weidenfeld & Nicolson, 2010).

Mendell, Capt. G. H., and Lieut. W. P. Craighill, trs. *The Art of War by Baron De Jomini* (Radford, VA: Wilder Publications, 2008).

Mettraux, Guénaël. *Perspectives on the Nuremberg Trial* (Oxford and New York: Oxford University Press, 2008).

Middlebrook, Martin. *Arnhem 1944: The Airborne Battle, 17–26 September* (Boulder, CO: Westview Press, 1994).

Middlebrook, Martin, and Patrick Mahoney. *The Sinking of the Prince of Wales & Repulse: The End of a Battleship Era?* (London: Leo Cooper, Ltd. 2004).

Middlemas, Keith, and John Barnes. *Baldwin: A Biography* (New York: Macmillan, 1969).

Mikesh, Robert C. *Japan's World War II Balloon Bomb Attacks on North America* (Washington, DC: Smithsonian Institution Press, 1973).

Miller, Donald L. *Masters of the Air: America's Bomber Boys Who Fought the Air War Against Nazi Germany* (New York: Simon & Schuster, 2007).

Miller, Edward S. *War Plan Orange: The U.S. Strategy to Defeat Japan, 1897–1945* (Annapolis, MD: Naval Institute Press, 1991).

Miller, Nathan. *War at Sea: A Naval History of World War II* (New York: Scribner, 1995).

Millett, Allan R., and Williamson Murray, eds. *Military Effectiveness*, Vol. 3: *The Second World War* (Boston: Allen & Unwin, 1988).

Milner, N. P., tr. *Vegetius: Epitome of Military Science* (2nd rev. ed.) (Liverpool: Liverpool University Press, 1996).

Milward, Alan S. *War, Economy and Society, 1939–1945* (Berkeley: University of California Press, 1977).

Mitcham, Jr., Samuel W. *Rommel's Greatest Victory: The Desert Fox and the Fall of Tobruk, Spring 1942* (Novato, CA: Presidio Press, 1998).

Mitchell, William "Billy." *Winged Defense: The Development and Possibilities of Modern Air Power—Economic and Military* (Tuscaloosa: University of Alabama Press, 2009). [New York and London: G. P. Putnam, 1925].

Mitter, Rana. *Forgotten Ally: China's World War II, 1937–1945* (Boston: Houghton Mifflin Harcourt, 2013).

Moorhouse, Roger. *The Devils' Alliance: Hitler's Pact with Stalin, 1939–1941* (London: Bodley Head, 2014).

———. *Killing Hitler: The Plots, the Assassins, and the Dictator Who Cheated Death* (New York: Bantam, 2006).

Moran, Charles McMoran Wilson, Baron. *Churchill Taken from the Diaries of Lord Moran: The Struggle for Survival, 1940–1965* (Boston: Houghton Mifflin, 1966).

Morgan, David. *The Mongols* (2nd ed.) (Malden, MA: Blackwell Publishing, 2007).

Morison, Samuel Eliot. *History of United States Naval Operations in World War II* [15 volumes: Vol. 1: *The Battle of the Atlantic, September 1939–1943*; Vol. 3: *The Rising Sun in the Pacific, 1931–April 1942*; Vol. 4: *Coral Sea, Midway and Submarine Actions, May 1942–August 1942*; Vol. 12: *Leyte, June 1944–January 1945*] (Boston: Little Brown, 1947–1962).

Morris, Eric. *Corregidor: The End of the Line* (New York: Stein and Day, 1981).

Morrison, J. S., J. F. Coates, and N.B. Rankov. *The Athenian Trireme: The History and Reconstruction of an Ancient Greek Warship* (2nd ed.) (Cambridge: Cambridge University Press, 2000).

Morton, Lewis. *Strategy and Command: The First Two Years* (Washington, DC: Center of Military History, US Army, 2000 [reprint of 1962 edition]).

Mosier, John. *The Blitzkrieg Myth: How Hitler and the Allies Misread the Strategic Realities of World War II* (New York: HarperCollins, 2003).

———. *Deathride: Hitler vs. Stalin: The Eastern Front, 1941–1945* (New York: Simon and Schuster, 2010).

Moskoff, William. *The Bread of Affliction: The Food Supply in the USSR During World War II* (Cambridge: Cambridge University Press, 1990).

Müller, Rolf-Dieter, and Gerd R. Ueberschär. *Hitler's War in the East, 1941–1945: A Critical Reassessment* (New York: Berghahn Books, 2009).

Murfett, Malcolm. *Naval Warfare 1919–1945: An Operational History of the Volatile War at Sea* (London and New York: Routledge, 2009).

Murray, Williamson. "Attrition and the Luftwaffe," *Air University Review* 34.3 (March–April 1983), 66–77.

———. *The Change in the European Balance of Power, 1938–1939: The Path to Ruin* (Princeton: Princeton University Press, 1984).

———. *Luftwaffe* (Baltimore: Nautical & Aviation Publishing Co., 1985).

———. *War, Strategy, and Military Effectiveness* (Cambridge: Cambridge University Press, 2011).

Murray, Williamson, and Tomoyuki Ishizu, eds. *Conflicting Currents: Japan and the United States in the Pacific* (Santa Barbara, CA: Praeger Security International, 2010).

Murray, Williamson, and Allan R. Millett, eds. *Military Innovation in the Interwar Period* (Cambridge: Cambridge University Press, 1996).

———. *A War to Be Won: Fighting the Second World War* (London: Belknap Press, 2000).

Murray, Williamson, and Robert H. Scales Jr. *The Iraq War: A Military History* (Cambridge: Belknap Press of Harvard University Press, 2003).

Murray, Williamson, and Richard Hart Sinnreich, eds. *Successful Strategies: Triumphing in War and Peace from Antiquity to the Present* (Cambridge: Cambridge University Press, 2014).

Murray, Williamson, Richard Hart Sinnreich, and James Lacey, eds. *The Shaping of Grand Strategy: Policy, Diplomacy, and War* (Cambridge: Cambridge University Press, 2011).

Myrvang, Folke. *MG-34–MG-42: German Universal Machine Guns* (Ian D. Skennerton, 2002).

Naimark, Norman M. *The Russians in Germany: A History of the Soviet Zone of Occupation, 1945–1949* (Cambridge, MA: Belknap Press of Harvard University Press, 1995).

————. *Stalin's Genocides* (Princeton: Princeton University Press, 2010).

Naimark, Norman, and Leonid Gibianskii. *The Establishment of Communist Regimes in Eastern Europe, 1944–1949* (Boulder, CO: Westview Press, 1997).

Neufeld, Michael J. *The Rocket and the Reich: Peenemünde and the Coming of the Ballistic Missile Era* (New York: Free Press, 1995).

Neumann, Hans-Joachim, and Henrik Eberle. *Was Hitler Ill? A Final Diagnosis* (Cambridge and Malden, MA: Polity Press 2013).

*New Yorker Magazine. The New Yorker Book of War Pieces* (New York: Reynal & Hitchcock, 1947).

Newcomb, Richard F., and Harry Schmidt. *Iwo Jima* (Nelson Doubleday, 1983).

Ney-Krwawicz, Marek. *The Polish Resistance Home Army 1939–1945* [Antoni Bohdanowicz, tr.] (London: PUMST, 2001).

Niestlé, Axel. *German U-Boat Losses During World War II: Details of Destruction* (Annapolis, MD: Naval Institute Press, 1998).

Norman, Andrew. *HMS Hood: Pride of the Royal Navy* (Stroud and Gloucestershire, UK: The History Press, 2009).

O'Brien, Phillips Payson. *How the War Was Won: Air-Sea Power and Allied Victory in World War II* (Cambridge: Cambridge University Press, 2015).

O'Callaghan, Joseph F. *Reconquest and Crusade in Medieval Spain* (Philadelphia: University of Pennsylvania Press, 2003).

O'Connell, Robert L. *Sacred Vessels: The Cult of the Battleship and the Rise of the U.S. Navy* (Boulder, CO: Westview Press, 1991).

O'Connor, Raymond G. *Diplomacy for Victory: FDR and Unconditional Surrender* (New York: W. W. Norton, 1971).

————, ed. *The Japanese Navy in World War II* (Annapolis, MD: US Naval Institute, 1969).

Odom, Thomas P. *Journey into Darkness: Genocide in Rwanda* (College Station: Texas A&M University Press, 2005).

Okumiya, Masatake, and Jiro Horikoshi. *Zero!: The Story of the Japanese Navy Air Force, 1937–1945* (London: Cassell, 1957).

Olive, Michael. *Steel Thunder on the Eastern Front: German and Russian Artillery in WWII* (Harrisburg, PA: Stackpole Books, 2014).

Olson, Lynne. *Those Angry Days: Roosevelt, Lindbergh, and America's Fight Over World War II, 1939–1941* (New York: Random House, 2013).

O'Neill, William. *A Democracy at War: America's Fight at Home and Abroad in World War II* (New York: Free Press, 1993).

Oosterman, Pieter. *M-1 Helmet of the World War II U.S. GI: A Reference Based on the M-1Helmet.com Collection* (Atglen, PA: Schiffer Military History, 2010).

Ormrod, W. Mark. *Edward III* (New Haven: Yale University Press, 2011).

Orr, Lt. Rob. "The History of the Soldier's Load," *Australian Army Journal* Vol. VII, No. 2 (2010), 67–88.

Orwell, Sonia, and Ian Angus, eds. *The Collected Essays, Journalism, and Letters of George Orwell,* Vol. 4: *In Front of Your Nose, 1945–1950* (New York: Harcourt, Brace & World, 1968).

Ostrogorsky, Georgije. *History of the Byzantine State* (New Brunswick, NJ: Rutgers University Press, 1969).

Overmans, Rüdiger. *Deutsche Militärische Verluste im Zweiten Weltkrieg* (Munich: R. Oldenbourg, 1999).

Overy, Richard. *1939: Countdown to War* (London: Allen Lane, 2009).

———. *The Bombers and the Bombed: Allied Air War over Europe 1940–1945* (Penguin Books, 2015).

———. *The Bombing War* (London: Allen Lane, 2013).

———. *Interrogations: The Nazi Elite in Allied Hands, 1945* (London: Allen Lane, 2001).

———. *The Origins of the Second World War* (2nd ed.) (London: Longman, 1998).

———. *The Twilight Years: The Paradox of Britain Between the Wars* (New York: Viking, 2009).

———. *Why the Allies Won* (London: Jonathan Cape, 1995).

Overy, Richard, and Andrew Wheatcroft. *The Road to War* (New York: Random House, 1989).

Pace, Steve. *Boeing B-29 Superfortress* (Marlborough and Wiltshire, UK: Crowood Press, 2003).

Paine, S.C.M. *The Wars for Asia, 1911–1949* (New York: Cambridge University Press, 2012).

Paret, Peter, Gordon A. Craig, and Felix Gilbert, eds. *Makers of Modern Strategy: From Machiavelli to the Nuclear Age* (Princeton: Princeton University Press, 1986).

Parker, Geoffrey, ed. *The Cambridge History of Warfare* [rev. ed.] (Cambridge: Cambridge University Press, 2009).

———. *Global Crisis: War, Climate Change, and Catastrophe in the Seventeenth Century* (New Haven, CT: Yale University Press, 2014).

———. *The Military Revolution: Military Innovation and the Rise of the West, 1500–1800* (2nd ed.) (Cambridge: Cambridge University Press, 1996).

Pasher, Yaron. *Holocaust versus Wehrmacht: How Hitler's "Final Solution" Undermined the German War Effort* (Lawrence: University Press of Kansas, 2014).

Paterson, Lawrence. *U-Boats in the Mediterranean, 1941–1944* (Annapolis, MD: Naval Institute Press, 2007).

Patterson, Robert P. *Arming the Nation for War: Mobilization, Supply, and the American War Effort in World War II* (Knoxville: University of Tennessee Press, 2014).

Patton, George S. *War As I Knew It* (Boston: Houghton Mifflin Company, 1947).

Payne, Stanley G. *Franco and Hitler: Spain, Germany and World War II* (New Haven: Yale University Press, 2008).

Perowne, Stewart. *The Siege Within the Walls: Malta 1940–1943* (London: Hodder & Stoughton, 1970).

Persico, Joseph E. *Roosevelt's Centurions: FDR and the Commanders He Led to Victory in World War II* (New York: Random House, 2013).

Philippides, Marios, and Walter K. Hanak. *The Siege and the Fall of Constantinople in 1453: Historiography, Topography, and Military Studies* (Routledge, 2011).

Piehler, G. Kurt, and Sidney Pash, eds. *The United States and the Second World War: New Perspectives on Diplomacy, War, and the Home Front* (New York: Fordham University Press, 2010).

Pimlott, John. *Luftwaffe: The Illustrated History of the German Air Force in WWII* (Osceola, WI: Motorbooks International, 1998).

———, ed. *Rommel: In His Own Words* (London: Greenhill Books; Mechanicsburg, PA: Stackpole Books, 1994).

Pleshakov, Constantine. *Stalin's Folly: The Tragic First Ten Days of World War II on the Eastern Front* (Boston: Houghton Mifflin, 2005).

———. *The Tsar's Last Armada: The Epic Journey to the Battle of Tsushima* (New York: Basic Books, 2002).

Poirier, Michel Thomas. "Results of the American Pacific Submarine Campaign of World War II" (Chief of Naval Operations, Submarine Warfare Division, 30 December 1999). http://www.navy.mil/navy-data/cno/n87/history/pac-campaigns.html.

———. "Results of the German and American Submarine Campaigns of World War II" (Chief of Naval Operations, Submarine Warfare Division, 20 October 1999). https://web.archive.org/web/20080409052122/http://www.navy.mil/navydata/cno/n87/history/wwii-campaigns.html).

Polmar, Norman. *Aircraft Carriers: A History of Carrier Aviation and Its Influence on World Events,* Vol. I: *1909–1945* (Washington, DC: Potomac Books, Inc., 2006).

Potter, John Deane. *Yamamoto: The Man Who Menaced America* (New York: Viking Press, 1965).

Prange, Gordon W. *At Dawn We Slept: The Untold Story of Pearl Harbor* (New York: McGraw-Hill, 1981).

Prince, Cathryn J. *Death in the Baltic: The World War II Sinking of the Wilhelm Gustloff* (New York: Palgrave Macmillan, 2013).

Prior, Robin. *When Britain Saved the West: The Story of 1940* (New Haven: Yale University Press, 2015).

Raeder, Erich. *Grand Admiral: The Personal Memoir of the Commander in Chief of the German Navy from 1935 Until His Final Break with Hitler in 1943* [Henry W. Drexel, tr.] (New York: Da Capo, 2001).

Rauch, Jonathan. "The Forgotten Millions: Communism Is the Deadliest Fantasy in Human History (But Does Anyone Care?)," *The Atlantic Monthly* (December 2003), (http://www.theatlantic.com/magazine /archive/2003/12/the-forgotten-millions/302849/).

Raus, Erhard. *Panzer Operations: The Eastern Front Memoir of General Raus, 1941–1945* [Steven H. Newton, tr.] (Cambridge, MA: Da Capo, 2003).

Ray, John. *The Battle of Britain, New Perspectives: Behind the Scenes of the Great Air War* (London: Arms & Armour, 1994).

Read, Anthony R., and David T. Fisher. *The Deadly Embrace: Hitler, Stalin, and the Nazi-Soviet Pact, 1939–1941* (London: Michael Joseph, 1988).

———. *The Fall of Berlin* (London: Hutchinson, 1992).

Recouly, Raymond. *Foch: Le Vainqueur de la Guerre* (Paris: Hachette, 1919).

Reid, Anna. *Leningrad: Tragedy of a City Under Siege* (New York: Bloomsbury, 2011).

Reinhold, Meyer. *From Republic to Principate: An Historical Commentary on Cassius Dio's Roman History, Books 49–52 (36–29 B.C.)*, APA Monograph Series, No. 34 (Atlanta, GA: Scholars Press, 1988).

Reischauer, Edwin O. *Japan: The Story of a Nation* (3rd ed.) (New York: Knopf, 1981).

Reiter, Dan, and Allan C. Stam. *Democracies at War* (Princeton: Princeton University Press, 2002).

Reynolds, David. *From World War to Cold War: Churchill, Roosevelt, and the International History of the 1940s* (Oxford: Oxford University Press, 2006).

———. "Fulcrum of the Twentieth Century," *International Affairs* 66.2 (1990), 325–350.

Reynolds, David, ed. *The Origins of the Cold War in Europe: International Perspectives* (New Haven: Yale University Press, 1994).

Reynosa, Mark A. *The M-1 Helmet: The History of the U.S. M-1 Helmet in World War II* (Atglen, PA: Schiffer Military History, 1996).

Rhodes, Richard. *Dark Sun: The Making of the Hydrogen Bomb* (New York: Simon & Schuster, 1995).

Rhys-Jones, Graham. *The Loss of the Bismarck: An Avoidable Disaster* (London: Cassell, 1999).

Ricks, Thomas E. *The Generals: American Military Command from World War II to Today* (New York: Penguin Press, 2012).

Ridley, Jasper Godwin. *Mussolini* (London: Constable, 1997).

Roberts, Andrew. *History of the English-Speaking Peoples Since 1900* (New York: Harper, 2007).

———. *The Holy Fox: A Biography of Lord Halifax* (London: Weidenfeld and Nicolson, 1991).

———. *Masters and Commanders: How Roosevelt, Churchill, Marshall and Alanbrooke Won the War in the West* (London and New York: Allen Lane, 2008).

———. *Napoleon: A Life* (New York: Viking, 2014).

————. *The Storm of War: A New History of the Second World War* (New York: Harper, 2011).

————, ed. *What Might Have Been: Leading Historians on Twelve 'What Ifs' of History* (London: Weidenfeld & Nicolson, 2004).

Roberts, Geoffrey. *Stalin's Wars: From World War to Cold War, 1939–1953* (New Haven: Yale University Press, 2006).

————. *Victory at Stalingrad: The Battle That Changed History* (Routledge, 2002).

Rohwer, Jürgen, and Mikhail S. Monakov. *Stalin's Ocean-Going Fleet: Soviet Naval Strategy and Shipbuilding Programmes 1935–1953* (London and Portland, OR: Frank Cass, 2001).

Rose, Lisle A. *Power at Sea*, Vol. 2: *The Breaking Storm, 1919–1945* (Columbia and London: University of Missouri Press, 2007).

Rosen, William. *The Third Horseman: Climate Change and the Great Famine of the 14th Century* (New York: Viking, 2014).

Rosenau, William. *Special Operations Forces and Elusive Enemy Ground Targets: Lessons from Vietnam and the Persian Gulf War* (Rand Corporation, 2001).

Rothwell, Victor. *War Aims in the Second World War: The War Aims of the Major Belligerents, 1939–45* (Edinburgh: Edinburgh University Press, 2005).

Rotundo, Louis C. *Battle for Stalingrad: The 1943 Soviet General Staff Study* (Washington, DC: Pergamon-Brassey's, 1989).

Ruge, Friedrich. *The Soviets as Naval Opponents 1941–1945* (Annapolis, MD: Naval Institute Press, 1979).

Rummel, R. J. "War Isn't This Century's Biggest Killer," *Wall Street Journal*, July 7, 1986.

Rutherford, Jeff. *Combat and Genocide on the Eastern Front: The German Infantry's War, 1941–1944* (Cambridge: Cambridge University Press, 2014).

Ruthven, Malise. "Hitler's Monumental Miscalculation," *New York Review of Books*, June 5, 2014.

Ryan, Cornelius. *The Last Battle* (New York: Simon and Schuster, 1966).

————. *A Bridge Too Far* (New York: Simon and Schuster, 1974).

Sabin, Philip, Hans van Wees, and Michael Whitby, eds. *Cambridge History of Greek and Roman Warfare*, Vol. I: *Greece, the Hellenistic World and the Rise of Rome* (Cambridge: Cambridge University Press, 2007).

————, eds. *Cambridge History of Greek and Roman Warfare*, Vol. II: *Rome from the Late Republic to the Late Empire* (Cambridge: Cambridge University Press, 2007).

Sadkovich, James J. *The Italian Navy in World War II* (Westport, CT: Greenwood Press, 1994).

Şahin, Kaya. *Empire and Power in the Reign of Süleyman: Narrating the Sixteenth-Century Ottoman World* (Cambridge: Cambridge University Press, 2013).

Saint-Exupéry, Antoine de. *Pilote de guerre* (New York: Éditions de la Maison Française, 1942).

Salerno, Reynolds M. *Vital Crossroads: Mediterranean Origins of the Second World War 1935–1940* (Ithaca, NY: Cornell University Press, 2002).

Salisbury, Harrison E. *The 900 Days: The Siege of Leningrad* (New York: Harper & Row, 1969).

Sanford, George. *Katyn and the Soviet Massacre of 1940: Truth, Justice and Memory* (London and New York: Routledge, 2005).

Sanford, William F. "The Marshall Plan: Origins and Implementation" (Washington, DC: United States Department of State, Bureau of Public Affairs, April 1987).

Sartre, Jean-Paul. *The Devil & the Good Lord, and Two Other Plays* [Kitty Black, tr.] (New York: Alfred A. Knopf, 1960).

Saunders, J. J. *The History of the Mongol Conquests* (New York: Barnes & Noble, 1971).

Savile, George. *The Complete Works of George Savile, First Marquess of Halifax* (Oxford: Clarendon Press, 1912).

Schain, Martin, ed. *The Marshall Plan: Fifty Years After* (New York: Palgrave, 2001).

Schäufler, Hans. *Panzer Warfare on the Eastern Front* (Harrisburg, PA: Stackpole Books, 2012).

Schifferle, Peter J. *America's School for War: Fort Leavenworth, Officer Education, and Victory in World War II* (Lawrence: University Press of Kansas, 2010).

Schopenhauer, Arthur. *The Collected Works of Arthur Schopenhauer* (Radford, VA: Wilder Publications, 2008).

Schramm, Percy Ernst. *Hitler: The Man & the Military Leader* [Donald S. Detwiler, tr.] (Chicago: Academy Chicago Publishers, 1999).

Schroeder, Paul W. *The Axis Alliance and Japanese-American Relations, 1941* (Ithaca, NY: Cornell University Press, 1958).

Scott, Wilbur J. "PTSD in DSM-III: A Case in the Politics of Diagnosis and Disease," *Social Problems,* Vol. 37, No. 3 (August 1990), 294–310.

Scullard, H. H. *The Elephant in the Greek and Roman World,* Aspects of Greek and Roman Life (Ithaca, NY: Cornell University Press, 1974; Cambridge: Thames and Hudson, 1974).

———. *Scipio Africanus: Soldier and Politician* (Ithaca, NY: Cornell University Press, 1970).

Sebag-Montefiore, Hugh. *Enigma: The Battle for the Code* (London: Weidenfeld & Nicolson, 2000).

Selden, Mark. "A Forgotten Holocaust: US Bombing Strategy, the Destruction of Japanese Cities and the American Way of War from World War II to Iraq," *The Asia Pacific Journal: Japan Focus,* Vol. 5, Issue 5 (May 2, 2007).

Senger und Etterlin, F. M. von. *German Tanks of World War II: The Complete Illustrated History of German Armoured Fighting Vehicles 1926–1945* [J. Lucas, tr.] (A & W Visual Library, 1969).

Senich, Peter R. *The German Assault Rifle: 1935–1945* (Boulder, CO: Paladin Press, 2008).

Seth, Ronald. *The Fiercest Battle: The Story of North Atlantic Convoy ONS 5, 22nd April–7th May 1943* (New York: Norton, 1961).

Setton, Kenneth M. *Papacy and the Levant, 1204–1571*, Vol. 4 (Philadelphia: American Philosophical Society, 1976).

Seymour, William. *Great Sieges of History* (Brassey's Ltd., 1992).

Shankland, Peter, and Anthony Hunter. *Malta Convoy* (New York: Ives Washburn, 1961).

Shaw, Stanford. *History of the Ottoman Empire and Modern Turkey*. Vol. I: *Empire of the Gazis: The Rise and Decline of the Ottoman Empire, 1280–1808* (Cambridge: Cambridge University Press, 1976).

Shillony, Ben-Ami. *Politics and Culture in Wartime Japan* (Oxford: Clarendon Press, 1981; New York: Oxford University Press, 1981).

Shirer, William L. *Berlin Diary: The Journal of a Foreign Correspondent, 1934–1941* (Baltimore: Johns Hopkins University Press, 2002) (originally published: New York: Knopf, 1941).

———. *The Rise and Fall of the Third Reich: A History of Nazi Germany* (New York: Simon & Schuster, 1959, 1960, 1990).

———. *The Sinking of the Bismarck* (New York: Random House, 1962).

Showalter, Dennis E. *Armor and Blood: The Battle of Kursk, the Turning Point of World War II* (New York: Random House, 2013).

———. *Hitler's Panzers: The Lightning Attacks That Revolutionized Warfare* (New York: Berkley Caliber, 2009).

Showalter, Dennis, and Harold Deutsch, eds. *If the Allies Had Fallen: Sixty Alternate Scenarios of World War II* (London: Frontline Books/New York: Skyhorse Publishing, 2010).

Showell, Jak P. Mallmann. *German Navy Handbook, 1939–1945* (Stroud, UK: Sutton Publishing, 1999).

———. *Hitler's U-Boat Bases* (Stroud, UK: Sutton Publishing, 2002).

Shrader, Charles R. *U.S. Military Logistics, 1607–1991* (New York: Greenwood, 1992).

Shtemenko, S. M. *The Last Six Months: Russia's Final Battles with Hitler's Armies in World War II* [Guy Daniels, tr.] (Garden City, NY: Doubleday, 1977).

Shulman, Milton. *Defeat in the West* (New York: E. P. Dutton, 1948).

Simpson, Emile. *War from the Ground Up: Twenty-First Century Combat as Politics* (London: Hurst & Company, 2012).

Sledge, E. B. *With the Old Breed, at Peleliu and Okinawa* (Novato, CA: Presidio Press, 1981).

Sloan, Bill. *The Ultimate Battle: Okinawa 1945—The Last Epic Struggle of World War II* (New York: Simon & Schuster, 2008).

Smith, Michael Llewellyn. *Ionian Vision: Greece in Asia Minor, 1919–1922* (New York: St. Martin's Press, 1973).

Smith, Truman. *Berlin Alert: The Memoirs and Reports of Truman Smith* (Stanford, CA: Hoover Institution Press, 1984).

Snyder, Timothy. *Bloodlands: Europe Between Hitler and Stalin* (London: Bodley Head, 2010).

Sommerstein, Alan H., ed. *Aeschylus Fragments* (Cambridge, MA: Harvard University Press, 2008) [Aeschylus III, Loeb Classical Library 505].

Sorel, Eliot, and Pier Carlo Padoan, eds. *The Marshall Plan: Lessons Learned for the 21st Century* (OECD, 2008).

Sowell, Thomas. *Intellectuals and Society* (rev. ed.) (New York: Basic Books, 2011).

Speer, Albert. *Inside the Third Reich: Memoirs* [Richard and Clara Winston, trs.] (New York: Macmillan, 1970).

————. *Spandau: The Secret Diaries* [Richard and Clara Winston, trs.] (New York: Macmillan, 1976).

Spilling, Michael, ed. *Weapons of War: Battleships and Aircraft Carriers, 1900–Present* (New York: Chartwell Books, 2013).

Stahel, David. *Operation Barbarossa and Germany's Defeat in the East* (Cambridge: Cambridge University Press, 2009).

Stanley, Roy II, Col. *Evolution of Airborne Operations 1939–1945 (Looking Down on War)* (Pen and Sword Military, 2015).

Steiger, Rudolf. *Armour Tactics in the Second World War: Panzer Army Campaigns of 1939–41 in German War Diaries* [Martin Fry, tr.] (New York: Berg, 1991; distributed exclusively in the US and Canada by St. Martin's Press).

Steinberg, Jonathan. *All or Nothing: The Axis and the Holocaust, 1941–1943* (London and New York: Routledge, 1990).

Steiner, Zara. *The Lights That Failed: European International History, 1919–1933* (Oxford and New York: Oxford University Press, 2005).

————. *The Triumph of the Dark: European International History, 1933–1939* (Oxford and New York: Oxford University Press, 2011).

Stoler, Mark A. *Allies and Adversaries: The Joint Chiefs of Staff, the Grand Alliance, and U.S. Strategy in World War II* (Chapel Hill: University of North Carolina Press, 2000).

Stone, David. *Shattered Genius: The Decline and Fall of the German General Staff in World War II* (Philadelphia: Casemate Publishers, 2012).

Stoye, John. *The Siege of Vienna* (new ed.) (Edinburgh: Birlinn, 2000).

Strachan, Hew, ed. *The Oxford Illustrated History of the First World War* (new ed.) (Oxford: Oxford University Press, 1998).

Stratigakos, Desmina. *Hitler at Home* (New Haven: Yale University Press, 2015).

Strauss, Barry. *The Battle of Salamis: The Naval Encounter That Saved Greece—and Western Civilization* (New York: Simon and Schuster, 2004).

Strawson, John. *Hitler as Military Commander* (London: B. T. Batsford Ltd., 1971).

Stubbs, D. "A Blind Spot? The Royal Air Force (RAF) and Long-Range Fighters, 1936–44," *Journal of Military History* 78 (April 2014), 673–702.

Sunderman, James F., ed. *World War II in the Air: Europe* (New York: Bramhall House, 1968).

———, ed. *World War II in the Air: The Pacific* (New York: F. Watts, 1962).

Suvorov, Viktor. *The Chief Culprit: Stalin's Grand Design to Start World War II* (Annapolis, MD: Naval Institute Press, 2008).

Syme, Ronald, Sir. *Sallust* (Berkeley: University of California Press, 1964 [2002]).

Symonds, Craig L. *Neptune: The Allied Invasion of Europe and the D-Day Landings* (Oxford and New York: Oxford University Press, 2014).

Tanaka, Toshiyuki. *Hidden Horrors: Japanese War Crimes in World War II* (Boulder, CO: Westview Press, 1996).

Taylor, A.J.P. *The Origins of the Second World War* (New York: Atheneum, 1961).

Thomas, Evan. *Sea of Thunder: Four Commanders and the Last Great Naval Campaign, 1941–1945* (New York: Simon & Schuster, 2006).

Thornton, Bruce S. *The Wages of Appeasement: Ancient Athens, Munich, and Obama's America* (New York: Encounter Books, 2011).

Tillman, Barrett. *The Clash of the Carriers: The True Story of the Marianas Turkey Shoot of World War II* (New York: NAL Caliber, 2006).

Tipps, G. K. "The Battle of Ecnomus," *Historia: Zeitschrift für Alte Geschichte* 34 (1985), 432–465.

Toland, John. *The Rising Sun: The Decline and Fall of the Japanese Empire, 1936–1945* (New York: Random House, 1970).

Toll, Ian W. *The Conquering Tide: War in the Pacific Islands, 1942–1944* (New York: W.W. Norton, 2015).

———. *Pacific Crucible: War at Sea in the Pacific, 1941–1942* (New York: W.W. Norton, 2012).

Tooze, Adam. *The Wages of Destruction: The Making and Breaking of the Nazi Economy* (London and New York: Allen Lane, 2006).

Treadgold, Warren. *A History of the Byzantine State and Society* (Stanford, CA: Stanford University Press, 1997).

Tucker, Spencer C., ed. *World War II at Sea: An Encyclopedia* (Santa Barbara, CA: ABC-CLIO, 2011).

Ulam, Adam B. *Stalin: The Man and His Era* (New York: Viking Press, 1973).

US Strategic Bombing Survey. *The Campaigns of the Pacific War* (Washington, DC: Naval Analysis Division, 1946).

———. *Summary Report (European War)* (Washington, DC: US Government Printing Office, 1945).

————. *Summary Report (Pacific War)* (Washington, DC: US Government Printing Office, 1946).

Van Creveld, Martin. *The Age of Airpower* (New York: PublicAffairs, 2011).

————. *Fighting Power: German and US Army Performance 1939–1945* (Westport, CT: Greenwood Press, 1982).

————. *Supplying War: Logistics from Wallenstein to Patton* (New York: Cambridge University Press, 1977).

Van der Vat, Dan. *The Pacific Campaign: World War II: The U.S.–Japanese Naval War, 1941–1945* (New York: Simon & Schuster, 1991).

Van der Zee, Henri A. *The Hunger Winter: Occupied Holland 1944–1945* (London: J. Norman & Hobhouse, 1982).

Vassiltchikov, Marie. *Berlin Diaries, 1940–1945* (New York: Vintage, 1988).

Villalon, I. J. Andrew, and Donald J. Kagay, eds., *The Hundred Years War: A Wider Focus* (Leiden: Brill, 2005).

Viroli, Maurizio. *For Love of Country: An Essay on Patriotism and Nationalism* (New York: Clarendon Press, 1995).

Vlahos, Michael. "Could Body Armor Have Saved Millions in World War I?" *The Atlantic* (April 30, 2013).

Voltaire. *The Complete Works of Voltaire*, Vol. 82 (Notebooks II) [Theodore Besterman, ed.] (Toronto: University of Toronto Press, 1968).

Walker, George K. "Sea Power and the Law of the Sea: The Need for a Contextual Approach," *Ocean Development & International Law* 7 (1979), 299–326.

Walker, Ian W. *Iron Hulls, Iron Hearts: Mussolini's Elite Armoured Divisions in North Africa* (Marlborough, UK: The Crowood Press, 2006).

Walker, John R. *Bracketing the Enemy: Forward Observers in World War II* (Norman: University of Oklahoma Press, 2013).

Walzer, Michael. *Just and Unjust Wars: A Moral Argument with Historical Illustrations* (New York: Basic Books, 2006).

Warlimont, Walter. *Inside Hitler's Headquarters, 1939–1945* [R. H. Barry, tr.] (New York: Praeger, 1965).

Warner, Denis, and Peggy Warner (with Sadao Seno). *Disaster in the Pacific: New Light on the Battle of Savo Island* (Annapolis, MD: Naval Institute Press, 1992).

Warren, Alan. *Singapore 1942: Britain's Greatest Defeat* (London: Hambledon and London, 2002).

Waterford, Van. *Prisoners of the Japanese in World War II: Statistical History, Personal Narratives, and Memorials Concerning POWs in Camps and on Hellships, Civilian Internees, Asian Slave Laborers, and Others Captured in the Pacific Theater* (Jefferson, NC: McFarland, 1994).

Watson, Alexander. *Enduring the Great War: Combat, Morale and Collapse in the German and British Armies, 1914–1918* (Cambridge and New York: Cambridge University Press, 2008).

Watson, Bruce Allen. *Sieges: A Comparative Study* (Westport, CT: Praeger, 1993).

Watt, Lori. *When Empire Comes Home: Repatriation and Reintegration in Postwar Japan* (Cambridge, MA: Harvard University Asia Center, distributed by Harvard University Press, 2009).

Webber, Bert. *Silent Siege: Japanese Attacks Against North America in World War II* (Fairfield, WA: Ye Galleon Press, 1984).

Weber, Eugen. *The Hollow Years: France in the 1930s* (New York: W. W. Norton, 1994).

Weeks, Albert L. *Russia's Life-Saver: Lend-Lease Aid to the U.S.S.R. in World War II* (Lanham, MD: Lexington Books, 2004).

Weidner, William. *Eisenhower and Montgomery at the Falaise Gap* (Xlibris Corporation, 2010).

Weigley, Russell F. *Eisenhower's Lieutenants: The Campaigns of France and Germany, 1944–45* (Bloomington: Indiana University Press, 1981).

———. *History of the United States Army* (New York: Macmillan, 1967).

Weinberg, Gerhard L. *Germany, Hitler, and World War II: Essays in Modern German and World History* (Cambridge: Cambridge University Press, 1995).

———. "Some Myths of World War II," *The Journal of Military History* 75 (July 2011), 701–718.

———. *Visions of Victory: The Hopes of Eight World War II Leaders* (New York: Cambridge University Press, 2005).

———. *A World at Arms: A Global History of World War II* (2nd ed.) (Cambridge: Cambridge University Press, 2005).

Weise, Christian, and Paul Betts. *Years of Persecution, Years of Extermination: Saul Friedlander and the Future of Holocaust Studies* (Bloomsbury Academic, 2010).

Wells, H. G. *The Complete Short Stories of H. G. Wells* [selected and edited by John Hammond] (London: J. G. Dent, 1998).

———. *The War in the Air* (Lincoln: University of Nebraska Press, 2002).

Wells, Mark K. *Courage and Air Warfare: The Allied Aircrew Experience in the Second World War* (London: Frank Cass, 1995).

West, Diana. *American Betrayal: The Secret Assault on Our Nation's Character* (New York: St. Martin's Press, 2013).

Westermann, Edward B. *Flak: German Anti-Aircraft Defenses, 1914–1945* (Lawrence: University Press of Kansas, 2001).

Whealey, Robert H. *Hitler and Spain: The Nazi Role in the Spanish Civil War, 1936–1939* (Lexington: University Press of Kentucky, 1989).

Wheeler, Keith. *Bombers Over Japan* (Alexandria, VA: Time-Life Books, 1982).

White, David Fairbank. *Bitter Ocean: The Battle of the Atlantic, 1939–1945* (New York: Simon & Schuster, 2007).

Whitehead, David. *Aineias the Tactician: How to Survive Under Siege, A Historical Commentary, with Translation and Introduction* (2nd ed.) (London: Bristol Classical Press, 2001).

Whitley, M. J. *Destroyers of World War II: An International Encyclopedia* (Annapolis, MD: Naval Institute Press, 1988).

Widen, J. J. *Theorist of Maritime Strategy: Sir Julian Corbett and His Contribution to Military and Naval Thought* (Farnham, Surrey, England: Ashgate Publishing Ltd., 2012).

Wieczynski, Joseph L., ed. *Operation Barbarossa: The German Attack on the Soviet Union, June 22, 1941* (Salt Lake City, UT: Charles Schlacks, Jr., 1993).

Wieder, Joachim, Einsiedel, Heinrich von Graf, and Helmut Bogler. *Stalingrad: Memories and Reassessments* (London: Arms & Armour, 1995).

Williamson, Gordon. *Kriegsmarine U-boats 1939–45* (Oxford: Osprey Publishing, 2002).

Wilmot, Chester. *The Struggle for Europe* (New York: Harper, 1952).

Winik, Jay. *1944: FDR and the Year That Changed History* (New York: Simon & Schuster, 2015).

Winkler, Heinrich August. *The Age of Catastrophe: A History of the West, 1914–1945* [Stewart Spencer, tr.] (New Haven: Yale University Press, 2015).

Woodhouse, C. M. *The Battle of Navarino* (London: Hodder and Stoughton, 1965).

World Peace Foundation. "The Staggering Burden of Armament," *A League of Nations* 4.2 (April 1921).

Wright, Patrick. *Tank: The Progress of a Monstrous War Machine* (New York: Viking, 2002).

Wright, Stephen L. *The Last Drop: Operation Varsity, March 24–25, 1945* (Harrisburg, PA: Stackpole Books, 2008).

Wünschmann, Kim. *Before Auschwitz: Jewish Prisoners in the Prewar Concentration Camps* (Cambridge: Harvard University Press, 2015).

Y'Blood, William T. *The Little Giants: U.S. Escort Carriers Against Japan* (Annapolis, MD: Naval Institute Press, 1987).

Yellin, Keith. *Battle Exhortation: The Rhetoric of Combat Leadership* (Columbia: University of South Carolina Press, 2008).

Yenne, Bill. *Hap Arnold: The General Who Invented the U.S. Air Force* (Washington, DC: Regnery History, 2013).

———. *Operation Cobra and the Great Offensive: Sixty Days That Changed the Course of World War II* (Pocket, 2004).

Zabecki, David T. *The German 1918 Offensives: A Case Study in the Operational Level of War* (London and New York: Routledge, 2006).

Zaloga, Steven. *Armored Thunderbolt: The U.S. Army Sherman in World War II* (Mechanicsburg, PA: Stackpole Books, 2008).

————. *The Atlantic Wall (1): France* (Oxford: Osprey Publishing, 2007).

————, ed. *Battleground: The Greatest Tank Duels in History* (Oxford: Osprey Publishing, 2011).

————. *Kamikaze: Japanese Special Attack Weapons, 1944–45* (Oxford: Osprey Publishing, 2011).

————. *Operation Cobra 1944: Breakout from Normandy* (Westport, CT: Praeger, 2004).

————. *Sicily 1943: The Debut of Allied Joint Operations* (Oxford and New York: Osprey Publishing, 2013).

Zeiler, Thomas W., and Daniel M. DuBois, eds. *A Companion to World War II* (Hoboken, NJ: Wiley-Blackwell, 2013).

Ziemke, Earl F. *Stalingrad to Berlin: The German Defeat in the East* (Washington, DC: Office of the Chief of Military History, 2011 [1968]).

Ziemke, Earl F., and Magna E. Bauer. *Moscow to Stalingrad: Decision in the East* (Washington, DC: Center of Military History, 1987).

Zimm, Alan D. *Attack on Pearl Harbor: Strategy, Combat, Myths, Deceptions* (Havertown, PA: Casemate Publishers, 2011).

Zuehlke, Mark. *Terrible Victory: First Canadian Army and the Scheldt Estuary Campaign: September 13–November 6, 1944* (Vancouver, BC: Douglas & McIntyre, 2007).

# Index

Photograph by the Hoover Institution

VICTOR DAVIS HANSON is the Martin and Illie Anderson Senior Fellow in classics and military history at the Hoover Institution, Stanford University. The award-winning author of several previous books, he lives in Selma, California.